DATE DUE

Gorbachev and Yeltsin as Leaders

How did Gorbachev and Yeltsin get away with transforming and replacing the Soviet system and its foreign relations? Why did they act as they did in pushing for such radical changes? And how will history evaluate their accomplishments? In this unique and original study, George W. Breslauer compares and evaluates the leadership strategies adopted by Gorbachev and Yeltsin at each stage of their administrations: political rise, political ascendancy, and political decline. He demonstrates how these men used the power of ideas to mobilize support for their policies, to seize the initiative from political rivals, and to mold their images as effective problem solvers, indispensable politicians, and symbols of national unity and élan. *Gorbachev and Yeltsin as Leaders* also compares these men with Khrushchev and Brezhnev, yielding new insight into the nature of Soviet and post-Soviet politics and into the dynamics of "transformational" leadership more generally. The book is an important contribution to the analysis and evaluation of political leadership. It is exceptionally well written and accessible to the nonspecialist.

Professor George W. Breslauer is Dean of Social Sciences and Chancellor's Professor of Political Science at the University of California, Berkeley. He is an author or editor of twelve books on Soviet and Russian politics and is Editor-in-Chief of the journal *Post-Soviet Affairs*. He is a member of the Council on Foreign Relations and in 1997 won the distinguished teaching award of the social science division of UC Berkeley.

Gorbachev and Yeltsin as Leaders

GEORGE W. BRESLAUER
University of California at Berkeley

CAMBRIDGE
UNIVERSITY PRESS

PUBLISHED BY THE PRESS SYNDICATE OF THE UNIVERSITY OF CAMBRIDGE
The Pitt Building, Trumpington Street, Cambridge, United Kingdom

CAMBRIDGE UNIVERSITY PRESS
The Edinburgh Building, Cambridge CB2 2RU, UK
40 West 20th Street, New York, NY 10011-4211, USA
477 Williamstown Road, Port Melbourne, VIC 3207, Australia
Ruiz de Alarcón 13, 28014 Madrid, Spain
Dock House, The Waterfront, Cape Town 8001, South Africa

http://www.cambridge.org

First published 2002

Printed in the United States of America

Typeface Sabon 10/13 pt.   *System* AMS-T$_E$X   [FH]

A catalog record for this book is available from the British Library.

Library of Congress Cataloging in Publication Data
Breslauer, George W.
Gorbachev and Yeltsin as leaders / George W. Breslauer.
p. cm.
Includes bibliographical references and index.
ISBN 0-521-81486-3 – ISBN 0-521-89244-9 (pbk.)
1. Soviet Union – Politics and government – 1985–1991.   2. Russia (Federation) – Politics
and government – 1991– .   3. Gorbachev, Mikhail Sergeevich, 1931– .   4. Yeltsin, Boris
Nikolaevich, 1931– .   I. Title.

DK288.B74   2002
947.085'4 – dc21   2001052443

ISBN 0 521 81486 3 hardback
ISBN 0 521 89244 9 paperback

I dedicate this book to my wife, Yvette Assia Breslauer, my daughter, Michelle, my son, David, my mother, Marianne Schaeffer Breslauer, and the memory of my father, Henry Edward Breslauer.

Contents

Preface

This book is about two men – Mikhail Gorbachev and Boris Yeltsin – who presided from 1985–1999 over the tumultuous transition from Soviet to post-Soviet politics. The speed of change during the first half of that period was remarkable. In 1985, the Soviet Union appeared to be an entrenched entity, capable of defending itself against all challenges to the Communist Party's right to rule at home and in Eastern Europe, and determinedly pursuing a policy of great-power competition abroad. By the end of 1987, *glasnost'* had broken out, the public media were increasingly challenging old doctrines, and the Soviet leadership was starting to make one-sided concessions to the United States on fundamental issues of national security. By the end of 1989, relatively free elections had taken place, Party officials were being voted out of office, communism had collapsed in Eastern Europe, the Soviet Army had retreated in defeat from Afghanistan, and the Cold War was coming to an end. By the end of 1991, an oppositional figure had been elected president of Russia, both communism and the Soviet Union had collapsed, and independent Russia had emerged as a seemingly helpless supplicant of the West. By the end of 1993, independent Russia had experienced two wrenching years of political and economic turmoil at home and was coming to realize the limits of Western willingness to assist its transition from communism. If one had gone to sleep in Moscow in 1985–1986 and woken up in 1992–1993, the change would have been unfathomable.

Without presupposing that Gorbachev and Yeltsin made all these things happen, it is fair to say that things would have happened quite differently had different individuals been in charge. Their acts of leadership were crucial. Both men will surely go down in history as having left a major mark on their country's condition as it approached the twenty-first century. The questions

I address in this book are: Why did these men act as they did? (Chapters 1, 2, 11) How did they get away with it – that is, how did they build support for their programs? (Chapters 3–10) And how might we evaluate their successes and failures as leaders? (Chapters 12–14)

My main concern is to document each man's leadership strategy. My theoretical approach emphasizes the dilemmas faced by leaders in building and maintaining their political authority (their credibility as problem solvers and politicians), the reasons they chose their political strategies and policy programs, and the consequences (intended and unintended) of those choices.

To tap into their authority-building strategies, I conduct a detailed analysis of their public rhetoric, backed up by analysis of the voluminous memoir literature – including memoirs by the two protagonists, Gorbachev and Yeltsin. From these texts and from related actions and signals, I reconstruct the given leader's program. I show how he used the diagnoses and prescriptions embedded in his public utterances to reach out to targeted audiences and constituencies whose support and involvement were essential to his purposes at each stage of his administration. I depict Gorbachev and Yeltsin as leaders of an ongoing and shifting political dialogue with friends and foes at home and abroad, a dialogue that helped to structure a fluid political scene. The immediate purpose of the dialogue was political communication; the larger purpose was to convince people that the speaker had a vision, ideas, and ideals worth supporting and that he also had the political skill, determination, and will to get his way. These were not "just words." They were words that shaped his reputation and credibility – and thereby mightily influenced his capacity to govern. As Richard Neustadt wrote about the American president: "He makes his personal impact by the things he says and does. Accordingly, his choices of what he should say and do, and how and when, are his means to conserve and tap the sources of his power."[1]

Given my purposes, the principal sources for such a study are the public statements of these leaders: their formal speeches at home and abroad, their press conferences, their press releases, and their unrehearsed comments in public forums. The memoirs of their political associates and advisors, in turn, give us insight into the relationship between the leaders' public and private utterances. The memoirs of Gorbachev and Yeltsin provide insight into their personal histories, their self-images, and the ways in which they wished to be remembered. Supplementary interviews with political actors – some by

---

[1] Richard E. Neustadt, *Presidential Power: The Politics of Leadership* (New York: Wiley, 1960), p. 179.

me, most by other scholars who have published on these leaders – allow me to check on the accuracy of published sources.

The public statements and memoirs of politicians must be interpreted with great care. They contain large doses of manipulative rhetoric and, presumably, factual falsehoods. But used judiciously, and with an eye to themes that are repeated in front of multiple audiences, they are an invaluable source of insight into what the leader was trying to accomplish during each stage of his administration. Similarly, memoirs of people who worked with these leaders must be approached with caution about the authors' private agendas. Some were written by people who bore grudges; others by people who idolized their former boss. Some strain to appear balanced in their judgments; others drip with contempt or glow with adoration. As with all historical documents, we must analyze them with a healthy dose of skepticism about their possible biases. But we may have confidence in our depictions to the extent that multiple sources – public and private communications, hostile and adulatory memoirs, published materials and interviews – converge in their testimony about each man's orientations and actions at given moments in time.

A word is in order about the provenance of these leaders' speeches and memoirs. Gorbachev and Yeltsin occasionally wrote their own speeches or statements; they also improvised during press conferences and impromptu encounters. But their major speeches were usually written by teams of speechwriters. This does not mean that such speeches may not be taken as indicators of their political strategies and policy preferences. On the contrary. Both men usually attended closely to the contents of the speeches they did not write,[2] and their speechwriters were very much aware of how the leader wished to represent himself in public. Both men frequently edited successive versions of speeches that were being written for them.

Yeltsin's three major memoirs appeared, respectively, in 1990 (before he became president of Russia); in 1994 (in the middle of his presidency); and in 2000 (after his resignation).[3] They provide valuable sources of insight into the man's personality, beliefs, and political strategy. All three books were ghost-written by Valentin Yumashev, an erstwhile journalist who became one of Yeltsin's closest aides, advisors, and confidantes. Yeltsin was intimately involved in shaping and editing the contents of the first memoir, somewhat less

---

[2] This may have been true of Yeltsin less often after his health took major turns for the worse in 1996–1997.
[3] Boris Yeltsin, *Against the Grain: An Autobiography*, trans. by Michael Glenny (New York: Summit, 1990); Boris Yeltsin, *The Struggle for Russia*, trans. by Catherine A. Fitzpatrick (New York: Random House, 1994); Boris Yeltsin, *Midnight Diaries* (New York: Public Affairs, 2000).

involved in shaping (but probably closely involved in editing) the second, and largely detached from the process of producing the third memoir. Nonetheless, Yumashev was so close to Yeltsin for so many years that we can take for granted that he came to know his boss's preferences and perspectives very well. He could have finished his sentences. And that is what he did, at a minimum, in writing the third memoir. For that very reason, we can take the third memoir, like the first two, as expressions of how Yeltsin wanted the public to remember him and his leadership. Factual details must still be treated with the usual skepticism, but that does not distinguish Yeltsin's memoirs from those of any other leader.

Gorbachev produced several books during and after his leadership of the USSR. From all accounts, he attended very closely to their contents. His book, *Perestroika,* which was not a memoir but a statement of Gorbachev's philosophy, appeared in 1987[4] and was written by a collective with which Gorbachev worked closely. His massive, two-volume memoirs[5] were written after his retirement from public office; he was deeply involved in their production as well. According to a personal communication to me from Professor Archie Brown (St. Antony's College, Oxford University), who received the information from aides of Gorbachev, Gorbachev talked about particular themes with his close associates. Those sessions were recorded and transcribed. He then read everything through and heavily annotated the transcript. Sometimes he resisted attempts by others to make him appear more far-sighted or "advanced" in his thinking at a given time than he believed himself to have been. Most of the words are his own – delivered orally and then confirmed and amended by him in typescript.

The difference in political context between 1985–1989 and 1991–1996 may explain why the memoirs of Gorbachev's colleagues tend to be political memoirs while those of Yeltsin's colleagues tend to be more personal memoirs. Gorbachev's colleagues worked or struggled with him on the resolution of fundamental policy issues. Some of them were fellow members of the Politburo; some were close aides. But both memoir-producing *aides* (such as Boldin, Chernyaev, Shakhnazarov, and Grachev) and memoir-producing *associates* (such as Politburo members Ligachev, Medvedev, Ryzhkov, Kriuchkov, Yakovlev, and Shevardnadze) observed him as he attempted to manipulate the Politburo and Central Committee – or, later, the Congress of People's

[4] Mikhail Gorbachev, *Perestroika: New Thinking for Our Country and the World* (New York: Perennial, 1987).
[5] Mikhail Gorbachev, *Zhizn' i reformy,* 2 vols. (Moscow: Novosti, 1996).

Deputies – to support him on the issues. Their memoirs expose us to Gorbachev the decisionmaker and coalition builder.

Most of the memoirs about Yeltsin, by contrast, were written by aides (Gaidar, Filatov, Korzhakov, Kostikov, Baturin, Satarov, Pikhoia), men and women who were not co-members of an authoritative decisionmaking body of which Yeltsin was chairman. They rarely observed him deliberating policy with authoritative politicians and reaching decisions based on consensus or majority rule. Yeltsin, unlike Gorbachev, was not accountable to a formal collective leadership. Hence, most of Yeltsin's key decisions as president were made by Yeltsin himself in closed counsel. The memoirs about his years in power, therefore, tend to stress his personality traits and the way he treated subordinates or antagonists. They are more revealing about Yeltsin the man than Yeltsin the decisionmaker and coalition builder.

For these reasons, when we use the memoir literature to explore Gorbachev's political personality, we must anticipate that those memoirs will tell us more about Gorbachev's political behavior in formal contexts than about his private, informal interactions and inclinations. Nonetheless, we can relate this evidence to other sources of information about Gorbachev, including many observers' interviews with people who knew him earlier in life, to paint a broad portrait of the man's private personality. Similarly, when we explore Yeltsin's decisionmaking processes, we must anticipate that his aides' memoirs will provide limited access. Even so, by analyzing Yeltsin's political rhetoric in varieties of forums at successive points in time – and by relating this to the self-image projected in his memoirs and the observations of associates about his shifting moods – we can reconstruct his rationales for the many important decisions he had to make.

From these varied texts, I specify each leader's domestic and foreign-policy programs and how these evolved over time. Through frequent comparison and contrast with analogous patterns of rhetoric and behavior by Khrushchev and Brezhnev, which I analyzed in an earlier study,[6] I attempt to deepen our understanding of continuity and change over the past fifty years of Soviet and Russian politics.

Passages and portions of selected chapters, now much revised, appeared previously in published form. Portions of Chapter 4 and passages within Chapter 5 appeared in "How Do You Sell a Concessionary Foreign Policy?" *Post-Soviet Affairs*, vol. 10, no. 3 (July–September 1994), pp. 277–90.

---

[6] George W. Breslauer, *Khrushchev and Brezhnev as Leaders: Building Authority in Soviet Politics* (London: Allen & Unwin, 1982).

Portions of Chapter 7 appeared in "Boris Yeltsin and the 'Invention' of a Russian Nation-State" (co-authored with Catherine Dale), *Post-Soviet Affairs*, vol. 13, no. 4 (October–December 1997), pp. 303–32. Portions of Chapter 8 appeared in "Boris Yel'tsin as Patriarch," *Post-Soviet Affairs*, vol. 15, no. 2 (April–June 1999), pp. 186–200. Portions of Chapter 9 appeared in earlier form in "Yeltsin's Political Leadership: Why Invade Chechnya?" in George Breslauer et al., *Russia: Political and Economic Development* (Claremont, CA: The Keck Center, 1995), pp. 1–24. Much of Chapter 13 appeared in earlier form in "Evaluating Gorbachev as Leader," *Soviet Economy*, vol. 5, no. 4 (October–December 1989), pp. 299–340. Portions of Chapter 14 appeared in "Personalism and Proceduralism: Boris Yeltsin and the Institutional Fragility of the Russian System," in Victoria Bonnell and George W. Breslauer (Eds.), *Russia in the New Century: Stability or Disorder?* (Boulder, CO: Westview, 2000), pp. 35–58. Portions of Chapter 12, as well as passages within Chapters 13 and 14, appeared in "Evaluating Gorbachev and Yeltsin as Leaders," in Archie Brown and Lilia Shevtsova (Eds.), *Political Leadership in the Russian Transition* (Washington, DC & Moscow: Carnegie Endowment for International Peace, 2001), pp. 45–66.

Many institutions have supported my research on this book during the past decade. I am grateful to the University of California at Berkeley, the Carnegie Corporation of New York, and The National Council for Eurasian and East European Research for research and travel grants. The Center for Slavic and East European Studies at UC Berkeley and its successor – The Institute for Slavic, East European, and Eurasian Studies – have unfailingly provided me with the ideal organizational and collegial contexts for sharing the ideas and generating the excitement on which all ambitious projects depend. Certainly, I could not have produced this book without the support of all these institutions. I hope I have justified their trust.

Many individuals assisted me with critiques of earlier drafts of the entire manuscript. It is a great pleasure to acknowledge and thank them here: Richard D. Anderson, Archie Brown, Valerie Bunce, Timothy Colton, Keith Darden, M. Steven Fish, James Goldgeier, Stephen Hanson, Jeffrey Kopstein, David Laitin, James Richter, Richard Samuels, Ilya Vinkovetsky, Edward W. Walker, Lucan Way, and Stephen White. I remain fully responsible for the end product.

I wish also to acknowledge the role of many graduate students at the University of California, Berkeley, whose research assistance helped me to gather materials over the years. Four graduate students did much more than gather materials; they assisted materially in analyzing them. My thanks to Catherine Dale, with whom I co-authored an article that became the basis for portions of Chapter 7. My thanks also to Matthew J. von Bencke, Leonid Kil, and Ilya Vinkovetsky. Ilya, in particular, deserves credit for both the huge numbers of hours he put in and the exceptional analytic subtlety he brought to our examination of speeches and memoirs.

Finally, I am indebted to my family for their patience, support, good cheer, and genuine enthusiasm over a long period. My children, Michelle and David, have grown up with "Gorby" and "Boris." My 25 years of marriage to Yvette have been distracted by four "best men" who stood constantly in the wings, begging for attention: Nikita, Leonid, Mikhail, and Boris. Throughout, the balance of life has been a good one. Soviet and Russian politics gave me objects of interest and stimulation as I pursued my intellectual curiosities. Yvette, Michelle, and David made every day a sweet one by giving me three best friends to come home to.

Leadership Strategies in Soviet and Post-Soviet Politics

In order to accomplish what they did, Gorbachev and Yeltsin had to overcome many obstacles to change. Doing so required them to exercise leadership, which I define as a process of stretching social constraints in the pursuit of social goals.[1] Those constraints are of several kinds: (1) organizations, institutions, and processes that structure politics and administration; (2) the material interests of individuals and groups; and (3) the identities, ideologies, and cultures of individuals and groups. Typically, in an established or entrenched system, these constraints reinforce each other. Ideologies and cultures come to justify the institutions and processes that structure both political life and the distribution of tangible rewards across the population. Those institutions and processes ensure the continuation of policies that cater to prevailing identities and that reproduce existing patterns of social and political inequality.

The Stalinist system came to be such an entrenched system, but certain features of that system did not survive for long after the death of its founder. Stalin's successors rejected a continuation of mass terror and economic austerity, rule by a despot, and perpetual confrontation with the capitalist world. Beyond that, they grappled with the challenge of reforming (Khrushchev, 1953–1964), adapting (Brezhnev, 1964–1982), or transforming (Gorbachev, 1985–1991) the Soviet system of monopolistic rule by the Communist Party–State and "anti-imperialist struggle" abroad, whereas Yeltsin (1989–1999) sought to destroy the system completely and to replace it with a workable alternative.

---

[1] For the definition of leadership as a process of "stretching constraints," see Warren Ilchman and Norman Uphoff, *The Political Economy of Growth* (Berkeley, CA: University of California Press, 1969).

In an earlier book, I examined the strategies deployed by Khrushchev and Brezhnev for reforming and adapting the Soviet system.[2] In the present volume, I switch the focus to their successors. Both volumes concentrate on the exercise of leadership, but this volume focuses on that most difficult and far-reaching variant called "transformational leadership."

Generalizations about transformational leadership can be found in the substantial literature on leadership in private corporations,[3] public bureaucracies,[4] and states.[5] The concept is defined in a variety of ways, but typically it involves a process of fundamental change in the culture and ordering principles of a unit. Bringing this about is a daunting challenge. To effect such change, the leader must do several things:

- Highlight publicly the incompatibility between emerging environmental demands, on the one hand, and current ordering principles and cultural assumptions, on the other.

---

[2] George W. Breslauer, *Khrushchev and Brezhnev as Leaders: Building Authority in Soviet Politics* (London: Allen & Unwin, 1982); see also James Richter, *Khrushchev's Double Bind* (Baltimore: Johns Hopkins University Press, 1994), and Richard D. Anderson, *Public Politics in an Authoritarian State: Making Foreign Policy during the Brezhnev Era* (Ithaca, NY: Cornell University Press, 1993). The studies by Richter and Anderson applied my framework to foreign policy under Khrushchev and Brezhnev and found that the patterns I had highlighted in domestic policy are equally observable in foreign policy. Moreover, Anderson elaborated and enriched the framework by synthesizing decisionmaking theory in a novel way, thereby reinforcing our findings through deductive logic. William J. Tompson published a political biography of Khrushchev using archival sources made available thanks to *glasnost'* (*Khrushchev: A Political Life* [New York: St. Martin's, 1995]). Tompson's book did not seek to test any theory, or even much to relate patterns and findings to existing Western literature on Khrushchev. Nonetheless, his periodization of Khrushchev's years in power tracks well with my findings, as does his depiction of Khrushchev's policy advocacy. Sergei Khrushchev's massive study–memoir (*Nikita Khrushchev and the Creation of a Superpower*, trans. by Shirley Benson [University Park: Pennsylvania State University Press, 2000]) concentrates on foreign policy and is a valuable source of information about Nikita Khrushchev's foreign policy values, world view, and emotions. But it does not provide much insight into the content and evolution of Khrushchev's political strategies and perceptions, perhaps because, as the author noted in an earlier volume, father did not often confide in his family about Kremlin politics (Sergei Khrushchev, *Khrushchev on Khrushchev: An Inside Account of the Man and His Era / by his son*, ed. & trans. by William Taubman [Boston, MA: Little, Brown, 1990], pp. 186–7).

[3] For example, Philip Selznick, *Leadership in Administration* (New York: Harper & Row, 1957); Noel M. Tichy and Mary Anne Devanna, *The Transformational Leader* (New York: Wiley, 1986).

[4] Jameson W. Doig and Erwin C. Hargrove, *Leadership and Innovation* (Baltimore: Johns Hopkins University Press, 1967).

[5] James MacGregor Burns, *Leadership* (New York: Harper & Row, 1978); Howard Gardner, *Leading Minds* (New York: Basic Books, 1995).

- Outline an alternative vision of political organization and culture that will restore a harmonious relationship between the transformed unit and its environment.
- Mobilize constituencies in support of that vision.
- Prevent defenders of the existing order from sabotaging transformation.
- Put specific programs in place that will result in the replacement of the existing order with one that is better suited to the environmental demands of tomorrow.

But leaders – be they adaptive, reformist, or transformational – must do more than just devise and sell a vision for a better tomorrow. They must also convince audiences that they, and they alone, possess the skills required to guide the country toward realizing that vision. Hence, their goals are both programmatic and personal. They attempt simultaneously to persuade large numbers of people that their program for change is desirable and realizable *and* that their occupancy of the highest office is necessary to bring about that change. These two emphases, the programmatic and the personal, are mutually reinforcing. The more a leader inspires people to believe in his program, the more those people will be inclined to believe in his competence as a leader. The more they believe in his competence, the more latitude he has to enact and implement his program. And the more effectively he implements his program, the more enthusiastically will people believe in both his vision and his leadership skills. I refer to this interactive process of persuasion, inspiration, and mutual identification as "building authority."

Building authority is not the same as consolidating power, though leaders in competitive political orders attempt to do both. As I use the term, "authority" is legitimized, credible power.[6] Building authority is the process by which leaders seek to legitimize their policy programs and demonstrate their competence or indispensability as problem solvers and politicians. A concern with building authority assumes that intimidation and bribery may not always be effective in mobilizing political support if the leader is broadly perceived to be incompetent or dispensable. A leader may consolidate his grip on power through intimidation and bribery. Such methods may be sufficient to retain that grip in such despotic and nonideological regimes as prevailed, say, in Cuba under Batista or Nicaragua under the Somozas. But intimidation and bribery, while features of the policy process in most systems, are usually

---

[6] This is not the standard Weberian definition of "authority"; instead, it follows Amitai Etzioni, *The Active Society* (New York: Free Press, 1968, p. 360), where authority is defined as "legitimate power."

insufficient to get one's way in nondespotic, ideological regimes, as in the Soviet Union after Stalin. Such regimes tolerate legitimate political competition (whether within an oligarchic elite or within an inclusive liberal democracy) and justify themselves in ideological terms. In such contexts, a leader's capacity to effect change cannot be increased beyond a certain point on the basis of bribery and intimidation alone. He must also build his authority by demonstrating a capacity to effect changes that will appeal to the beliefs, identities, and cultural orientations of targeted constituents.

In order to elaborate further on the process of building authority, to generate hypotheses to consider when examining Gorbachev's and Yeltsin's leadership, and to set the backdrop for understanding the constraints that Gorbachev faced when he came to power, I will begin by reviewing Khrushchev's and Brezhnev's leadership strategies. Although neither of these men was a transformational leader, their exercise of leadership illustrates two distinct strategies of authority building in a Soviet-type system. And the limitations they shared provided object lessons for both Gorbachev and Yeltsin in the 1980s.

AUTHORITY BUILDING AFTER STALIN

If it was to move beyond Stalinism, the Soviet system required a leader who was committed to significant change. Whatever Stalin's political successors might have thought about the desirability and necessity of "high Stalinism," most of them did not think it feasible to maintain following his death. They viewed as unsustainable the level of tension within society as a result of the police terror, the Gulag camps that were bulging with political prisoners, the exhausting pace of life, and the extreme material austerity. Most of them viewed as undesirable a situation in which the secret police – a state within a state – might be used against them by a new Stalin. Most of them feared that perpetual confrontation with the capitalist world could lead to nuclear war.

The result of these intense, shared fears was a series of quick decisions to reduce the level of tension at home and abroad: arrest and execution of the head of the secret police and his top associates; proclamation of a new deal for the Soviet consumer; and a series of conciliatory offerings to the United States and its allies. This was a watershed that reflected a rapidly emerging and growing sentiment within the leadership. It comprised something I have called the "post-Stalin consensus."[7] That consensus remained in force right through the collapse of the USSR. As far as we know, at no time in the subsequent 38 years was serious consideration given in Politburo deliberations to

---

[7] Breslauer, *Khrushchev and Brezhnev*, p. 18.

the option of returning to the extremes of Stalinism. The new deal was political and economic, domestic and international; it gave reassurance both to the population at large and to the ruling elite.

The post-Stalin consensus, however, was largely a negative one. True, it promised the population a new era of physical and material security. It also partially based the legitimacy of the regime on improvements in the standard of living of the population. But it did not specify much more than that. It left plenty of room for fundamental disagreement among Soviet leaders about the vision to be pursued, the price to be paid by varied domestic interests in pursuit of that vision, and the sacrifices in traditional values to be suffered for the attainment of new goals. It also left unclear how competing politicians would justify the break with Stalinism and their programs for moving beyond Stalinism.

For this was a regime in which ideas mattered greatly. The Communist Party of the Soviet Union (CPSU) for decades had depicted all of Soviet history as the implementation of a grand design for building a utopian society at home and abroad.[8] The Party had legitimized its political monopoly by claiming exclusive insight into how to achieve that utopian goal. Hence, if there was to be a break with Stalinism, it would be necessary to explain why, at this point in time, a change of course was required. It might not have been necessary to blacken the historical image of Stalin in order to undermine the entrenched Stalinist interests and identities that impeded changing course. But it certainly was necessary to explain the change in ideological terms, and to spell out the reasons that the Stalinist legacy had become a brake on forward movement toward the good society. This tension between the perceived requirements of forward movement and allegiance to traditional values would be a focus of political conflict for decades thereafter.[9]

---

[8] For good demonstrations of this, see Mikhail Heller and Aleksandr Nekrich, *Utopia in Power: The History of the Soviet Union from 1917 to the Present* (New York: Summit, 1986), and Martin Malia, *The Soviet Tragedy: A History of Socialism in Russia, 1917–1991* (New York: Free Press, 1994).

[9] The extraordinary importance of doctrinal justifications in communist regimes is the key reason we focus so carefully on leaders' public statements in studying politics in those regimes. Because of Stalin's canonization of Lenin's thoughts and words, the leaders' words in these societies became central as acts of political communication and coordination. All officials and most citizens knew this; officials in particular therefore read the words of leaders very carefully for small variations in meaning and text. They parsed small nuances of phrase for deeper meaning. When Western Kremlinologists used the same technique to document changes in policy and politics, they were often ridiculed in the West. Those critics mistakenly assumed that one could read leaders' speeches in communist regimes essentially as one reads leaders' speeches in liberal democracies. In fact, Kremlinologists were treating those speeches much as communist officials did. It is striking how many memoirs published during the past decade refer to speeches and newspaper articles as key moments in Soviet politics.

As the leadership made its break with the extremes of Stalinism, deeper issues about the Leninist legacy came to the fore. How to prevent criticism of
Stalinism from evolving into criticism of that system's origins in Leninism?
How to prevent expanded political participation from challenging the leading
role of the Party and its monopoly of political, economic, and social life? How
to rein in the secret police, and to narrow the definition of political crime,
without justifying the substitution of a system based on rule of law? How to
improve the economy without a genuine decentralization of economic power
that might challenge the sanctity of central planning and the right of Party officials to intervene, at will, in administrative affairs? How to strike deals with
the "imperialists," in order to manage the nuclear balance of power, without
forsaking one's commitments to leadership of the "anti-imperialist struggle"
and the world communist movement?

These tensions between the goals of the post-Stalin era and the deeper
legacy of Leninism were not immediately obvious to Soviet leaders. But as
liberalization of speech and publication expanded under Khrushchev and
Brezhnev, more members of the critical intelligentsia could be heard raising
questions about the compatibility of certain features of Soviet Leninism with
the attainment of the new goals. Hence, political conflict under Khrushchev
and Brezhnev rarely concerned whether or not to pursue those new goals.
Rather, it centered on the costs to be borne – in terms of traditional values –
when pursuing them. As a result, in building his authority, the Party leader
rarely chose between traditional values and new goals; he instead sought to
synthesize the two, or to put together packages that borrowed from each. Both
Khrushchev and Brezhnev sought to demonstrate their political skills and programmatic vision by forging policies that would allegedly attain post-Stalin
goals without undercutting the legitimacy and stability of the monopolistic,
Party-led system.

It was not difficult to justify such amalgams. The Soviet political tradition
was multifaceted and contradictory, containing both "reformist" and "conservative" strands.[10] Yet there were limits to the degree of diversity easily
legitimized by that tradition. Marxism–Leninism could not justify a social
system based on political freedom, the dominance of market coordination and
private property in the economy, or a permanent accommodation with imperialism on the global stage. Hence, Stalin's successors faced the challenge of
devising innovative policies that would move beyond Stalinism without embracing classical liberal approaches to the domestic organization and foreign
relations of the country. Only after 33 years of experimentation with efforts to

---

[10] See Stephen F. Cohen, "The friends and foes of change: Reformism and conservatism in the
Soviet Union," *Slavic Review*, vol. 38, no. 2 (June 1979), pp. 187–202.

reform and adapt the system within these limits did leaders emerge within the Politburo who were willing to press for something more far-reaching – something that challenged the Party's monopoly at home and its anti-imperialist mission abroad. That was the point at which reform evolved into transformation of the system and, eventually, its replacement with an alternative. It was also the point at which the system itself started to come apart.

STRATEGIES FOR SQUARING THE CIRCLE

Khrushchev sought initially to demonstrate that increased consumer satisfaction could be realized without massive reallocation of funds out of the military and heavy-industrial sectors. He also sought to prove that a reduction of bureaucratic centralism could be achieved without a loss of administrative control, and that expanded criticism of officialdom could be reconciled with the maintenance of tight political control and strict censorship. The key to synthesizing these conflicting priorities, in his eyes, was to combine partial political liberalization with a reduction in the socioeconomic privileges of Party officials, expansion of the role of Party activists at the expense of full-time Party officials, and the generation of nationwide fervor through ambitious campaigns for social transformation and economic growth. However, restructuring political relationships within the system required a confrontation with powerful political interests, which was one reason that Khrushchev pressed his campaigns against Joseph Stalin and his legacy. By the time Khrushchev was overthrown in 1964, the Soviet Union had broken decisively with the extremes of Stalinism. But Khrushchev had much less to show for his efforts to provide the Soviet people with material abundance, social equality, and a sense of authentic political participation.

Brezhnev based his authority within the political establishment on a program that replaced Khrushchev's political and social reforms with patriotic appeals ("Soviet patriotism") and budgetary redistributions. Rather than restructure authority relations, Brezhnev proposed to accelerate economic growth by pouring enormous resources into agriculture, wages, Siberian development, and imports of foreign goods. He sought to reconcile political control with "socialist legality" by squelching the anti-Stalin campaign and cracking down on dissidents while simultaneously creating a more predictable and less pressured environment for politically conformist experts. Brezhnev defined his role as an intra-establishment consensus builder who would not confront (or radically deprive) the major institutional interests in the system.

Whatever their differences, Khrushchev and Brezhnev were both "Party men." Neither of them believed in, or advocated, democratic pluralism or an end to the "leading role of the Party." Both men forged programs that relied heavily on Party activism and political intervention in economic and social affairs for their realization. Both men sought to create a sense of nationwide fervor on behalf of their programs. The turn away from utopian values after Khrushchev did not mean abandoning efforts to generate mobilizational fervor per se. (Recall that, under Brezhnev, construction of the Baikal–Amur railroad was dubbed "The Project of the Century.") The difference was that Khrushchev sought to redefine the character of Party mobilization in an anti-elitist direction, thereby challenging the prerogatives of the Party *apparatchiki*. He advocated new methods of mobilization with active Party members and specialists taking the lead. In contrast, Brezhnev advocated methods of mobilization that would further the achievement of post-Stalin goals without challenging the prerogatives and privileges of full-time officials of the Party–State.

The two leaders differed less in their foreign policies than in their domestic policies. They both pursued strategies of "offensive détente."[11] They both opted to build their authority by demonstrating that they could compete globally with "imperialism" and simultaneously strike deals with the United States that would manage the nuclear relationship. They both promised to do so from a position of strength and to secure Washington's recognition of the USSR as a co-equal and global superpower. In sum, they both promised to deliver peace through strength. Khrushchev, however, promised far more than he could deliver in the near term and sought to compensate for the shortfall through bluff: for example, public exaggeration of Soviet missile capability that was meant to intimidate Western leaders into making concessions. When his bluff was called by Western governments, he was thrown onto the political defensive, both at home and abroad, and sought new ways to recoup his credibility. During 1963–1964, frightened by the close brush with nuclear war during the Cuban Missile Crisis and desperate for a success that would bolster his credibility within the Central Committee, Khrushchev pursued a foreign policy that came close to abandoning the Soviet commitment to allies in the world communist movement. He was so desperate for "peace" that he was willing to abandon "strength."[12]

This policy was dropped by Khrushchev's successors, partly out of national pride and partly because the U.S. military escalation in Vietnam strengthened hardliners within the leadership.[13] Brezhnev abandoned bluff and sought deliberately to build the military strength required to play the role of a co-equal

---

[11] The term was coined by Jack Snyder in "The Gorbachev revolution: A waning of Soviet expansionism?" *International Security*, vol. 12, no. 3 (Winter 1987/88), pp. 93–131, at p. 103.

[12] See Richter, *Khrushchev's Double Bind*, ch. 7.

[13] Ibid., ch. 8.

superpower and interventionist global power. Only then did he reenter into a détente relationship with the United States. Brezhnev also recommitted the Soviet Union to its communist allies and promised to build a détente with the imperialist camp that would actually advance the goals of the world communist movement.

Khrushchev was ousted from office in October 1964, criticized for both his policies and his leadership style; Brezhnev died in office, but only after a lengthy period that would subsequently be dubbed "stagnation" at home and abroad. Thus, neither of them succeeded in squaring the circle: how to combine the Communist Party's monopoly on power with policies that could revitalize an entrenched, overbureaucratized system at home and keep pace with the United States abroad. Their policy programs – and the fallback positions they adopted after their initial programs were discredited – proved incapable of improving all-round economic performance, public élan, or Soviet standing abroad.

TACTICS FOR GETTING ONE'S WAY

Khrushchev, the reformer, embraced a leadership style that was anti-establishment and confrontational – what might be called "Leninist populism." He mobilized the masses against the "bureaucrats." Brezhnev, the conservative, adopted a leadership style that was establishmentarian and consensual. These were distinct approaches to leadership within a post-Stalinist, Leninist system.

Khrushchev's strategy was to exploit the atmosphere of crisis after Stalin to make common cause with the masses against intransigent forces within the establishment. He played upon elite fears of social unrest by intentionally raising popular expectations, or prematurely publicizing policy proposals, and then arguing within the political elite that growing popular disaffection made the acceptance of these proposals a necessity. He leaked Politburo deliberations to selected, interested audiences in order to intimidate other actors in the policymaking process. He invited members of the intelligentsia to join him in criticizing the inherited order. He invited nonmembers to be present, or to give speeches, at meetings of the Party's Central Committee in order to bias the discussions in a particular direction and to intimidate skeptics. When his policies started to falter, and when he could no longer deliver on his inflated promises, Khrushchev intensified the anti-Stalin campaign, blamed officials of the Party and state for the shortfalls, purged many of them, and launched an assault on Party organs at all levels of the hierarchy.

Brezhnev's rejection of political populism, as well as his greater emphasis on throwing money at problems, were consistent with his posture as a consensus builder and political broker among interests within the establishment.

His goals were conservative and his leadership strategy was tailored to them. He eschewed appealing to the masses over the heads of his colleagues, avoided playing upon elite fears of the masses, and shunned raising consumer expectations for personal political gain. Instead, Brezhnev presented himself as the leader best qualified to build coalitions that would induce the most powerful institutional interests to reorient their operations and to make the system, as structured, work more effectively. And he promised to do all this without political purges.

AUTHORITY BUILDING AND PUBLIC POLITICS

The contrast in authority-building strategies between these two men highlights a feature of the Soviet system that becomes crucial to understanding the dilemmas and opportunities facing Gorbachev and Yeltsin. The Soviet political order was based on a heavily defended system of *private politics.* Important deliberations and decisionmaking took place within the upper reaches of the Party–State hierarchy, in arenas that were dominated by the trustees of a privileged class of full-time officials of the Communist Party, the economic bureaucracy, the military, and the security services. Secrecy and a façade of unanimity were the prevailing norms. A leader like Brezhnev, who was comfortable with brokering relations among these elite interests, could easily respect the prevailing norms. But a leader like Khrushchev, who wanted to reform the system and challenge some of its fundamentals, would have to defy the norms of secrecy and unanimity. He would have to mobilize new social forces to challenge the prerogatives of entrenched interests. He would have to propose doctrinal revisions and challenge some of the sacred cows of Stalinist doctrine. This was not a matter of choice. If he wanted to reform the system (which *was* a matter of choice), his authority-building strategy would have to challenge the notion that politics is entirely a private affair. Otherwise, he would remain too much a captive of the interests that dominated the Soviet political establishment.

Leaders who sought to go beyond reform and to *transform* the system would have to embrace even more far-reaching strategies for building political leverage. They would have to defy the norms of private politics to an even greater extent than Khrushchev had. Indeed, one of the central dramas of the Gorbachev and Yeltsin eras was the creation of an autonomous public realm: the transformation of politics from a private affair into a public affair. Gorbachev eventually viewed freer speech (*glasnost'*), greater freedom of association, a freer press, and competitive elections as necessary to revitalize the system, awaken society, and neutralize entrenched interests that might obstruct the transformation of the Soviet system into some sort of "social-ist democracy." For Yeltsin, that public arena became his ticket to political resurrection in 1989 and the avenue through which he later became president of Russia. Gorbachev's authority-building dilemma was how to open a public arena without destroying the system he was seeking peaceably to transform. Yeltsin's authority-building *opportunity* in the 1980s lay in his exploitation of that public arena, to Gorbachev's political disadvantage. But Yeltsin's authority-building dilemma after the collapse of the Soviet Union became: how to build a new system in a context of intense, public political competition?

Expansion of the arenas of political conflict may be a necessary condition for both reform and transformation of the system, but such expansion is far from a sufficient condition; indeed, it can be used as easily for reactionary purposes. Mao Zedong, for example, mobilized Red Guards during the Cultural Revolution as a way of smashing bureaucratic conservatism and repressing nonconformist thought. Only when expansion is combined with liberalization of political expression is it capable of serving the cause of progressive reform or transformation of the system. Only when some degree of autonomy is granted to public arenas can political conflict within those arenas advance the progressive transformation of the system. Under such conditions, dissident or "revisionist" ideas come to play a causal role in making change possible and in shaping the direction of that change.

Leaders who wish to seize the political initiative in order to reform or transform the system need allies outside the political establishment. They need to mobilize new social forces in order to use them as a wedge against entrenched conservative forces. For those regimes in which ideas are important, activation of such social forces must be legitimized while channels are created through which their voices can be heard. Hence, Soviet leaders who sought to reform or transform politics since Stalin had to transform both the *language* and the *arenas* of contestation.

For example, Khrushchev's anti-Stalin campaign, beginning in 1956 and extending through the end of his reign, sought to break through the "bureaucratism" that he claimed to be a fundamental constraint on progress. His campaign emboldened journalists and members of the cultural intelligentsia to disseminate public critiques of the existing state of affairs. Many of these works bordered on critiques of the system of rule – the ordering principles of the polity – as opposed to the traditional tendency to blame all problems on the individual deficiencies of specific officials. Under Khrushchev, then, the permissible explanation for failure was allowed to ascend to a much higher level of abstraction. His doctrinal innovations at Party Congresses in 1956,

1959, and 1961 provided intellectual space for members of the newly reborn "critical intelligentsia" to push still further their critiques of the system. Eventually, they went further than Khrushchev could abide, both personally and politically. Periodically, Khrushchev cracked down and tried to rein in the scope of permissible criticism – only to expand it again when pushing his reformist agenda.

Brezhnev's purposes as a consolidator of the system did not require him to expand either the arenas of politics or the level of generalization of criticism. To the contrary, Brezhnev made top-level policymaking less transparent and permeable than it had been under Khrushchev and worked faithfully within established arenas. He also put an end to the anti-Stalin campaign, rescinded earlier doctrinal changes, and reduced the scope of permissible criticism to within-system levels. This approach to the structure and language of politics was tailored to conservative and consolidative purposes.

Gorbachev, in turn, sought to transform the system more fully than even Khrushchev. His campaign for *glasnost'* therefore allowed the scope of permissible criticism to rise to unprecedented levels. While Gorbachev, as we shall see, feared that excessive criticism of the Stalinist past might undermine him politically, he nonetheless encouraged the critical intelligentsia to run with his doctrinal innovations and to develop an increasingly systemic critique of current problems. Expanded public criticism, he hoped, would stimulate the initiative of educated youth, expose bureaucratic obstruction, and build legitimacy for an emerging political order. That criticism would also build a constituency to support Gorbachev politically and to which he could point in order to intimidate advocates of a political backlash.

Boris Yeltsin exploited the new arenas and publics called forth by Gorbachev and helped to radicalize them far beyond what Gorbachev desired. Moreover, he founded new arenas himself, such as the Russian presidency, and helped turn criticism of the old regime into rejection of the entire communist system. In the process, he outflanked Gorbachev politically and, intentionally or not, helped to bring down Gorbachev, the Soviet system, and the USSR.

Both reformist and transformational leadership in a monopolistic, Leninist system require a leader to propagate heretical new ideas, create new public arenas, and mobilize previously intimidated social forces into politics. Such leadership requires strategically focused public criticism to undermine the enemies of change, and it requires new constituencies to provide a new political base for a new political order. All this is counterintuitive in several respects. It is extremely risky to subject your *own* system to criticism and to bring new, unpredictable social forces and radical ideas into politics. No leader can easily predict or control the consequences. For a leader concerned with nothing more than retaining power, there are other (and much safer) ways of conducting politics. But at a certain point, when a political system is mired in stagnation, standing pat may fail as an authority-building strategy despite the very same possibilities for intimidation, patronage allocation, and coalition building around material interests that allowed previous leaders to resist change. When that point is reached, the winning political strategy is to propagate an "idea whose time has come."

In sum, reforming or transforming the Soviet political order required changes in policy, political organization, and the language of politics; changing just one by itself would be insufficient. In established systems, reigning ideologies and structures tend to be mutually reinforcing. Leaders who wish to overcome constraints on change therefore must operate at two levels: (1) they must build coalitions of material interests to support needed changes in policy and organization; and (2) they must propagate new ideas that both delegitimize the old way of doing things and create legitimacy for new ways of doing things. The core of the challenge is how to change the system, or build a new one, without sacrificing your authority and power in the process.

STAGES OF ADMINISTRATION

I have noted similarities and differences between Khrushchev and Brezhnev in their approaches to problem solving and politics. I have only alluded to the fact that both of their administrations passed through at least three distinct stages. Each stage reflected the authority-building challenges facing the leader at that point during his tenure in office, and each stage was marked by a distinct approach to problem solving and political self-justification by the leader. The three-stage rhythms of change within each administration are suggestive of shifting political incentives and opportunities as politicians exercise leadership. This will become relevant as we analyze the dilemmas that Gorbachev and Yeltsin encountered at analogous stages of their administrations.

When we look back on the Khrushchev and Brezhnev years, we find in each administration that a stage of political succession struggle and power consolidation was followed by a period of ascendancy of the Party leader, which in turn was followed by the frustration of his programmatic goals and a decline in his authority. Each stage posed a distinct authority-building challenge to the leader. In the first stage – before he had consolidated his power, outflanked his rivals, or expanded his role to become chief architect of domestic and foreign policy – the Party leader concentrated on putting together a coalition that was biased in the direction of traditional interests. Thus, in this initial stage, both Khrushchev and Brezhnev most strongly advocated the development of heavy industry and defense. Both men pointed to threats from the "imperialists" and emphasized the protection of traditional values more than the adoption of new approaches. Both leaders also introduced policy innovations to clean up some of the mess inherited from their predecessors. In particular, both came forth with large-scale programs for agricultural development that were justified as necessary to ensure reliable supplies of food for the urban population. At the same time, both men tried to seize the initiative by pinning the "extremist" label on their political rivals, suggesting that those rivals were either too conservative or too radical to protect traditional values and simultaneously move the country forward.

Yet after consolidating their power and purging (Khrushchev) or outflanking (Brezhnev) their rivals, both men expanded their roles and selectively incorporated into their programs elements of the policies associated with the more reformist of their defeated rivals. Each of them presented a comprehensive program for forward-looking changes in both domestic and foreign policies that constituted a more balanced synthesis of traditional values and new approaches than they had advocated earlier. Both leaders now claimed to speak for "all the people."

In both cases, however, the synthesis proved overly optimistic and unworkable. Brezhnev's synthesis was arguably less ambitious and optimistic than Khrushchev's, a fact that reflected Brezhnev's conservatism, his political dependence on a self-protective political establishment, and lessons learned from the Khrushchev experience. But Brezhnev's program remained highly optimistic nonetheless, promising to expand production in both heavy and light industry and simultaneously to deliver both détente with the imperialists and intensified competition in the Third World.

Because of the gap that resulted between promises and achievements, the credibility of both Khrushchev's and Brezhnev's claims came to be doubted. Each man then tried to reestablish his credibility, reshuffle his support coalition, and redefine his program. Each leader went through several bouts of such changes during his remaining years in office.[14]

---

[14] Some people argue (in passing and without elaboration or documentation) that Khrushchev did not perceive himself to be on the political defensive in 1960–1964 and that the changes he introduced in that period were efforts to salvage his *program,* not his political authority (Richard Ned Lebow and Janice Gross Stein, *We All Lost the Cold War* [Princeton, NJ: Princeton University Press, 1994], pp. 403–4, fn. 57). I have also received personal communications from a reader to this effect. And it is at the basis of all literature that treats the Soviet general secretary as politically unassailable (as in, for example, Dmitrii Volkogonov, *Autopsy for an Empire: The Seven Leaders Who Built the Soviet Regime* [New York: Free Press, 1998]). This objection cuts to the heart of my approach to the study of politics and is worth rebutting. The interpretation does not explain why Khrushchev was so devoted to his program (pure idealism?). And it assumes implausibly that he had sufficient power to be oblivious to the prospect that his mistakes and shortfalls could immediately be held against

Gorbachev's and Yeltsin's years in power can be divided into three analogous stages. Indeed, that is the basis for the organization of this book. Each of these leaders went through a stage of succession and consolidation, followed by a stage of ascendancy, which gave way to a stage of decline. Even so, with the emergence of an autonomous public arena in the 1980s and 1990s and with the collapse of the Soviet system, the political incentives facing Gorbachev and Yeltsin differed dramatically from those facing Khrushchev and Brezhnev. Hence, we will find some novel twists on the conclusions of my earlier study – twists that reflect the difference between the task of reforming or adapting the Soviet system, on the one hand, and the task of transforming or replacing it, on the other.

AUTHORITY-BUILDING STRATEGIES: AUDIENCES, SOURCES, AND RESONANCE

Authority building is a process of establishing and maintaining one's credibility among constituencies that have the power to make or break one's hold over either policymaking or office. It is a process that is universal to contexts marked by competitive politics. And it is all the more important in the context of *ideological* politics, in which the struggle over ideas bears on the very identity of the political community. But where do authority-building strategies come from? What are the audiences for one's authority-building strategies? What determines whether one's ideas resonate with those audiences? Let us address these issues in the established Soviet context under Khrushchev and Brezhnev before exploring how things changed under Gorbachev and Yeltsin.

him by others in the leadership – an especially implausible assumption in a regime in which political struggle had been so intense and so costly to the losers. By contrast, I treat leaders in politically competitive regimes as actors who view both power preservation and authority maintenance as prerequisites for the realization of their programs, and I view them as living with constant uncertainty about the state of their power, authority, and credibility. They may or may not be faced with crystallized factional opposition: I am persuaded by the evidence that Khrushchev and Brezhnev did not face such overt, sustained opposition. But they had to be constantly attentive to the possible reactions of associates who could undermine their political security. Hence, even if they did not proclaim publicly, "I am on the political defensive!" (which would not be smart politics), defensive rhetoric and counteroffensive behavior when their programs are faltering is a good indicator of leaders' efforts to re-seize the political initiative when the ambitious programs they sponsored have been discredited. They enjoyed a great deal of power to define policy, even during the third stage of their administrations. But their perceived level of political insecurity rose as the credibility of their programs and promises declined. Ultimately, my claims may have to be treated as an assumption of this study, rather than a fully documented demonstration, since the private perceptions and fears of leaders – whatever they might have said openly in a recorded Politburo meeting now in the archives – are things they would have experienced but kept to themselves.

We are trying to understand the factors that entered into the calculations of Soviet politicians as they competed for the highest office in the land.
Clearly, the first consideration on their minds was: What strategy is most
likely to work? How can I mobilize powerful supporters in greater quan-
tity, and more effectively, than my competitors? In thinking about this, a
politician in any competitive system will focus on what is important to the
(s)electorate: its interests and identities. He will think about the coalitions
that might be built among existing interest groups, the promises that could
be made to induce them to support him, and the more diffuse ideas and symbols he could invoke that would resonate with his (s)electors' notions of social
progress.

In scanning the array of interests in the political establishment at a given
moment in time, our hypothetical competitor would certainly want to avoid
alienating the most powerful, entrenched interests in the system. Nonetheless, he could not afford to be identified with a "stand-pat" position, as he
would also sense a yearning among the elite for ways of getting the country
out of the mess bequeathed by his predecessor. This is the point at which we
reach the limits of a structural approach to the prediction of leadership behavior. The leading roles of the Communist Party, the military–industrial
complex, the economic planners, and the security organs were constants
throughout the post-Stalin era. But leadership strategies for combining interests across institutions, for selectively defying the interests of some of those
institutions, and for constructing diffuse appeals to broader identity considerations varied greatly.

That variation was more a product of the personal ideas and strategies
of competing politicians than of institutional structures: ideas about how to
combine the old and the new; political strategies formulated under conditions
of immense uncertainty about what was likely to work; ideas and strategies
propagated with the intention of defining a political niche for oneself and
denying that niche to one's competitors. The value of an authority-building
approach is that, without denying the constraining impact of structures, it
highlights the tendency of leaders to forge and justify programs that cannot
be predicted from knowing solely the structure of political organization and
the content of dominant interests in the polity.[15] And the structural approach
is particularly ill-suited to predicting the effectiveness of leadership strategies
once the system is in crisis – as was the case after Gorbachev began his efforts to transform the system. At that point, the interaction among leadership

---

[15] As Keynes once wrote: "I am sure that the power of vested interests is vastly exaggerated compared with the gradual encroachment of ideas" (John Maynard Keynes, *The General Theory*
[New York: Harcourt Brace, 1936], p. 383).

strategies, crumbling structures, and newly mobilized social forces was much more open-ended.

Another ideational factor that cannot be predicted simply from knowing the structures and interests of the regime is the *climate of opinion within the political establishment* at the point of political succession. That climate influences the strategies adopted by political competitors. After Stalin, a widespread (though far from unanimous) yearning existed within the political establishment and intelligentsia for restoring to the people and the elite a sense of physical security; this sentiment coexisted with a yearning within many quarters of the political establishment for restoring a sense of dynamism, for "getting the country moving again." The coexistence of these palpable sentiments meant both that "movement" should not be in the direction of a continuation of Stalinism and that promising physical security to cadres should not be equated with stagnation in policy. Khrushchev sensed these yearnings, shared them, played upon them, and worked to shape their policy expression. By contrast, after Khrushchev, officials of the Party and state yearned primarily for a period of tranquility and predictability that would regularize and guarantee their material privileges, their job security, and their autonomy from both unregulated mass criticism and arbitrary leaders. At the same time, they hoped for leadership that would clean up the economic and administrative disarray of Khrushchev's last years in office. Brezhnev sensed, shared, and responded to these yearnings.

Political competitors also appeal to ideas, not just interests, when they attempt to build clientele networks based on a sense of shared identity. The symbols leaders invoke in packaging their programs are chosen to resonate with the identities of audiences within the political elite. Leaders attempt to plug into traditional notions of national glory, need, or international standing, into notions of societal progress, solidarity, and élan, and into core ideas of the ideological tradition. Even in a regime like Brezhnev's, where the conservative and consolidative thrust of policy seemed to pander only to material and status interests, the leader framed his policy choices in ways that played to audiences' concern for national élan: Brezhnev's large-scale agricultural programs of 1965–1966; his programs for development of the Non-Black-Earth Zone and Siberia; accelerated construction of the Baikal–Amur railway and territorial–industrial complexes; and his "Peace Program" of 1971. All these projects were presented as glorious means of moving the country toward transcendant domestic and international goals.[16]

---

[16] On Marxist–Leninist elites as believers in the capacity of their systems to transcend historical constraints, see Stephen Hanson, *Time and Revolution* (Chapel Hill: University of North Carolina Press, 1997).

But they had to do so credibly. Targeted individuals will calculate whether the appeals being sent their way are likely to yield the promised results and likely to prevail in any subsequent power struggle. To the extent that proposals are not credible, they can be dismissed as empty promises, wishful thinking, or the desperate rhetoric of a political loser. The winning strategy is for a politician to craft a set of appeals that link the past to the future in ways that are plausible and in ways that allow him to seize the policy initiative, throw his rivals onto the political defensive, and thereby induce potential clients to support the man who is likely to win (a bandwagoning effect). Brezhnev and Khrushchev were able to fashion programs that credibly (to Party–State officials) combined selected traditional values with new solutions to problems and that, they claimed, would move the country forward, aggrandize the material interests of certain constituencies, and do so skillfully under the leadership of patrons likely to prevail in the power struggle. Thus, authority building in Soviet politics involved making a credible claim to possessing scarce problem-solving and political skills.

The initial reliance of Khrushchev and Brezhnev on hardline constituencies appears to validate a structural explanation for their behavior as political competitors. It may, in fact, validate the notion that the autonomous role of personal ideas is diminished when the stakes involved are of the highest order: political survival or demise.[17] Both men initially appealed more to the material interests of key constituencies, and to traditional features of the reigning ideology, than they would after they had won the power struggle. But why did these leaders expand their coalitions and programs once they had achieved ascendancy in the leadership? Why did they not simply stick with the coalition with which they had won the power struggle – a coalition that, in both cases, allied them with the two most powerful interests in the system: the Party apparatus and the military–industrial complex?

One answer is cognitive: a stand-pat strategy was not credible to those who believed in the post-Stalin consensus; elite audiences came to perceive the contradictions within the system as urgently in need of being addressed, however gingerly (Brezhnev) or boldly (Khrushchev). Another answer is ideological and emotional: the regime's optimistic ideological tradition encouraged an expansive vision of the system's capacity to build a society of abundance for all the people. A third answer is political: this was still a Leninist system, and the leader was accorded no fixed term of office. Hence, post-Stalin leaders

---

[17] "[T]he lower the cost of expressing one's convictions the more important the convictions will be as a determinant of choice" (Douglass C. North, *Institutions, Institutional Change and Economic Performance* [Cambridge University Press, 1990], p. 43).

experienced a felt need for *political overinsurance,* even after they had consolidated their power. The political uncertainty about procedures and term of office gave the leader an incentive to build outsized (rather than minimal) winning coalitions, which in turn led him eventually to sponsor programs that appealed to constituencies located across a wide band of the political spectrum.[18] Having won the power struggle by appealing to concentrated interests that had exceptionally intense preferences, he acquired the power to become more inclusive as well as the incentive to insure himself politically by drawing previously excluded interests and identities into his coalition. Whether his personal goal was to hedge against risk through insurance or to increase his political independence by reducing his reliance on a small coalition, the behavioral result was the same: an expanded coalition.

Whatever the reasons for promulgating so ambitious a program, the leader found himself on the political defensive after the shortcomings of that program became manifest. This is a point at which personality became an especially important determinant of the leader's behavior. His response to frustration was far less dictated by a clear perception of what the political traffic would bear. Khrushchev became extraordinarily erratic during his last four years in office. In both domestic and foreign affairs, he searched frantically for panaceas that would help him regain lost authority, and he confronted the most powerful and entrenched interests in the system. Brezhnev instead adopted a deliberate strategy of returning to the coalition on which he had ridden to the top in the 1960s and of using whatever resources he could marshal to try to salvage as much of his comprehensive program as possible.

AUTHORITY BUILDING AND POST-SOVIET POLITICS

Comparison of Khrushchev's and Brezhnev's authority-building strategies allowed me to generalize about the nature of Soviet politics. But is the framework applicable to a system that is crumbling or being replaced, as was the case from 1988 through 1999? In this book, I intend to demonstrate that it is in fact relevant to the new context. In good measure, that relevance stems from the framework's initial derivation from the study of democratic regimes. The idea of leadership as a process of stretching social constraints – and of authority building as a necessary precondition for acquiring the leverage to do so

---

[18] This point was made in Richter, *Khrushchev's Double Bind.* Lack of a fixed term of office is also a feature of parliamentary regimes. However, in Leninist regimes, the felt need for political overinsurance is reinforced mightily by the unattractiveness of political retirement and the lack of autonomous arenas in society in which to build alternative careers or to launch a political comeback.

successfully – is a universal of politics in competitive regimes, whether these are competitive oligarchies or pluralist democracies. Indeed, I first developed the idea when reading Neustadt's classic study of the American presidency, in which he argued that "Presidential power is the power to persuade."[19] The Soviet regime in the post-Stalin era, it seemed to me, had become a competitive oligarchy within which political competition was expressed publicly as a contest of ideas. While coercion and patronage remained key bases for political compliance in Soviet politics, ideas had grown in importance as the price to be paid for political failure had declined.[20] I concluded that something useful could be learned about Soviet politics by looking at policy advocacy as more than just a game of power maximization and by looking at political leverage as more than just the power to command and coerce. It follows logically that the basic framework is eminently applicable to successor regimes that embrace public and democratic modes of political contestation, for that framework derived originally from the study of a democratic regime.

There are still other reasons to apply the framework to post-Soviet Russia. First, seizing the initiative and thus throwing one's competitors onto the political defensive is a widely used strategy among competing politicians in competitive oligarchies as well as in public, democratic politics. Second, the division of administrations into stages reflects something more general, though such stages will vary in length and character in different systems. The stages of struggle for succession (the electoral campaign in liberal democracies) followed by "honeymoon" or ascendancy periods followed by declining authority form a familiar pattern. It is striking, for example, how many British prime ministers (even the "great" ones) ended their careers in office on a note of failure or repudiation.[21] Finally, there is a commonality in the tendency of politicians to promise more than they can deliver and then to struggle with a loss of credibility when their inability to deliver becomes obvious. This phenomenon is hardly restricted to Soviet politics, though huge gaps between aspirations and capacity are certainly characteristic of communist regimes. For all these reasons, we shall see that an authority-building framework helps

---

[19] Richard Neustadt, *Presidential Power: The Politics of Leadership* (New York: Wiley, 1960), p. 10.
[20] Put differently, politicians were more likely to speak their minds in private and political venues once they no longer had to fear being shot for being on the wrong side of an argument or political struggle.
[21] See Richard Rose, *The Prime Minister in a Shrinking World* (Cambridge, U.K.: Polity Press, 2001); on governing cycles in communist and democratic systems, see Valerie Bunce, *Do New Leaders Make a Difference?: Executive Succession and Public Policy under Capitalism and Socialism* (Princeton, NJ: Princeton University Press, 1981).

to illuminate the evolution of Boris Yeltsin's presidency, even though his leadership was no longer being exercised within a Marxist–Leninist Party–State.

Thus far, I have been discussing the context within which political choice takes place; I have said less about the personalities and personal beliefs of the leaders in question. Such was also the case with my book on Khrushchev and Brezhnev, in which I was more interested in highlighting features of the system that led to a number of similarities across their administrations. The personal factor, however, must loom larger – much larger – in a book about Gorbachev and Yeltsin. Khrushchev's reformism and Brezhnev's conservatism had long pedigrees within Soviet history, as did Gorbachev's initial strategy of reformism during 1985–1987. But Gorbachev's subsequent decision to push for transformation of the system, and Yeltsin's decision to try to destroy and replace the Leninist system, were unprecedented acts by political leaders of the system itself. One cannot explain these choices without reference to these leaders' personalities and beliefs before they came to power, which is the focus of the next chapter.

2

Gorbachev and Yeltsin: Personalities and Beliefs

Most of the time they were in power, both Gorbachev and Yeltsin were less constrained by formal political structures than Khrushchev and Brezhnev had been. We must therefore understand the personalities and beliefs of Gorbachev and Yeltsin if we hope to specify the determinants of many of their policy choices.

GORBACHEV AS A POLITICAL PERSONALITY

There is nothing in Gorbachev's biography to suggest the personality of a rebel. Rather, Gorbachev comes across as an organization man, one who joined the Communist Party at a younger age than did Yeltsin and who found his greatest honors and satisfactions in life within that organization.[1] Gorbachev came to Moscow as a young man from the provinces who was eager to "make it" in the capital and to rise within the political hierarchy. One of the first things he did after matriculation at Moscow State University was to become a Young Communist League (Komsomol) activist. He applied for candidate membership of the CPSU at the youngest age allowable. Gorbachev's career took him through the law faculty at Moscow State University, during which time he became head of his class's Komsomol, followed by a conventional career climbing the ladder of the political hierarchy – first in the Young Communist League, then in the Party apparatus. Once in the Party apparatus, he never left it. Whereas some analysts treat this career path as predicting the mentality of a "conservative" *apparatchik,* it is more accurate to

---

[1] This distinction first appeared in Dmitry Mikheyev, *Russia Transformed* (Indianapolis, IN: Hudson Institute, 1996), pp. 49ff.

treat it as predicting faith in the "leading role of the Party" within Soviet "socialist" society, and belief in proper organization and Party-led mobilization as the guarantor of progress toward "realizing the full potential of socialism." Gorbachev's attraction to Party work derived from the possibility of doing *political* work as a leader of people. He was repelled by the deskwork of bureaucrats and rejected a career in the procuracy when it was offered to him.

Like Gorbachev, Yeltsin was repelled by formal, bureaucratic deskwork and preferred to work directly with people involved in solving concrete problems. Both men prided themselves on their motivational skills. But Yeltsin, unlike Gorbachev, was drawn to complex, *technical* tasks of construction engineering and prided himself on the mastery of technical skills that would allow him to reach new heights in grandiose acts of construction. He worked in economic administration for many years before being recruited into the Party apparatus. During his rise within the Party–State apparatus, Yeltsin was evaluated in terms of the construction projects put up under his leadership. Gorbachev, as the Komsomol leader in Stavropol, was evaluated by his superiors according to more abstract, subjective, and political criteria.

Gorbachev's personality as a well-adjusted organization man within a political bureaucracy mirrored the well-adjusted relationship he enjoyed with his family. Gorbachev had a friendly, affectionate relationship with his father. The father and son worked together around the clock to bring in the harvest when Mikhail was a teen-ager; they discussed news and confided in each other. The father treated the son like an equal. In the summer of 1948, as they worked side by side, Mikhail earned a medal, *Orden' Trudovogo Krasnogo Znameni* (The Order of the Red Banner of Labor), and his father received the more prestigious *Orden' Lenina* (The Order of Lenin). Gorbachev took pride in this accomplishment for the rest of his life; in his memoirs, written in the 1990s, he still described this as his greatest honor.[2] Throughout most of his political life within the *nomenklatura* hierarchy, Gorbachev seems to have believed in the system and to have been committed to improving its functioning.

Gorbachev knew how to get ahead by getting along. In one-on-one conversation, he was the type of man who could "read" the orientations and preferences of his interlocutors, shift his own posture to accord with theirs, and get them to believe that he was sympathetic to their position – even when his goal was to change their mind.[3] This trait served him well as he rose

---

[2] Mikhail Gorbachev, *Zhizn' i reformy,* vol. 1 (Moscow: Novosti, 1996), p. 56.
[3] These were impressions an American journalist reached from interviewing people who knew Gorbachev as a young man (Hedrick Smith, *The New Russians* [New York: Random House, 1990], pp. 41, 49). Archie Brown (*The Gorbachev Factor* [Oxford & New York: Oxford

within the hierarchy. He greeted many Politburo members who visited and vacationed in Stavropol in the 1970s, socializing with them in informal settings.[4] He managed to impress them both as politically reliable and as an intelligent, dynamic regional leader with interesting new ideas about how to make the system perform better. As D'Agostino pithily summarizes it, "Gorbachev's various patrons might often have been at odds with each other, but Gorbachev seems somehow not to have accumulated enemies, not even the enemies of his friends."[5] There is no evidence either of the seething resentment toward superiors in Moscow or of the severe impatience that Yeltsin appears to have suppressed, at times imperfectly, during the early 1980s.

Once co-opted into the Brezhnev Politburo, Gorbachev seated himself as far from Brezhnev as possible and avoided showing his disgust when Brezhnev made a gaffe.[6] He notes in his memoirs that, in Brezhnev's Moscow, the most important thing was to "know one's place": never to overstep the boundaries of one's position and rank.[7] Once in power, Gorbachev's tactical caution remained a defining characteristic of his political personality, even as he was attempting to change the system. Fyodor Burlatskii, on the basis of interviews with many of Gorbachev's aides and associates, argues that Gorbachev was "prone to compromise" and preferred to play "the sure hand," which "irritated the direct and passionate Yeltsin," who was more inclined to take risks.[8]

Colleagues describe Gorbachev as a man of immense energy, passion, intelligence, and eagerness to solve problems.[9] One aide describes Gorbachev's

---

University Press, 1996], p. 37) makes the more limited claim that Gorbachev possessed "an ability to get along with people of different views and dispositions." Reportedly, psychologists who worked for the U.S. Central Intelligence Agency, and who were observing Gorbachev during his years in power, concluded that "he is keenly intuitive; he senses the situation and reads people on the spot, managing his inner reactions so that he can shift from charming to tough to malleable to menacing in the space of moments" (reported in Gail Sheehy, *The Man Who Changed the World* [New York: HarperCollins, 1990], p. 10).

[4] V. I. Boldin, *Krushenie p'edestala: Shtrikhi k portretu M.S. Gorbacheva* (Moscow: Respublika, 1995), p. 127; see also Brown, *The Gorbachev Factor*, pp. 49–51.

[5] Anthony D'Agostino, *Gorbachev's Revolution* (New York: NYU Press, 1998), p. 58.

[6] Gorbachev, *Zhizn'*, vol. 1, pp. 182–3.

[7] Ibid, p. 182.

[8] Fyodor Burlatskii, *Glotok svobody*, vol. 2 (Moscow: RIK Kul'tura, 1997), pp. 122, 129–30. Admittedly, this is tricky terminology. One could also argue that Gorbachev, while in power, was "risk-acceptant" in seeking to transform the system and that Yeltsin, in 1985–1989, was "reckless." The distinction among terms like "caution," "risk-acceptance," and "recklessness" often hinges on the observer's values or on his perception of the magnitude of constraints on change.

[9] Anatolii Chernyaev, *Shest' let s Gorbachevym* (Moscow: Progress, 1993) pp. 8–9; Pavel Palazchenko, *My Years with Gorbachev and Shevardnadze: The Memoir of a Soviet Interpreter* (University Park: Pennsylvania State University Press, 1997), p. 107. Both Boldin and Ligachev,

ability to become genuinely fascinated by new things, a trait that hardly characterized older members of the Brezhnev Politburo in the 1970s.[10] Another aide, Anatolii Chernyaev, accompanied Gorbachev to Western Europe in 1972 and was mightily impressed by how effectively Gorbachev briefed Belgian communists on the "battle for bread" that was then being conducted in the USSR, as well as by his enthusiasm and liveliness: "he clearly stood out in comparison to other regional Party leaders with his extraordinariness (*nyeordinarnost'*) and his passion."[11] When he returned to Moscow, Chernyaev told his boss, Boris Ponomarev (head of the International Department of the Central Committee), that Gorbachev was just the right kind of Party official "to uphold the 'image' of the CPSU among fraternal parties," adding that he had never before met anyone as good as Gorbachev at impressing foreigners.[12]

Gorbachev's passion and enthusiasm were not just for show. Chernyaev also reports that, while driving through the Belgian and Dutch countryside in 1972, Gorbachev "almost did not look outside .... [Instead], he grabbed me by the elbows and 'proved,' 'proved,' 'proved' how important it was to do this or that in Stavropol."[13] Gorbachev would "prove" that something needed to be done – or could be done – and would thereby convince his audiences that it *had* to be done. Here we see a preview of the general secretary whose leadership style was based on convincing people that *perestroika* was desirable, necessary, and feasible: "there is no other way." Indeed, Gorbachev was a self-confident debater, a man who took pride in his capacity for logical argumentation and impressive self-presentation. In his memoirs he claims that, by his junior year as a law student, he could debate as well as the very best of his classmates. He prided himself on not being afraid to show weakness by asking questions; this honed his skills as a debater.[14]

Many political leaders are self-confident and have strong egos; indeed, that may be a prerequisite for achieving "greatness." But Gorbachev's self-confidence was joined to a genuinely *optimistic* mind-set. Many observers

antagonists of Gorbachev when they wrote their memoirs, recall Gorbachev's workaholic tendencies (Yegor Ligachev, *Inside Gorbachev's Kremlin* [New York: Pantheon, 1993], p. 148; Boldin, *Krushenie,* p. 34); see also the sources used in Brown, *The Gorbachev Factor,* pp. 31–43, and Smith, *The New Russians,* pp. 41, 44ff., 59ff. Sheehy (*The Man,* p. 136) quotes the Soviet Ambassador to the United States, after his first meeting with Gorbachev, as calling him "an insatiable hurricane of a person."

[10] Palazchenko, *My Years,* p. 107; for testimony to this effect by people who knew him during his days at Moscow State University, see Smith, *The New Russians,* pp. 46–7.

[11] Chernyaev, *Shest' let,* p. 8.

[12] Ibid.

[13] Ibid.

[14] Gorbachev, *Zhizn',* vol. 1, p. 61.

recall the young Gorbachev as an optimist, which is all the more remarkable considering the apocalyptic circumstances of his youth (collectivization, the Great Terror, and World War II). His official translator reports that General Secretary Gorbachev was intensely optimistic about the realizability of the reforms he had begun.[15] Others witnessed this trait but did not share the optimism. As one close advisor is reported to have said in the late-1980s: "I know we can't succeed. But when I get in front of that warm and charming man who wants so much to do something for the country, I have no heart to tell him that we can't succeed."[16] Whether at the level of local campaigns in Stavropol or with respect to reform of the Soviet system as a whole, Gorbachev was clearly an idealist whose beliefs and actions were sustained by a passionate and optimistic, yet carefully controlled, personality.

Optimism, passion, intensity, curiosity, egocentrism, insatiable energy, and self-confidence – combined with risk control, prudence, and calculating other-directedness – are personality traits that Gorbachev brought to the table as he chose his political strategy for reforming the system, once he had the power to do so. But such traits do not reveal the *content* of a person's beliefs: just what are they optimistic, passionate, and energetic about, and toward what ends do they exercise prudence and risk control? For these questions, we must explore Gorbachev's political beliefs.

GORBACHEV'S POLITICAL BELIEFS

Gorbachev's political rise was likely facilitated by his combination of demonstrated political reliability and personal dynamism, both in "selling" the system to external audiences and in experimenting with the system to make it work better. Indeed, these traits lent credibility to his claims, once appointed general secretary, that he would make the system realize its full potential. But what did he believe in? And why did he become a *reformist* general secretary?

There is considerable disagreement in the scholarly literature about Gorbachev's ideological commitments. Most of the debate, however, concerns how far Gorbachev's beliefs and attitudes evolved during his years as general secretary of the Central Committee of the CPSU. One view has it that, through a combination of domestic and international influences, he evolved by 1989–1990 into a social democrat and an anti-Leninist – akin, in these respects, to

---

[15] Palazchenko, *My Years*, p. 123.
[16] Dusko Doder and Louise Branson, *Gorbachev: Heretic in the Kremlin* (New York: Viking, 1990), p. 304.

the leadership of the Socialist Party of Spain.[17] A contrary view argues that he evolved into a "socialist democrat" akin to the Mensheviks of 1917, as opposed to having become a Bernsteinian socialist or a social democrat.[18] Still others view Gorbachev as either confused, bungling, or consistently despotic.[19]

There is less disagreement about Gorbachev's political and ideological commitments before he came to power in 1985. Gorbachev shared the sense of patriotic fervor that many members of his generation experienced in the wake of World War II and the period of reconstruction that followed. Thereafter, as he built his career, his views on policy were heavily influenced by Khrushchev's de-Stalinization campaign and by the widespread corruption and socioeconomic stagnation of the late-Brezhnev era.[20] Moreover, his travels in Eastern and Western Europe during the late 1960s exposed him to the relative opulence of the West – all the more so when compared to conditions in Stavropol[21] – while the invasion of Czechoslovakia in 1968 left him ambivalent about the wisdom and justice of suppressing the "Prague Spring."[22] These points of attraction and repulsion combined to make him susceptible to new ideas about how to reform the system – or how to assist the system to realize its potential – once he had a chance to make a difference in the late 1970s.[23]

According to associates and aides, by the early 1980s Gorbachev was already an anti-Stalinist and a reform communist who was convinced that the

---

[17] See Brown, *The Gorbachev Factor*, and Robert D. English, *Russia and the Idea of the West: Gorbachev, Intellectuals and the End of the Cold War* (New York: Columbia University Press, 2000).

[18] Ken Jowitt, *New World Disorder: The Leninist Extinction* (Berkeley: University of California Press, 1992), ch. 6; Stephen E. Hanson, *Time and Revolution: Marxism and the Design of Soviet Institutions* (Chapel Hill: University of North Carolina Press, 1997), ch. 6; D'Agostino, *Gorbachev's Revolution*.

[19] On Gorbachev as a despotic bungler who sought to strengthen the socialist system, not fundamentally transform it, see Donald Murray, *A Democracy of Despots* (Boulder, CO: Westview, 1995); on Gorbachev as a confused Leninist who sought to democratize socialism but had little idea how to do so, see Jerry F. Hough, *Democratization and Revolution in the USSR, 1985–1991* (Washington, DC: Brookings Institution, 1997).

[20] On this score, Hanson and Brown are in agreement (Hanson, *Time and Revolution*, p. 183; Brown, *The Gorbachev Factor*, pp. 39–41 and ch. 3). There are also incidents from Gorbachev's earlier years that reveal a streak of resentment against those who enjoyed undeserved privilege; see the incidents reported in D'Agostino, *Gorbachev's Revolution*, p. 53, and Sheehy, *The Man*, pp. 74–5.

[21] Dmitry Mikheyev, *The Rise and Fall of Gorbachev* (Indianapolis, IN: Hudson Institute, 1992), p. 32; Brown, *The Gorbachev Factor*, pp. 41–3.

[22] Brown, *The Gorbachev Factor*, p. 41; English, *Russia and the Idea*, pp. 181–2.

[23] Brown (*The Gorbachev Factor*, pp. 40–1) documents the ambivalence-enhancing impact of these revelations on Gorbachev's thinking. Moreover, in Stavropol Gorbachev participated in the resettlement of populations that had been deported by Stalin but were allowed by Khrushchev to return to their native lands (D'Agostino, *Gorbachev's Revolution*, p. 53).

Soviet system needed to change ("we cannot go on living in this way"[24]) but who imagined such change to be much more modest than the transformations he would eventually sponsor in the late 1980s.[25] Consistent with his upbringing within the Party apparatus, Gorbachev came to power believing that the root of most problems lay in corrupted cadres and that a necessary (though not sufficient) condition for solving most problems was the recruitment of uncorrupted cadres. He thought that reform would succeed and the system would realize its potential only if the right personnel were recruited into key positions in the Party apparatus.[26] According to his closest aide, Gorbachev's initial goal was to replace personnel and then to build "businesslike, comradely, and honest" relations within the Communist Party.[27] This vision required him to purge the corrupted cadres and mobilize the uncorrupted cadres by persuading them to join him in building a reformed Leninist political order. It called for restructuring authority relationships, though it did not anticipate the extent of restructuring that would be required to restore the legitimacy and effectiveness of the political order.

With respect to international relations, Gorbachev also shed some fundamental beliefs and predispositions of the Brezhnev era. Before he came to power, Gorbachev had already concluded that an end to the Cold War was a necessary condition for restoring the Soviet Union's health at home and prestige abroad, that Soviet foreign policy had to be demilitarized (including withdrawal from Afghanistan), that Soviet domination of Eastern Europe by military means had to end, and that the Soviet Union had to develop close ties with West European governments.[28] Moreover, he articulated a commitment to nonviolence as a principle of political order (*"nye streliat'"*: "no more shooting"[29]) that would eventually have portentous consequences for his control of processes of change within Eastern Europe and the Soviet Union as well. It is doubtful that he was a committed pacifist, but he clearly much preferred that the renewal of socialism be based on persuasion and not on violence. Thus, rather than viewing Gorbachev as an "uncommitted thinker,"[30] it is more fruitful to think of him as starting his general secretaryship as an

---

[24] Cited in Brown, *The Gorbachev Factor*, p. 81.

[25] Ibid., ch. 3; Smith, *The New Russians*, pp. 68–72.

[26] Chernyaev, *Shest' let*, p. 123; Gorbachev, *Zhizn'*, vol. 1, pp. 286–92 (chapter entitled: "Cadres decide everything"); Boldin, *Krushenie*, pp. 45–7.

[27] Chernyaev, *Shest' let*, p. 23.

[28] For documentation, see English, *Russia and the Idea*, pp. 183–4, 194, 199–200.

[29] Andrei Grachev, *Kremlevskaia khronika* (Moscow: EKSMO, 1994), p. 113.

[30] Janice Gross Stein, "Political learning by doing: Gorbachev as uncommitted thinker and motivated learner," *International Organization*, vol. 48, no. 2 (Spring 1994), pp. 155–83.

anti-Stalinist, a "reform communist," and an anti-militarist who was already committed to creating a less militarized international order and a reformed socialist political order at home. Beyond that, the evidence suggests that Gorbachev was actively searching and feeling his way and was indeed a highly "motivated learner."[31]

Such beliefs were not incompatible with being an organization man who enjoyed good relations with his superiors. Many journalists, academics, and officials were "within-system" dissidents who had come to view Brezhnevism as an embarrassment and were searching for a reformist alternative. Khrushchev's de-Stalinization had been a formative experience for them, just as it was for Gorbachev. Moreover, the Marxist–Leninist tradition held out the vision of a one-party socialist democracy, which allowed these people to rationalize that (a) the alternative to Stalinism was not capitalism but rather reform Leninism and (b) "socialism" could be made consistent with procedural democracy.[32]

Gorbachev viewed the achievement of such a goal as requiring more than just organizational measures. It also required painstaking doctrinal justification. He placed great stock in the power of ideas, both oral and written, as a means of mobilizing support and demobilizing potential opponents. This reflected his education and belief in Marxism–Leninism, his training in legal studies, and his self-confidence as a debater. While a regional Party leader, he placed great stock in logical argumentation as a means of justifying policy choices. Colleagues in Stavropol recall his knowledge of Party history, the works of Lenin, and Marxism–Leninism.[33] In the first years of *perestroika*, Gorbachev again immersed himself in Lenin's works, which he re-read; he had a complete set of Lenin's works in his office and often read passages aloud to his chief of staff, V. Boldin. According to Boldin, Gorbachev believed that publications made possible the spreading of the word, which was crucial to progress: "he considered his words to be the main thing, one of the most important instruments of accomplishment (*metodov raboty*)."[34] But to Gorbachev this was more than just political justification; his attention to "the word" was also part of an active, intellectual search within the record of Lenin's last years for relevant truths about how to reform Soviet socialism.

---

[31] Ibid.
[32] For a book-length exposition of this thesis by one such within-system dissident, see Roy Medvedev, *On Socialist Democracy* (Nottingham, U.K.: Spokesman, 1977); a good source of insight into the reformist mentality in the Politburo after Gorbachev came to power is Chernyaev, *Shest' let*, passim.
[33] Brown, *The Gorbachev Factor*, pp. 31–2.
[34] Boldin, *Krushenie*, p. 12; also see pp. 132, 133, 293, 378.

As general secretary, Gorbachev edited and re-edited texts of articles and speeches with great passion. He devoted his vacation of August 1987 to completion of his book, *Perestroika: New Thinking for our Country and the World*.[35] As late as 1988, Gorbachev read transcripts of the first Party congresses after 1917 in connection with his desire to reorganize the apparatus.[36] Thus, Gorbachev sought political rhetoric that would provide compelling slogans, extended theoretical justification of policy changes, and a guide to programmatic development.

Gorbachev was not an impulsive or extemporaneous debater. He liked to mull issues; he developed his thoughts through contemplation, discussion, and writing. He searched constantly for evidence of success or failure in public policy and simultaneously searched for new theoretical formulations or generalizations to reconcile empirical reality with socialist theory. He was, then, a contemplative man who, by Leninist standards, kept an open mind and was eager to learn. He liked to go for long walks in the woods with his wife or his colleagues to talk about issues and develop his ideas.[37] When he visited Canada in 1983, during Andropov's time in power, Gorbachev abandoned the official program and spent hours talking with then-Ambassador Aleksandr Yakovlev about the future of Russia.[38] In both Stavropol and Moscow, Gorbachev sought out informed, cultured people – including foreigners – for extended discussions, during which he worked out his own ideas.[39] It was during a long stroll with Eduard Shevardnadze in 1984 that the two men came to agreement that "everything has gone rotten."[40]

Given his combination of idealism, optimism, energy, intelligence, demonstrated political reliability, and cautious, manipulative political tactics, Gorbachev was perhaps ideally suited to the task he set for himself: to break the Soviet Union out of the Brezhnevite mold at home and abroad before wouldbe opponents could mobilize to prevent him from doing so. It is more difficult to conceive of Boris Yeltsin successfully doing the same had he been general secretary in 1985–1987.

---

[35] New York: Harper & Row, 1988.

[36] Chernyaev, *Shest' let*, p. 223.

[37] In his memoirs, he credits nature with "forming" him and his views (Gorbachev, *Zhizn'*, vol. 1, p. 173; see also p. 172).

[38] Grachev, *Kremlevskaia*, p. 140; see also the documentation and discussion in English, *Russia and the Idea*, p. 184.

[39] Grachev, *Kremlevskaia*, pp. 177–8; English, *Russia and the Idea*, pp. 180–6.

[40] Brown, *The Gorbachev Factor*, p. 81; Carolyn McGiffert Ekedahl and Melvin A. Goodman, *The Wars of Eduard Shevardnadze* (University Park: Pennsylvania State University Press, 1997), p. 30.

YELTSIN'S POLITICAL PERSONALITY AND BELIEFS

In 1985, after he had been in power only a few months, Gorbachev brought to Moscow to work in the Central Committee apparatus a provincial Party leader, Boris Yeltsin, who had headed the Sverdlovsk Party organization, one of the largest in the country, for almost a decade. As we now know, neither Gorbachev nor most other members of the Politburo anticipated the trouble they were buying.[41]

Within the ranks of regional Party first secretaries in the late-Brezhnev era, several types of leaders could be found. The distinction was not generational. All of them, for reasons of either identity or material interests, shared a common commitment to the "leading role of the Party" in the political system. But beyond that, their political personalities diverged. Some, such as Grishin (Moscow) and Romanov (Leningrad), were the aristocrats of Brezhnevite infamy; they reflected and reinforced the personal corruption of the era and stood for continuity in policy. Others, such as Ligachev (Tomsk), were the puritans who found corruption to be shameful and who honed their skills on trying to crack down on corruption within their province. Still others, such as Bogomiakov (Tyumen), were technocratic in their orientation and sought to integrate rational, scientific expertise and orderly procedure into problem solving within their domains. And a few others, such as Shevardnadze of Georgia, were gutsy reformists who sought ways to decentralize aspects of the command system in order to devise a Party-led system that would be more efficient and more legitimate. The puritans, technocrats, and reformists would eventually part ways, but they all initially thought of themselves as opponents of corrupt Brezhnevism and as believers in *perestroika*.

Yeltsin had been first secretary of the Sverdlovsk Party organization since 1976. Before that, most of his professional life had been spent as a construction engineer and supervisor of construction projects. His love of construction comes through in his first autobiography and was clearly a passion of his during early adulthood.[42] There is no evidence that Yeltsin was corrupt

---

[41] Gorbachev's prime minister, Nikolai Ryzhkov, claims in his memoirs that he warned Gorbachev and Ligachev against appointing Yeltsin as first secretary of the Moscow city Party committee. According to Ryzhkov, he advised them about Yeltsin that "even though he is a builder, by his nature he is a destroyer" (Nikolai Ryzhkov, *Desiat' let velikikh potriasenii* [Moscow, 1995], p. 139). Ryzhkov had worked with Yeltsin for many years in Sverdlovsk.

[42] Boris Yeltsin, *Against the Grain: An Autobiography*, trans. by Michael Glenny (New York: Summit, 1990), pp. 43–56, 78–9, 108; for details of Yeltsin's work in construction, see Leon Aron, *Boris Yeltsin: A Revolutionary Life* (London: HarperCollins, 2000), ch. 2.

as Party leader in Sverdlovsk; like Ligachev, whose recommendation was the trigger for drawing him into the central Party apparatus, Yeltsin lived a relatively austere personal life and fought against political corruption. He used his powers as Party leader in Sverdlovsk to prosecute campaigns against corrupt members of the *nomenklatura* and some of the socioeconomic privileges they enjoyed. He thus combined the technical skills of a technocrat with the personal and political orientation so valued by the puritans.[43]

As for his accomplishments as local Party leader, the central Party leadership had every reason to expect that he would fulfill their hopes. His record during almost nine years as head of the Sverdlovsk *obkom* (provincial Party committee) indicated that he was a tough, effective taskmaster. Yeltsin himself referred to his leadership as analogous to that of a tsar, in total control of his province.[44] In dealing with officials, "[w]hether I was chairing a meeting, running my office, or delivering a report to a plenum – everything that one did was expressed in terms of pressure, threats, and coercion."[45]

Had this been all, Yeltsin might have satisfied Brezhnev but not Gorbachev and Ligachev. But there was more. He is said to have been relatively popular among the population of this large, important province. He is said to have improved the economic situation and the standard of living in Sverdlovsk province, pushing his subordinates hard but never asking them to work any harder than he – a workaholic's workaholic – was himself prepared to work. He was personally involved in supervising construction projects in the province, not defining his role as that of a paper-pusher. He lobbied the authorities in Moscow for large sums of money to fund major new projects in the province. He pressed for greater regional autonomy in industrial administration, so that campaigns for restructuring of enterprises could yield results.[46]

This was the CPSU's ideal of a leader: someone capable of effectively leading campaigns of *shturmovshchina* (storming) while gaining some popularity among the bulk of the population. Yeltsin apparently believed in the system

---

[43] See Aron, *Boris Yeltsin,* pp. 45–6, 86, 88, 104–5; Mikheyev, *Russia Transformed,* pp. 52–7; John Morrison, *Boris Yeltsin: From Bolshevik to Democrat* (New York: Dutton, 1991), pp. 31–42; Yeltsin, *Against the Grain,* pp. 43–70, 88–9. Yeltsin was also very fond of alcohol, which distinguished him from Ligachev. And Gorbachev cursed frequently during private discussions with aides, in contrast to Yeltsin. (Neither Gorbachev nor Yeltsin nor Ligachev was a smoker.) "Puritanism," as here used, merely means uncorrupted.

[44] Yeltsin, *Against the Grain,* p. 70; Boris Yeltsin, *The Struggle for Russia,* trans. by Catherine A. Fitzpatrick (New York: Random House, 1994), p. 179.

[45] Quoted in Morrison, *Boris Yeltsin,* p. 40.

[46] For documentation of the claims in this paragraph, see Aron, *Boris Yeltsin,* ch. 3.

and was skilled at making it work. In sum, he found ways of selectively over-coming "stagnation" without challenging the leading role of the Party.[47] This was the traditional ideal of the Party leader who was tough, bright, informed, relentless, and respected – except among the corrupt officials whom Yeltsin tried to purge. But presumably that was fine with Gorbachev and Ligachev, who shared this goal and who brought Yeltsin to Moscow and, eight months later, put him in charge of cleaning up corruption in the huge Moscow city Party organization.

Yeltsin also appeared to be politically reliable. His speeches as regional Party leader were often critical of central planning organs for paying insuf-ficient attention to regional needs.[48] But such was the case, more generally, with speeches by the most dynamic and influential regional first secretaries, including Gorbachev before he came to Moscow in 1978.[49] On politically sensitive issues, Yeltsin apparently toed the line – and then some. When an anthrax epidemic broke out in the province in April 1979, Yeltsin did an excel-lent job of preventing the outside world from learning of it.[50] When, in 1978, the Politburo ordered the bulldozing of the house in which the Tsar Nicholas and his family had been executed by the Bolsheviks in 1918, Yeltsin carried out the orders immediately, fully, and efficiently.[51] When the cultural intelli-gentsia pushed too far to circumvent the censors, Yeltsin cracked down.[52] In sum, there was no reason for the authorities in Moscow to believe that Yeltsin was a maverick or a loose cannon, much less a liberal.

Yeltsin's leadership style in Sverdlovsk was idiosyncratic for the region, and this could have caught the eye of the Central Committee apparatus. Re-searchers have found that, in contrast to his predecessors, he had an open style

---

[47] Studies of Yeltsin's earlier career that reach conclusions roughly equivalent to those in this paragraph include Aron, *Boris Yeltsin,* chs. 1–3, and Mikheyev, *Russia Transformed,* ch. 3. For a more critical view, see Pilar Bonet, "Lord of the manor: Boris Yeltsin in Sverdlovsk *oblast'*," Occasional Paper no. 260 (Washington, DC: Kennan Institute, 1995), p. 1, and Pilar Bonet, "Nevozmozhnaia Rossiia. Boris Yeltsin, provintsial v Kremlye," translated from the Spanish by G. Luk'ianova in *Ural* (Yekaterinburg), no. 4 (April 1994), pp. 24, 141.

[48] See Aron, *Boris Yeltsin,* pp. 60–78.

[49] For a content analysis of the speeches of regional Party leaders in the late 1970s, see George W. Breslauer, "Is there a generation gap in the Soviet political elite?" *Soviet Studies,* vol. 36, no. 1 (January 1984), pp. 1–25.

[50] Aron, *Boris Yeltsin,* pp. 52–3.

[51] Ibid., pp. 111–13.

[52] Ibid., pp. 118–25; for other examples of Yeltsin's political conformism in those days, see Yu. M. Baturin, A. L. Il'in, V. F. Kadatskii, V. V. Kostikov, M. A. Krasnov, A. Ya. Livshits, K. F. Nikiforov, L. G. Pikhoia, and G. A. Satarov, *Epokha Yel'tsina: Ocherki politicheskoi istorii* (Moscow: Vagrius, 2001), pp. 38, 40.

of leadership: he met regularly with groups and held lengthy, candid question-and-answer sessions with them. He addressed the public regularly on local television. During the Andropov era, he led "raids" on local retail stores to force them to expose hoarded goods and release them for public purchase. He often came to work by public transportation, not always using the limousines available to regional Party first secretaries.[53] None of this, however, would necessarily have alarmed members of the Politburo who were considering him for promotion. As long as Yeltsin remained in firm control of his region, maintained social stability, and fulfilled the economic Plan, then an open, accessible style of leadership was a plus, for it demonstrated that Party leadership could simultaneously be exacting, effective, and, if not popular, at least respected. Yeltsin's use of public transportation both reinforced his anti-corruption campaign and muted popular resentment of Party privileges. Indeed, Gorbachev himself, when head of the Stavropol Party organization, frequently walked to work.[54]

Some questions might have been raised by a glance at Yeltsin's résumé. He had never served as a second-in-command. In Mikheyev's opinion, Yeltsin's meteoric rise within the Party organization "allowed him to skip a critically important part of the process of integration into the Party's organizational culture: he was never forced to adopt the humiliating posture of total submissiveness and the denigrating requirement to please one's superiors by all possible means."[55] This, according to Mikheyev, allowed him to retain both some independence of mind and some self-confidence and identity,[56] which may have been one of the roots of Yeltsin's maverick qualities in Gorbachev's Politburo. But assuming it was noticed by those considering his promotion in 1984–1985, it would not necessarily have raised eyebrows. For the new Soviet leaders were looking for uncorrupted and talented officials who could improve and selectively reform the system without challenging its essential features. They were not looking for Brezhnevite aristocrats, whose independence of mind and initiative (if they ever possessed them) had been fully ground down

---

[53] Mikheyev, *Russia Transformed,* p. 56; Vladimir Solovyov and Elena Klepikova, *Boris Yeltsin: A Political Biography* (New York: Putnam, 1992), pp. 152–4; Aron, *Yeltsin,* pp. 79–92. Yeltsin's chief of staff during 1993–1995 reports in his memoir that he saw a television program about Yeltsin during his years as Party leader in Sverdlovsk province in which Yeltsin came across as a loyal Party functionary, but even then he "exhibited a kind of openness, energy, and good knowledge of the subject about which he spoke freely" (Sergei Filatov, *Sovershenno nesekretno* [Moscow: Vagrius, 2000], pp. 421–2).

[54] Donald Morrison (Ed.), *Mikhail S. Gorbachev: An Intimate Biography* (New York: Time, 1988), p. 98.

[55] Mikheyev, *Russia Transformed,* p. 57.

[56] Ibid., p. 58.

by the Party's personnel mechanisms. The fact that Yeltsin had a background that prevented him from becoming complacent and corrupt would have been viewed as an asset; it was not necessarily a sign that he would become a disruptive force within the Politburo.

What the central Party leaders probably did not know was that Yeltsin had other personality traits that, when combined with his lack of submissiveness, would indeed make him a loose cannon. Yeltsin was impulsive, temperamental, easy to offend, and very sensitive to slights. He did not imagine himself just a construction engineer who had become a Party boss; he thought of himself as a turnaround artist, capable of undertaking wholesale cleanup operations that would break most men. When momentous results were not forthcoming, Yeltsin became frustrated and angry.[57]

Moreover, and more seriously, Yeltsin chafed in positions of subordination and was upset, as Sverdlovsk Party leader, that his peers (Gorbachev and Ligachev) had risen farther and faster within the Party apparatus than he had. He admitted as much in his first autobiography, written and published in 1990.[58] Central Party leaders would not have known, in 1984, just how resentful he was on this score. Nor would they have known that when Central Committee secretary Ligachev had earlier come to visit Sverdlovsk for an inspection tour, Yeltsin had to exit the car in which they were riding together in order to contain his rage at Ligachev's demeaning questions about why things allegedly were not done in Sverdlovsk the way Ligachev had done them in Tomsk. Yeltsin summoned his deputy in the car behind them to take his place in the car with Ligachev, lest Yeltsin say or do something impulsive.[59] None of this boded well for Yeltsin's containing his emotions in Moscow and being a team player.[60]

In addition to being impulsive and impatient, Yeltsin had been a risk-taker – indeed, a risk-seeker – all his life. It may not be an exaggeration to say that he was genetically programmed for risk, and developmentally he became addicted to it. His brother Mikhail wrote that Boris always "lived on the edge

[57] On Yeltsin's self-image, see Yeltsin, *Against the Grain*, pp. 76–80, 108–10, 114, 118–25, 231.

[58] Ibid., pp. 72–3.

[59] Bonet, "Nevozmozhnaia Rossiia," pp. 105–6; presumably Ligachev did not learn of this, because John Morrison reports that Ligachev was extremely enthusiastic about Yeltsin when he returned to Moscow (Morrison, *Boris Yeltsin*, p. 42). Aron (*Yeltsin*, pp. 116–17) reports on something like this incident but does not have Yeltsin exiting the car – just grinding his teeth.

[60] A source that cannot be cited also told me that, when Yeltsin was in Texas in 1989, he became so angry at something said by his American host that he ordered the chauffeur to stop the car, exited it in the middle of the ride, and began running down the street to contain his anger. An analogous example is found in Yeltsin's walking out of a televised interview with Leslie Stahl in Moscow in June 1992 (Associated Press, June, 1992).

of possibilities."[61] Yeltsin's first two autobiographies are littered with examples, from early childhood through 1993, of his inclination to live on the edge. His risk-seeking did not find expression in the technological realm: as a construction engineer, he engaged in careful study before tackling complex tasks. Rather, it found expression in his personal and political life. Yeltsin reports several instances of his talking back to hierarchical superiors during the Stalin era and getting away with it.[62] As a child of only 11 years, he claims to have used the primary school graduation ceremony to denounce publicly a teacher who, he felt, was treating the students unfairly.[63]

Yeltsin's adventuresome spirit often led him into close brushes with death and, in a few cases, with political ruin. As a child, he insisted on trying to defuse a hand grenade that he and his friends had stolen from an ammunition depot. As his friends stood back at his insistence, he handled the grenade; it exploded and blew off two of his fingers.[64] I count nineteen such incidents in the two autobiographies, not all of them quite as dramatic but several of them equally so.[65] Even if some of the stories are apocryphal, no literature on Yeltsin has attempted to refute the general pattern. Someone who has led this kind of life and always survived close brushes develops an enormous confidence in his survival capacities, if he did not have it to begin with. That confidence, in turn, further fuels the inclination to succumb to impulse and to continue taking risks. In the case of Yeltsin, it even led him to believe in his own predestination: "It always seems as if someone is rescuing me. I've even begun to believe that I'm under some mysterious protection."[66]

Many of Yeltsin's traits were not unique to him among post-Stalinist leaders. Indeed, they bore some striking resemblances to Nikita Khrushchev. Khrushchev was also a risk-taker (though not a self-destructive one). Khrushchev also had an impulsive streak and was hugely impatient to see results. He too was temperamental and very sensitive to slights. Indeed, more than many

---

[61] Mikheyev, *Russia Transformed*, p. 66.
[62] Yeltsin, *Against the Grain*, pp. 27, 50, 53.
[63] Ibid., p. 27.
[64] Ibid., p. 29.
[65] Ibid., pp. 22, 29, 36, 45, 46, 47, 258–9; Yeltsin, *The Struggle for Russia*, pp. 30, 46–7, 61, 93, 117–19, 191–2, 194, 195–6, 239.
[66] Yeltsin, *The Struggle for Russia*, p. 197 (see also pp. 84, 120, 142, 193, 205, 211); Yeltsin, *Against the Grain*, pp. 19, 154, 162. In his most recent memoir, published nine months after he resigned from the presidency, Yeltsin writes that, in a golf cart, "I like to zoom downhill and aim for a tree, then turn at the last moment. That's how I relax" (Boris Yeltsin, *Midnight Diaries* [New York: Public Affairs, 2000], p. 311). It is doubtful that, in his present physical condition, Yeltsin engages in this practice; his use of the present tense in this passage more than strains credulity.

others in the late-Stalinist Politburo, Khrushchev chafed under the humiliation of Stalin's rule, though he was astute enough not to risk his life by
challenging the despot. And Khrushchev, too, proved to be a loose cannon
in the post-Stalin leadership, first in launching his anti-Stalin campaign and
later in reacting to the frustration of his program. Eventually, his capricious-
ness cost him his job. The difference was that, in the 1950s and early 1960s,
Khrushchev was on top, while in the 1980s, Yeltsin was a junior member of
Gorbachev's Politburo.[67]

Ironically, Gorbachev, who was on top in the 1980s, was haunted by the
prospect that, if he moved too fast with his reforms, he might suffer Khrushchev's fate and be forced out of office. It appears not to have occurred to
him that a man with some of Khrushchev's personality traits and perspectives
would join the leadership team and complicate his own political life – precisely because Gorbachev's caution, embraced to avoid Khrushchev's fate, so
frustrated the neo-Khrushchevian, Yeltsin!

In addition to being of almost identical age, Yeltsin shared with Gorbachev a number of personality traits: enormous energy, passion, intensity,
self-confidence, egocentrism, workaholic tendencies, and a highly retentive
memory. He also shared Gorbachev's disillusionment with Brezhnevism and
his urge to improve the socialist system, initially by purging corrupt cadres.
Both men were provincials of peasant background, men whose families had
suffered greatly during collectivization and the Great Terror and who were
offended by corruption and unearned privilege. Both came from austere backgrounds – Yeltsin more so than Gorbachev – but made their careers by dint
of extraordinarily hard work.[68] As regional Party leaders, both men were

---

[67] Reading in Aron's book about Yeltsin's style of leadership in Sverdlovsk, I am struck by other
parallels with Khrushchev: (1) Yeltsin's leadership of construction projects (Aron, *Yeltsin*, p.
31) is reminiscent of Khrushchev's hands-on, no-nonsense, workaholic style in supervising
construction of the Moscow subway in the 1930s (see William J. Tompson, *Khrushchev: A
Political Life* [London: St. Martin's, 1995], ch. 2); (2) both men abhorred leadership "from the
desk," wanting to get personally involved in the construction (Aron, p. 38; Tompson, p. 45);
(3) both men sought to strengthen the disciplinary responsibility of the work collective and
the effect of collective material rewards (Aron, p. 67; George W. Breslauer, *Khrushchev and
Brezhnev as Leaders* [London: Allen & Unwin, 1982], chs. 2, 4); (4) Yeltsin put forth a proposal for the regional deconcentration of industry during the Brezhnev era that was strikingly
similar to Khrushchev's *sovnarkhoz* scheme of 1957 (Aron, p. 76 – Aron remarks on this parallel with Khrushchev); and (5) both men were quick to blame local officials for setbacks and
to call immediately for their dismissal (Aron, p. 83; Breslauer, *Khrushchev and Brezhnev*,
chs. 3, 6).

[68] Indeed, they both wore (and wore out) only one suit throughout their college years, which in
both cases ended with graduation in 1955. But Gorbachev grew up in better material conditions than Yeltsin. The Stavropol *krai* is part of the productive Black Earth (*chernozem*)

ambitious, hard-working, relatively uncorrupted, and innovative in devising local experiments that might improve the operations of the local economy and that might also (they claimed) fruitfully be generalized to the national economy.[69] Both men devised a more populist, consultative style of leadership of their provinces than was standard under Brezhnev. And, of course, both men had to temper their dissatisfactions by engaging in the dissimulation and doublespeak that were requisites for political survival.

But beyond all this, the two men diverged. One type of divergence was in their educational and career paths. Gorbachev had been on a "political" track during his college years, whereas Yeltsin was on an engineering track. Gorbachev studied ideology in great depth and with seeming belief in the genius of the Marxist–Leninist tradition. Yeltsin focused his learning on the concrete engineering tasks of the construction trades, studying Marxism–Leninism only insofar as required by the curriculum or by his later application for Party membership.[70] Both men came to be skeptical of received wisdoms that did not accord with the realities they witnessed around them; Gorbachev was fond of quoting to his classmates the Hegelian notion that "truth is concrete." But Gorbachev's mind was geared toward melding empirical observations with the discovery of abstract theoretical generalizations about the system as a whole, whereas Yeltsin's was geared toward the discovery of everyday, scientific, and administrative practices that would solve concrete problems.

Gorbachev sought out Komsomol and Communist Party membership at the earliest moments of eligibility, whereas Yeltsin had to be approached by the Party when he reached the limit of upward mobility within his trade beyond which advancement required that one be a member of the Party. Hence, though he was born in the same year as Gorbachev, Yeltsin joined the Party nine years later than had Gorbachev (1961 versus 1952). Yeltsin worked in construction for thirteen years after university before being recruited into the

---

region. The Urals, where Yeltsin grew up, are significantly poorer. In addition, by virtue of being in the village – and having a grandfather who was the collective farm chairman – Gorbachev's family had better access to food than Yeltsin's. It may or may not be indicative, but if one looks at Yeltsin's photographs as a teen-ager and college student at Ural Polytechnic, he is tall but thin as a stick. In contrast, Gorbachev in photographs from his college years begins to acquire a pudgy round face; note the contrast between the earlier pictures and his engagement photograph with Raisa in Sheehy's *The Man*. For Yeltsin's photographs, see the Russian version of Yeltsin's last autobiography, *Prezidentskii marafon* (Moscow: AST, 2000). I am grateful to Ilya Vinkovetsky for drawing my attention to this contrast.

[69] Compare Brown, *The Gorbachev Factor* (pp. 45–6) with Aron, *Boris Yeltsin* (pp. 64–9, 75–6).

[70] Yeltsin's former advisors and associates write: "A builder by profession, he sought out projects that could yield tangible and possibly quick results. He was little interested in theory or abstract discussions on general themes" (Baturin et al., *Epokha*, p. 803).

Party apparatus; even then, he spent his first eight years within the apparatus supervising construction in the province. He did not assume a nonspecialist rank within the Party apparatus until 1976, when he was catapulted into the position of first secretary of the regional Party organization. Gorbachev, by contrast, joined the Komsomol and then the Communist Party apparatus almost immediately after graduating from the university, and he worked his way up each hierarchy almost entirely in political generalist (rather than economic specialist) positions.

One of the most striking differences between the biographies of Gorbachev and Yeltsin lies in the timing of their exposure to international, cosmopolitan influences. One might refer to this as the timing of their "deprovincialization." Gorbachev came to Moscow in 1950, at the age of 19, and spent the next five years exposed to the culture of the capital and to students from Eastern Europe. Yeltsin did not leave the provinces for any extended period of residence until 1985, when he was 54 years of age!

Whether for reasons of nurture or nature, the two men's personalities and mentalities also differed considerably in ways that would influence the choices they made as leaders in Moscow. Yeltsin's impatience, impulsiveness, envy, and sensitivity to slight made him an unpredictable force within the Gorbachev Politburo. Nobody who has studied Gorbachev attributes such traits to him. Whereas Yeltsin was a demanding and at times brutish "boss" by temperament, Gorbachev was more comfortable accepting criticism from his subordinates and associates. Whereas Yeltsin was a provincial who was eager to learn new technical skills, Gorbachev was a would-be cosmopolitan who was eager to expand his understanding of the world beyond the borders of the USSR.[71] Yeltsin was by temperament a risk-seeker; Gorbachev, though not averse to risk, was more cautious. It is hard to imagine Yeltsin fashioning for himself the cautious political strategies that Gorbachev devised as general secretary had Yeltsin, not Gorbachev, become Party leader in 1985. Yeltsin's personality and mentality were better suited to the role of angry and utterly determined revolutionary hero, which he adopted in 1988–1989 and pursued until he had helped to bring down both Gorbachev and the system that Gorbachev was trying to construct.

CONCLUSION

I began this book by noting that its central focus is the authority-building and authority-maintenance strategies of Gorbachev and Yeltsin as they sought

---

[71] See English, *Russia and the Idea*, p. 330, fns. 112–13.

variously to reform, transform, destroy, and replace the Soviet system. Strategies are the means by which leaders seek to stretch the social constraints in their environment, both to realize their visions of social progress and to secure their credibility as effective problem solvers and politicians. The choices that leaders make are, in part, a function of how they define their visions and how they calculate the malleability of constraints on the realization of those visions. But those choices are also products of their attitudes toward conflict, risk, and compromise.

The choice of a political strategy is not a one-time thing; strategies vary over the course of a leader's administration. During the stage of political succession, political conflict is intense and rivals jockey for position. This constrains a competitor's choices to those that seem most likely to win the power struggle – to the extent that he is able to predict which strategy will be a winning one. During a leader's stage of ascendancy, he tends to have greater room for political maneuver and greater latitude to allow his personal preferences and predispositions to reshape his program. During the stage of decline, the leader is embattled but approaches this struggle from a position of ascendancy and relative strength when compared to his political leverage during the earlier stage of struggle for succession. Personal factors loom large in determining the choices a leader makes for how to combat the decline in his authority.

Though both Gorbachev and Yeltsin grew up within the Soviet system and though both believed in the "leading role of the Party" until at least 1987, their personalities and political mentalities differed in significant ways. In Chapter 11, I will address how these idiosyncratic factors influenced the ways in which each man exercised power and leadership.

3

The Rise of Gorbachev

The formal context of Soviet politics had not changed significantly by the time Gorbachev came to power in March 1985. He was chosen general secretary by a secret vote of the Politburo with consultative input from some of the most influential regional Party leaders in the Central Committee.[1] The reigning ideology remained Marxism–Leninism, and the audiences for authority-building strategies remained the elite representatives of the institutional pillars of the system. The short-term material interests and political identities of patrons and clients within those institutions remained essentially as they had been for decades. For these reasons, quite a few observers – while intrigued by the prospect of a young and articulate general secretary – did not harbor very high hopes that he would be inclined or able to transform the system. He was, after all, a product of that system and a man who had been chosen for advancement by the aged guardians of the Leninist system. If Suslov, Brezhnev, and Andropov could all endorse his meteoric rise into the highest reaches of power, how much of a free thinker could he possibly be?

What *had* changed, however, was the climate of opinion within the Soviet political establishment. That climate was quite different from the one that prevailed at the time of Khrushchev's ouster and was, in many ways, analogous to the one that had prevailed at the time of Stalin's death. Both 1953 and 1985 were marked by a widespread sense within the Politburo and Central Committee that something had to give, that things could not continue in the old way. Each period was marked by a collective loss of self-confidence about

---

[1] Archie Brown, *The Gorbachev Factor* (New York: Oxford University Press, 1996), pp. 82–8; Jerry F. Hough, *Democratization and Revolution in the USSR, 1985–1991* (Washington, DC: Brookings Institution, 1997), pp. 76–9.

the elite's ability to sustain enforcement of its formula for domination.[2] In both eras, there was a widespread sense that the main trajectory of both foreign and domestic policy was leading the country into a cul-de-sac or worse. Many officials in both periods feared domestic unrest if the situation were allowed to fester. In the 1950s and also in the 1980s, the Politburo and Central Committee were gripped by a sense of imminent threat from abroad. In both periods, many officials experienced not just a sense of fear but also a sense of bewilderment or embarrassment at the stagnation – both economic and ideological – into which the country had lapsed. In sum, in both periods a *negative consensus* prevailed within the political establishment: a widespread view that things could not continue as they had, that new approaches to solving problems were needed. Even though there was no positive consensus in either period as to the preferability of any set of alternative policies (other than a consensus in 1953 that the regime needed to deliver a higher standard of living to the populace), there was a growing sense of urgency about the need to "get the country moving again." In 1982 (after the death of Brezhnev) and again in 1984 (after the death of Andropov), the Old Guard held off this sentiment. By 1985, enough of them had departed the scene that the sentiment could prevail.[3]

Of course, more than thirty years separated the two successions; we would expect many things to have changed in the interim. There was no "Stalin question" in 1985, no need to demystify the exalted authority of the previous leader as a precondition for breaking with his policies. Likewise, there was no collective yearning to rein in the Party leader in order to avoid repetition of a murderous regime. In 1985 there was rather a sense of the need for vigorous leadership to push the country in new directions. Another difference

---

[2] I first advanced this proposition regarding 1985 in George W. Breslauer, "How do you sell a concessionary foreign policy?" *Post-Soviet Affairs*, vol. 10, no. 3 (July–September 1994), p. 280; it is also argued in Hough, *Democratization and Revolution*, p. 15. See also Paul Hollander, *Political Will and Personal Belief: The Decline and Fall of Soviet Communism* (New Haven, CT: Yale University Press, 2000).

[3] For good examples of these sentiments among men who would be leading members of Gorbachev's Politburo or leading aides to the general secretary, see Anatolii Chernyaev, *Shest' let s Gorbachevym* (Moscow: Progress, 1993), pp. 10–13, 27–9, 31–2, 55–6, 62–3; Nikolai Ryzhkov, *Perestroika: Istoriia predatel'stv* (Moscow: Novosti, 1992), p. 42; Nikolai Ryzhkov, *Desiat' let velikikh potriasenii* (Moscow: Assotsiatsiia "Kniga. Prosviashchenie. Miloserdie," 1995), pp. 42–6; Yegor Ligachev, *Inside Gorbachev's Kremlin: The Memoirs of Yegor Ligachev* (New York: Pantheon, 1993), pp. 15–16, 35. These men display a common alienation from the Brezhnev legacy, though specific points of alienation differed among them, as did their emotional reactions. Chernyaev, for example, emphasizes the shame and humiliation he experienced. Ryzhkov emphasizes his disgust with the Brezhnev administration's blocking of economic reform; Ligachev emphasizes his disgust with corruption among cadres.

was cognitive, as three decades of experimentation in domestic and foreign policies had led to a good deal of individual and collective learning about the feasibility of policies and programs. To solve the dilemmas in domestic and foreign relations, programs that had "sold" in the 1950s could not credibly be sold to the bulk of the political elite in the 1980s – just as programs successfully sold in the 1980s could not have been sold in the 1950s. A leader who tried to build his authority in 1985 by promising to achieve grandiose visions of rapid progress toward the "full and final victory of communism" at home and abroad would probably have been met by skepticism at best and by derisive laughter at worst.

By the mid-1980s, Stalin's successors had already attempted many variants of "minor reform" of the Soviet command economy, but to little effect. They had tried varied methods of improving the agricultural situation, except for genuine decentralization of authority – again to little effect. The pace of economic growth had slowed to a crawl, and in some sectors had reached zero- or negative-growth levels. Soviet leaders had achieved several "détentes" with the United States, but all had unraveled. They had built a huge military establishment but still were not being treated as an equal by the United States in global affairs. They had achieved nuclear parity but now were threatened by Ronald Reagan's Strategic Defense Initiative ("Star Wars"). Their alliance system had expanded to many corners of the globe, but it was embattled and very costly. After the Vietnam War, it appeared that the United States had lost the initiative in world affairs, only to manage a resurgence under Reagan. The vaunted Soviet Army was mired in Afghanistan, taking heavy losses.

Loss of self-confidence is a mood. A sense that things cannot continue in the old way, and that old visions of progress have been discredited as unworkable, are negative lessons. Moods and negative lessons do not lead logically to specific solutions for malaise. Indeed, given the diversity of material interests within the Soviet political establishment, we would expect no easy consensus to form on how to overcome the crisis. Most officials had few concrete ideas about what was likely to make the system as a whole deliver the goods more reliably. As is so often the case in such circumstances of collective insecurity and uncertainty, they were looking for leadership. Gorbachev promised to provide it.

Behind the scenes during Brezhnev's years in power, much searching for viable alternatives to both Khrushchevian utopianism and Brezhnevite conservatism – some of it published underground owing to censorship – took place among reformist intellectuals in the academic and journalistic worlds. Reformist experiments in domestic and foreign policy that had taken place sporadically under Khrushchev, that had been advocated unsuccessfully by

Brezhnev's prime minister (Aleksei Kosygin), and that had improved the Hungarian economy in the 1970s helped to keep alive and legitimize the vision of a "renewed socialism" and a workable East–West accommodation.[4] Gorbachev heard of these discussions and sought to tap into them privately when he was promoted to the position of Central Committee secretary in late 1978. His mentality was open-minded and empirically oriented, seeking to absorb experiences that might work better than had Brezhnev's policies (see Chapter 2). He had been attentive and receptive to events in Eastern Europe and to the lessons of Eurocommunism. His learning was steadily advanced by consultations with reformist specialists as he rose within the leadership between 1978 and 1982. Once exposed to data about the real state of the economy in the early 1980s, he agreed with Eduard Shevardnadze in 1984 that "[e]verything has gone rotten."[5] He told his wife on the eve of assuming the general secretaryship that "we cannot go on living in this way."[6]

But Gorbachev was more than just an amateur scientist seeking solutions to societal problems. He was also a politician on the rise. The two roles merged with urgency after Brezhnev died in 1982 and a series of political successions raised the stakes associated with expressing new ideas. As he aspired to become general secretary, he would have to think about solutions that he could sell politically and that would build his authority – his legitimacy and credibility – as a leader.

A democratic socialist vision at home, combined with an accommodationist strategy abroad, was only one of several approaches that had not yet been tried and discredited in the USSR. One alternative to radical reformism treated the main problem as a moral one: the extensive corruption of Soviet officialdom during the Brezhnev years. The solution appeared to be a policy of replacing corrupt personnel with a new cohort of uncorrupted cadres. Doing so would require a certain measure of *glasnost'* in order to train the public spotlight on the problem and enlist the public in campaigns to expose corrupt bureaucrats. The traditional Party "aristocracy" of the Brezhnev years would

---

[4] For analyses of the published discussions of alternatives, see Elizabeth Valkenier, *The Soviet Union and the Third World: An Economic Bind* (New York: Praeger, 1983); Jerry F. Hough, *The Struggle for the Third World: Soviet Debates and American Options* (Washington, DC: Brookings Institution, 1986); Franklyn Griffiths, "The sources of American conduct: Soviet perspectives and their policy implications," *International Security*, vol. 9, no. 1 (Fall 1984), pp. 30–50; Matthew Evangelista, *Unarmed Warriors: The Transnational Movement to End the Cold War* (Ithaca, NY: Cornell University Press, 1999).

[5] Brown, *The Gorbachev Factor*, p. 81; Carolyn McGiffert Ekedahl and Melvin A. Goodman, *The Wars of Eduard Shevardnadze* (University Park: Pennsylvania State University Press, 1997), p. 30.

[6] Brown, *The Gorbachev Factor*, p. 81.

be replaced by Cromwellian puritans who would no longer use public office for private material gain. The traditional Red Directors, or at least those corrupted by the Brezhnevite experience, would be replaced by honest and efficient technocrats whose rise to positions of authority had been partially frustrated in the 1970s. Under this alliance of puritans (such as Party secretary Yegor Ligachev) and technocrats (such as Prime Minister Nikolai Ryzhkov), more decisionmaking responsibility could be devolved to lower levels of the administrative hierarchy without fear that it would be abused. As a result, the economy would be managed more effectively and more productively, authentic social and work discipline would be enhanced, and hence the authority of the CPSU would rise. This was the approach that had been championed by Yuri Andropov during his short time as general secretary. It is the approach (and the man) lauded by both Ryzhkov and Ligachev in their memoirs.[7]

In foreign relations, one alternative to an East–West accommodation was the exploitation of Soviet nuclear capability to convince the West of the need to "do business" with the USSR on equal terms. This would have been a confrontational variant of the strategy of "offensive détente" that had informed Brezhnev's strategy in East–West relations. But to those who concluded that Brezhnev's approach had proven unworkable, there remained an alternative to confrontation: retrenchment from Soviet positions of overextension abroad. This was a feasible alternative to continuing in the old way. It required finding a way to get out of Afghanistan, even if the goals of the invasion had not been achieved. It required a reduction of commitments to Third World allies, and to some allies within the world communist movement, in order to bring Soviet global policy more into line with a newfound appreciation of the limits of Soviet capability. It entailed exploitation of the potential of the peace movement in Western Europe and North America, in the hope that these societies would force their leaders unilaterally to stop building and deploying new missiles and space-based weapons systems. In fact, these were the policies followed by Yuri Andropov during his fifteen months at the helm (November 1982–February 1984).[8]

Nor would this approach necessarily be vulnerable to the charge that it was antithetical to the Soviet tradition. Throughout Soviet history, there had been periods when the leadership had opted for a "breathing spell" in its global offensive in order to consolidate gains and attend to domestic problems.

---

[7] Ryzhkov, *Desiat' let,* pp. 43, 186, 188; Ligachev, *Inside Gorbachev's Kremlin,* pp. 16–17, 27–30, 51–2. Hough, *Democratization and Revolution,* also invokes the concepts of "puritans" and "technocrats," albeit in passing.

[8] Ryzhkov (*Desiat' let,* p. 50) also praises some of these features of Andropov's foreign policies.

Likewise, the strategy of playing upon contradictions within the imperialist camp (and among forces within capitalist countries) had a long pedigree in Soviet history.

Thus, while acknowledging that both Khrushchev and Brezhnev had promised far more than they could deliver, the anti-accommodationist and anti-liberal forces within the Soviet Politburo and Central Committee could credibly claim to possess alternative visions that had not yet been discredited. Those who had least credibility within this context were the "stand-patters": traditional Brezhnevites (such as Party secretaries Grigorii Romanov, Viktor Grishin, and Vlodimir Shcherbitsky) who protected their material interests and pretended that things could indeed continue in the old way. The strength of those material interests and Leninist identities within the Central Committee and Politburo was such that Gorbachev would be chosen general secretary only after two other successors to Brezhnev (Yuri Andropov and Konstantin Chernenko) had died in office. Obviously, during the early 1980s, radical reform was not perceived to be the only alternative to Brezhnevism.

IN ANTICIPATION OF POLITICAL SUCCESSION

When Gorbachev was chosen general secretary in March 1985, Foreign Minister Andrei Gromyko, in his nomination speech, is said to have described him as a man with "a nice smile but iron teeth."[9] The implication was that Gorbachev was a new, more flexible, kind of leader – but no fool. He could hold his own with the best of them, at home and abroad. He would be able to get the country moving again without sacrificing core interests or values of the system. Little did Gromyko know that ultimately Gorbachev would falsify that prediction. At the time, however, Gorbachev may not have known it, either.

During the first year and a half that Gorbachev was in power, he presented himself as much the kind of leader that Gromyko had suggested. He did not conceal the fact that he stood for breaking with the old way of doing things. But he did so gingerly as he built his power base and forced the retirement of more leaders among the Brezhnevite stand-patters.

Domestic Policy and Politics

Members of the Politburo, as well as leading members of the Central Committee, knew that Gorbachev had been consulting and consorting with radical

---

[9] Dusko Doder in *The Washington Post* (March 17, 1985). Hough claims that this remark attributed to Gromyko may have been the product of a mere rumor (Hough, *Democratization and Revolution*, p. 77).

reformist academics and journalists during his years in Moscow.[10] They also knew that, in his years as head of the Stavropol province Party organization, he had sponsored some innovative measures for reorganizing economic production at the provincial level.[11] But they had little reason to suspect at the time that he would eventually sponsor a complete overhaul of the system. For Gorbachev was also correctly perceived as someone who had played by the Leninist rules of the game for decades. His speeches during 1976–1981 had been unexceptional by contemporary standards.[12] In rising from a provincial position to one in Moscow, Gorbachev had been sponsored – and thereby vouched for – by the likes of Suslov and Andropov, who were among the most influential members of the Old Guard. His speeches as a Politburo member from 1980 until late 1984 had not gone much beyond the policy consensus prevalent at the time, which was consistent with an Andropovite experimental approach to improving the performance of the economy and replacing corrupt cadres.[13] Moreover, he had reinforced the image of being a team player by properly biding his time after the death of Andropov and not contesting the choice of a stand-patter, Konstantin Chernenko, as general secretary.[14] Puritans and technocrats in the Central Committee also knew him

---

[10] Robert D. English, *Russia and the Idea of the West* (New York: Columbia University Press, 2000), p. 183.

[11] Brown, *The Gorbachev Factor*, pp. 45–7.

[12] A content analysis of speeches and published articles by provincial Party leaders in the RSFSR during 1976–1981 showed the post-Stalin generation of officials to be divided between those who made very few demands for change (less so even than their counterparts in the older generation of such leaders) and those who were very much more demanding and impatient in their rhetoric than all others. On this scale, Gorbachev (like Yeltsin) was in the latter group but had one of the lower scores within that group; notably, his rhetoric was demanding in content but not impatient in style. He did not stand out in any way. See George W. Breslauer, "Is there a generation gap in the Soviet political establishment: Demand articulation by RSFSR provincial Party first secretaries," *Soviet Studies,* vol. 36, no. 1 (January 1984), pp. 1–25. On other indicators, such as innovations introduced in Stavropol province or his muted advocacy of the decentralized link (*zvenevaia*) system in Soviet agriculture in the late 1970s (Brown, *The Gorbachev Factor*, pp. 45–6), Gorbachev comes across as experimental but not iconoclastic, much less strident, which is consistent with his placement in my content analysis of speeches. On Yeltsin's published demands of the center while Party leader in Sverdlovsk, see Leon Aron, *Boris Yeltsin: A Revolutionary Life* (London: HarperCollins, 2000), ch. 3.

[13] Hough (*Democratization and Revolution,* pp. 73–4) argues that Gorbachev's ceremonial speech of April 22, 1983, on the anniversary of Lenin's birth, was iconoclastic in presenting "an unmistakable endorsement of Lenin's New Economic Policy (NEP) and was followed by his ideas about taking objective economic laws more firmly into account ... [and about] a skillful use of money–goods relations." Yet at that time Andropov was general secretary and the speech was quite consistent with suggestions found in the general secretary's published addresses. It would certainly have been compatible with laying the groundwork for a program modeled on Chinese or Hungarian reforms, which Andropov is said to have been considering at the time (Hough, *Democratization and Revolution,* p. 96–7).

[14] Brown, *The Gorbachev Factor*, p. 69.

to be both uncorrupted by Brezhnevite standards and a competent adminis-
trator, hence someone who fit their mold. In sum, Gorbachev projected the
image (whether manipulatively or not) of someone who could lead without
being overly threatening to core interests and identities within the political
establishment. He could advance new goals without threatening cherished
traditional values.[15]

But the question of the day was: Which traditional values were the most
cherished? The basic Leninist heritage, with its emphasis on the leading role
of the Party? Or the more recent opportunities for the *nomenklatura* to en-
rich itself? Gorbachev made clear where he stood on this issue even before
the death of Chernenko. As Chernenko's health started to fade in late 1984,
Gorbachev moved quickly to seize the initiative from the stand-patters and
to occupy a distinct ideological niche in the succession struggle. The time
had passed for being deferential and self-denying in the face of aspirations
of other, more senior members of the leadership. Gorbachev was ready for a
campaign speech. He defined himself publicly as someone who would revive
the best features of the Leninist heritage by pursuing political and economic
reforms at home and accommodation abroad.

He chose the occasion of a closed Party conference on ideology in December 1984 to make his move. His was the most radical single speech by a leading member of the Politburo since Khrushchev.[16] It was analogous in content
(though not in its timing) to Khrushchev's "secret speech" denouncing Stalin
in 1956, for Khrushchev had used that speech as a way of breaking through political deadlock and seizing the political initiative by defining radical change
in doctrine and policy as a moral and practical necessity. In December 1984,
Gorbachev, though not yet Party leader, signaled that he was prepared to
transform Soviet doctrine – the language of Soviet politics – in order formally
to delegitimize the Brezhnevite way of doing things. He did not yet challenge
the traditional arenas of politics. His speech was given in a private arena and
did not call for the creation of new public arenas; that would come later.
Still, Gorbachev's rivals among the Brezhnevite stand-patters understood the
implications of Gorbachev's words and felt threatened by them. Chernenko
himself tried to prevent Gorbachev from delivering the speech, but Gorbachev stood firm. Chernenko and his allies succeeded only in preventing the
speech from appearing in full in *Pravda*.[17]

---

[15] Ryzhkov (*Desiat' let*, p. 200) writes that only in 1987 did he realize just how different were his
and Gorbachev's views on economic issues.

[16] The speech was reprinted in Mikhail S. Gorbachev, *Izbrannye rechi i stat'i*, vol. 2 (Moscow:
Izdatel'stvo politicheskoi literatury, 1987), pp. 75–108; citations are from this source.

[17] See Hough, *Democratization and Revolution*, p. 73; Brown, *The Gorbachev Factor*, p. 82.

The address was phrased in abstract terms – as doctrinal speeches typically are – and did not elaborate on the specific policies that would follow from the doctrines endorsed. But it contained most of the code-words that would later become the hallmarks of Gorbachev's transformations: *perestroika, glasnost', reforma, demokratizatsiia,* the "human factor," and the need for cadres to "trust" people and to "respect their intellect." Like Khrushchev's speeches at the 20th Party Congress in February 1956, it was notable for the remarkable number of criticisms that bordered on "systemic" as well as for the rhetoric of impatience and urgency that filled the text.[18] Indeed, when Gorbachev spoke of production relations in the USSR having come into conflict with the mode of production, he was repeating the traditional Marxist definition of a pre-revolutionary situation.

This speech was an unmistakable assault on Brezhnevite "stand-pattism." Beyond that, it was an endorsement of not just one alternative to the policies prevailing under Chernenko. Rather, it created an umbrella of concepts and ideas under which representatives of all three alternatives to Brezhnevism could huddle: puritans (anti-corruption fighters), technocrats (rationalizers of the planned economy), and political reformists. Puritans and technocrats in the Central Committee could draw the conclusion that Gorbachev was advocating a policy of widespread replacement of corrupt and incompetent cadres, a policy with which they agreed. They could conclude that Gorbachev's rhetoric – which extolled the communist system, Marxist–Leninist ideals, and social discipline – simply implied a determination to purge the apparatus of corrupt cadres, to staff it with uncorruptible people such as themselves, and thereby to release the untapped potential of the socialist system. This would not necessarily have been threatening to them; nor would it presage any loss of political control over society. Indeed, Gorbachev's emphasis on the growing "contradictions" in Soviet society echoed Andropov's justification for his disciplinarian policies and anti-corruption campaign.[19] Similarly, Gorbachev's critique of Soviet methods of rule could have implied varied policy prescriptions. Khrushchev had pressed for similar goals without abandoning political centralization, the leading role of the Party, or Leninist anti-liberalism.

Puritans and technocrats could have viewed Gorbachev as simply saying that the situation had become too urgent to ignore – not an especially

---

[18] Khrushchev had not only criticized Stalin in his secret speech; in his published speech to the 20th Party Congress, he had criticized the "bureaucratism" of Soviet society and had called for a frontal assault to overcome it (*Pravda,* February 15, 1956).

[19] On the Andropov model in this regard, see Ernst Kux, "Contradictions in Soviet socialism," *Problems of Communism,* vol. 33, no. 6 (November–December 1984), pp. 1–27.

outrageous claim in light of the revolutionary workers' movement ("Solidarity") in fraternal Poland, which had almost brought down communism in that country in 1981. But compared with Gorbachev's prior caution in public speeches, and given his introduction of so many concepts associated with Khrushchev's anti-Stalin campaign of 1956, the Kosygin reforms of 1965, and the Prague Spring of 1968, this speech was also intended to appeal to, and activate, reformists within the Party and the critical intelligentsia. In the vision expressed to this heterogeneous audience, the puritans were promised a return to revolutionary rectitude, the technocrats were promised modernization and efficiency, and the critical intelligentsia were promised more opportunities to express themselves. All of them were promised a more efficient and productive economic system, a stronger Soviet Union, and a more consensual polity.

The ideas expressed by Gorbachev served as an umbrella for a wide range of groups whose interests often did not overlap. This is a crucial function performed by leaders who propagate new ideas. Gorbachev was not simply playing the role of a "political entrepreneur" who identifies the common "contract space" between established interests and defines a program that secures their support.[20] Rather, Gorbachev was creating a new set of political symbols that were ambiguous enough that puritans, technocrats, and radical political reformists could all assign their favored interpretation to those symbols. This ambiguity allowed Gorbachev to exercise the authority to make changes that in some ways would not have met with the approval of these groups.[21]

---

[20] For this view of leadership, see Oran R. Young, "Political leadership and regime formation: On the development of institutions in international society," *International Organization*, vol. 45, no. 3 (Summer 1991), pp. 281–308, esp. p. 288; see also James MacGregor Burns, *Leadership* (New York: Harper & Row, 1978), on "transactional leadership."

[21] It is noteworthy that two analyses of Gorbachev's politics that treat him as more power-hungry than principled entirely ignore this speech: Dmitry Mikheyev, *The Rise and Fall of Gorbachev* (Indianapolis, IN: Hudson Institute, 1992); and Anthony D'Agostino, *Gorbachev's Revolution* (New York University Press, 1998). By contrast, three analyses that treat Gorbachev as a committed radical reformer already in 1984 attach importance to this speech as an indicator or harbinger of Gorbachev's beliefs (Brown, *The Gorbachev Factor*, pp. 78ff.; Hough, *Democratization and Revolution*, p. 74; Robert D. English, *Russia and the Idea of the West: Gorbachev, Intellectuals and the End of the Cold War* [New York: Columbia University Press, 2000], p. 199). I treat this speech as an indicator of Gorbachev's authority-building strategy, whatever might have been his inner convictions at the time. The authority-building approach treats public statements as exercises in political impression management and political communication, though it also presumes that leaders come to be hostage to the political identities they define publicly for themselves.

Foreign Relations

Gorbachev's public statements on East–West relations at the time also suggested that he was capturing a broad ideological niche in the struggle to succeed Chernenko while simultaneously presenting himself as the man who could lead the country responsibly in new directions. He combined a vigorous defense of Soviet status in world affairs with an endorsement of flexibility and accommodation. He suggested that Chernenko's policies were leading the country into a dead end and that new ideas and postures were needed to avoid that fate. In his speech to the ideological conference of December 10, 1984, he had little to say about foreign affairs, but what he did say combined ritualistic rhetoric with a criticism that the USSR had allowed its opponents to steal from it the initiative on the global scene. Re-seizing the initiative would lead not to an escalation of the Cold War but rather to "constructive dialogue and practical measures leading to the lessening of international tension." [22]

Only eight days later, in a speech before the British parliament on December 18, 1984, that was reprinted in full in *Pravda,* Gorbachev elaborated on the meaning of flexibility.[23] There he foreshadowed many of the concepts that would later come to mark his accommodationist foreign policy. He called for a "healing" (*ozdorovlenie*) of international relations. He mentioned the need for "new thinking in the nuclear age" and the need for accommodations based on "a balance of interests" between East and West. He referred to *both* sides' interests as "legitimate" (*zakonnye*) and called for "sensible compromises" and trust based on "compatible (*sovpadaiushchie*) interests." He referred to Europe as "our common home." And he abandoned the traditional aversion to showing weakness by repeating several times that the USSR needed peace in order to pursue its domestic goals. Gorbachev did criticize the United States and tried to draw a distinction between the United States and Europe, but he did not dwell on it.

Similarly, Gorbachev's visit to Great Britain in December 1984 combined conciliatory rhetoric, a relaxed style, and a flexible way of thinking with tough-mindedness and a blunt, self-confident, articulate defense of Soviet pride and interests when challenged directly by members of parliament. Margaret Thatcher, at least, had seen beyond the latter and appreciated the potential implicit in the former, proclaiming: "I like Gorbachev. We can do business

---

[22] Gorbachev, *Izbrannye,* vol. 2, p. 103.
[23] Ibid., pp. 109–16.

together."[24] By contrast, Andrei Gromyko, in his nomination speech on behalf of Gorbachev less than three months later, may have viewed Gorbachev's
performance in England as the harbinger of a more effective pursuit of "offensive détente."[25]

In sum, even before he became general secretary, Gorbachev signaled his
intention to lead the Soviet Union out of what he defined as a cul-de-sac.
He offered his own vigorous leadership to defuse East–West tensions and to
overcome the crisis at home. While he made clear that he was entertaining
reformist proposals for domestic change and that he was endorsing a greater
measure of Soviet flexibility and conciliation in East–West relations, it was by
no means clear how far he would push each of these tendencies. More specifically, his public statements left unclear the price in traditional values he would
be willing to pay in order to advance these goals. Whereas his general posture as a new kind of leader was clear, his concrete policy positions were
sufficiently ambiguous that they could have received explicit or tacit endorsement from a wide range of political types within the Politburo and Central
Committee. This was a clever formula for seizing the initiative in a political competition. Only the stand-patters would be alienated. But their loss of
self-confidence and dwindling numbers (with the passing of older members
of the Politburo) made them increasingly ineffectual as a blocking coalition.

GORBACHEV IN POWER

Once he became general secretary in March 1985, Gorbachev's level of caution, traditionalism, and ambiguity suddenly increased. The one exception
was cadres policy, in which Gorbachev moved rapidly, consolidating his power
perhaps faster than any Party leader in Soviet history. Steadily and quickly,
he enlarged his political machine and consolidated his power base by firing members of the Politburo, as well as stand-pat officials of the central
and regional Party apparatuses, and replacing them with people he knew, respected, or trusted. But regarding actual policy changes, he moved slowly and
cautiously; his rhetoric, though still novel, was less far-reaching than in his

---

[24] *The New York Times* (December 23, 1984).
[25] Gorbachev reiterated several of these themes in a more restrained speech before a domestic
audience on February 20, 1985 (Gorbachev, *Izbrannye*, vol. 2, pp. 117–28, esp. pp. 125–6).
This speech before his nominal electorate for the Supreme Soviet endorsed a perspective on international affairs that contrasted markedly with that endorsed by Gorbachev's Brezhnevite
rival, Grigorii Romanov, in his own electoral speech (see *Leningradskaia pravda,* February 15,
1985).

December 1984 speech to the ideology conference. This led some observers at the time to assume that Gorbachev was little different in orientation from the Brezhnev generation. But that assumption ignored the impact on Gorbachev's behavior of politics, power consolidation, and authority-building imperatives. Gorbachev was building a political machine and temporarily deferring in policy to the more conservative forces within the Politburo and Central Committee.

Gorbachev's domestic policies from March 1985 to the fall of 1986 were noteworthy more for their traditionalism than for their reformism; they were more reminiscent of Andropov's policies than of Khrushchev's. As such, they must have appealed greatly to such puritans as Yegor Ligachev, whom Gorbachev was both promoting to the Politburo and drawing into the inner circle of the leadership. The economic policy of acceleration (*uskorenie*), for example, called for budgetary redistributions to the benefit of the machine-building sector, increased pressure on managers to economize on materials, and campaigns against lack of discipline among workers and managers alike. Administrative reorganizations that took place at the time did not challenge the principles of the command economy, much less introduce elements of a market economy. Instead, they intensified pressure on economic administrators. Anti-corruption campaigns were launched or expanded, increasing the opportunity for Gorbachev to build his political machine. Similarly, the anti-alcoholism campaign launched in May 1985 resembled traditional Soviet campaigns; in fact, we now know that it was supervised by Ligachev, though there is disagreement as to whether he was a driving force in adopting the policy.[26]

It remains unclear to what extent Gorbachev believed at the time that these policies would suffice to reenergize the economy – or to what extent his deferral to the puritans was driven by political calculation.[27] What is clear,

---

[26] According to Yegor Ligachev (*Inside Gorbachev's Kremlin*, pp. 335–9), he supported the campaign as a member of the Politburo and became "actively involved with the cause" (p. 336), but he was not its initiator. Yeltsin (Boris Yeltsin, *Against the Grain: An Autobiography*, trans. by Michael Glenny [New York: Summit, 1990], p. 127) presents a picture of a fanatical Ligachev running the campaign. Politburo member Nikolai Ryzhkov (*Perestroika*, pp. 93–5) depicts Ligachev and Solomentsev as the driving forces behind the campaign, a depiction that is supported by the memoirs of Gorbachev (*Zhizn' i reformy*, vol. I [Moscow: Novosti, 1995], p. 341).

[27] Gorbachev (*Zhizn' i reformy*, vol. I, p. 336) claims that he believed in 1985 that these policies, along with replacement of cadres, would indeed suffice. I find this hard to accept at face value, given the degree of radicalism of his speech to the Ideology Conference in December 1984 and the speed with which he jettisoned "acceleration" in 1986 and replaced it with radical

however, is that he used this time to prepare the ground for the possibility of more radical policies. For though his speeches during 1985 and through early 1986 were, on balance, less radical than those delivered during December 1984–February 1985, they included phrases and formulations that were associated with political and economic reform. On the one hand, we find themes such as "acceleration," discipline, the need for both workers and cadres to learn to think differently, and the need for greater "socialist democracy" (a favorite theme of Chernenko's). These themes were traditionalist in thrust, or at least could have been interpreted in traditional terms, and they tended to predominate quantitatively in his speeches of March 1985 through mid-1986. Yet, at the same time, Gorbachev continued to talk about the need for economic reform – a theme that was especially important to technocrats.[28] Gorbachev took back nothing he had said in December 1984. His speeches continued to note the need for *glasnost'*, *perestroika,* and democratization, themes that were especially important to radical reformists.[29] Thus, at the 27th Party Congress (February 1986), Gorbachev spoke of the need for "radical reform," his first such reference.[30] In July 1986, he equated *perestroika* with a "real revolution."[31] As before, though, he remained vague about the specific policies that would flow from these principles, and their encasement in more traditionalist rhetoric allowed puritans and technocrats to feel less threatened by the radical phrases than they might otherwise have been.

For example, at the 27th Party Congress, Gorbachev proclaimed that "[a]ny restructuring of the economic mechanism ... begins with the restructuring of consciousness, the giving up of formed stereotypes of thinking and practice, [and a] clear understanding of new challenges."[32] Puritans could have understood this to mean that purging corrupt cadres and intensified

changes that assumed the causes of dysfunctions to be systemic. Moreover, closer inspection of this passage in his memoirs reveals the following. He writes that in 1985 his team ("we," never "I") really did initially hope to overcome stagnation through "acceleration." However, he also says that, having engaged in substantial analytical work in 1982–1984, he and his team were even then cognizant of the fact that a more substantial economic reform would "eventually" be necessary. Thus, acceleration was a needed jolt, to be followed by something more radical.

[28] See Ryzhkov, *Desiat' let* (pp. 44–5, 69, 83, 120, 255) for examples of the prime minister's urge for reforms that would diminish the Party's intervention in the operation of the economy. He even had a good word for Bukharin at the expense of Lenin (p. 255).

[29] Examples include Gorbachev, *Izbrannye,* vol. 2, pp. 130–1, 142–3, 150, 158, 433; vol. 3, pp. 235–43; vol. 4, pp. 37–8, 48, 50.

[30] Gorbachev, *Izbrannye,* vol. 3, p. 212.

[31] Ibid., vol. 4, p. 37.

[32] Gorbachev, *Izbrannye,* vol. 3, p. 217.

Party educational work among the workers were preconditions for changes in institutional structure. Gorbachev's "revolution," then, could have been interpreted as a cultural revolution, not a political revolution against the prerogatives of the Party apparatus. Similarly, in his speeches of March–April 1985, Gorbachev frequently cited the Party's paternalistic role as an educator (*vospitatel'*) of the Soviet people. In his speech upon being elected general secretary, for example, he argued that

[t]he deepening of socialist democracy is inextricably tied to the heightening of social consciousness.... We must continue to expand *glasnost'* in the work of Party, Soviet, state and social organizations. V. I. Lenin said that the state is rich because of the consciousness of the masses. Our practice has completely corroborated this conclusion. The better informed are the people, and the more consciously they act, the more actively they support the Party, its plans and programmatic aims.[33]

This was a decidedly elitist statement that could easily be interpreted by audiences within the Central Committee as assurance that, although changes were needed, they would not challenge the leading role of the Party.

Reassurance notwithstanding, the persistent inclusion of reformist phrases in speeches by the general secretary had potentially far-reaching implications in an ideocratic regime.[34] Those phrases amounted to a tacit repudiation of the self-congratulatory doctrinal formulations that had previously justified standing pat (or what Gorbachev would call "stagnation"). They thereby opened up intellectual and political space for reformist members of the journalistic community, academia, and the cultural intelligentsia to become publicly involved in the debate about alternatives to Brezhnevism. They allowed would-be political activists to point to statements by the general secretary as political cover for risky efforts to stretch the boundaries of legitimate public discourse and association. At this early stage in his administration, Gorbachev gingerly opened the space (and provided the cover) by combining traditionalist with reformist rhetoric while pursuing largely traditionalist policies. He was challenging the formal doctrines of Brezhnevism, but without yet challenging the primacy of private arenas of power and without alerting puritans and technocrats within the leadership to the potentially threatening implications of what was to come.

[33] Gorbachev, *Izbrannye*, vol. 2, pp. 130–1.
[34] An "ideocratic" regime is one in which the status and privileges of the ruling elite are justified with reference to a sacred ideological heritage of which the elite is the current trustee and embodiment.

To take another example, at this early stage Gorbachev did not yet treat *glasnost'* as an end in itself. Rather, he defined it as a necessary instrument for exposing bureaucrats who were hiding their malfeasance or incompetence. *Glasnost'* was a necessary searchlight and the beam now needed to be intensified. He also described it as a mechanism by which the Party would heighten its credibility with the masses and thereby induce them to contribute to realization of the Party's goals. But he had not yet crossed the divide between elitism and populism; the central authorities still needed to control the scope and focus of "openness." This was implicit in his coupling of *glasnost'* with traditional, elitist concepts.[35] Indeed, in June 1986, at a private meeting with leaders of the USSR Writers' Union, Gorbachev urged writers not to make the Stalin issue the centerpiece of their definitions of *glasnost'*. Why dissipate all our energies on arguments about the past, he asked, when we need to concentrate our attention and energies on the present and the future![36] Here too, Gorbachev's emphasis was on caution and on presenting himself as a leader who could balance and mediate conflicting intellectual agendas, political orientations, classes, and generations.

Words are important in a regime that seeks to legitimize itself with reference to a sacred ideological heritage. The populace may not believe in the tenets of the ideology, but the regime's constant defense of those tenets is meant to signal officialdom's collective unassailability. When a leader wants to change things significantly, he can mobilize new sources of support for his efforts by changing the doctrine and thereby signaling that representatives of the established order – and perhaps the order itself – are no longer unassailable. This is what Khrushchev's anti-Stalin campaign signaled. This also explains why it was so important for the conservative Brezhnev regime to put an end to the anti-Stalin campaign and to introduce new doctrinal formulations in order to re-defend the established order. Gorbachev was following Khrushchev's (not Brezhnev's) lead, though in a less confrontational way at this point. But in the 1980s, as in the 1950s, journalists, academics, and the critical intelligentsia took up the cause.

A similar pattern is observable in foreign relations. During the initial period of his administration, Gorbachev prepared the ground intellectually

---

[35] At the 27th Party Congress, he defined *glasnost'* as a vehicle for facilitating "political creativity of the masses" (*Izbrannye,* vol. 3, p. 241); in April 1986, he bundled *glasnost'* with "criticism and self-criticism" as prerequisites for forward movement (ibid., p. 352). *Glasnost'* only becomes an end in itself in Gorbachev's speeches beginning in January 1987 (*Izbrannye,* vol. 4, p. 358).

[36] See the account of this meeting in "Gorbachev meets Soviet writers: A Samizdat account," *Radio Liberty Research Report,* no. 399/86 (October 23, 1986).

for later foreign policy initiatives. We have seen that, from December 1984 through February 1985, Gorbachev had already signaled his identification with "new thinking" and other concepts that were harbingers of a more flexible posture in international affairs. This did not change during his first year in office, though his policies remained cautious and his rhetoric could be read both ways. At the 27th Party Congress in February 1986, for example, he referred to the war in Afghanistan as a "running sore," thus providing the first critical appraisal of that war in public by a Soviet general secretary.[37] Yet his comments on East–West relations at the same Congress combined a strongly accommodationist thrust with an equally strong denunciation of "U.S. imperialism."[38]

Similarly, in relations with the communist governments of Eastern Europe, Gorbachev proceeded with caution and ambiguity. One month after his election as general secretary, he reaffirmed the basic principles of the "Brezhnev Doctrine" (sanctioning Soviet use of force to prevent the overthrow of socialism) in a published speech on the renewal of the Warsaw Pact Treaty.[39] In the same month, however, he reportedly told some East European leaders privately that the USSR would not rescue them should their populations repudiate them.[40] During 1985–1986, Gorbachev addressed the issue of Eastern Europe very infrequently, concentrating on other matters. But in his speech to the 27th Party Congress, he did not endorse the Brezhnev Doctrine or its associated concepts and instead enunciated a more cooperative vision of Soviet relations with Eastern Europe.[41] Likewise, in a private speech to staff of

---

[37] *Izbrannye*, vol. 3, p. 251. Gorbachev was the fourth general secretary to preside over the war in Afghanistan. Andropov had called for an in-house, private policy review of the war but had not criticized the military effort in public.

[38] See Gorbachev's address to the Congress in *Pravda*, February 26, 1986, section I ("The Present-Day World: Basic Tendencies and Contradictions") and section IV ("The Basic Goals and Directions of the Party's Foreign-Policy Strategy"); see also the discussions of this speech in English, *Russia and the Idea*, pp. 209–10, and Brown, *The Gorbachev Factor*, pp. 221–2. The speech was marked by a tense and inconsistent coexistence of accommodative offerings and essentialist depictions of "U.S. imperialism," which traditionally implied the inability to ease tensions with that country. Thus: "Imperialism is impelled by its mainsprings and its very social and economic essence to translate the competition of the two systems into the language of military confrontation. Because of its social nature, imperialism continually generates aggressive, adventuristic policies.... This is especially typical of U.S. imperialism" (as translated in *Current Soviet Policies: The 27th Congress of the CPSU* [Columbus, OH: Current Digest of the Soviet Press, 1986], p. 13).

[39] *Pravda*, April 28, 1985.

[40] Brown, *The Gorbachev Factor*, p. 249, citing testimony by Chernyaev, Medvedev, and Gorbachev.

[41] *Pravda*, February 26, 1986; see also the discussion in Karen Dawisha, *Eastern Europe, Gorbachev, and Reform: The Great Challenge*, 2nd ed. (Cambridge University Press, 1990), p. 207.

the Ministry of Foreign Affairs in May 1986, Gorbachev insisted on the need for a more respectful Soviet attitude in dealing with Eastern Europe.[42]

The concepts that Gorbachev endorsed in both the Congress and the Ministry speeches were far less radical than those he would articulate later. They resembled innovations introduced by Khrushchev at the analogous stage of his administration when he, too, was trying to overcome a legacy of coercive domination and alienation in Soviet–East European relations, hoping to place those relations on a more cooperative and consensual basis but without encouraging anti-communist tendencies. Indeed, Khrushchev and Gorbachev, in the first stages of their administrations, may have shared the optimistic belief that an intermediate, stable equilibrium could be reached in Soviet relations with Eastern Europe – one that entailed neither coercive Soviet domination nor forced Soviet abdication.[43]

It is also noteworthy that Gorbachev did little at this stage to reduce the rate of growth of the Soviet military budget. He even increased Soviet military assistance to some clients in the Third World and briefly escalated the Soviet military offensive in Afghanistan, if only to improve the Soviet bargaining position in withdrawal negotiations.[44] He did not depart from his predecessors' strategy of offering incremental Soviet concessions in arms-control negotiations and of demanding equivalent, reciprocal concessions from the United States. Yet he did meet with President Reagan in Geneva (October 1985) and Reykjavik (October 1986), thus breaking the Soviet government's announced determination to avoid such meetings until the United States had abandoned its Strategic Defense Initiative. Although nothing concrete resulted from those two summits, Gorbachev and Reagan impressed each other and Gorbachev felt free thereafter to endorse the notion of total abolition of nuclear weapons as well as the principle of on-site inspection. Thus, in foreign as well as domestic policy, Gorbachev was both embracing traditional approaches and preparing the ground – intellectually and politically, but less so in policy – for more radical initiatives later on.

---

[42] Brown, *The Gorbachev Factor*, p. 242.

[43] Lévesque, in a comprehensive study, refers to these early years as a period of "Soviet immobilisme" in East European policy, which contrasted with the evolution of foreign policy concepts in other realms (Jacques Lévesque, *The Enigma of 1989: The USSR and the Liberation of Eastern Europe* [Berkeley: University of California Press, 1997], ch. 3).

[44] Raymond Garthoff, *The Great Transition: American–Soviet Relations and the End of the Cold War* (Washington, DC: Brookings Institution, 1994), p. 727.

4

Gorbachev Ascendant

The radicalization of Gorbachev's program and political strategy began in late 1986, with a signal going out that an expanded definition of *glasnost'* was now the "Party line." This indicated to editors of journals that censorship was to be relaxed and that they would be much freer to criticize. This was also the point at which Gorbachev started to extol the virtues of voluntary associations ("informals"). To dramatize, both at home and abroad, this expansion of the right of social forces to mobilize themselves autonomously, in December 1986 Gorbachev personally saw to the release from house arrest of the heroic symbol of dissidence, Andrei Sakharov. The following month he introduced to a plenary session of the Central Committee a wide-ranging program of "democratization," which included proposals for multicandidate, secret elections of Party, soviet, and managerial officials. In the same month, he announced that the Soviet Union would open up to the world economy by allowing joint ventures with foreign enterprises on Soviet soil.

In short order there followed new laws on cooperatives and "individual labor activity," which presaged new opportunities for legal entrepreneurial activity, and, in June 1987, a "Law on the State Enterprise" that signaled a push to dismantle the command economy. Almost all these initiatives in domestic policy were only first steps, a "foot in the door" approach, steps that delegitimized old values and justified in principle entirely new approaches to economic organization and the world economy. Almost all of them would be radicalized still further in the course of 1987–1988. Most dramatically, an extraordinary Party Conference in June 1988, which was televised nationally, laid plans for internal democratization of the CPSU, for the transfer of major decisionmaking authority from Party organs to the legislative councils (soviets) at all levels, and for the creation of a popularly elected legislature –

the Congress of People's Deputies – for which competitive, public elections would be held in March 1989. Indeed, one scholarly observer treats June 1988 as the point at which Gorbachev made the transition from being a reformer to being a transformer of the Soviet system.[1]

Unveiled within a few short months, these fresh initiatives vastly expanded Gorbachev's earlier programs. He was now establishing his political identity: a reformist (not a puritan or technocratic) vision of the future.

Gorbachev radicalized foreign policy as well. Building upon policy changes announced in 1986, Gorbachev made a series of stunning unilateral concessions that abandoned almost all Soviet negotiating positions in order to make possible completion of the INF ("Euromissile") Treaty in Washington, D.C., in December 1987. He announced in January 1988 that the Soviet Union would withdraw its troops from Afghanistan by May 1989 regardless of the consequences. He forced a breakthrough on the reduction of conventional forces in Europe by announcing at the United Nations, in December 1988, a large, unilateral reduction of Soviet forces. He assured his audiences that this would take place even if the United States and NATO failed to reciprocate in kind. He pledged in the same speech that the Soviet Union would not intervene militarily again in Eastern Europe. And, also in 1988, he began to urge conservative East European elites to accommodate liberalizing forces within their societies and to implement their own *perestroika* before it was too late.[2]

In sum, further radicalization of *glasnost'*, *perestroika*, democratization, and "new thinking" became the basis of Gorbachev's authority-building strategy during his stage of ascendancy. They marked his comprehensive program and the vision of the future he propounded. He was engaged in a relentless process of public desacralization and partial destruction of the Brezhnevite political-economic and sociopolitical orders. By desacralizing the established order, he was in effect stripping the *apparat* and the official classes of immunity from public, systemic criticism and thereby also emboldening the intelligentsia and the masses to believe that such forceful criticism could now be safely advanced in public. Televising the debates among Party officials at the June 1988 Party Conference was a means of simultaneously demystifying politics, subverting the notion that the "monolithic" Party had unique insight

---

[1] Archie Brown, *The Gorbachev Factor* (Oxford & New York: Oxford University Press, 1996), ch. 6.

[2] On the last point, see Karen Dawisha, *Eastern Europe, Gorbachev, and Reform: The Great Challenge*, 2nd ed. (Cambridge University Press, 1990), pp. 219–20, and Jacques Lévesque, *The Enigma of 1989: The USSR and the Liberation of Eastern Europe* (Berkeley: University of California Press, 1997), ch. 4 (entitled "The Second Half of 1988: The Turning Point").

into the "correct line," educating the population about alternative ways of thinking, and allowing people to believe that political initiative and involvement might be rewarding.

Such public criticism also assisted Gorbachev in his efforts to maintain the initiative against neo-Brezhnevite and newly conservative forces within the Central Committee and Politburo. Puritans such as Ligachev, and technocrats such as Prime Minister Ryzhkov, found themselves increasingly disillusioned with Gorbachev during this stage of his leadership. Their alienation from Gorbachev's evolving definitions of *perestroika* only deepened as the general secretary permitted civil liberties to expand in the areas of religion, travel, emigration, speech, and mass media.[3] As the bounds of the permissible grew, so too did the boldness of journalists, academics, writers, artists, and political activists. Their actions, and the autonomous social organizations they helped to create or enlarge, pushed beyond the degrees of freedom of speech and association that Gorbachev had formally and publicly sanctioned. Increasingly, Gorbachev's unwillingness to draw and enforce limits alienated those members of the Central Committee who had always assumed that the alternative to order would be anarchy.

There is a striking parallel between Khrushchev's behavior in 1958–1960 and that of Gorbachev during 1987–1989. In both periods, these men achieved positions of ascendancy within the leadership. Both of them put forth comprehensive programs for attaining a hugely ambitious goal based on a progressive, transcendant vision.[4] Khrushchev, like Gorbachev, expanded the arenas of politics and the scope of generalizable criticism of the system in order to overcome entrenched obstacles to change.

The content of their visions was quite different, however. Khrushchev advocated and promised no less than the "full-scale construction of communism,"

---

[3] See Nikolai Ryzhkov, *Desiat' let velikikh potriasenii* (Moscow: Assotsiatsiia "Kniga. Prosviashchenie. Miloserdie," 1995), pp. 77, 86, 185–8, 200. Yegor Ligachev (*Inside Gorbachev's Kremlin: The Memoirs of Yegor Ligachev* [New York: Pantheon, 1993]) devotes many pages to denunciation of Politburo member Aleksandr Yakovlev as an evil force within the Politburo who was pushing Gorbachev's reforms in increasingly radical and unacceptable directions. On Ligachev's alienation, see also Anatoly Chernyaev, *Shest' let s Gorbachevym* (Moscow: Progress, 1993), pp. 97, 201–5; on Ligachev's and Ryzhkov's joining together against certain forms of radicalization, see ibid., p. 236. Ryzhkov (*Desiat' let*, p. 199) also writes that in 1987 there were passionate meetings of the Politburo, "hot, ferocious (*iarostnykh*), endlessly long" meetings that "went as far as cussing (*do rugani dokhodivshikh*)."

[4] For the argument that, throughout Soviet history, ascendant leaders have been driven by an ideological urge to "transcend" real-world constraints, see Stephen E. Hanson, *Time and Revolution: Marxism and the Design of Soviet Institutions* (Chapel Hill: University of North Carolina Press, 1998).

based on "overtaking and surpassing capitalism" in growth and consumption indicators, as well as a decisive shift in the international "correlation of forces" in favor of socialism and, before too long, the "full and final victory of socialism" on a global scale. But Khrushchev did not seek to bridge, much less cross, the divide between Leninism and procedural democracy. He sought only to make the Leninist system somewhat more open and significantly less bureaucratized, which, he claimed, would energize the population and help to build a society of material abundance and political consensus. There was no room in his programs of 1958–1960 for competitive, secret elections, publicity for anti-system criticism, pluralism as an ideal, or voluntary associations that were independent of Party control. Khrushchev's vision was of a process of sociopolitical and socioeconomic homogenization, whereas Gorbachev was endorsing and expanding pluralism and heterogeneity (though not individualism per se) in these spheres. Khrushchev's vision of politics was plebiscitarian and populist, with himself as the uncontested leader. Gorbachev's was institutional and representative, with Gorbachev as the leading political broker and guarantor of progress – but not someone who should be treated as immune to criticism or challenge.

Both men recognized that reforming the system required organizational and ideological challenges to the heritage within which they were operating. But only Gorbachev was ready to synthesize Leninism with a variant of procedural democracy by subjecting officialdom to autonomous mechanisms of public accountability.[5] And only Gorbachev was ready to abandon the "anti-imperialist struggle" abroad.

JUSTIFYING AND STEERING DOMESTIC TRANSFORMATION

During 1987–1989, Gorbachev transformed both the ideology and organization of Soviet politics – what I have called the language and arenas of politics. He radicalized and elaborated the reformist concepts that he had advanced only gingerly during 1984–1986. Now he criticized "the dogmatic,

---

[5] Khrushchev would move in an even more radical direction – though nothing approaching Gorbachev's level of radicalism – during his last years in office, when he was politically embattled and searching for ways simultaneously to make the system work and to keep potential rivals off balance. See, for example, Alexander Yanov, *The Drama of the Soviet 1960s: A Lost Reform* (Berkeley: University of California, Institute of International Studies, 1984), and William Zimmerman, *Soviet Perspectives on International Relations, 1956–1967* (Princeton, NJ: Princeton University Press, 1969), pp. 99–101, 152, 196–205, 222ff., 259–69.

bureaucratic and voluntaristic inheritance"[6] and basically gave notice to those who were unable or unwilling to adapt to a new sociopolitical order.[7] But he did not jettison those components of his public statements that had appealed to puritans and technocrats. Nor did he ignore other officials who had internalized Marxist–Leninist categories and assumptions but who accepted the need for significant change in light of the crisis in which the country found itself. Instead, Gorbachev shifted the weights among these emphases within his speeches, consistently trying to demonstrate that, while a reformist, he remained faithful to the ideological tradition. In a sense, he did a remarkable job of appearing to straddle, but not cross, the divide between Leninism and procedural democracy.

One way in which Gorbachev did this was by articulating a vision of a reformed Soviet socialist society: one that remained faithful to traditional, Marxist socialism, to the romantic Leninism of "State and Revolution" (published in 1917), and to the reformist Leninism of the "New Economic Policy" (1921–1927) but that broke with the elitist and dictatorial features of the system as it had developed since then. Thus, his speeches and writings during 1987–1988 consistently extolled and quoted Lenin to justify his most radical proposals. In equal measure, they extolled the virtues and potential of "socialism" – a potential, he claimed, that his policies would reveal and realize. At times, this resulted in formulations that, to an outside observer, might have appeared to be arcane and convoluted: "The essence of *perestroika* lies in the fact that it unites socialism with democracy and revives the Leninist concept of socialist construction both in theory and in practice."[8] But to members of the Central Committee, these words could have lent a familiar ring to a potentially threatening policy.

Such familiarity might not have resulted in enthusiasm for the changes among those officials who were nervous about the implications of public criticism, decentralization, and competitive elections. But that familiarity may have allowed many officials, already somewhat intimidated by Gorbachev's assertiveness and lacking in self-confidence to begin with, to rationalize that the processes being unleashed were in principle controllable. It also allowed

---

[6] Mikhail S. Gorbachev, *Izbrannye rechi i stat'i*, vol. 6 (Moscow: Izdatel'stvo politicheskoi literatury, 1987), p. 64 (February 1988 Central Committee Plenum). "Voluntaristic" here refers to the ability of Party officials to conduct themselves with impunity; it implies the need to make them formally accountable for their actions.

[7] See e.g. ibid., p. 394 (June 1988 CPSU Conference).

[8] Mikhail Gorbachev, *Perestroika: New Thinking for Our Country and the World* (New York: Perennial, 1987), p. 22.

them to rationalize that Gorbachev himself was committed to holding those processes within bounds. Gorbachev sought to reassure them: the intent, he averred, was to "deepen people's socialist self-government.... We are not talking about, obviously, any kind of sabotage (*lomka*) of our political system. We must use all of its possibilities with maximal efficiency."[9] Democracy, after all, was to be *socialist* democracy; pluralism was to be *socialist* pluralism. Nothing he was proposing was meant to invalidate the "socialist idea" and the Soviet peoples' "socialist choice."

Gorbachev also assured his audiences that he respected the achievements of Soviet history – even as he was seeking a "sharp break" with past practice – and would preserve the best features of the inherited system. Thus, alongside his calls for criticism of the past and the filling in of "blank spots" in history and literature, he defended the historical record of the Party under very difficult circumstances (World War II, the Cold War) and lauded Soviet accomplishments.[10] He presented his reforms as a continuation of the earlier efforts of progressive forces within the Party who had attempted unsuccessfully to realize the potential of socialism back in 1953, 1956, and 1965.[11] In like manner, when discussing decisions during the *perestroika* period, he always referred to them as collective, not individual, decisions by the leadership. And he reassured his audiences, using Marxist language, that the leadership remained firmly in charge of an evolutionary process that would not get out of control:

I want to emphasize ... that *perestroika* is not a negation, and even if it is a negation, it is a dialectical one. Affirming our line for acceleration, for *perestroika,* we stand not on some slippery swamp, but on firm ground that has been formed through the efforts of many generations of Soviet people, as a result of our struggle as pioneers (*pervoprokhodtsy*).[12]

For the technocrats, Gorbachev also had choice ways of framing the changes he proposed. He appealed to scientific rationalism, which has deep roots in both Marxism and Soviet history. Reminiscent of Lenin's fascination with

---

[9] Gorbachev, *Izbrannye,* vol. 4, p. 317 (speech at January 1987 Plenum of Central Committee). For representative examples of Gorbachev's extolling of socialism and Leninism in 1987–1988, which marked almost every speech he gave, see Gorbachev, *Perestroika,* pp. 18–19, 22, 36, 72, 82; Gorbachev, *Izbrannye,* vol. 5, p. 411 (November 1987 anniversary speech); vol. 6, pp. 61–7 (February 1988 Plenum of Central Committee), and pp. 335, 394, 395 (June 1988 CPSU Conference).

[10] Gorbachev, *Izbrannye,* vol. 4, pp. 373–4 (February 1987 meeting in Central Committee).

[11] Ibid., vol. 6, pp. 351, 383, 399–400 (June 1988 CPSU Conference).

[12] Ibid., vol. 5, p. 210 (July 1987 meeting in Central Committee); see also vol. 4, p. 327 (January 1987 Central Committee Plenum).

American efficiency and industrialization, he proclaimed that *perestroika* "is the attachment to socialism of the most modern forms."[13] Modernity had institutional forms, but socialism had political and cultural content! *Perestroika* would "attach" one to the other without corrupting the essence – the soul – of the system. Similarly, "*Perestroika* means a resolute shift to scientific methods .... It means the combination of the achievements of the scientific and technological revolution with a planned economy."[14]

Gorbachev's emphasis on a "law-based state" (*pravovoe gosudarstvo*) could also have been appealing to would-be rationalizers of the Soviet economy. These people yearned to create a more predictable, procedural grounding for public administration. And, like their puritan brethren, they viewed official corruption and arbitrariness as enemies of administrative rationalization. Both puritans and technocrats wanted to avoid a return to autocratic leadership of the Politburo – whether Stalinist despotism or Khrushchevian arbitrariness. To the extent that legality constrained arbitrariness among their leaders (i.e., "provided reliable guarantees against a return to the cult of personality," as both Khrushchev and Gorbachev put it), it too was desirable.[15] A law-based state, to technocrats and puritans, was not intended to replace an authoritarian regime with mass democracy. But, to the extent that legal codification fosters administrative rationalization and nonarbitrary leadership, these types of officials could find something appealing in Gorbachev's democratization program.[16]

Even as he defined *perestroika* as a revolution, Gorbachev spoke the language of evolution, defining change as a long-term process that requires acclimatization to continuous change. Leninists must be creative, he would say, just as Lenin was. On the one hand, he was providing reassurance that the system would not collapse but would instead "realize its potential." On the other hand, he insisted that accommodation to the "stagnation" of the late-Brezhnev era was unacceptable and was in fact a surer recipe for systemic demise. Progressive change was an idea that also had deep roots in the Marxist and Leninist traditions. Indeed, those traditions were rooted in a theory of

---

[13] Ibid., p. 410 (November 1987 anniversary speech).

[14] Gorbachev, *Perestroika*, p. 21.

[15] This is the phrase Khrushchev used at the Party Congress in 1961 to justify intensification of the anti-Stalin campaign. Gorbachev broadened the idea to encompass guarantees of *perestroika* as a whole against regression. Thus, at the 19th Party Conference in June 1988, he averred: "the task of renewal requires guarantees .... We need such guarantees, to strengthen them" (Gorbachev, *Izbrannye*, vol. 6, p. 392).

[16] On the law-based state, see Gorbachev, *Perestroika*, pp. 91–5; Gorbachev, *Izbrannye*, vol. 6, pp. 354–7, 373–6 (June 1988 CPSU Conference).

historical change, within which stasis was viewed as regressive and change was treated as the normal condition of human affairs.[17] To be sure, the ideological tradition assumed that the transition from one system to another (as from capitalism to socialism) would require a violent revolution from below. But Gorbachev did not define *perestroika* as that kind of a transition; instead, socialism was still "developing" and *perestroika* would assist in the realization of socialism's potential. It would result not in a new historical system but rather in a more progressive, moral, and liberating variant of socialism.[18]

Gorbachev's comprehensive program was premised on the notion that culture must be transformed even more quickly than political and economic organization if structural changes were to take root and result in new patterns of behavior. This was the rationale for his emphasis on what he called "the human factor," which he had brought up already in December 1984 and on which he elaborated at the 27th Party Congress in February 1986.[19] In April 1986, he argued that cultural change – among both the elite and the masses – was a precondition for successful economic reform: "We have to begin, first of all, with changes in our attitudes and psychology, with the style and method of work.... I have to tell you frankly that, if we do not change ourselves, I am deeply convinced that there will be no changes in our economic and social life."[20] This was an argument that resonated positively during the stage of political succession, for it appealed to the puritans and technocrats as well – as long as the content of the proposed changes in attitude and style of work were not specified. The Soviet tradition had included a stage and concept of "cultural revolution." And the CPSU had always been touted as an organization whose activists would continuously educate and mold (*vospitat'*) the less-conscious masses. Hence, when Gorbachev called for more attention to the consciousness of the masses and to the role this might play in forging a more vibrant, dynamic, and efficient society, he struck a chord that was familiar to officials of the Party–State.

---

[17] Robert C. Tucker, *The Marxian Revolutionary Idea* (New York: Norton, 1969); Hanson, *Time and Revolution*.

[18] See Gorbachev, *Izbrannye*, vol. 4, pp. 370, 371 (February 1987 meeting in Central Committee); vol. 5, pp. 410–11 (November 1987 anniversary speech); vol. 6, p. 63 (February 1988 Central Committee Plenum), p. 395 (June 1988 CPSU Conference); Gorbachev, *Perestroika*, p. 37 ("*Perestroika* is a revolutionary process for it is a jump forward in the development of socialism, in the realization of its essential characteristics"). Brown quotes from an interview Gorbachev gave in 1992 in which he described the process of *perestroika* as having been intended to be "revolutionary in its essence but evolutionary in its tempo" (Brown, *The Gorbachev Factor*, p. 94).

[19] Gorbachev, *Izbrannye*, vol. 3, p. 217.

[20] Gorbachev speech, April 8, 1986, as quoted in Dusko Doder and Louise Branson, *Gorbachev: Heretic in the Kremlin* (New York: Viking, 1990), p. 137.

During his stage of ascendancy, Gorbachev would retain the commitment to cultural change but give it a radical, transformative content. Now the educated masses were treated as the source of wisdom, not simply clay to be molded by Party officials. Now officials would be held formally accountable to the conscious public, with secret-ballot elections and multiple candidacies. Now a "pluralism of opinions" and systemic criticism were defined as healthy phenomena that would better assist society as a whole to discover "truth." *Glasnost'* and democratization now implied an equalization of status between officials and masses as well as a process of formal accountability of those officials to the masses. It was difficult to disguise the threatening implications of these ideas and practices to officials of a Leninist regime, whatever their orientation. Gorbachev tried to reduce opposition by instituting procedures that allowed officials a disproportionate influence over the nomination process and that ensured a certain degree of corporate representation in the new parliament. Yet Gorbachev also obscured the more radical implications behind a veil of continuity.

One way he did this was periodically to declare that criticism and mass initiative, while prerequisites for the success of *perestroika,* were not absolutes. The goal must be "conscious discipline."[21] Criticism must combine "bravery" with a "principled orientation" – that is, *printsipial'nost',* which in Soviet lexicon means respect for the "correct [Party] line."[22] In February 1987, he addressed the issue of how far criticism should go in the era of *perestroika.* He declared that it must not be baseless; it must be *"partiinoi* (Party-minded), based on truth ... the sharper it is, the more responsible it should be."[23] A "law-based" *(pravovoe)* state creates a framework for "responsible" citizenship, not for unlimited license.[24] In like manner, Gorbachev echoed his predecessors' commitment to normative definitions of the public interest: "we support and will continue to support that which serves socialism, and will reject everything that is against the interests of the people."[25] This was a far cry from the tenets of *liberal* democracy, for it presumed that the public interest had to be defined by an enlightened elite and defended by that elite against citizens who were not principled, disciplined, or responsible.

---

[21] Gorbachev, *Perestroika,* p. 18.

[22] Gorbachev, *Izbrannye,* vol. 4, p. 326 (January 1987 Plenum).

[23] Ibid., p. 371 (February 1987 meeting in Central Committee); see also ibid., p. 359 (January 1987 Central Committee Plenum), and vol. 5, p. 415 (November 1987 anniversary speech).

[24] Gorbachev, *Perestroika,* pp. 93–4.

[25] Gorbachev, *Izbrannye,* vol. 6, p. 61 (February 1988 Central Committee Plenum); see also vol. 4, p. 327 (January 1987 Central Committee Plenum), and vol. 6, p. 393 (June 1988 CPSU Conference).

Gorbachev also reassured members of the Central Committee that, as long as they themselves got on the *perestroika* bandwagon, they had nothing to fear from the masses. The people, he argued repeatedly, are loyal to the Party, to *perestroika*, and to the system. They have been well educated by Soviet institutions and therefore have much expertise to offer. They need not be distrusted. Their activation need not be feared.[26]

For those who doubted the loyalty of the masses, Gorbachev provided assurance that a mighty and fundamentally legitimate Party–State, led by a determined general secretary, remained willing and able to enforce limits: "Is it possible that we, with such a powerful Party, such a patriotic people, which is dedicated to the ideas of socialism, to its Motherland, will not be able to cope if someone decides to use the wide-ranging *glasnost'*, the democratic process for self-serving and anti-societal aims, for the aim of blackening?"[27] Considering that the cohesion and capacity of the KGB and other control mechanisms remained high during Gorbachev's stage of ascendancy, many officials of the Party–State must have found this assurance to be credible.

In addition to reassurance, Gorbachev played upon the elite's lack of self-confidence to intimidate fence-sitters into cooperating with his policies. In his December 1984 "campaign" speech, he had defined the need for fundamental change as a national security imperative if the USSR was to "enter the 21st century as a great power," and he had implied that the country was on the brink of a prerevolutionary situation.[28] Once in power, he toned down such dire warnings, but they reappeared as his program became more radical. "We are living in a critical time," he warned in September 1986.[29] The "destiny of socialism" hinges on avoiding a repetition of the mistakes of the 1970s and early 1980s.[30] There is "no alternative"; *perestroika* is simply "an objective necessity."[31]

The result of these efforts, Gorbachev assured his audiences, would be satisfying and familiar to those who joined the *perestroika* bandwagon. He

[26] Gorbachev, *Izbrannye*, vol. 2, p. 235 (27th Party Congress of February 1986); vol. 4, pp. 35–6, 50–1 (July 1986); vol. 4, p. 359 (January 1987 Central Committee Plenum); vol. 5, p. 130 (June 1987 Central Committee Plenum); vol. 6, p. 70 (February 1988 Central Committee Plenum); vol. 6, pp. 394–5 (June 1988 CPSU Conference). See also Gorbachev, *Perestroika*, pp. 54–7.

[27] Gorbachev, *Izbrannye rechi*, vol. 4, p. 358 (January 1987 Central Committee Plenum).

[28] Ibid., vol. 2, p. 86.

[29] Ibid., vol. 4, p. 88.

[30] Ibid., p. 300 (January 1987 Central Committee Plenum); see also vol. 5, p. 130 (June 1987 Central Committee Plenum); vol. 6, p. 77 (February 1988 Central Committee Plenum); vol. 6, pp. 326, 394 (June 1988 CPSU Party Conference: "The fate of the country, the fate of socialism is at stake. We are obligated to make clear the sharpness of the situation to those who have yet to acknowledge it" [p. 394]).

[31] Ibid., p. 300 (section heading of address to January 1987 Central Committee Plenum).

could not specify in detail what that system would look like. But he assured them that it would meet the highest ideals of the Marxist tradition. As he put it toward the end of his speech to the June 1988 Party Conference:

> Yes, we do reject everything that deformed socialism in the 1930s and led it to stagnation in the 1970s. We want the type of socialism that has been cleansed from the encrustations (*nasloenii*) and perversions of past periods, but that retains everything that is best that came from the founders of socialist teaching.... We see socialism as a system of high culture and morality. It retains and reproduces the best accomplishments of the spiritual development of humankind, its rich moral experience. This is a society in which the life of working people is saturated with material and spiritual fulfillment, rejecting consumerism, lack of spirituality, and cultural primitivism.[32]

Although men like Ligachev and Ryzhkov were increasingly alienated by Gorbachev's radicalization, their ability jointly to oppose Gorbachev's initiatives was inhibited by the fact that they were alienated by different features of his program. Puritans were most concerned about affirming the leading role of the Party – and of orthodox values – in culture, politics, and administration. Technocrats were most concerned about rationalizing public administration by getting Party officials to interfere less in the workings of the ministerial bureaucracy and by rationalizing plan indicators. Thus, taking Chernyaev's informative memoir as a guide, we learn that Ryzhkov and Ligachev squared off in a December 1986 Politburo meeting about the desirability and necessity of retail price increases.[33] We also learn that, in November 1987, Ryzhkov blew up at Ligachev over economic reform policy: "Yegor Kuzmich personalizes the gross output, slave-driving, shock-work approach.... [T]he prime minister's reaction is understandable, he blew up.... It's been obvious for some time now that he [Ligachev] elicits a deep and barely concealed personal hostility, and not only from Ryzhkov."[34] And Ryzhkov delivered "the most forcefully emotional speech" against Ligachev over the Nina Andreeva affair (Spring 1988). Ryzhkov "even suggested relieving Ligachev of his control of ideology."[35]

But Ryzhkov's memoirs also reveal his alienation from both Ligachev and Gorbachev over an issue that is key to technocratic thinking: the calculation of what is possible. Ryzhkov denounces the anti-alcohol campaign as an example of a policy that placed ideology over practical considerations: "The tragedy of the campaign was in attempting to speed up and bring about the [immediate] achievement of what should have been a long-term program.

---

[32] Ibid., vol. 6, pp. 395, 396.
[33] Chernyaev, *Shest' let*, pp. 122–3.
[34] Ibid., p. 202.
[35] Ibid., pp. 205–6; see also Ryzhkov, *Desiat' let*, pp. 96–7, 102.

This demonstrated the personalities of Gorbachev and Ligachev – to solve problems immediately and quickly, without regard for real possibilities."[36] Yet it was Gorbachev's sponsorship of a campaignist approach to all of his policies, including *perestroika,* that made him appear to embody less of a break with the past than he would prove actually to be. As a result, during 1987–1989, Gorbachev was able to position himself as a liaison among shifting coalitions of supporters and dissenters within the Politburo. By shifting his political support among reformists, puritans, and technocrats, Gorbachev was able to forestall the creation of a stable coalition of opponents to his domestic policies.

JUSTIFYING A CONCESSIONARY FOREIGN POLICY

A similar pattern of justification of fundamental changes by cleverly linking them to the Marxist–Leninist tradition, and by presenting himself as an enlightened Marxist, can be found in Gorbachev's authority-building strategy in the realm of foreign policy.

Gorbachev used his proclaimed "new thinking" about international relations as justification for a concessionary foreign policy. The new thinking amounted to a new theory of international relations – one closer to liberal internationalism than to power politics, isolationism, or proletarian internationalism, which were its main competitors behind the scenes. The premises of the theory allowed Gorbachev to argue that his policies were not a sellout but a salvation, that they amounted to concessions to *reality* but not concessions to the imperialists per se. Given the cognitive and emotional condition of the elite, Gorbachev's audiences were predisposed to entertain these explanations as, at least, plausible. The plausibility of the claims, then, allowed Gorbachev to seize the initiative from rivals who argued that he was selling out the ideological heritage of the regime.

The power of the new thinking as justification can best be appreciated by comparing it to the "old thinking." Bear in mind that the Brezhnevite theory of international relations had been deployed to justify a nonconcessionary foreign policy, one that sought to collaborate and compete simultaneously – and to do each from a position of relative strength (or at least acknowledged equality) vis-à-vis the "imperialists." This was the meaning of the idea that "peaceful coexistence" was a form of class struggle. The collaborative urge under Brezhnev had been genuine, but it was not intended or allowed

---

[36] Ibid., p. 102.

to supplant or compromise the commitment of the Soviet leadership to the "anti-imperialist struggle," to Soviet hegemony in Eastern Europe, or to the continued division of Europe. What Gorbachev sought to justify was a policy that decisively subordinated or even abandoned the anti-imperialist struggle to the higher imperatives of great power collaboration, a policy that sought to eliminate inter-bloc competition on the European continent – indeed, to create a community of friendly states "from Vancouver to Vladivostok."

The basic tenets of the "old thinking" justified combining inter-bloc competition with collaborative management of the nuclear relationship.[37] However much Soviet doctrine had evolved since the death of Stalin, it was still based on a two-camps (or two-blocs) image of the international system in which an ongoing struggle between imperialist and anti-imperialist forces was shaping the future of international relations and was fostering – at some indeterminate point in the future – the "final crisis of capitalism." Class interests, though set within the existing state system, were still the driving force of international politics. Peaceful coexistence was a necessary concession to the realities of the nuclear age, but it sought to create a safe umbrella under which the competitive struggle could proceed and not to sacrifice class struggle on the altar of collaboration. Peaceful coexistence, then, was meant to make the world safe for the spread and defense of socialist values.

All of this was consistent with the two primary normative commitments that had been embedded in the Leninist–Stalinist heritage since 1918. The Bolshevik Party had a historical responsibility to maintain the power of the CPSU in the USSR *and* to assist the eventual global victory of socialism over imperialism. In practice these desiderata often conflicted with each other. In the nuclear age, they led to a constant wariness of the escalatory potential inherent in competitive or confrontational initiatives. However, with the possible exception of Khrushchev in 1963–1964,[38] they never led to the abandonment of one or the other normative commitment.

The commitment to anti-imperialist struggle was sustained, despite periodic setbacks and sobering experiences, by philosophical assumptions built

[37] Studies that specify the content of foreign policy doctrine under Brezhnev include: John Lenczowski, *Soviet Perceptions of U.S. Foreign Policy* (Ithaca, NY: Cornell University Press, 1982); R. Judson Mitchell, *Ideology of a Superpower* (Stanford, CA: Hoover Institution, 1982); Franklyn Griffiths, "The sources of American conduct: Soviet perspectives and their policy implications," *International Security*, vol. 9, no. 1 (Fall 1984), pp. 30–50; Zimmerman, *Soviet Perspectives*; Richard D. Anderson, *Public Politics in an Authoritarian State: Making Foreign Policy during the Brezhnev Years* (Ithaca, NY: Cornell University Press, 1993); S. Neil MacFarlane, *Superpower Rivalry and 3rd World Radicalism: The Idea of National Liberation* (London: Croom Helm, 1985).

[38] See Zimmerman, *Soviet Perspectives*, pp. 99–101, 152, 196–205, 222ff., 259–69.

into the ideological heritage. A Marxist–Leninist treated conflict and change as the normal conditions of international politics, as indeed of history and matter more generally. Hence setbacks and struggles were to be expected, but discouragement was prevented by the assumption that time is on the side of socialism and that eventual victory is assured. This assumption did not have to be demonstrated empirically. Indeed, the philosophy of knowledge on which the ideology was based presumed that, in any given era, only the process of struggle itself would reveal the scope of currently attainable gains. This reinforced the commitment to struggle, just as belief in the inevitability of eventual victory served to maintain morale. Once that belief was irretrievably lost, morale – or the stomach for sustained anti-imperialist struggle in the face of rising costs – plummeted as well.

Gorbachev's new thinking was crafted in this context of lost belief and damaged self-confidence. It substituted for the old precepts a quite different perspective on international politics.[39] In place of two-camp struggle based on class interests, Gorbachev touted the "interdependence" of the world community, the commonality of interests among states of North America, Europe, and the USSR, and the transcendant threats to "all-human interests" posed by nuclear competition, the militarization of international relations, the proliferation of weapons of mass destruction, Third World poverty, and environmental hazards. Peaceful coexistence, his spokespersons argued, must no longer be viewed as a form of class struggle. Rather, it is an end in itself, essential to avert threats to the survival of humankind inherent in unrestrained competition. It was therefore imperative that the great powers, and especially the superpowers, put an end to their military competition and collaborate on the resolution of transnational existential threats.

The new thinking was especially critical of the use of military force as a means of dealing with threats to states. Since violence contains the greatest escalatory potential in interstate relations, and since global interdependence ensures that violent disruptions may reverberate throughout the international order, demilitarization of relations among states was a priority. From this it followed that great-power relations could not be built upon mutual intimidation; rather, the goal was a "mutual security" in which neither side tried to base its own security on the other side's insecurity.

---

[39] Studies of the doctrinal content of Gorbachev's new thinking include: Allen Lynch, *Gorbachev's International Outlook: Intellectual Origins and Political Consequences* (Boulder, CO: Westview, 1989); Margot Light, *The Soviet Theory of International Relations* (New York: St. Martin's, 1988); V. Kubalkova and A. A. Cruickshank, *Thinking "New" about Soviet New Thinking* (Berkeley: University of California, Institute of International Studies, no. 74, 1989); Robert D. English, *Russia and the Idea of the West: Gorbachev, Intellectuals and the End of the Cold War* (New York: Columbia University Press, 2000).

An important tactical component of the new thinking was the entreaty to "deny the imperialists their 'enemy image'." On this score, the new thinking proclaimed that, in order to build a collaborative relationship with the West, it was necessary to reshape the politics of foreign policy decisionmaking in the West. If hardliners remained ascendant in Western capitals, then Soviet overtures would not be reciprocated and the prospect of great-power collaboration would not be realized. Accordingly, the USSR's historical responsibility was to make offers the West could not refuse in order to delegitimize the hardliners' claim that the communist enemy could never be trusted. Thus, Soviet policies would assist the transformation of both public and elite opinion in Western countries, helping thereby to create the political basis for the kind of sustained collaboration required to defuse threats to civilization.

As we documented in Chapter 3, Gorbachev's speeches of December 1984 had already endorsed concepts associated with new thinking and new thinkers in foreign relations. However, as in his address to the 27th Party Congress in February 1986,[40] such endorsement had coexisted – not very peacefully – with traditional rhetoric about the "world revolutionary process" and the "anti-imperialist struggle." At that time, new themes were present but not prominent in his speeches. In 1987, however, Gorbachev largely eliminated the traditionalist rhetoric. Themes of the new thinking occupied center stage in his major address of February 1987 to an international conference of peace activists gathered in Moscow.[41] Implications of the new thinking were elaborated extensively in the book Gorbachev published that year, which was intended for both internal and external audiences.[42]

SELLING SALVATION OR SELLING OUT?

In what ways could these doctrinal substitutions justify a concessionary foreign policy? How could they gain credibility among audiences beset by self-doubt concerning their own political staying power at home and abroad? Perhaps most striking about the content and tone of the new thinking was its resonance with certain features of the Marxist–Leninist ideological heritage, which allowed many "romantic Leninists" to relate to it even if they were ambivalent about its content. Thus, as Kubalkova and Cruickshank have nicely demonstrated,[43] the new thinking, like the Leninist heritage in Soviet foreign policy, was highly moralistic, missionary, and self-righteous in presenting the

---

[40] *Izbrannye*, vol. 3, esp. pp. 245–52.
[41] *Izbrannye*, vol. 4, pp. 376–92.
[42] Gorbachev, *Perestroika*.
[43] *Thinking "New."*

Soviet Union as a beacon for world public opinion. It presented the image of a radiant future to be brokered by a progressive USSR that possessed special insight into historical necessity and was mobilizing global social forces to discredit militarist "old thinkers" in all countries. In this respect, the new thinking could appeal as well to "Soviet patriots," who were primarily interested in Western acceptance of the USSR as a co-equal great power; they were being promised a future in which their country would play a leading role in the promised transformation of international relations.

This perspective fed nicely into traditional Soviet optimism as well as Leninist ontology. It presented the newly defined radiant future as a potential that is latent within the current international system – but a potential that can be realized only through conscious action and determined consciousness-raising. In this respect, global interdependence and a "common European home" were latent conditions and also policy goals. At the same time, the new thinking presented interdependence as an autonomously growing trend within international relations, one that could be resisted only at growing cost and with potentially catastrophic consequences. All of this echoed precisely a key philosophical premise of Marxism–Leninism: the inevitability of the desirable. The victory of socialism at home and abroad was historically inevitable, but only if enlightened elites struggled to realize the socialist potential latent within the current order of things.

The idea of "robbing the imperialists of their enemy image" was also an ingenious update of a traditional Soviet perspective on East–West competition. Leninist and Stalinist foreign policy had always looked to influence or ally with potentially progressive forces in Western societies against militarist elites within those countries. After Stalin, this tendency continued but was supplemented by a more differentiated image of Western elites, which led Khrushchev and Brezhnev at times to urge policies that would help the "moderates" or "bourgeois realists" in their policy struggles with the "madmen."[44] Thus, Gorbachev's strategy of helping to raise the consciousness of global masses about the need for transnational cooperation, as well as his strategy of undercutting the credibility of hardliners in policymaking circles, resonated with important tactical components of the Leninist heritage.

In a practical sense, Gorbachev's deprecation of the utility – and magnification of the dangers – of the military instrument in global affairs provided a justification for undercutting the political weight of powerful constituencies

---

[44] Zimmerman, *Soviet Perspectives*; Franklyn Griffiths, "Images, politics, and learning in Soviet behavior toward the United States" (Ph.D. dissertation, Columbia University, New York, 1972).

in contemporary Soviet politics. Moreover, his redefinition of security as having to be "mutual" challenged the unilateralism and self-sufficiency inherent in Soviet military doctrine. Surely, elite audiences who lacked self-confidence about their ability to continue in the old way, who were intimidated by the prospect of another arms race, and who realized to their chagrin that the arms buildup under Brezhnev had not, after all, shifted the correlation of forces to the advantage of socialism, were susceptible to an alternative way of thinking about global politics. Similarly, conservative elites who realized that repeated Soviet invasions had not reduced the endemic instability of East European regimes were susceptible to an alternative vision of political order on the European continent. Gorbachev's redefinitions could provide solace to these audiences even as they angered the unreconstructed militarists.

To a lesser degree (but still substantially), this redefinition also resonated with the Leninist heritage, for the "correlation of forces" doctrine had roots in a tradition that never measured power in purely military terms. In contrast to some balance-of-power notions in Western "realist" thought, the Leninist correlation of forces insisted that the sources of power are multidimensional. Gorbachev was thus plausibly emphasizing some of those other dimensions, including moral authority. Then too, the correlation of forces doctrine was always explicitly *dynamic* in its thrust; as Seweryn Bialer has noted, it focused on the correlation of *trends*.[45] Hence audiences who had a sense of foreboding about the future could receive reassurance from the new thinking. Its emphasis on other sources of power, and on conscious struggle to realize the potential latent within the international system, could shift the correlation of trends back to the advantage of the Soviet Union in world affairs – or at least could stop the anti-Soviet tide. The outcome might not be socialist revolution or victory in the anti-imperialist struggle, both of which Gorbachev either wrote off or downplayed, but it would be a new era of Soviet co-leadership in world affairs that would help to avert catastrophes facing the global village.

Another strength of the new thinking as an act of political salesmanship was that elements of it had already been legitimized in Soviet politics in earlier decades. The dangers of nuclear war, and the implicit "all-human" stake in avoiding it, had been central to doctrinal innovations that Malenkov (and, later, Khrushchev) had introduced in the 1950s and 1960s.[46] Those doctrinal changes survived Khrushchev's overthrow more or less intact, facilitating the

---

[45] Seweryn Bialer, *Stalin's Successors: Leadership, Stability, and Change in the Soviet Union* (Cambridge University Press, 1980), p. 246.

[46] In addition to Zimmerman, *Soviet Perspectives,* and Griffiths, "The Sources," see Evangelista, *Unarmed Warriors.*

détente of the early 1970s. Likewise, notions of global interdependence had entered official Soviet rhetoric, albeit tentatively, under Khrushchev and even before him, as these notions had typically been emphasized for tactical purposes during traditional Soviet "breathing spells" in foreign policy. To be sure, Gorbachev was now elaborating these concepts to an unprecedented extent and was drawing conclusions for Soviet global power that by far exceeded those of his predecessors. Yegor Ligachev, for example, was correct to complain in 1988 that the regime's Leninist identity was threatened by the recent substitution of "all-human interests" for class interests as the top priority of Soviet foreign policy.[47] But precisely because the concepts were familiar ones, and because they could be used to justify either a breathing spell or a more fundamental reevaluation, they afforded Gorbachev the tactical advantage – whether he planned it this way or not – of postponing awareness among the fence-sitters and ambivalents in the Central Committee of the full implications of what he was doing.

There was more than just formal doctrinal change involved in the process of justifying Gorbachev's giveaways. There were also tactical maneuvers with which he supplemented the new doctrine. Consider, for example, his behavior in Washington, D.C., in December 1987, when he made concessions that allowed him and President Reagan to finalize and sign the INF Treaty. After the signing, Gorbachev and Shevardnadze stood up, beaming, and raised their arms straight up in a victory gesture.[48] Victory? Gorbachev, in the course of 1987, had abandoned every negotiating position upon which Soviet leaders had been insisting since 1979. But this was victory according to a different set of criteria. Moscow had made Reagan an offer he could not refuse and robbed him of his "enemy image" of the USSR. Gorbachev had delivered the presumably irreconcilable author of Star Wars missile defense and "evil empire" rhetoric to the temple of negotiation and collaboration. Gorbachev and Shevardnadze had proven that one could do business with Reagan – or better, that Reagan could be induced to do business with them. The U.S. missiles would not be deployed after all!

This was an entirely different set of "success indicators" from those traditionally employed by Soviet negotiators. Until then, the cost of achieving the goal had been the issue; but as Gorbachev redefined the game, the cost was to be downplayed if not ignored. The goal of delivering Reagan and of ending the deployment of Pershing and cruise missiles on land in Europe had been accomplished.

---

[47] *Pravda,* August 6, 1988, p. 2.
[48] "The CBS Evening News," December 8, 1987.

This conception of reciprocity – and of equivalence of exchange in the East–West relationship – was new to Soviet bargaining behavior. It could only have been sold in terms that played to the elite's loss of self-confidence. At the theoretical level, the new thinking did just that, making a virtue of proclaimed necessity. Yet even below the level of theory, at the very practical level of everyday political rhetoric, Gorbachev played to the loss of self-confidence with the much-applied proclamation: "there is no alternative!"[49]

Consider the implications of this claim. In effect, it argues that the appropriate success indicator for judging Soviet negotiating behavior is not conformance of the deal to some preconceived notion of equal sacrifice by each superpower. "There is no alternative" is an implicitly dynamic concept, one that invites the audience to consider the consequences of intransigence and of the failure to reach agreement. It stands in contrast to the static conceptions of quantitative parity and equivalent exchange that marked U.S.–Soviet negotiations throughout the 1970s. Gorbachev was telling his audiences that intransigence would allow the emergence of a reality still more disagreeable than the reality he proposed to negotiate with the United States. In the INF negotiations, for example, the implication was that the deployment of Pershing and cruise missiles in Europe, faced by a large and growing Soviet arsenal of SS-20s and by other countermeasures against the U.S. deployments (and then by U.S. reactions to those countermeasures), would be more disagreeable than intrusively verified elimination of all these missiles by both sides.[50]

When we consider tactical advantages, no catalog of the times would be complete without mention of the term "new thinking." The connotations of the phrase squared with a climate of opinion that was eager to "get the country moving again" after the geriatric leadership's debacles of the early 1980s. But the term also facilitated seizure of the political initiative and disabling of one's opponents by its progressive and optimistic connotations. Doubters were waved off as "old thinkers." New thinking was a sign that you had understood the requirements of historical necessity, that you recognized the

---

[49] Already in April 1985, Gorbachev had been arguing that "there is no other way" when proclaiming that a decisive break with Brezhnevism was needed (Gorbachev, *Izbrannye*, vol. 2, p. 155; see also p. 212 [May 1985]). The argument, of course, had been implicit in his December 1984 speech, when he suggested that Russia could lose its great-power status or could face a revolutionary situation at home if it did not change course. What changed in 1987 was the application of the claim ("there is no alternative") to a specified, transformational program for breaking out of the constraints of the culture and institutions (ideology and organization) bequeathed by Brezhnev.

[50] Although speculative, it is not difficult to imagine discussions in which Gorbachev countered the defiant negotiating proposals of militant colleagues with the challenge: *"nu, i potom, chto?"* ("yes, and what *then?*").

direction in which history was moving. Old thinkers had allowed themselves to become myopic about their "historical responsibility." Who would want to be so dubbed?

None of this is to claim that clever argumentation alone was sufficient to sell a concessionary foreign policy. Surely, both the message and the messenger had an impact. Gorbachev built up his power base before launching his foreign policy revolution. Moreover, his strong personality, capacity for complex debate in small groups, and magnificent sense of political timing and surprise during his rise to ascendancy (though not thereafter) reinforced the image projected by his power – thereby giving his audiences a motivation to follow him, or at least not to defy him. The content, tone, and form of the new thinking then became an important reinforcement of both power and personality, helping Gorbachev to build his authority as a foreign policy decisionmaker even as (by traditional standards) he was "giving away the store."

Thus, in both domestic and foreign policy, Gorbachev built authority by first consolidating his power while cultivating the image of a "responsible" innovator and then pushing to the fore with a comprehensive, radical program that he managed to present as a novel synthesis of Leninism and procedural democracy: "socialist democracy." This strategy was ingenious as long as his political audiences were unable to calculate the magnitude of the threats to their interests and identities that lurked below the surface. It did not take long before these became obvious.

5

Gorbachev on the Political Defensive

The twelve months between mid-1989 and mid-1990 were one of those turning points in a leader's administration when suddenly things start to go very wrong. Khrushchev experienced this from mid-1960 to mid-1961. For Brezhnev, the tide did not turn so suddenly; his domestic program faltered in 1972, his foreign policy only during 1974–1976. For Gorbachev, as for Khrushchev, one year highlighted the contradictions within both his domestic and foreign policy programs. This also meant that both men suddenly experienced a crisis of credibility. Both of them had promised a great deal and had pushed themselves to the fore as sponsors of a transformative vision.[1] Hence, they could not credibly diffuse responsibility for failure onto the leadership collective. Their authority was on the line. In Gorbachev's case, he found himself at the mercy of domestic and international forces he himself had unleashed as he introduced an autonomous public arena into Soviet politics and as he pursued a conciliatory foreign policy. This chapter analyzes the vulnerabilities of Gorbachev's domestic and foreign policies and his efforts to retain and recoup his political authority as those vulnerabilities became obvious.

VULNERABILITIES OF PERESTROIKA

During 1988–1989, the contradictions within Gorbachev's program for *perestroika* started to become obvious. His strategy of giving the official class a

---

[1] Khrushchev's transformative vision of 1959–1960 was of a Leninist system that had achieved its utopian goal. Since Khrushchev was not seeking to destroy the Leninist system, however, I have been referring to his leadership as "reformist" and to Gorbachev's as "transformational." This should not be confused with my use here of "transformative vision" to refer to both men's programs during their stages of ascendancy.

stake in the new order by only gradually shifting authority from Party executive organs to soviet legislative organs, while a boon for democracy, created a situation in which officials of the Party and the state had both the incentive and the opportunity to instead "steal the state": privatizing and stealing the assets of their agencies and contributing thereby to a collapse of public administration that was becoming increasingly evident in 1990.[2] Similarly, his strategy of giving officials the opportunity to become businessmen, while it gave them a stake in the new order, also gave them the opportunity to use their continuing official power to monopolize business activity in the budding private sector that they were entering.

Glasnost' revealed the contradictions between Leninism and liberalism. Gorbachev had attempted to expand the functions of *glasnost'* from a limited "searchlight" role – selectively exposing incompetence and malfeasance among officials – to a broader, more systemic critique. But he tried to do so gradually in order to avoid driving moderates into the ranks of the extremists on both ends of the political spectrum. Indeed, during 1987–1988, while increasingly removing the shackles of censorship, he also tried to keep journal and newspaper editors from going too far, tried to strike a balance between the old and the new in his public statements, and tried to maintain the fiction of there being a "correct Party line" to which agents of the regime were expected to conform.[3]

All of this was easier said than done. During 1988–1989, the forces of radicalism within the cultural intelligentsia, the journalistic community, and the Academy of Sciences were publishing increasingly bold and systemic critiques; they did so within the very public arenas that Gorbachev had created for them.[4] Whereas Gorbachev was willing to criticize Stalin, they were willing to criticize Lenin also. Whereas Gorbachev was willing to denounce the

---

[2] Steven L. Solnick, *Stealing the State: Control and Collapse in Soviet Institutions* (Cambridge, MA: Harvard University Press, 1998).

[3] See, for example, his speech on the 70th anniversary of the 1917 Bolshevik Revolution, November 7, 1987 (Mikhail Gorbachev, *Izbrannye rech'i i stat'i* [Moscow: Izdatel'stvo politicheskoi literatury, 1987], vol. 5, pp. 386–436).

[4] For studies of the evolution of *glasnost'* and of this tension between Gorbachev and the radicals, see Alec Nove, *Glasnost' in Action: Cultural Renaissance in Russia* (Boston: Unwin Hyman, 1989); Roy Medvedev and Giuletto Chiesa, *Time of Change: An Insider's View of Russia's Transformation* (New York: Random House, 1989); Stephen F. Cohen and Katrina vanden Heuvel, *Voices of Glasnost: Interviews with Gorbachev's Reformers* (New York: Norton, 1989); William & Jane Taubman, *Moscow Spring* (New York: Summit, 1989); Andrei Melville and Gail W. Lapidus (Eds.), *The Glasnost Papers: Voices on Reform from Moscow* (Boulder, CO: Westview, 1990); Jack F. Matlock, Jr., *Autopsy on an Empire* (New York: Random House, 1995).

corruption of many officials and the Party apparatus for acting as a "braking mechanism" on the implementation of *perestroika*,[5] the radicals were willing to argue that the system of single-party rule itself was the problem – that it created and protected a class of corrupt officials and that it was incapable of being reformed. Whereas Gorbachev countenanced a far-reaching yet only partial review of the crimes of Soviet history, the radicals insisted on a complete review of that history. Whereas Gorbachev was willing to institute parliamentary elections, the radicals called for public election of the president and an end to the exclusive nominating procedures employed during the first parliamentary elections. Gorbachev, both to protect his power and to regulate the process of transformation in order to keep it peaceful, wanted to retain the ability to modulate free expression. The radicals wanted an absolute commitment to free speech. As a result, the rate of radicalization of the active, mobilized public during 1989–1990 was decidedly outpacing Gorbachev's strategy for maintaining a balance between the "moderate right" and the "moderate left" while retaining for himself an indispensable political role as balancer between the two poles.[6]

In economic policy, Gorbachev moved cautiously and with half-measures, thus heightening the contradictions. He reduced the prerogatives of ministries and central planners, but went slow on (or entirely avoided) the construction of market institutions, de-monopolization of the economy, and liberalization of prices. The consequence was that, by 1989–1990, the capacity of the command system to coordinate exchange relationships within the economy had been crippled, but a market economy had not yet been created as a substitute. Perhaps Gorbachev rationalized that opening the economy to the world market, as he began to do with his unprecedented joint-ventures legislation in January 1987, would offset these deficiencies. But that would take time as well as a further loosening of restrictions on joint ventures. In the near term, this left the economy with the worst of both worlds, suffering from extreme disequilibrium and lack of coordination.

[5] Mikhail Gorbachev, *Perestroika: New Thinking for Our Country and the World* (New York: Perennial, 1987), pp. 97–8.

[6] For a penetrating analysis of the contradictions that emerged as political space was opened to autonomous political expression, see Michael Urban (with Vyecheslav Igrunov and Sergei Mitrokhin), *The Rebirth of Politics in Russia* (Cambridge University Press, 1997), chs. 3–6. For other excellent case studies of this rebirth of political society, see Kathleen E. Smith, *Remembering Stalin's Victims: Popular Memory and the End of the USSR* (Ithaca, NY: Cornell University Press, 1996); Jane I. Dawson, *Eco-nationalism: Anti-Nuclear Activism and National Identity in Russia, Lithuania, and Ukraine* (Durham, NC: Duke University Press, 1996); M. Steven Fish, *Democracy from Scratch: Opposition and Regime in the New Russian Revolution* (Princeton, NJ: Princeton University Press, 1995).

For example, Gorbachev's strategy of gradually increasing the opportunities for private commercial activity, while leaving such activities only semi-legitimized and under heavy regulatory restrictions, provided the opportunity for corrupt officials and organized crime to extort from, and ultimately control, the budding, small-scale private sector – and to ensure against the emergence of a truly competitive market. Moreover, Gorbachev's refusal to tackle macroeconomic stabilization by liberalizing price controls led him to borrow money abroad and spend money desperately to counter disequilibria in the economy, which exacerbated hidden inflation, shortages, and a severe budgetary shortfall. By mid-1990, the shelves of foodstores were largely empty in Moscow at a time when people had the newfound freedom to complain loudly and to seek electoral revenge against Party officials for the situation.[7]

This points to still another contradiction. Gorbachev, consistent with the Marxist tradition, defined Soviet socialism as a salvageable system. He promised to realize the potential of that system by demonstrating that a "good" society (a "socialist democracy") lay latent within Soviet society. In order to accomplish this, he needed to mobilize the "human factor" – the young, the educated, and the idealistic – by removing the shackles imposed on them by a corrupted Party apparatus. Like Khrushchev earlier, Gorbachev argued that Party activists, not Party bureaucrats, would become the leadership core of a future socialist society. They would lead by example, and they would help to bring out the best in people. Gorbachev argued that cultural transformation would be a product of persuasion and inspiration and that conscious mobilization of the population, led by the best and the brightest among Party activists, was the route toward that end. By contrast, the regulatory institutions and incentive structures typical of highly competitive, capitalist societies were based on the assumption that human beings can be motivated only by coercion and greed – that human nature is ultimately egoistic and invidious, and that discipline needs to be imposed from without. Instead, Gorbachev's program was based on the premise that human beings in a socialist society are essentially charitable and collectivistic, if properly inspired.

Such an optimistic vision may or may not be intrinsically realistic, but that is beside the point. In the Soviet case, it is clear that realization of the vision required both time and improvements in everyday material conditions. However, Gorbachev found himself with very little "political time" on his hands. He could not demonstrate the collectivistic potential latent within Soviet citizens on short order (if ever). And, given the contradictions in his

---

[7] On the contradictions within Gorbachev's approach to economic reform, see Marshall I. Goldman, *What Went Wrong with Perestroika* (New York: Norton, 1991).

economic policy, material conditions deteriorated. Hence, many Soviet citizens, anxious about material conditions and unshackled by *glasnost'*, became cynics and/or critics, rapidly losing faith in *perestroika* and becoming vocal opponents of Soviet leaders in Moscow. Gorbachev could hardly recoup his authority in 1990–1991 by pointing to this mobilized opposition (such as the "Democratic Russia" movement) as an example of the new socialist citizen, for they were already rejecting him as insufficiently radical.

In 1989–1990 as well, centrifugal forces within the federation at large threatened to reach a point of no return. Secession was already on the front burner in the Baltic states, inter-ethnic violence was starting to sweep the Caucasus and portions of Central Asia, and the Nagorno–Karabakh issue between Armenia and Azerbaidjan had already resulted in open warfare. Here Gorbachev fell victim to his program's lack of appreciation of the depth of nationalist sentiment in the republics. *Glasnost'* had created an autonomous public arena in which to press nationalist and secessionist demands. Disintegration of the command economy undercut the ties that bound together the economies of the republics within the Soviet Union. Economic nationalism reinforced growing civic and ethnic nationalism in those union republics. Democratization introduced competitive elections to republican legislatures that fundamentally undermined the centralized system of cadre control that Gorbachev had inherited. Henceforth, republic-level officials would know that their political careers hinged as much, and perhaps more, on satisfying constituents "below" as on catering to political bosses "above" in Moscow. The combination of all these policies, together with Gorbachev's reluctance to use force to define strict limits to republican initiatives, further angered and demoralized officials of the military and the KGB – the very institutions that would be needed to prevent disintegration from resulting in dissolution of the USSR. In sum, the weakening of central control and the transformative policies embraced by Gorbachev brought to the fore a series of contradictions within Soviet ethnofederalism, contradictions that Soviet leaders had previously managed through a combination of strict political controls and economic benefits to the politically conformist.[8]

---

[8] On the evolution of tensions between the republics and the center during 1988–1990, see Gail W. Lapidus, "Gorbachev and the 'national question': Restructuring the Soviet Federation," *Soviet Economy*, vol. 5, no. 3 (July–September 1989), pp. 201–50, and Gregory Gleason (Ed.), *Federalism and Nationalism: The Struggle for Republican Rights in the USSR* (Boulder, CO: Westview, 1990). On the contradictions within Soviet ethnofederalism, see Ronald Suny, *The Revenge of the Past: Nationalism, Revolution, and the Collapse of the Soviet Union* (Stanford, CA: Stanford University Press, 1993), and Valerie Bunce, *Subversive Institutions: The Design and Destruction of Socialism and the State* (Cambridge University Press, 1999).

Gorbachev had no realistic strategy for keeping nationalism within bounds once his policies removed both the incentives and the threats on which Soviet central power had rested. He assumed that negotiations among leaders of the republics, plus a nationwide referendum, would lead to a middle ground on which a stable federation would rest. He further assumed that he could rein in the forces of both reaction and secession. He proved capable of doing neither, though he did prevent a full-blown reactionary backlash against centrifugal tendencies. But he was unwilling or unable to join forces fully with either extreme to save his political hide.

Thus, Gorbachev's policies crippled the ability of the old system to defend itself *as a system* against the very social forces his policies had unleashed. The result was not the creation of a stable equilibrium on which a middle way could rest. Instead, the result was systemic disintegration, public mobilization of opposition to that system, and a relentless slide toward collapse. Gorbachev never advocated abolition of the Communist Party or collapse of the Soviet Union. But that is what he got, and the speed with which this occurred discredited his leadership, leaving him little time to recoup his political authority.

VULNERABILITIES OF THE NEW THINKING

Even as Gorbachev's domestic policies were foundering, one could discern vulnerabilities within the new thinking that would make it susceptible to counterattack. Here, in the foreign policy realm, contradictions were increasingly being revealed between the new thinking's idealistic liberal internationalism and the *realpolitik* that still informed the foreign policies of the United States. The new thinking, as a way of conceptualizing international politics and thereby of justifying Soviet concessionary behavior, was both intrinsically vulnerable and losing credibility in light of events abroad.

One such vulnerability was intrinsic to the tension in Marxist–Leninist theory between the potential and the actual. Khrushchev and Brezhnev had touted the traditional Leninist claim that the twentieth century was indeed the era of the "final crisis of capitalism" and that the global correlation of forces was shifting in favor of socialism. It was the historical responsibility of the USSR to assist those forces that would effect the final crisis and the decisive shift. But one could not know in advance whether such assistance was on the verge of making the difference. It remained only an article of faith that victory was "inevitable."

In like manner – but with very different purposes and much greater urgency – Gorbachev had predicted that the contemporary world was becoming so interdependent and dangerous that all reasonable people would recognize the need for an anti-militarist, cooperative world order. He further predicted that, as a result of Soviet concessionary foreign policies, international public opinion and (accordingly) the leaders of major governments would acknowledge the moral force of the USSR and treat that country as a leading power within the emerging world order. Having based his foreign policies on this prediction, Gorbachev had to search for evidence that the potential he so loudly touted was indeed being realized. He had to worry about his ability to demonstrate that his concessionary behavior was in fact helping to transform the adversary (by robbing him of his "enemy image") and helping to actualize the potential for a new world order inherent in the "fact" of global interdependence. (This authority-maintenance imperative was, I take it, in part responsible for his triumphant posturing at the December 1987 summit in Washington.) Thus, the credibility of Gorbachev's authority-building strategy in the foreign policy realm was hostage to the behavior of the United States and to events (in Afghanistan, Europe, the United States, and elsewhere) that were largely beyond his control.

Unfortunately for Gorbachev, he was not able to demonstrate much more actualization of potential than the willingness of Ronald Reagan and George Bush to sign deals that involved Soviet acceptance of maximal U.S. terms. Nor was Gorbachev able to claim that his idealistic, self-denying internationalism was being reciprocated by the United States. The U.S. invasion of Panama in 1989 and the Persian Gulf confrontation (1990) and war (1991), although not threatening to Soviet national security, provided fuel for arguments that U.S. politics were not changing at all, that *realpolitik* remained the driving perspective behind U.S. foreign policy, that military force remained the primary instrumentality of U.S. foreign policy, and that the U.S. goal was a unipolar world, not an East–West collective security system. The Persian Gulf war demonstrated this contradiction at work. On the one hand, Gorbachev accepted and endorsed the use of military force against Saddam Hussein if the Iraqi leader did not withdraw his troops from Kuwait. On the other hand, Gorbachev tried desperately to avoid the war, attempting last-minute Soviet mediation of the conflict between Washington and Baghdad. It was a measure of the political dilemma in which he found himself that the Soviet leader left town (Moscow) when President Bush expressed irritation at Soviet efforts and launched the ground offensive against Iraq.[9]

A further vulnerability of the new thinking revealed itself in Eastern Europe during 1989. Gorbachev assumed that an all-European security community

---

[9] *Pravda*, February 25, 1991, p. 1, and March 1, 1991, pp. 1–2.

could eventually emerge as the Soviet Union and the socialist states of Eastern Europe transformed themselves into socialist democracies and sought a joint, Soviet-backed rapprochement with Western Europe and the United States. Toward this end, he even encouraged reformist forces within Eastern Europe to assert themselves against recalcitrant communist elites – in the faith that this would lead to the construction of socialist democracies rather than revolutionary overthrow of the entire political order. Just as Gorbachev assumed that a democratic–internationalist equilibrium could develop in interrepublican relations within the USSR, so he assumed that such an equilibrium could develop in Eastern Europe. Both assumptions proved illusory. The alternative to state socialism in Eastern Europe was not socialist democracy and a foreign policy of equal friendship with both East and West. Rather, it was either revanchist nationalism or liberal democracy and an effort to join Western Europe at the expense of relations with the USSR. Gorbachev's search for a stable equilibrium was frustrated by a cascade of revolutions against both Communist Party rule and alliance with the USSR.

The collapse of communism in Eastern Europe not only discredited Gorbachev's promise to reconcile transformation and stability, it also undercut his promise to reconcile transformation with Soviet national security. Gorbachev's eagerness to claim that traditional definitions of national security had become obsolete was here put to its most severe test. Panama and Iraq damaged the credibility of Gorbachev's claims about the broader international order. But events in Eastern Europe hit even closer to home: collapse of the Warsaw Pact, reunification of Germany within NATO, demands from Poland, Hungary, and Czechoslovakia that Soviet troops depart their country as soon as possible, a Conventional Forces in Europe Treaty in which the West secured asymmetrical deep cuts in Soviet armed forces, and the sudden emergence of Western rhetoric about "victory" in the Cold War. All these events cascaded in less than a year, between late 1989 and late 1990. They bolstered the credibility of counterclaims that the international order had not essentially changed for the better and that the shifting correlation of trends internationally actually posed a direct threat to Soviet national security and, indeed, to the survival of the USSR as a state.

Such a critique was compelling, as communist states collapsed *seriatim* throughout Eastern Europe during the second half of 1989. But Gorbachev could not bring himself to use force to stem the tide. In his mind, the prospective costs of doing so exceeded by far the costs of living with the consequences of these anti-communist revolutions. Gorbachev had built his authority at home *and abroad* by arguing against the continued militarization of state–society relations and relations among states. By 1989, he would have had to renounce everything he had stood for publicly if he had sent the tanks back into

Eastern Europe. This would have cost him the good relations he had developed with Western leaders as well as the prospects of material benefit and international integration ("Europe – our Common Home") that those relations held. Remilitarization would also have undercut the stated rationale for continued democratization of his own country. Of course, it would also have deeply undercut his credibility as a leader among the audiences to which he had directed his authority-building appeals. Furthermore, by 1989, it might also have run counter to the self-image and values he had internalized during 1985–1989.[10]

Hence, Gorbachev acquiesced in the East European revolutions and tried to make the losses more palatable to his political audiences. He negotiated a deal with the United States and Germany that provided for substantial material assistance to the USSR and for a phased (rather than precipitous) withdrawal of Soviet troops from eastern Germany. In exchange, he accepted what had fast become a fait accompli: the reunification of Germany within NATO. But material assistance, in the eyes of most Soviet politicians, was scant compensation for national humiliation and national-security perils. Not surprisingly, when Foreign Minister Shevardnadze resigned in December 1990, he complained specifically about those deputies who were accusing him of a sellout in the Persian Gulf and Eastern Europe.[11] Thus, well before the collapse of the USSR and the end of Gorbachev's days in power, both nationalists and advocates of *realpolitik* had defected from the dominant foreign policy coalition or had become more vocal in expressing their ambivalence.

How did Gorbachev respond to the growing gap between promise and performance? Simultaneously, he sought to reconsolidate his political power and to recoup his depleted credibility and authority as leader.

THE RECONSOLIDATION OF POLITICAL POWER

A Soviet Party leader could not take his power for granted; he was not elected to a fixed term of office and had to begin his years in office in the midst of a struggle for power. (By contrast, the succession struggle in electoral regimes precedes the assumption of formal power.) For this reason, Soviet leaders did not present comprehensive programs until their stage of ascendancy, following their victory in the power struggle. In the meantime, they sought not only to shape the climate of opinion within the Central Committee in their favor but also to build networks of supporters within the Central Committee, its apparatus of rule, and regional Party organs.

---

[10] For a masterful demonstration of how Gorbachev came to be incapable of bringing himself to use force in Eastern Europe, see Jacques Lévesque, *The Enigma of 1989: The USSR and the Liberation of Eastern Europe* (Berkeley: University of California Press, 1997).

[11] *Izvestiia*, December 29, 1990.

Gorbachev followed this conventional route during the first stage of his administration. During 1985–1987, he placed supporters in the Politburo, the central Party apparatus, and the regional Party organs, while purging many incumbents from those institutions. He also replaced the editors of major media outlets and the directors of major cultural institutions (Union of Writers, Union of Theatre Workers, etc.). These outlets and institutions were the instruments of *glasnost'* that bolstered his ability to mobilize a social base for significant change.

Although Gorbachev consolidated his power exceptionally quickly by historical Soviet standards, the radical policies he adopted during his stage of ascendancy undermined the loyalties of his erstwhile clients within the Party apparatus. The democratizing policies he enacted in 1988 clearly (and predictably) threatened the material interests of Party officials, who were sensitive to being criticized in public and completely unaccustomed to being replaced through public elections. The radicalization of Gorbachev's policy program, therefore, led him to both weaken and purge the institutions through which he had prevailed in the succession struggle. Thus, in October 1988, he abolished almost all the branch economic departments of the Central Committee, diminished the role of the Central Committee Secretariat in top-level decisionmaking, and set up six new Central Committee commissions (of dubious power) to perform functions previously exercised by the Secretariat. In April 1989, Gorbachev pressured 98 members and candidate members of the Party's Central Committee to resign from that body; several of these were Politburo-level holdovers from the old regime, including former Foreign Minister Andrei Gromyko and former Prime Minister Nikolai Tikhonov.

But even as Gorbachev was sapping the very bodies of the Party apparatus within which he enjoyed the power of patronage allocation, he was building up the power of alternative institutions within which he did not have such hierarchical powers. His program called for the steady transfer of political power from the Party apparatus to newly created legislative institutions. The Congress of People's Deputies was founded by competitive, popular election in April 1989. It chose a Supreme Soviet as its primary working body. Gorbachev was elected chairman of that Supreme Soviet by a vote of the deputies.

Gorbachev had taken the step of undermining the institutions through which he had consolidated his power only two years earlier. He had then sponsored the creation of an institution in which accountability of the parliamentarians would be to the people, rather than to a political boss at the top of the political hierarchy. His chairmanship of this institution, and his effort to foster the image of a strong leader within that institution (through cajoling as well as persuasion), were attempts to build alternative sources of power through which he could ensure that democratization, which was genuine, did not lead to his overthrow.

Such was also the case ten months later (in February 1990) when Gorbachev asked the Central Committee to abrogate Article 6 of the Soviet Constitution, which stipulated that the CPSU play the "leading role" in the political order. This was a move long since demanded by radical political movements under the umbrella of Democratic Russia, which mobilized tens of thousands of supporters in public demonstrations. Abrogation of the CPSU's right to be the only legal political Party was a precondition for legalization of multiparty (not just multicandidate) competition in the electoral process. Gorbachev compensated for this further weakening of the Party by engineering his own selection as president of the USSR. Rather than submit to a public election, he allowed himself to be elected president by a vote of the Congress of People's Deputies. And rather than resign as Party leader, which he feared would cede the entire Party structure to hostile forces that might deploy resources of the institution to undermine both him and his reforms, he decided to serve simultaneously as general secretary of the CPSU and president of the USSR.[12]

Thereafter, Gorbachev continued to weaken the central organs of the Party. He purged and reorganized the Politburo in July 1990, after which he called meetings of that body with decreasing frequency. He set up two new bodies for top-level deliberations – a "Presidential Council" and a "Federation Council" – neither of which had independent sources of power through which to defy him. The new Politburo became a marginalized policymaking body. Without seats for leaders of the state, military, or police bureaucracies, the Politburo ceased to be an oligarchy of elites that could pretend to dictate policy in all sectors or that could attempt to subject Gorbachev to the discipline of the collective leadership. With a trusted deputy in charge of day-to-day Party affairs, Gorbachev could concentrate on affairs of state, confident that the Politburo could not become either a unified or an assertive force. Finally, by having himself elected general secretary by the Party Congress, not the Central Committee, Gorbachev established the precedent that he would not be held accountable to the Central Committee.

We should not succumb to the impression that Gorbachev was oblivious to the need for a reserve of raw power to fend off political enemies. He was not so naïve as to believe that a high-wire act of persuasion and rhetoric could continue to "balance" opposing forces in the political elite and society. The wild card in his mind may have been the KGB, which he treated gingerly during 1985–1989 (perhaps recalling the key role that the KGB played in the

[12] For documentation of Gorbachev's reasoning at the time, based on the memoirs of associates, see Brown, *The Gorbachev Factor*, pp. 195–6.

removal of Khrushchev).[13] His purges and restructuring of the Party, ministerial, and military commands did not extend to the KGB, though he did replace the chairman of that organization in 1988 after Chebrikov supported the
Nina Andreeva manifesto against *perestroika*. Although many KGB officials
lamented the "excesses" of *glasnost'* and democratization, their functions
were actually expanded in other areas: foreign intelligence and counterintel-
ligence and especially economic intelligence-gathering.[14]

In sum, Gorbachev tried to strengthen the legislative organs of the state
as he weakened the executive and legislative organs of the Communist Party,
simultaneously bolstering his formal executive powers within each and relying on the KGB as insurance against the collapse of the state. In the case
of the new legislative structures, however, his ability to protect himself from
defiance was complicated by his lack of patronage powers within those institutions. Gorbachev had initiated and then accelerated the transfer of power
from "kings" (the Party) to "people,"[15] and he thus made his formal power
increasingly dependent on his capacity to maintain legitimacy and credibility
as a problem solver and politician. This was perilous for a leader who was
already suffering a crisis of authority. The KGB command proved faithful to
him only as long as he strengthened that institution to prevent the collapse
of the USSR. Once Gorbachev swung back into an alliance with the radicals
in spring 1991, KGB Chairman Kriuchkov initiated preparations for the coup
attempt of August 1991.[16]

THE REDIRECTION OF GORBACHEV'S MANAGEMENT STYLE

Whatever their strategies for building authority and consolidating power, Soviet leaders can also be distinguished by the extent to which they exercise

[13] See William J. Tompson, *Khrushchev: A Political Life* (New York: St. Martin's, 1995), ch. 10.
[14] On Gorbachev's relations with the KGB during 1985–1989, see Amy Knight, *The KGB: Police
      and Politics in the Soviet Union* (Boston: Unwin Hyman, 1990); Alexander Rahr, "Gorbachev
      and the post-Chebrikov KGB," *Radio Liberty Report on the USSR*, vol. 1, no. 51 (December
      22, 1989), pp. 16–20.
[15] I borrow the image from Reinhard Bendix, *Kings or People* (Berkeley: University of California
      Press, 1978).
[16] Gorbachev's behavior in fall 1990 is usually referred to as a swing to the "right," and his
      switch in April 1991 as a move back to the "left." I have tried thus far to avoid left–right ter-
      minology, but it becomes increasingly difficult as the political situation polarizes. Hence, let
      me clarify my use of the terms. In Soviet history prior to Gorbachev, Soviet literature used
      "right wing" to refer to the reformists (e.g. Bukharin) and "left wing" to refer to the ortho-
      dox Leninists. In Western literature during the Gorbachev era, however, the Soviet political
      scene was assimilated to Western categories of analysis: the "right" referred to traditional-
      ists of one kind or another who were opposing Gorbachev's radicalization; the "left" referred
      to those seeking democratization and marketization at home and accommodation abroad. I
      will use the Western parlance in this book.

personalistic leadership vis-à-vis their advisors and the collective leadership. Stalin's personalism was the extreme case: despotic and deadly. Khrushchev's personalism was arbitrary and nonconsultative, but it was neither despotic nor deadly. At all stages of his administration, Khrushchev frequently announced public initiatives without consulting the collective leadership and occasionally humiliated other members of the Politburo in public. By contrast, Brezhnev – while "first among equals" (because of the powers of his office) and while exercising leadership that steadily enhanced his status within the collective – behaved more like a chairman of the board than like a personalistic leader. He worked through, rather than around, the collective.

Where does Gorbachev fit along this spectrum from a highly personalistic to a highly executive operating style? For the first two stages of his administration (1985–1989), I would place him somewhere in the middle of the continuum but closer to the executive end. His radical associates and aides claim that he displayed a relatively consultative style of leadership and tolerance of criticism.[17] Even though he exercised innovative leadership, he respected the norms of collective leadership by subjecting himself to the discipline of the collective – for example, by having speeches and policy initiatives cleared in advance. Gorbachev combined self-confidence and egocentricity with self-control, prudence, and restraint; he exhibited both personal assertiveness on policy and deference to the leading role of the Politburo. He did not generally succumb to impulse and did not humiliate members of his Politburo in public. His capacity to hide his real thoughts and to lead diverse members of the leadership to believe he supported them was manipulative but nonconfrontational. He often mediated tensions within the Politburo. In December 1986, for example, Gorbachev adjourned a meeting of the Politburo without decision, claiming that the debate had become so heated that he feared a split in the Politburo. Sometime after the Nina Andreeva affair of spring 1988, Ligachev was being so harshly criticized in a Politburo meeting that Gorbachev started to defend him and to "try to reconcile the two sides."[18]

At the same time, we would expect also to find personalistic elements in Gorbachev's leadership style. We know (from his biography) that he was a natural leader in his Komsomol days, self-confident and assertive but also a good listener. His self-confidence and egocentricity may account for some of the more paternalistic components of his private discourse once he became general secretary. Thus, Gorbachev typically used the informal *"ty"* ("you")

---

[17] Archie Brown, *The Gorbachev Factor* (Oxford & New York: Oxford University Press, 1996), p. 389, fn. 9.

[18] Anatolii Chernyaev, *Shest' let s Gorbachevym* (Moscow: Progress, 1993), pp. 122–3, p. 207.

in addressing colleagues, subordinates, and even people he did not know.[19] He frequently referred to himself in the third person.[20] These practices plainly irritated associates and aides who later parted company with Gorbachev, and they led his main rival (Yegor Ligachev) to conclude that Gorbachev was attracted to the aura of an "enlightened monarch."[21]

Memoirs by Gorbachev's aides and associates, both hardliners and moderates, agree that he often would play people off against each other.[22] Gorbachev is said (by a close supporter) to have pitted Ligachev against Yakovlev and vice versa: they were each given about half of the responsibility for doctrinal affairs that, until January 1982, had been held by Mikhail Suslov.[23] In like manner, Gorbachev allegedly preferred to have others do kamikaze work for him; they were assigned to advocate policies and then take the political heat, while Gorbachev sat back and assessed the situation, deciding whether to intervene on their behalf or disown them.[24] He also preferred to have several teams working in parallel on the same task.[25] Consistent with these tactics was Gorbachev's tendency to dissimulate. Boldin claims that, on difficult issues, Gorbachev almost never said a definite "yes" or "no" to his associates. Rather, his tactic was to resort to interjection (*mezhdometie*), silence, or changing of the topic.[26] All these elements of his operating style were manipulative, but they were not manifestations of arbitary rulership.

Yet the political system, and the policy circumstances under which he came to power in Moscow in 1985, demanded of Gorbachev that he be more than

---

[19] Ibid., p. 7; V. I. Boldin, *Krushenie p'edestala: Shtrikhi k portretu M.S. Gorbacheva* (Moscow: Respublika, 1995), pp. 221–2; Fyodor Burlatskii, *Glotok svobody*, vol. 2 (Moscow: RIK Kul'tura, 1997), p. 126.

[20] Chernyaev, *Shest' let*, p. 104; Andrei Grachev, *Kremlevskaia khronika* (Moscow: EKSMO, 1994), p. 181. The practice appears as well in Gorbachev's memoirs, written after his forced retirement (Mikhail Gorbachev, *Zhizn' i reformy*, vol. 1 [Moscow: Novosti, 1996], pp. 269, 281, 369, 371).

[21] Yegor Ligachev, *Inside Gorbachev's Kremlin* (New York: Pantheon, 1993), pp. 98, 124.

[22] Grachev, *Kremlevskaia*, p. 132; Boldin, *Krushenie*, pp. 163, 208, 240. These authors differ, however, in their interpretation of Gorbachev's motives. Grachev sees this as a means of gaining multiple sources of information and interpretation; Boldin views it as a way of avoiding personal responsibility for failure. I do not find the two interpretations to be mutually exclusive, as I assume that politicians seek, when they can, to reconcile rational decisionmaking with political self-interest.

[23] Grachev, *Kremlevskaia*, p. 95.

[24] On this point as well, Grachev (a supporter of Gorbachev) and Boldin (a protagonist in the coup of August 1991) are agreed; see ibid., p. 133, and Boldin, *Krushenie*, p. 208. See also Ligachev, *Inside Gorbachev's Kremlin*, p. 307, on Gorbachev's allegedly opportunistic use of Yakovlev in the Nina Andreeva affair of spring 1988.

[25] Grachev, *Kremlevskaia*, p. 132.

[26] Boldin, *Krushenie*, p. 17. Many coup plotters claim that Gorbachev gave them mixed signals in 1991, leading them to believe that he would welcome their imposition of emergency rule as long as Gorbachev himself could not be implicated (ibid., p. 19).

just a skilled and manipulative chairman of the board. The political system encouraged both power consolidation by the Party leader and adulation of the general secretary as the font of wisdom and initiative. Gorbachev tried to resist such adulation and even denounced it in one public forum, fearing that a traditional "personality cult" would undermine public belief that his democratic reform program was serious.[27] But bolstering the image of the Party leader went hand-in-hand with far-reaching policy innovations – and Gorbachev was expected to provide leadership to a demoralized political elite. Hence, at televised meetings of the Congress of People's Deputies in 1989, Gorbachev used the powers of the podium to criticize and praise speakers, projecting the image of a founding father who was responsible for ensuring that the children did not get out of control. This behavior did not win him points with those who disagreed with his policies, but it did convey the message that, democracy or not, Gorbachev considered himself indispensable as a leader.

Once Gorbachev was thrown onto the political defensive, personalistic elements in his management style increased proportionately. His reconsolidation of political power effectively neutered the Politburo as a check on the behavior of the general secretary. He consulted less and less with advisors like Chernyaev, who had stood with him throughout the first stages of his administration. Indeed, in 1990–1991, he lamented to his aides that he could trust only two men: Defense Minister D. Yazov and KGB Chairman V. Kriuchkov.[28] Ye. Primakov, a top advisor to Gorbachev, advised him at the time that he ought not trust information received from the KGB as much as he did.[29] Both his radical and reactionary associates felt betrayed as he manipulated them constantly into believing that he agreed with them. In the end, Gorbachev's heightened personalism lacked both the raw power and the political credibility to head off his demise.

GORBACHEV'S AUTHORITY-MAINTENANCE DILEMMA

During 1989–1990, Gorbachev became increasingly defensive about the policies he was advocating and about his performance as a leader. Under growing challenge from critics on the left and the right, Gorbachev tried to maintain his authority by arguing that his basic conception of the middle way remained the only desirable and feasible alternative to either totalitarian restoration or

---

[27] Dusko Doder and Louise Branson, *Gorbachev: Heretic in the Kremlin* (New York: Viking, 1990), pp. 119–20.

[28] Boldin, *Krushenie*, p. 386; Chernyaev, *Shest' let*, p. 401.

[29] Chernyaev, *Shest' let*, p. 452.

systemic collapse and anarchy. He struggled to maintain his image as an effective leader, and he frequently reminded political audiences of the price he
would *not* pay in seeking to transform the Soviet Union.

From 1988 onward, critiques of *perestroika* appeared in increasingly au-
tonomous public arenas: the mass media, Central Committee meetings, the
Party Conference of June 1988, the Party Congress of July 1990, the Supreme
Soviet, the Congress of People's Deputies, demonstrations in the streets of
Moscow, the newfound (1990) Communist Party of the RSFSR (i.e., Russia),
and wildcat strikes by coal miners throughout the country (1989 and 1991).
Although many of these criticisms and events stemmed from the very social
forces that Gorbachev had unleashed in order to drive forward the process of
transformation, he now felt the need to define limits. He strove to balance
transformation with traditional values and political stability.

Thus, at the First Congress of People's Deputies (1989), at which some
speakers defined the Communist Party as the main obstacle to democratization, Gorbachev called the Party "the guarantor of this revolutionary process"
(i.e., *perestroika*) and its defender against "both conservative and ultra-leftist
elements."[30] When *glasnost'* was becoming radicalized in 1988, he told representatives of the media that "we need order, responsibility, and initiative
as we need the air we breathe" and proclaimed that "*glasnost'* in the interests of the people and socialism should be without limits. I repeat – in the
interests of the people and socialism."[31] In the face of challenges to the Communist Party's "leading role," he proclaimed that "without the Party, without
its fundamental influence on every aspect of social life, *perestroika* will not
succeed."[32] In the same speech, he summed up his position as follows:

> We say that *perestroika* means renewal but not dismantling of socialism. We say that
> *perestroika* is a revolutionary transformation, remedying deformations of socialism
> but not amounting to a restoration of capitalism. We say that *perestroika* is the re-
> vival of creative Marxism, the fresh realization of Lenin's ideas, the assertion of new
> approaches and methods of work.[33]

Similarly, when republics were defying Moscow's authority by passing
laws on sovereignty that conflicted with those passed by central authorities,
Gorbachev insisted on the importance of "the Union," held together by a

---

[30] M. K. Gorshkov, V. V. Zhuravlev, and L. N. Dobrokhotov (Eds.), *Gorbachev–Yel'tsin: 1500
dnei politicheskogo protivostoiania* (Moscow: Terra, 1992), p. 131. This book is a compen-
dium of speeches by Gorbachev and Yeltsin from 1986 to 1991.

[31] *Pravda*, September 25, 1988 (Gorbachev, *Izbrannye*, vol. 6, pp. 572, 575).

[32] *Sovetskaia Rossiia*, September 30, 1989.

[33] Ibid.

"transformed Communist Party."[34] When leaders of the Russian republic demanded sovereignty from the center's diktat, Gorbachev argued that "an isolated Russia" is not the solution.[35] When radicals called for abolishing Party cells in the army and in security organs, Gorbachev insisted that communists had the "right" to organize autonomously.[36] When radicals pushed for the legalization of private land ownership, Gorbachev declared his opposition and argued that collective and state property should limit the scope of purely private enterprise.[37] Even after the coup of August 1991, Gorbachev returned to Moscow and urged that the sins of the Party apparatus not be visited on the millions of rank-and-file Party members.[38] He also insisted that the "socialist choice" and the "socialist idea" had not been discredited and that these remained the core of both his political philosophy and of the only viable, good society.[39]

Throughout 1990–1991, as centrifugal pressures grew, Gorbachev warned repeatedly that the Soviet Union, in some renegotiated form, simply had to be preserved. After April 1991, he became more tolerant of confederal formulas as he observed that federalism ("strong center–strong regions") was no longer acceptable to regional leaders, whether or not he believed, in his heart, that confederalism could ever constitute a stable equilibrium. "New, unprecedented" forms of statehood were tolerable, even desirable, as long as they avoided formal secession and disassociation of the constituent units of the pre-existing state. Anything to retain formal continuity and the juridical existence of the state; anything to avoid formal disintegration and the conflicts that, he claimed, would ensue; and, of course, anything to retain the office he occupied and the state without which his office would cease to exist.[40]

---

[34] Gorshkov et al., *Gorbachev–Yel'tsin*, pp. 208–9; see also *Sovetskaia Rossiia*, September 30, 1989.

[35] Gorshkov et al., *Gorbachev–Yel'tsin*, p. 209.

[36] Ibid., pp. 215–16, 221.

[37] *Izvestiia*, August 19, 1990; *Sovetskaia Rossiia*, September 22, October 9, and December 1, 1990. See also TASS, September 17, 1990: "Not the nationalization of all and sundry, but the creation of free associations of producers, joint stock companies, production and consumer cooperatives, associations of leaseholders and entrepreneurs – that is the high road to a genuine socialization of production on the principles of free will and economic expediency. It is here that the roots of the true socialization of our economy lie."

[38] *Pravda*, August 23, 1991.

[39] Ibid.; see also *Sovetskaia Rossiia*, May 25, 1990, and October 9, 1990.

[40] Gorbachev's emphasis on (indeed, obsession with) statehood runs through his speeches even when his logic comes across as forced. On March 29, 1991, he warned that calls to close down the Communist Party would mean the "disruption of all elements of statehood" (Moscow Radio Rossii Network, March 29, 1991). On July 24, 1991, he warned representatives of the republics against confrontations that could lead to "the breakdown of Soviet statehood" (TASS, July 24, 1991). On August 2, 1991, shortly before the abortive coup, he justified the new Union Treaty as "a reform of Soviet statehood" and pointed to the institutional mechanisms it would

Gorbachev's defense of Soviet statehood contained more than just the defense of a political–organizational form; it also contained advocacy of a valued political community. He clearly articulated a conception of political community that was internationalist and ethnically inclusive and that constituted a "unique civilization" with a "common fate." His rhetoric both extolled the Soviet Union as a civilization worth preserving and warned of the dire consequences of trying to decouple the components of an organic entity. Retention of common statehood, then, was a prerequisite for binding together the peoples residing in the USSR. As he remarked in February 1991:

> In approaching the referendum and thinking about our position, each of us should understand that, essentially, what is at stake is the fate of our state and of each of its peoples, our common fate.... One can justifiably say that a unique civilization has developed in this country, one that is the result of many centuries of joint efforts by all of our peoples.[41]

When he resigned from office begrudgingly on December 25, 1991, Gorbachev spoke to the nation about his greatest fears: "The worst aspect of this crisis was the collapse of statehood. I am alarmed at our people's loss of their citizenship of a great country – the consequences of this could be severe for everybody."[42]

In Defense of Transformation

During this period, Gorbachev also felt the need to respond to a reactionary challenge, for this threatened to scuttle *perestroika* and to halt the processes of

provide for combining division of powers with coordinating functions (Moscow Central Television Network, "Vremia," August 2, 1991). On November 20, 1991, Gorbachev complained that one consequence of the coup had been to destroy the prospects for signing the Union Treaty. Hence, the authorities would have to start over in the face of "the threat of destruction of our statehood" (Moscow All-Union Radio Maiak, November 20, 1991). Two weeks later (*Izvestiia*, December 3, 1991), he declared to the Supreme Soviet that the number-one issue is the "crisis of our statehood," which is paralyzing official action while threatening the economy and morality. He placed his hopes in revival of the Union Treaty to save the country from disintegration. The Union Treaty would offer a "new, unprecedented statehood," but "any loss of time may be catastrophic." (See also Moscow Central Television Network, December 5, 1991: "the question of statehood is the vital question.") As late as December 18, Gorbachev sent a message to leaders of the "sovereign states" (before a scheduled December 21 meeting) in which he urged an emphasis on continuity as they move to "the creation of a new form of statehood" (TASS, December 19, 1991).

[41] *Pravda* and *Izvestiia*, February 7, 1991; see also Moscow Central Television Network, First Channel, "Vremia," August 2, 1991.

[42] *Nezavisimaia gazeta*, December 26, 1991. Throughout 1990–1991, Gorbachev had spoken in apocalyptic terms about the consequences of collapse of the Soviet Union, calling it a "crime" with consequences that would be "ruinous" and that would result in escalating civil conflict. For examples, see *Pravda*, February 15, 1990; *Pravda*, June 20, 1990; *Pravda*, December 11, 1990; *Pravda*, December 18, 1990; TASS, March 16, 1991; *Pravda*, April 27, 1991.

transformation entirely. Thus, he rejected the rationality of those people who have "panicked" in the face of increasingly autonomous social forces, who claim that "democracy and *glasnost'* are all but a disaster," who "are losing confidence and surrendering their positions," who "see a threat to socialism," who "regard these changes as the downfall, disintegration and collapse of everything – as a real apocalypse," or who have succumbed to "needless fear."[43]

As Gorbachev explained it, such people did not understand that *perestroika* is the roadmap to a more just, humane system in which the most cherished goals of socialism would be achieved and sustained. But the Communist Party could only retain its leading role – de facto, if not de jure – if it transformed itself. A consensus on behalf of such a leading role could only be reached if the Communist Party changed its methods of rule. Such self-transformation would ensure that the Party and its cadres retain their hegemony within the political order.

Now, when all of society is on the move, when the process of democratization has expanded in depth and in breadth, when it is bringing to the surface of public life both new strengths and new problems that require discussion and resolution, on this path we more and more often run into the inertia of old thinking, into a desire to resort to old methods, to slow down the processes that are under way. This is where the contradiction arises.

Some people are even beginning to panic, all but seeing a threat to socialism, to all our gains, from the development of democratic processes in the country.

No, comrades, today we should not concern ourselves with slowing popular initiative and grass-roots activity. The Party's task is to head up the process of the growth of the people's public activeness, to set the tone of this process and to strengthen its constructive elements in the interests of the revolutionary renewal of socialist society, in the interests of restructuring. This is the heart of the matter.[44]

The stakes were high. If the Party proceeded along this path, it "will receive even more support from the working people." If it failed to do so, then "irreparable damage will be done."[45] In response to those who viewed this as a weakening of the Party's leadership role, Gorbachev was blunt:

The dialogue between the Party and the working people is not a weakness, not the transformation of the CPSU into a debating club. If it is a weakness to conduct a dialogue with all strata of society, then I do not know what courage is.... We must not

---

[43] *Pravda*, September 25, 1988 (Gorbachev, *Izbrannye*, vol. 6, p. 568); also, vol. 7, p. 477, 487–90 (April 25, 1989); TASS, September 17, 1990; *Pravda*, December 18, 1990.

[44] Gorbachev, *Izbrannye*, vol. 7, pp. 489–90 (April 25, 1989: concluding speech to the CPSU Central Committee Plenum).

[45] Ibid., p. 490.

operate according to the pattern: permit or not permit, allow or not allow. All that is in the past.[46]

Gorbachev employed the same logic with respect to economic reform. Facing audiences of Party cadres, he insisted that the transition to a market economy simply had to be accelerated. This would not constitute a restoration of capitalism; nor would it forsake socialist values. It was an objective necessity if the standard of living was to rise. And it could not wait.

> We regard an accelerated transition to a regulated market economy as a way out of the current situation. We should finally overcome fluctuations in this respect.... We need the transition to the market not for its own sake but in order to reach new forms of economic life.... We should understand well the essence of the transition to a market economy and agree on this issue. There is no other choice....
>
> Attempts are being made to impose an opinion on society that *movement* towards the market means a return to capitalism. One could not have invented anything more absurd.[47]

But even as Gorbachev warned the radicals not to tolerate secession from the USSR, he also warned reactionaries and conservatives that the Soviet Union could no longer afford to remain a unitary, totalitarian state. An intermediate solution, he told the Ukrainian Communist Party in September 1989, would defuse many inter-ethnic tensions. That solution would have to be based on "democracy and equality, mutual respect and free development of peoples"; it would have to "shape a new image of our Soviet federation that harmoniously combines the interests of national sovereignty and development and the common interests of the union of peoples of our country."[48] Stopping the conflicts that threatened to tear the country apart required "accelerating the radical transformation of the Soviet federation" – combined, he admitted, with "resolute measures" (i.e., coercion in the face of violence).[49]

Gorbachev as Embattled Centrist: The 28th Party Congress, July 1990

Gorbachev had built his authority by claiming the ability to bridge moderate forces on the left and right wings of the Soviet political spectrum. As the

[46] Ibid., p. 491; for similar statements, see also *Sovetskaia Rossiia,* September 30, 1989 (speech to Ukrainian Party Plenum); *Pravda,* December 13, 1989; *Pravda,* June 20, 1990 (speech to Conference of RSFSR Communist Party); *Pravda,* December 18, 1990 (speech to Congress of People's Deputies).

[47] *Pravda,* June 20, 1990; see also TASS, September 17, 1990; *Pravda,* April 27, 1991.

[48] *Sovetskaia Rossiia,* September 30, 1989.

[49] *Pravda,* February 15, 1990. For later examples of this intermediate position, see Gorbachev in *Pravda,* December 18, 1990; TASS, March 16, 1991; *Pravda,* April 27, 1991.

level of political polarization rose and as more and more centrists defected to the more extreme wings of the political spectrum, Gorbachev's political base grew weaker. It was in his interest as a politician to create the perception that there was no desirable alternative to the continued existence of a strong, centrist coalition. The 28th Party Congress of July 1990 illustrated Gorbachev's efforts (a) to prevent a formal split in the Communist Party, in order to retain his centrist role, and (b) to move the Party and its policies in a more radical direction in order to keep pace with the growing polarization.

The delegate selection process had been dominated by regional Party committees, yielding a Congress that was far more conservative than the Party membership as a whole. As a result, during the first days of debate, Gorbachev and his reformist allies were subjected to widespread, frequent, and harsh criticism, while Yegor Ligachev led the conservative charge. When viewed in light of the reactionary tide that had dominated the Congress of the RSFSR Communist Party just one month earlier, it appeared to outside observers that Gorbachev might be forced to abandon his plans to further restructure the Party's leading organs. It even appeared that he could be forced out as general secretary, or have to share power with a hardline opponent. At a minimum, it appeared that hardliners would consolidate their power to obstruct Gorbachev and his transformational agenda.

By the end of the Congress, however, Gorbachev had stemmed and reversed the conservative tide. He was overwhelmingly reelected as general secretary, and his chosen candidate, V. A. Ivashko, trounced Yegor Ligachev for the position of Deputy Chairman of the CPSU. The Politburo was totally reconstructed – expanded to include the first secretary of every republic plus a series of nonentities. Ligachev retired to Siberia after failing even to win reelection to the Central Committee. One exultant delegate concluded: "The monster of conservatism has been slain!"[50]

At the same time, Gorbachev appeased conservatism by refusing to abolish democratic centralism, to disband Party cells in the workplace, army, and police, or to accede to other such demands of the Democratic Platform, a radical faction within the CPSU and Congress. The result was that Boris Yeltsin and many radical deputies, including the mayors of Moscow and Leningrad, withdrew from the CPSU in order to challenge the Party order from without.

Gorbachev had apparently hoped to avoid the defection of the radicals. His tactic called for neutralizing or purging the puritans and technocrats, as represented and rallied by Ligachev, moving the Party's center of gravity to the center-left and encouraging the radical left to believe that he would use

[50] Roy Medvedev, as quoted in *The Pittsburgh Press*, July 15, 1990, p. A4.

his new powers to the benefit of radicalizing reforms. He succeeded on the first two scores but lost the radicals in the process. Still, if there really existed a threat that conservative forces would dominate this Congress, then the first two purposes were more important to Gorbachev than the third.

As for the substance of policy, this Congress reflected a struggle among three major organizational tendencies within the Party. One tendency, represented by Ligachev, was willing to fight to maintain the *monopolistic* position of the Party in society, economy, and polity. A second tendency, represented by Boris Yeltsin, was *abolitionist,* demanding that the Party abdicate its leading role, politically and organizationally, by dissolving Party cells in nonpolitical institutions and by ceding the Party's organizational resources to an autonomous state that would redistribute them to diverse social and political forces. Gorbachev adopted the centrist position: anti-monopolistic *and* anti-abolitionist. As he put it, "[t]he question of whether there should or should not be Party organizations at enterprises can be answered very simply: there should be. This naturally fully applies to members of other parties."[51] Gorbachev was calling for the Party to adopt a *competitive* posture and for the population to decide which organizations to join. "Let society decide," seemed to be his message. In the meantime, he would retain his posture and his political role as an *antidisestablishmentarian.*

In both his opening and closing speeches, and in shorter statements in between, Gorbachev played upon the dominant fears of conservative and uncommitted delegates: that society would decide against them, and deal with them accordingly, in the absence of successful reform. This was a credible warning, coming as it did on the heels of the collapse of communism in Eastern Europe. Gorbachev presented himself as the sole indispensable leader who could steer the Party and country away from such a fate. When delegates threatened a vote of "no confidence" in the leadership, Gorbachev warned them that such a rebellion could so divide the Party that it would never recover: "If you want to bury the Party, to divide the Party, just continue this way. But think seriously about it!"[52] Leninists in particular understood this principle of political life – that division within the elite invites challenges from below. When wrapping up his reelection as general secretary, Gorbachev made clear his demand that the Party allow further radicalization of reform. The only real choice lay between de-monopolization and marginalization: "The Party's success depends on whether it realizes that this is already a different society. Otherwise other political forces will crowd it out and we

---

[51] TASS, July 2, 1990; *The New York Times,* July 3, 1990, p. A5.
[52] TASS, July 7, 1990; *The New York Times,* July 8, 1990, p. A4.

will lose our position."[53] He called on delegates to "put an end to this monopoly forever."[54] This posture likely helped to foster a bandwagon effect among Congress delegates, who apparently more feared a marginalized future without Gorbachev than a radicalized, competitive future with him at the helm. By contrast, for radical democratizers within the Party, the fear of staying inside apparently exceeded their fear of being isolated from the Party's organizational resources.

Gorbachev in Defense of his Leadership Capacity

Gorbachev was more than a national problem solver, scientifically seeking the happy medium that would balance transformation and stability as well as new goals and selected traditional values. He was also a politician, faced with defending his authority against those who could argue that the growing contradictions in society proved his incompetence and liability – and even his dispensability – as a leader.[55] Like his predecessors, Gorbachev had built his authority by trying to present himself as an indispensable problem solver and builder of political coalitions. As the vulnerabilities of his program unfolded, he had to worry, like any politician, about the impact of those contradictions on his political credibility. This preoccupation was evident in his speeches during 1989–1991, the third stage of his administration, when (like his predecessors) he was on the political defensive. It took the form of ongoing efforts to defend himself against accusations that he had made a mess of things.

During 1988–1989, Gorbachev frequently defended *perestroika* against its critics on the right and the left. But it was only in 1990 that a tone of genuine alarm entered Gorbachev's speeches, reflective of the growing polarization that posed a threat to both social peace and Gorbachev's political standing. In his speech to the first Conference of the Communist Party of the RSFSR (a hostile, reactionary audience) in June 1990, Gorbachev felt the need to justify himself and his policies quite fully. He began by expressing alarm at the growth of political polarization:

Some favor *perestroika,* while others already anathematize it. But this is not all. The desire is being witnessed recently to go over from statements to actions. Attempts

[53] Radio Moscow, July 10, 1990; *The Wall Street Journal,* July 11, 1990, p. A10.
[54] *The New York Times,* July 11, 1990, p. A6.
[55] In the given time period, Gorbachev was no longer *building* his authority. Rather, he was desperately trying to *recoup* it.

are being made to muster dissatisfaction ... and to exploit the acuteness of the situation as a ram against *perestroika*.... No matter from what positions such attacks are launched, their true purpose is destructive.[56]

However, Gorbachev followed these warnings with a more defensive summary of the successes of his administration. The basic theme was: Look how much we have accomplished in such a short period of time!

Within just one year, 1987, we created prerequisites for reforms that greatly surpass everything achieved previously. And then, within two years of the implementation of the reform, we have actually finished a "preparatory school" which brought us to the shaping of a market economy, regulated in its social aspects. Thus, within three years we have fully achieved everything that has been debated and experimented with for more than thirty years.

And now, two years since the 19th Party Conference, we have achieved what the most progressive people of our country have been striving for for decades. The Party has decided not to assume the functions of the state any longer. The division of power is now actual fact. Elections have become truly free. We are actually on the threshold of true political pluralism. *Glasnost'* has become an effective tool of progress. The notion of "social democracy" is no longer a mere propaganda phrase. It is a reality ....

We can say now that what whole generations were striving for and could not achieve has been achieved in the ideological and political sphere within five years. Thus, despite all drawbacks, extremes, negative phenomena and losses, including those of an ideological and moral nature, the way has been cleared for the spiritual rebirth of man and society.[57]

Gorbachev did not leave it at that. He was willing to admit, in the spirit of "self-criticism," that he had made mistakes. Rather than revert to the traditional Soviet tendency to blame dysfunctions on local cadres and "anti-state behavior," he accepted some of the responsibility himself.

Speaking of recent years, the Party, its Central Committee and Politburo were unable to avoid miscalculations and even mistakes, as they sought to overcome the heavy

---

[56] *Pravda*, June 20, 1990. For subsequent, analogous expressions of alarm, see Gorbachev in *Pravda*, December 11, 1990; *Pravda*, December 18, 1990 ("We are in a dire situation"); *Trud*, December 21, 1990 ("the main thing is not to panic"); TASS, March 16, 1991; TASS, April 7, 1991 (in Japan); *Pravda*, April 27, 1991; and sources cited in note 12. In his speech of April 26 to the Central Committee Plenum, published in *Pravda* the next day, Gorbachev portrayed himself as a latter-day Lenin: "The situation resembles the social and psychological atmosphere that arose within the Party during the period when V. I. Lenin had abruptly turned the Party and the country towards NEP .... Lenin was accused of reneging on the cause of October and the interests of workers and peasants and of deviation from the principles of socialism .... In the end, the Stalinist dictatorship with all the well-known consequences asserted itself in the Party and the country .... So let us all together try to prevent emotions from pushing our plenum away from positions of political common sense" (*Pravda*, April 27, 1991).

[57] *Pravda*, June 20, 1990; see also *Pravda*, December 18, 1990.

legacy of the past and launched transformations to renew society. We did not always catch up with developments or find unequivocal political solutions to various
problems....

As a matter of self-criticism, one has to admit that we underestimated the forces of
nationalism and separatism that were hidden deep within our system and their ability
to merge with populist elements, creating a socially explosive mixture.[58]

After 1989, Gorbachev was also on the defensive about the results of his
foreign policies, but he appears to have been less embattled in this realm. For
one thing, he was being attacked from only one end of the political spectrum –
the reactionary extreme. The radical democratic forces generally approved of
his concessionary foreign policies and the "new thinking" about international
relations. For another thing, the spectre of civil conflict within the USSR or
of the country's dissolution was far more threatening than even such foreign
policy setbacks as the collapse of communism in Eastern Europe. Hence,
Gorbachev's foreign policy commentary during this period lacked both the
sense of alarm and the self-criticism that marked Gorbachev's defense of his
record on domestic policies. Instead, the Soviet leader simply insisted that
the new thinking was working, that the world was still conforming to the expectations inherent in the new thinking, and that the potential latent within
the international order was being realized – in good measure because of the
leadership he had supplied.

For example, on August 1, 1989, Gorbachev reported to the USSR Supreme
Soviet on his recent trips to the West and the recent meeting of Warsaw Pact
countries. He noted the importance of his own role as a leader in helping to
build a new world order: "I sense how quickly our relations with the Western
world are changing.... As is now clear to everyone, the personality element
is of enormous importance for present-day politics."[59] Speaking to the Conference of the RSFSR Communist Party in June 1990, Gorbachev proclaimed
that "[p]rofound transformations in international relations are quite apparent and widely known. The epoch of exhausting and pointless confrontation
is over. As a result, the entire world situation has improved considerably. Our
security has been strengthened and conditions have been created for cutting
our defense spending in order to use those funds to improve people's standard
of living." Lest there be any talk of these changes having reduced Soviet security by emboldening would-be antagonists, Gorbachev added: "we shall never
allow anyone to interfere in our affairs." And lest this hardline audience forget

---

[58] *Pravda,* June 20, 1990. For subsequent, analogous self-criticisms, see Gorbachev in *Pravda,*
    December 18, 1990; Associated Press, September 10, 1991.
[59] BBC, August 3, 1989.

the basic principle of "mutual security" and unilateral restraint that underlay the "new thinking," Gorbachev continued: "we unconditionally recognize the same right of choice of every people."[60] Compared to the growing alarm in Gorbachev's speeches about domestic matters, however, this was tepid fare.

PENDULAR DEFENSE OF AUTHORITY

Gorbachev's apparent victory at the 28th Party Congress in July 1990 was Pyrrhic. He had managed to defeat the conservatives and to strengthen his control over the top-level organs of power, but leaders of the most radical wing of the CPSU (Boris Yeltsin, A. Sobchak, G. Popov) handed in their Party membership cards. Moreover, reactionary forces concentrated on capturing the newfound Communist Party of the RSFSR. The CPSU had actually split after all, despite Gorbachev's best efforts.

Surely, the days of a radical transformational leader employing "centrist" political tactics were numbered if the level of political polarization reached the point that there were few "centrists" (i.e., moderates) remaining in the political establishment and among mobilized social forces.

Within these limits, however, Gorbachev tried to cope with the polarization taking place around him. Earlier, during the initial stages of his authority crisis (late 1989 to mid-1990), he had made ongoing concessions to radicalism while trying to hold those concessions within bounds. He had been a reluctant accommodator. After the 28th Party Congress, Gorbachev's advisors presented him with a program for radical reform of the Soviet economy and for the creation of a functioning market economy within 500 days. Other advisors, however, presented him with a counterproposal for reform that did not go as far in the direction of decentralization and that had less chance of reinforcing centrifugal forces within the union republics. After deliberating several days, Gorbachev told the dueling teams of economists to work together to reconcile their proposals with each other: an intellectual and practical impossibility.[61] In the absence of such reconciliation, Gorbachev was unwilling to push through any radical program for economic reform.

This was a sign that Gorbachev was shifting tactics, perhaps in confusion as to what might work. He decided that he had cast his lot too fully with the radicals. Thus began the pendular phase of Gorbachev's authority-maintenance

---

[60] *Pravda,* June 20, 1990; see also Gorbachev's address to the Fourth Congress of People's Deputies (*Pravda,* December 18, 1990).

[61] For Gorbachev's comments on earlier and later versions of these plans, see Official Kremlin International News Broadcast, September 4, 1990, and TASS, September 17, 1990.

tactics. He now sought to shore up the power of conservatism. He fired several of his most liberal advisers and associates and appointed conservatives in their place, many of whom would help to organize the coup against him in August 1991. It was in this context that Eduard Shevardnadze resigned, in December 1990, after making an impassioned speech in which he charged that reactionary forces were seizing the initiative and after criticizing Gorbachev for not having done enough to protect him against their accusations.[62] Gorbachev also reinforced conservatism in his approach to maintaining the cohesion of the Soviet Union. He broke with the radicals with whom he had been negotiating a decentralized union and adopted a hold-the-line posture there as well. Whether he was complicit in the use of violence against separatists in Latvia and Lithuania in January 1991 remains a matter of historical dispute.[63] But it is probably not coincidental that this happened during Gorbachev's course correction of September 1990–April 1991. For if he did not order it himself – which is plausible, given his distaste for the use of force – then he certainly created a political context in which those more inclined to use force felt at greater liberty to do so behind his back.

Gorbachev admitted to this shift of political strategy in his speech to the Fourth Congress of People's Deputies in December 1990. It was time, he argued, to strengthen executive power at all levels of the system and to restore order:

The most essential thing needed to get over the crisis is to restore order to the country. This hinges on the issue of power. If we have strong government, tight discipline, and control over the fulfillment of decisions, then we shall be able to ensure normal food supplies, rein in crime and stop inter-ethnic strife. If we fail to achieve this, a greater discord, the rampage of dark forces and a breakup of statehood would be inevitable....

It is precisely for the sake of attaining these goals that a strong executive power at all levels is necessary – from the head of state to executive committees in town and countryside – an executive power able to secure the observance of laws, the implementation of decisions and to maintain proper and discipline....

The president bears full responsibility for the country's security.

None of this furthered the cause of either economic reform or maintenance of cohesion within the USSR. Instead, Gorbachev's move to the right only infuriated the radicals and reinforced centrifugal forces in both the center and the republics. A "war of laws" intensified between the center and the

---

[62] *Izvestiia,* December 29, 1990.

[63] Brown (*The Gorbachev Factor,* pp. 279ff.) makes the case for Gorbachev's noninvolvement in these decisions.

periphery concerning who had legal jurisdiction in the republics and regions. In March 1991, Gorbachev sponsored a nationwide referendum to register popular sentiment on whether maintenance of the union should remain a top priority. And while he secured majority support in all voting republics for the ideal of retaining the USSR, the wording of the referendum was so misleading that many radicals claimed it to be a poor measure of the public's actual preferences.

Then, suddenly, Gorbachev decided that his swing to the right had been ineffective, perhaps even counterproductive. In April 1991 he swung back to the left on the issue of the union (but not on economic reform), making common cause with the radicals and this time on their terms. Thus, rather than move back toward a middle-of-the-road position and try to broker a compromise between extremist forces, as he might have done in 1989–1990, Gorbachev instead rejoined negotiations for a confederal relationship between the center and the republics. This meant "strong regions–weak center," a major retreat from his earlier defense of a more balanced, federal formula.

Gorbachev remained consistent in his strategic determination to maintain the existence of the USSR, to search for a "third way" between state socialism and capitalism, and to synthesize collectivistic and individualistic conceptions of democracy. What changed during his last year and a half in office was his perception of the political strategy required to maintain his power and recoup his authority while pursuing these goals. In the face of a rapidly polarizing situation, he reverted to a pattern of allying himself sequentially with those extreme forces that he viewed to be ascendant at the moment.

We had earlier seen this pattern of pendular swings as a means of recouping authority. Khrushchev embraced one political base in 1961–1962 but abandoned it after October 1962, when the shock of the Cuban Missile Crisis led him to reevaluate the risks, both at home and abroad, of continuing down that road. He then swung in the opposite direction, confronting the military–industrial complex at home and pursuing a concessionary détente with the United States. Similarly, Gorbachev abandoned the hardline coalition when he concluded that the risks of a prolonged alliance were too great, and the rewards too few, in the context of a rapidly polarizing society and a rapidly disintegrating USSR. He rejoined the camp of the radicals in hopes of salvaging a confederal compromise.

It was two years before Khrushchev's revised strategy failed; he was ousted by a cabal of his associates in October 1964. Things moved more quickly in 1991. Within four months of Gorbachev's shift back to the left, a cabal of his reactionary associates placed him under house arrest and seized the reins of government.[64] The coup failed ignominiously within three days. When Gorbachev returned to the capital, he spent several months trying to restore an effective political role for himself and working to prevent dissolution of the USSR.

But events overtook him. In Ukraine, polarization had advanced so far that, on December 1, 1991, an overwhelming majority of the population voted for independence. Shortly thereafter, the presidents of Russia (Yeltsin), Ukraine (Kravchuk), and Belorussia (Shushkevitch) met in the forest outside Minsk and plotted the formal dissolution of the USSR. Gorbachev learned about it after the fact; he was furious but helpless. He accepted the inevitable and resigned his office on December 25, 1991. Like Khrushchev, he had been forced out of office by a conspiracy. But Gorbachev's case was unique in that he was the victim of two conspiracies – one from the right and one from the left. First he suffered house arrest by the "establishmentarians" and later he suffered abolition of his country and his political office by the "disestablishmentarians." This sequence of cabals was a vivid reflection of the degree of polarization made possible by Gorbachev's policies. It also mirrored the declining size of the centrist political base on which Gorbachev had rested his political authority.

---

[64] Most of the coup plotters claim that Gorbachev misled them into believing that he wanted them to impose a state of emergency, from which he would dissociate himself but from which he would also eventually benefit. This was a theme argued by several of the coup plotters who were interviewed in Moscow in June 1999 at a conference in which I participated. Some Western scholars also believe that Gorbachev was no innocent victim of the coup; see, for example, Amy Knight, *Spies without Cloaks: The KGB's Successors* (Princeton, NJ: Princeton University Press, 1996), pp. 12–37, and John B. Dunlop, *The Rise of Russia and the Fall of the Soviet Empire* (Princeton, NJ: Princeton University Press, 1993). But Brown, *The Gorbachev Factor* (pp. 294ff.), persuasively refutes these claims, as does Anatolii Chernyaev in his "Afterword to the U.S. Edition" of the English-language Anatolii Chernyaev, *My Six Years with Gorbachev* (University Park: Pennsylvania State University Press, 2000), pp. 401–23; see also the "Foreword" to this edition by Jack F. Matlock, Jr., then U.S. Ambassador to the Soviet Union (ibid., pp. vii–xiv).

6

Yeltsin versus Gorbachev

The collapse of Gorbachev's efforts to steer a middle course toward a mixed system at home and abroad was in large measure a product of the social forces his policies had unleashed in the USSR and Eastern Europe. But if there was one individual who acted as an independent causal force in the unfolding of this process, it was Boris Yeltsin. Initially, during 1986–1988, Yeltsin merely complicated Gorbachev's authority-building efforts. During 1989–1991, however, he effectively scuttled Gorbachev's attempts to recoup lost credibility. When Gorbachev first tapped Yeltsin for a leadership position in Moscow in 1985, raising him from the ranks of first secretary of the Sverdlovsk Party organization, he had little idea of the trouble he was buying. Gorbachev's authority-building strategy at that point was still fairly conservative, and in 1986–1987 it would come to combine radicalization with a *controlled* and *evolutionary* pace of change. It sought to expand the arenas of politics and transform the language of politics, but at a pace to be dictated by the general secretary. Yeltsin, it turned out, found the pace in each realm to be intolerably slow.

YELTSIN, GORBACHEV, AND THE STAGE OF
POLITICAL SUCCESSION, 1985–1986

The Politburo brought Yeltsin to Moscow in April 1985, appointing him first as head of the Central Committee construction department and then as Central Committee secretary for construction. By his own admission, he hated the experience, for the central Party apparatus left him much less leeway to run things as he saw fit. Though he worked long, hard hours and drove his staff to distraction with his workaholic tendencies, he felt like a caged animal at this desk job.[1] Gorbachev and Ligachev learned of Yeltsin's dissatisfaction and decided to reassign him. They saw to his appointment, in December 1985, as first secretary of the Moscow city Party committee, one of the most powerful positions in the country; simultaneously, they made him a candidate member of the Politburo. Run for many years by Viktor Grishin, the Moscow Party organization had sunk into a swamp of corruption during the Brezhnev years. Gorbachev wanted someone in that job who could purge the Grishin political machine and turn the Moscow Party into a force for administrative and political rationalization. Yeltsin's track record in Sverdlovsk suggested he could do just that.

Yeltsin took to the job with the alacrity of the turnaround artist he imagined himself to be. Though self-conscious about being a provincial bumpkin in elite circles of the country's capital,[2] he did not let this deter him; he was determined to turn Moscow around. He was given the job, he would write later, because Moscow was "in need of a rescue operation."[3] According to Yeltsin, Gorbachev "knew my character and must have felt certain I would be able to clear away the old debris, to fight the mafia, and he knew that I was tough enough to carry out a wholesale cleanup of the personnel." And Gorbachev was right, because "[w]e had to rebuild practically from zero" for "[a]bsolutely everything was in a state of neglect."[4] It is far from clear whether Gorbachev or Ligachev wanted Yeltsin to turn Moscow upside down. But Gorbachev did signal that he was looking for a no-nonsense turnaround artist.[5] Ever the passionate "stormer," Yeltsin tackled the job at full throttle.

Yeltsin's leadership style in Moscow mimicked his populist style in Sverdlovsk, though his populism became still more far-reaching – and threatening to traditional values – in the context of Gorbachev's policy of "acceleration." He rode the busses and subways, raided stores in search of goods being hoarded under the table, and held public meetings with lengthy question-and-answer periods. He dragged around the city members of the municipal Party and

---

[1] Boris Yeltsin, *Against the Grain: An Autobiography,* trans. by Michael Glenny (New York: Summit, 1990), p. 91; see also the lengthy memoir by nine of Yeltsin's former advisors, staff members, and government ministers: Yu. M. Baturin, A. L. Ilin, V. F. Kadatskii, V. V. Kostikov, M. A. Krasnov, A. Ya. Livshits, K. F. Nikiforov, L. G. Pikhoia, and G. A. Satarov, *Epokha Yel'tsina: Ocherki politicheskoi istorii* (Moscow: Vagrius, 2001), pp. 40–1.

[2] Yeltsin, *Against the Grain,* p. 90; Baturin et al. (*Epokha,* p. 41) report that he was widely referred to by Moscow officials as *chuzhak* (stranger, interloper, alien).

[3] Yeltsin, *Against the Grain,* p. 108.

[4] Ibid., pp. 109, 110, 114, 118–25.

[5] Gorbachev said in July 1986 that Moscow needed "a large bulldozer to clear the way" (as quoted in Leon Aron, *Boris Yeltsin: A Revolutionary Life* [London: HarperCollins, 2000], p. 134).

governmental leadership, both on inspection tours and to respond to questions from the public. He called for more unrestrained, public criticism of shortcomings. He even publicized the fact that he was using a public health clinic for his medical services, rather than the Kremlin hospital to which he was entitled.[6] In these ways, the provincial puritan signaled that a "man of the people" had arrived in town, one who did not accept the traditional ways of doing things, one who would not treat politics as an entirely private affair, one who did not accept the system of privilege through which the loyalty and cohesion of the ruling elite had been purchased, and one who did not accept the notion that Moscow's corrupt nobility of Party and state officials was entitled to immunity from exposure and accountability. This was new for Moscow and was a breath of fresh air for those of its citizens who were hoping for a new deal. It was also combustible political material that went beyond what Gorbachev was saying and doing during his stage of political succession.

Yeltsin's populism as leader in Moscow was Leninist, analogous to that which Khrushchev had embraced after the death of Stalin. In Chapter 2, reflecting on Yeltsin's earlier life and tenure of rule in Sverdlovsk, I noted many similarities between Khrushchev's and Yeltsin's leadership styles. Yeltsin's rule in Moscow further highlights the similarities. Both men were a distinctive personality type within a Leninist system: the "stormer." The stormer professes to hate bureaucracy, deplores the ability of lower-level officials to evade responsibility for nonperformance, attempts to solve problems by intensified pressure on (and purge of) cadres, and uses a combination of controlled publicity and mass mobilization to expose underachieving or corrupt officials. In a position of political leadership, the stormer becomes responsible for getting things done, which only increases his sense of urgency about delivering results. That sense of urgency leads him to become increasingly autocratic, to try to galvanize people in pursuit of seemingly unattainable plan targets, to reorganize bureaucracies with abandon, and to seek panaceas for the solution of practical problems. In the end, as was the case of both Khrushchev's Soviet Union and Yeltsin's Moscow, the stormer eventually discovers the limited ability of such methods to improve systemic performance or to deliver the goods.[7]

Khrushchev came to power prepared to shake things up and to force the *nomenklatura* to change their ways. In the process, during 1953–1956, he displayed many of the tendencies just described. So, too, did Yeltsin in Moscow

---

[6] Timothy Colton, *Moscow* (Cambridge, MA: Harvard University Press, 1997), pp. 572–8; Aron, *Boris Yeltsin,* pp. 135–70.

[7] Aron (*Boris Yeltsin,* p. 170) sums up six-month results of Yeltsin's storming: "the yield was startlingly, pitifully, and confoundingly puny." The result was little better on most fronts after eighteen months (ibid., pp. 197–8).

in 1986–1987.[8] Each man used storming additionally as a means of intimidating associates in the leadership to do things his way. Thus, Khrushchev would go out among the people and urge them to be more demanding of public officials; then he would return to official meetings of the elite and urge them to adopt his policies lest they face the wrath of the people – who, he said, had become more demanding![9] So too with Yeltsin, who told a meeting of the city's Party elite in January 1986 – one month after his appointment as Moscow's Party first secretary – that the people of Moscow "are no longer simply complaining. They are indignant."[10] Such allusions to the threatening mood of the masses were risky and incendiary tactics. They could raise consumer expectations, deepen popular alienation, and be interpreted as invitations to the people to assert themselves against the regime. But such a strategy was one option for getting things done and building one's political leverage in a Leninist system.

Both Khrushchev and Yeltsin were a particular type of stormer: the egalitarian populist. They were both inexhaustible workaholics who despised routine deskwork and preferred to be out among the people, urging them on and even working alongside them. They also professed to despise corruption, invoked the egalitarian rhetoric of the ideological heritage, and criticized the socioeconomic privileges accorded to underachieving officials.[11] A stormer of this type has the potential, when frustrated, to become a critic of the *nomenklatura* system itself. Both Khrushchev and Yeltsin, albeit under very different circumstances, evolved in this direction – though Khrushchev, unlike Yeltsin, never crossed the line.

Yeltsin's efforts to revitalize Moscow presaged (as with Khrushchev) a search for ways to circumvent the corrupt bureaucracy by enlisting the broader public against the bureaucrats. Calls for greater criticism amounted to calls for the public to expose wrongdoing. Yet such calls, in and of themselves, were unlikely to shatter or even jar the wall of mutual protection that shielded entrenched officials, so a leader might feel the need to go farther: to expand

---

[8] In a parallel with Khrushchev that is striking for its unreality, Yeltsin in 1986 "pledged, by 1990, to have telephones installed within a year of request ... [and] ... promised to double the length of the Metro routes in the next five years" (Aron, *Boris Yeltsin*, p. 149).

[9] George W. Breslauer, *Khrushchev and Brezhnev as Leaders: Building Authority in Soviet Politics* (London: Allen & Unwin, 1982), pp. 37–8.

[10] John Morrison, *Boris Yeltsin: From Bolshevik to Democrat* (New York: Dutton, 1991), p. 47; see also Aron, *Boris Yeltsin*, pp. 136–8.

[11] "Egalitarian" here refers to revulsion at the extremes of *nomenklatura* privileges. It does not mean endorsement of a radical egalitarian "leveling" approach to worker compensation, though it often means a preference for collective material rewards over purely individual material rewards.

both the scope of criticism and the arenas in which it took place. In Khrushchev's case, the initial calls for criticism ran into immediate resistance from self-protective officials. Khrushchev responded by launching his anti-Stalin campaign; then he started publishing the proceedings of Central Committee meetings and inviting non–Party members to attend. At the same time he launched a campaign for transferring functions to public organizations independent of officialdom. There followed his more radical doctrinal innovations ("Party of all the people"), his policy of limiting the tenure of Party officials to a fixed term in office, and his tentative consideration of multi-candidate elections.[12]

Yeltsin soon discovered the limits of what he could accomplish by traditional methods. Gorbachev had charged him with cleaning out Grishin's large network of corrupt political clients. That was fairly straightforward. Yeltsin immediately started firing high-ranking officials of Moscow's municipal Party apparatus. But the more people he fired, the more people he claimed needed to be fired. Networks stretched throughout the city in both vertical and horizontal directions. One man's client was another man's patron at a lower level or in a different bureaucracy. A corrupt director of a retail outlet had to have many protectors in different sectors and levels of the Party and state apparatus. Within a year and a half Yeltsin had purged about 60 percent of all district Party chiefs in the large Moscow Party organization – a staggering figure.[13] At a public meeting in April 1986, Yeltsin revealed his dismay that, despite the purges, corruption was proving to be a bottomless pit as well as a problem more tenacious than he had anticipated. He would fire people and replace them, and then the replacements would turn out to be corrupt as well.[14] In this forum, Yeltsin did not go so far as to define corruption as a systemic problem, but an observer could have reached that conclusion. Instead, Yeltsin simply expressed his dismay as well as his determination to keep purging all those people who succumbed to temptation.

Yeltsin had already sensed that there were deeper causes to the problem, ones that would require qualitatively new policies to eliminate. In Sverdlovsk he had conducted limited campaigns against both corruption and the socioeconomic privileges of officialdom. These privileges allegedly offended his conception of social justice and ran counter to his own way of living; he

---

[12] Breslauer, *Khrushchev and Brezhnev*, chs. 2, 4, 5, 6.
[13] Mikheyev, *Russia Transformed* (Indianapolis, IN: Hudson Institute, 1996), p. 57; Aron, *Boris Yeltsin*, p. 166.
[14] "Vypiska iz vystupleniia t. Yeltsina B.N. pered propagandistami g. Moskvy," Radio Liberty, Arkhiv Samizdata, no. 5721 (April 11, 1986); for Yeltsin's retrospective account, see Yeltsin, *Against the Grain*, pp. 115–19.

claimed to be uninterested in personal material luxuries.[15] He may or may not have understood fully the link between privilege and corruption, though doing so did not require much of an intellectual leap.[16] Institutionalized privilege was a system of rule. It ensured both the loyalty of the elite *and* the impunity of officialdom against challenge from below. By contrast, corruption was not officially sanctioned; it was treated as deviant in principle, even when the leadership in Moscow cast a blind eye to it. But the corruption of officialdom under Brezhnev became so entrenched precisely because the Politburo protected officials against challenges to their prerogatives and perks. Were a new leader to allow attacks on the privileges of the elite, it would signal an end to that impunity. Hence, it was not accidental that, even as Khrushchev was expanding the arenas and scope of criticism in order to undercut the bureaucracy and increase his own political leverage, he was also adopting policies to reduce the socioeconomic privileges of the *nomenklatura.*

If not in Sverdlovsk, then quickly in Moscow, Yeltsin drew the link between the two. And he did not hesitate to express it in the highest and most public of Party forums. His speech at the 27th Party Congress in February 1986, only two months after he was appointed head of the Moscow Party organization, was the most iconoclastic of all the speeches delivered at that meeting.[17] Like Khrushchev in February 1956, and like Gorbachev in December 1984, he not only criticized "some cadres" for poor performance (which would have been routine) but also generalized the criticism to imply that the problem went beyond "some cadres" and was more of a systemic deformation that needed to be confronted: "an inert layer of time-servers with Party cards." But unlike Gorbachev at the time, Yeltsin was prepared as well to strike at the privileges that allowed this "layer" to be "inert time-servers." Yeltsin made this incendiary issue – what was being called at the time the issue of "social justice" – the centerpiece of his address to the Party Congress and warned that, if problems were not overcome, political stability could not be guaranteed.[18]

Rooting out corruption and reducing official privileges in Sverdlovsk was hard enough; doing so in Moscow was a virtually insurmountable challenge. Moscow was much larger and was located in the midst of the central organs of power. The Central Committee's apparatus, headquartered in Moscow,

---

[15] Boris Yeltsin, *Ispoved' na zadannuiu temu* (Sverdlovsk: Sredne-Ural'skoe knizhnoe izd-vo, 1990), p. 87 (the claim is greatly tempered in the English-language version of this book [*Against the Grain*, p. 90]); *Toronto Star*, November 12, 1987.

[16] Baturin et al. (*Epokha*, pp. 43–4) suggest that Yeltsin well understood this link and that this understanding contributed to his zeal.

[17] *Pravda*, February 27, 1986, pp. 2–3.

[18] Aron, *Boris Yeltsin*, p. 143.

could easily protect its political clients against a maverick leader of the Moscow Party organization. Yeltsin was accustomed to being fully in charge and, as noted in Chapter 2, chafed in positions of subordination.[19] He soon learned that appeals to the apparatus of the Central Committee and to patrons within the Politburo could actually help the corrupt bureaucrats evade his thrusts or reverse his decisions. This might explain why his speech at the Party Congress also included a demand that the Central Committee apparatus "butt out" so that Yeltsin could do his job. This was a less incendiary remark than his other ones, because it was not a form of systemic criticism. But it was not likely to win Yeltsin many allies within the Politburo and Central Committee apparatus as then constituted. And it was sure to alienate the very man – Central Committee Secretary Yegor Ligachev – who had been instrumental in having Yeltsin promoted to a position in Moscow in the first place.

This may have been the point at which Gorbachev and Ligachev realized that they had misjudged the man from Sverdlovsk. Gorbachev, who combined reformist and puritanical traits, might have been comfortable in principle with what Yeltsin was saying, and he might have found it politically useful to have someone push for radicalization without the general secretary himself having to take responsibility should a backlash set in. But Gorbachev might have wondered whether Yeltsin would push the process of public radicalization faster than he and the Politburo could control. Gorbachev might also have worried that the measured introduction of radical ideas and doctrines, which was his strategy at the time, would be discredited by Yeltsin's extension of them into a prematurely systemic critique.

Even more so than Gorbachev, however, Ligachev must have realized that the man for whom he had expressed such enthusiasm in September 1984 was not cut from the same cloth as he. They both fit the puritanical mold of the ascetic anti-corruption fighter who found ways to make the system work better while maintaining social stability. They both possessed the mentality of a stormer who places inordinately high pressure on subordinates to get things done. But Ligachev had little patience for systemic critiques that might undercut the public legitimacy of the leading role of the Party.[20] In his personal life, Ligachev might have been an ascetic, but he understood that the system

---

[19] Former Politburo member Aleksandr Yakovlev reportedly said that, as a candidate member of the Politburo, Yeltsin did not have much of a presence, adding: "He is energetic when he is first, but if he is not first he goes sour right away" (quoted in Sergei Filatov, *Sovershenno nesekretno* [Moscow: Vagrius, 2000], p. 418).

[20] Although he does not discuss Yeltsin in his memoir, Ligachev does note that he himself supported *perestroika* and *glasnost'* until it started to allow systemic critiques in public forums (Yegor Ligachev, *Inside Gorbachev's Kremlin* [New York: Pantheon, 1993], pp. 91, 96–7, 131,

of institutionalized privilege could not be challenged without potentially undercutting the larger system of *nomenklatura* domination.[21] Indeed, in his
own speech to the Party Congress, Ligachev criticized the CPSU's daily newspaper, *Pravda*, for publishing an article that aired popular discontent with the
socioeconomic privileges of the *nomenklatura*.[22]

Moreover, Ligachev could not have been happy to be advised that the central Party apparatus, of which he was the top-ranked Central Committee
secretary, should abdicate its right to intervene in the affairs of the most important regional Party organization in the country! Ligachev was a puritan
and could cooperate during this early stage with those technocrats (such as
Ryzhkov) who appeared to respect a system based on central planning and
control and also to respect official privileges.[23] Hence, he considered himself a "reformer" and endorsed *glasnost'* and *perestroika* in principle; but he
was not an egalitarian populist. Yeltsin was pushing well beyond Ligachev's
conception of tolerable reform.

YELTSIN AND GORBACHEV'S STAGE OF ASCENDANCY, 1987–1989

Once Gorbachev began to radicalize his program in late 1986, Yeltsin would
feel vindicated and emboldened by the new direction and pace of policy
change. *Glasnost'* and democratization looked to Yeltsin like the kind of
societal self-expression required to outflank the bureaucracy and mobilize
new energies to revitalize the country. *Perestroika* suggested a license to rethink authority relationships between the Party and the state, between the
central and regional Party apparatuses, and between the central planners and
regional executives. Yeltsin did not yet possess a complete, anti-systemic critique, much less a crystallized vision of what might replace the Leninist system. By his own testimony, he was still very much a Leninist in 1986, a man
who saw no clear alternative to the leading role of the Party and state ownership of production. But Yeltsin – like Gorbachev, Shevardnadze, and Yakovlev

---

287, 295); notable in this regard is Ligachev's contention that iconoclasm in policy was more
tolerable than iconoclasm about the public interpretation of the history of the USSR.

[21] Ligachev's personal asceticism is amply evident from his memoir; it is also noted in Fyodor
Burlatskii, *Glotok svobody*, vol. 2 (Moscow: RIK Kul'tura, 1997). I have also been told that
a former Soviet cultural figure who toured the country and performed in Tomsk, where Ligachev was then *oblast'* first secretary, was taken to see Ligachev, who began by taking the
measure of his interlocutor thusly: "Do you smoke? Do you drink?" An aide of Ligachev told
this cultural figure that, if either question was answered in the affirmative, Ligachev had no
further use for the person. But on Ligachev's preference for keeping the system of privileges
for *nomenklatura* officials, see *The Washington Post*, March 3, 1986.

[22] *Pravda*, February 28, 1986.

[23] Ligachev, *Inside Gorbachev's Kremlin*, pp. 350–1.

in 1984 and like Khrushchev in 1956 – had concluded that "we cannot go on like this" and was searching for more radical measures to deal with the manifold obstacles to change.

Initially, Yeltsin was both enthusiastic about the radicalization of Gorbachev's program and admiring of Gorbachev for having done so.[24] Moscow started to experience a cultural renaissance, as scores of voluntary associations ("informals") emerged to claim their right to space in an autonomous public arena. Cautiously, but with determination, the informals challenged official dogmas and asserted their right to dramatize demands in public arenas not dominated by Soviet officialdom. Yeltsin did not cause this renaissance to happen, but he also did little to discourage it. He was neither a democrat nor a cultural eccentric, but he understood that it would be impossible simultaneously to resist both the corrupt bureaucracy and the awakening society. He cast his lot with the latter.

The puritans and the technocrats, however, experienced such an awakening with apprehension. They appreciated the utilitarian approach to *glasnost'*: as an instrument for exposing malfeasance and for providing a safety valve for pent-up public frustrations with Brezhnevite stagnation. But members of the educated, activated public did not care to be used for such limited purposes. They soon pushed for still further expansion of the public arena and the scope of critical public discourse. All this was taking place to the greatest extent in Moscow itself, within eyesight and earshot of the Kremlin. Yeltsin was willing to tolerate it and even allowed a congress of informal associations to meet in Moscow – a major event in those tenuous, early days of *glasnost'*. Ligachev presumably was not amused.

Nor was Ligachev likely to have been amused by Yeltsin's continuous purges of the Moscow Party organization, withdrawal of socioeconomic privileges from people who worked for him, and public criticism of the central Party apparatus for obstructing these efforts. There was, of course, truth to Yeltsin's complaints about the Central Committee Secretariat's intervention on behalf of some of the people he had targeted.[25] But there was also something quixotic about his reaction to the frustration of his initiatives. Like Khrushchev in 1961, who experienced similar frustrations in trying to combine frequent and far-reaching purges and administrative reorganizations with an insistence on quick results, Yeltsin had a short fuse and a penchant for turning up the heat in response to resistance. Occasionally, he complained at

---

[24] Yeltsin, *Against the Grain*, p. 139; Aleksandr Korzhakov, *Boris Yel'tsin: Ot rassveta do zakata* (Moscow: Izd-vo "Interbuk," 1997), pp. 52, 64–5; Aron, *Boris Yeltsin*, p. 192.

[25] Baturin et al., *Epokha*, p. 48.

Politburo meetings about his frustrations. He also complained privately to Gorbachev, on the assumption that Gorbachev would be both sympathetic and a potential ally. But within months, and despite a January 1987 Central Committee plenum at which Gorbachev launched his radical program for "democratization," Yeltsin began to conclude that Gorbachev was a compromiser who would never throw down the gauntlet against those who were obstructing or slowing *perestroika*.[26]

Later, in retrospect, Yeltsin would write bitterly about meetings of the Politburo during this period. He criticized Gorbachev for being long on words and short on actions, for dominating the formal sessions of the Politburo with long-winded speeches that resulted only in (what he considered to be) half-measures. It galled him that he was only a candidate member of this Politburo (unlike his predecessor, Viktor Grishin), without the full voting rights of those – Gorbachev and Ligachev – who were his contemporaries but who had risen much farther and faster than he and now dominated the proceedings. Indeed, these pages of Yeltsin's first memoir read like they were written by a newly elected member of a board of directors who has been emboldened by his membership but has not yet learned that the most critical decisions are made not by the board but rather by the executive committee of the board.[27]

Yeltsin's memoir of this period hardly does justice to the unprecedented radicalism of Gorbachev's program of democratization. Perhaps Yeltsin was alienated by the fact that, at the January 1987 plenum, Gorbachev settled for a closing resolution that was less radical about intra-Party democratization than Gorbachev had proposed in his opening speech. Perhaps he was upset that Gorbachev's public rhetoric was still somewhat less iconoclastic than was his own. Perhaps Yeltsin was so focused on problems inside Moscow that the gap between central Party resolutions and actual changes on the ground was foremost in his mind. Or perhaps Yeltsin was galled by, indeed obsessed with, Ligachev's ability to frustrate some of his initiatives behind the scenes. Whatever the precise cause, in 1987 Yeltsin was apparently torn between concluding that Gorbachev was insufficiently committed to change and concluding that Gorbachev simply lacked the courage to confront Ligachev and abandon his "go slow" tactics. Yeltsin was not seeking to bring Gorbachev down in early 1987; he was seeking rather to bring him around. He wanted Gorbachev to become as bold as he in publicly challenging the sclerotic organs of the Party and the state at all levels. He was trying to stiffen Gorbachev's spine.

[26] Burlatskii, *Glotok svobody*, vol. 2, pp. 129–30, 193.
[27] Yeltsin, *Against the Grain*, pp. 130–1.

In the face of continuing frustration, however, Yeltsin came to the conclusion that his leadership of the Moscow Party organization was a lost cause. He felt like an isolate within the Politburo[28] and decided to resign. When Gorbachev failed to accept his resignation and was unavailable to discuss the matter further, Yeltsin's frustration grew.

Just before adjournment of a meeting of the Central Committee membership – called on October 21, 1987, to discuss Gorbachev's proposed draft of his important anniversary speech – Yeltsin let his impulses get the best of him and asked to speak. He had not gone into the meeting determined to do so, and he had only a few notes written down in case he did. But, as the meeting was about to conclude, this lifelong risk-seeker (see Chapter 2) could not resist the temptation. He then delivered a disjointed but utterly blunt attack on the slow pace of *perestroika,* on the obstructionist behavior of Yegor Ligachev and the central Party apparatus, and even on Gorbachev's allegedly hesitant, self-congratulatory leadership of the entire process. He reiterated his criticisms of Party privilege and his warning that political stability was at risk if conditions did not improve. *Perestroika,* he was suggesting, was not only insufficiently radical and far-reaching; it was threatening to mire the country again in stagnation. He repeated his offer to resign from the Politburo.[29]

Only a speech delivered before the mass public would have been more of a challenge to the leadership. As it was, this challenge was great enough, not just for what it said but also for where and when it was delivered. Yeltsin was denouncing the Politburo in front of the "Party public," the 300-odd members of the Central Committee to whom the Politburo was nominally (but not actually) accountable.[30] This was a challenge both to the leaders being criticized and to the Politburo as an institution. It was a breach of institutional discipline in that it was not discussed by the collective leadership beforehand in private session and approved in advance for discussion before the broader clientele. It was an unsanctioned effort to force an expansion of the arenas and language of legitimate criticism far beyond those Gorbachev had already sanctioned. It was the very definition of "loose cannon" behavior within the Leninist institutional context. Only a direct appeal to the mass public would have been more intolerable.

---

[28] Baturin et al., *Epokha,* p. 48.
[29] For the text of Yeltsin's speech, see M. K. Gorshkov, V. V. Zhuravlev, and L. N. Dobrokhotov (Eds.), *Gorbachev–Yel'tsin: 1500 dnei politicheskogo protivostoianiia* (Moscow: Terra, 1992), pp. 23–5.
[30] For the concept of Party members as the "citizens" and "public" of Leninist regimes, see Ken Jowitt, "An organizational approach to the study of political culture in Marxist–Leninist systems," *American Political Science Review,* vol. 68, no. 3 (September 1974), pp. 1171–91.

In response, Gorbachev opened the floor to denunciations of Yeltsin by reformists and conservatives alike. If, before this, Gorbachev might have rationalized that Yeltsin could be useful within the leadership as a counterweight to those opposed to the further radicalization of *perestroika*, now he saw Yeltsin as someone who might actually discredit the cause of radicalizing reform.[31] Politburo members Eduard Shevardnadze, Aleksandr Yakovlev, and perhaps Vadim Medvedev were pushing the cause of radicalization within the leadership, but they were doing so largely at the pace demanded by Gorbachev. The general secretary presumably did not want to frighten the puritans and technocrats into mobilizing against his program. Apparently, he wanted them to think, for as long as possible, that there was a legitimate place for them in the new order and no need to become obstructionist. Yeltsin's behavior, however, was threatening to give them a case in point of what further radicalization might engender, much as Dubček's Czechoslovakia in 1968 worked to the disadvantage of reformists within Brezhnev's Politburo and Central Committee. At least within the Party, Yeltsin's penchant for egalitarian populism and his disrespect for the norms of proper procedure might prematurely antagonize the "centrists" and fence-sitters on whom Gorbachev was banking for support. The cruel and sustained hazing of Yeltsin – especially later on, in the Moscow Party organization meeting at which Gorbachev saw to his removal from office – was apparently Gorbachev's concession to his own perceived coalition-maintenance needs.

Perhaps because he felt guilty about the cruelty of the exercise (Gorbachev had had Yeltsin dragged from his hospital bed after a heart seizure to experience a vicious verbal assault by associates in the Moscow Party organization), Gorbachev gave Yeltsin a dignified position within the state bureaucracy as deputy minister for construction.[32] But he also advised Yeltsin privately that he would never let him back into politics.[33] There followed a period of many months during which Yeltsin put himself through a wrenching self-examination. He was determined to draw fundamental conclusions from what he had been through.[34] He had experienced the full force of an

---

[31] Archie Brown, *The Gorbachev Factor* (Oxford & New York: Oxford University Press, 1996), p. 171.

[32] The chorus of denunciations at the meeting of the Moscow city Party committee was especially vicious, perhaps more so than Gorbachev had anticipated. Aron (*Boris Yeltsin*, p. 215), based on memoirs by and interviews with participants, writes: "As the meeting progressed, Gorbachev began to look strangely uncomfortable, even 'embarrassed.' He fidgeted. He grew red in the face. His eyes crisscrossed the hall 'restlessly.' A few times, he shook his head, as if 'struck by the fury and the spite he had unleashed.' By contrast, next to him Egor Ligachev sat with arms crossed on his chest staring 'triumphantly' at the hall below."

[33] Burlatskii, *Glotok svobody*, p. 135; Yeltsin, *Against the Grain*, p. 14.

[34] Yeltsin, *Against the Grain*, pp. 204ff.

inquisition by the Party apparatus, unlike anything seen within the Central Committee since 1961, and had even been denounced by some people he thought were his friends. He had fought against the corruption and privilege of the Party apparatus as a whole and against the domination of regional Party and state organs by the central Party apparatus. Instead of being thanked for his efforts to improve the situation in Moscow, he was purged and nearly driven to his death. Despite all this, he continued to believe (in principle at least) in the "leading role of the Party" and a better future for the Soviet people under the leadership of the CPSU.[35] How could he reconcile these conflicting beliefs? Never one to shirk a personal challenge, Yeltsin was searching for answers. He had not yet realized that he would have to jettison one or the other set of beliefs.

This agonizing reappraisal was taking place in a political context that was changing by the month. The battle between radical reform and "hold the line" conservatism was heating up. The Nina Andreeva affair of March 1988, supported by Yegor Ligachev, was a blatant effort by those opposed to further radicalization to dramatize their conviction that *perestroika* was turning out to be a threat to the entire system of Party rule.[36] Radical reformists within the leadership, supported by Gorbachev, counterattacked and managed to throw the conservatives back onto the defensive. In the meantime, radical reformist editors of journals and newspapers were allowing or encouraging further expansion of the scale of criticism – to the extent that many of the things Yeltsin had said at the 27th Party Congress were by now standard fare in large-circulation publications. The informal organizations were growing exponentially in number and assertiveness. The Soviet intelligentsia, including young and old alike, was losing its fears and inhibitions and was increasingly acting on its convictions, confident in its growing strength as a social movement. A huge public demonstration on Yeltsin's behalf took place in Sverdlovsk. Some people demanded publicly to know what had happened in the Central Committee meeting at which Yeltsin had defied the Politburo. Letters of support reached him from around the country, greatly bolstering his spirits,[37] and perhaps also influencing his intellectual development. Yeltsin had earlier viewed societal awakening as a healthy manifestation of vitality and a useful ally against the bureaucracy, but now he was starting to realize also that "the people" might become the core of a political strategy through which he could resurrect himself politically.

---

[35] On the timing of Yeltsin's final break with these beliefs, see Aron, *Boris Yeltsin*, p. 366.

[36] Nina Andreeva, a chemistry teacher from Leningrad, published in a nationwide Party newspaper a manifesto denouncing *perestroika* as a betrayal of Soviet history. The publication was facilitated, if not instigated, by Yegor Ligachev.

[37] Aron, *Boris Yeltsin*, p. 227.

The June 1988 Party Conference provided an unanticipated forum for Boris Yeltsin to continue his struggle with the Party's establishment. He had decided to resume the battle for his political resurrection and rehabilitation, as well as for his increasingly radical vision for the future of the Soviet political order. And the circumstances of this conference – its televising nationwide – allowed him to turn what had been an intra-Party war into a public battle. This forum would allow Yeltsin's grievances to be aired before an audience of all the people, not just the Party citizenry or the nobility of the *nomenklatura* that sat within the Central Committee. Gorbachev, too, was trying to expand both the scope and the arenas of criticism as a way of transforming the Soviet system into a more democratic form of political organization. He had his own reasons for doing so, unrelated to the challenge from Yeltsin. He did not intend for Yeltsin to speak at the conference, but the irrepressible Boris Nikolaevich forced his way to the podium toward the very end of the conference and Gorbachev, for reasons best known to himself, allowed Yeltsin to speak. Gorbachev also allowed Yegor Ligachev to respond, and the combative Politburo member took up the challenge.

Millions of television viewers were provided, for the first time, with a close-up view of uncensored intra-Party debate and struggle. It was both an enlightening and a mesmerizing experience for most of them. They witnessed the diverse orientations toward Party life that were put on display: the puritan who was proud of "building socialism" during the so-called "era of stagnation"; technocrats discussing the limits of economic decentralization and market-oriented reforms; radical reformers seeking a fundamental democratization of the Party. They also witnessed Boris Yeltsin: not yet clear as to what democracy looks like, and humbly begging the Party to rehabilitate him, but increasingly convinced that the Party apparatus was the problem and not the solution.[38]

At least as important as the conference debate were the resolutions of the conference that called for creating a national legislature based on nationwide elections to be held in March 1989. Yeltsin had about six months to survey the political landscape and decide whether this was a channel of political mobility he might wish to exploit. At some point, he decided that it was. Consistent with both his lifelong search for huge challenges and his determination to show Gorbachev and the Politburo that he was their equal, Yeltsin refused to run for parliament in his home town of Sverdlovsk. That would have been too easy a win. If he was to reemerge as a national figure in politics and not

---

[38] For Yeltsin's speech at the conference, see Gorshkov et al., *Gorbachev–Yel'tsin*, pp. 75–82; for a brilliant analysis of how Yeltsin's rhetorical style at the conference may have resonated with the Russian mass public, see Aron, *Boris Yeltsin*, pp. 245–6.

just as one of several thousand parliamentary deputies, then he would have to beat the greatest of odds. Yeltsin decided to run for the citywide seat in the city of Moscow itself.[39] This was by far the largest electoral district in the USSR, which greatly increased the vote's importance as a bellwether of public opinion.

Officials in control of nominating processes did their best to obstruct Yeltsin's running and then threw their weight behind the director of a large limousine factory as his opponent. They smeared Yeltsin in the newspapers with charges that were variously political and personal. Nothing worked. The more they smeared him, the more his popularity and credibility rose. Yeltsin ran on a program that condemned corruption and privilege and called for radical democratization of the Party.[40] In the end, he blew away his opponent, winning an astonishing 89.4 percent of the vote.

At some point during late 1988 or early 1989, Yeltsin's personal reevaluation of his political philosophy led him to a conclusion that the founders of liberal democratic theory had reached hundreds of years earlier: democratization requires a transfer of power and authority from "kings" to "people."[41] In the case of the communist system in its post-Stalin era, the "king" was the Party, a collectivity that claimed a secular variant of "divine right." Whereas once Yeltsin had been a true believer in the right of the Party to embody and express truth and legitimacy, now he transferred those traits to another collectivity: the "people." And whereas once the Party spoke *for* the people, now that Party would answer *to* the people, and Yeltsin would be their standard-bearer. Gorbachev's reforms made this possible. To Gorbachev's surprise and distress, Yeltsin seized the opportunity to get back into politics – precisely what Gorbachev had warned him he would never allow – and to turn those new arenas against the Party and, later, against Gorbachev. Whereas Gorbachev viewed these new channels (elections and a parliament) as an expansion of the public arena that would result in a form of democratic socialism, Yeltsin treated them as instruments for destroying the power of the Party apparatus. Whereas the new language of politics under Gorbachev now routinely included amalgams of socialist and liberal democratic precepts (e.g., "socialist pluralism" and "socialist market"), Yeltsin used the new public forums to reject those amalgams as unworkable and to trump them with both liberal democratic and anti-system doctrines. The stage was set for Yeltsin to

---

[39] Yeltsin writes about his reasons for running in Moscow in Yeltsin, *Against the Grain,* pp. 83–5.
[40] See, for example, the campaign speech that was reprinted in *Moskovskaia pravda,* March 21, 1989.
[41] Reinhard Bendix, *Kings or People* (Berkeley: University of California Press, 1978).

seize the political initiative at the very moment at which Gorbachev, for reasons other than Boris Yeltsin, had been thrown onto the political defensive.[42]

GORBACHEV DECLINING, YELTSIN RISING, 1989–1991

There is general agreement among observers that 1989 was the year during which Gorbachev lost control of the social forces that his policies of *glasnost', perestroika,* and *demokratizatsiya* had unleashed. That is to say, at about this time the mobilization of anti-system forces by sociopolitical organizations (such as *Democratic Russia* in Russia and the ethno-national popular fronts in other republics) was pushing for radicalization of policy at a rate that exceeded Gorbachev's preferences and efforts. Earlier, Gorbachev had followed a strategy that sought to push policy in a radical direction but without driving moderates into opposition. Now he found himself in a position of trying simultaneously to keep up with rapidly radicalizing social forces (to avoid losing his radical base) and of restraining them as best he could (to avoid losing the moderates). Gorbachev's main fear, as we shall see, was irretrievable polarization. It frightened him as a citizen because he believed that it presaged social instability; but it also should have frightened him as a politician, for it threatened to make him irrelevant as a political actor. His distinctive political competence lay in his tactical skills as a bridge between the wings within the Communist Party. Total polarization would mean collapse of the center of the political spectrum, in which case no such bridging would be possible: the wings would be too far apart from each other. The political role with which he had built his authority would become irrelevant.

Yeltsin, by contrast, would play a polarizing role by catering to and gathering around him the very anti-system forces that Gorbachev was seeking to restrain. To the extent that Yeltsin succeeded in building his authority by embracing the forces of radical maximalism, Gorbachev's task would become harder and perhaps impossible. In sum, Yeltsin was building his authority with a platform that, if successful, might diminish the probability that Gorbachev would succeed in recouping his own political authority. Both Khrushchev and Brezhnev had been thrown onto the political defensive and had sought to recoup authority by redesigning their programs. In both cases they faced intra-Party skeptics and low-key critics who wondered whether their latest initiatives were any more likely than previous ones to succeed at an

---

[42] Yeltsin was certainly ambitious. But it is not my purpose to determine whether his policy positions were driven by pure political ambition or by genuine belief. Leaders seeking to build their authority are not required necessarily to believe in the ideas they are propagating.

acceptable price. But Gorbachev's situation was unique, precisely because he had opened up Soviet politics to *public* political competition. He now faced an open political struggle, one marked by mobilized mass constituencies that included anti-communist social forces and explicit counter-elites. This was no longer "Leninist politics." But it was a variant of competitive politics that contained its own logic of authority building and authority maintenance and its own stages of development. Gorbachev's stage of decline was coterminous with Yeltsin's stage of political succession, during which the latter would strive to consolidate a new political base.

Yeltsin rose steadily to prominence in the new public arenas. Within the USSR Congress of People's Deputies, he had a forum for his speeches that was initially televised to a nationwide audience. He was elected to membership in the policymaking Supreme Soviet, which was scheduled to meet in continuous session. Within the Supreme Soviet he became a prominent member of the Interregional Group of Deputies, chaired initially by the distinguished physicist and dissident democrat, Andrei Sakharov, and then by Yeltsin himself after Sakharov's sudden death in December 1989. In March 1990, Yeltsin won public election as a delegate to the newly created parliament of the RSFSR and became a member of its Supreme Soviet. One month later, in May 1990, he won a tense, close battle for chairmanship of the Supreme Soviet. In July 1990, he announced to the 28th Congress of the Communist Party of the Soviet Union that he was turning in his Party card; he then dramatically marched up the aisle to the exit. In March 1991, using his position as Chairman of the Supreme Soviet, he engineered a public referendum that endorsed the establishment of a Russian presidency freely elected by the citizens of Russia. Three months later he won that election in a landslide. Thus, Gorbachev's efforts to recoup his political standing took place in a context in which a rising political star, more radical than Gorbachev himself, was increasingly dominating the very public arenas that Gorbachev had created to channel public initiative and to control the rate of polarization.

Yeltsin played a polarizing game of politics during these last two to three years of Gorbachev's leadership. No matter what Gorbachev proposed in domestic policy, Yeltsin criticized the Party leader for conservatism and half-measures. He supported centrifugal forces in the union republics at a time when Gorbachev was trying to contain them through a combination of threats and rewards. He defined the "center" (i.e., the Kremlin and the Soviet authorities in Moscow) as the main obstacle to Russia's achieving a decisive transition to a new political and socioeconomic order. He initiated a "war of laws," contesting or blocking the enforcement of Soviet laws on the territory of the Russian republic. He sponsored a declaration of Russian "sovereignty" and supported other republics that were doing the same. He dictated terms for a proposed "Union Treaty," being negotiated throughout 1990–1991, that would have turned the USSR into a confederation of largely independent states – leaving the center with few powers that the republics did not explicitly and consensually cede to it. He sided with the coal miners who suddenly rose up in strikes against economic conditions (1989) and, later (1991), against Gorbachev and the communist regime itself, endorsing the legitimacy of their demands and taking the opportunity to have jurisdiction over the mines transferred to the Russian republic. He told representatives of Russia's regions, who were also declaring their "autonomy" in relation to central power *in Russia,* to "take all the autonomy you can swallow."[43]

When Gorbachev accommodated radicalizing forces, Yeltsin typically upped the ante by endorsing a still more radical option. And when Gorbachev moved back toward the center of the political spectrum – seeking compromises between gradualist and rapid programs for economic reform, and between federalist and confederalist terms in the Union Treaty – or when the regime used violence against anti-system forces in Georgia, Azerbaidjan, or the Baltics, Yeltsin denounced Gorbachev for being conservative, reactionary, or worse. It was a classic polarizing game, designed to put Gorbachev in "no-win" situations and to create the conditions for a decisive break with the old order. Yeltsin, over time, became increasingly determined to destroy both Gorbachev's authority and the Kremlin's powers.

Yeltsin was not the only major political actor mobilizing against Gorbachev during this period. In response to such shocks as the collapse of communism in Eastern Europe (1989), miners' strikes, removal of the leading role of the Communist Party from the Constitution (1990), disintegration of all-union power structures (1990–1991), proto-secessionist tendencies in Russia, Ukraine, the Caucasus, and the Baltics, and the apparent unwillingness of Gorbachev to stand up against the tide, the forces of conservative reaction began to mobilize in public and behind the scenes. Gorbachev initially tried to accommodate them and, as we have seen, moved partially to the right on domestic policy during the period from September 1990 to April 1991. But this was little more than a holding action, for the social forces that held the

[43] Foreign Broadcast Information Service, Daily Report, Soviet Union (hereafter, FBIS-SOV), August 13, 1990, p. 84; seven months later, however, he qualified this admonition: "the autonomies can take as much sovereignty as they can administer. We can agree to all of that. But they will have to answer independently, of course, for the well-being of their people. We make one condition: they will have to take part in a federation treaty with Russia. I underline: we will not let anyone pull Russia down" (*Komsomol'skaia pravda,* 14 March 1991). My thanks to Philip Roeder for this citation.

initiative in day-to-day politics were the radical, anti-system forces – or at least those forces whose behaviors furthered the disintegration of the system. Gorbachev could prevent the promulgation of a radical and rapid decentralization of the economy, but he could not impose a gradualist program of reform when the leadership of the Russian republic refused to implement it. He could prevent the adoption of a confederalist Union Treaty, but he could not impose a federalist alternative when the major republics, including Russia, refused to honor it. In the meantime, the economy was experiencing a steady decline in performance that was commensurate with a steady decline in the cohesion of public administration.

When, in April 1991, Gorbachev decided to shift camps once again and to negotiate the transformation of the USSR into a confederation, he predictably infuriated the conservatives and reactionaries who had joined his government in recent months and who expected some reassertion of the Kremlin's authority over the country. When instead Gorbachev scheduled a ceremony in August 1991 for signing the radical version of a Union Treaty, leaders of all-union institutions – the KGB, military, and central planners – took things into their own hands. Their coup of August 19, 1991, was hastily and poorly planned, had only limited support among military commanders, and was not energized by any collective sense of self-confidence. Moreover, while the plotters had succeeded in holding Gorbachev under house arrest in his vacation home far from Moscow, they had not succeeded in so isolating Boris Yeltsin. This was Yeltsin's finest hour. He risked his life by standing on a tank and demanding, as the duly elected president of Russia, that the troops not take part in this anti-democratic infamy, warning that they would be held accountable if they cooperated with the treasonous plotters.

The subsequent history of Russia, and perhaps also of the Soviet Union, might have been quite different had Yeltsin not survived his defiance. It would have taken but one sniper's bullet to end his life as he stood on that tank. And it would have taken just one determined platoon commander to open artillery fire on the White House and to kill off much of the leadership of the anti-system forces assembled there that day. Although mobilized social forces may push a country's politics in a given direction, they do not always determine how far the push will go and how long it will last. Yeltsin's role in further polarizing Russian politics, and in frustrating Gorbachev's efforts to recoup his political role, is undeniable. Absent Yeltsin after August 1991, and even if the coup had ultimately failed after such a bloodletting, the political landscape would have been quite different. But the flip side is also true: Yeltsin's successful defiance of the coup plotters turned his high popularity into a condition of almost legendary charisma. Seemingly, he had single-handedly faced down the coup, a feat at least as large and awe-inspiring as his successful political resurrection through electoral politics in 1989.[44]

Yeltsin had performed a seeming miracle, which is precisely what charismatic leaders are viewed by their followers as capable of doing. Thereafter, he had Gorbachev at his mercy – and he was rarely merciful, much less magnanimous. Yeltsin may not have decided until November–December 1991 to work behind the scenes with the leaders of two other republics to dissolve the Soviet Union and to transfer the Kremlin (and the all-union institutions it controlled) to the jurisdiction of the Russian republic. He may not have decided in August–September whether he preferred to replace Gorbachev as leader of a new, confederal Union of Sovereign States. But it was increasingly clear by fall of 1991 that Gorbachev was finished as a serious political force and that the future of Russia would be shaped by the decisions of President Yeltsin.

THE POLITICS OF "INBIDDING" AND OUTBIDDING

In established democratic regimes in which levels of social conflict and polarization are relatively low, and when the electoral contest is "winner-take-all," political competitors on the campaign trail typically compete for the votes of the moderate middle of the electorate. When social conflict and polarization rise, a reverse process sets in. The moderate middle declines in size and candidates must compete for the allegiances of the swelling extremes of the political spectrum. Under such conditions, the language of politics becomes more extremist in both directions. Moreover, competitors on the same side of the ideological spectrum often seek to outbid each other for the allegiances of the extremist voters. In contexts marked by polarizing ethnic or racial conflict, the reactionary strategy is sometimes referred to as "playing the ethnic (or race) card." This will take a dual form: denouncing one's ideological opponents for their position on the issue and outbidding one's rivals on the same side of the political spectrum by showing that one is more intensely committed to the value than they are.

In situations of rising electoral polarization, competitors on each side of the political spectrum may attempt to seize the initiative from rivals within their ideological camp by trumping each other's policy advocacy – or, to use still other metaphors from card games, by "upping the ante," "raising the

---

[44] This, in any case, was the public perception. There are those who argue that Yeltsin was not in danger of losing his life during the coup – that the plotters chose not to try to kill him. I leave the resolution of this matter to future historians.

stakes," or "outbidding each other." This often takes the form of trying to exaggerate the competitor's compatibility with the opposite wing of the political spectrum. Whether this proves to be a winning strategy depends on the type of election in question (party primary versus general election), the electoral rules (proportional representation versus winner-take-all), and the size and dispositions of the "moderate" bloc among the voting public. In Yeltsin's case, the special circumstances created by Gorbachev's reforms provided him a propitious opportunity for building his political standing through such outbidding.

Soviet politics before Gorbachev was certainly not electoral politics, but it was a form of competition for the allegiance of intra-elite constituencies. In this competition, the higher the level of issue polarization within the establishment, the greater the temptation to up the ante in order to seize the initiative from rivals. This was the case during the political succession struggle that followed Stalin's death and before the "Stalin question" had been resolved. It was Khrushchev who successfully played the game of outbidding. The post-Stalin consensus called for breaking with the terroristic atmosphere and improving the consumer situation. But Khrushchev threw his rivals onto the political defensive with his unexpected denunciation of Stalin. In socioeconomic policy, he accused his rivals of failing to understand the magnitude of the food emergency, as he sponsored a campaign (the "Virgin Lands" project) for rapidly cultivating new lands in order to alleviate the grain shortage – thus trumping Malenkov's more sober (and more expensive) long-range plan for the further development of traditional agricultural regions. Khrushchev then upped the ante further, touring the country and calling on peasants to commit to extraordinary levels of meat and milk production within a three- to four-year period. Khrushchev's rivals in the leadership were consistently caught flat-footed by this intentional effort to raise popular consumption expectations and to shatter political icons. By the time they tried to oust Khrushchev in 1957, however, his patronage network in the Central Committee had grown to the point that he was able to turn the tables and purge his competitors instead.

When Khrushchev was finally ousted in 1964, the leadership was far more consensual than it had been after Stalin's death. The anti-Stalin campaign was brought to a halt to prevent the intelligentsia from continuing to cast doubt on the wisdom of the Communist Party and its "correct line." Khrushchev's extraordinary promises about the "full and final victory of communism" in the USSR and about "overtaking and surpassing the United States" in industrial production and standard of living were also tacitly retracted. Collectively, the leadership had developed a better appreciation of the incapacity of the system to deliver on such promises. Given these changes, the level of issue polarization within the leadership had declined to the point that "inbidding," or building a coalition that coopted the moderate middle of the political spectrum, became the winning formula. Khrushchev most recently, and Stalin before him, had demonstrated to the political leadership the dangers "from above" when a leader gains too much power and can use it against his nominally "collective" leadership. Under such circumstances, political competition under Brezhnev became constricted: confined within narrower arenas of politics and always sensitive to the need to avoid challenges to the political prerogatives of the Party leadership, whether from "above" (an autocrat) or "below" (forces outside the Party–State). Maintenance of a façade of unity within the leadership was a way of heading off such challenges; it interacted with, and reinforced, the moderate issue consensus within the leadership. The result was that political competition became more a matter of inbidding than outbidding. This went on for some twenty years and contributed to a condition that Gorbachev and his allies would characterize as "stagnation."

Gorbachev, like Khrushchev, faced a situation in which the climate of opinion within the political establishment had shifted toward a diffuse sense that "we cannot go on like this." There was no consensus regarding how to cure the malaise, but there was a widespread yearning for change. The stand-pat mentality of Brezhnev's and Chernenko's heirs (Tikhonov, Grishin, Romanov, Kunaev, et al.) was the analog of the neo-Stalinist sentiment in 1953 – and was as easily outflanked. Gorbachev's "campaign speech" of December 1984 was analogous to Khrushchev's de-Stalinization campaign. It threw down the gauntlet and announced that continuing in the old way was no longer acceptable. After consolidating his power base in 1985–1986, Gorbachev again seized the initiative by beginning a process of continuous radicalization of policy, which found expression in his *glasnost'* and *demokratizatsiya* programs of 1987–1988. But in sponsoring these initiatives, Gorbachev was not trying to outbid rivals within the leadership. Those who agreed with his program, such as Shevardnadze and Yakovlev, were not his rivals but his allies; he did not need to outbid them. Gorbachev was simply trying to lead the country in the direction he preferred. He preferred to radicalize in piecemeal fashion, trying to keep social forces from pushing too far and too fast in a direction that might bring down the system or create a powerful backlash by forces within the establishment.

These were the conditions under which Yeltsin tried to outbid Gorbachev, first in order to force him to radicalize more fully and more quickly (1986–1987) and then in order to outflank Gorbachev in the struggle for the allegiances of newly mobilized social forces (1988–1991). Yeltsin lost the first of these struggles because it took place within the confines of the Party establishment and at a time when the level of issue polarization within the Politburo and Central Committee was still relatively low. However, he won the second struggle because it took place in a public arena that extended to a newly empowered (and quickly radicalizing) electorate. In effect, Yeltsin was able to outbid Gorbachev once two conditions obtained: (1) political polarization had risen greatly; and (2) the game of political competition was taking place in new arenas and with new rules – arenas and rules that, ironically, had been called into being by Gorbachev himself.

At the 27th Party Congress (February 1986), Yeltsin revealed that he was now more radical than any other member of the Politburo, criticizing the central Party apparatus and the socioeconomic privileges of the *nomenklatura* and doing so in front of a broad Party membership in a speech that would be published in *Pravda* the next day. Yeltsin did much the same in a number of Politburo meetings, where he criticized the pace of *perestroika* (and thereby criticized Gorbachev's leadership), causing Gorbachev at one point to storm out of the meeting.[45] At some points in time, Gorbachev might have found it convenient to have a Politburo member advocating things that were even more radical than what Gorbachev was advocating. That would enhance Gorbachev's image as a *responsible* reformer and, at least temporarily, increase the puritans' and technocrats' sense of dependence on Gorbachev for political protection against "wild-eyed radicals" within the elite.

But when, in 1987, Yeltsin took his critique of *perestroika,* Ligachev, privilege, and Gorbachev's leadership to a meeting of the Central Committee – and did so without clearing his speech in advance with the Politburo – he had violated some of the most cherished rules of Politburo politics. He was tearing down the façade of unanimity that the Politburo preferred to show to broader audiences, even those within the political establishment, and was seeking to mobilize members of the Central Committee against his rivals within the Politburo. He was, in short, trying to discredit Gorbachev by "reporting" him to the Central Committee, accusing him of lack of courage and accusing Ligachev of seeking to sabotage *perestroika.* The vitriolic denunciation he received for his efforts, and his subsequent firing from positions in the Politburo and regional Party leadership, were demonstrations that outbidding in a still-Leninist regime is best conducted from a position of strength. Lacking a strong constituency for his views within the Central Committee, and lacking the institutional channels through which to mobilize a broader public constituency, Yeltsin's challenge was easily beaten back.

---

[45] Yeltsin, *Against the Grain*, pp. 128–9.

Such was not the case in 1988–1989, when Yeltsin seized the opportunity to outbid Gorbachev before broader, more sympathetic audiences. The process began at the televised 19th Party Conference of June 1988, which was precisely the forum at which Gorbachev introduced his most radical proposals. Absent Yeltsin's intervention, Gorbachev might have left this conference with a public image as a great democratizer. Instead, Yeltsin's unscheduled speech, for which he literally had to force himself to the microphone, raised the stakes to the point that Gorbachev came away looking like a moderate – or, at worst, like a conservative – in the eyes of the most radical forces. Some of Yeltsin's criticisms and proposals were merely tactical and could well be characterized as carping, as follows.[46]

- The Party Conference should have taken place much earlier.
- The election of delegates to the conference was not always conducted in a democratic fashion.
- Current members of the leadership who served under Brezhnev and who were tolerant of stagnation and corruption should be dismissed from the Politburo.
- When a general secretary leaves office, many other members of the Politburo should depart with him.
- The designers of *perestroika* did not prepare the ground for it properly; they did not sufficiently analyze the reasons for "stagnation."

But other proposals and criticisms staked out a more radical and egalitarian conception of democratization.

- Gorbachev's proposal to combine the functions of first secretaries of Party committees and heads of soviet delegations should be put to a popular referendum.
- The general secretary should also be subjected to direct, secret-ballot public election.
- Leaders of all political institutions should have term limits of two terms for each office and an age limit of 65 years.
- The Politburo should produce accounts of its activity – the biographies of its members, how much money they earn, what they do, etc.
- The budget of the Central Committee should be discussed openly.
- Corruption and privileges among the upper *nomenklatura* are intolerable and a violation of "social justice"; access to resources should be based on

---

[46] The following proposals are found in Yeltsin's speech as reprinted in Gorshkov et al., *Gorbachev–Yel'tsin*, pp. 78–82.

the principle that material shortages must be experienced by everyone, including officials of the Party apparatus.

- The Party apparatus is too large and strong; it can frustrate democratization. Reduce the apparatus of regional Party organizations by 2–3 times and of the Central Committee by 6–10 times, and liquidate various departments of the Central Committee apparatus.
- Socialism has failed "to resolve the main issues – to feed and clothe the people, to provide for the service sector, to solve social problems."

By any definition of the term, both Gorbachev and Yeltsin were proposing radical, democratizing changes in June 1988, beyond anything heard in Party forums since the 1920s. Soviet doctrine under Brezhnev had justified the hegemony of the CPSU by claiming that only the Party was capable of aggregating interests in society and of preventing tensions within society from becoming "antagonistic contradictions." Competitive elections and a multiparty system were not needed, so the doctrine read, because only the CPSU had sufficient understanding of the public interest to mediate and contain social conflict. It was unnecessary to expand the political rights of the masses, since such rights were only needed in systems in which an antagonistic relationship obtained between the interests of the "people" and the interests of their rulers.[47]

When Gorbachev began trying to introduce new mechanisms of intra-Party democracy in 1987 and new mechanisms of official electoral accountability in 1988, he marched well beyond the previous doctrinal limits. For he was now claiming that the Party, as constituted, could not be trusted to smooth contradictions, to aggregate interests properly, and to defend the public interest rather than solely the personal interests of the official class. Hence, genuine accountability to "the people" required more than merely a stated commitment to be responsive to popular needs; it required that one give power to the people directly to sanction or remove unresponsive officials.

Boris Yeltsin's egalitarian populism while Party first secretary in Moscow had led him toward an antagonistic view of the relationship between the *nomenklatura* and the populace. At the time, he thought of the *nomenklatura* as a set of corrupted officials in need of being replaced. After 1987, however, he came increasingly to define the *nomenklatura* in systemic terms: not as an

---

[47] For fuller discussion and documentation, see Breslauer, *Khrushchev and Brezhnev*, pp. 174–5; for the work of an intra-establishment liberal who was trying to extend the Brezhnevian definition of political participation to include "expanded political rights," see Fyodor Burlatskii, *Lenin, gosudarstvo, politika* (Moscow: Nauka, 1970).

aggregate of individuals but as a system of rule. This was consistent with Gorbachev's public statements at the time. But Yeltsin pushed things farther and faster than Gorbachev on the theoretical plane. His outbidding was both an expression of his evolving beliefs and an act of political competition that motivated him to seek increasingly radical positions to endorse.[48]

By June 1988, what distinguished Gorbachev from Yeltsin was not the endorsement of democratization but rather the degree to which each man defined democratization as consistent with maintenance of the "leading role of the Party." Both men continued formally to endorse the desirability and necessity of the Party's leading role. But Yeltsin was increasingly defining the Party apparatus as standing in antagonistic *and irremediable* contradiction to the public interest. Gorbachev's proposals would have made Party officials increasingly accountable to an electorate; Yeltsin's proposals would have done this and, additionally, would have made the daily operations of the Party apparatus more open to public scrutiny and more easily subject to angry public mobilization. Yeltsin, then, was one large step closer than Gorbachev to the position that the CPSU needed to be abolished because it was incapable of being transformed.

After June 1988, as Soviet democrats pushed to further radicalize the reforms, Gorbachev accommodated the pressures. Until fall 1990 he acceded incrementally, and often with protest, to increasingly radical demands – either because he believed in radicalization as an end in itself or because he calculated that the cost of resistance exceeded the cost of acquiescence. He was playing a political game of selective accommodation while trying to contain the pace of political polarization.

Yeltsin, however, was playing a different game, using newspaper interviews and public speeches to dog Gorbachev by continuously outbidding him for the allegiance of the people and, in the process, further radicalizing the perspectives and perceptions of the populace. If Yeltsin's public statements had had no impact on the rate of polarization, we would not need to refer

---

[48] Outbidding is a calculated act of political competition. In any given case, it may or may not be hypocritical. Yeltsin's beliefs radicalized over time in response to learning, as during his trip to the United States in September 1989 (Aron, *Boris Yeltsin*, ch. 7). But Yeltsin's "views" also happened to radicalize at key points in the political competition with Gorbachev – in the run-up to the 1989 and 1990 parliamentary elections, for example. Given the speed with which human beings are able to rationalize their behavior as being in line with their principles, it may be a futile exercise to try to determine the degree to which Yeltsin's radicalization was opportunistic. Nor is it a necessary exercise, for the approach to authority building and political competition employed in this book focuses largely on impression management and the public presentation of self. It is enough to demonstrate the process of outbidding and to consider its impact on political audiences.

to this as outbidding; we would simply argue that he chose a different constituency than did Gorbachev within a rapidly polarizing electorate. Under
such circumstances, Yeltsin's behavior would have mimicked the rate of social polarization, not influenced it. We would need an ambitious and careful
study of the interaction between Yeltsin's actions and the behavior of social
forces to decide the matter conclusively. But the available evidence suggests
to me that Yeltsin in 1988–1989 became a focal point for social forces.

To be sure, there were forces more radical than he. But the bulk of the
population that came eventually to support him had not developed a revolutionary consciousness by 1988–1989. Yeltsin articulated for them, in intelligible form, that which they felt in their guts. He helped them to explain the
precise sources of their condition. He raised their consciousness about what
was necessary to reverse their misery. And, importantly for a focal point,
he demonstrated by his succession of political victories that peaceful revolutionary change was not only desirable and necessary but also *feasible*. This
set him apart from deputies in several public forums who advanced proposals
that were fully as radical as his were. Yeltsin was able to outbid Gorbachev because he did so persistently and on all domestic issues,[49] in numerous venues,
and with a plausible claim to compete with Gorbachev for the allegiance of
the populace (whether he denied this intent or not).

We have already witnessed Yeltsin's outbidding of Gorbachev at the televised June 1988 Party Conference. But the conference ended with numerous
speeches that roasted Yeltsin for his iconoclasm, and the leadership rejected
his request to be "rehabilitated" by the Party. All this caused him to fall into
prolonged despondency.[50] Yet after absorbing the lessons of the Party Conference and buoyed by a torrent of letters and telegrams of support, Yeltsin
decided to run for a seat in the new parliament, the Congress of People's
Deputies, elections to which would be held in March 1989. The intellectual
and emotional bruising he had recently suffered – combined with the prospect
of a political competition in which he could settle scores and regain power –
caused him to up the rhetorical ante still further. In his electoral platform,
published in *Moskovskaia pravda* on March 21, 1989,[51] Yeltsin called for a
comprehensive decentralization of power to all those who wished to receive it:
the "people," the soviets, enterprises, would-be landowners, even republics.

---

[49] I discern no pattern of outbidding on foreign policy issues, unless one chooses to define inter-
republican relations as such.
[50] Aron, *Boris Yeltsin*, p. 249.
[51] *Moskovskaia pravda*, March 21, 1989, reprinted in Gorshkov et al., *Gorbachev–Yel'tsin*; cited
demands are on page 118.

Although Yeltsin did not yet articulate a coherent alternative to the existing system, he was moving in that direction. This platform implied (though it did not say it) that "the leading role of the Party" in the country's political, economic, and cultural life should be abolished.

Similarly, at the televised First Congress of People's Deputies on May 31, 1989, Gorbachev referred to the CPSU as the "guarantor of democracy," whereas Yeltsin characterized the Party as the main obstacle to democratization.[52] Yeltsin also demanded "greater political rights, greater economic and financial independence ... for each republic of the USSR," and he supported a deputy's proposal that some republics be allowed to have two state languages.[53] In a clearly demagogic bid for support of the "little man," Yeltsin suggested that Gorbachev's years in power had been a "do-nothing" period: "Even at this congress we should solve at least one concrete question, otherwise people will not understand us. For example, institute free supply of medications and free [public] transport in the cities for invalids and people living below the poverty line, solve the question of pensions, at least in part."[54] Yeltsin claimed that in one realm, however, Gorbachev had done too much. He had concentrated too much power in his own hands: "We could find ourselves again, without realizing it, in the grip of a new authoritarian regime, a new dictatorship." Yeltsin proposed a yearly popular referendum on the question of trust in the chairman of the Supreme Soviet of the USSR.[55]

Two months later, in a published interview, Yeltsin commented that the congress should abolish Article 6 of the Constitution (which protected the monopoly role of the Communist Party in the political system), with power being exercised only by organs elected by the people.[56] In the same month, he called for a "drastic reduction" in the KGB, a topic on which Gorbachev continued to exercise reserve in public comments.[57] In December 1989, his speech at the Congress of People's Deputies upped the ante on economic reform, calling for a more complete economic decentralization than he had ever advocated before and demanding a *rapid* transition to the market – much more rapid than the six years that the Ryzhkov government was proposing.[58] In the same month, a rare direct exchange took place between Gorbachev and

---

[52] Ibid., p. 134.
[53] Ibid., p. 138.
[54] Ibid., p. 139.
[55] Ibid.
[56] Ibid., p. 146.
[57] Soviet television, July 14, 1989 (FBIS-SOV, July 17, 1989), as noted in Marc Zlotnik, "Yeltsin and Gorbachev: The politics of confrontation" (unpublished manuscript, 1999).
[58] Soviet television, December 15, 1989 (FBIS-SOV, December 18, 1989).

Yeltsin regarding their political identities. Yeltsin told a Greek newspaper: "Those who still believe in communism are moving in the sphere of fantasy. I regard myself as a social democrat." Gorbachev responded several days later at a meeting of the Supreme Soviet: "I am a Communist, a convinced Communist. For some that may be a fantasy. But for me it is my main goal."[59]

Matters continued to escalate thereafter. The year 1990 saw the outbidding encompass: (1) matters of intra-Party reform (should the CPSU split into two parties? Should the conservatives be purged and the Party turned into a social democratic party? Should a multiparty, liberal democratic political order replace the current system?); (2) direct attacks on Gorbachev's fitness to continue in power; (3) relations between Moscow and the republics of the USSR; and, most consequentially, (4) the right of Russia to run its own affairs, irrespective of the wishes of the Soviet "center." This extension of outbidding, which both mirrored and further emboldened radicalizing forces in society, set the USSR on a course toward its eventual dissolution.

In January 1990, Yeltsin told a Latvian youth newspaper that the Baltic republics needed real sovereignty; he also accused Gorbachev of having become a rightist in view of his reluctance to pass fundamental laws on property, land, and the media and of his "unconcealed wish" to retain Article 6 of the Constitution.[60] In an interview eleven days later, Yeltsin implied his intention to split the Party at its forthcoming Congress unless there is "a serious renewal."[61] At the Central Committee plenum on February 5, 1990, Yeltsin elaborated on the meaning of such a renewal. Morrison summarizes it well:

His demands included the abandonment of democratic centralism and a guarantee of freedom of opinion for individual members; the abolition of the full-time *apparat*; a multiparty system; the formal recognition of internal Party factions; the abolition of article six of the Soviet constitution ...; a change in the Party structure from vertical to horizontal; democratic Party elections; an end to the *nomenklatura* system of Party control over appointments; decentralization of the Party finances; the transformation of the Party into a federal structure of parties from individual republics, including Russia .... [62]

On February 17, Yeltsin declared that Russia should be "autonomous in internal and international relations."[63] On February 20, he declared that the

---

[59] The exchange is noted and translated in Morrison, *Boris Yeltsin*, p. 108.

[60] Gorshkov et al., *Gorbachev–Yel'tsin*, pp. 164–5.

[61] Ibid., p. 169.

[62] Morrison, *Boris Yeltsin*, p. 118.

[63] Moscow radio, February 17, 1990 (FBIS-SOV, February 20, 1990), as depicted in Zlotnik, "Yeltsin and Gorbachev."

purpose of his seeking the chairmanship of the soon-to-be-elected Supreme Soviet of Russia was to force a "radicalization of all reforms."[64] In the course of this election campaign, Yeltsin made explicit what he had only hinted at earlier: that the USSR needed a liberal democracy based on total freedom of choice, without the limits that Gorbachev continued to advocate.[65] Yeltsin was making a virtue of the centrifugal forces that were straining the seams of the Soviet Union, endorsing them without equivocation and, in effect, equating disintegration with "freedom of choice" and "democracy." Gorbachev, by contrast, was defining centrifugal forces as portents of anarchy and trying to rein them in and buy them off.

In May 1990, things escalated further – again at Yeltsin's initiative. At the First Congress of People's Deputies of the Russian Federation, where he was elected as chairman by a narrow margin, Yeltsin defined "sovereignty" for the republics as the right to decide what rights the "center" should enjoy. Legally, he argued, the Russian constitution should supersede the all-union constitution. On May 30, he announced that laws were being prepared for the popular election of a Russian Federation president.[66] In June 1990, Gorbachev and Yeltsin polemicized with each other on the matter of republican sovereignty, with Yeltsin supporting "strong republics" and Gorbachev upholding the importance of the union (an "isolated" Russia is not the solution, Gorbachev insisted).[67] In July 1990, the fateful 28th Party Congress took place at which (as we have seen) Yeltsin took an abolitionist position concerning the organizational powers of the CPSU and Gorbachev countered with a position that was both anti-monopolistic and anti-abolitionist. This did not satisfy Yeltsin, who raised the stakes once again by exiting the congress and handing in his Party card.

And so it went, on issue after issue. Gorbachev would move incrementally in more radical directions and then Yeltsin would trump him, denounce him for caution or lack of commitment, and force a public confrontation. As revolutionary forces within the intelligentsia and within the union republics gained strength, Yeltsin ensured that he kept up with them (or stayed ahead of them), leaving Gorbachev in the unenviable position of trying to restrain them and being denounced as a conservative – or, alternatively, of casting his lot with hardline forces within the Party. Thus, Yeltsin, in summer 1990, forced Gorbachev prematurely to endorse the 500-day program for radical reform

[64] *Sovetskaia Estoniia*, February 20, 1990, as quoted in Aron, *Boris Yelstin*, p. 364.
[65] See Aron, *Boris Yeltsin*, pp. 366–70.
[66] Gorshkov et al., *Gorbachev–Yel'tsin*, p. 200.
[67] Ibid., pp. 204–9.

of the economy by threatening to implement it within Russia. In January 1991, Yeltsin called on Russian soldiers sent to the Baltics to consider refusing to follow the illegitimate orders of their commanders.[68] The next day, Yeltsin announced that Russia, Kazakhstan, Belorussia, and Ukraine might sign a four-sided treaty – ahead of the Union Treaty being negotiated at the time – that other republics and the center would be welcome to sign later on.[69] On February 19, 1991, Yeltsin for the first time called on Gorbachev to resign.[70] In March, when Gorbachev sponsored a nationwide referendum on whether Soviet citizens wanted to maintain the union, Yeltsin inserted onto the Russian republic's ballot the question of whether a popularly elected Russian presidency should be created. After Yeltsin's election as president, he signed a decree ending the activity of political parties within Russian state organs, an action that provoked both the communists and Gorbachev.[71]

Yeltsin began the year 1991 with a public position that sought to reconcile Russian autonomy with maintenance of a confederal variant of the USSR. It was not initially a call for Russian secession from the existing state. Indeed, on March 17, 1991, he called upon voters to *endorse* Gorbachev's referendum on behalf of a "renewed union." Yet in contrast to Gorbachev's position, Yeltsin called simultaneously for "the strengthening of Russia's statehood." Moreover, he defined such strengthening as a prerequisite for effective membership in the proposed "Union of Sovereign States." He discussed the ambiguities publicly:

I support the union. But only one that the republics would join of their own free will and not by force.... Even today there are several republics that have declared their intention to secede from it.... The only power that is strong is power based on the support of the people. Therefore, we believe that the president of Russia should be elected not by a narrow circle but by all citizens of the republic, by the whole people. The introduction of the post of president will make it possible to strengthen the sovereignty of the republic.... The election of a president of Russia by means of a vote of all the people is only the start of the strengthening of executive power in the republic.... I view your "Yes" [vote] as support for reforms in our republic, as your personal contribution toward strengthening Russian statehood, which will enable Russia to be a full participant in a renewed union of sovereign states.[72]

Yeltsin got what he had asked for: a presidential election in Russia that he won handily in June 1991. He was now in a position to act upon his calls

[68] Ibid., p. 295.
[69] Ibid., p. 296.
[70] Ibid., p. 314.
[71] Ibid., pp. 375–7.
[72] Moscow Radio Rossii Network, March 17, 1991.

for "strengthening executive power in the republic" as a means of further "strengthening Russian statehood," albeit within the context of a "renewed union." As events unfolded, it became clear that Yeltsin's commitment to a renewed union was far weaker than were his commitments to executive power within the republic and independence of the republic from any imperative co-ordination by the union's central authorities. At the same time, while unwilling publicly to advocate dismemberment of the USSR, he depicted a Russian state that would be the core of a redefined union of sovereign states.[73]

As time went on, events would force Yeltsin to choose between this flowering of Russian executive power and statehood relative to the union "center" on the one hand and, on the other hand, his avoidance of publicly advocating dissolution of the USSR. That would lead to his final act of outbidding Gorbachev, in December 1991, when he conspired reluctantly (but successfully) to abolish both the Soviet Union and Gorbachev's presidency.

CONCLUSION

In sum, Gorbachev's reforms unleashed forces that eventually he could not control. He was playing a political game that required him to maintain support among moderates even as he tried to push those moderates toward increasingly radical positions. However, the level of polarization among politically mobilized citizens was increasing more rapidly than Gorbachev had anticipated. Into this breach jumped an aggrieved and determined Boris Yeltsin. He sensed intuitively that the USSR was experiencing a peaceful revolution, not a controlled transformation. He sensed that the winning political strategy in such a situation was to keep up with – and stoke the passions of – radicalizing forces and simultaneously to frustrate the efforts of political rivals to contain the pace of change. He played this game relentlessly, perhaps relishing the opportunity to gain revenge against Gorbachev for the agony of 1987.

This explains why occupying the middle ground in competitive politics is viewed sometimes as a rational strategy and sometimes as folly. When the level of issue polarization among those with the right to participate in politics is low, and when "moderates" predominate numerically within the active (s)electorate, occupying the middle ground can be a winning strategy. But when the level of polarization is high and rising, when "moderates" are moving toward one or the other extreme, and when counter-elites raise the

---

[73] See, for example, his statement at a press conference on June 26, 1991 (Official Kremlin International News Broadcast, June 27, 1991).

expectations of popular audiences, occupying the middle ground becomes a losing strategy: one gets caught in a cross-fire, accused by both extremes of selling them out.

Gorbachev had risen skillfully within the Soviet political establishment. Once in the position of general secretary, he had demonstrated his capacity to initiate a peaceful transformation of the system. But in the end, and precisely because of the institutions Gorbachev had created, Yeltsin was able to play the game of public politics better than Gorbachev himself. Gorbachev proved more skilled at authority building within a Soviet political structure. Yeltsin proved more skilled at exploiting the public politics that Gorbachev had called into being.

7

Yeltsin Ascendant

Yeltsin had won the power struggle. He would now enter his own stage of ascendancy, when he would be expected to take political responsibility for solving the problems facing Russia – in particular, a collapsing state and an economy on the verge of collapse. The expectations of him were shaped in large part by the public image he had forged in the course of outflanking Gorbachev. Yeltsin had built his authority and seized the political initiative on the basis of an expanding but largely negative program: anti-corruption, anti-privilege, anti-Party apparatus, anti-communist, anti-Gorbachev, and, finally, anti-"the center" (i.e., the Kremlin's Soviet authority). The apogee of this accumulation of authority came in August 1991 when, in the eyes of many citizens, he assumed almost legendary heroic status by mounting a tank in front of the White House and facing down the coup plotters, seemingly through the sheer force of his will. The positive features of Yeltsin's program were real, but they were neither elaborated nor implemented at the time. Throughout 1991 and especially during his presidential election campaign of Spring 1991, Yeltsin promised Russia that he would build a market economy on the Western model, integrate the country into the global capitalist economy, and see Russia take its place among the "normal" and "civilized" liberal democracies of the world. But he did not have to specify a strategy for accomplishing all this, since Russia was not yet autonomous of the Kremlin's dictates.

All he needed to do in order to win the power struggle (no mean feat, of course) was to identify himself publicly with these visionary goals and lambaste Gorbachev at every turn for failing to adopt a program that would accomplish them swiftly on a nationwide basis. During the period of radicalization and revolutionary polarization made possible by Gorbachev's transformation of Soviet politics, this was a winning strategy. It allied Yeltsin with the most mobilized, self-confident, and energetic forces within society: anti-system voters and protesters in all republics; educated, urban youth; and "Westernizers" among the technical and critical intelligentsia. It permitted him to paint his main rivals as either spent forces (Gorbachev), conservatives (Ligachev), or restorationists (the coup plotters). It allowed him to build his own authority by playing the revolutionary's game of undercutting the authority of incumbents and state institutions alike. And it allowed him to accumulate political support without having to specify a positive program and take responsibility for policy results.

Each of the Soviet leaders on whom we have focused – Khrushchev in 1958–1959, Brezhnev in 1970–1971, and Gorbachev in 1986–1987 – followed his victory in the political succession struggle with a brief period during which he emerged ascendant within the leadership and had the authority and power to sponsor a comprehensive program for change in domestic and foreign policies. This was the leader's "honeymoon" period, when his authority was at its greatest and many skeptics deferred to his right to specify a vision.[1] Yeltsin, too, emerged ascendant after his victory in the Russian presidential election of June 1991, and his authority soared even higher after August 1991. Moreover, in many ways he was even more unconstrained at this point than the earlier leaders had been, both because he had secured a huge electoral mandate and because there was no longer a powerful collective leadership – backed by clients within a Central Committee apparatus – to which he had to report. And in October of that year, his parliament (the Russian Supreme Soviet), which would later become antagonistic to his program, accorded him special powers to rule by decree for a one-year period. His honeymoon had begun, but like his predecessors', it would not last long.

RUSSIA'S POST-SOVIET POLICY AGENDA

Yeltsin's ascendancy took place in a context that looked quite different from those that Khrushchev, Brezhnev, and Gorbachev faced at analogous stages of their administrations. The Communist Party no longer enjoyed a "leading role" or the opportunity to impose its "correct line" on the country; instead, it was struggling to avoid expropriation of its assets and abrogation of its right to exist. Politics, of course, was no longer a private affair; instead, the mass public was now the arena for contested electoral politics, while civil liberties – freedom of speech, religion, organization, press, and movement – were

---

[1] Gorbachev, however, faced more resistance to his domestic policy radicalization in 1987 than had Khrushchev and Brezhnev at comparable points in time.

widespread. The command economy had been destroyed, though an institutionalized free market had not been created. Internationally, communism had ceased to rule in Eastern Europe, the Warsaw Pact had been dissolved, and there was no longer a Soviet Union to serve as ideological and organizational center of the world communist movement.

Whatever program Yeltsin intended to forge, it was not going to be Leninist. At the analogous stage of their administrations, his predecessors in the Kremlin had come forth with programs that sought to adapt, reform, or transform the Party–State apparatus; Yeltsin instead faced a crumbling Party–State and the challenge of building a new one. His immediate predecessor sought to transform the Communist Party; Yeltsin proposed to destroy it and to replace it with new bases of political organization and ideology. Gorbachev had sought to transform the command economy; Yeltsin sought not only to cope with a rapidly disintegrating, no longer commanding economy but also to *build* an economic system to replace it. His predecessor had tried to define a new mission and ethos for the "Soviet people"; Yeltsin had to cope with the disorientation and identity void following the collapse of Soviet civilization while helping to build a Russian nation to replace it. Gorbachev had been challenged to provide a formula for dealing with the "nationalities problem" within the USSR; Yeltsin had to define a strategy for ordering Russia's now-foreign relations with the fourteen other successor states of the former Soviet Union. His predecessors had to specify a program for simultaneously maintaining or extending the global power of the USSR and keeping the peace between the two nuclear superpowers. Yeltsin had to define from scratch what were to be *Russia's* roles and responsibilities in the post–Cold War international system. In sum, Yeltsin was challenged to be simultaneously a state builder, a nation builder, the designer of a new economic order, and a statesman. He had built his authority as an oppositional leader but would have to maintain it as a creator.

In fall 1991, when Yeltsin began to anticipate and prepare for his country's independence from Soviet authorities, the Russian leader set to work on these general issues as well as on the numerous practical matters that still faced him in the rush of daily decisionmaking. The latter were not inconsiderable. He still had to deal with Gorbachev, who was working furiously to recoup some political standing following the August 1991 coup and its aftermath and who put much of his energy into trying to save the Soviet Union from extinction. Yeltsin also had to put together a team of advisors, aides, and cabinet members to help him design new programs. He had to decide how to handle autonomist pressures in Russia's regions, now that some were starting to claim greater sovereignty than most politicians in Moscow could countenance; indeed, the Chechen-Ingush Republic formally announced its secession from Russia in November 1991. Yeltsin had to decide whether to allow new local elections to take place as scheduled in Fall 1991 or rather to alter the schedule of elections in light of new political realities. He had to respond, one way or the other, to pressures on him to call unscheduled elections for the Supreme Soviet and to sponsor a "presidential political party" to compete in those elections – in order to seize this unique opportunity to elect a more radical deputy corps within the legislature. And he had to decide whether to capitalize on his charismatic authority to increase the formal powers of his office.

Whereas Gorbachev in 1988–1989 had come forth with a comprehensive program for transforming the Soviet Union without inducing systemic collapse, Yeltsin now had to deal with the aftermath of a collapse he had helped to bring about. He also had to come forth with a comprehensive program for transforming newly independent Russia into the kind of "normal," "civilized" country that he had been touting. Gorbachev had tried to transform the Soviet system on the territory of the USSR; Yeltsin now had to replace that system on the territory of Russia, presumably in ways consistent with the vision he had propounded on his way to the top. There was, at this point, plenty of room for political creativity. Yeltsin's personal preferences could hold sway – at least for the moment – as he decided how to attain the vision. Constraints would pile up soon thereafter, however, as the costs of his policy initiatives became evident.

YELTSIN AS STATE BUILDER

Several weeks after the abortive coup of August 1991, Yeltsin held a press conference for foreign journalists (September 7) at which he said the following about his image of what kind of a state Russia needed:

> The country is now devoid of all "isms." It isn't capitalist, nor communist, nor socialist; it's a country in a transitional period, which wants to proceed along a civilized path, the path along which France, Britain, the United States, Japan, Germany, Spain and other countries have been and still are proceeding. It's an aspiration to proceed precisely along this path, that is, the decommunization of all aspects of society's life, the deideologization of all aspects of society's life, an aspiration to democracy ....[2]

Four days later, at the Conference on Security and Cooperation in Europe (CSCE), he would add still more evocative imagery: "Our democracy is like

[2] Moscow Russian Television Network, September 7, 1991 (FBIS-SOV-91-174, p. 66).

a sickly child. But the main choice has already been made. We have the determination to go the whole way, climbing up the ladder to civilization."[3]

Yeltsin proposed to emulate Western "civilization" in many of its specifics. At the news conference, he indicated that a new presidential service had to be created and, toward that end, his associates were studying the organization of the White House staff in the United States, "where this system has simply been refined right down to the details ...."[4] Subsequently, he spoke of the need for creating an independent judiciary and legal profession,[5] the normality of political opposition[6] and of mutual criticism between the executive and legislative branches,[7] the need to create a rule of law,[8] the desirability of allowing Gorbachev to retire from office "with dignity,"[9] the "shaping and development of a civil society," "a strong and united democratic federative state," and the need for civil service reform and the rooting out of corruption.[10]

But how to bring these about? How to root out corruption, build a reliable civil service, and foster rule of law? How to protect the independence of the judiciary? How to create a strong civil society? And precisely what form of representative democracy did he have in mind? What degree of separation of powers between the executive and legislative branches – and how much criticism of himself and his policies – would he put up with? What would be the relative powers of the federal authorities and the regions of Russia?

Yeltsin depicted strong executive power as a prerequisite for building a new order on the ruins of the old. The man who had chafed in positions of subordination, and who would admit that he always wanted to be the "boss,"[11] was prepared to capitalize on his extraordinary political momentum by maximizing his powers to the extent possible. Thus, he demanded (and received) from the Supreme Soviet emergency powers to rule by decree for twelve months. He moved quickly to bring the military and secret police under the control of trusted associates. He brought in former associates from Sverdlovsk to run his presidential administration.[12]

---

[3] Moscow Radio Rossii Network, September 11, 1991 (FBIS-SOV-91-177, p. 1).
[4] Moscow Russian Television Network, September 7, 1991 (FBIS-SOV-91-174, p. 69).
[5] Moscow Radio Rossii Network, October 17, 1991.
[6] Ibid.
[7] Moscow Russian Television Network, February 19, 1992.
[8] Deutschlandfunk Network, November 17, 1991; *Der Spiegel,* November 18, 1991, pp. 253–62.
[9] Moscow All-Union Radio Maiak Network, December 23, 1991.
[10] Moscow Russian Television Network, April 5, 1992 (FBIS-SOV-92-066, p. 23).
[11] Boris Yeltsin, *Against the Grain: An Autobiography,* trans. by Michael Glenny (New York: Summit, 1990), pp. 72–3.
[12] When asked about this in a televised interview on February 19, 1992, he denied that this is untoward ("it is one-tenth the number Bush brought from Texas") yet then argued that it

But Yeltsin depicted strong executive power as more than a way to maximize his personal political security. He also depicted it as a prerequisite for holding Russia together as a territorial entity. Thus, he announced that autonomist pressures in the regions would be offset by the appointment of presidential representatives to serve as "heads of administration" in each region. He postponed plans for new local elections and the election of regional governors. And when the Chechen-Ingush Republic declared its independence, he tried to use military force to overturn the decision, though his action was rescinded by the parliament.[13]

Yeltsin's approach to executive power was plebiscitarian. In fall 1991 he did more than demand that parliament accord him the power to rule by decree; he also rejected the request of leaders of Democratic Russia that he sponsor a presidential party, opting instead to be president of "all the people." The "people" had been his ticket to resurrection in 1989; they had validated him further as president in June 1991; he had appealed to them in August 1991. His state-building and authority-building strategies would rest on his capacity to mobilize popular support directly without the mediation of a partisan political organization.[14]

Moreover, Yeltsin presented himself as a man who possessed the unique set of skills required to steer Russia through the difficult passage before it. Whereas he described Gorbachev as timid and inclined toward "half-measures," Yeltsin depicted himself as possessing "the courage to take this severe step" (i.e., the unfreezing of prices).[15] His image was that of a tough, self-made man who demands of others that they be willing to tackle the Herculean challenges he

---

was necessary in light of the political insecurity surrounding him: "Do you think I want to find myself in Gorbachev's position? At such a difficult moment on 19 August everyone from his personal bodyguard to the prime minister acted as traitors. They all betrayed him. I do not want to find myself in that position" (Moscow Russian Television Network, February 19, 1992 [FBIS-SOV-92-034, p. 51]). He repeated the latter rationale in an interview televised on June 11, 1992, while adding that his strategy had already proven itself: "if you recall the time of the putsch, on 19 and 20 August, none of the comrades in arms selected by me defected" (Moscow Russian Television Network, June 11, 1992 [FBIS-SOV-92-114, p. 22]).

[13] On October 28, 1991, several weeks before the fiasco in Chechen-Ingushetia, he proclaimed to the Congress of RSFSR People's Deputies: "there is a point beyond which we cannot go under any conditions. This point is Russia's territorial integrity and its state and legal unity. We cannot allow and will not allow the breakup of Russia, or its fragmentation into dozens of principalities that are at war with each other" (Moscow Russian Television Network, October 28, 1991 [FBIS-SOV-91-209, p. 54]).

[14] See Lilia Shevtsova, *Yeltsin's Russia: Myths and Reality* (Washington, DC: Carnegie Endowment, 1999), p. 16; Peter Reddaway and Dmitri Glinski, *The Tragedy of Russia's Reforms: Market Bolshevism against Democracy* (Washington, DC: U.S. Institute of Peace, 2001), ch. 6.

[15] Moscow Russian Television Network, October 28, 1991.

himself was willing to tackle.[16] He was a man of action who depicted himself as a revolutionary hero. Following the anti-communist revolution, he presented himself as the man who would cure Russia of its diseases and then lead it along the road to "civilization."

YELTSIN AS NATION BUILDER

State building requires the formal definition of constitutional relationships and the construction of formal institutions. Nation building, by contrast, is a more symbolic process of instilling in a population a sense of "we feeling" that is based on a common sense of history and destiny. But it also has a formal dimension in that building a nation-*state* (as opposed to an oppositional social movement) also entails constitutional specification of the boundaries of the political community: who "the people" are and what their rights and obligations are as citizens. In Russia, for example, where prior notions of a "Soviet people" no longer applied, do "the people" include all residents of the Russian Federation, regardless of ethnicity, or only those of Russian ethnic ancestry? Whichever definition is chosen, what will be the terms of responsiveness between the people and the state? Will this relationship be defined in civic and procedural terms that are based on universalistic and liberal democratic conceptions of accountability to empowered individuals? Or will the legitimacy of the state be based on more exclusive and substantive criteria, such as the material and symbolic goods that it "delivers" to the population?

Yeltsin's emphasis on gaining Russia's independence coexisted in his political rhetoric with a liberal definition of the people whom those institutions would serve. He eschewed nostalgic, invidious, imperial, and ethnic designations of the character of the state and promoted instead a non-ethnic definition of citizenship within Russia. While his state-building rhetoric can justifiably be depicted as endorsing civil liberties, strong executive authority, and plebiscitarian accountability, his approach to Russian nationhood can be characterized as liberal, de-ethnicized nation building.

Yeltsin's rhetoric on this score was consistent during both the struggle with Gorbachev and his subsequent period of ascendancy. He addressed the issue in terms that contrasted sharply with those of both ethnic nationalists and imperialist restorationists within Russian politics. His speeches eschewed references to *Rus'* (the lands of the Russians), in favor of *Rossiia* (the country, Russia). He referred consistently to *Rossiiskie*, not *Russkie*, state interests.

---

[16] See interview in *Trud*, December 14, 1991 (FBIS-SOV-91-241, p. 36).

He referred to citizens of Russia as *Rossiiane* (citizens of the country, Russia), not *Russkie* (ethnic Russians). He referred to the people as the *narod* (people), not the *natsiia* (nation, a term used largely by the most extreme nationalists).

A corollary of this choice of vocabulary was Yeltsin's consistent underscoring of the multinational character of the Russian Federation. When not referring to the secularized entity of "the Russian (*Rossiiskii*) people," he referred to "the interests of the peoples of the state of Russia."[17] Yeltsin cautioned against any policies that could stoke inter-ethnic strife, and he warned frequently of the need to construct a political order within which all the peoples of the country would feel represented.[18] In this connection he explicitly renounced the Russian imperial heritage and rejected the notion of a tyranny of the ethnic majority: "Russian statehood, which has chosen democracy and freedom, will never be an empire, or a big or small brother, it will be an equal among equals."[19] Ethnic minorities within Russia and their constituent republics within the Russian Federation, he averred, possessed laws of their own that Moscow was obliged to "respect."[20] One of his "priorities," he proclaimed to a nationwide television audience, was "the revival of the traditional values of all the peoples of Russia and the development of their culture."[21] The state, he later declared, must not "impinge on the spiritual and cultural specificity of nations [within Russia]." Indeed, that same state has an obligation to "assist in preserving the native language, culture, and traditions of the peoples of Russia." But lest he be accused of ignoring the concerns of the majority ethnicity within the Russian Federation, he added: "That fully applies to the Russian (*russkii*) people as well."[22]

Yeltsin also attempted to refute his opponents' appropriation of Russian history. He insisted that Russia's historical traditions were not necessarily antithetical to the new values of freedom and democracy, citing the democratic experiments in Russian history as the traditions to be revived. In the late nineteenth and early twentieth centuries, he declared,

Russia was confidently modernizing herself; she was moving toward the market and democracy, and her culture was forcefully asserting common human values, while

---

[17] Moscow Domestic Service, "Congress Diary," June 22, 1990.
[18] Moscow Domestic Service, December 11, 1990; TASS, March 29, 1991; Moscow Russian Television Network, October 6, 1992; Moscow Ostankino Television Network, November 9, 1993.
[19] TASS, September 3, 1991; see also Moscow Central Television, "Vostok," December 29, 1991.
[20] TASS, March 29, 1991.
[21] Moscow Russian Television Network, April 5, 1992 (FBIS-SOV-92-066, p. 23).
[22] Moscow Ostankino Television Network, November 9, 1993.

naturally retaining national specifics. [As a result], it is all the more strange to hear accusations of our betraying the national tradition.[23]

Yeltsin's imagery of Russia as a nation was of a wounded country with an unspecified, spiritual sense of unity based on geography, history, and the very multinational character of its citizenry.[24] He defined these features as strengths to be mobilized in order to heal the wounds of the past and construct a revitalized, but new, nation. He called for "patriotism" and "pride" but warned against chauvinism and restoration.[25] He refurbished the Kremlin to restore the unifying, historical symbols of statehood.[26] He proposed a role for the Russian Orthodox Church in helping to unify Russia, but without either exclusionary or invidious references to other religions.[27]

Yeltsin combined this conception with his oft-stated vision of a civic political order. The Russian people were depicted in his speeches as a collectivity of individuals who possessed democratic rights derived from universal principles of human rights: "Neither the Communist Party, nor the nation, nor any other party, but rather the individual himself, is the supreme value."[28] He declared to the United Nations in February 1992 his intention to renounce all statist and coercively collectivist ideologies in favor of "democracy, human rights and freedoms, legal and moral standards, and political and civil rights."[29] Later that year, Yeltsin declared to the Supreme Soviet that "we do not need a new 'ism' " to solve Russia's problems.[30]

Nevertheless, recurrent themes in Yeltsin's speeches loosely described the new order as predicated on certain substantive ideas other than the procedural commitment to "democracy" and "individualism." In the same speech to the Supreme Soviet, Yeltsin defined these as a "sense of duty and patriotism."[31] Indeed, in defending his economic reforms earlier that year, Yeltsin

---

[23] *Rossiiskie vesti*, April 21, 1993; see also Moscow Russian Television Network, June 7, 1993, where he defined the past pillars of Russian statehood as Novgorod, Peter I, Alexander II, and the *zemstva* [local councils], concluding that procedural democratic statehood is therefore not at all at odds with the traditions of Russia.

[24] See Moscow Domestic Services, December 4, 1990; Radio Rossii, April 1 and June 4, 1991; Moscow All-Union Radio Maiak, August 29, 1991; Moscow Russian Television Network, April 7 and November 30, 1992; and *Rossiiskie vesti*, April 21, 1993.

[25] TASS, September 3, 1991; Moscow Central Television, "Vostok," December 29, 1991.

[26] TASS, September 1, 1992.

[27] TASS, October 6, 1992, and February 5, 1993.

[28] TASS, November 2, 1991; see also Radio Rossii, May 21 and June 1, 1991, as well as *Rossiiskaia gazeta*, February 3, 1992.

[29] *Rossiiskaia gazeta*, February 3, 1992.

[30] TASS, October 6, 1992.

[31] Ibid.

had argued that those reforms were compatible with his own "vision of patriotism," a view of a "united, revitalized Russia ... a civilized country capable
of providing high standards of living and strict observance of human rights
for its citizens."[32]

When we combine these rhetorical positions with Yeltsin's plebiscitarian
approach to executive power, we conclude that Yeltsin was offering the office
of the presidency, and himself as its occupant, as the symbol and protector
of that proud, multi-ethnic nation. To be sure, the president must be regularly accountable to the people and must justify their trust. He must respect
the laws that restrict the discretion of the state vis-à-vis its citizens. But as a
centralized symbol, in both rhetoric and constitutional wording, Yeltsin offered the president as the personification of the Russian (*Rossiiskii*) people.
Moreover, he defined the Russian people as unified by their common sense of
duty and by the loose binding power of a democratic patriotism – not by their
ethnicity.[33]

DEFINING THE BOUNDARIES OF THE RUSSIAN NATION AND STATE

Two specific dilemmas of state building and nation building arose immediately upon the collapse of the USSR. One concerned the territorial borders
of the new Russian state. The Russian Federation had been a circumstantial
construction of Soviet power. The borders of the heartland of the Russian
empire in 1913 and 1917 were not identical to the borders of the Russian
Federation in 1991. Adjustments had been made at numerous times, including (most recently) Khrushchev's whimsical transfer of Crimea to Ukraine in
1954. Hence, there remained plenty of reason for competing politicians to
differ credibly over the desirability and feasibility of again revising the borders of the Russian Federation.

A second dilemma concerned the obligations of the Russian state to the
20–25 million ethnic Russians living in the newly independent former republics of the Soviet Union. Formally, they were now residents or citizens
of other sovereign states. But given the role Moscow had played for at least
sixty years in protecting their interests and guaranteeing their security, they
seemed to warrant treatment by the Russian state somewhat different from
the relative lack of interest accorded twentieth-century Russian diasporas in
distant lands. Did Russia's protection or proselytizing of this newest diaspora constitute interference in the internal affairs of independent states?

---

[32] *Rossiiskaia gazeta,* April 7, 1992.
[33] In this respect, Yeltsin's position was consistent with Soviet-era ideology, which embraced
"Soviet patriotism" and eschewed ethnic "nationalism."

Alternatively, were these Russians in the "Near Abroad" tacit or would-be citizens of the Russian state? And if the latter, should the boundaries of Russia be redrawn to incorporate those lands currently occupied largely by Russians?

Boris Yeltsin was both consistent and insistent in presenting a de-ethnicized and civic conception of the political order he promised to construct within the Russian Federation. However, the question of how to define Moscow's obligations to Russians in the Near Abroad was one that split the democratic camp immediately upon the collapse of the USSR. Angry rhetoric emanated from the mouths of some individuals, such as St. Petersburg mayor Anatolii Sobchak, who had been leaders of the anti-communist and democratic revolution in Soviet and Russian politics.[34] At the other end of the political spectrum, both ethnic nationalists and imperial restorationists could use the issue as justification for the most revanchist proposals, while imperial institutions – such as the Soviet Army, which remained entrenched in the Near Abroad – could serve as an instrument for revanchist actions. Whatever his predispositions in such a context, it would have been difficult for Yeltsin to avoid eventual political isolation if he advocated a policy of laissez-faire toward governments in the successor states or if he ignored the alleged plight of new Russian diaspora.

Yeltsin responded by attempting to combine the universalism of his state-building and nation-building strategies within Russia with a qualified defense of Russians in the Near Abroad. It was a tense and, in some respects, incompatible coexistence of policy orientations, a reflection of one of the most intractable dilemmas of democratic nation building in a post-imperial and diasporic context. From late 1990 onward, more than a year before the dissolution of the USSR, Yeltsin spoke out clearly on behalf of the ethnic Russian and "Russian-speaking" populations in the increasingly autonomous, and then independent, republics of the USSR.[35] Clearly and consistently, he articulated concern for these "compatriots" (*sootechestvenniki*) and committed the Russian government to protect their rights against discrimination or persecution.[36]

---

[34] In an interview with *Le Figaro* on December 4, 1991, responding to the recent Ukrainian vote for independence, Sobchak stridently opposed "the threat of forced Ukrainianization in Crimea, with its Russian majority." He argued that Russia "would immediately raise territorial claims" if Ukraine refused to join in a political union (*Report on the USSR*, December 13, 1991).

[35] See TASS, November 13, 1990; *Argumenty i fakty*, no. 3, 1991, pp. 4–5; TASS, February 9, 1991; Reuters, September 30, 1991; *Komsomol'skaia pravda*, May 27 and July 3, 1992; *Trud*, October 6, 1992; TASS, March 17 and March 22, 1993.

[36] See *Pravda*, September 26, 1990; *Izvestiia*, December 25, 1990; *Krasnaia zvezda*, June 11, 1992; TASS, September 7, October 6, and November 5, 1992.

He held a centrist (i.e., moderate) position within the debate of the time. He insisted, in contrast to the extreme nationalists and imperial restorationists,[37] that pursuit of the rights of compatriots should take place through "legal" and "political" means.[38] Rhetorically, he rejected the use of armed force and indicated his desire that Russians in the Near Abroad stay put, rather than emigrating back to Russia.[39] He treated the issue of the political rights of Russians within those countries as one to be negotiated through state-to-state bargaining and the conclusion of interstate treaties.[40] He appealed to Western governments and international organizations to join in protecting these allegedly stranded and persecuted populations, invoking international conventions on human rights as justification.[41]

There were, to be sure, counter trends within Yeltsin's own cabinet. Defense Minister Grachev made occasional vitriolic statements that stretched or contradicted the moderation of Yeltsin's remarks.[42] Furthermore, Moscow's actual policies in the Near Abroad occasionally leaned on the threat or use of force and material coercion.[43] Yeltsin himself wavered between an ethnic

[37] See Official Kremlin International News Broadcast, September 20, 1991; *Literaturnaia Rossiia*, no. 42, 1991; Russian Press Digest, December 11, 1991; *Komsomol'skaia pravda*, January 17, 1992; TASS, January 17, 1992, January 21, 1992, February 27, 1992, July 1, 1992, October 8, 1992, October 15, 1992, October 17, 1992, January 31, 1993, and February 20, 1993; *Moskovskie novosti*, February 12, 1992; Reuters, February 13, 1992; Official Kremlin News Broadcast, January 28, 1993. For example, just after the Soviet collapse, Vladimir Lukin (chair for foreign affairs of the Russian Supreme Soviet) wrote a letter to Supreme Soviet Chair Ruslan Khasbulatov in which he argued that Ukraine should give up either the Black Sea Fleet or Crimea (*Toronto Globe and Mail*, January 23, 1992).

[38] See *Izvestiia*, December 25, 1990; Reuters, September 30, 1991; *Komsomol'skaia pravda*, May 27, 1992; *Krasnaia zvezda*, June 11, 1992.

[39] *Pravda*, September 26, 1990; TASS, November 13, 1990; *Argumenty i fakty*, no. 3, 1991; *Komsomol'skaia pravda*, May 27, 1992.

[40] See *Krasnaia zvezda*, January 15, 1991; *Argumenty i fakty*, no. 3, 1991; TASS, February 9, 1991; *The New York Times*, June 22, 1992; *Trud*, October 6, 1992; and TASS, June 29, 1993.

[41] See TASS, July 10, 1992, April 30, 1993, June 29, 1993; see also Reuters, November 6, 1992.

[42] As early as mid-June 1992, Grachev declared that the use of force against Russians would be answered with force (*The New York Times*, June 22, 1992). By late 1993, Kozyrev had articulated the possibility of a strong response. He stated that Russia would "protect the Russian population and Russia's interests in a tough manner wherever it is needed and whoever is concerned, even if it be our friends" (Reuters, November 24, 1993). Given Kozyrev's known views on interstate relations, however, we may assume that Kozyrev was posturing when he made this statement. Nonetheless, the fact that he felt the need to posture is a good indicator of the changing climate of opinion within Russian politics.

[43] For example, Russia stopped delivery to Estonia of natural gas, for which Estonia is completely dependent on Russia (*The New York Times*, June 26, 1993). While the nominal reason was Estonia's backlog of unpaid debt, the move closely followed the introduction of Estonia's new Law on Foreigners, which, Yeltsin stated, "crudely violates the legal, civil, property, social and vital interests of Russians and the Russian-speaking population" (TASS, June 25, 1993).

definition of the purported constituency within the Near Abroad and a definition that included many millions of non-Russians (the "Russian-speaking population") as well.[44]

Thus, there was a continuous tension between Yeltsin's extension to ethnic Russians and Russian speakers in the Near Abroad of tacit rights to protection by Russia and his simultaneous insistence that, within Russia, citizenship was to be defined in territorial, not ethnic, terms. The tension reflected the intellectual and political dilemmas of fashioning a de-ethnicized strategy of nation building within this post-imperial context of dispersion and competing nation-building strategies. It might have been the best amalgam of incompatible premises that any liberal politician at the time could have hoped to come up with. But Yeltsin promised to balance and manage those tensions as he pushed to the fore.

BUILDING A NEW ECONOMIC ORDER

One of the most urgent challenges that Yeltsin faced in the fall of 1991 was to decide on his strategy for rescuing the sinking Russian economy. He interviewed several economists and economic administrators, seeking their advice and evaluating their credentials for positions in his administration. He settled on a previously obscure economist named Yegor Gaidar, who sold him on the idea that, without strong medicine, the Russian economy would collapse. Gaidar offered to prevent that collapse with a strategy for rapid transformation that had been called "shock therapy" when adopted in Latin America and Poland. He proposed to end price controls, balance the state budget through severe cuts in subsidies to industry and agriculture, and de-monopolize the economy through rapid privatization of state-owned assets. The result, he argued, would be economic "stabilization," the introduction of a competitive market economy, and the eventual production in large quantities of goods that consumers actually wanted to buy. Such was the theory.[45]

Yeltsin bought it – for reasons that may have been personal and political. He was a witness to the economic disarray in the country at the time, but he was also attracted to a breakthrough strategy for building a new economic

---

[44] Yeltsin regularly interspersed his more numerous references to "Russian-speaking populations" (see TASS, February 9, 1991; *Komsomol'skaia pravda*, May 27 and July 3 1992; *Trud*, October 6, 1992; Reuters, October 8, 1992; TASS, October 27, 1992; Reuters, November 6, 1992; TASS, March 17, April 30, and June 25, 1993) with references to "ethnic Russians" (see *Argumenty i fakty*, no. 3, 1991; Reuters, September 30, 1991; TASS, March 17, 1993; Reuters, April 4, 1993).

[45] See Gaidar's account of his fall 1991 job interview with Yeltsin in Yegor T. Gaidar, *Dni porazhenii i pobed* (Moscow: Vagrius, 1996), p. 105.

order in Russia. Shock therapy promised quick results at the macroeconomic level, with none of the procrastination and compromise he had criticized in Gorbachev's policies.[46] It was consistent with the campaignism, commandism, and "struggle" that had been common features of the Stalinist and post-Stalinist administrative cultures in which Yeltsin grew up and that had defined his leadership style in both Sverdlovsk and Moscow. As Fyodorov notes, it filled the cognitive vacuum left by the disappearance of any confidence in the previous ideology and also appealed to the campaignist mentality: it was simple, was clear-cut in its principles, and required resolve and political decisiveness to implement.[47]

Moreover, shock therapy was reductionist in that it focused attention on transformation of the individual citizen; it promised to "cure" Russians of the lethargy into which they had fallen. As much as the strategy was a prescription for macroeconomic stabilization, it was also based on an implicit theory of behavioral and cultural change. It was a cultural revolution of sorts. If people were put in situations where survival depended on their exercising entrepreneurial initiative, and if the state ended its practice of dictating to people what kind of initiative to exercise,[48] then they would finally overcome their lethargy and search for those opportunities. As Yeltsin put it in retrospect: "Sometimes it takes a sharp break or rupture to make a person move forward or even survive at all";[49] this observation was based on personal experience, for he had put himself through such a wrenching cognitive and value transformation during 1988 after being purged from the Soviet leadership.[50] Presumably, sustained behavioral change would ultimately lead attitudes to conform with the new behavior, transforming the culture of lethargy and envy into one of initiative and achievement.

---

[46] As he put it in introducing the reform (*Sovetskaia Rossiia,* October 29, 1991): "The time has come to act decisively, firmly, without hesitation.... The period of movement with small steps is over .... A big reformist breakthrough is necessary" (as quoted and translated in Anders Åslund, *How Russia Became a Market Economy* [Washington, DC: Brookings Institution, 1995], p. 64).

[47] Valentin Fyodorov, *Yel'tsin* (Moscow: "Golos," 1995), pp. 27–8, 55. See also Gaidar, *Dni,* p. 105; Yu. M. Baturin, A. L. Il'in, V. F. Kadatskii, V. V. Kostikov, M. A. Krasnov, A. Ya. Livshits, K. F. Nikiforov, L. G. Pikhoia, and G. A. Satarov, *Epokha Yel'tsina: Ocherki politicheskoi istorii* (Moscow: Vagrius, 2001), pp. 173–4.

[48] Yeltsin called this "freedom ... from the bureaucratic straitjacket" (Moscow Russian Television Network, October 28, 1991 [FBIS-SOV-91-209, p. 47]).

[49] Boris Yeltsin, *The Struggle for Russia,* trans. by Catherine A. Fitzpatrick (New York: Random House, 1994), p. 149.

[50] Yeltsin, *Against the Grain,* pp. 203–10; 216–39. Observation of this parallel between societal shock therapy and his own personal reappraisal was noted in Dmitry Mikheyev, *Russia Transformed* (Indianapolis, IN: Hudson Institute, 1996), p. 89.

As Yeltsin presented it, cultural transformation would also be a product of generational change. Those who would not (or could not) adapt to the stringent new requirements would be replaced by the new generations reaching their twenties and thirties in the 1990s. He projected himself as the leader of a revolution that would bring those new generations into positions of authority in the polity, economy, and society. For the most part, he assumed the older generation of citizens to be relatively hopeless as would-be capitalists, having been ruined by the old system. But his candor also revealed his Leninist "campaign" mentality. As head of the Moscow City Committee, for example, Yeltsin says he strove to replace compromised workers in Moscow shops with "young, 'uninfected' (*nezarazhennaya*) staff."[51] When he discusses shock therapy in the second memoir, he praises tough, independent, ambitious young people who possess "an entirely new psychology."[52] Russia's backwardness cannot be overcome until generational change has taken place: "We must finally admit that Russia comprehends democracy poorly – not merely for global, historical reasons but for rather prosaic ones: the new generation cannot break its way into power. The Socialist mode of thinking has left its imprint on all of us .... The new generation must come to the forefront as quickly as possible."[53] There are no fortresses that "uninfected" young people cannot storm, once you give them an electoral voice, hire them in large numbers, liberate them from the command economy, and allow money to be the focus of economic ambition and exchange.

Yeltsin knew that he was running a huge risk. This breakthrough strategy promised to impose severe pain on the population in the near term, and at a time when institutions of democratic accountability existed that could subject Yeltsin to public criticism, legislative censure, impeachment, or electoral defeat. Moreover, for all his charisma and for all the legal authority garnered

---

[51] Yeltsin, *Against the Grain*, p. 118 (the Russian original is in Boris Yel'tsin, *Ispoved' na zadannuiu temu* [Sverdlovsk: Sredne-Ural'skoe knizhnoe izdatel'stvo, 1990], p. 112). On the other hand, it should be noted that, in both the Russian and English versions, Yeltsin was sufficiently self-conscious about the connotations to put the word "uninfected" in quotation marks.

[52] Yeltsin, *The Struggle*, p. 146.

[53] Ibid., pp. 290–1. For other references in Yeltsin's memoirs to the crucial role of the younger generation, see *Against the Grain*, pp. 183, 234, 253; *The Struggle*, pp. 126–7, 151–2, 291; Boris Yeltsin, *Midnight Diaries* (New York: Public Affairs, 2000), pp. 23, 27, 28, 39, 63, 79–83, 103, 114, 274. Shortly after the August 1991 coup, Yeltsin proclaimed as follows: "no matter how difficult it is, each of us should aim to do whatever we can to restructure ourselves in a fundamental way, so that we can follow a civilized road. This will be difficult, very difficult .... It will be easier for young people, whose hearts, minds, and heads have not been drawn into the system" (news conference for Russian and foreign journalists hosted by Russian President Boris Yeltsin at the Russian Soviet Federated Socialist Republic House of Soviets in Moscow on September 7, 1991, as transcribed in FBIS-SOV-9-174, p. 68).

from his victory at the polls in June 1991, Yeltsin knew that Russia's nascent democracy was a fragile one. In August 1991, after all, a coup d'etat had been attempted. Although he had defeated the attempt, Yeltsin continued to govern under a pall of uncertainty about the possibility of another coup attempt, this one perhaps more successful than the last. He had been told by the architect of the shock therapy (Gaidar) that the pain would be severe, and that he – Gaidar – might have to be sacrificed politically as a result.[54] One could observe the apprehensions of Yeltsin in late 1991, therefore, when he repeatedly tried to reassure audiences that the pain from shock therapy would last only six months, or one year at most.[55]

YELTSIN AS STATESMAN

The emergence of an independent Russia forced Yeltsin also to address East–West relations and their relationship to both Russian security and Russian prosperity. He inherited a drastically altered position in the world, as Russia was shorn of the USSR's East European alliance system and its global power status. Gorbachev's concessionary foreign policy had tried to make the best of this situation by making a virtue of necessity, by attempting to integrate into Western multilateral organizations, by doing the bidding of the West on most issues in contention, and by seeking as much economic assistance from the West as he could hope to secure. Yeltsin, while in opposition to Gorbachev, did not dissent from these aspects of his foreign policy.[56] He did not try to outbid Gorbachev on East–West relations.

But after the August coup, when Yeltsin started to define an independent foreign policy for Russia, he went beyond what even Gorbachev had advocated. He called for "substantial cuts in defense expenditures," cuts that soon (1992) assumed enormous magnitudes.[57] He volunteered to adopt "a more radical stance on the destruction of nuclear, bacteriological, and chemical weapons, on the ending of underground testing of nuclear weapons."[58] He

---

[54] Gaidar, *Dni,* p. 105.

[55] *Sovetskaia Rossiia,* October 29, 1991; Official Kremlin International News Broadcast, November 20, 1991; Moscow Central Television, November 20, 1991.

[56] With the exception of the Kurile Islands dispute with Japan, on which Yeltsin insisted in 1991 that Gorbachev no longer had authority to negotiate the return to Japan of territory that was formally part of the Russian Republic; see Tsuyoshi Hasegawa, *The Northern Territories Dispute and Russo-Japanese Relations,* 2 vols. (Berkeley: University of California, International and Area Studies, 1998), vol. 2, pp. 374f.

[57] Moscow Central Television First Program Network, September 3, 1991 (FBIS-SOV-91-171, p. 10); Åslund, *How Russia Became,* p. 66.

[58] Moscow Russian Television Network, September 7, 1991 (FBIS-SOV-91-174, p. 66).

curried favor with European audiences by announcing that Russia would move toward full repeal of the death penalty.[59] In December 1991, Yeltsin publicly announced Russia's interest in joining NATO.[60] He accepted the applicability to Russia of the terms of the Conventional Forces in Europe Treaty (1990), even though the restrictions had been tailored to the geography of the Soviet Union, not Russia.

After January 1992, when Russia was formally an independent state, Yeltsin established a firmly pro-Western foreign policy. He outdid Gorbachev's arms-reduction race, announcing in June 1992 that Russia had already begun unilaterally destroying SS-18 intercontinental ballistic missiles. He ended his country's continuing – and very large – subsidies to Cuba and Afghanistan.[61] Yeltsin's Russia assumed responsibility for Soviet debt, supported U.S. containment of Iraq, stated that it was willing to renegotiate the Anti-Ballistic Missile Treaty and to consider developing a joint global ballistic missile defense with the United States, agreed to ambitious cooperation in space exploration, and opened secret archives to Americans investigating prisoners of war and the downing of Korean Air Lines flight 007.[62]

In June 1992, Yeltsin addressed a joint session of the United States Congress, where he received thirteen standing ovations and promised that "the idol of communism, which spread social strife, enmity, and unparalleled brutality everywhere, which instilled fear in humanity, has collapsed. It has collapsed never to rise again. I am here to assure you. We shall not let it rise again in our land."[63]

Yeltsin was not subtle. The explicit quid pro quo for this consistent support of U.S. foreign policy objectives was financial aid. Democracy in Russia, Yeltsin told the joint session, has only one chance:

there will be no second try.... The reforms must succeed.... If we [that is, you Americans] do not take measures now to support Russia, this will not be a collapse of Russia only, it will be a collapse of the United States, because it will mean new trillions of dollars for the arms race.[64]

---

[59] Moscow Radio Rossii Network, September 11, 1991.

[60] Press conference in Rome, TASS, December 23, 1991.

[61] In fall 1991, he had already declared his intention to do this.

[62] Baturin et al. (*Epokha*, p. 467) write that Yeltsin and his foreign minister, Andrei Kozyrev, largely continued Gorbachev's and Shevardnadze's course in foreign policy, adding: "There was even a kind of competition between the two teams – who can appeal to the West the most."

[63] Michael Dobbs, "Yeltsin Appeals for American Aid," *The Washington Post*, June 18, 1992, p. 1.

[64] Ibid.

Back at home, Yeltsin sold his foreign policies as the harbinger of Russia's integration into the civilized, Western world, which would also provide the financial aid and security umbrella that Russia would need during this transition.

During the days immediately following the dissolution of the USSR, Yeltsin presented the "Commonwealth of Independent States" (CIS), which he co-founded in December 1991, as a sign that Russia was breaking decisively with the imperial past and behaving like a "normal, civilized" state, even as it sought responsibly to offset the political and economic disarray caused by the dissolution of the USSR. When, on December 12, he discussed the CIS at Russia's Supreme Soviet, he explained that the choice of Minsk (Belarus) as the center of the CIS did not mean that city was the capital of a new union "but – and this is very important – it does mean the end of speculation that Russia aspires to take the place of the union center and cherishes some kind of imperial ambitions."[65] Two days later, in an interview in *Trud,* he explained that this was the civilized way to handle relations among friendly states: "There was only one way – to unite, but not within the framework of a single state but within a community of states. Just as, for example, the European countries are now doing." In a speech to the Russian Supreme Soviet on December 25, Yeltsin also made clear that there was an important practical rationale for such a decentralized organization as the CIS: "The Commonwealth of Independent States is today the optimum and perhaps the only option to preserve stability both in Russia and in the other states. Our principle is: Not the states for the sake of the Commonwealth but, on the contrary, the Commonwealth for the sake of the peoples, citizens and states."[66]

BIG PROMISES AND MEASURES OF PROGRESS

Leaders during periods of transformation or crisis typically try to mobilize support for their visions by holding out the prospect of a better tomorrow, to be made possible by near-term exertions and/or the endurance of considerable pain. Winston Churchill promised that wartime victory would follow the expenditure of much "blood, sweat, and tears." Closer to home, Khrushchev promised the full-scale construction of communism if all Soviet citizens exerted themselves to the fullest in the directions and ways he had specified. Gorbachev promised a third way between capitalism and statist socialism if

---

[65] Moscow Russian Television Network, December 12, 1991 (FBIS-SOV-91-239, p. 40).
[66] Moscow Radio Rossii Network, December 25, 1991 (FBIS-SOV-91-248, p. 38).

all citizens restructured themselves psychologically and responsibly exercised the rights he was extending to them. Yeltsin propounded a vision of a free, peaceful, and prosperous society, integrated into Western civilization. But he never said it would be easy.

The metaphorical structure of Yeltsin's speeches in fall 1991 is indicative of his effort both to legitimize a great leap forward and to warn his audiences of how far they had to go, especially with regard to economics. Not coincidentally, this also served to protect him against accusations that he was inflicting unnecessary pain. We might call this the "from hell to heaven" metaphor, based on an image of ascent from the lowest depths. Thus, in a speech of September 11, 1991, he announced that Russia was about to "begin the process of the most difficult ascent to normal life"; to understand the magnitude of the challenge, one "has to take account of the abyss in which we found ourselves." But, with courage and endurance, "we have the determination to go the whole way, climbing up the ladder to civilization."[67] Doing so requires freedom from communism, which had put people in a "bureaucratic straitjacket."[68] Only such freedom will permit the country finally "to get on its feet" in order to begin the ascent.[69] A related metaphor was that of illness and life-threatening conditions, which require strong medicine and bold action to bring the patient back from the brink. The legacy of communism, he argued, had left the country "sick."[70] "We have undertaken these actions in order to save ourselves from drowning."[71] Given the gravity of the condition, "there was no other way" than to adopt such measures.[72]

But lest his apocalyptic rhetoric be interpreted as unnecessarily frightening, Yeltsin also reassured his audiences that the pain would be rewarded. At the metaphorical level, he continued the imagery of disease but classified the

---

[67] Moscow Radio Rossii Network, September 11, 1991 (FBIS-SOV-91-177, p. 1). Other examples of the metaphor include: "we will finally begin to haul ourselves out of the quagmire that is sucking us in deeper and deeper" (Moscow Russian Television Network, October 28, 1991 [FBIS-SOV-91-209, p. 47]); and "we have a chance to climb out of this ditch in which we have found ourselves" (Moscow Central Television, "Vostok," December 29, 1991 [FBIS-SOV-91-250, p. 27]).

[68] Moscow Russian Television Network, October 28, 1991 (FBIS-SOV-91-209, p. 47).

[69] Moscow Radio Rossii Network, September 11, 1991 (FBIS-SOV-91-177, p. 1).

[70] Moscow Radio Rossii Network, September 11, 1991 (FBIS-SOV-91-177, p. 2).

[71] *Trud,* December 14, 1991, pp. 1–2, as translated in FBIS-SOV-91-241, p. 36. See also "Russia is gravely ill, its economy is ill" (Moscow Central Television, "Vostok," December 29, 1991 [FBIS-SOV-91-250, p. 29]).

[72] Ibid. Not coincidentally, "there is no alternative" was also an argument that Gorbachev used against conservatives who were skeptical of his political radicalization.

present disease as curable: "as distinct from human ailments, there are no in-
curable diseases in the economy."[73] At the concrete level, Yeltsin hastened
to assure his audiences that the pain would be relatively short in duration:
"If we embark on this path," he announced on October 28, 1991, "then we
will see real results by the autumn of 1992.... Everyone will find life harder
for approximately six months. Then, prices will fall and goods will begin
to fill the market. By the autumn of 1992, as I promised before the elections, the economy will have stabilized and people's lives will gradually get
better."[74]

Or so Yeltsin promised and, presumably, hoped. In interviews toward the
end of the year, he was very eager – too eager – to convince journalists that
the pain would be short-lived. "Six months, six months," he repeated.[75] He
was in the difficult situation of trying to protect himself politically by shaping the indicators by which his success as a political leader would be judged.
Yeltsin was also aware of both the unpredictability of the situation and the
link between his promises and his political authority. As he declared on February 19, 1992: "I believe that the reforms will win and this year this victory
will already be obvious. There is no doubt about it. I will not go back on my
word, which I gave during the election campaign. I will not go back on it!"[76]

During the months following defeat of the August 1991 coup, Yeltsin
worked feverishly both to undercut Gorbachev and to formulate a comprehensive program for independent Russia. He succeeded on both scores, but
the program was filled with vulnerabilities. Like the programs of all his predecessors at the helm in Moscow, and like many a comprehensive program put
forward by presidents and prime ministers in liberal democracies, Yeltsin's
program was extremely ambitious, quickly met reality, and was in need of
adjustments. From mid-1992, Yeltsin began making those adjustments. He
did not abandon the basic premises for which he had stood; he only reconsidered the costs and risks, shifting his politics somewhat toward the center.
After taking two steps forward, Yeltsin took one step back while continuing
to point the country in the general direction he had promised all along.

---

[73] *Trud,* December 14, 1991, pp. 1–2, as translated in FBIS-SOV-91-241, p. 38; see also Yeltsin's
December 29, 1991, State of the Republic Address (televised by Moscow Central Television)
for the same argument. And, continuing the metaphor, one year later he would refer to bankruptcy as a sometimes useful "surgical procedure" (December 1, 1992 address to 7th Congress
of the Congress of People's Deputies).

[74] Moscow Russian Television Network, October 28, 1991 (FBIS-SOV-91-209, p. 48).

[75] Moscow Central Television, November 20, 1991.

[76] Moscow Russian Television Network, February 19, 1992 (FBIS-SOV-92-034, p. 53).

Backlash Sets In

The crunch hit very soon, as the abolition of most price controls in January 1992 led to an immediate tripling and quadrupling of prices, a continuing inflation, and the wiping out of the value of the life savings and pensions of many Russian citizens.[77] The spectre of civil unrest hung over the country as spiraling inflation rapidly impoverished a people who had for decades been accustomed to price stability. In like manner, the sharp cuts in budget subsidies to enterprises led to a howl of protest from enterprise directors, their lobbying organizations, and their patrons in the Supreme Soviet. These hardships induced a widespread anti-Yeltsin mobilization within the Supreme Soviet itself, led by former Yeltsin ally and parliamentary speaker Ruslan Khasbulatov and soon thereafter joined by Aleksandr Rutskoi, Yeltsin's own vice-president.

Moreover, a "red-brown" coalition of Russian nationalists, neocommunists, and imperialist restorationists began to coalesce during 1991–1992, even as Yeltsin had his hands full dealing with the daily conflicts with parliament over politics and policy. The red-browns were united in their support for authoritarianism and their opposition to building a Westernized liberal democracy. They denounced democratic proceduralism, unbridled individualism, and a secular, civic definition of the Russian state. For them, the state was a moral community, not simply a set of formal organizations and procedures. This gave them an advantage in the struggle with liberals, who found it difficult to integrate liberal nationalism and the virtues of individualism with a moral content that transcended the democratic proceduralism itself. Yeltsin's definition of the nation as "multinationality" plus "democratic individualism," his insistence that Russia did not need a new collectivist ideology, and his apparently self-serving definition of himself as the guarantor of the new secular nation allowed opponents rhetorically to seize the initiative on the issue.

In the realm of interstate relations, a growing chorus of voices started to be heard – even among many earlier supporters of Gorbachev's "new thinking" – calling for some hard-headed thinking about Russia's "national interest." Now that Russia and the Soviet Union had made unilateral concessions and asymmetrical deals on almost all foreign policy issues, where was the government prepared to draw the line? Of that which remained, what would it *not* give away? If Russia was a reemerging nation-state and no longer either

---

[77] The first round of savings wipeouts, however, had occurred in spring 1991 under Gorbachev's prime minister, Valentin Pavlov, whose "reforms" had no redeeming positive consequences.

a Russian or a Soviet empire, what were the national interests it was to pursue as it made its own place in the world? Groups of policy influentials and parliamentarians discussed and debated these issues in 1992, producing memoranda and publications that insisted upon the need for Russia to craft an international identity – other than that of a supplicant – and to take a stand in defense of that identity and the interests that flowed from it. The phrase that invariably accompanied these elaborate and intelligent pronouncements was that Russia is, and must be treated as, a "great power" (*derzhava*). The people associated with this "realist" perspective on international affairs came to be known as "statists" (*gosudarstvenniki*). While most of the statists were not part of the emerging red-brown coalition, they were a powerful dissenting voice from the concessionary foreign policy that Yeltsin had intensified after the collapse of the USSR.

"... And One Step Back"

In a speech delivered on April 5, 1992, we see the first signs that Yeltsin had perceived the need for an adjustment. He defended his economic reforms and predicted that, at the forthcoming meeting of the Congress of People's Deputies, "an attempt at revanche will be made [which must receive] a decisive rebuff."[78] But he also conceded that his government had made mistakes and that corrections were now in order:

Not even the most precise calculations and the most well thought-out models are capable of taking into account all the very complex areas of life with its multifarious surprises. Not a single program can be implemented if it is not constantly subjected to adjustments and corrections. The past months have taught the government a great deal.[79]

But a correction was not the same thing as abandonment of previous policy:

If we stop the reforms, we'll never emerge from poverty. To achieve a breakthrough is incredibly difficult .... Only one path today has the right to existence – that of the continuation of radical reforms .... I will not shift from that path. And, in my opinion, there is simply no other way.[80]

In the same speech, Yeltsin rebuffed the nostalgics among the defeated communists and nationalists:

---

[78] Moscow Russian Television Network, April 5, 1992 (FBIS-SOV-92-066, p. 20).
[79] Ibid.
[80] Ibid.

We will not have a continuation of the isolation of our country under the pretext of preserving Russia's original character. That would mean once again driving Russia into a historical impasse, condemning it to backwardness and its people to a meager existence.[81]

Yeltsin closed by reiterating that the matter of Russia's Westernization was not an issue for negotiation: "History cannot be turned back."[82] He repeated many of these themes in his speech the next day to the Congress of People's Deputies.

Having admitted that he had made mistakes, Yeltsin also felt the need to alter the concrete indicators of success by which his effectiveness as a leader would be judged. In November 1991, he had promised six months of pain to be followed by a turnaround. On May 27, 1992, he altered the assessment. Asked whether he wished to retract any of his earlier promises, he said "No" but revised what those promises had actually been:

I said back at the time of the Russian presidential campaign that the end of 1992 would see the beginning of stabilization in the economy. I did not simply say that the situation would improve. First, you get the stabilization of the economy and then, as a consequence, improvement in people's lives.[83]

Yeltsin then went on to elongate the time frame under which his success should be judged:

The reform cannot be completed in a single year.... [We] are seeking to ... define the stages: What can be done now, what in three years' time, and what is possible only after ten years. We have had to go through this most critical period of 1992. And I think we are now perhaps past the most dangerous point.[84]

Being now "past the most dangerous point" was of course a prediction, but it bought time. As time went on and economic hardships deepened, Yeltsin's political rhetoric turned to still other justifications of his record. In his August 19, 1992, televised speech on the anniversary of the putsch attempt, he congratulated the government and the nation for merely surviving the treatment: "Over the past six months, Russia has developed the basis of a market system. As the saying goes, we stepped into the water without knowing how to swim. But we have not choked in water or drowned."[85] He went on immediately to lengthen still further the time frame for judgment of results: "It is

[81] Ibid., p. 23.

[82] Ibid.

[83] *Komsomol'skaia pravda*, May 27, 1992, p. 2, as translated in FBIS-SOV-92-103, May 28, 1992, p. 28.

[84] Ibid.

[85] Moscow Russian Television Network, August 19, 1992 (FBIS-SOV-92-162, p. 19).

precisely now that we are gaining the unique experience that will benefit us and even more so our children and grandchildren."[86] Thereafter, as his confrontation with parliament escalated, so too did his explanations for failure evolve. On April 14, 1993, he declared that "it is the legislature that is responsible for the hardships associated with reforms";[87] later, he further broadened his attribution of responsibility, defining the culprit as the institutional and cultural legacy of communism.[88]

Yeltsin did not merely change his rhetoric; he also made concrete changes in policy. In spring 1992, about five months after the initiation of Gaidar's program, Yeltsin shuffled his cabinet and appointed four representatives of the managerial and defense lobbies to key positions. He also tolerated the pumping of new monies into the economy in order to maintain subsidies that would prevent bankruptcies of major enterprises that might trigger social unrest among the newly unemployed. He embraced a mass privatization program ("we need millions of owners and not hundreds of millionaires" – April 7, 1992, and August 19, 1992) that was nonetheless biased toward selling most shares to insiders (managers and workers of the enterprise) rather than to outside investors (whether domestic or foreign), in order to prevent mass layoffs (which would threaten social stability) and the large-scale dismissal of managers (which would threaten Yeltsin's ties with the managerial lobby).

The conflicting goals of Yeltsin's economic policy were coming into focus. He pursued macroeconomic stabilization through freeing prices and slashing the budget, and he rapidly privatized the economy – including a strong push to get parliamentary approval for privatization of land. But he pushed further with his reforms in ways that least threatened social stability or the interests of the "Red Directors." This was the meaning of his newfound incantation, beginning in June 1992, that the "principal task" is "to halt the drop of production."[89] Such a hybrid policy would not lead to a great deal of enterprise restructuring or many bankruptcies,[90] but it could provide a bulwark against communist restoration by creating a widespread stake in the prevention of re-nationalization. And it could be sustained only if new infusions of loans and credits from the International Monetary Fund, the World Bank, and foreign governments allowed Moscow to buy off discontent at home.

---

[86] Ibid.

[87] Moscow Ostankino Television First Channel Network, April 14, 1993 (FBIS-SOV-93-071, p. 13).

[88] *The Herald* (Glasgow), April 30, 1993, p. 4.

[89] *Vreme*, June 15, 1992, as translated in FBIS-SOV-92-132, p. 35.

[90] See Joseph Blasi et al., *Kremlin Capitalism* (Ithaca, NY: Cornell University Press, 1997), ch. 4.

But those loans and credits were not easy to secure, for the conditionality attached to them actually increased the risk of social instability in Russia. Hence, on July 4, 1992, in a televised news conference in the Kremlin, Yeltsin adopted the mantle of protector of the Russian people against unreasonable and dangerous demands by Russia's benefactors and creditors:

I will state plainly that during discussions there were voices calling for us to freeze wages. Of course, this would have produced great exhilaration at the International Monetary Fund, but we cannot embark on this. You see? Then, by this step, we will immediately open up, I would simply say, some local conflicts, or ones at the level of industries or regions. There will definitely be tension. There will definitely be dissatisfaction among people. There will definitely be quite widespread strikes....

If we free fuel prices today, there will be a tenfold increase in all other prices, including prices for bread and food products and so on. Will the people bear it? They will not .... When the people's patience snaps, their trust in the president will be exhausted and then chaos will begin.[91]

Yeltsin was willing to admit that he was backtracking: "we resorted to a certain moderation of the reforms, even when it meant the loss of a certain dynamism."[92]

His July 4, 1992, lecture also permitted Yeltsin to assume a nationalist mantle and thereby blunt some of the criticism coming from statists and nationalists:

So today, Mr. Camdessus ... will insist on us freeing fuel prices. This is now the main subject of disagreement between us. We cannot embark on this and I will tell him so today .... If that's the case, we can do without the 24 billion, all the more so because it is not some sort of charity handout. We will have to pay for it later. The sum is a credit, civilized credit. We should not be forced onto our knees for it. No, Russia is a great power and will not allow itself to do that....[93]

We know the mood of the people. But the International Monetary Fund and Mr. Camdessus do not know the limits of the people's tolerance.[94]

DEFENDING THE NATIONAL INTEREST

This effort to assume a nationalist mantle was indicative of the direction in which Yeltsin was edging in other realms of policy. In response to the efforts

---

[91] Moscow Russian Television Network, July 4, 1992 (FBIS-SOV-92-129, p. 24).

[92] *Vreme,* June 15, 1992 (FBIS-SOV-92-132, p. 35).

[93] Moscow Russian Television Network, July 4, 1992 (FBIS-SOV-92-129, p. 25).

[94] Ibid.; see also his June 15, 1992 interview with *Vreme,* in which many of these themes are previewed. In the latter he had also said: "It is our principal task to halt the drop of production before the end of the year .... The main condition for achieving that goal is preservation of stability in society."

of statists and chauvinists alike, Yeltsin sought to counter radical nationalism
not by adopting its message but rather by attempting to supplement his liberal
internationalism with a nonprovocative and nonexclusionary state centrism.

In response to criticisms of Russia's concessionary foreign policy, Yeltsin
shifted toward the center. In 1992–1993, Yeltsin moved Russia toward a more
assertive position. He canceled his visit to Japan and shelved the idea of making concessions on return of the southern Kurile Islands. Moscow began to
insist on a special status for Russia within the Partnership for Peace, organized by Washington as an omnibus military adjunct to NATO that included
all post-communist states. Moscow became more insistent on Western deference to its association with Serbian interests in the Yugoslav civil war. Both
politically and militarily, Russia became more assertive on the ground in the
Near Abroad, and it announced to the West that the CIS was an area of exclusive Russian interest. As noted previously, the Russian government used
economic coercion and military threats against Estonia in response to its discriminatory citizenship law of 1992. A push began in 1993 for CIS states
to allow "dual citizenship" to their ethnic Russian populations and to increase the range and depth of economic and political integration within the
Commonwealth. In February 1994, the Foreign Ministry drafted a program
for the protection of Russian speakers in former republics that included the
use of economic sanctions to protest rights violations. According to a Foreign Ministry spokesperson, that measure was included because "we feel that
diplomatic measures are not enough."[95] Thus, in response to the discrediting of idealist thinking about international relations, Yeltsin moved toward
a *realpolitik,* spheres-of-influence approach to Russia's international "neighborhood" and toward a somewhat more insistent posture in the Far Abroad.

Yet beyond these shifts Russia remained a cooperative partner with Western
Europe and the United States in arms control and other realms of East–West
relations. Yeltsin was furthermore decidedly accommodative in relations with
the two largest successor states after Russia: Ukraine and Kazakhstan. The
correction of 1992–1993 was a search for a synthesis of liberal internationalism and realist statism – or, put differently, a search for a relationship based
on elements of both cooperation and competition. Yeltsin's hope was that
such a combination would satisfy Russia's statists while retaining good will
in Western capitals. The dominant goal of his East–West policy remained: to
enlist maximal Western cooperation in easing the socioeconomic, political,
and military transitions within Russia.[96]

---

[95] *Rossiiskaia gazeta,* February 18, 1994; *Moscow Times,* February 18, 1994.
[96] He reiterated the goal many times and was gushing about the prospects for European integration in a speech in Brussels on December 9, 1993.

CONSTITUTIONAL CRISIS AND THE STATE-BUILDING CONUNDRUM

The one realm in which Yeltsin did not change his position concerned his re-lations with parliament and the power of the presidency. True, during much of 1992 he tried to reach accommodations with the Congress of People's Deputies, but to little avail.[97] By fall 1992, Yeltsin's extraordinary powers to rule by decree had expired; the parliament was disinclined to renew them and was even seeking to scale back the president's formal powers. Some deputies were also calling for Yeltsin's impeachment.[98]

That seems to have been a point of no return in Yeltsin's eyes. He had built his authority as an advocate of benevolent but personalistic leadership. He had in fact pushed himself hard to build coalitions and forge compromises among disparate forces while serving as Chairman of the RSFSR Supreme Soviet in 1990–1991,[99] but that behavior reflected the narrow (four-vote) mar-gin by which he had been elected chairman in a closed, intra-parliament vote. Once Yeltsin had received validation of his leadership by the mass public (in the June 1991 presidential election), he asserted himself. Opposition to his lead-ership during 1992 from the Congress of People's Deputies – and from his own vice-president, who joined the anti-Yeltsin forces – threatened his political au-thority and contradicted his definition of the principles of political order. The Congress, he argued, was a holdover from Soviet days that had never been subjected to a truly free and fair election. It was all the more intolerable that, because of the constitutional impasse, the Supreme Soviet claimed to be the

---

[97] The scholarly literature on the battles of 1992–1993 is divided over whether Yeltsin or the par-liament and its speaker (Ruslan Khasbulatov) was more to blame for the impasses – or whether this was an impersonal, inter-institutional conflict that was bound to escalate to a schism. For the "institutional" argument, see Yitzhak M. Brudny, "Neoliberal economic reform and the consolidation of democracy in Russia: Or why institutions and ideas might matter more than economics," in Karen Dawisha (Ed.), *The International Dimension of Post-Communist Transitions in Russia and the New States of Eurasia* (Armonk, NY: M.E. Sharpe, 1997), pp. 297–321, and Nikolai Biriukov and Viktor Sergeyev, *Russian Politics in Transition* (Alder-shot, U.K.: Ashgate, 1997), pp. 176–87. Leon Aron (*Boris Yeltsin: A Revolutionary Life* [New York: HarperCollins, 2000], pp. 495, 510) blames the deadlock on Khasbulatov's personality; Jerry F. Hough (*The Logic of Economic Reform in Russia* [Washington, DC: Brookings In-stitution, 2001], pp. 138–42, 159–61) blames the outcome on Yeltsin's personality; and Lilia Shevtsova (*Yeltsin's Russia: Myths and Realities* [Washington, DC: Carnegie Endowment, 1999], pp. 38–40, 59–61, 76, 90) assigns equal responsibility to both sides, blaming individ-uals and bemoaning missed opportunities – not treating the gridlock as an inevitable product of institutional rivalry. For a riveting, on-the-spot journalistic account of the siege of parlia-ment in September–October 1993, see Veronika Kutsyllo, *Zapiski iz Belogo doma* (Moscow: "Kommersant," 1993).

[98] *The Independent* (London), September 24, 1992; *Los Angeles Times*, December 2, 1992.

[99] Associated Press, July 16, 1990; see also the observations of John Morrison, *Boris Yeltsin: From Bolshevik to Democrat* (New York: Dutton, 1991), ch. 13.

"supreme authority" within the polity, as written in the banal but still unrepealed Brezhnev Constitution of 1977. The "people" were the supreme authority, according to Yeltsin's plebiscitarian conception of authority, and he – but not the parliament – had passed that test.[100] Hence, when parliamentarians began to call for his impeachment, the Russian president was ready to rumble.

In a speech delivered on February 11, 1993, Yeltsin admitted that the economic reform policies of 1992 had been marked by "quite a few mistakes."[101] But rather than getting defensive about his personal responsibility, Yeltsin shifted the blame to the legislative branch: "growing tension in the sphere of government inflicted huge damage last year, including economic damage. Today, this is liable simply to blow up the country, to torpedo any, even the very best, action program."[102] The following week, he railed about the intolerability of the standoff between the legislative and executive branches, demanding a new constitution and a public referendum.[103] On February 28, his strategy was becoming clear. He pushed his political rhetoric to the extreme, defining the choices as binary oppositions. He accused the Supreme Soviet of trying to impose a "return to the absolute power of the Soviets." This stood in sharp contrast to the "normal division of power [between executive and legislative branches] that is accepted throughout the world." The result of this split was political paralysis, which threatened "an explosion of counterrevolution in the country ... which would ruin not only the reforms and democracy, but Russia itself." His conclusion was predictable, but stated for the first time in public: "I can no longer tolerate such a situation."[104]

But Yeltsin was not willing to isolate himself politically. In the same speech, he appealed to his audience – the middle-of-the-road coalition of industrialists, "The Civic Union" – to join him in a broad centrist coalition that would isolate the extremists.[105] He reiterated the theme in a televised interview on March 7, 1993.[106] Four days later, at the 8th Congress of People's Deputies, he insisted that Russia must be a presidential republic and warned that "the Congress must choose between consensus or confrontation – one or the other."[107]

---

[100] Of course, the "people" are the font of legitimacy in any notion of popular sovereignty, be it plebiscitarian or representative. But as Yeltsin presented it, only he had received true validation by all the people in a free and fair election.

[101] Ostankino Television First Channel Network, February 11, 1993 (FBIS-SOV-93-029, p. 18).

[102] Ibid.

[103] Moscow Russian Television Network, February 18, 1993 (FBIS-SOV-93-032, pp. 13–15).

[104] Moscow Russian Television Network, February 28, 1993 (FBIS-SOV-93-038, p. 20).

[105] Ibid., pp. 21–2.

[106] Moscow Ostankino Television First Channel Network, "Itogi," March 7, 1993 (FBIS-SOV-93-043, pp. 9–12).

[107] Moscow Ostankino Television First Channel Network, March 11, 1993 (FBIS-SOV-93-046, p. 18).

Yeltsin apparently decided to further polarize the situation by demonizing his opponents, thereby presenting himself as the man who would take the measures required to save the country from reactionary restoration and inevitable destruction. In a televised address to the Russian people on March 20, he defined the Congress of People's Deputies as a holdover from the "former Bolshevik, anti-popular system ... that aspires again today to recoup its lost authority over Russia."[108] He described the recent 8th Congress as "a dress rehearsal of revenge on the part of the former Party *nomenklatura.*"[109] Moreover, "imperial ideology reigned supreme at the Congress."[110] If allowed to run the country, such forces would foment "armed conflicts with all the former Union republics, ... a return to the arms race, growing military expenditures, and a global confrontation with the whole world."[111] Reverting to the "hell to heaven" metaphor, Yeltsin reversed the direction of travel, warning that, if the revanchists came back to power, "this would be plunging into the abyss."[112] As the elected representative of all the people and the guardian of Russia's well-being, Yeltsin announced that he was signing a decree suspending the authority of parliament, giving the president emergency powers to rule, scheduling a public referendum – on support for the president, the Congress, and Yeltsin's social policies – and anticipating new parliamentary elections. Yeltsin was going the plebiscitarian route once again. As he put it on March 26, "I leave my fate in the hands of the most just and supreme judge: the people."[113]

Within days, Yeltsin rescinded his threat to impose emergency rule. But he got the public referendum he had been seeking, and he got the public validation as well, winning the plebiscite (held in late April) rather handily. Although he had rescinded the emergency regime, he still felt the need to resume negotiations with the parliament over the terms of a new constitution and federation treaty. In subsequent months, these negotiations remained deadlocked over incompatible conceptions of executive–legislative and center–periphery relations. Yeltsin grew increasingly impatient. He escalated the rhetoric once again, accusing parliament and its local soviet branches of seeking to restore communism ("a process of repression against dissidents

---

[108] Moscow Ostankino Television First Channel Network, March 20, 1993 (FBIS-SOV-93-053, p. 13).
[109] Ibid.
[110] Ibid.
[111] Ibid.
[112] Ibid., p. 14.
[113] This quotation is from Russian Television Network, March 26, 1993 (FBIS-SOV-93-057, p. 23); see also Official Kremlin International News Broadcast, April 15 and 16, 1993; *Rossiiskie vesti*, April 16, 1993; *Argumenty i fakty*, April 22, 1993.

within the whole system of the soviets is under way. The aim is to exterminate everything that is alive"[114]). Finally, in September 1993, he did what he had been contemplating all year.[115] He dissolved the Supreme Soviet by decree and announced that new elections would take place in December. This was an acknowledged violation of the existing Constitution, which specifically prohibited any attempt to dissolve or even suspend the Russian parliament. But Yeltsin justified the action as a national-security imperative: "These measures are essential to protect Russia and the whole world against catastrophic consequences of the disintegration of Russian statehood, again recurring in a country that has an enormous arsenal of nuclear weapons."[116]

In early October 1993, when deputies refused to leave the parliament that Yeltsin had declared dissolved, the situation turned violent. This is not the place to assign degrees of responsibility for the escalation; clearly, from a humanitarian standpoint, both sides share in the blame. Yeltsin turned off the electricity in the parliament; not long thereafter, armed and unarmed resistance to the dissolution triggered violence on the streets of Moscow between pro-executive and pro-parliament supporters. After a tense period of several days, Yeltsin managed to convince military commanders to support him. He brought in overwhelming – some would say disproportionate – military force and used powerful artillery against the parliament building to ensure the exit and arrest of deputies lodged therein. Hundreds of Russian citizens are said to have died during those days of violence. But Yeltsin prevailed. This cleared the field for Yeltsin to define the terms of the new Constitution and to call elections for a new parliament.[117]

Those elections took place in December, along with a referendum on whether or not the country should adopt Yeltsin's preferred constitution. That constitution reflected the strong version of the position that Yeltsin had been fighting for throughout 1992–1993. It was super-presidentialist in the relations among branches of government in Moscow. The president was accorded wide powers to rule by decree, while the parliament and the constitutional court enjoyed only limited powers. The proposed constitution provided for no vice-presidency, so that no future VP could turn against the president the way Yeltsin's vice-president, Aleksandr Rutskoi, had done during 1992–1993.

---

[114] Moscow Maiak Radio Network, August 12, 1993 (FBIS-SOV-93-154, p. 14).
[115] Aleksandr Korzhakov (in *Boris Yel'tsin: Ot rassveta do zakata* [Moscow: Izd-vo "Interbuk," 1997], pp. 158–9) claims that Yeltsin had made preparations for the parliament to be gassed and seized by the army in the spring of 1993 had it supported his impeachment at that time.
[116] Moscow Ostankino First Channel Network, September 21, 1993 (FBIS-SOV-93-182-S, p. 2).
[117] For divergent assessments of responsibility for the violent outcome, contrast Aron, *Boris Yeltsin*, pp. 540–50, with Reddaway and Glinski, *The Tragedy of Russia's Reforms*, pp. 370–429.

Moreover, by the terms of the constitution, it was almost impossible to impeach the president and equally difficult to amend the constitution itself. The constitution reflected Yeltsin's "boss" mentality and plebiscitarian conception of accountability. The document was designed to ensure that the president would be by far the highest authority in the land, largely unaccountable to institutions and primarily answerable only to the voters at the subsequent presidential election.[118]

As for center–periphery relations, the new Constitution was based on a mix of unitary and federal principles. This, too, was the strong version of the position Yeltsin had been pushing during 1992–1993 in negotiations over the Federation Treaty. The task had been complicated by both the powerful centrifugal forces at play in 1990–1991, which Yeltsin had encouraged at the time, and the institutional legacy of Soviet rule. There remained a hierarchy of status that differentiated among the territorial units within Russia and accorded some of them (the ethnic "republics") greater autonomy, privilege, and political rank than others. During the negotiations, republics sought to maximize their autonomy from the center while provinces (oblasts and krays) sought to attain no less autonomy than republics would be granted. Yeltsin's constitution sought to rein in both of these tendencies, to define both republics and provinces as equally "subjects of the Federation," and to expand the formal powers of the center to impose its will on the regions. At the same time, in a significant bow to federal principles, it gave the regions formal representation by their leaders in the upper house of the new parliament and scheduled the direct election of regional governors. This mix of unitary and federal principles stood in sharp contrast to the de facto confederalism (strong regions–weak center) that existed at the time.[119]

Thus, as a state builder, Yeltsin's democratic rhetoric of 1989–1991 evolved thereafter toward a mix of liberal and illiberal principles. He attached low priority to construction of a strong system of political parties, to a balanced separation of powers between the executive and legislative branches, to checks and balances among the branches of government, and to the further encouragement of regional autonomy. Instead, super-presidentialism,

---

[118] Yeltsin's chief of staff at the time reports that Yeltsin personally edited a draft of the constitution only days before it was to be made public; perhaps his most significant revision, according to Filatov, concerned the status of the presidency: "additions that specify that presidential decrees are normative and that the president may chair government sessions" (Sergei Filatov, *Sovershenno nesekretno* [Moscow: Vagrius, 2000], p. 329).

[119] Filatov (ibid., pp. 333–4) quotes Yeltsin as saying, at the time of finalization of the draft constitution, that the adjective "sovereign" should no longer be attached to "republics" in that document because "the position of the president is to protect the rights of nations, on whatever part of the territory of Russia they happen to live, not to protect the rights of 'sovereign' national states."

plebiscitarianism, populism, and a center strong enough to prevent regions from ignoring the writ of Moscow were the features of Yeltsin's evolving program of state building. Civil liberties and electoralism in state–society relations, and a still-to-be-negotiated relationship between center and periphery, remained as the principal liberal features of his state-building program.

CONCLUSION

During his period of ascendancy, Yeltsin worked out programs in the major realms of policy that were geared toward transforming independent Russia into a new, decisively post-Soviet polity, economy, and international actor. The program unfolded over the course of 1992–1993. Yeltsin broadened his coalition beyond the intense but narrow political base on which he had built his authority during the struggle for power of 1989–1991. That anti-communist and anti-statist political base supported his "shock therapy" for the economy, his liberal strategy of nation building, his willingness to dissolve the USSR, and his concessionary foreign policies. But already in mid-1992, as the costs of these policies were rising, it became clear that Yeltsin was making adjustments to accommodate forces and ideas that otherwise might be mobilized against him.

From mid-1992 through the end of 1993, Yeltsin fashioned an appeal that promised: (1) to sustain his economic reform efforts while averting threats to social stability; (2) to build a secular Russian nation without sacrificing Russian ethnic traditions or the interests of the Russian diaspora in the Near Abroad; (3) to integrate Russia into Western international organizations without sacrificing Russia's autonomy as an international actor or its ability to defend its national interests as a "great power"; (4) to maintain the territorial integrity of Russia without resorting to military force against the regions; and (5) to construct a presidential republic in which the president would be the guarantor of the accomplishment of all these goals.

Yeltsin made the transition from a predominantly oppositional figure within Soviet politics to the president of an independent Russian state, and he forged a comprehensive program for leading his country into the promised land. That program was a complex mix of orientations, but each realm of policy excluded deference to the unreconstructed communists and extreme nationalists. Yeltsin settled on a formula for co-opting the center of the political spectrum while continuing to pursue the agenda he had laid out in late 1991. It was by no means clear that such an amalgam of policies would yield the intended results. If it did not, Yeltsin would find himself on the political defensive once again, and he could not diffuse responsibility for failure. His personalistic leadership style – and his insistence on being granted emergency powers to rule by decree – meant that others could not credibly be blamed if the synthetic program failed. If he wanted credit for accomplishments then he would also have to accept responsibility for failure. Or so people would judge him, whether he accepted their judgment or not. As with Khrushchev and Gorbachev before him, that is precisely what happened.

8

Yeltsin on the Political Defensive

In December 1993, Yeltsin should have been riding high. He had eliminated the old Supreme Soviet and imprisoned his nemeses, Ruslan Khasbulatov and his former vice-president, Aleksandr Rutskoi. He had secured passage of his Constitution, which accorded him extraordinary powers vis-à-vis all other political institutions, made him virtually unimpeachable, and enshrined the approach to center–periphery relations and nation building for which he had been pushing. But that is not quite how Yeltsin saw it. Although he celebrated passage of the Constitution, he was apparently surprised by the results of the elections to the Duma: the anti-regime nationalists and communists won a substantial plurality. Yeltsin did not comment on the December 12 election results until ten days later. Then he criticized the "democrats" for their disunity, the opposition for their extremism, the government for the way in which it had implemented policy, and himself for having lost touch with the people.[1]

The memoir literature gives us a fuller understanding of Yeltsin's reaction to this frustration. The Russian president was very pleased with his accretion of formal powers and with the adoption – at long last! – of his preferred Constitution. But he was distressed by the dramatic deflation of his popularity with the mass public. He had exerted great energy to gain military support for subduing the Supreme Soviet by force – and even then it was a close call. He knew that he might not be able to count on such support in the future. Moreover, public opinion polls revealed a backlash against him for having used military force in October 1993.[2] The Duma elections brought

---

[1] Moscow Ostankino Television First Channel Network, December 22, 1993 (FBIS-SOV-93-244, pp. 1–8).
[2] Associated Press, October 30, 1993.

into power another set of oppositional forces (radical nationalists and communists), this time mobilized by political parties better organized than the parliamentary factions that had supported Khasbulatov and Rutskoi. Within two months, the new Duma declared an amnesty for all those political figures arrested in October 1993 and for the coup plotters of August 1991 as well.

Yeltsin was enraged by the amnesty and by the failure of his staff to prevent it, apprehensive about the loyalty of the military, and disappointed by the electoral verdict. He disappeared for several weeks in January 1994 and, in the eyes of some of his staff members, returned a changed man. Memoirs reveal that his most immediate reaction to these frustrations, other than depression and hitting the bottle, was to retreat into a more authoritarian and reclusive management style. Study of the evolution of his leadership reveals that his always personalistic operating style had earlier been accessible, open to suggestion, and consultative. After 1993, however, Yeltsin allowed an exclusionary and neo-tsarist component, which I will refer to as "patriarchal," to reign ascendant in relations with his staff. He retreated into himself.[3] The present chapter focuses on Yeltsin's behavior during this stage of political defensiveness. I first examine the transformation of Yeltsin's management style in dealings with his staff and cabinet and then analyze the change in Yeltsin's authority-maintenance strategy after 1993.

YELTSIN AS PATRIARCH

I noted in Chapter 5 that the management styles of Soviet leaders varied from highly personalistic to "executive," as measured by the degree to which they worked through (or, alternatively, around and over) their "cabinets" and staffs. Gorbachev combined some personalistic traits with a largely executive style of management. But after he was thrown onto the political defensive, he became more arbitrary and less consultative than he had been before. Yeltsin had always been much more of a personalistic leader than Gorbachev, but he became even more so when on the political defensive.

---

[3] I first developed this periodization and conceptualization in George W. Breslauer, "Boris Yeltsin as patriarch," *Post-Soviet Affairs*, vol. 15, no. 2 (April–June 1999); since then, several books have appeared that examine this period using diverse methodologies (interviews, documents, memoirs, and insider information). It is reassuring to note that they all point to a turn of this sort after December 1993 and they all view Yeltsin as having reverted at this time to a more reclusive, monarchical style of leadership. See Leon Aron, *Boris Yeltsin: A Revolutionary Life* (New York: St. Martin's, 2000), pp. 564–77; Lilia Shevtsova, *Yeltsin's Russia: Myths and Realities* (Washington, DC: Carnegie Endowment, 1999), pp. 99–100; Peter Reddaway and Dmitri Glinski, *The Tragedy of Russia's Reforms: Market Bolshevism against Democracy* (Washington, DC: U.S. Institute of Peace, 2000), ch. 8.

Personalism is not necessarily the same as despotism – though all despots are, by definition, personalistic. Personalism is a form of rule in which the leader is not held accountable – formally, regularly, and frequently – to institutions that can substantially constrain his discretion. Beyond that, personalistic rulers *can* be generous, proper, and temperate; they are not necessarily tyrannical, capricious, or corrupt. Patriarchalism is a form of personalism that treats the political community as a household within which the leader is the *pater familias*; patriarchs typically rely on tradition, rather than charisma or rational–legal norms, to validate their right to rule as they please.[4] But the concept does not prejudge how the ruler distributes benefits, be these material or honorific, and whether he is generous or stingy and responsive or unresponsive to his staff's personal feelings.

Examination of the memoir literature, bolstered by the author's personal interviews with some of Yeltsin's subordinates, offers insight into the nature of Yeltsin's self-conception as a leader. As shown in Chapter 2, Yeltsin always ruled over his administrative domains like a tsar and master; Yeltsin always had a patriarchal self-image as well. Thus, even before 1994, within his inner circle he viewed himself as head of the household, as a leader who demanded total loyalty to himself and his commands, and who had the right to exercise maximal discretion over the public and (at times) private lives of his subordinates. There was nothing impersonal about these relationships, nothing based on procedural propriety or the prerogatives of office – except his own. The staff and officials of the presidential administration were his retainers, not his lieutenants. He treated his entourage as a family with himself as its head rather than as a corpus of professionals of which he was chief executive. This is not a mere academic distinction; it had striking behavioral consequences.

Yeltsin compelled his subordinates to try to improve themselves along the lines he dictated. According to Bonet's research on Yeltsin's tenure in Sverdlovsk, he insisted that all his assistants wear formal clothes.[5] When they were not dressed formally enough for him, he made them return home to change their clothes. He also "turned the obkom [the regional Party committee] into a

---

[4] Max Weber, *The Theory of Social and Economic Organization* (New York: Free Press, 1947), p. 346; Reinhard Bendix, *Max Weber: An Intellectual Portrait* (Garden City, NY: Doubleday, 1960), pp. 330–60; H. E. Chehabi and Juan J. Linz (Eds.)., *Sultanistic Regimes* (Baltimore: Johns Hopkins University Press, 1998), ch. 1. Note that, as used by Weber and his followers, patriarchs are male; however, this usage does not correspond to the usage in current feminist literature, which treats male domination of women as a product or distinguishing characteristic of patriarchy. In the usage employed in this article, a patriarch is a leader who dominates subordinates of both sexes.

[5] Pilar Bonet, "Lord of the manor: Boris Yeltsin in Sverdlovsk oblast'," Occasional Paper no. 260 (Washington, DC: Kennan Institute), 1995, p. 8.

volleyball league," dividing it into five teams in which members of the provincial Party committee (*obkom*) were required to participate, both to foster bonhomie and to improve the physical fitness of his political elite.[6] As president of Russia, Yeltsin continued the pattern. After the August 1991 coup, he ordered a house to be built where he, his wife, and his daughters' families, as well as all the top officials in his administration and their families, would reside. He insisted that one apartment be held in common by residents of the apartment building, so that joint celebrations could be held there. Similarly, Yeltsin insisted that members of his entourage share his passion for playing tennis and that they display proper deference by losing to him on the court. He organized a "Presidential Club" into which members of his staff and cabinet were selectively initiated. He demanded that, in his presence or at the Presidential Club, associates not use swearwords.[7]

Former press secretary Vyacheslav Kostikov notes in his memoirs that Yeltsin considered himself "something like the father of an extended family (*semeystvo*)." He enjoyed flaunting his patriarchal authority and liked it when he had the opportunity to demand that somebody apologize for a bureaucratic inadvertence: "ask Papa for forgiveness." He liked a good meal with vodka, during which he would offer long toasts and enjoy his role as head of the family.[8]

Memoirs by associates – as well as Yeltsin's own memoirs – are laced with additional examples of this attitude. Kostikov affirms that Yeltsin harbored a great deal of sentimentality, almost love, for Gaidar and says that, for Yeltsin, Gaidar was his "alter ego" (*vtorym ya*).[9] Yeltsin is reported to have referred to Chubais and Nemtsov as being "like sons to me."[10] Yeltsin's ghost-writer (and eventual chief of staff) Valentin Yumashev appears in a photograph with Yeltsin in one memoir; the caption reads: "For the President, V. Yumashev is almost like a son. It is not for nothing that his patronymic is Borisovich."[11]

---

[6] Pilar Bonet, "Nevozmozhnaia Rossiia: Boris Yel'tsin. Provintsial v Kremle," trans. by G. Luk'ianova, in *Ural* (Yekaterinburg), no. 4 (April 1994), pp. 80–3; Fyodor Burlatskii, *Glotok svobody* (Moscow: RIK Kul'tura, 1997), vol. 2, p. 123.

[7] On the communal apartment building, see Korzhakov, *Boris Yel'tsin*, pp. 134–50; on tennis, see Yeltsin, *The Struggle*, pp. 234–6; on Yeltsin's need to win on the court, see Korzhakov, *Boris Yel'tsin*, p. 61; on the Presidential Club, see Viacheslav Kostikov, *Roman s prezidentom: zapiski press-sekretaria* (Moscow: Vagrius, 1997), p. 319, Korzhakov, *Boris Yel'tsin*, pp. 24–5, and Yeltsin, *The Struggle*, pp. 236–7; on swearwords, see Yeltsin, *The Struggle*, p. 237, and Korzhakov, *Boris Yel'tsin*, p. 309.

[8] Kostikov, *Roman*, pp. 8, 25.

[9] Ibid., pp. 157, 278.

[10] *Financial Times*, September 16, 1997.

[11] Valerii Streletskii, *Mrakobesie* (Moscow: Detektiv-Press, 1998), last page of book (unnumbered). Note also the following observation by a Russian journalist: "Presidential policy has

Kostikov's memoir (1997) is entitled *Love Affair with a President*. An interviewee and former Yeltsin aide avers that, in the early 1990s, Yeltsin "loved" his young advisors and they "loved" him in return.[12]

During the 1980s, Yeltsin's relationship with his bodyguard, Aleksandr Korzhakov, was intimate to the point that the two exchanged blood from their fingers on two occasions to affirm their eternal loyalty to each other as "blood brothers."[13] (Yeltsin was in his mid-fifties at the time.) Korzhakov refers to a vacation that he and Yeltsin took in 1986 as our "honeymoon."[14] Yeltsin was the designated "wedding patriarch" at the marriage of Korzhakov's daughter.[15] Streletskii writes of the psychology of those responsible for guarding Party and governmental officials under Yeltsin: "bit by bit they are turned into 'members of the families' of those they are guarding."[16] Tellingly, when Yeltsin rebuked Korzhakov in May 1996 for getting involved in politics, the blood brother proclaimed to Yeltsin's daughter that "it would be mild to say that I do not love Boris Nikolaevich." Tatyana flew into a rage at this statement.[17]

In such an administrative context, the key to both political longevity and political influence was to capture the attention and the ear of the leader. But this had to be done with all proper deference. Indeed, when seven members of Yeltsin's staff wrote a joint letter to their boss in 1994 – urging him not to repeat his embarrassing and apparently drunken performance in Berlin – Boris Nikolaevich was livid. His reaction, however, was that of a patriarch, not an executive: he demanded that each of them, individually, admit to him their "guilt" and express "repentance."[18]

Yeltsin's patriarchal self-conception extended beyond his immediate entourage and economic ministers. It also encompassed members of the military leadership. On this score, the detailed study – part memoir, part research project – by Baranets (1998) is useful and has an air of credibility, though of course it is only a single source and was written by a man quite alienated by

long been a family business, in which Yumashev is admitted with the rights of a relative" (Aleksandr Gamov, in *Komsomol'skaia pravda*, July 8, 1998); see also Baturin et al., *Epokha*, pp. 732, 780.

[12] See also Oleg Poptsov, *Khronika vremyon "Tsaria Borisa"* (Moscow: Sovershenno sekretno, 1996), p. 269.

[13] Korzhakov, *Boris Yel'tsin*, p. 223.

[14] Ibid., p. 63.

[15] Ibid., p. 243.

[16] Streletskii, *Mrakobesie*, p. 24.

[17] Korzhakov, *Boris Yel'tsin*, p. 358.

[18] Ibid., pp. 220–3; Kostikov, *Roman*, pp. 328–31. Yeltsin eventually calmed down, however; see Baturin et al., *Epokha*, pp. 523–4.

Yeltsin's treatment of the Russian military. Here too we encounter the use of intimate, familial metaphors. Defense Minister Grachev "loved" Yeltsin, and the two men once declared their "eternal friendship and love" for each other.[19] When he awarded Grachev a special presidential gold medal in a public ceremony, Yeltsin declared that this "is my personal gift to you."[20]

The Patriarch as Abusive Parent

The language of familial intimacy and love is one discursive indicator of a patriarchal self-conception. But Yeltsin, like Khrushchev, also reserved to himself the right to abuse verbally members of the executive branch. As Baranets documents, in October 1993, when Yeltsin sought military support against the Supreme Soviet, one of the participants at the meeting remarked that "[w]e were sitting there and feeling as if our strict and enraged father had come to our school in order to listen to the principal's complaining about our bad behavior."[21] Several years later, after having decided to fire Defense Minister Igor Rodionov and Chief of the General Staff Viktor Samsonov, Yeltsin first harassed them verbally in front of their subordinates.[22]

Nor were the military the only victims. Other members of Yeltsin's cabinet were subjected to open, verbal abuse: Foreign Minister Kozyrev, Interior Minister Yerin, and Nationalities Minister Yegorov are specifically mentioned in memoirs as having gotten the treatment, while Kostikov implies that Prime Minister Viktor Chernomyrdin was victimized as well.[23]

Yeltsin also felt at liberty to be physically abusive. He could be very cruel to the most loyal of his aides, especially when he had been drinking. Whatever the foibles of presidents and prime ministers elsewhere, it is difficult to imagine them "playing the spoons" on the heads of their ranking assistants and, when the others in the room responded with laughter, increasing the speed and force of the spoon-pounding, as well as the number of heads being pounded.[24] It is also difficult to imagine them emulating Yeltsin's behavior on a boat on the Yenisei River, when he lost patience with the interruptions of his press secretary and ordered his bodyguards to toss the man overboard.

---

[19] V. N. Baranets, *Yel'tsin i ego generaly: zapiski polkovnika genshtaba* (Moscow: "Sovershenno sekretno," 1998), pp. 170, 230.

[20] Ibid., pp. 248–9.

[21] Ibid., p. 26.

[22] Ibid., pp. 77, 122.

[23] Yegor T. Gaidar, *Dni porazhenii i pobed* (Moscow: Vagrius, 1996), pp. 107–8, 333–4; Korzhakov, *Boris Yel'tsin*, pp. 52–3; Kostikov, *Roman*, p. 347.

[24] Korzhakov, *Boris Yel'tsin*, pp. 81–2.

When his bodyguards hesitated, on the assumption that he was kidding, he reiterated that he was serious and saw that the hapless press secretary went over the side.[25]

Nor did Yeltsin's abuse of his most dependent and servile subordinates cease at the boundary of the Russian executive and presidential branches. We also learn that he played the spoons on the head of the president of Kyrgyzstan, Askar Akayev![26] Unless this was mutual, good-natured play (not clear from the memoir account), it is a stunning indicator of the extent to which Yeltsin may have considered portions of the Commonwealth of Independent States (CIS) to be part of his political household.

The Patriarch as Generous Benefactor

Although Yeltsin frequently abused his subordinates and those most dependent upon him, he could also be generous toward members of the political family. He enjoyed giving gifts (usually expensive watches) to his staff.[27] The gestures reached beyond the inner circle as well. He became the focus of innumerable requests for special favors – tax exemptions, in particular – from representatives of regional and sectoral interests. Reportedly, he found it difficult to say "no" in the face of opportunities to assist friends, maddening his budget-conscious economics minister in the process, though he also used such dispensations as a conscious strategy of "buying" political support.[28] Moreover, such tendencies extended beyond the borders of the Russian Federation. Yegor Gaidar reports in his memoir his fear that Yeltsin, if left alone with the leaders of Belarus, would concede more than Russia could afford in economic policy.[29] An interviewee added that such fears were well-founded, but not because of Yeltsin's (very real) ignorance of economics or an ideological

---

[25] Ibid., pp. 253–4.

[26] Ibid., p. 82. This was corroborated by others (none of them admirers of Korzhakov) interviewed by me in Moscow in June 1998.

[27] Ibid., p. 54. As Korzhakov notes, this notion of *shef darit* (the chief or patron gives a gift) was one that Yeltsin enjoyed practicing in his Sverdlovsk days as well.

[28] Kostikov, *Roman*, pp. 216–17; Baturin et al., *Epokha*, pp. 339, 340, 435. See also Eugene Huskey, *Presidential Power in Russia* (Armonk, NY: M.E. Sharpe, 1999), pp. 137–8; Anatol Lieven, *Chechnya: Tombstone of Russian Power* (New Haven & London: Yale University Press, 1998), p. 171; Victor M. Sergeyev, *The Wild East: Crime and Lawlessness in Post-Communist Russia* (Armonk, NY: M.E. Sharpe, 1998), pp. 117–18. Huskey reports that Finance Minister Livshits lamented that Yeltsin does not understand the economy "and tries to help everyone … but some people need to be imprisoned rather than helped" (p. 57) and that Economics Minister Yasin complained that Yeltsin has "his favorite directors who can open any doors" (p. 137).

[29] Gaidar, *Dni*, pp. 183–4.

commitment to CIS integration. Rather, what drove Yeltsin in such conversations was paternalism and a sense of communalism. As this interviewee put it, Yeltsin's expressed sentiment was: "We're a family here. Let's dispense with the formalities! Why should we wrangle? Here, I'll give you this!" This extended beyond the Russia–Belarus relationship, according to this insider, and helps to explain Russia's flexibility in relations with Ukraine and Kazakhstan (the latter regarding Caspian Sea oil). The same interviewee averred that, in CIS relations, Yeltsin "could be generous to a fault."[30]

Yeltsin also thought in generous patriarchal terms about his relationship with the Russian population, even as his policies caused great suffering to a majority of the population. He thought of himself in 1992–1993 as "Director of all of Russia" whose election as president had validated his right to interpret the will of the people.[31] Because of his overwhelming victories in confrontations with the old system and in free elections, he believed that he didn't have to account, or explain himself, to anyone.[32] But he also thought of himself as a "people's tsar": benevolent and caring, though strict when necessary.[33] When he would offer reassurances to the populace that their pain would shortly ease, he felt like a Russian priest lifting the spirits of his flock.[34] On a tour of Russia in 1992, he brought along hundreds of millions of rubles for "gifts to the working people." He knew that this violated the prevailing economic policy, "but he considered it possible for himself to make tsarist gestures."[35]

The Evolution of Yeltsin's Management Style

Yeltsin entertained a personalistic self-conception throughout his political career; he always wanted to be "in charge." He was an extremely demanding boss, one who expected all his subordinates to work and play as hard as he did.

---

[30] Although I have no evidence on the matter, such an attitude may have informed Yeltsin's relations with Tatarstan's President Shaimiev and the generous terms Yeltsin offered to secure the treaty of February 1994, which accorded that republic substantial autonomy within the Russian Federation. For an admission that many people accuse him of being too generous to the CIS leaders – and for his self-justification for doing so, see Boris Yeltsin, *Midnight Diaries* (New York: Public Affairs, 2000), pp. 247–8.

[31] Kostikov, *Roman,* pp. 306–7; Poptsov, *Khronika vremyon,* p. 283.

[32] Kostikov, *Roman,* p. 304.

[33] Burlatskii, *Glotok svobody,* vol. 2, p. 315.

[34] Kostikov, *Roman,* pp. 21–2.

[35] Ibid., pp. 42–3. In *Presidential Power,* Huskey argues that Yeltsin conceived of the presidency as "the country's primary institutional patron" (p. 119) and of the president as standing above all branches of government and sending "emissaries" (p. 81) to them. The evidence displayed in this chapter supports Huskey's characterizations.

In Sverdlovsk, he expected subordinates to give up their weekends to play volleyball or to go fishing and hunting whenever he so demanded.[36] In Moscow, they were called to the tennis court. But Yeltsin's operating style evolved over time. He always combined personalism with a patriarchal self-conception; a reclusive, monarchical style became dominant only after 1993. Memoirs by two of his close aides from the late 1980s, while he was an oppositional leader in Gorbachev's Soviet Union, make little mention of the traits I have been emphasizing to this point, stressing instead Yeltsin's charismatic personalism at the time.[37] Several memoirs by people who worked with Yeltsin both before and after 1993 distinguish between the early President Yeltsin and the late President Yeltsin, with the breakpoint coming sometime in late 1993. Before then, Yeltsin was a populist who, these memoirists claim, was confident of his ability to mobilize the masses against his political adversaries. He also enjoyed enormous charismatic authority within his entourage and rational–legal authority derived from his public election as president in June 1991. In addition, within his inner circle, while demanding the deference due a patriarch, he was also accessible, consultative, and receptive to a range of policy advice.

By late 1993, however, Yeltsin had lost confidence in his ability to rally the masses, a conclusion reinforced mightily by the results of the December 1993 parliamentary elections.[38] This was not only a blow (presumably) to his ego; it was also a threat to his authority-maintenance strategy. For a plebiscitarian approach to getting one's way assumes that "the people" will side with the leader against his political enemies. In 1988–1989, Yeltsin had turned to the people for defense against the Communist Party–State. In 1989–1992, he had risen to ascendancy on waves of popular affirmation and reaffirmation. In 1993, the costs of his policies were piling up and the populace lost faith in their hero. Yeltsin was still in power – formally, stronger than ever – but found himself in new political territory.

Gaidar writes that, around this time, Yeltsin began to present himself as a benevolent tsar surrounded by a huge court.[39] Increasingly over time, Kostikov reports, Yeltsin referred to himself in the third person.[40] According

[36] Burlatskii, *Glotok svobody*, vol. 2, p. 123.
[37] Lev Sukhanov, *Tri goda s Yel'tsinym* (Riga: "Vaga," 1992); Viktor Yaroshenko, *Ya otvechiu za vsyo* (Moscow: Vokrug sveta, 1997).
[38] Kostikov, *Roman*, pp. 151–2; Gaidar, *Dni*, pp. 230–1, 313–14; Korzhakov, *Boris Yel'tsin*, p. 330.
[39] Gaidar, *Dni*, p. 295.
[40] Kostikov, *Roman*, p. 308.

to Korzhakov, Yeltsin began to be heavily preoccupied with his personal security.[41] He also narrowed the circle of those to whom he would turn for advice and allowed the security personnel in his entourage to have a major influence on policy.[42] As Kostikov lamented, "we ['democrats'] were pained that, in relations with Boris Nikolaevich, a steady disappearance of democratism, accessibility, and relations of trust was occurring."[43] One former associate explains this trend as a joint product of the physical pain and exhaustion Yeltsin experienced at this time and the emotional anguish of having "lost" the December 1993 parliamentary elections after having expended so much energy to prevail over the Supreme Soviet in 1993. He had been expending so much "negative energy" for so many years that, by 1994, his entourage could bring him "bad news" only when it was packaged with three times as much "good news."[44]

The change led Gaidar to remark to Kostikov in January 1994 that "we must return Yeltsin to Yeltsin," which meant that they must find a way to curb Yeltsin's authoritarian impulse, reinforce his consultative strain, and prevent him from relying excessively on alcohol as an escape.[45] Yeltsin had evolved from a "people's tsar"[46] into an increasingly reclusive monarch. His personalism – though a constant throughout his years as president – had evolved from a populist, consultative, and accessible variant into a more reclusive and exclusionary one.

The Patriarch as System Manager

Yeltsin's sense of political vulnerability and his withdrawal into a more exclusionary operating style were accompanied by a demonstrable shift in his authority-maintenance strategy as well. From 1994 onward, Yeltsin presented himself publicly as a leader whose primary goal was to consolidate the new

---

[41] Korzhakov, *Boris Yel'tsin*, p. 133.

[42] Gaidar, *Dni*, p. 300.

[43] Kostikov, *Roman*, p. 322. Yeltsin's chief of staff at the time, Sergei Filatov, reports that Yeltsin became relatively reclusive and traveled little around Russia in 1994–1995 (*Sovershenno nesekretno*, p. 401).

[44] Interview by the author, Moscow, June 1998; see also Korzhakov, *Boris Yel'tsin*, p. 251.

[45] Kostikov, *Roman*, p. 296. In his post-retirement memoir, Yeltsin admits that alcohol got the best of him during 1994–1995 (Yeltsin, *Midnight Diaries*, pp. 318–19), though he denies being an alcoholic either before then or since then; for a somewhat different view of Yeltsin's reaction to the December 1993 votes, see Baturin et al., *Epokha*, p. 402. Curiously, the "author's collective" that produced *Epokha* included V. Kostikov.

[46] Burlatskii, *Glotok svobody*, vol. 2, p. 315.

order he had built and to manage the contradictions within that new order. He presented himself more as a system manager than a system builder. The change led him to distance himself further from the radical reformers and to shore up his ties with the centrists. This was consistent with his earlier reactions to political challenge.

When his popularity fell and criticism rose after the economic reforms of early 1992, he shifted toward currying support from centrists in many realms of policy. After his military victory over the parliamentarians and their paramilitary allies in October 1993, but before the elections of December, Yeltsin began to emphasize the theme of "normalization" and the need for a long-term process of cultural adaptation to the new system.[47] At his press conference following the elections, he declared that "the whole of Russia craves stability. Russia needs peace."[48] The memoir he signed for publication in early 1994 ends with the prosaic promise to give the Russian people "stability and consistency in politics and the economy" and with the declaration that "the only definite guarantor of calm is the president himself."[49] After he calmed down following his anger at the amnesty of February 1994, Yeltsin proposed and brokered a "memorandum on social accord" geared toward inducing all moderates to agree formally to work within the system, to avoid inflaming public passions, and to help him isolate the extremists within the Duma.[50] The Constitution, he suggested, had put an end to the contradictions of dual power, and it would open up a civilized basis for lasting peace and rational development.

Structural transformations were no longer the leitmotif of Yeltsin's administration. The emphasis would now fall on consolidation of gains, rationalization of administration within the new structural context, political isolation of anti-system forces, and popular adaptation to the system as constructed.[51]

A good indicator of the change in policy priorities was the newfound emphasis in Yeltsin's speeches on consolidative themes and a relative downplaying of the transformative themes that had predominated in 1992–1993. His first

---

[47] Interview in *Izvestiia*, November 16, 1993.

[48] Moscow Ostankino Television First Channel Network, December 22, 1993, as transcribed in FBIS-SOV-93-244, p. 2.

[49] Yeltsin, *The Struggle*, p. 292.

[50] Also, in an interview on April 5, 1994, he made clear that another priority had entered his goal-set: "I believe that one of my main accomplishments by 1996 will have been to create the guarantee that prevents the country from falling into totalitarianism .... Our shared duty is to isolate the extremist forces in parliament (*La Republica*, April 5, 1994, p. 14 [FBIS-SOV-94-065, pp. 11–12]).

[51] See Baturin et al., *Epokha*, pp. 16–17, 379–80, 397, 412.

speech to the Federation Council, on January 11, 1994, stressed the need to firm up the market economy by giving it a legal infrastructure.[52] On February 24, his landmark "State of the Federation" address to the Federal Assembly was titled "On Strengthening the Russian State" and declared: "The important stage of Russia's transformation into a democratic state is now coming to a close. A democratic system of power is being shaped on the basis of the Constitution."[53] The section on economic reform itself, the priority in earlier days, was now located in the middle of a long address. This speech and subsequent ones – while still touting the need to continue and deepen the reform process – placed much greater emphasis on the maintenance of social peace (that is, among "all healthy forces in society") and the creation of order, with new attention to courts, crime, social programs, administrative reliability, an orderly relationship between Moscow and the regions, the population's long-term adaptation to the new system, and the need for civil service reform as a means of reducing the level of corruption. Following the amnesty, Yeltsin summarized the new orientation nicely in a speech to the government on March 4, 1994: "Today in Russia democracy means first and foremost stability, order, cooperation."[54] Gaidar sensed the shift coming and resigned from his position as a member of the government's cabinet in January 1994.[55]

Yeltsin had been a competent manager and Party leader in Sverdlovsk from the 1950s through the 1970s, when he had been undisputed master of his domain and when the communist system enforced a social peace and political conformity that kept conflict within bounds. He had then evolved into a tactically brilliant revolutionary figure during Gorbachev's last years in power.

---

[52] Moscow Radio Rossii Network, January 11, 1994.

[53] *Rossiiskaia gazeta,* February 25, 1994, p. 1, as translated in FBIS-SOV-94-039, p. 37.

[54] Moscow Maiak Radio Network, March 4, 1994 (FBIS-SOV-94-043, p. 16).

[55] In an interview published in *Izvestiia* on March 26, 1994, Yeltsin was challenged to explain the fact that he had noticeably distanced himself from the "democrats and radical reformers." He denied that he had done so, claiming that he had instead "broadened the spectrum of cooperation.... Precise, thorough, patient work is essential here. Passions must not be further intensified.... The main idea ... – strengthening the state on the basis of the Constitution – is cherished by everyone whose common sense has not failed them.... I feel that the main demand now being voiced by people and by all strata of society is that stability is strengthened and our life rendered more peaceful" (*Izvestiia,* March 26, 1994). In August 1995, he went even further: "Time is changing the meaning of the word 'democrat.' Until recently it had been used primarily for radicals, hardline opponents of the former system, and dedicated rally participants. Now, in my view, it primarily refers to professionals able to create. People who recognize only the constitutional method of coming to office and leaving office. Democrats are the people who are prepared to ensure that the country moves toward a normal life" (*Komsomol'skaia pravda,* August 19, 1995).

As president of independent Russia he had led the country, for better or for worse, through a radical rupture with the legacy of communist institutions. But now – weakened by age, illness, and the sheer fatigue of having battled for so long – Yeltsin faced still another social role: the leader as system manager.

The course of the privatization program reflected this new stage in Yeltsin's administration. As previously scheduled, a second round of privatization, based on a new set of rules, took place during 1994–1995. Whereas the rules governing the first round ("voucher privatization" in 1992–1994) favored insider workers and managers, the second round amounted to one of the largest and most blatant cases of plutocratic favoritism imaginable. Huge industries, potentially worth many billions of dollars, were "sold" to a few wealthy individuals for a nominal sum – in some cases, less than one percent of their real value. It is doubtful that Yeltsin either understood the intricacies or cared to learn them. As he confessed in his second memoir, "I do not pretend to understand the philosophy behind our economic reforms."[56] But his advisors convinced him that rapid transfer of large assets into the hands of monopoly capitalists would help create a class of wealthy property owners who would be potent allies in the ongoing struggle against communist restoration. Those capitalists would then have a great deal to lose from the communists coming back to power and would accordingly be willing to use all means to prevent that from happening. And, with the presidential election only one year away, their financial and political (i.e., media) support for Yeltsin would be assured. Yeltsin, in this stage of political defensiveness, could thus use the new round of privatization simultaneously to shore up his personal power and to redefine his authority-maintenance strategy by presenting himself as the guarantor against communist restoration, whatever the price.

In December 1994, Yeltsin made the fateful decision to invade the republic of Chechnya. I will discuss the rationale for that decision in Chapter 9. In this chapter, I will briefly examine the aftermath as an indicator of Yeltsin's reaction to the frustration of his policies. Following the invasion, members of the political, military, and journalistic establishments criticized Yeltsin forcefully. They challenged him to justify his strategy for maintaining the integrity of Russia. The goal itself was unobjectionable, and he touted it in his State of the Federation speeches of February 1995 and February 1996; indeed, in the 1996 speech, he defined the most important accomplishment (the "first success") of four years of reform as prevention of the disintegration of Russia.[57]

---

[56] Boris Yeltsin, *Zapiski prezidenta* (Moscow: Ogonyok, 1994), p. 235; the admission was omitted from the English-language version, *Struggle*, p. 145.

[57] TASS, February 23, 1996.

But beyond that, how could he justify the price paid in Chechnya to achieve that goal? How do you convince Russians that it is worth losing thousands of soldiers to keep largely Muslim Chechnya within the ostensibly liberal Russian Federation and yet not worth a drop of blood to protect ethnic Russians in the so-called Near Abroad? Yeltsin did not have a ready answer, a reflection of the (perhaps intractable) dilemma of nation-state construction in a post-imperial but diasporic context.

Instead, Yeltsin fell back on nationalistic discourse. He lectured journalists about their alleged obligation to promote the spiritual and religious rebirth of Russia,[58] much as Gorbachev and Khrushchev had tried to keep journalists from going too far in response to the campaigns for *glasnost'* and de-Stalinization. Yeltsin called on the younger generations not to "disgrace the glory of their fathers," to appreciate the importance of defending the Motherland.[59] He publicly courted Cossack organizations – both to secure their loyalty and to make rhetorical use of their historical and current roles in guaranteeing Russian statehood and nationhood.[60]

Yeltsin also took the opportunity to crack down on the most extreme anti-system forces among the Russian nationalists. On March 23, 1995, he issued a decree against "fascist" organizations and activities.[61] This was an effort to lay down the law, to establish boundaries to anti-regime activity, to construct a right-wing enemy of the Russian nation, and to warn that the Yeltsin

---

[58] Moscow Russian Television Network, February 16, 1995; *Rossiiskaia gazeta,* February 20, 1995.

[59] TASS, June 13, 1995.

[60] It seems that the first war in Chechnya (1994–1996) triggered a growing romance between Yeltsin and Cossack organizations. When the war began, Cossacks were drawn in immediately, as historically Cossack villages came under fire and were destroyed. Self-organized battalions immediately volunteered their services, and on January 30, 1995, Cossack leaders asked Yeltsin to "severely punish" Chechen president Dudaev for bringing conflict into Russia and pledged their assistance in protecting Russian territorial integrity (TASS, January 30, 1995). In May 1995, the Extraordinary Council of Cossack Atamans declared its readiness to serve loyally and to defend the security and territorial integrity of Russia (TASS, May 19, 1995). Yeltsin reciprocated with a decree "On the state registry of Cossack societies" (*Moskovskie novosti,* August 25, 1995) and later with the decree "On the main directorate of Cossack troops under the President of the Russian Federation" (TASS, January 20, 1996), both of which recognized the Cossacks officially and also organized them for state service. In September 1995, Yeltsin publicly praised the role of Cossacks in Russian history (TASS, September 7, 1995). In 1996, he expressed his confidence that the Cossacks would continue to set a good example by "defend[ing] the borders and interests of Russia as in ancient times" (TASS, April 17, 1996). Correspondingly, he noted that he would continue to assist the irreversible revival of the Cossack community, a "pillar of Russian statehood" (TASS, June 6, 1996).

[61] It was published in *Rossiiskaia gazeta* on March 25, 1995.

government was willing and able to defeat that enemy. Thus, as all radical nationalists had long warned, this decree acknowledged that the "nation" was under threat, but it uniquely declared the nation to be under threat from the most extreme nationalists themselves. And the decree pointed to Yeltsin's government as the force that would save the nation from that threat.

Nonetheless, Yeltsin resisted ethnicization of the rhetoric of nation building. Thus, in appealing for unity behind his Chechnya policy, he proclaimed that "the citizens of Russia, regardless of their nationality [read: ethnicity], are dying there."[62] Moreover, Yeltsin supplemented his remarks about citizen obligations with a reiteration of the democratic principles of freedom of speech and freedom of the press. His anti-fascism decree was apparently aimed at those radical nationalists who were prepared to call militias into the streets, rather than at the Ziuganovs, Baburins, and others who were expressing their opposition within the legitimate political institutions created by the December 1993 Constitution.

In sum, Yeltsin redefined his priorities and political strategies after December 1993. But the transition from system builder to system manager did not relieve him from having to manage the contradictions built into that system of rule.

THE SYSTEM MANAGER AS STATESMAN

Yeltsin's pro-Western foreign policy of 1992 came under criticism at the time, leading the Russian president to explore the possibility of synthesizing a pro-Western, liberal international policy with one that attempted to advance and defend Russia's national interest as a "great power." After the Duma elections of 1993, however, Yeltsin felt the need to respond with ever greater sensitivity to perceived setbacks or shortfalls on the international scene. In 1994, Yeltsin became less of an assertive leader who was building bridges to the West and more the defensive manager of a fragmented and often incoherent foreign policy. Initially, he had oversold his pro-Western foreign policy. Thereafter, he promised the best of both worlds. By 1994, Western powers were acting in ways quite divergent from the ways Yeltsin had promised they would. Critics – led by Zhirinovskii's Liberal Democratic Party of Russia and the Communist Party, which held sway in the newly elected Duma – turned up the rhetorical heat on Yeltsin for allegedly kow-towing to the West and to the United States in particular.

Yeltsin the authority builder had created unrealistic expectations. Now his critics, combined with his personal isolation and unhelpful international

---

[62] TASS, February 23, 1996.

events, made his optimistic vision of a Russia–West "marriage" seem both less desirable and less feasible. The result of this process was the transformation of Yeltsin into a defensive statesman who was struggling not only to manage the contradictions between these expectations and reality but also to defend his political authority as an effective foreign policymaker.

Russia and the West, 1994–1996

A search for Western assistance to help finance the Russian transition had been a constant throughout Yeltsin's years as president of the Russian Federation. In the early years, hopes were high in Moscow that the rich democracies would provide huge sums, both in appreciation of the anti-communist credentials of the Yeltsin government and in fear of what might replace it. Those hopes were soon disappointed, and the "game" thereafter became one of playing upon Western fears of Russian revanchism to induce the extension of whatever credits, loans, guarantees, and policy concessions the West might be persuaded or cajoled to deliver. Jerry Hough, in a recent study, demonstrates how Yeltsin and his government played upon the Western identification of Yeltsin's political survival with the continuation of something called "reform." The rhetorical characterization of opponents within Russia, and the timing of alleged threats to "reformism," often coincided with moments when the International Monetary Fund was deliberating the extension of new loans. Those loans, Hough argues, were largely counted upon to help pay the wages of workers in the urban state sector of the economy and thereby to avert potential social unrest.[63]

Clinton and Yeltsin met in Moscow in January 1994. In the news conference held jointly with Clinton, Yeltsin, though upbeat and ebullient, gave voice to a long list of Russia's concerns about U.S. deficiencies as a partner of Russia in international affairs, complaining of discriminatory trade restrictions and the treatment of Russians in the Baltics ("There should be no double standards here, whether it is taking place in Haiti or in the Baltic area").[64] In his dinner toast to Clinton following the summit, Yeltsin extended the laundry list of complaints, signaling irritation and impatience with his American partner and suggesting that the United States was not doing its part to help Russia.[65]

---

[63] Jerry Hough, *The Logic of Economic Reform in Russia* (Washington, DC: Brookings Institution, 2001).

[64] Moscow Russian Television Network, January 14, 1994 (FBIS-SOV-94-011, p. 7).

[65] ITAR-TASS, January 14, 1994 (FBIS-SOV-94-011, pp. 12–13); "we need to be sincerely supportive of each other's success .... It is not enough to mouth these values. It is necessary to bring one's actions into line with them" (ibid., p. 13).

After the pro-Western romanticism of early 1992 had worn off, Yeltsin felt the need to elicit Western financial support without giving away too much in return. His revised authority-building strategy called for him to manage the contradictions among an array of goals. In his State of the Federation address on February 24, 1994, Yeltsin went farther than ever before in identifying the sheer number of conflicting goals he was promising to advance:

It is in Russia's interests to create favorable external conditions for the country's development. This must be achieved by a proper and friendly but at the same time firm and consistent foreign policy, in which the desire for cooperation does not conflict with the country's national interests and Russian citizens' sense of national pride.[66]

That was a tall order, indeed!

Issues other than trade, credits, and arms reductions also conspired to complicate the realization of this vision. Most immediately at the time, the war in former Yugoslavia caused a crisis in U.S.–Russian relations. Beginning in late 1993, NATO threatened to bomb Serbia if it failed to respect United Nations "safe havens." However, Serbian President Slobodan Milosevic proved recalcitrant. When NATO responded by bombing the Bosnian Serbs – despite Russia's protests and without the imprimatur of the UN Security Council – Yeltsin temporarily postponed his State of the Federation address and thereafter complained repeatedly in public about both a Western double standard in Yugoslavia and Western unilateralism.[67] After much international maneuvering, Russian troops served side-by-side with NATO troops, but under UN command, in what proved to be a failed attempt to secure the safe havens from attack. However, they did so with mixed support from Russia's Ministry of Defense. The NATO leaders became increasingly frustrated with Milosevic and were poised to begin airstrikes on the night of February 17, 1994. But that day the Russians surprised NATO by unilaterally brokering a cease-fire and landing Russian troops in and around Sarajevo. Yeltsin released a statement that touted the Russian "triumph," and he later called for a Russia-led summit of the United States, Britain, France, and Germany to resolve the Serb–Bosnian crisis. The summit never took place.

Coterminous with the Yugoslav crisis was the matter of NATO's enlargement, which held out the prospect of adding East European states to the

---

[66] "Poslanie Prezidenta Rossiiskoi Federatsii Federal'nomu Sobraniiu: Ob ukreplenii rossiiskogo gosudarstva. (Osnovnye napravleniia vnutrennei i vneshnei politiki.)," *Rossiiskaia gazeta,* February 25, 1994, pp. 1, 3–7, quoted from p. 1.

[67] Moscow Ostankino Television First Channel Network, October 4, 1994 (FBIS-SOV-94-193, pp. 7–10), quoted from p. 9; *Rossiiskaia gazeta,* August 10, 1995, p. 1; Moscow Radio Rossii Network, September 8, 1995; ITAR-TASS, September 8, 1995.

alliance. The issue further complicated Yeltsin's efforts to deliver on the multiple goals of his redefined foreign policy vision, and it reinforced the credibility of anti-Western forces within Russia's political establishment and intelligentsia. Several compromises were offered by the Western powers: a "Partnership for Peace," in which Russia and all formerly communist states would participate; a temperate pace of NATO expansion, sensitive to Yeltsin's political predicament; and, ultimately, a NATO–Russia Charter, institutionalizing forms of cooperation between an enlarged NATO and an excluded Russia. Even though these compromises were ultimately agreed upon, they were viewed in Moscow as little more than palliatives. The issue of NATO's enlargement eastward (which Moscow could not prevent) and of Moscow's likely exclusion from membership severely complicated Yeltsin's authority maintenance throughout 1994–1996.

In October 1993, U.S. Secretary of State Warren Christopher presented to Yeltsin the idea of the Partnership for Peace, which Yeltsin misunderstood to be an *alternative* to NATO expansion. Christopher recalled the misunderstanding in his memoir:

> Yeltsin became quite animated when I described the Partnership proposal. The Russians had been very nervous about the NATO issue in the run-up to our visit.... He called the Partnership idea a "stroke of genius," saying it would dissipate Russian tensions regarding the East Europeans and their aspirations toward NATO .... "This really is a great idea, really great," Yeltsin said enthusiastically. "Tell Bill that I am thrilled by this brilliant stroke." In retrospect, it is clear that his enthusiasm was based upon his mistaken assumption that the Partnership for Peace would not lead to eventual NATO expansion.[68]

Within months, however, it became clear to Russian officials and to Boris Yeltsin that they had either misunderstood or been misled. Foreign Minister Kozyrev did his best during 1994 to push for a revitalized Organization for Security and Cooperation in Europe in lieu of an expanded NATO.[69] But during the second half of 1994, the United States intensified its efforts to build support for NATO enlargement.[70] Moscow reacted with indignation. At a meeting of European heads of state in Budapest in December 1994, Yeltsin and Kozyrev angrily denounced NATO expansion and refused to sign on to the Partnership for Peace.[71] At a Clinton–Yeltsin summit meeting in Moscow

---

[68] As quoted in James M. Goldgeier, *Not Whether but When: The U.S. Decision to Enlarge NATO* (Washington, DC: Brookings Institution, 1999), p. 59.

[69] *Segodnia,* February 25, 1994; TASS, March 2 and June 22, 1994; UPI, March 10 and August 17, 1994; Official Kremlin International News Broadcast, August 17, 1994.

[70] Goldgeier, *Not Whether,* pp. 71–5.

[71] Ibid., pp. 85–7.

in May 1995, the rhetorical heat subsided but no final agreement was reached, as "Clinton and Yeltsin agreed to disagree on enlargement" and Clinton rebuffed Yeltsin's demands for a substantial delay in the admission of new members to NATO.[72] Although Clinton thought he had persuaded Yeltsin at that summit to join the Partnership for Peace,[73] it was not until December 1996 that Kozyrev's successor, Yevgeny Primakov, agreed for the last time to join NATO's Partnership – and even after that, Russia participated only fitfully.

Given this thicket of contradictions, during 1994–1995 Yeltsin found it increasingly difficult to reconcile with reality his previous vision of friendly and benevolent U.S.–Russia relations. After a September 1994 summit with Clinton, Yeltsin declared: "There are people in my country, though few, who say that our relationship with the U.S. is transient and that an era of confrontation will return. But I would like to tell you that we have never fought the U.S. and I believe, and I can say as President of Russia, that we will never fight the U.S."[74] By that December, Yeltsin was less optimistic, warning of a "cold peace" in place of the Cold War.[75] In spring 1995, Foreign Minister Kozyrev announced that "[t]he honeymoon is over" in U.S.–Russian relations.[76]

Of course, Yeltsin very often put a positive spin on the "results" of his meetings with leaders of the rich democracies. In his news conferences and dinner toasts at summits, he frankly summarized the remaining areas of disagreement and often sternly lectured his Western counterpart on the deficiencies of his policies. But he also spoke of the progress made in discussions and in mutual understanding of each other's positions. And he frequently spoke ebulliently of their personal relationship. This was an important component of his authority-maintenance strategy. If he could not deliver concrete, laudatory results on issues like Yugoslavia, NATO, trade, and the like, he could at least hold out the prospect of future progress that would result from continuation of his close, personal relationships with Western leaders. This was the likely rationale for his constantly referring to "my friend Bill," "my friend Helmut," and, later, even "my friend Ryu," the Japanese leader whom he was meeting for the first time. Thus, in January 1996, after a one-hour telephone conversation with Clinton, Yeltsin proclaimed a "second honeymoon" in U.S.–Russia relations, proudly declaring that "I remained loyal to my friend and he remained loyal to me."[77] The message was consistent. Russia and the

---

[72] Ibid., p. 92, 93.
[73] Ibid., p. 93.
[74] *Financial Times*, September 24, 1994.
[75] *Los Angeles Times*, December 6, 1994.
[76] *Financial Times*, March 24, 1995.
[77] *The Washington Post*, January 28, 1996.

West might be as far apart as ever on the issues that divide them, but Boris Nikolaevich can still manage this as a disagreement among close friends – and can hold out the prospect of bridging the divide in the future.[78]

The Commonwealth of Independent States

Already in 1993, Russia had begun to move toward an increasingly interventionist policy in the Near Abroad. Progress toward some degree of economic reintegration of states of the former Soviet Union became a goal of Russian foreign policy. Better yet, demonstration of enhanced political and military cooperation among those states, coerced or otherwise, became a means by which Yeltsin tried to assuage his nationalist critics. Thus, as early as January 1994, the *Financial Times* reported that Russia was negotiating a secret deal to merge its economy with that of Belarus.[79] Yeltsin confirmed these rumors in a speech in February, when he also publicly signed a military cooperation treaty with Georgia.[80] In ensuing months, Yeltsin announced several treaties and agreements deepening ties with Belarus, Georgia, Kazakhstan, Ukraine, Tadjikistan, and Armenia. During 1993–1995, Russia pressured states of the Commonwealth to adopt "dual citizenship" laws. Yeltsin also made increasingly nationalistic statements about Russia's "moral and political" responsibility to provide security and currency for CIS countries,[81] turned up the rhetorical heat on European governments to punish Estonia and Latvia for their restrictive citizenship laws (which disadvantaged resident Russians), and proclaimed Russia's right to police the Near Abroad when threats of instability on Russia's borders appeared.[82] Kozyrev ratcheted up the patriotic rhetoric in parallel, announcing by April 1995 that Russia was prepared to use force to "defend our compatriots abroad."[83]

Much of this rhetoric proved to be bluster. Economic and political unions with Belarus were on the Russian policy agenda from 1991 onward, yet none were implemented to a degree that would force Moscow to pay significant

---

[78] In his post-retirement memoir, Yeltsin discusses his final summit meetings with Western leaders in precisely these terms. He presents himself as a great leader who brought the world back from the precipice by forgiving Western leaders their challenges to Russian security and pride (*Midnight Diaries*, ch. 23).

[79] *Financial Times,* January 7, 1994, p. 1.

[80] ITAR-TASS, February 3, 1994.

[81] Radio Free Europe/Radio Liberty Daily Report, no. 126, Part I, June 29, 1995.

[82] Moscow Russian Television Network, January 14, 1994 (FBIS-SOV-94-011, pp. 6–7); *Rossiiskaia gazeta,* February 25, 1994 (section on foreign policy); *Rossiiskaia gazeta,* April 29, 1994, p. 3; *Izvestiia,* July 21, 1994, pp. 1, 3.

[83] *Izvestiia,* April 20, 1995.

material costs. Yeltsin and presidents Kravchuk and Kuchma of Ukraine announced several compromise resolutions of their conflicts over control of the
Black Sea Fleet during 1994–1996, only to see these resolutions fall apart
and the negotiations reopened. The issue of dual citizenship was quietly
dropped when widespread governmental resistance to the idea arose in the
Near Abroad.[84] European pressure on Estonia resulted in a change in that
country's laws, as a result of which Russia withdrew her troops by the announced deadline. Throughout, Russian officials tried to increase the level
of economic integration within the Commonwealth, but they avoided using
a heavy hand and typically backed off when they met resistance. On the
other hand, Russian military assertiveness, both covert and overt, intensified
in the affairs of the more defenseless successor states: Georgia, Moldova, and
Tadjikistan.

Yeltsin used the prospect of CIS integration to co-opt nationalist sentiment and maintain his broad, centrist coalition. His commitment to defend
Russians in the Near Abroad may or may not have been genuine, but his
hardline rhetoric was certainly an easy way to score points with nationalist
constituencies. He declared his preference that Russians in those countries
not emigrate back to Russia and that the issue never torpedo his relations
with the rich democracies. Similarly, Yeltsin was attentive to instability along
Russia's borders. He declared it right and proper that Russia use its military,
political, and economic leverage to reduce or contain the instability in ways
that were consistent with Russia's long-term interests. Yet when discussing
these issues with European and U.S. leaders, he was willing to balance his
"spheres of influence" approach with invitations to European institutions to
provide peacekeeping forces and good offices on the territory of the former
Soviet Union.

CONCLUSION

When Yeltsin's initial promises lost credibility, he tried to deepen his appeal
to moderates and centrists in order to expand his coalition. His "system management" posture constituted a step back from the transformative thrust of
his comprehensive program; it represented an effort to consolidate gains. One
of his main, stated priorities now came to be the (negative) goal of isolating
the extremists and preventing communist restoration. Toward that end, he
tried to maintain his appeal to the broadest possible range of moderate forces.

---

[84] Igor Zevelev, "Russia and the Russian diasporas," *Post-Soviet Affairs,* vol. 12, no. 3 (July–
September 1996).

This choice, while rational as a means of retaining power, forced Yeltsin to present himself as a man who could manage the contradictions within both his domestic and foreign policies. It required him to demonstrate simultaneously that consolidation did not mean stasis and that continued reform did not mean a radical disruption of the lives of the people. Similarly, on the international front, he had to demonstrate that cooperation with the West did not mean capitulation and that the advancement of Russia's interests abroad would not lead the rich democracies to deny economic and political assistance to Russia. It was a precarious balance to strike. None of Yeltsin's predecessors had managed to recoup their authority and realize their policy priorities once their comprehensive programs faltered. Yeltsin kept trying, for he had a mechanism – popular reelection – that was unavailable to his predecessors. But that reelection was imperiled by a momentous decision Yeltsin had made in December 1994: the decision to invade Chechnya.

9

Yeltsin Lashes Out

The Invasion of Chechnya (December 1994)

Yeltsin's political defensiveness and his search for means to recoup lost authority were decisive determinants of the fact and timing of his decision to invade Chechnya. By late 1994 – with his personal approval ratings plummeting, the economy in a precarious state after the crash of the ruble on October 11, 1994, a hostile (albeit less powerful) Duma, charges of corruption swirling around his government, powerful centrifugal forces still asserting themselves in the regions of Russia, Western assistance and investment at a small fraction of earlier expectations, integration into Western institutions proceeding at a snail's pace, and NATO expansion on the table – Yeltsin found himself severely challenged to justify the quality of his leadership. He was very much on the defensive politically, even though he had secured popular ratification of a Constitution that, formally at least, largely shielded him from threats of impeachment or legislative vetoes of his decrees. Moreover, already in 1995, "election season" would begin in anticipation of parliamentary elections scheduled for December 1995 and presidential elections scheduled for June 1996.

It was in this context that Yeltsin tackled the Chechnya problem. His first State of the Federation address, in February 1994, was significantly entitled "The Strengthening of the Russian State."[1] A treaty relationship was struck with Tatarstan in February 1994 that gave that region within Russia an exceptional level of autonomy, far more than that accorded regions within Switzerland, Spain's Catalonia, or states within the United States. But the president

---

[1] "Poslanie Prezidenta Rossiiskoi Federatsii Federal'nomu Sobraniiu: Ob ukreplenii rossiiskogo gosudarstva. (Osnovnye napravleniia vnutrennei i vneshnei politiki.)," *Rossiiskaia gazeta*, February 25, 1994, pp. 1, 3–7.

of Chechnya would not accept the same terms; he insisted on independence from Russia and on pursuing policies that threatened Russia's internal security. In May 1994, Yeltsin gave a speech to officers of the border guards in which he proclaimed that "we will firmly defend the territorial integrity of the Russian Federation. We do not have any spare, unneeded land in Russia!"[2]

Thus, a continuing challenge to the territorial integrity of Russia accompanied a sharp decline in Yeltsin's political popularity and credibility. Unable to deliver on many of his other promises, Yeltsin apparently felt the need to demonstrate that, at a minimum, he could defend Russia's statehood. This was the promise – the authority-recouping strategy – implicit in his February and May 1994 speeches. He succeeded with respect to Tatarstan but was not successful with respect to Chechnya. First he tried negotiations; after six months of fruitless effort, they failed. Then, in summer–fall 1994, he tried covert military action. When that failed, he invaded.[3]

The first crucial variable in my reconstruction is authority maintenance: the timing of the invasion was a function of Yeltsin's declining popularity. The second variable is the nature of the issue: a potentially serious challenge to the state's integrity or security. It is this combination that explains the fact and the timing of the invasion.

This squares with the findings of a major study by Richard Ned Lebow of great-power crisis initiation in the nineteenth and twentieth centuries. Lebow found that, when a threat of international reversal coincides with a threat to regime stability or leadership authority, the threshold for risk-taking is lowered dramatically, as is the threshold for wishful thinking. This argument is consistent with considerable theoretical literature on the psychology of risk-taking, which demonstrates that acceptance of risk grows in the face of a threat of loss more than it does in the face of opportunities for gain.[4] Moreover, Lebow's findings suggest an exceptional incentive for risk-taking and wishful thinking: the threat of a *double loss* – the coincidence of an external threat to state interests and an internal threat to regime stability or leadership authority. When we apply this approach to a comparison of Khrushchev,

---

[2] Quoted in Yu. M. Baturin, A. L. Il'in, V. F. Kadatskii, V. V. Kostikov, M. A. Krasnov, A. Ya. Livshits, K. F. Nikiforov, L. G. Pikhoia, and G. A. Satarov, *Epokha Yel'tsina: Ocherki politich-eskoi istorii* (Moscow: Vagrius, 2001), p. 457.

[3] By contrast, Peter Reddaway and Dmitri Glinski (*The Tragedy of Russia's Reforms: Market Bolshevism Against Democracy* [Washington, DC: U.S. Institute of Peace, 2001], p. 439) interpret Yeltsin's rhetorical stress on "strengthening the state" as doctrinal cover for strengthening his personal grip on the machinery of the central government.

[4] Yaacov Y. I. Vertzberger, *Risk Taking and Decisionmaking* (Stanford, CA: Stanford University Press, 1998), pp. 36–7.

Brezhnev, Gorbachev, and Yeltsin, we find parallels that help us better to explain the timing of the invasion of Chechnya.

SOVIET AND POST-SOVIET COMPARISONS

If we think of Khrushchev's years in power, the Brezhnev administration, and Gorbachev's time at the helm, we find a pattern that is strikingly similar to that observed under Yeltsin. In all four cases, we witness a similar act of initiating crisis or war at an advanced stage of the leader's years in power: the Cuban Missile Crisis in 1962; the invasion of Afghanistan in December 1979; the assaults on Vilnius and Riga in January 1991;[5] and the invasion of Chechnya in December 1994.

In all four cases, we observe a leader who had built his authority with an ambitious program that promised much more than it could deliver. In all four cases, the act of violence took place shortly after the unworkability of the leader's program had become evident. In all four cases, the initiation of war or crisis took place at a time when the leader was suddenly faced with having to prevent or counter precisely what he had promised he would not let happen: an imminent challenge to fundamental state interests.

In Khrushchev's case, during the twelve months preceding the October 1962 crisis, the United States exposed Soviet strategic inferiority and implied a determination to exploit it. These revelations and U.S. policy undercut Khrushchev's optimistic claims that the correlation of forces was shifting decisively in favor of socialism. In Soviet eyes, the Kennedy administration was claiming a decisive shift in the balance of power. Khrushchev's Cuban adventure was designed to thwart the American challenge.[6]

The second half of 1979 held analogous implications for Soviet interests. The SALT II arms-control treaty was seemingly headed for defeat in the U.S. Congress. The Cuban brigade crisis (August) and American disinterest in according Moscow "most favored nation" status – despite record levels of emigration from the USSR that year – further suggested to Soviet leaders that anti-détente forces had reemerged ascendant in American politics. Worse, all this coincided with a year-long rapprochement between the United States and

---

[5] To this day, Gorbachev denies personal responsibility for this tragedy, while others claim he initiated or allowed the action. I will not enter that debate here but will instead assume the action was not taken against Gorbachev's expressed will.

[6] The best study of the crisis, which accumulates mountains of evidence leading to precisely these conclusions, is Richard Ned Lebow and Janice Stein, *We All Lost the Cold War* (Princeton, NJ: Princeton University Press, 1994).

China, which was rapidly assuming the dimensions of an anti-Soviet military relationship. And only days before the decision to invade Afghanistan was finalized, NATO announced its decision to proceed with the deployment of U.S. Pershing-2 and cruise missiles in response to the Soviet deployment of SS-20s in 1977. The mood within the Soviet political establishment at the time, sensed by Robert Legvold during a visit to Moscow in December 1979, was that it was time to "show the Americans."[7]

In 1990, Gorbachev faced the consequences of his contradictory policies as centrifugal forces within the USSR intensified greatly. Declarations of sovereignty by several republics became harbingers of separatism and secession. The Baltic republics in particular had already insisted upon full independence. Gorbachev's promise to forge a "renewed Union," with strong republics and a strong center, was encountering powerful challenge. The attacks on Vilnius and Riga took place in January 1991.

On this score, the timing of the invasion of Chechnya is analogous. Having proclaimed that 1994 would be a year for strengthening the Russian state, and with the rest of his domestic and foreign policy programs under serious challenge, Yeltsin addressed the threat from Grozny in analogous fashion: with a determination to demonstrate that he could enforce state power on the territory of Russia and thereby at least fulfill the promises associated with his fallback authority-maintenance strategy.

There is still another similarity among the cases. In all four, the leader responded to an authority crisis by narrowing or redefining the circle of his advisers and associates, or by ceding control of policy to hardliners in the leadership. Khrushchev did not consult widely about the necessity or advisability of putting missiles in Cuba. And, as his programs were exposed as failures, he became increasingly arbitrary during 1961–1962 in purging central and local officials, in circumventing the top leadership, in revealing his preferred solutions publicly, and in railroading the Presidium into accepting his schemes.

Brezhnev had neither the health nor the incentive to mimic Khrushchev's political style. But we know that the decision to invade Afghanistan was initiated and pushed by a small subset of the Politburo with very little consultation among the broader political or specialist elites. The decision was largely a product of forceful initiatives by Andropov, Ustinov, and Gromyko – respectively, the heads of the KGB, the armed forces, and the Ministry of Foreign

---

[7] Robert Legvold, "Caging the bear: Containment without confrontation," *Foreign Policy*, no. 40 (Fall 1980), p. 82.

Affairs – with strong support from Suslov (the ideological secretary of the Central Committee) and with Brezhnev's acquiescence or approval.[8]

Gorbachev initiated his famous "shift to the right" precisely four months before the January 1991 events in Vilnius and Riga. He broke with the radical democrats in September 1990 over the "500 days" plan for marketization of the economy, arguing that it would result in the collapse of the USSR. In November 1990, he co-opted hardliners into key leadership positions, fired several liberal advisers, and reorganized institutions to the advantage of the imperial "power ministries."[9] This was the context within which Eduard Shevardnadze angrily announced his resignation as Foreign Minister, only weeks before the crackdown in the Baltics.

Yeltsin's pattern of consultation during 1994 went in a similar direction. His advisors report in their memoirs and newspaper exposés that, during this year, Yeltsin narrowed the circle of his advisers to the hardline group within the Security Council that is generally considered to have been the decision-making body for the Chechnya invasion. He also drastically curtailed his earlier practice of soliciting a wide array of options and viewpoints before making his choice.[10]

The narrowing of consultative patterns, or the ceding of control of policymaking to hardliners, reinforces another attribute of at least three of these cases: wishful thinking about the feasibility or cost of heading off reversal. From all accounts, Khrushchev convinced himself that Kennedy would back down and was genuinely surprised, confounded, and frightened by Kennedy's actual reaction.[11] From all accounts, Brezhnev and his associates

---

[8] See the revealing newspaper memoir by Oleg Grinevskii, "Kak my 'brali' Afghanistan [How we 'took' Afghanistan]," *Literaturnaia gazeta*, no. 31 (August 2, 1995), p. 14. Grinevskii, who headed the Foreign Ministry's Middle East Department at the time of the invasion, presents minutes of several Politburo meetings, quotations from several participants whom he interviewed, as well as verbatim quotations of statements at the time by Foreign Minister Gromyko. His reconstruction is ambiguous as to the extent of Brezhnev's involvement, but is consistent with a view of Brezhnev as a backstage vetoer or approver of initiatives by associates in the Politburo.

[9] Gorbachev's close aide, Anatolii Chernyaev, reports that this was the point at which Gorbachev stopped soliciting the advice of his liberal advisors, consciously isolating himself from their viewpoints (A. S. Chernyaev, *Shest' let s Gorbachevym* [Moscow: "Progress," 1993], p. 401).

[10] Vyacheslav Kostikov, *Roman s prezidentom* (Moscow: Vagrius, 1997), pp. 284–5, 296–7, 303–7, 325–6; Emil Pain and Arkady Popov in *Izvestiia*, February 7–10, 1995 (article in four installments); Mark Urnov in *Segodnia*, March 22, 1995; Baturin et al., *Epokha*, pp. 598–9, 626, 635; Sergei Filatov, *Sovershenno nesekretno* (Moscow: Vagrius, 2000), pp. 236, 254; Valery Tishkov, *Ethnicity, Nationalism, and Conflict in and after the Soviet Union* (London: Sage, 1997), pp. 212–16. Most of these authors were among those who were marginalized at the time.

[11] Lebow and Stein, *We All Lost the Cold War*, p. 80.

greatly underestimated the risks and costs of sending the Red Army into Afghanistan.[12] Gorbachev's calculations in January 1991, like his decision-making involvement, were less transparent. We know he was frightened by the prospect of an uncontrolled fragmentation of the union and determined, at least in principle, to prevent it – especially in the wake of the collapse of communism in Eastern Europe in late 1989. But we also know that he was opposed to the use of force to achieve his goals. We know less about whether he believed a show of force in Vilnius, Riga, or elsewhere could reverse the centrifugal processes in motion at the time.

Yeltsin expected the invasion of Chechnya to be much smoother and cleaner than it turned out to be, in part because the Chechen opposition had come so close (with covert Russian assistance) to prevailing in November and in part because Defense Minister Grachev promised an easy victory.[13]

It is difficult to measure a subjective phenomenon like wishful thinking. But there does seem to be a pattern in our cases. Leaders on the political defensive initiate or tolerate efforts to reverse a highly adverse trend by means of a dramatic show of force. That creates a politically motivated predisposition to believe that the initiative will succeed.

A POLITICAL–COALITIONAL PERSPECTIVE

My comparison of the four cases has located patterns that transcend the unique features of each leader's personality and that also transcend differences among them in the amount of political power they had accumulated while leading the country. Of the four cases, Khrushchev and Yeltsin garnered more personal power – that is, autonomy to make choices once their authority had begun to decline – than had Brezhnev and Gorbachev. Both Khrushchev and Yeltsin made the key decisions to use force.

By contrast, Brezhnev was ill in March 1979 when Gromyko, Andropov, and Ustinov first tried to push through the Politburo a decision to intervene militarily in Afghanistan. When informed of the decision, Brezhnev vetoed it, arguing that he did not want to spoil his forthcoming summit meeting with President Carter in Vienna (in June) at which he looked forward to signing the SALT II arms-control treaty. Later that year, when prospects for improvement in U.S.–Soviet relations had dimmed, the three Politburo heavyweights

---

[12] Sarah E. Mendelsohn, *Changing Course: Ideas, Politics, and the Soviet Withdrawal from Afghanistan* (Princeton, NJ: Princeton University Press, 1998), pp. 63–4.

[13] Anatol Lieven, *Chechnya: Tombstone of Russian Power* (New Haven & London: Yale University Press, 1998), pp. 89ff.

tried again; this time Brezhnev acquiesced, perceiving little to lose. Thus, Brezhnev played the role first of vetoer and then approver, rather than initiator, of decisive action.[14]

In the case of Gorbachev, who was certainly healthy and involved in high politics, we are still not sure whether he made the final decision to use military force in the Baltics (while retaining "plausible deniability" of responsibility), allowed it to happen while pretending not to know, simply tolerated it, or was surprised by it. Although some scholars believe the answer to be fairly clear and to be consistent with Gorbachev's distaste for the use of force,[15] the record is ambiguous. And well it might be, for Gorbachev frequently dissimulated in front of his colleagues in the leadership in order to maintain plausible deniability of his responsibility if things went wrong (see Chapter 5).

If Khrushchev and Yeltsin clearly initiated action on the decision, but Brezhnev did not and Gorbachev may or may not have, how can we theorize about the nature of Soviet and post-Soviet politics in a way that would explain all four of these choices? Perhaps an authority-maintenance perspective, with its focus on an individual leader making a clear choice with an eye to shoring up his political position, is too restrictive when dealing with specific decisions by leaders who enjoyed varying degrees of personal power and accountability to a collective leadership or competing institutions. However, instead of replacing this perspective with a political–sociological or interest-based approach that denies leadership autonomy and attributes outcomes solely to impersonal institutional forces (the "military–industrial complex," the "Party apparatus," the "party of war," and the like), we can merge an approach based on ideas and choice with a political–coalitional perspective. Such a synthesis highlights both the political constituencies on which leaders base their policies and the relative autonomy of the leader from that political base.

Under Khrushchev, Brezhnev, and Gorbachev, the leader initially consolidated his power and authority by appeasing the interests of the dominant hard-line constituents: the Party–ideological apparatus and the military–industrial complex. This was true of Khrushchev in 1953–1954, of Brezhnev in 1965–1968, and of Gorbachev in 1985–1986. Once each was confident of having consolidated his position and having outflanked his rivals within the Politburo, all three men offered comprehensive programs that appealed to a wider range of constituencies than had their earlier programs. But after each of

---

[14] See Grinevskii, "Kak my 'brali' Afghanistan."
[15] Archie Brown, *The Gorbachev Factor* (Oxford & New York: Oxford University Press, 1996), pp. 279ff.

these comprehensive programs failed, each leader again contracted his coalition by selectively playing to hardliners in hopes of maintaining a political base. This is how Khrushchev behaved in domestic (economic and administrative) and foreign policy from mid-1960 through the Cuban Missile Crisis; it describes Brezhnev's realignment on domestic policy during 1973–1975; and it describes Gorbachev's behavior on domestic policy from September 1990 to April 1991. The interventions discussed here all took place during these periods of contracted political coalition and appeasement of hardline forces.

When his comprehensive program lost credibility by early 1994, Yeltsin narrowed his coalition, moving still farther in a hardline direction and relying more on the statists (*gosudarstvenniki*). This period of contraction coincided with his upgrading of state building as a priority task by which his leadership should be judged and also coincided with his redefinition of Chechnya as an urgent matter.

Thus, all four leaders met the challenges to state interests at a time when they had contracted their coalitions and advantaged hardline political constituencies. Of course, they were not simply prisoners of others who were actually in charge. The extent to which each political leader retained freedom to maneuver and relative autonomy from his political constituents varied among the four. But they shared a political field within which hardliners either had seized the initiative or were encouraged or allowed to do so. The mobilized audience for the redefined authority-maintenance strategy was a more hardline constituency than that appealed to during the middle stage of the leader's administration.

From this perspective, Brezhnev's incapacitation and Gorbachev's denial of responsibility do not invalidate my theory. Each of these two interventions was facilitated by the leader's *prior* decision to contract his political coalition and to cede some of the political initiative to hardliners.

IN SEARCH OF COVARIATION

My argument thus far draws upon three sources: (1) comparability to patterns of great-power brinksmanship in the nineteenth and twentieth centuries (as studied by Lebow) and consistency with psychological theories of risk-acceptance; (2) multiple sources of comparability to other cases of the use of force by post-Stalin Soviet leaders during analogous stages of their administrations; and (3) a specific theory of coalition maintenance in Soviet and post-Soviet politics that predicts variations in leaders' reactions to threats to state interests, depending on the fragility of their political authority at the time.

In the social sciences, few tests are definitive and conclusive. We can only add additional tests to see whether our tentative conclusions are reinforced or undermined by those tests. The next step in my analysis of the Chechnya case and its earlier analogs is the most challenging: to explore empirically whether comparable acts occurred during earlier stages of the administrations of these leaders. If such were the case then it would undermine the claim that such acts are products of the political circumstances of the stage of "decline" that follows the discrediting of the leader's program. It would require volumes of research in Soviet archives to document covariation or its absence. Some of that research is currently being conducted (and soon to be published) by scholars such as Mark Kramer, Hope Harrison, and others. For present purposes, I will just discuss some possibilities.

Soviet invasions and crisis initiation certainly had taken place during earlier stages of administrations. The invasions of Hungary (1956) and Czechoslovakia (1968) took place during the stage of political succession struggle. Khrushchev's ultimatum to the West regarding Berlin (November 1958) occurred after he had consolidated his political ascendancy. Thus, political defensiveness per se is not a prerequisite for military intervention or crisis initiation.

This counterargument is challenging. However, one could argue that the interventions in Eastern Europe were fairly predictable – both because political protest in Eastern Europe tended to intensify during periods of Soviet collective leadership and because those collective leaderships (before Gorbachev) were unprepared to "lose" Eastern Europe, defined loss of control by the Communist Party as unacceptable (with factionalization of the Party and the collapse of censorship as key indicators), and had not lost their collective will to use force.[16] Similarly, settlement of the German problem under Khrushchev, by threat and confrontation if necessary, may equally have been a matter of

---

[16] Christopher Jones argued (before Gorbachev came to power) that collapse of the "leading role of the Party" was the trigger for Soviet interventions in Eastern Europe (Christopher D. Jones, *Soviet Influence in Eastern Europe: Political Autonomy and the Warsaw Pact* [New York: Praeger, 1981]). The Soviet archives on the Hungarian and Czech invasions have been available for some years now and demonstrate that the Soviet leadership was hoping to avoid invasion and launched numerous diplomatic initiatives to avert the need. But those archives also show that Soviet leaders were determined to prevent, by one means or another, either factionalization of the Communist Party or renunciation of the Warsaw Pact. They sought to induce local authorities to regain control of the situation, by military means if necessary, and only invaded after they lost hope of such an outcome (personal communications from Professor Andrew Janos of UC Berkeley, Dr. Charles Gati of Johns Hopkins SAIS, and Professor Hope Harrison of George Washington University). In his memoir, former Politburo member Anastas Mikoyan claims that there was no need to invade Hungary in 1956, because he "had already negotiated a peaceful exit from the crisis" (*Tak bylo: Razmyshleniia o minuvshem*

substantial (though not unanimous) consensus – or deference to Khrushchev's optimism – within the leadership.[17] By contrast, military intervention of the sort employed in our four cases was less readily predictable in terms of these usual considerations and involved much less consensus within the leadership. The Cuban Missile Crisis, the invasion of Afghanistan, the assaults on Vilnius and Riga, and the invasion of Chechnya took most outside observers by surprise and were far from consensual decisions of the leadership as a whole.

Another way to look for covariation is to ask whether there were times when similar conditions of political authority existed but the response to threats to state interests was different. Put differently, were there cases during the *late* stages of administrations when such challenges occurred but the response was not to intervene?[18] The two examples that come to mind are Poland in 1980–1981 and Eastern Europe in 1989. The case of Poland hinges on whether the Politburo was willing to invade that country had General Jaruzelski refused to impose martial law. This remains a matter of contention.[19] But even if the Politburo had proved unwilling to invade Poland in 1981, this would

[Moscow: Vagrius, 1999], p. 598; my thanks to Hope Harrison for suggesting this source). See also Sergei N. Khrushchev, *Nikita Khrushchev and the Creation of a Superpower* (University Park: Pennsylvania State University Press, 2000), pp. 195–7. But Mikoyan apparently did not have many (if any) supporters for his position in the Soviet leadership, and there is no way of knowing whether the "peaceful exit" he negotiated would have slowed the revolutionary tide in Hungary. My concern is not whether there was ambivalence, uncertainty, agonizing, an urge to find peaceful exits, or selective political disagreement in the Soviet leadership; the issue is whether the leadership – in the 1950s through the 1970s – ever displayed a collective willingness to tolerate a collapse of the "leading role of the Party" in a Warsaw Pact state. The only exception to this generalization may be the archival evidence presented by Mark Kramer to the effect that, for one day (October 30, 1956), the CPSU Presidium apparently did unanimously decide to let Hungary go and become a noncommunist country. The decision was reversed the following day (Mark Kramer, "The Soviet Union and the 1956 crises in Hungary and Poland: Reassessments and new findings," *Journal of Contemporary History,* vol. 33, no. 2 [April 1998], pp. 163–215) and seems to have reflected confusion rather than loss of commitment.

[17] As claimed by Michael J. Sodaro (*Moscow, Germany and the West from Khrushchev to Gorbachev* [Ithaca, NY: Cornell University Press, 1990]) and Hannes Adomeit (*Soviet Risk-Taking and Crisis Behavior* [London & Boston: Allen & Unwin, 1982]); by contrast, Hope Harrison (personal communication) notes that Mikoyan was also a dissenter on the decision of fall 1958 (see Mikoyan, *Razmyshleniia,* p. 598). Mikoyan's memoir, however, does not indicate that he had allies on this issue.

[18] I exclude from consideration Stalin's failure to invade Yugoslavia in 1948–1949, as my theory extends only to politically competitive regimes.

[19] See Mark Kramer, "Jaruzelski, the Soviet Union, and the imposition of martial law in Poland: New light on the mystery of December 1981," *Cold War International History Project Bulletin,* no. 11 (Winter 1998). Kramer will soon publish a book on the matter, using the fullness of available archival evidence. Kramer shows that the Soviets were telling Jaruzelski that they

not necessarily refute the theory because the Soviet Union was already mired in war in Afghanistan. War on two fronts simultaneously would have been unprecedented for post-Stalinist leaders.

The second example is more challenging. Gorbachev's failure to use military force to prevent the collapse of communism in Eastern Europe and the reunification of Germany within NATO was certainly inconsistent with past Soviet patterns of behavior. The case would not undermine our theory, however, if one interpreted Gorbachev's comprehensive program of 1987–1989 as already precluding the use of force to retain control of Eastern Europe and interpreted his fallback position of 1990 as retaining the right to use force to prevent the disintegration of the USSR. Moreover, Gorbachev's political authority did not plummet until 1990 – well after the collapse of communism in Eastern Europe – and he was winning accolades abroad for not using military force.[20]

One other case of the use of force contradicts my theory. In November 1991, at an earlier stage of his administration – indeed, at a time when his authority was extremely high – Yeltsin mobilized police (MVD) forces for use against Grozny in the wake of Dudaev's coup d'etat and declaration of Chechnya's independence from (what was then called) the RSFSR. Given that Yeltsin was not then on the political defensive, we have here still another instance of lack of covariation of the first type discussed previously.

Although the case is striking in that it also concerns military intervention by Yeltsin in Chechnya, it does not challenge the theory as much as it would seem to. Yeltsin's level of commitment to this action at the time was quite low, and the action itself barely got off the ground. A fairly small contingent of MVD troops were sent to Grozny in the expectation that their very presence would restore order. The troops did not initiate action; they were unexpectedly fired upon by Chechen troops and did not escalate in response. When his parliament objected to the police action, and in the face of Chechen gunfire, Yeltsin immediately backed off and recalled the contingent – even though he

would not invade. They were telling him to take care of Solidarity on his own and that they would limit themselves to a show of force. However, had Jaruzelski not taken the advice and not cracked down, or had the crackdown gone awry, the Soviet leadership would likely have reconsidered the decision not to invade, assuming there was such a decision and it was not expressed just for its rhetorical impact on the Polish leader. My thanks to Mark Kramer (personal communication) for a synopsis of his book's argument on this point.

[20] On Gorbachev's unwillingness to use force in Eastern Europe and the path through which he came to this sentiment, see Jacques Lévesque, *The Enigma of 1989: The USSR and the Liberation of Eastern Europe* (Berkeley: University of California Press, 1997). However, Gorbachev publicly (in 1990–1991) neither advocated nor ruled out the use of force to prevent disintegration of the USSR.

had the juridical right to follow through (despite parliament's disapproval), even though his troops had been shot at, and even though his vice-president, Aleksandr Rutskoi, strenuously advocated escalation.

It is difficult to imagine Yeltsin behaving the same way once he had committed to action in November–December 1994. His determination to respond in kind to provocation, to follow through with an initiated action, and to ignore parliamentary protests in the later period stood in sharp contrast to the ease and rapidity of decommitment in the earlier period. In the meantime, Yeltsin's perceived political authority and level of political defensiveness had changed markedly.

ALTERNATIVE EXPLANATIONS FOR THE INVASION OF CHECHNYA

Let us now return to an exclusive focus on the invasion of Chechnya and consider several alternative explanations for that specific decision. To the extent that such explanations prove deficient, they increase the persuasiveness of my preferred, political explanation. The scholarly and journalistic treatment of the decision offers a range of interpretations. Some of these treat the outcome as largely inevitable, given Dudaev's unwillingness to compromise on a matter of fundamental Russian interest. Others view the outcome as far from inevitable and as largely a reflection of Yeltsin's combative personality. In between stand those who view the outcome as the product of a process of incremental commitment in which uncertainty and unanticipated consequences accumulated to the point where the leadership unwittingly stumbled into a desperate situation.

Invariant State Interests

One might simply argue that reference to domestic politics is unnecessary, since vital state interests were in question. States do not tolerate secessions, and that is what Dudaev was trying to do. Whatever the condition of Yeltsin's political authority, he would have felt the desire or need to eliminate separatism. The territorial integrity of the state and the territorial reach of state power are "first principles" for decisionmakers, whatever their levels of political legitimacy or defensiveness.

While superficially appealing, this strikes me as an overgeneralization. For one thing, this theoretical perspective is inconsistent with the peaceful dissolution of the USSR in 1991 and of Czechoslovakia in 1993. For another, it cannot explain most of the previous three years of Moscow's relations with

Chechnya before the invasion. Yeltsin's initial response to the Chechen declaration of independence in November 1991 was as this theory would have predicted: he called on Russian security forces to quell the secession. But his parliament's response did not conform to such predictions; nor did Yeltsin's quick reversal of his decision.

Thereafter, Chechnya remained on the back burner for more than two years. Dudaev continued to proclaim his republic's independence from Russia and Moscow did not press the issue, instead striking deals with other republics and regions that granted them varying degrees of autonomy short of secession. Why did Moscow essentially ignore Dudaev for so long? Perhaps because the threat from a Chechen declaration of independence was not perceived as particularly great. The international community refused to recognize it, and the Chechen authorities could not ally with other states to affirm their independence from Moscow. Many elites in Moscow considered the existing level of Chechen defiance to be quite tolerable, while others even advocated divesting Russia of the burden of holding onto a poor, small, peripheral, rebellious Muslim region. And why did Chechnya come to the fore of politics in 1994? Why did Moscow suddenly end its tolerance? Without factoring in considerations other than invariable, "objective" state interests, one cannot persuasively answer these questions. Whether the Chechnya situation was tolerable or threatening depended ultimately on subjective considerations: one's vision of Russia and, in the case of the top leaders, the extent to which one's political authority was hostage to an articulated vision.

Incremental Engagement

From this perspective, the Russian leadership was incrementally "sucked into" an ever-deepening commitment in Chechnya. Whereas the "invariant state interests" perspective eliminates contingency, the incrementalist raises contingency to a high level.

According to this viewpoint, the following facts are salient. Moscow had already (at the beginning of 1994) engaged Dudaev in intensive negotiations as part of a larger effort to develop treaty relations with the most autonomy-seeking ethnic republics. However, in contrast to the government of Tatarstan, Dudaev was unwilling to accept maximal autonomy within Russia. The negotiations lasted for about six months, at which time Moscow had the option of dropping the issue or of escalating the pressure. Moscow chose to help arm and supply the resistance to Dudaev and to engage in covert operations in an attempt to topple him – but to deny involvement if the covert operations became public. These operations almost succeeded in November 1994 but then suddenly failed at the end of that month. At that point again, Yeltsin could have dropped the issue. But the media in Moscow seized upon the issue and publicized Russian military involvement in the Chechen resistance. This publicity challenged the government to demonstrate that it could finish a job it had started and could avoid defeat at the hands of a secessionist force.

This interpretation cannot explain why, after the failure of negotiations in summer 1994, Moscow decided to escalate. What prevented Moscow from returning the issue to the back burner, where it had stood throughout 1992–1993? Why could Moscow not have continued to live with Dudaev's criminal challenges – as long as he did not engage in frontal assaults against Russian vital interests, such as sabotage of the oil pipeline or pogroms against ethnic Russian citizens of Chechnya? The argument that Chechnya had become the center of a vast criminal underworld – running arms and drugs, hijacking trains, and stealing oil and gas – may have weighed on the minds of Russian decisionmakers, all the more so because the incidence of such crimes had grown during 1991–1994. It is plausible that the growth and spread of Chechnya's intrusion on Russian economic and social interests raised the cost to Russian decisionmakers of temporizing. But it would still need to be demonstrated that the decisionmakers considered it urgent to end those challenges as soon as possible, rather than to live with and contain them or to blunt them by means that stopped short of invasion.

Similarly, after the defeat of covert operations, it is difficult to believe that the media provoked Yeltsin and his associates to do what they were otherwise disinclined to do. They could have disengaged and tried to contain the Chechnya problem; they could have blockaded the region; they could have attempted further covert operations, including perhaps further efforts to assassinate Dudaev; they could have stepped up their efforts to bolster the political opposition in anticipation of Chechen elections scheduled for October 1995. Instead, they chose to invade. Rather than blame publicity, anger, or embarrassment for their decision, I am more inclined to seek an explanation that accounts for the entire, year-long pattern of events. And while the testimony of one decisionmaker cannot necessarily be taken as definitive, it is noteworthy that Deputy Premier Nikolai Yegorov, who was Minister for Nationalities and Regional Affairs and one of the hardliners urging Yeltsin to invade, commented privately that "we now need a small victorious war, as in Haiti. We must raise the president's rating."[21]

---

[21] Valery Tishkov, *Ethnicity, Nationalism, and Conflict*, p. 218. Tishkov, an advisor to Yeltsin on nationalities issues, believes that "[t]he Chechnya crisis could have been resolved without using the army by various means and methods. Such possibilities continued to exist right up

Personality: The Need for Struggle

According to this interpretation, the invasion of Chechnya was simply a reflection of Yeltsin's personality. From this perspective, Boris Nikolaevich is predisposed to attack problems and conquer them through a titanic struggle. Chechnya was simply one in a series of such campaigns.

Certainly there is truth in the claim that the invasion was consistent with a behavioral tendency that Yeltsin displayed throughout his life. As noted in Chapter 2, his first autobiography reveals a risk-seeker who was inclined to attack problems in traditional Bolshevik fashion. The invasion of Chechnya, by this accounting, was simply Yeltsin's issue of choice in 1994 and reflected his typical way of solving problems. The extreme variant of this explanation would treat Chechnya as Yeltsin's annual dose of intense struggle, which he needed to achieve psychodynamic catharsis; had there been no Chechnya, he would have invented one.

The problem with the interpretation just outlined is that it sells Yeltsin vastly short and ignores the other side of his personality and his record of achievement. He was far more complex than a mere recitation of his most titanic struggles would suggest. His communist upbringing instilled in him a measure of prudence and pragmatism that constituted a competing set of predispositions within his personality. His experience during 1989 interacting with democrats, and with Andrei Sakharov in particular, gave him a clearer sense of what he stood *for* to supplement his sense of what he was struggling *against*.[22] His maturation included growth of tolerance for ambiguity, which often checked or competed with his authoritarian dispositions. Indeed, we have already noted many aspects of Yeltsin's policy record that reflect prudence, pragmatism, tolerance of ambiguity, and conscious avoidance of a "struggle" mentality: his efforts at nation building in Russia, his stance toward the Near Abroad, and his attempts to nurture Russian relations with the West.

Moreover, the reality of Yeltsin's personalistic urge, and the memory of his titanic struggles against opponents, should not blind us to his ability to strike a multiplicity of leadership postures depending on the context in which he was operating and the political strength of his opponent or interlocutor. I count at least "six Yeltsins" in evidence since 1987. Three of them are egocentric and inflexible; three, to varying degrees, are accommodative and interactive.

---

until December 1994" (p. 226). Tishkov is also of the opinion that "the President's principal reason [for invading Chechnya] was to bolster his own declining popularity" (p. 218).

[22] Timothy J. Colton, "Boris Yeltsin, Russia's all-thumbs democrat," in Timothy J. Colton and Robert C. Tucker (Eds.), *Patterns in Post-Soviet Leadership* (Boulder, CO: Westview, 1995), ch. 3.

In the first grouping is Yeltsin the *awesome antagonist,* who unleashed thunder on Ligachev, Gorbachev, the coup plotters, the Supreme Soviet, and Chechnya when his patience had run out or his relationship with them had reached the point of no return. There is also Yeltsin the *heroic mobilizer of the people,* who won almost 90 percent of the vote in the 1989 elections and who stood on the tank during the August 1991 coup. Then there is Yeltsin the *patriarch,* who treats his political dependents as his extended family – within which he demands obedience and dispenses absolution to those who have "sinned" – and who treats Russia as his patrimony within which he dispenses both sanctions and rewards.

In the second grouping of postures (wherein Yeltsin's autocratic tendencies are restrained or repressed) is Yeltsin the *hard but flexible bargainer,* who alternately implores, cajoles, threatens, and accommodates in order to strike deals, as in his annual struggles with the Duma over the budget. Then there is Yeltsin the *respectful, businesslike interlocutor,* a posture he adopted (when healthy and sober) in his dealings with heads of state of lesser powers over which Russia had little control: China, Eastern Europe, and small or mid-size powers elsewhere.[23] Finally, there is Yeltsin the *chummy pal,* the posture he adopted when dealing with heads of state of the G-7 nations ("my friend" Bill, Helmut, and even Ryu).

Undeniably, Yeltsin's personality played a role in his decisionmaking. Specifically, with respect to 1994, Yeltsin's sensitivity to slight made him less willing to negotiate a compromise with Dudaev. President Shaimiev of Tatarstan related the following to Valery Tishkov:

"While visiting Tatarstan in March 1994, Yeltsin told me that, in spite of not all at the Security Council agreeing with him, he was ready for talks with Dudayev on the Tatarstan model. But then suddenly the press reported (probably it was done deliberately) that Dudayev was speaking negatively of him." Apparently from that moment on, Yeltsin (undoubtedly under the influence of aides and some members of the government who were nursing the presidential ego) crossed Dudayev off the list of those with whom he could somehow communicate.[24]

Nonetheless, negotiation of a compromise is one thing; invasion is another. There were many intermediate alternatives. That Yeltsin chose the most extreme variant in December 1994 cannot be explained with reference to his personality alone.

---

[23] A subcategory of this might be *awed interlocutor,* evident in his earlier behavior when meeting with Patriarch Aleksi; for examples, see Kostikov, *Roman,* pp. 134, 240.

[24] Tishkov, *Ethnicity, Nationalism, and Conflict,* p. 187.

Power versus Authority

Still another alternative to my political interpretation would contest the extent to which Yeltsin felt himself to be politically on the defensive in 1994. We know that relations between parliament and executive during that year were far more stable than they had been during the year preceding adoption of the December 1993 Constitution, which provided for a strong presidency and a weak legislature and which formally shielded the president against easy impeachment. If Yeltsin believed in the reliability and durability of these formal arrangements, then he should not have felt himself exceptionally on the political defensive and could have faced Chechnya with a lower sense of urgency. Presumably, he could have reacted differently to the failure of negotiations with Dudaev and/or the failure of covert operations. He was in an "objectively" strong position.

This argument assumes that politics in weakly institutionalized regimes works in roughly the same way as politics in strongly institutionalized regimes. I would vigorously contest that assumption. Politics in Moscow, both Soviet and post-Soviet, was marked by unusually large measures of uncertainty about the tenure of leaders in office. Leaders constantly worried about how to insure themselves against premature political demise. In contrast to leaders in more strongly institutionalized (or constitutionalized) regimes who may seek only "minimal winning coalitions" on policy, both Soviet and post-Soviet leaders felt the need to substantially *over*insure themselves. This may explain why they all embraced programs that promised a great deal to almost everybody and hence proved impossible to fulfill. In the presence of dashed promises, the insecurity of tenure looms still larger and the leader becomes ever more sensitive to a growingly hostile or skeptical climate of opinion within the political establishment. The leader's time horizons become shorter and his threshold for risk-taking declines. As we have seen in Chapter 8, the memoir evidence supports such an interpretation of Yeltsin's mood in 1994. Even though he (unlike his predecessors) had been elected to a fixed term of office, he, like they, could never take his political security for granted. He feared extra-constitutional acts by elite actors as well as public opinion polls showing his popularity plummeting. Having based his relations with military commanders on personalistic ties, he could not take for granted their loyalty to a procedurally correct, constitutional order. Yeltsin might still have had the power, but he was losing authority – and he knew it.

A political explanation does not deny the role of personality, incremental engagement, and the magnitude of threats to state interests in decisionmakers' choices. Rather, it treats these as insufficient to explain the timing and outcome of this case or to explain variation among analogous cases. It argues that an intervening political variable – the condition of authority maintenance – may make the difference between the choice of militarized versus nonmilitarized responses to threats against state interests. For leaders on the political defensive often overreact to challenges.[25]

---

[25] Boris Yeltsin is not fond of this interpretation. In his latest memoir, he delicately expresses his dissent: "Some have claimed that I aggravated the Chechen situation in order to strengthen my own authority and make the presidential regime more brutal. But that's nonsense, total delirium!" (Boris Yeltsin, *Midnight Diaries* [New York: Public Affairs, 2000], p. 58).

Yeltsin's Many Last Hurrahs

Yeltsin invaded Chechnya in part to recoup political authority. It proved instead to be an unmitigated disaster. One year later, the parliamentary elections of December 1995 yielded a Duma that was even more dominated by radical nationalists and communists than the earlier one had been. Yeltsin's popularity plummeted to unprecedented lows: the percentage of respondents (in a public opinion poll of January 1996) who would have chosen him that day for president was in the low single digits.[1] Presidential elections loomed in June 1996, and it remained unclear whether Yeltsin could recoup his authority with the electorate sufficiently to prevail in that election.

THE PRESIDENTIAL ELECTIONS OF 1996

Yeltsin had to decide what posture to strike in the presidential election campaign. Should he try to co-opt the constituents of his opponents by running on a patriotic, hardline platform? Or should he try to differentiate himself from his opponents by mobilizing moderate and anti-communist constituencies? Initially, Yeltsin was inclined to run on a nationalistic platform as defender of the integrity of the Russian state and nation. In March 1996, however, new advisors persuaded him to switch course. He replaced his old advisory team and decided to present himself as the candidate of peace, order, stability, and progress. He decided to depict his main opponent in the election, Gennadii Ziuganov, as a totalitarian restorationist and himself as the savior of the nation from a return to Stalinism. He had killed communism and now

---

[1] *Vecherniaia Moskva,* January 24, 1996, p. 1, reports the results of a reliable opinion poll that placed Yeltsin in sixth place among prospective candidates, with 4% of respondents.

he would ensure that it stayed dead. He promised to end the war in Chechnya and opened negotiations during the election campaign itself. He used his control of governmental resources, and the support of business tycoons, to dominate the airwaves and smear his opponents. He violated campaign finance laws with impunity. He co-opted the moderate nationalist electorate by drawing General Aleksandr Lebed' into his governmental team before the second-round runoff against Ziuganov. He worked with international organizations on the timing of announcements of economic assistance to Russia. It was a brilliant and successful strategy, albeit one that was riddled with procedural violations of electoral law. As a result, Yeltsin won the election handily.[2]

In 1989–1991, Yeltsin had successfully played a polarizing political game, outbidding Gorbachev at every turn for the energies, votes, and approval of anti-establishment forces. In 1996 he also played a polarizing game, but of a different sort. He successfully defined the campaign as a choice between steady, peaceful "progress" and violent totalitarian restoration. To the extent that media manipulations allowed him to imprint this choice in the mind of the average voter, he was able to appeal to both the radical, anti-communist voters and the moderate, "median" voters who – however much alienated by Yeltsin's policies – feared totalitarian restoration more than they feared a continuation of the status quo. Whereas Yeltsin had helped to bring down communism in 1989–1991 by playing to the most revolutionary forces in society, he defended his position of power in 1996 by dominating the moderate middle of the political spectrum.

Unlike his predecessors, Yeltsin had recouped political authority. He was able to do so only because the electoral system provided a public channel for the revalidation of authority. These channels differed fundamentally from the political structures within which his predecessors had exercised leadership. Gorbachev could have gone this route in 1989 but, by the time he realized how fragile his program had become in the face of centrifugal forces, he lacked the self-confidence to test his authority by organizing a public presidential election.

Having rebuilt his shattered authority, Yeltsin faced a four-year term during which he would be expected to deliver on that promise of a stable and brighter future. In domestic policy, he stood for both stability and marked progress toward a more prosperous future; in foreign affairs, he stood both for the defense of Russia's interests as a "great power" and for cooperation with

---

[2] This summary of the presidential campaign is based on Michael McFaul, *Russia's 1996 Presidential Election: The End of Polarized Politics* (Stanford, CA: Hoover Institution, 1997).

the West. In order to deliver on the mandate of his reelection, Yeltsin had to continue managing the contradictions between his policies and the tensions in the system he had built – and to do so, this time, with better results.

But he had to do so in a much weakened physical condition. In 1995 he suffered a heart attack; several more heart seizures followed in July 1996. In November 1996, he underwent a quintuple bypass operation on his heart, followed by a lengthy bout with pneumonia. He was not able to function consistently again until February 1997. Nor would he ever be consistently healthy again. During the years leading up to his voluntary resignation on December 31, 1999, Yeltsin periodically was hospitalized with bronchitis, pneumonia, or heart troubles. He was never really healthy, but he was periodically functional. And during those periods of functionality he sought to advance the program for which he stood while ensuring that his personal grip on power was firmly maintained.

In retrospect, watching Yeltsin simultaneously pursue his contradictory goals made for high drama – with moments of tragedy, moments of heroism, and many elements of farce. Yeltsin had many "last hurrahs" as well as many embarrassments, but in the end, he had the last laugh.

THE CHANGING MEANING OF "REFORM"

After the "loans for shares" program of 1995, many sectors of the Russian economy were dominated by some 15–20 extraordinarily wealthy men who controlled the largest "financial-industrial groups" and their associated banks.[3] Close ties with high governmental officials allowed these men to siphon off huge sums from the state, including grants and loans from international organizations. Some of the names of these plutocrats are familiar to readers of Western newspapers: Boris Berezovskii, Vladimir Gusinskii, Vladimir Potanin, Pyotr Aven, Mikhail Khodorkovskii, and Rem Vyakhirev, to mention but a few. This new, crony-capitalist economy reflected a symbiosis of state and private interests that effectively re-monopolized key sectors of the economy. Some of these so-called oligarchs, in return for having bankrolled Yeltsin during the presidential election, received cabinet-level positions in Yeltsin's government. A good case has been made that the access some of these men (especially Boris Berezovskii) enjoyed during 1994–1999

---

[3] For a detailed overview, see Juliet Johnson, "Russia's emerging financial–industrial groups," *Post-Soviet Affairs*, vol. 13, no. 4 (October–December 1997).

corrupted Yeltsin's family and left him forced to choose between tolerating the corruption or cracking down on his own family.[4]

Yeltsin's government and circle of influence also included self-proclaimed "reformers" whose stated goals were to fight corruption, bolster tax collection, marketize the economy, restructure industry, and foster competition within re-monopolized sectors.[5] The men associated with this label included Yegor Gaidar, Boris Fyodorov, Anatolii Chubais, Sergei Kirienko, Boris Nemtsov, and others. Prime Minister Viktor Chernomyrdin, until he was fired in 1998, floated between the camps. Yeltsin consciously stood above the two main factions within his presidential and governmental "courts." He shifted back and forth between them and played them off against each other, reserving for himself the role of "ultimate arbiter." Both factions wanted Russia to remain open to the West, not least because the interests of both factions required continuing loans from the IMF and World Bank. Hence, they united in opposition to isolationist and revanchist forces within the parliament. But when these forces were weak or irrelevant to the circumstances of the moment, the "oligarchs" and "reformers" were, more often than not, at each other's throats.[6]

As a result of this new constellation of political forces, "radical reform" came to assume a new meaning. In 1992–1994, during Yeltsin's stage of ascendancy, it stood for a breakthrough into a new system. In 1996–1997, however, Yeltsin redefined his program to emphasize incremental progress within the contours of the new system he had constructed. In this context, "radical reform" meant specific policy measures – legalization of land ownership, improved tax collection, reduced corruption, budgetary restraint, stabilization of the ruble's exchange rate – that seemed to meet the requirements for IMF loans and that sometimes (but not always) ran counter to the entrenched material interests of the oligarchs. Because both the oligarchs and the reformers

---

[4] For the best demonstration of this process of enmeshment, see Peter Reddaway and Dmitri Glinski, *The Tragedy of Russia's Reforms: Market Bolshevism against Democracy* (Washington, DC: U.S. Institute of Peace, 2000), ch. 8.

[5] I place the word "reformers" in quotation marks because some of them allegedly used their power just to feather their own nests at the expense of the plutocrats and were not interested in reducing corruption or de-monopolizing the economy. "Oligarchs" is the term that the "reformers" applied to the plutocrats as a group. For the most forceful statement of this perspective, which targets Anatolii Chubais as the leading wolf in reformer's clothing, see Janine Wedel, *Collision and Collusion: The Strange Case of Western Aid to Eastern Europe* (New York: St. Martin's, 1998).

[6] I am grateful for this insight to Leonid Kil, a doctoral candidate in UC Berkeley's Department of Political Science.

favored IMF subsidies, one observer has even gone so far as to conclude that differences among them were staged in order to manipulate audiences in the international arena.[7]

Given the entrenchment of the oligarchs and their connection both with government officials and with organized criminal elements, reformist measures were much less likely to reshape the economic order than had the macroeconomic stabilization programs of 1992 and the privatization programs of 1992–1995. This led observers to treat Yeltsin's second term in office as principally a farce. Much as Brezhnev during his last six years in power had used progressive rhetoric while presiding over growing stagnation, so Yeltsin has been depicted as cynically mouthing all the right words while doing nothing to try to change the actual situation.[8]

While we cannot know for sure just what was on Yeltsin's mind, it is unlikely that he thought of his actions in this way. As discussed in Chapter 2, Yeltsin had always lived his life on the edge, had always been a risk-*seeker,* possessed a sense of his own predestination to lead his country toward the promised land,[9] detested Brezhnev's period of stagnation, and loathed Gorbachev's "half-measures." He was unlikely to have settled for simply hanging onto power and presiding over systemic stagnation and personal decrepitude. True, he was tired and unhealthy in his last years. But he had also been tired and ill when he decided to run for a second term as president. Nor was he in it for the money; personal material possessions seem never to have motivated this man. In his own mind, and to judge by the rhetoric of his presidential campaign, he still viewed himself as both the guarantor against communist restoration and the guide to a progressive future.[10]

---

[7] See Jerry F. Hough, *The Logic of Economic Reform in Yeltsin's Russia* (Washington, DC: Brookings Institution, 2001).

[8] This too is a theme in Hough, *The Logic of Economic Reform,* as also in Reddaway and Glinski, *The Tragedy of Russia's Reforms.*

[9] Boris Yeltsin, *The Struggle for Russia,* trans. by Catherine A. Fitzpatrick (New York: Random House, 1994), pp. 84, 197; Boris Yeltsin, *Against the Grain: An Autobiography,* trans. by Michael Glenny (New York: Summit, 1990), p. 19. For additional examples by associates and observers, see Valentin Fyodorov, *Bez tsenzury: Yel'tsin* (Moscow: "Golos," 1995), p. 58, and Lev Sukhanov, *Tri goda s Yel'tsinym* (Riga: "Vaga," 1992), p. 225.

[10] For examples, see ITAR-TASS in English, March 6, 1996 (FBIS-SOV-96-045, p. 24); Moscow Russian Television Network, April 6, 1996 (FBIS-SOV-96-068, p. 22, 25, 26); *Rossiiskie vesti,* April 30, 1996 (FBIS-SOV-96-084, p. 26); Moscow Russian Public Television First Channel Network, May 19, 1996 (FBIS-SOV-96-098, p. 5). His self-image as guarantor against communist restoration is a repeated theme also in his last memoir (Boris Yeltsin, *Midnight Diaries* [New York, Public Affairs, 2000], pp. 17, 24, 187, 211–13, 218, 240, 268, 333). These memoirs are largely self-serving and cannot be used to validate claims about what happened and why. But, as with most documents of this sort, they can be useful for what they reveal about

This should not surprise us; leaders tend to develop a self-image and a vision of some sort. Yeltsin once viewed and presented himself as a great revolutionary and then as a great system builder. He was probably not aware of the limits of his ability to change the structure of interests after 1995. But he had campaigned for reelection on a platform of both stability and progress, albeit within the system that he had built. His pattern of observable behavior in 1997–1998 can be viewed as that of a confused but determined leader who was trying to deliver on that promise – but who had only a limited understanding of policy and a narrow repertoire of intuitive responses to frustration.

At the same time, Yeltsin was a political animal operating within a weakly institutionalized system. He could not assume that he was safe from removal from office just because he had revalidated his power in a public election. Nor could he assume that retirement would be a pleasant experience if he could still be prosecuted in court for crimes allegedly committed while president. Hence, during his heart surgery, he relinquished control over the "nuclear button" to Prime Minister Chernomyrdin. But one of his first acts after regaining consciousness was to retake control of that button and to reaffirm that an Acting President was no longer needed; another was to fire Aleksandr Lebed', his national security advisor. In sum, Yeltsin's entire second term was preoccupied both with the management of policy dilemmas and with the protection of his personal political security.

Following his exit from the hospital in early 1997 after a bout with pneumonia, the rest of Yeltsin's second term can be divided into two periods that are separated by the August 1998 financial crash. During the first period, Yeltsin pursued policies that balanced "forward movement" with stability. During the second period (September 1998 through December 1999), he focused principally on maintaining stability, largely conceded his ineffectuality at further reforming the system, and intensified the search for a personal exit strategy. In the wake of the financial crash, threats to his personal security escalated: threats of impeachment, forced retirement, and prosecution of him and his family for corruption. Yeltsin's exit strategy sought to maintain social stability while creating the political conditions that would ensure him a dignified retirement and immunity from prosecution.

---

underlying assumptions or perspectives of the author and about what he most wants to be remembered for. In addition, they can be taken at face value when they reveal facts that are unflattering to the author, as when Yeltsin revealed that he almost canceled the presidential elections and almost banned the Communist Party in 1996 (ibid., pp. 24–5) or that he became alcohol-dependent in 1994–1995 (ibid., pp. 318–19). Even though Yeltsin did not write this memoir (or earlier ones) himself, we have every reason to believe that his ghost-writer, Valentin Yumashev, was keenly attuned to how Yeltsin wanted himself depicted.

BALANCING STABILITY AND REFORM, FEBRUARY 1997—AUGUST 1998

During fall 1996, Yeltsin's incapacitation led prominent politicians to start positioning themselves for another presidential race. Aleksandr Lebed', Gennadii Ziuganov, and others spoke publicly as if the demise of the president were imminent. The political atmosphere seemed to recapitulate the extremist rhetoric of the first round of the 1996 presidential election. Thus, Lebed and Ziuganov publicly called upon Yeltsin to resign. Both of them spoke in apocalyptic terms about prospective labor unrest, mutiny in the armed forces, confrontation with Ukraine, and U.S. intentions vis-à-vis Russia.[11] Another would-be presidential aspirant, Moscow Mayor Yuri Luzhkov, joined the fray as well, making highly provocative declarations about Russia's rights in Crimea.[12] The cat was away and the mice did play, spurred by a combination of ambition and incentives built into the electoral system: the requirement of a new presidential election within 90 days after the death or incapacitation of the president.

When Yeltsin recovered from heart surgery and pneumonia, he came out swinging. He seemed determined to demonstrate that he was in charge and capable of energizing the system and overcoming sources of stagnation. At his annual State of the Federation speech to parliament on March 6, 1997, the BBC observer noted that "the president looked quite well and his voice was strong. He walked unaided and quite briskly to the lectern and delivered the address standing."[13] The speech was hard-hitting; it conceded a host of problems, declared that the "people's patience is at breaking point," and blamed corrupt, privileged "authorities" and "high-ranking officials" – indeed, everybody but himself – for the crisis. He announced that he was about to replace high-ranking governmental officials with "competent and energetic people." And he proclaimed that he was taking some of these matters under his personal control. Taxes needed to be collected, corruption attacked, privileges rescinded, pensions and wages paid on time, social services improved – a litany of formidable tasks.

---

[11] Moscow television stations NTV and RTR, August 5, 1996; *Izvestiia*, September 7, 1996; ITAR-TASS, September 9, October 1, and October 14, 1996; ORT (television), October 8, 1996; *Vecherniaia Moskva*, September 25, 1996; *Flag Rodiny*, October 5, 1996. Sources were located through a Lexis-Nexis Internet search.

[12] *Izvestiia*, October 3, 1996.

[13] "BBC Summary of World Broadcasts," March 7, 1997; a group of former Yeltsin advisors and governmental officials writes that the president's double recovery – first from heart surgery and then from pneumonia – "gave him an illusion of a return to former form" (Yu. M. Baturin, A. L. Il'in, V. F. Kadatskii, V. V. Kostikov, M. A. Krasnov, A. Ya. Livshits, K. F. Nikiforov, L. G. Pikhoia, and G. A. Satarov, *Epokha Yel'tsina: Ocherki politicheskoi istorii* [Moscow: Vagrius, 2001], p. 732).

As a link to his identity as a system builder, Yeltsin referred to many of these policy changes as "reform": tax reform; reforms to the pension system; reform of housing and municipal services; military reform; reforming the social sphere. But the solutions he proposed were largely within-system policy changes, and they were largely statements of aspiration, not strategies for overcoming the constraints on change presented by the existing configuration of bureaucratic, economic, and political power. The main strategy was to replace slothful officials ("[t]he fundamental causes of our problems lie here") and to "impose order." He ended his speech with the anodyne declaration: "together we shall introduce order – order in Russia, for Russia, for the sake of Russia."[14]

Within days, Yeltsin shook up the highest reaches of his government. He brought back Anatolii Chubais and brought in Boris Nemtsov, a reformist young governor of the Nizhnii Novgorod region; each man was given the title of "first deputy prime minister." He fired the minister of agriculture and the minister of energy, both of whom had been close to Prime Minister Chernoymrdin. He also replaced the minister of defense. Chubais and Nemtsov, in the name of radical "reform," began an assault on some of the oligarchs – though not on the oligarch (Vladimir Potanin) most closely allied with Chubais himself. Prime Minister Chernomyrdin, often viewed as a protector of the oligarchs because of his close ties to the energy–export lobby, was being counterbalanced by a powerful alliance of actors whose main goals did not include protecting Chernomyrdin's favored oligarchs.

The struggle continued throughout 1997 with gains for both sides. Yeltsin stood largely above the fray, allowing the contending forces to battle it out and playing them off against each other. This suited his purposes as ultimate arbiter, and it did not seem to be inhibiting economic progress, for 1997 was marked by a relatively stable economic situation and the first signs of an economic turnaround. Yet by late December, Prime Minister Chernomyrdin had reasserted his power within the government and had re-established himself as the main pacemaker of Russia's economic policy. He convinced Yeltsin to relieve Chubais and Nemtsov of their portfolios as minister of finance and minister of energy and fuel (respectively), even as they remained in the cabinet.

The growth statistics of 1997 were deceptive, however, and signs were accumulating of impending economic and political crises. Even in his unhealthy state, Yeltsin surely was aware that some oligarchs were claiming publicly to be more powerful than the political leadership. Nor could he have been oblivious to the fact that his rhetorical calls for increasing the autonomy of the

---

[14] Yeltsin later wrote of this speech: "It was time to bring order to the government and elsewhere. I would impose it. The government had proven that it was unable to work without being shouted at by the president" (Yeltsin, *Midnight Diaries*, p. 74).

state from the tycoons, to increase tax collection, and to effect a transition from "oligarchic capitalism" to something called "people's capitalism" were having little practical effect.[15] By March 1998, he must have known that the previous year's successes in paying wages had been reversed and that arrears were piling up again. He was certainly informed that worker protests were planned for April 9 and that communist and nationalist parties would try to use that day's events to build momentum toward the parliamentary elections of 1999 and presidential election of the year 2000. In fact, the Duma was planning a vote of "no confidence" in his government. The collapse of oil prices, along with the spread to Russian stock markets of the "Asian flu," only exacerbated economic woes and threatened to reverse progress toward an economic turnaround.

Yeltsin did not need to understand all the complexities; he needed only to sense a trend that held ominous economic and political implications. When younger and healthier, Yeltsin the decisionmaker had combined political intuition with complex calculation. Now that he was older and less healthy, the intuitive sense remained even as the calculative faculties declined. Yeltsin sensed during the first months of 1998 that things were no longer going as he had planned. In his State of the Federation address of February 17, 1998,[16] he acknowledged improvements in the rate of economic growth but reiterated many of the downbeat themes of his 1997 address, demanding that the government "put a stop to the rise in nonpayments" and warning ominously that "[i]f the government is unable to accomplish these strategic tasks, we shall have a different government."

Under analogous circumstances in the past, Yeltsin had typically kept his own counsel and, after a period of either despondency or calculated personal absence, returned with a plan to re-seize the initiative. That is what happened in March 1998. Out of public view for many weeks,[17] he returned with the surprise announcement that he was dismissing the top governmental figures charged with economic administration: Chubais; Anatolii Kulikov, head of the tax police; and, most strikingly, Viktor Chernomyrdin himself, the veteran prime minister. With such an abrupt and complete housecleaning, Yeltsin presumably hoped to demonstrate that he was still in charge and to be feared; presumably he hoped also to build a new team and new policies that were geared toward breaking the stalemate in economic administration and

---

[15] See his speech of September 24, 1997, in which he called for the transfer of state revenues to a soon-to-be-established state bank as a means of reducing the dependence of the state on the tycoons (*Rossiiskie vesti*, September 25, 1997).

[16] BBC Worldwide Monitoring, Former Soviet Union – Political, February 17, 1998, Internet edition, "Yeltsin warns government must reduce public indebtedness or be replaced."

[17] According to *The New York Times*, March 24, 1998.

delivering on his claim of pushing history forward with more vigorous "reformist" policies. Or at least that is the image he tried to project in public.[18]

To replace Chernomyrdin, Yeltsin tapped Sergei Kirienko, the deputy minister of fuel and energy. Kirienko had several traits to recommend him: he was professional, knowledgeable about Russia's macroeconomic situation, forthright, pragmatic, and willing to claim that he knew what was needed to rescue the economy from renewed stagnation.[19] Moreover, Kirienko was young (only 36 years old), had been successful in building his own business (thus he understood both the old and the new systems), and was from the provinces (thus, not yet under the thumb of any of the Moscow-based oligarchs). Kirienko was a protégé of First Deputy Prime Minister Nemtsov but still too young and lacking in stature to threaten the president politically; hence, he was likely to prove both capable and politically deferential. In Kirienko, Yeltsin appeared to have found an intelligent, loyal, energetic, professional technocrat who was willing and ready to play by the political rules set by the president and capable of perhaps attaining positive economic results. He could instill fresh energy into an increasingly stagnant governing regime and possibly prepare it for the major political tests of 1999–2000.[20] And he could do all this without pretending to force the Russian president into early retirement. Thus, Yeltsin made a choice that seemed simultaneously to advance his political power and economic policy goals. The choice certainly appeared to fit with his electoral mandate to combine economic progress with social stability.

Moreover, Yeltsin was prepared to run genuine political risks in order to ensure Kirienko's ratification by the Duma. It took him a full month to prevail – and then only on the third and final vote. Yeltsin alternately threatened, cajoled, sweet-talked, co-opted, and bribed members of the parliament to comply with his choice. After losing on the first two votes, he could have proposed an alternate candidate. But he decided instead to play a game of brinksmanship, daring the Duma to reject his candidate a third time and thereby bring about its dissolution and early parliamentary elections. This was as much a threat to Yeltsin as it was to the Duma, for the Russian president – scorned again in popularity polls – had to fear that new elections would return a parliament still more hostile than the present one. Nonetheless, Yeltsin stuck with Kirienko, made very few policy or personnel concessions to the opposition in the Duma, and ultimately prevailed. Kirienko formed a cabinet of

---

[18] Baturin et al. (*Epokha*, pp. 732, 795) argue that Yeltsin was motivated by a sense of mission, wanting to go down in history as a successful reformer.

[19] On these points, see D. Gornostaev in *Nezavisimaia gazeta*, March 27, 1998, pp. 1–2; see also Yeltsin's discussion of Kirienko in *Midnight Diaries*, pp. 103–14.

[20] For further evidence on these points, see Ye. Grigorieva in *Nezavisimaia gazeta*, April 8, 1998, pp. 1, 3.

economic officials who were primarily young technocrats drawn largely from the provinces. Yeltsin's "coup" of March–April 1998 had been successful. He had reasserted and enhanced his power, re-seized the initiative, and installed a government that held hope of breaking through some of the constraints on economic progress.

Little did Yeltsin know, however, that he had only bought himself a few months' respite.

BALANCING STABILITY AND PERSONAL POWER: AUGUST 1998–DECEMBER 1999

In the first years of his second term as president, Yeltsin sought to combine political stability, personal power, and economic progress. In the last year and a half before his resignation, he tried to ensure stability and personal power while seeking immunity from prosecution after his retirement from office. This search for personal protection dovetailed with Yeltsin's concern for social stability. If a "social explosion" occurred, it might well sweep Yeltsin away. The search for immunity also dovetailed with his self-image as guarantor against communist restoration, for no guarantee of immunity would be worth the paper on which it was written if the communists won the parliamentary and presidential elections of 1999–2000. What Yeltsin dropped from his priorities during this period was the earlier focus on economic progress. This omission was a circumstantial product of the August 1998 financial crash, which displayed the hollowness of the economic system Yeltsin had created and which discredited the "oligarchs" and "radical reformers" alike. Having no idea how to correct the economic situation, Yeltsin concentrated on finding a governmental team that would re-create some modicum of economic and political stability while protecting him from the impeachment threats and charges of corruption that were accumulating around him.[21]

Yeltsin's renewed focus on "stability" led him to fire Kirienko after the August financial crisis and to call back Chernomyrdin.[22] Twice, Yeltsin nominated Chernomyrdin to be prime minister; twice, the Duma rejected the

[21] Baturin et al. (*Epokha*, p. 778) argue that, whereas Yeltsin had been driven by a reformist mission before August 1998, thereafter he was dedicated fully to the search for a successor.

[22] In *Midnight Diaries* (pp. 176, 181) Yeltsin claims that he saw in Chernomyrdin a "heavyweight" who could engineer the compromises that would stabilize the situation. Yeltsin had argued that a younger generation was needed to push history forward when he explained his firing of the cabinet in March 1998 and its replacement with a new team of young reformers, led by 36-year-old Sergei Kirienko (*Komsomol'skaia pravda*, April 1, 1998). When this renewed, "breakthrough" strategy led instead to the crash of the ruble in August 1998, Yeltsin tried to go back to an emphasis on social stability. His nomination of Chernomyrdin for this

nomination. Earlier in 1998, when he nominated Kirienko, Yeltsin had been willing to play brinksmanship with the Duma; this time, he lost his nerve. For the third nomination, he begrudgingly proposed Foreign Minister Yevgenii Primakov, whose professionalism gave him an aura of competence to handle the job, whose efforts to assert Russia's "national interests" made him acceptable to the nationalists in the Duma, and whose background in the Communist Party (along with his experience in the security services) made him acceptable to many communist parliamentarians.[23]

Yeltsin's nomination of Primakov – and the Duma's enthusiastic approval – meant that the Russian president had lost the political initiative. But at least Primakov might be able to figure out some way to stabilize the reeling financial system, and he might use his contacts abroad to help Russia secure continuing Western assistance. Equally important, Primakov might prove capable of inducing Yeltsin's antagonists in the Duma to withdraw their impeachment resolutions, end their corruption investigations against Yeltsin's family, and grant the Russian president blanket immunity from prosecution after his retirement.

Primakov labored for more than half a year as prime minister, attempting with some success to stabilize the domestic situation but without much progress toward guaranteeing Yeltsin's political security. The political temperature rose both at home and abroad. NATO bombed Serbia, despite Russia's objections, shortly after NATO had admitted three East European states to membership – also despite Russia's displeasure. Yeltsin's economic program at home was in shambles, his relations with the West were at a low point, and his personal political security was again threatened. How would he deal with the fact that his authority had plummeted ever further and his power was increasingly under threat?

In April 1999, Yeltsin delivered his annual State of the Federation address. This was a short, disjointed, somewhat incoherent, and decidedly defensive statement.[24] He began by denying the importance of the foreign policy setbacks. He attempted to dismiss them in a few sentences, making a virtue of necessity and stressing instead his role as a beacon of stability:

purpose squares with the pattern of discussion in his 1994 memoir (*The Struggle*, pp. 126–7, 155, 168, 169, 200–1, 222–3), where young cadres are praised for their contributions to transformative goals while "experienced" cadres are praised (and recruited) for their contributions to consolidative goals: efficiency and the maintenance of social stability.

[23] One can well understand Primakov's appeal to a wide range of oppositional and establishment forces by reading his memoir (Yevgenii Primakov, *Gody v bol'shoi politike* [Moscow: Sovershenno sekretno, 1999]).

[24] East European Press Service, Russian Political Monitor, April 2, 1999, Internet edition, "Text of Yeltsin's address to the federal assembly."

Russia has made its choice. We will not allow anybody to drag us into an armed conflict. Preventing schisms and discord within the country is our number one task. Of course Russians worry about Yugoslavia, but they worry about their own country even more. Our prestige in the international arena depends on how effectively we solve our own problems.

What really matters, he argued, is the maintenance of order, stability, and security for all, himself included: "order in the corridors of power is needed, as is consent and stability in the economy and the social sphere." But some people were seeking to undermine these conditions: "Some irresponsible and nervous statements are being made. People in the corridors of power are not hiding their irritation with one another."

Yeltsin then tried to diminish the claim that August 1998 had proven the complete bankruptcy of his leadership. But he was clearly on the defensive about this: "August 17 is the only thing that everybody chooses to remember. But there was July before that, wasn't there? A hot month, when the government adopted an anti-crisis program and the International Monetary Fund resolved to give us the first installment of the loan." Then he shifted the blame, suggesting that the August crash might have been averted had the Duma itself acted more responsibly: "The Duma rejected the [anti-crisis] program, and neither Kirienko's government nor I were able to defend it. The Duma sent a bad signal to investors."

Having disclaimed personal responsibility, Yeltsin then shifted to Primakov the responsibility for resolving the current dilemma: "Primakov's government has to take ... decisive steps now." Those steps could not include ceding the initiative to revanchist policymakers. Indeed, Yeltsin resurrected the revanchist spectre with which he had ridden to victory in the 1996 presidential election. He spoke of "enemies of reform" whose "ideas are old," who embrace a "program of revenge," and who "are still calling for directives and plans in the economy, for censorship in media, and for another round of the Cold War and refusal to integrate into the global economy ...." He declared that "another round of centralization would only wreck fragile market institutions." He averred that "[w]e have to prevent the opposition from acting without regard for the law" and from pushing the "swinging pendulum ... into the danger zone."

After resurrecting this binary opposition between the forces of good and evil, Yeltsin declared that he would entertain no amendments to the Constitution before new elections to the Duma were held in December 1999. He thereby undercut a process that Primakov was trying to orchestrate behind the scenes: constitutional amendments to reduce the powers of the presidency in exchange for an end to impeachment proceedings and a grant of immunity to the president. Moreover, Yeltsin ominously proceeded to predict the results of the December parliamentary elections, declaring that a new, younger political elite would assume power to lead the country forward: "the new Duma will consist of decent and uncorrupt people – not professional patriots but patriotic professionals .... Let's give them a chance to decide for themselves whether or not amendments [to the Constitution] are needed." Such a prediction might have been the rhetoric of a democratic politician seeking to create a bandwagon effect. More likely, they were the statements of a leader who was trying to intimidate both the opposition and regional governors by implying that he might rig the elections.

Primakov was on notice: stabilize the economic situation, deliver Western assistance, and get the parliament to rescind its impeachment resolutions. Moreover, he had to do so without promising constitutional amendments to the parliamentary opposition. Primakov was given little time to deliver and probably could not have done so in any case. A familiar pattern therefore repeated itself: very shortly after his March 1997 State of the Federation speech, Yeltsin had reshuffled the government. In the month following his February 1998 speech, he had fired Chernomyrdin. True to form, a month after his April 1999 address, Yeltsin fired Primakov. Whereas he had caved in to parliamentary opposition in September 1998 – when he had accepted Primakov rather than force a third vote on Chernomyrdin – he was now, more characteristically, ready to rumble. He nominated Sergei Stepashin, former head of the Interior Ministry, to replace Primakov. Yeltsin all but dared the Duma to defy him.

The rhetorical heat in Moscow intensified immediately. Outraged parliamentarians expressed their indignation at the firing of Primakov and vowed that Stepashin's nomination would never be ratified. Their rhetoric proved to be a poor predictor of their own behavior. By nominating Stepashin, who symbolized the security agencies, Yeltsin was signaling his possible willingness to resort to force or declare a state of emergency should the nomination fail on all three votes. He was clearly signaling that he would not back down on the third vote, as he had in September 1998. He would dissolve the Duma and force early parliamentary elections, which might or might not change the political balance within the Duma but could certainly deprive many incumbents of their seats and privileges. All this was in the spirit of his speech a month earlier, which must have added credibility to his threats. In the end he prevailed, intimidating the Duma into ratifying his nominee.[25]

---

[25] Circumstantial support for the proposition that Yeltsin was seeking, after August 1999, primarily to combine economic stabilization with personal political protection can be found in

Stepashin lasted but a few months. He labored valiantly at home and abroad to stabilize the economy and deliver Western economic assistance. But in August 1999, Yeltsin struck again, suddenly replacing Stepashin with an even more shadowy figure, Vladimir Putin, then a 46-year-old former KGB spy who was a seemingly loyal member of the national security establishment within Yeltsin's presidential circle. Yeltsin declared that Putin represented a new generation of leaders and would likely succeed Yeltsin as president when new elections were held in June 2000. A weary Duma narrowly ratified Putin's nomination on the first ballot on August 16, 1999. Why force early elections when the regularly scheduled elections were coming up within four months?

YELTSIN'S VERY LAST HURRAH

During summer 1999, the level of tension in southern Russia escalated rapidly. Armed incursions into neighboring Dagestan by militant Chechen forces threatened to destabilize that multi-ethnic (but largely Islamic) republic of the Russian Federation. Indeed, some Chechen leaders proclaimed their intention to establish an Islamic state within Dagestan. The Russian army, working with local police forces of Dagestan, tried to beat back these incursions. Then apartment buildings began to explode in Moscow, claiming the lives of some 300 Muscovites and terrorizing the city. We do not know who set those explosives. Was it the work of Chechen terrorists, seeking to demoralize the Russian people and to exact revenge for Russia's military reaction to the events in Dagestan? Or was this a provocation by Russia's national-security establishment, intended to create the political pretext for a renewed invasion of Chechnya?

Whatever the case, Yeltsin and Putin cited the explosions as rationales for reinvading Chechnya *en masse*. Perhaps this was a "normal," consensual reaction to provocation or setback in an area of vital interest. More likely, the second war in Chechnya was as "political" as the first. Putin embraced nationalist rhetoric and presented himself as the sponsor of the effort ("we will wipe them out in their outhouses"). A fledgling pro-government political coalition called "Unity" was quickly formed to compete in the parliamentary elections in December. There was little content to the party's program except patriotic (though not ethnically chauvinist) discourse, boilerplate statism, and revenge against the Chechen terrorists. The government unleashed a devastating and

Midnight Diaries, where Yeltsin interprets Primakov as in tacit alliance with nefarious forces to gain power and destroy presidential rule (pp. 202–5, 211–13, 218, 268) and where Yeltsin interprets Mayor Luzhkov's actions in analogous fashion (pp. 227, 229–31, 244, 290ff.).

relentless assault on Chechen guerrillas and civilians by Russian airpower, artillery, and ground troops.

The political strategy worked. Through a combination of electoral fraud and genuine appeal to a frustrated electorate that was seeking strong leadership, "Unity" garnered 23.8 percent of the party-list votes for the new Duma, largely at the expense of a coalition led by former prime minister Primakov and Moscow mayor Luzhkov. Yeltsin and Putin were elated. In a televised spot, Yeltsin congratulated Putin and excitedly praised the Russian people for their wisdom.[26]

The vote took place on December 19, 1999. In the days following, Yeltsin pondered the implications and reached the decision to resign. He announced it to a surprised nation in his New Year's Eve address. It was a brilliant stroke. He had been proclaiming for years that he would serve out his full term and be the first freely elected president of his country to turn over power peacefully to his successor. He had been predicting that the communists would not succeed him and that he would retire as the successful guarantor of the country against communist restoration, though he never made clear just how he intended to ensure this. Undoubtedly, Yeltsin's self-image as a state builder inclined him toward realizing this vision; ideally, he would have preferred to serve out his term. But after August 1998, a higher priority arose: that of guaranteeing his personal security – and that of his family – after retirement. The tug between the idealist goals and Yeltsin's personal security was real, but he was not about to sacrifice the latter in pursuit of the former.

The results of the parliamentary elections, together with public opinion polls showing that Putin's popularity was high and rising, shaped the timing of Yeltsin's resignation. By resigning at the end of December, Yeltsin forced new presidential elections within 90 days – a constitutional requirement. Putin's popularity would not likely plummet within three months. By contrast, waiting until June to hold elections might provide time for military setbacks to take place in Chechnya and for the electorate to reconsider its support for Putin. Moreover, Putin was more likely than any of his prime ministerial predecessors to pave the way for Yeltsin to live a secure and comfortable retirement.

Putin did not disappoint him. His first act as Acting President was to grant Boris Yeltsin lifetime immunity from prosecution. The scramble to succeed Yeltsin began, but the outcome looked to be a foregone conclusion. Yeltsin had had the last laugh. As things looked to him on the eve of the new millennium,

---

[26] ORT television carried their joint appearance from the Kremlin on Wednesday, December 22, 1999, three days after the Duma elections (Interfax, December 22, 1999).

he had outmaneuvered his opponents, secured his personal future, prevented communist restoration, built a new system, maintained the territorial unity of Russia, and sustained the vision of integrating Russia into the global capitalist economy. The cost to the country may have been enormous, for which he apologized in his resignation speech.[27] But the alternative, he continued to argue, would have been worse.

CONCLUSION

Yeltsin's second term as Russia's president looks, in retrospect, like a string of initiatives geared toward keeping political opponents and political allies continuously off-balance. This image, in turns, leads one easily to the conclusion that all Yeltsin was interested in was maintaining power. However, as I have argued throughout this book, that is a shortsighted way of thinking about politics, for politicians usually have more on their minds than just power maintenance. The temptation to conclude that power is all that matters is still greater when we observe leaders on the political defensive. They tend to pay more attention to shifting their political alliances or firing would-be rivals during that last stage than during their stage of ascendancy. It is worth recalling, for example, that Khrushchev launched continuous purges of high-level personnel throughout the third stage of his administration. Both Brezhnev and Gorbachev also mimicked this pattern. Yeltsin was no exception. It may be difficult to think back past the image of Yeltsin as a doddering old man engaged in Byzantine political maneuvers. But when we think of the length and breadth of his political strategies from 1985 to the present, we see a man who developed a series of ambitious policy programs on which he staked his political authority – and in which he presumably invested his political identity. By 1996, he was probably a spent force as a transformational leader.[28] Even so, he continued to try (when he had the energy) to combine a larger policy project with a strategy of undercutting actual and potential political rivals. Only after August 1998 did he strike the appearance of a leader whose almost sole concern was for his personal political security.

---

[27] For an English translation of the resignation speech, see Yeltsin, *Midnight Diaries*, pp. 386–7.
[28] For lengthy argumentation of this point, see Reddaway and Glinski, *The Tragedy of Russia's Reforms*, chs. 8–9.

11

Explaining Leaders' Choices, 1985–1999

The main purpose of this book has been to identify Gorbachev's and Yeltsin's evolving strategies for building, maintaining, and recouping their authority as leaders. In the present chapter, I turn from description and analysis to explanation. Why did Gorbachev and Yeltsin choose these strategies at each stage of their administrations? That these two men occupy center stage in the book should not lead us to assume that their personalities and personal beliefs were always the primary – much less, sole – determinants of their choices. Other factors delimited and shaped their behavior at given points in time: (1) the political organization of the regime and the interests that dominated within it; (2) the regime's ideological traditions and legitimizing credos; (3) the prevailing climate of opinion within the political establishment; (4) the process of political competition for power and authority among elite actors; (5) mobilized social forces within the country; and (6) direct and indirect pressures from abroad.

When Khrushchev and Brezhnev were in power, these factors were relatively limited, stable, and predictable. Politics was a private affair and was dominated by the political and organizational interests of the Party–State apparatus and the budgetary interests of the military–industrial complex. Marxism–Leninism's hostility to liberalism defined the limits of winnable political advocacy. Political competition for power and authority took place within the narrow confines dictated by the political organization and ideological anti-liberalism. Social forces within the country were dominated by the Party–State apparatus; they could affect indirectly the climate of opinion within the political elite but could not mobilize autonomously against that elite. Pressures from abroad could influence individual decisions and the

stability of political coalitions in Moscow.[1] But the influence of foreign governments on Soviet policy choices was limited by Soviet determination to avoid
dependency on global capitalism and to lead an alternative, autonomous
world system: the "socialist international division of labor" and the "world
communist movement."[2] It remains an open historical question as to whether
the trajectory of Soviet policies at home and abroad would have been different
had U.S. policies been different at key turning points in superpower relations.
But it is striking how much greater was the impact of direct and indirect
international pressures on Gorbachev and Yeltsin than on Khrushchev and
Brezhnev.

The influence of many of these factors grew dramatically as Gorbachev's
radical policies took effect. As traditional Soviet organization and ideology
crumbled, the influence of autonomous social forces, direct and indirect international pressures, new rules of political competition, and new political
actors rose sharply. This was a fluid field. The old constraints were not
immediately replaced by new constraints of a different kind. Social and international forces did not immediately rush in to replace Soviet ideology and
organization. Rather, the period from 1987–1993 was one in which many
things were possible. This is the point at which the personalities and beliefs
of Gorbachev and Yeltsin loom large in any explanation of choices – more so
than had been the case with Khrushchev and Brezhnev. For as the structures
of Soviet rule disintegrated, leaders had greater latitude to act as they wished.
Yet these two leaders also played major roles in causing those structures to
crumble in the first place.

Personality and individual beliefs played larger roles at some stages of administration than at others. Soviet organization and ideology, for example,
continued to shape Gorbachev's behavior in the early years of his administration. His personality and personal beliefs played a more decisive role in the
middle stage of his administration. Social forces and direct international pressures played a greater role in the last stage of his administration. Yeltsin exploited, encouraged, and selectively channeled those social forces to assist his
rise to power. Subsequently, Yeltsin's personality and personal beliefs shaped
the choices he made in response to domestic and international pressures

---

[1] See Jack Snyder, "International leverage on Soviet domestic change," *World Politics,* vol. 42,
no. 1 (October 1989), pp. 1–30. For tests of the impact of international events on turning
points in Soviet politics and policy during 1953–1966, see James Richter, *Khrushchev's Double
Bind* (Ithaca, NY: Cornell University Press, 1994).

[2] See Ken Jowitt, *The Leninist Approach to National Dependency* (Berkeley: University of California, Institute of International Studies, 1978).

during the second stage of his administration. By the third stage, however, Yeltsin largely caved in to accumulating interests at home and abroad, interests and pressures that he himself had previously encouraged.

Political competition was a constant during 1985–1999, even as its rules changed several times during those years. Thus, while pressures from domestic social forces and international actors grew as Soviet institutions and ideology crumbled, the impact of those pressures was filtered through a game of politics played by competitors with distinctive personalities and beliefs. In Chapter 9, I attempted to demonstrate how this political game influenced leaders' thresholds for lashing out at threats. In the present chapter, I discuss the extent to which personality, beliefs, politics, social forces, and international pressures may have influenced the *choice of political strategies* at each stage of the Gorbachev and Yeltsin administrations.

Such an exercise is necessarily more speculative than has been the analysis presented in the empirical chapters of this book. Weighing the relative impact of numerous causal influences requires more evidence than I have collected as well as different kinds of tests in order to rule out competing explanations. Absent that research, my judgments must remain far from conclusive. But it makes little sense to avoid making causal claims owing simply to their inconclusiveness. It makes more sense to build upon the evidence presented in this book – including comparisons among our four leaders – to enlarge our supply of credible hypotheses as to why things happened as they did.

GORBACHEV, 1985–1986

Similarities between the behavior of Gorbachev during the first stage of his administration and the behavior of Khrushchev and Brezhnev during their stages of struggle for succession alert us to organizational and ideological constraints on their choices. During the first stage of their administrations, both Khrushchev and Brezhnev built their authority by allying with relatively hardline constituencies (the Party *apparatchiki* and the military–industrial complex), even as they sponsored innovations to lead the country out of the morass into which it had fallen. Both men also worked vigorously to enlarge their political machines and to expand their patronage base within the Party–State apparatus. In all these respects, Gorbachev's strategy resembled the strategies of his major predecessors. Gorbachev deferred to the puritans and technocrats in most realms of domestic policy – and to the hardliners in much of foreign policy – during 1985–1986, even as he built his power base, raised some hard questions about Soviet foreign and defense policy, and began altering the language of politics to legitimize a forthcoming radicalization of policy at home and abroad.

In all three cases, the Party leader managed to occupy a political niche that combined the pursuit of dynamic new goals with the protection of cherished traditional values. Of course, the specific content of those amalgams varied, reflecting both the conditions at the time and the distinctive personalities and beliefs of the leaders in question. But the parallels are striking for what they tell us about the impact of the political and ideological context on choices during this first stage of their administrations. The "private" structure of political organization (which had not yet begun to crumble in 1985–1986), the dominant interests within the political establishment, the process of political competition, the dominant biases of the ideological heritage, and the climate of opinion at the time go farther to explain the political strategies of all three leaders than do their respective personalities or beliefs. At this stage, all three men were deferring to dominant interests and ideals within the establishment at the time. Within this context, Gorbachev (like Khrushchev) fashioned for himself an image as a responsible reformer; Brezhnev projected the image of an enlightened conservative.

GORBACHEV, 1987–1989

Once they had consolidated their power, built their authority, and emerged ascendant within the leadership, all three leaders changed direction – although to greatly varying degrees. All three of them came forth with comprehensive programs for progress at home and abroad, though Brezhnev's definition of "progress" (consistent with the climate of opinion within the Central Committee at the time) was not reformist. The contents of those programs differed greatly, but all were highly ambitious, optimistic, and forward-looking. Khrushchev and Gorbachev promised a "great leap forward" toward a utopian ideal, though they tapped into different strands of the utopian heritage.[3] Brezhnev abandoned both utopianism and reformism, but he did promise significant progress toward the reconciliation of numerous contradictory domestic and foreign policy ambitions. All three programs were touted as consistent with key elements of the Marxist–Leninist tradition.

We do not need to invoke personality to explain the fact that all three programs were ambitious. Rather, this similarity reflected the Soviet regime's

---

[3] On diverse utopian strands within the Marxist and Leninist heritages, see Stephen Hanson, *Time and Revolution* (Chapel Hill: University of North Carolina Press, 1998).

ideological heritage; Soviet political organization facilitated assertive leadership and generated the expectation that a leader, having consolidated power, would outline a program for comprehensive progress at home and abroad. The ideological heritage, in turn, fostered an expectation that the winner would provide dynamic and far-reaching leadership that would propel the country forward through large-scale campaigns. The "leading role of the Party" was enhanced and validated by the conduct of such campaigns. Soviet leadership of the world communist movement, combined with that country's great-power status, further reinforced the expectation of ambitious, demonstrative leadership at home and abroad.

More idiosyncratic factors must be invoked, however, to explain differences in the contents of these comprehensive programs. For example, Gorbachev's program built on the beliefs he had developed as a reform communist in the two decades preceding his selection as general secretary (see Chapter 2). A hypothetical "Ligachev program" would have looked quite different. Khrushchev's program reflected his eagerness to realize many elements of Marx's social vision and of Lenin's political vision (as propounded in Lenin's essay, "State and Revolution"). Brezhnev's program reflected his (and his cohorts') disillusion with Khrushchevian utopianism as well as his political allies' disillusion with reformism.

But there was another difference between Khrushchev's and Brezhnev's stage of ascendancy, on the one hand, and Gorbachev's, on the other. Both Khrushchev and Brezhnev sponsored comprehensive programs that *selectively reincorporated* elements of the programs of their defeated, reformist political rivals. Having denounced Malenkov's emphasis on light industry and chemicals along with Malenkov's sense of urgency about forging a détente relationship with the United States, Khrushchev incorporated both of these goals into his program of 1959–1960 even as he also continued to pursue the goals he had endorsed during the succession struggle. Similarly, having conducted the succession struggle by supporting heavy industry and a militant posture toward the West, Brezhnev incorporated a program for light industry, as well as a major program for détente, into his policy advocacy of 1970–1971 even as he continued to pursue traditional goals.

Selective reincorporation may have been the product of a felt need to expand one's coalition in light of the political insecurity faced even by an ascendant Party leader in a system that promised no fixed term in office and that provided dismal retirement prospects.[4] Whatever the precise motive, it had

---

[4] Parliamentary regimes provide no fixed term of office. But a prime minister can lose a reelection bid and still hope to make a political comeback later on – or pursue a lucrative career

the effect of making the leader's program still more ambitious by promising a great deal to almost all audiences.

Notably, Gorbachev did not engage in selective reincorporation. When faced with the failure of "acceleration" (*uskorenie*) to improve economic performance in 1985–1986 and when faced with continued deadlock in East–West relations, Gorbachev did not propose a comprehensive program based on a mix of "acceleration" and reform, hardline foreign policies and selective concessions. Instead, he abandoned both "acceleration" and traditionalist foreign policies and proposed a comprehensively radicalized program. True, as we saw in Chapters 5 and 6, Gorbachev increasingly tried to hold the line against too rapid or far-reaching a radicalization of domestic policy. But this only means that Gorbachev feared that excessive radicalism could prove counterproductive. It is also true that Gorbachev railed consistently against a vision of the future that was purely market capitalist or *liberal* democratic; but this only means that he was presenting himself throughout his years in office as neither a capitalist nor a liberal democrat. Relative to what he proposed in 1985–1986, Gorbachev's radical programs of 1987–1988, though elaborated with some tactical caution, yielded relatively little to the perspectives of traditionalists within the regime, which is why many conservatives broke with him politically in 1988–1989. He refused to yield to the temptation, in 1987–1988, to seek political security in a compromising, inclusive program. Instead, he yielded to the conclusion that comprehensive progress toward a New Deal at home and abroad was impossible without a transformation of the political system. If one admires Gorbachev's program, one could argue that this was part of his "greatness" as a transformational leader.

The patterns just outlined suggest the following generalizations. The *fact* of Gorbachev's proposing a comprehensive and ambitious program for progress toward an idealized future should not be ascribed principally to his unique personality or beliefs, because the ideology and organization of the regime would have pushed any leader in the direction of an idealized comprehensive program. But the *specific content* of Gorbachev's program, and its comprehensive radicalism at home and abroad, certainly can be ascribed to the man's personality and personal beliefs. Nor do other candidates for causal status make a strong case. Gorbachev's radical policies were not a consensual

---

in the private sector or otherwise maintain his social status. A deposed Soviet leader enjoyed no such opportunities, vanished from top-level political life and publicity, and faced the possibility of criminal prosecution. This was not a "law" of communist regime politics, for some leaders have made comebacks in Eastern Europe and China. But no Soviet Politburo member managed to do so in Soviet times.

response of the Politburo to objective circumstances; in fact, they were highly controversial. Radical social forces were not sufficiently mobilized in 1986–1987, and were too easily cowed, to assign them causal responsibility for the origination of Gorbachev's program.[5] The climate of opinion within the political establishment was impatient for change – and was thus a contributory and permissive factor – but did not specify the scope or content of desirable policy changes. The ideological tradition could have supported diverse approaches to "getting the country moving again."

International influences were both indirect and direct. Indirectly, the attraction of Western prosperity and the magnet of cultural Westernization had grown as Soviet elite self-confidence in the superiority, or even workability, of their system had declined. Directly, governments abroad approved of Gorbachev's political reforms, while U.S. military policy under Ronald Reagan highlighted the inability of an unreformed Soviet Union to continue to compete as a global superpower. Yet none of these influences goes far to explain Gorbachev's domestic political reforms of 1987–1988. Gorbachev's comprehensive program held out the promise of a "socialist" democracy and rejected specific emulation of Western liberal capitalist democracy. Western governments at the time were not pressuring Gorbachev to democratize the Soviet system. Moreover, the conclusion that the Soviet Union needed to reform itself in a more liberal direction in order to compete in the modern world was one that Gorbachev and other "reform communists" had drawn before Ronald Reagan ever came to power.

In short, we could have predicted with confidence that any leader, including Yegor Ligachev, would consolidate power and present a program for comprehensive progress at home and abroad. We could also have predicted that the program would seek to reverse the decline of the Soviet economy. But the way Gorbachev used the power he had accumulated by 1987 can be

---

[5] Note, for example, that as late as spring 1988 – when the Nina Andreeva letter calling for a rollback of *perestroika* was published – the critical intelligentsia of Moscow ducked for cover, expecting a KGB-led crackdown. They only regained courage after Gorbachev and his associates forced through the Politburo a published rebuttal of the Andreeva letter (William & Jane Taubman, *Moscow Spring* [New York: Summit, 1989], pp. 146–86; Michael Urban [with Vyacheslav Igrunov & Sergei Mitrokhin], *The Rebirth of Politics in Russia* [Cambridge University Press, 1997], p. 90). Moreover, Urban and his colleagues, in a thorough study of the emergence of informal organizations and *glasnost'* in 1986–1988, conclude that social forces did not enjoy the political initiative against the authorities until the elections of March 1989: "Until the onset of the electoral process, the informal movement in Russia had remained a marginal phenomenon ... these elections revived the flagging movement" (pp. 121–2); a rally in Moscow on March 22, 1989, "marked the turning point at which political society felt itself sufficiently strong to challenge openly the repressive party–state" (p. 135).

traced to his prior commitments to end the Cold War, to revitalize Soviet society (preferably by nonviolent means), and to build a socialist democracy in
the USSR – along with his commitment to do all this by means that salvaged
both core "socialist" values and his own political role.[6]

---

[6] The Western literature on Gorbachev's leadership presents diverse explanations for the radicalization of his program. Brown, Hough, Lévesque, and English treat the turn as an expression
of Gorbachev's beliefs and as a reflection of his accumulated political power, though they
do not distinguish the fact of the program's ambitiousness, comprehensiveness, and utopianism from its specific contents. Hence, they do not search for alternative causal factors to
explain the form versus the content of the program. See Archie Brown, *The Gorbachev Factor*
(Oxford & New York: Oxford University Press, 1996); Jerry F. Hough, *Democratization and
Revolution in the USSR, 1985–1991* (Washington, DC: Brookings Institution, 1997); Jacques
Lévesque, *The Enigma of 1989: The USSR and the Liberation of Eastern Europe* (Berkeley:
University of California Press, 1997); Robert D. English, *Russia and the Idea of the West: Gorbachev, Intellectuals and the End of the Cold War* (New York: Columbia University Press,
2000). Mikheyev, Volkogonov, and Malia also depict Gorbachev as exceptionally powerful
by 1987; they, too, treat the abandonment of "acceleration" as a choice dictated principally
by Gorbachev's frustration with the results of that program. But their depiction of Gorbachev's comprehensive program stresses the limits more than the scope of its radicalism. What
all these works have in common, however, is a focus on Gorbachev's personality and beliefs as
the proximate determinants of the change in course. See Dmitry Mikheyev, *The Rise and Fall
of Gorbachev* (Indianapolis, IN: Hudson Institute, 1992); Dmitri Volkogonov, *Autopsy for an
Empire: The Seven Leaders Who Built the Soviet Regime* (New York: Free Press, 1998), ch. 7;
Martin Malia, *The Soviet Tragedy: A History of Socialism in Russia, 1917–1991* (New York:
Free Press, 1994).

By contrast, D'Agostino's ambitious and original study (Anthony D'Agostino, *Gorbachev's
Revolution* [New York: NYU Press, 1998]) treats ideas as important in Soviet elite political
culture but treats them entirely as instruments of power struggle. They are effective as instruments because they resonate within the political culture, but they are embraced entirely for
reasons of political power. D'Agostino therefore views radicalization as part of a historical pattern: Stalin, Khrushchev, and Gorbachev all "escaped forward" when challenged politically.
Hence, he views political challenges to Gorbachev in 1987, led by Politburo member Yegor Ligachev, as the impetus for the general secretary to radicalize his program in order to throw his
opponents off balance and to prevent their placing limits on his power. Although this bears
a resemblance to my framework, which also takes seriously the role of ideas within the political culture and which treats a leader's ability to seize and maintain the political initiative as
crucial to authority building and authority maintenance, the resemblance is only superficial.
D'Agostino asserts that a Soviet leader must escape the constraints of collective leadership but
does not explain *why* he must do so; never does he claim that the alternative is to be overthrown, nor does he explain why Brezhnev accepted a much more constrained position than
did Stalin, Khrushchev, or Gorbachev. D'Agostino treats power as primary and "principle" as
a disposable instrument in the power struggle. He writes, for example, that neither Gorbachev
nor Yeltsin "held any position for which he was willing to suffer the slightest loss of political
leverage" (p. 295). Given the massive uncertainty under which the two leaders had to make
hard choices (an uncertainty that is conceded when D'Agostino later [pp. 341–3] argues that
Gorbachev had no blueprint with which to anticipate the consequences of his choices), and
given the political risks each of them accepted at several points in time, this statement about

The radicalization of Gorbachev's foreign policy during this period may also be ascribed to his personality and beliefs. There was no specified political consensus driving the choice of a concessionary foreign policy; nor did social forces, ideology, or the logic of political competition dictate the choice. Westernizers within the intelligentsia supported Gorbachev and urged him on, but they were relatively few in number and did not have the power to sanction him for not following their advice. He chose to heed their advice and to learn from them. The ideological tradition allowed Gorbachev to justify the choice in idealist, even utopian, terms, but that tradition was hardly biased toward abandoning the anti-imperialist struggle. Political competition might have given Gorbachev an incentive to seize the initiative. In the past, however, such competition had led to selective reincorporation and an inclusive program, rather than the far-reaching radicalization that Gorbachev now advocated.

Most Western observers credit Gorbachev with making these choices; some observers, however, qualify the credit by arguing that the strategy of the Reagan administration had left the Soviet leader with little alternative. These people argue that forces *in the international environment* forced Gorbachev to choose between the policies he adopted and intransigent policies that would have been even less in his interest.[7] There is something to be said for this interpretation. Gorbachev unsuccessfully tried to induce President Reagan to accept compromise solutions in 1985–1987. Thereafter, Gorbachev decided that radical concessions were more advantageous than living with the consequences of no agreement. Given his conviction that an end to the Cold War was a necessary precondition for successfully reforming Soviet society,

Gorbachev's and Yeltsin's power fixation strikes me as empirically indefensible. Moreover, I see no purpose in trying to assign weights to the causal role of power and principle. I treat politicians as seeking to have it both ways: to find and defend a credible, principled political niche and political identity from which they will build (and try to maintain) their authority and power. D'Agostino writes, for example, that "[r]eform ideas grew more radical in their implications as the struggle with the opposition intensified" (p. 343). I would reverse this equation and argue instead that opposition intensified as reform ideas grew more radical. Part of the difference here is that I, like the other group of scholars, view Gorbachev as a very powerful, ascendant leader by 1987–1988. D'Agostino is able to downgrade the causal role of personality and personal beliefs because (like Mikheyev, Volkogonov, and Malia) he deprecates the radicalism of Gorbachev's program by contrasting it to a liberal democratic, capitalist, and internationally capitulationist ideal. Finally, D'Agostino confuses the reader (or, at least, this reader) by employing a framework that treats ideas as merely instruments of power struggle while at several points characterizing Gorbachev as an idealist (pp. 9, 349).

7 For this viewpoint, see Beth A. Fischer, *The Reagan Reversal: Foreign Policy and the End of the Cold War* (Columbia: University of Missouri Press, 1997).

he conceded to Reagan's maximalist demands on several fronts. But there was still a major role played here by Gorbachev's personality and beliefs, for many other members of the Soviet leadership were unenthusiastic about Gorbachev's foreign policy decisions. They would not have made the same choices, had they been in control. It follows that Gorbachev had degrees of political freedom to choose otherwise. He could have engaged in "selective reincorporation" in his foreign policy program and yet, as in domestic policy, he chose not to do so.

Thus, whereas political constraints appear to have shaped Gorbachev's choices during 1985–1986, his personality and individual beliefs appear to have been the more decisive determinants of his choices during 1987–1988.[8]

GORBACHEV, 1989–1991

When Gorbachev's programs started to falter in 1989, he might have reacted as Khrushchev and Brezhnev initially had: seeking renewed support from traditionalist constituencies he had appeased during the first stage of his administration. But this was not the way Gorbachev initially reacted to frustration. Instead, while continuing to try to enforce limits on radical change, he pushed forward with radicalization rather than trying to reverse it. He accommodated radical forces by abrogating the "leading role of the Party," conducting republican elections in spring 1990, creating a Soviet presidency independent of the Communist Party, and politically disenfranchising the *nomenklatura*. He further liberalized joint-ventures legislation to open the Soviet economy to the world economy, and he further liberalized policy on emigration, dissent, freedom of association, and freedom of religion. Abroad, he withdrew Soviet forces from Afghanistan and tolerated the collapse of communism in Eastern Europe. There is no reason to ascribe all this to political pressures from within the Party–State establishment; most officials would have counseled holding the line against further radicalization. The KGB remained intact at the time (1989–1990) and could have cracked down if ordered to do so. Soviet tanks

---

[8] Let me here dispose of a straw man. This interpretation does not suggest that Gorbachev's ideas were products of either revelation or omniscience. He was influenced in his thinking by radical reformist advisors and associates both at home and abroad, and he was acting under conditions of uncertainty about what was needed and what would work. But these conditions (influence and uncertainty) are universals of political decisionmaking. Within the context of such universals, some leaders forge ambitious, transformative programs while others yield to constraints and adopt "lowest common denominator" programs. It was Gorbachev's personality and beliefs that led him in the direction of the former rather than the latter.

could have rolled into Eastern Europe; or, at a minimum, Gorbachev could have threatened action. But the Soviet leader chose not to take that route.[9]

Why he chose initially to radicalize rather than to contract his coalition is a different question. An idealist explanation would have it that Gorbachev fervently believed (or had come to believe) in his vision of a demilitarized international order and a consensual polity at home. Hence, he plowed forward despite the risks and uncertainties of doing so. But a purely idealist explanation ignores changes in the social context at home and abroad.[10] An explanation that combines idealism with materialist calculation would argue that, by 1989, active social forces both in Russia and in the other republics of the USSR – along with social forces in Eastern Europe and governmental forces in the West – had so raised the price to be paid for cracking down that Gorbachev perceived the cost of repression to exceed the cost of toleration. He therefore decided to align himself with the less intransigent of those social forces, to make the best of an uncontrolled situation, to make a virtue of necessity, and hopefully to maintain his authority as the "man who changed the world."[11]

---

[9] Mikheyev (*The Rise and Fall*) does not perceive Gorbachev radicalizing in response to the frustrations of 1988–1989. Rather, he views him as shifting to the right (hardline), on domestic issues at least, already in fall 1988 and remaining there. But much of the evidence he brings forth is equally consistent with Gorbachev's efforts to enforce limits to radicalization, which does not distinguish his behavior of 1987–1988 from his behavior of 1989–1991. Similarly, D'Agostino (*Gorbachev's Revolution*) sees Gorbachev "escaping forward" in 1989–1990 by seeking absolute power, purging rivals, and attempting to destroy the capacity of the Party to constrain him. But this undeniable power consolidation strategy is only different in degree from what Gorbachev was doing in 1985–1988; all general secretaries had built a political machine in order to prevail in the succession struggle and sought to expand that machine – and purge rivals – in response to the frustration of their programs. What distinguished Gorbachev was his determination both to consolidate further his personal grip on power and to further radicalize policy through the transfer of power from Party to electorally accountable state institutions.

[10] Brown (*The Gorbachev Factor*) and English (*Russia and the Idea*) offer idealist explanations and approve of Gorbachev's decision; Hough (*Democratization and Revolution*) also focuses on Gorbachev's vision but expresses bafflement that Gorbachev could have been so naïve as to assume that his refusal to use force would not lead to chaos and collapse. None of these authors, however, ignores social and international forces; hence, none could properly be labeled "pure idealists."

[11] I advanced this interpretation in George W. Breslauer, "Evaluating Gorbachev as leader," *Soviet Economy*, vol. 8, no. 4 (October–December 1989), pp. 299–340, which was written in July 1990 (as the journal was behind schedule). The "man who changed the world" phrase, of course, is from Sheehy's volume of that title (Gail Sheehy, *The Man Who Changed the World* [New York: HarperCollins, 1990]). Without explicit endorsement, this explanation of Gorbachev's behavior seems also to inform Lévesque's study (*The Enigma of 1989*).

This combined idealist–materialist explanation gives equal weight to Gorbachev's personality and beliefs, on the one hand, and social forces at home and abroad, on the other. For it was the radicalization of domestic social forces – through self-mobilization and through encouragement by Gorbachev, Yeltsin, and other leading politicians – that raised the cost of repression to such a high level. And it was the deepening Soviet economic crisis that so raised the cost of alienating Western governments, as Gorbachev increasingly counted on those governments to provide material assistance (including arms-reduction treaties) to weather the crisis. But it was Gorbachev's ideals that kept him from attempting a counterrevolutionary restoration to stem the tide. He evidently cared about his image abroad and about the kind of society he was trying to build at home, for he retained in 1989–1990 the institutional capacity to crack down.

As we know, in fall 1990 Gorbachev abandoned further radicalization and allied himself with conservative forces. Events of September 1990 through March 1991 ominously suggested that an effort might be underway to roll back societal radicalization. It is not likely that this shift was forced upon Gorbachev by hardliners in the Central Committee or Supreme Soviet. Only two months earlier, in July 1990, he had purged Ligachev and many other conservatives from the leadership and the Central Committee. Rather, the explanation for this shift is likely to reside in the interaction between Gorbachev's beliefs and the accelerating pace of social mobilization and polarization. An explanation cast entirely in terms of personality would suggest that Gorbachev lost his nerve in the face of cascading failures (at home and abroad) and great uncertainty as to what might stem the tide. An explanation cast at the level of beliefs would point out that social mobilization now clearly threatened to bring down the Soviet Union itself – a value that Gorbachev had never been willing to entertain losing. Hence, when the level of social mobilization threatened disintegration of the USSR, the calculus shifted. The perceived cost of toleration had grown to the point that the cost of repression seemed marginally more acceptable.[12]

And yet this shift to the right lasted only six months, after which Gorbachev shifted back to support for the radicals on the issue of center–periphery relations. Hence, we should not settle too quickly for an explanation of Gorbachev's behavior that is rooted entirely in the interaction between his ultimate beliefs and the level of radicalization of social forces. But nor should

---

[12] By contrast, D'Agostino (*Gorbachev's Revolution*, pp. 280–97) argues that this shift was actually an effort by Gorbachev to bolster his personal power.

we succumb to explanations based purely on power maximization.[13] Gorbachev was indeed determined to protect his power position. He resisted calls by radical associates in 1990 for him to break with the Communist Party and base his power exclusively on the soviets and the presidency. He feared that this would leave powerful institutions in the hands of people who would use those institutions to destroy him and his policies.[14] In addition to maintaining his power and authority, however, Gorbachev was trying to prevent the collapse of the USSR. It was entirely uncertain just how he could do both.

Moreover, when it came to the choice of policies for doing all this, Gorbachev was both internally conflicted and externally cross-pressured. The cost of repression was severe. Internally, he experienced value conflict and ambivalence; externally, he feared the reactions of Western governments if he resorted to repression.

Gorbachev had expressed his distaste for the use of force (*ne streliat'* ["no more shooting"]) as early as 1985. When this conflicted, in 1990–1991, with both the maintenance of his political authority and his ability to contain polarization, Gorbachev was forced to choose between values of importance to him. His ambivalence may have expressed itself in the fact that the Baltic crackdown was limited in both scope and duration. Whether or not Gorbachev gave the order for troops to attack Vilnius and Riga, he *had* created a permissive political context for such a crackdown and yet prevented the repression from escalating to the point that it might have been effective in intimidating secessionist forces.

Gorbachev was also cross-pressured in that the costs of repression would also be felt in foreign relations. A repressive strategy might have led Gorbachev to be censured severely by the governments on which he most counted for economic assistance. He also needed the goodwill of those governments to be able to demonstrate at home that he remained an indispensable link to the international community, which many Soviet citizens hoped would provide material assistance and psychological comfort to their beleaguered country. Repression could also have led to his condemnation by political leaders abroad whom he had come to respect greatly. Indeed, it may not be too strong to say that Gorbachev had developed international referents (George Bush,

---

[13] D'Agostino, for example, writes: "Gorbachev's hard line ... was no longer bolstering his personal power. So he proceeded to discard it like an old coat. Indeed, now he could only save himself by another abrupt turn" (ibid., p. 297).

[14] Brown, *The Gorbachev Factor*, pp. 195–6.

Margaret Thatcher, Felipe Gonzalez, leaders of the Italian Communist Party) whose opinions of him he valued greatly irrespective of their ability to do him harm.

Thus, Gorbachev's shift back to support for the radicals on federal policy in April 1991 appears to have been a reaction to the fact that his support for conservatives had yielded little or nothing – from either an ideal or a material standpoint. The radicals, unlike the conservatives, had social forces mobilized behind them and seemed receptive to the idea of negotiating a treaty that, on paper at least, would retain some sort of unity among the republics of the USSR. The conservatives had only the threat of repression – with all the psychic, political, and material costs this might entail both at home and abroad. It was worth another try to return to negotiations on a treaty.

All of this helps us to understand one of the most extraordinary features of 1991: Gorbachev's acquiescence in the collapse of the state he had served all his life. As we have seen, this was not his preferred outcome. He struggled constantly to prevent it during 1990 and 1991. He was torn between *ratifying and containing* collapse by sponsoring a confederal formula that he feared would not hold and *preventing* collapse by sponsoring a widespread and bloody crackdown against separatist forces. He found himself between a rock and a hard place and responded by sequentially tacking in each direction without going fully to either extreme. Even when he acquiesced in the confederal formula in July 1991, he expressed his ambivalence by dropping hints to associates about the need for emergency rule. He never resolved this ambivalence.

Thus, Gorbachev's zigs and zags during 1990–1991 resulted from a combination of three things: (1) loss of nerve as he witnessed, successively, the potential costs of each policy extreme; (2) confusion as to what would succeed in reconciling his conflicting substantive and political goals; and (3) efforts to reposition himself to maintain credibility and to recoup authority with "healthy forces" of all persuasions. As it turned out, moderates represented a declining percentage of the mobilized and self-confident forces in Soviet politics and society. Gorbachev could no longer position himself as a liaison *between* the forces of the right and the left. The level of polarization had reached the point that Gorbachev's pendular strategy only highlighted to both sides the fact that he had become an eminently dispensable leader. After the failed coup of August 1991, Gorbachev was indeed a spent political force. Had he wished, in fall 1991, to employ force to prevent the juridical dissolution of the Soviet Union, he would have had few takers. All he could do was angrily acquiesce in his forced retirement.

YELTSIN, 1985–1991

Yeltsin comes across as a "larger than life" figure during the Gorbachev years. It is tempting to explain his behavior during 1985–1991 entirely with reference to his personality: his risk-seeking, extraordinary willpower, passion for struggle, and unusual "feel" or intuition for how to relate to the masses when public politics became an option in 1988. Indeed, personality is certainly a large part of the explanation for many of Yeltsin's choices. Absent those personality traits, it is difficult to imagine a regional Party secretary and candidate member of the Politburo reacting to frustrations as Yeltsin did in 1987. It is also difficult to imagine a different personality "crashing" the June 1988 Party Conference and forcing his way to the podium. Personality would also explain the decision to seek a seemingly hard win in Moscow in the March 1989 parliamentary elections rather than the easy win that would have awaited him in Sverdlovsk. Yeltsin's personal attributes were also necessary conditions for sustaining the challenge to Gorbachev during 1989–1991, for attaining the chairmanship of the Russian Supreme Soviet in May 1990, for creating and then winning the Russian presidency in June 1991, for facing down the coup of August 1991, and for dissolving the USSR in December 1991. Moreover, Yeltsin's rhetorical style – and his intuition for finding words, modes of expression, and actions that resonated with mass audiences – well explain his effectiveness in the game of public politics throughout 1988–1991.[15]

Yeltsin's personal beliefs were also sufficiently unusual in the Soviet leadership at this time that, along with his willful personality, they reinforce idiosyncratic explanations of his choices. Many officials combined a "storming" mentality with a predisposition to purge corrupt cadres; each of these traits had deep roots in the Soviet political tradition. Many officials also understood that a "populist" strategy was needed to circumvent bureaucratic constraints on change. Less frequent was the combination of populism and egalitarianism that targeted elite privileges as unjust and an impediment to progress. Khrushchev and Yeltsin were similar in drawing this linkage. Initially, both men defined the problem of bureaucratic corruption in discrete terms, as a "cadres problem": purge the corrupted, replace them with "uninfected" personnel, and the system will work. But as their responsibility for performance grew and their frustrations deepened, each man moved toward a systemic critique. To be sure, both men had the personality traits

---

[15] Reporters for the *London Times*, after interviewing Yeltsin in 1990, wrote with admiration of "his instinctive grasp of another vital ingredient of politics: 'street credibility'" (quoted in Leon Aron, *Boris Yeltsin: A Revolutionary Life* [London: HarperCollins, 2000], p. 364).

required to move in that perilous direction: impatience for results and political courage.

Once we concede that Yeltsin's personality and beliefs were decisive determinants of his behavior during 1985–1991, is there anything left to say about the contribution of Soviet ideology, the climate of opinion, politics, social forces, and international factors toward an explanation of his choice of political strategy? Yes, to some degree; these factors were contributory and permissive, but not decisive. Let me address them in turn.

Soviet Ideology. The Marxist–Leninist ideological tradition contained an egalitarian vision ("the workers' state"; "to each according to his needs"; "all power to the soviets"; the "classless society") that fueled both Khrushchev's and Yeltsin's sense of self-righteousness as they attacked the privileges of the *nomenklatura*. These features of the tradition allowed Yeltsin in 1985–1987 to present himself as a leader in the struggle for "social justice" and to claim simultaneously that he was acting fully in accord with the Leninist tradition. The multifaceted, internally contradictory ideological tradition thereby contributed to the formulation of Yeltsin's political strategies – and facilitated their implementation, though not their effectiveness – during his 23 months as head of the Moscow Party organization.

After 1988, traditional Soviet ideology became less and less of an influence on Yeltsin's choices, except in the negative sense that it provided a menu of doctrines that Yeltsin was rapidly rejecting. Yeltsin was searching at this time for a counter-ideology to explain his frustrations and to deploy in the public struggle over ideas. He was assisted in his search by liberal democrats like Andrei Sakharov and other radicals within the Congress of People's Deputies. His conversion was hastened by his encounter in September 1989 with the abundance of American capitalism. By 1990, Yeltsin had come to embrace the rhetoric of liberal democratic and then market democratic theory. Soviet ideology played a causal role for Yeltsin after 1988 only in defining the undesirable "other" against which he was helping to mobilize, embolden, or ally with growing numbers of social forces.

Climate of Opinion. The climate of opinion within the Soviet establishment in 1985–1987 also may have influenced certain of Yeltsin's choices in those years. On the one hand, the widespread urge to "get the country moving again" led him to believe that drastic measures would be tolerated (and even welcomed) toward that end.[16] Once he was responsible for delivering results

---

[16] Recall that, at the 27th Party Congress in February 1986 – where Yeltsin delivered a quite radical speech – he explained his failure to deliver as radical a speech five years earlier (under Brezhnev) by saying that he had lacked political courage at the time.

for his leadership in Moscow, his awareness of the climate of opinion lent political reinforcement to his natural impatience. On the other hand, the mixed and ambiguous content of the prevailing climate – its yearning to find a way to make the system work without threatening the system's existence – heightened Yeltsin's frustration at the slow pace of change. In such an ambiguous climate, Gorbachev initially fashioned for himself the image of a responsible reformer. In the same climate, Yeltsin lost patience with the ambiguities and found himself being dubbed irresponsible.

Political Organization and Political Competition. Politics also was an independent causal force in several senses. The political organization of the regime during 1985–1987 was still highly constricted. Yeltsin's frustrations in trying to "cleanse" Moscow politics during this time were to some extent products of a system of mutual protection among officials of the central and Moscow Party apparatus. Yeltsin's decision to offer his resignation was in large measure impelled by a recognition that, in such a regime, he would be made the scapegoat for his failure to turn Moscow around. His personality and beliefs might have driven his decision to appeal to the Central Committee in 1987, but political organization explains both the source of his frustration and the ease with which he was defeated.

Political organization changed after 1987 as a result of Gorbachev's reforms, which allowed politics to become a still weightier causal force, albeit in a different way. The definitions of "politics" and of "political organization" had changed. The fact that political competition was now public increased the scope for political outbidding by allowing the rate of *societal* political polarization, not just intra-establishment polarization, to determine the niches that politicians could aspire to occupy. Moreover, by opening new avenues for political competition, Gorbachev – intentionally or not – allowed his own stage of ascendancy to become, in effect, a new stage of political succession struggle. His reforms allowed counter-elites to appeal to newly formed constituencies and thereby to build themselves up into genuine rivals for the votes of the citizenry. No previous Party leader had used his stage of ascendancy in this way. Hence, the fact of public political competition, and the polarizing effects of that process in a context of systemic transformation, created a continuously expanding field of opportunity for Boris Yeltsin and others. Yeltsin's decisions to exploit the opportunities were products of his personality and beliefs, but the existence of the opportunity was a product of the changed structure of political competition. Yeltsin's decisions to outbid Gorbachev repeatedly in that context were only in part expressions of his personality; they were also reflections of the logic of public political competition in a polarizing context. Similarly, Yeltsin's embrace of a liberal democratic and market democratic counter-ideology was speeded by the intensified struggle over ideas that public political competition encouraged.

Social Forces. Yeltsin's decisions of 1985–1988 were not choices dictated by any effort to keep up with radicalizing social forces; he was ahead of them at the time.[17] During 1989–1991, however, the balance between leadership and autonomous social radicalization shifted greatly. Some of Yeltsin's actions during this period were responses to sudden bursts of social defiance he had not anticipated, such as the miners' strikes of 1989 and the radicalization of demands for autonomy or independence in the Baltic states. But many instances of Yeltsin's public outbidding during 1988–1989 (see Chapter 6) were anticipatory, not reactive, and had the effect of emboldening radical forces to mobilize and express themselves without fear. Yeltsin became a focal point for social activists who viewed his political resurrection as a sure sign that nonviolent revolutionary change was actually possible. Moreover, Yeltsin's response to unanticipated outbursts of social rebellion – in sharp contrast to Gorbachev during 1990–1991 – was typically to accommodate and praise them, thereby encouraging them to continue their defiance of the Kremlin.

Social forces and political competition were permissive factors, not determinants of Yeltsin's behavior. Most other politicians at the time, lacking Yeltsin's personality traits and beliefs, would have behaved quite differently in response to the opportunities.

International Factors. Yeltsin's choices during 1985–1991 were only minimally or indirectly affected by factors in the international environment. He was, of course, influenced indirectly by the decline of the Soviet economy relative to its capitalist competitors. Judging by his autobiographies and his statements at the time, however, Yeltsin was no more focused on the international context than were other regional Party secretaries. Indeed, Gorbachev was more of a reform communist and more attentive to international comparisons than was Yeltsin in 1976–1985. During Yeltsin's tenure as Party first secretary in Moscow (1985–1987), he displayed very little interest in the international context of Soviet policy.

During Yeltsin's political resurrection of 1988–1989, and again during his direct rivalry with Gorbachev of 1990–1991, international comparisons

---

[17] From his first days as first secretary of the Moscow city Party organization, Yeltsin was predicting social and political instability if the authorities did not change their ways and improve the consumer situation. He might genuinely have believed that there would be a reckoning down the road, but he was not (in 1985–1988) responding to concrete manifestations or outbursts of social discontent. If anything, he was trying to encourage people to express their dissatisfactions as a way of pressuring officials or as a justification for purging those officials.

became more salient to Yeltsin. His search for a worldview to substitute for Leninism led him to endorse the alternative – market democracy and liberalism – that had become ideologically hegemonic in the international system during the second half of the 1980s. More concretely, his visit to a Houston supermarket in 1990, he claims, was a traumatic experience; it led him to conclude that socialism was a pipe dream and that capitalism might be the only realistic path to prosperity. Yet there were many other political actors in and around the leadership who had already drawn these conclusions. The hegemony of market democracy internationally, then, was a factor that influenced all those who were rejecting Leninism to consider liberalism as the only feasible alternative. Given his political competition with Gorbachev, however, Yeltsin would have outbid Gorbachev in the anti-system direction whether or not a salient international alternative existed. There is too little reference to international considerations in Yeltsin's public political rhetoric of 1989–1990 to suggest otherwise.

As for direct international pressures, these had even less impact on Yeltsin's political choices. Indeed, it was a source of intense frustration to him in 1989–1990 that Western governments refused to acknowledge him as a legitimate political leader of the USSR. The United States and its West European allies at this time were trying to shore up support for Gorbachev and viewed Yeltsin as an inconvenience, if not a troublemaker. As late as fall 1991, President Bush was trying to forestall the juridical collapse of the Soviet Union. Yeltsin's fundamental political choices during 1989–1991 were largely taken in spite of, not in response to, direct pressures from international actors.

YELTSIN, 1991–1993

The fall of 1991 is generally considered to have been a turning point in Soviet and Russian history. This was Yeltsin's honeymoon period at the beginning of his political ascendancy. His level of charismatic authority had risen to new heights in August 1991, and he seized that moment to begin crafting a comprehensive program for coping with the disintegrating situation he had inherited and for creating the foundations of a new order. The country's spiraling economic crisis, centrifugal forces in the republics, and the further disintegration of state institutions were circumstantial factors that forced Yeltsin's attention, but they did not force him to respond as he did. Moreover, organized social and political forces within Russia proved powerless to compel Yeltsin to respond as they preferred. Actors in the international arena had little direct impact on Yeltsin's *political* choices, but they did influence his decisions on economic reform. In all, Yeltsin was as unconstrained in fall 1991 as he would ever be. He had the opportunity to choose for himself how to respond to the crisis. Accordingly, his personality and beliefs loomed large as determinants of his choices. His decision to seek the right to rule by decree, his resistance to founding a presidential political party, and his decision to distance himself from democratic forces were choices forced on him by no one. They reflected his personal preferences.

Yeltsin's decisions regarding economic reform were shaped by a wider constellation of forces and circumstances. Something had to be done to gain control of the disintegrating economy. Neoliberal advisors (both Russian and foreign) backed by international financial institutions strongly advocated a particular course of action; still other options were being suggested by Russian economists. Yeltsin's receptivity to the neoliberal advice still needs to be explained.

That receptivity reflected his socialization in the Soviet system and a personality that drew him to the role of "stormer" within that system. Given the testimony in his autobiographies, along with the testimony of those who worked for him (see Chapter 7), we can see why "shock therapy" appealed to Yeltsin at the time. He was attracted to a breakthrough strategy for clearing away obstacles to the construction of a new socioeconomic system – a strategy that would contrast with the "half-measures" for which he criticized Gorbachev. Shock therapy, as Yeltsin defined it, resembled a large-scale campaign to transform society, a painful but necessary cure for the lethargy of Russian citizens; it resembled a cultural revolution. It required that all citizens resolve to overcome their slothful ways – or suffer extreme deprivation. It placed its bets on young people.

These preferences were more than just an expression of Yeltsin's personality. They had roots in a Marxist–Leninist tradition that was missionary, progressive, and optimistic. Stalin, Khrushchev, and Gorbachev had all sought to transform society by reshaping (or realizing the potential of) "the human factor" and by explicitly appealing to the younger generation. They, too, had launched nationwide mobilizations to construct an unprecedented social order. Indeed, Yeltsin justifed his economic revolution in terms that were strikingly similar to the justifications of his predecessors. In Hanson's terms, Yeltsin mimicked the Marxist–Leninist search to "transcend historical constraints"[18] – a search that, in this specific and limited sense, did not distinguish him from Stalin, Khrushchev, or Gorbachev. Even though Yeltsin had explicitly rejected Marxism–Leninism, there was something about that tradition's way of thinking that stayed with him. "Building capitalism" under Yeltsin rejected the content of socialism even as it mimicked the approach to "primitive

---

[18] Hanson, *Time and Revolution.*

accumulation" that had marked both early capitalism and the building of socialism in the USSR.

Although organized social and political forces within Russia did not force Yeltsin to adopt this economic strategy, international influences did have an important impact on the choices he made. Indirect international influences included the post–Cold War zeitgeist of the triumph of market democracy and the extraordinary attraction of "Western civilization" as both model and savior. These indirect pressures would have existed whatever the policies of Western governments and international financial institutions at the time, but direct pressures from abroad also played a role. Russia's finances were in dire straits, and Western governments were promising large-scale assistance if Russia adopted the orthodoxy of the International Monetary Fund. Hence, while Yeltsin was predisposed by personality and beliefs to embrace a revolutionary economic strategy, he was also aware that carrots and sticks abroad were pushing him in this direction. He may have felt boxed in by circumstances. But other political actors – including Gorbachev before him – had avoided conceding to Western advice. Rather than viewing Yeltsin as a leader who was forced by the West to do its bidding, we should instead view him as a man whose personality and beliefs predisposed him to accept Western urgings. The "stormer" found "shock therapy" to be the appropriate cure for his country's ills.[19]

Nonetheless, from spring 1992 onward, the "stormer" began to backtrack. The social, economic, psychic, and international costs of his breakthrough strategy had begun to accumulate. Hyperinflation, mass impoverishment, collapse of production at home, and continuing retreat abroad all led to the mobilization of anti-Yeltsin sentiments within the intelligentsia, the managerial corps, and the Congress of People's Deputies. The Russian population largely suffered in silence, but apocalyptic forecasts of how long their patience would last appeared in myriad newspaper articles and public speeches by prominent figures. This was the point at which Yeltsin had to decide whether to persist with the fullness of his program or instead modify and moderate it. He could have persisted – he had the power to do so and Western governments and international organizations promised to reward Russia for doing so – yet he decided to engage in a course correction.

What accounts for this shift? One interpretation would be idiosyncratic: that Yeltsin the Soviet-style "stormer" was also Yeltsin the neo-Leninist who

---

[19] By contrast, Jerry Hough (*The Logic of Economic Reform in Russia* [Washington, DC: Brookings Institution, 2001], p. 129) believes that Yeltsin chose "shock therapy" because it was most consistent with his goal of quickly achieving Russia's independence from the USSR.

understood the need to consolidate gains after an initial thrust. According to this interpretation, Yeltsin was exercising political prudence not because he was forced to do so but rather because he anticipated or feared the consequences of not doing so. The argument would continue as follows.

Having been at the forefront of a revolution that brought down both communism and the USSR, and having advocated immediately thereafter a revolutionary approach to "building capitalism," Yeltsin considered it prudent not to push his luck. He did not know at what point popular patience might snap.[20] He knew how he had come to power, and he knew that he had helped to destroy Gorbachev politically by outbidding him for the allegiance of an aroused populace. He also knew that the forces of restoration were seeking to employ the same strategy against him. He did not want to drive the moderates into the arms of his antagonists within the Supreme Soviet; neither did he want to strengthen the communists' and chauvinists' credibility with the populace. He did not want to remain vulnerable to the charge that he had no strategy for protecting Russia's national interests abroad or for protecting the interests of Russians in the Near Abroad. In short, Yeltsin's behavior was driven by a perception that the accumulating costs of his revolutionary strategy might come back to haunt him unless he engaged in a course correction.[21]

Thus (according to this interpretation), organized political forces within the parliament, the climate of opinion in the country and in the mass media, the pleas of directors of suffering enterprises, and the political insecurity of being president in a weakly institutionalized and highly unruly regime triggered a reaction of prudence by Yeltsin. Prudence, of course, is not the same as capitulation. Yeltsin persisted with the general trajectory of his policies at home and abroad; he simply introduced a course correction.

Another way to interpret this behavior is as an act of political coalition building. It bears resemblance to the kind of selective reincorporation in which Khrushchev and Brezhnev (but not Gorbachev) had engaged at their

---

[20] Recall his anxious promises of November 1991 that things would start to improve in six months (Chapter 7).

[21] A number of observers and associates have noted Yeltsin's political intuition about impending shifts in the mood of the masses (Oleg Poptsov, *Khronika vremyon tsaria Borisa* [Moscow: Sovershenno sekretno, 1996], pp. 55, 107, 167, 384; Fyodor Burlatskii, *Glotok svobody* [Moscow: RIK Kul'tura, 1997], vol. 2, p. 259; Yegor T. Gaidar, *Dni porazhenii i pobed* [Moscow: Vagrius, 1996], pp. 106–7). Whether or not their perceptions were accurate, the observations imply that Yeltsin made these decisions after keeping his own counsel and that he sought to anticipate the reactions of potential antagonists when making his choices. Moreover, in his second memoir (published in early 1994), Yeltsin acknowledges the course correction and justifies it in prudential terms (Boris Yeltsin, *The Struggle for Russia*, trans. by Catherine A. Fitzpatrick [New York: Random House, 1994], pp. 164–7).

stages of ascendancy. This explanation is not antithetical to the one just sketched, but it places somewhat less emphasis on the idiosyncratic and ideological sources of Yeltsin's behavior and more emphasis on politics as a process of political competition. From this perspective, Yeltsin was positioning himself to occupy a political niche in which he would not be isolated at the extreme end of the domestic political spectrum. Instead, he was positioning himself to dominate both the "center" and the "radical wing" of the spectrum. His program remained radical on balance in that it was consistent with maintaining the breakthrough thrust of fall 1991, and it conceded nothing to the unreconstructed communists he had defeated in 1991 or to the Russian chauvinists and imperial restorationists that were growing in strength.[22] One explanation for Khrushchev's and Brezhnev's acts of selective reincorporation was their felt need for outsized coalitions in the face of political insecurity. Yeltsin, in this interpretation, also would have viewed his partial move toward the center as an act of political self-insurance in a highly contentious political context. Even the considerable differences in the structure of politics in the 1990s (as compared to the 1950s–1970s) would not be enough to erase this common response to political insecurity.[23]

Of course, as with both Khrushchev and Brezhnev, selective reincorporation only increased the ambitiousness of the comprehensive program, for it promised to deliver on the new goals with less disruption to traditional concerns and interests than had earlier been anticipated. Nonetheless, Yeltsin's course correction did not have the effect of moderating the rate of political polarization between the legislative and executive branches.

[22] Analogously, Khrushchev and Brezhnev, when fashioning their comprehensive programs, had abandoned the extreme hardline positions once articulated by Molotov and Shelepin. They instead selectively reincorporated reformist positions articulated by Malenkov and Kosygin.

[23] Peter Reddaway and Dmitri Glinski (*The Tragedy of Russia's Reforms: Market Bolshevism against Democracy* [Washington, DC: U.S. Institute of Peace, 2001], pp. 167–72, 234–5), by contrast, argue that Yeltsin "moved to the middle" already in spring 1990, seeking an alliance with the managers of large industrial firms and distancing himself from the extremists of Democratic Russia. The authors then interpret "shock therapy" as based on a coalition of neoliberals and the managerial elite at the expense of the democrats, the communists, and the radical nationalists. This argument would be consistent with a view of Yeltsin as a man who rose to the position of chairman of the Russian Republic Supreme Soviet (May 1990) as an oppositional extremist and then sought to broaden the coalition on which he would base his "rule" in Russia. Reddaway and Glinski offer what amounts to a political interpretation of Yeltsin's behavior at his stage of ascendancy (i.e., a search for political security). Though they do not propose a "stage analysis" of Yeltsin's administration, it is worth noting that their periodization of the stage of political succession and the stage of ascendancy tacitly differs from my periodization. On the other hand, Reddaway and Glinski (p. 288) also argue that Yeltsin moved still further to the middle in mid-1992 and for reasons similar to those I have specified here.

As policy deadlock continued well into 1993, Yeltsin decided to resolve it through confrontation. This was a decision made by Yeltsin himself – encouraged by advisors but mandated by no social forces, international actors, or political imperatives. It was a choice dictated by the combination of his personal threshold for responding to prolonged frustration and by his long-held belief in the higher virtue of personalistic leadership. Therefore, the Constitution that he put to the voters in December 1993 was a close reflection of the super-presidentialist, plebiscitarian, and anti-centrifugal vision of political order he had been touting since fall 1991.

YELTSIN, 1994–1999

As we have seen, Yeltsin was delighted by the passage of his Constitution but shocked by the victory of communists and chauvinists in the parliamentary elections of December 1993. He was disheartened by the decline of his personal popularity and angered by the amnesty accorded (in February 1994) to the leaders of the parliamentary resistance of October 1993. Yeltsin's response to this frustration was to become more reclusive, authoritarian, and patriarchal. If the thrust of his authority-building strategy during 1991–1993 had been transformative, the thrust of his subsequent strategy for maintaining and recouping that authority was consolidative.

Why did he react in this way? Given what we know about Yeltsin's personality, and given the emphasis on personality factors in his aides' memoirs, we might be tempted to ascribe the reaction entirely to idiosyncratic factors. Yeltsin, by this accounting, was predisposed to personalistic leadership and to a patriarchal self-conception. In that respect, he was a product of Soviet socialization, like so many other *apparatchiki* of this type in the post-Stalin era. In the face of frustration, he allowed this orientation to become dominant; he reverted to his roots.

While such an argument has some plausibility, it seems incomplete. Yeltsin's personality, after all, also included a passion for facing challenges and an aversion to stasis. These were also features of a particular type of Soviet *apparatchik*. Furthermore, his self-image – as well as his authority-building strategy – rested on a promise to construct a new political and economic order, which was far from complete in 1994.

An alternative explanation for Yeltsin's reversion to a reclusive political style is political – specifically, political insecurity. Although he had been freely elected as president of Russia and enjoyed enormous charismatic authority after August 1991, these sources of political popularity are wasting assets. During his struggle with the Supreme Soviet in 1992–1993, he could never be certain that he would not be removed from office by force; the abortive coup attempt of 1991 was a very recent memory. Nor, in October 1993, did Yeltsin find it easy to gain military support for assaulting the parliament; many commanders were reluctant to implement his orders. He could never be confident that his administrative staff was devoted to implementing his declared policies; in fact, one memoirist claims that Yeltsin drew the conclusion that parliament had declared amnesty for his political enemies only as a result of the negligence or perfidy of his own staff.[24] Hence, even if he were not already so inclined (which he was), circumstances would have nudged Yeltsin toward suspicion: a heightened insistence on personal loyalty, a growing tendency to test the loyalties of his associates and appointees, a more pronounced urge to show them who was boss, a simultaneous urge to ensure his personal security by developing intimate personal relationships with his defense minister (Pavel Grachev) and his bodyguards, and a decision that divided government just doesn't work.[25]

Thus, political uncertainty was a constant throughout his years as Russian president whereas political self-confidence, authority, and credibility were variables. As Yeltsin's own confidence declined in his ability to solve the country's problems, to mobilize the masses, to control the "force ministries," and to maintain his authority and credibility as an effective leader, his level of reclusive authoritarianism increased. The Constitution might have given the president enormous formal powers, but Russia was a young republic. Yeltsin still had to worry constantly about whether he might become a victim of extra-constitutional acts. Though elected to a five-year term of office in 1991, he could not be confident that – in the face of plummeting popularity among the masses – forces within the political establishment would not seek to remove him from office before the end of his term. And he could not take for granted that the electorate would grant him a second term in the election scheduled for June 1996.

As argued in Chapter 9, Yeltsin's sense of political insecurity in 1994 made a significant contribution to his decision to invade Chechnya at the end of that year. More broadly, however, Yeltsin's reaction to frustration after 1993 was to attempt to consolidate the system he had started to build, rather than to

---

[24] Viacheslav Kostikov, *Roman s prezidentom: zapiski press-sekretaria* (Moscow: Vagrius, 1997), pp. 286–7, 290–3.

[25] On the last point, see Yeltsin, *The Struggle*, p. 238, where (writing in early 1994) he declares his disenchantment with a division of powers among the branches of government.

finish the construction. He touted himself as the man who would never allow the disintegration of Russia. Beyond ensuring territorial integrity, Yeltsin defined his main role as guarantor against communist or revanchist restoration, which led him to marshal a coalition of interests that included moderates and what he called "reformists." He turned a blind eye to the growing corruption within his administration. He endorsed the "loans for shares" privatization scheme of 1995, which created a small class of powerful tycoons who would fight against communist restoration and claim a stake in Yeltsin's reelection. He flirted with the idea of canceling the 1996 presidential election and banning the Communist Party of the Russian Federation. To be sure, he continued attempts to cooperate with the United States and Western Europe, to integrate Russia into Western international institutions, and to secure loans and credits from the West. Increasingly, however, he treated these goals as preconditions for successful consolidation of the new order at home, as guarantees against the instability that could lead to communist restoration, and as markers of his indispensability as a leader who, through his relationships with Western leaders, could bring home the goods.

Yeltsin's choice to react to frustration in this way was not dictated by political "necessity." There was no constellation of political forces after 1993 that was forcing him down this path. Neither the Duma nor social organizations had the power either to compel Yeltsin to adopt a consolidating strategy or to prevent him from adopting a more radical set of policies. The Duma was a more docile organization than the Congress of People's Deputies, in part because of the latter's forced dissolution and in part because of the new rules of the game dictated by the December 1993 Constitution.[26] Social organizations, though numerous, were less powerful than they had been during 1990–1991; this resulted from an ebbing of the revolutionary wave, the reassertion of some political controls, and the impoverishment of much of society owing to shock therapy.[27] Governments abroad were not pushing Yeltsin in this direction, though they did define his continuance in power as an indispensable alternative to communist restoration.

In short, Yeltsin had the option to pursue different policies. He might have pushed forward with radicalization, as Gorbachev and Khrushchev (eventually) had done, but he lacked the inclination, the energy, the health, and the residual political self-confidence to do so. Instead, he tried to manage the

---

[26] See Michael McFaul, *Russia's Troubled Transition from Communism to Democracy: Institutional Change during Revolutionary Transformations* (Ithaca, NY: Cornell University Press, 2001), chs. 6–7.

[27] See Urban et al., *The Rebirth of Politics in Russia,* part IV.

incomplete system he had built, to shore up his grip on power, and to tout himself as the man whose longevity would ensure that the communists could never dismantle the foundations of that system.

Yeltsin was also a victim of constraints he had helped to create; hence, he lacked many of the instruments for completing the edifice on which he had begun construction. Yeltsin was increasingly burdened by decisional overload that often paralyzed policymaking. In this respect, he was partially the victim of his own success in destroying the communist system, for he ruled as president without the benefit of an established apparatus of officials to organize the flow of information to him and the implementation of his requests. Even a healthy leader would have been burdened by this deficiency, but Yeltsin was not a healthy man. He suffered from a weak heart, a painful back injury incurred in Spain in 1990, alcohol dependency, and a regimen of medications that exacerbated his seemingly manic-depressive mood swings. Over time, his press secretary reports, the burden of decisional overload took a further toll, leading Yeltsin to avoid documents, appointments, and (increasingly) decisions.[28] Moreover, given his political insecurity, Yeltsin resisted the obvious conclusion – that he delegate more decisionmaking responsibility to others – perhaps fearing a dilution of his authority or the crystallization of threats to his power.[29]

Yeltsin's emphasis on consolidation rather than continuing transformation (e.g., helping to build a rule of law) was reinforced by his fatalism about the impossibility of reforming the Russian bureaucracy. In his second memoir, which reflected on the lessons of his stage of ascendancy, Yeltsin argued that the Russian bureaucracy was a quagmire out of which little of use could be expected to emerge. He wrote that both the Russian bureaucracy and the Russian people required a "strong hand" to budge them from their inertial and nihilistic behavioral patterns. Unified, strong command was more important than rule of law, for "[e]veryone knows that we Russians do not like

---

[28] Kostikov, *Roman*, pp. 306–7: "Coming into his office, I often found him seated behind an empty table in deep, morose thought. He missed his earlier role of 'Director of all of Russia.' And it seemed that [he] was losing his head in the face of the scale of the deeds he enumerated for himself in his Constitution." Kostikov also reports that, during his entire period as president of Russia, Yeltsin was in physical pain from a variety of ailments, including severe back and leg pain (ibid., p. 196), an observation that is supported by Aleksandr Korzhakov, *Boris Yel'tsin: Ot rassveta do zakata* (Moscow: Izd-vo 'Interbuk,' 1997), p. 202.

[29] Korzhakov (ibid., p. 310) reports that, in the fall of 1993, Prime Minister Chernomyrdin tried to persuade Yeltsin to grant him more responsibilities and duties in order to relieve the presidential workload. Yeltsin, according to Korzhakov, viewed this with deep suspicion, fearing that Chernomyrdin might be seeking more formal power or might be planning to run against him in 1996.

to obey all sorts of rules, laws, instructions, and directives ... rules cut us like a knife."[30] "Somebody had to be the boss," he wrote in his second memoir. "Russia's main paradox was that ... [t]here had not been any real powerful leader in the Republic of Russia." At present, people "are almost incapable of doing anything themselves." Two or three presidencies will have to go by, he claimed, before this situation will change.[31] In this memoir, Yeltsin's very occasional references to rule of law were either ritualistic incantations or were accompanied by a befuddlement about how to make the Russian bureaucracy procedurally accountable: "Unfortunately, the law enforcement agencies are adapting very slowly and poorly to this new crime phenomenon. That's the typical Russian style."[32]

Fatalism about "the system" over which he ruled may also explain the blind eye he increasingly turned to the growing corruption of his government. This is a curious feature of Yeltsin's presidency. Few observers believe that Yeltsin held office largely for his personal material gain. In Sverdlovsk, he was not personally corrupt and he waged campaigns against corruption and privilege. In fact, he was advanced to a position in Moscow precisely because he was "clean" and a proven anti-corruption fighter. When he was first secretary of the Moscow Party committee in 1985–1987, he was famous for his anti-corruption campaigns and for his criticism of the formal privileges of the *nomenklatura*. Yet, despite regular speeches as president about the need to root out corruption, memoirists report a tendency for him increasingly to avoid following up on reports of corruption in his own administration.[33] His attitude of resignation about the unreformability of the Russian bureaucracy and about Russian cultural opposition to rule-driven behavior may also explain his failure to crack down on corruption. Resignation, sheer fatigue, and a lack of ideas about how to reduce corruption without further increasing his political vulnerability may have combined to deter him from tackling the task.

There are other, equally plausible explanations. One would be that Yeltsin cared about corruption only as a means of rising to power and dropped the concern once he became president of Russia. A second interpretation is that Yeltsin actually sought the corruption of all those around him in order to keep them loyal to him and dependent upon him for political protection against

---

[30] Yeltsin, *The Struggle*, pp. 139–40.

[31] Ibid., pp. 6, 7, 18–19.

[32] Ibid., p. 148.

[33] Valerii Streletskii, *Mrakobesie* (Moscow: Detektiv-Press, 1998), pp. 155–6; Kostikov, *Roman*, p. 216.

prosecution.[34] A third interpretation is that Yeltsin could not crack down on corruption without harming his own family – and especially his daughters and their husbands. While the evidence for Yeltsin's personal corruption after 1994 is scant, the evidence for the growing corruption of his children's families from 1994 onward is voluminous.[35] In particular, the business tycoon Boris Berezovskii appears to have enmeshed Yeltsin's family in unearned wealth and illicit associations of which Yeltsin may well have been aware. This raised the personal cost to Yeltsin of cracking down on corruption in his midst.

Whichever interpretation is correct (and they are not all mutually exclusive), the net result was that – for psychological, physical, political, or personal reasons – Yeltsin fought against corruption only rhetorically. This was consistent with his general posture toward transformative change in the period after 1993.

Yet even as he emphasized stability and consolidation during 1994–1999, Yeltsin periodically behaved as if it mattered that he demonstrate his ability to keep pushing history forward toward completion of the capitalist project. Periodically (1995, 1997, 1998), Yeltsin would suddenly emerge from seclusion, fire or demote members of his government, and appoint ministers – such as Boris Nemtsov, Sergei Kirienko, and Sergei Stepashin – who were young, independent of the oligarchs, and inclined to build a market-regulating state. He mandated them to break through constraints on the construction of a capitalist society (see Chapter 10). Whether Yeltsin actually believed what he was saying is impossible to discern. This may have been his way of convincing himself that he had not succumbed to Brezhnev-like stagnation. It may have been his way of trying to convince others, at home and abroad, that he was not a spent political force. It may have been his way of trying to convince the International Monetary Fund that he would not waste its money. Or it may have been a simple strategy of power maintenance: keeping all officials constantly off-balance and bringing in young people who did not have the stature or the connections to threaten his authority. Only when Yeltsin genuinely feared that he or his family could be prosecuted after his retirement from office did he drop the pretense of launching reformist breakthroughs. Even then, in retrospect, he tried to convince readers of his latest memoir that his main purpose in firing ministers during 1998–1999 had not been to protect himself but rather to find the man who would have the ability to prevent the communists from ever coming back to power.[36]

---

[34] This argument is made in Jerry Hough, *The Logic of Economic Reform*.
[35] See Reddaway and Glinski, *The Tragedy of Russia's Reforms*, ch. 8.
[36] Boris Yeltsin, *Midnight Diaries* (New York: Public Affairs, 2000), ch. 24.

CONCLUSION

In Chapter 1, I argued that structural explanations of leadership behavior in Soviet-type systems take us only so far. Those explanations highlight the constraining effects of political organization and Marxist–Leninist ideology on the scope of discretion available to the would-be authority builder. Within those parameters, however, leaders could fashion diverse authority-building strategies.

Structural explanations of leaders' choices become even less compelling once Gorbachev comes to power and especially after he consolidates power and begins to implement a comprehensive program. After 1986, the personalities and beliefs of individual leaders became ever more determinant of the fundamental choices they made. To be sure, many of their personal beliefs had roots in the Soviet ideological tradition, and their leadership styles mirrored distinctive types of *apparatchik* operating styles within the post-Stalin generations of regional Party officials. Hence, my focus on idiosyncratic factors is not meant to suggest that Gorbachev or Yeltsin were genetic mutations or alien bodies that somehow seized power in the Soviet system. Not at all. In fact, the authority-building and authority-maintenance framework employed in this book focuses our attention on precisely the opposite. It explores the ways in which leaders fashion appeals to political audiences and then use those appeals to build up their credibility and hence their leverage as leaders.

Once we concede that multiple appeals may resonate with the same audiences, and once we acknowledge that authority building is also an act of manipulation of audiences by leaders, then we are back to asking *how much* latitude leaders had to alter the structural constraints (organizational and ideological) of the system. From this perspective, Gorbachev and Yeltsin were less and less constrained as their efforts to transform the Soviet system moved forward in the 1980s. As the organization and ideology of the Soviet system cracked and then crumbled, Gorbachev's and Yeltsin's personalities and mentalities became that much more determinant of the choices they made.

The role of increasingly autonomous social forces also grew steadily during 1987–1993. Gorbachev released those social forces and then relied on them as a base of support for intimidation of the Old Guard within the establishment. By 1989 we can speak of autonomous social forces as being in perpetual interaction with leaders in reshaping the context of Soviet and post-Soviet politics – and in "co-producing" their leadership strategies. Ultimately, Gorbachev would trail in this process. Yeltsin seized the leadership of the process in 1989, but he too would sometimes be surprised by new levels of radical self-assertion by groups in society.

By 1993, radical social mobilization had subsided or had been channeled into legislative arenas. Under those circumstances, Yeltsin opted for an authority-maintenance strategy that appealed to a particular combination of reformist and conservative forces within both the political establishment and the broader society. By 1996, Yeltsin had built the foundations of a new system. To some extent, that system created structural constraints that, during Yeltsin's second term in office, may have limited his discretion to almost the same degree that the established Soviet system had limited the discretion of Brezhnev in his last years in office. President Putin's tortured efforts to fashion a program for significant change appear to be testimony to the resilience of those constraints. But that is a subject for another book.

12

Criteria for the Evaluation of Transformational Leaders

I have devoted most of this book to *analysis* of the political strategies of Gorbachev and Yeltsin. Chapters 9 and 11, however, were devoted to the challenge of *explaining* their choices. There remains an additional exercise of core relevance to the study of leadership: *evaluation*. How should we evaluate Gorbachev and Yeltsin as leaders? This is by far the most difficult task, for it subsumes the other two. We must determine what those men were trying to do and specify how much latitude they had to pursue those goals before we can evaluate the effectiveness of their leadership. And we must employ counterfactual reasoning ("what might have been") to ask whether their actions led to outcomes that would not have happened in the absence of their leadership. The exercise is made even more challenging by the normative component of any evaluation.[1] I begin the exercise with a short chapter that specifies criteria for the evaluation of transformational leaders. I then devote the last two chapters of the book to evaluations of Gorbachev and Yeltsin as transformational leaders.

REQUISITES OF EFFECTIVE TRANSFORMATIONAL LEADERSHIP

Transformational leadership is a process of what Schumpeter called "creative destruction": dismantling of the old system in a way that simultaneously creates the foundations for a new system.[2] This is a tall order for the most talented of leaders. As I argued in Chapter 1, leaders who seek to accomplish creative destruction must:

---

[1] Recall that the root for the word "evaluation" is "value."

[2] Joseph Schumpeter, *Capitalism, Socialism, and Democracy* (New York & London: Harper & Brothers, 1942), pp. 81–6.

- highlight publicly the incompatibility between emerging environmental demands, on the one hand, and current ordering principles and cultural assumptions, on the other;
- outline an alternative vision of political organization and culture that will restore a harmonious relationship between the transformed unit and its environment;
- mobilize constituencies in support of that vision;
- prevent defenders of the existing order from sabotaging transformation; and
- implement specific programs that will result in the replacement of the existing order with one that is better suited to the environmental demands of tomorrow.

When the point of departure is a monopolistic Leninist system, a transformational leader must:

- create and legitimize autonomous public arenas;
- disperse social, economic, political, and informational resources into those arenas;
- construct new institutions for coordination of decentralized social exchange and integration of the new social order; and
- plant the seeds of a new political–economic culture that is consonant with the new social order.

Thus, he must destroy the structures and culture of the old order, put new structures in their place, and help articulate a new culture. That, in any case, is the ideal. Rare is the leader who is able to succeed in both system destruction and system building. Gorbachev and Yeltsin tried to be successful on both counts.

STANDARDS FOR LEADERSHIP EVALUATION

In both journalism and academic scholarship, leadership evaluation takes place all the time – but usually without reflection on the standards being applied. Consequently, different standards may be applied to the same leader by different observers, leading to divergent bottom-line evaluations.

One standard is purely normative, with the norms determined by the observer: Do I agree or disagree with the values and goals being pursued by the leader? If I agree with his values and goals, I call him "great." If I dislike his values and goals then he cannot qualify as "great." A normative approach might also focus on the results of a leader's policies. If I approve of those results, I render a positive evaluation; if I disagree, my judgment will be negative. (As Hoffmann puts it, "a man who is a hero to my neighbor may be a calamity to me."[3]) More often than not, a normative approach to evaluation will conflate intentions and results, treating the latter as a product of the former.

For example, those who disliked what Gorbachev stood for often brought great passion to their negative evaluations, while those who liked what he stood for often displayed "Gorbymania." *Time* magazine might proclaim Gorbachev its "Man of the Decade," but Soviet reactionaries were damning his Westernization of the country while Soviet free-marketeers were damning his stubborn retention of a commitment to the "socialist idea." People at both ends of the Soviet political spectrum expressed dismay that Gorbachev eventually came to be so much admired abroad yet so little admired at home. When the debate over a leader's "performance" hinges largely on acceptance or rejection of the values he pursued or realized, the debate need not detain us long. It is not amenable to resolution through the marshaling of evidence. The debate may take a detour into a philosophical discussion of the relative merits of different values, but that is a different task than evaluating leadership per se.

Although a purely normative approach is too limited, we still need a standard by which to judge a leader's performance. Hence, a second approach to leadership evaluation hinges principally on judgments about *effectiveness*. Since effectiveness can only be determined relative to a set of goals (effective at achieving *what?*), goals and values must be part of the equation. But taking as our standard the *observer's* values does not get us very far if these differ from the values of the leader in question. It makes no sense to evaluate a leader's effectiveness in achieving goals he was not pursuing. Performance evaluation that is based on a standard of effectiveness must take *the leader's* goals and values as the standard and judge his effectiveness in advancing those goals. This is the approach I adopt in the final chapters of this book. How well did Gorbachev and Yeltsin perform as leaders in pursuit of the goals they embraced?

This approach need not entail approval of the leader's goals. An observer who disagrees with the leader's goals may nonetheless begrudgingly concede that he was highly effective in achieving them. Conversely, an observer who agrees with the goals may sadly concede that the leader proved ineffective in achieving them. And to fill out the possibilities: an observer may disagree

---

[3] Stanley Hoffmann, "Heroic leadership: The case of modern France," in Lewis J. Edinger (Ed.), *Political Leadership in Industrialized Societies* (New York: Wiley, 1967), p. 113.

with the goals and celebrate the leader's ineffectiveness in pursuing them, or the observer may agree with the goals and celebrate the leader's effectiveness in achieving them.

Effectiveness typically comes at a price. Leaders may achieve their goals at high or low cost to other values. Stalin is an obvious case in point. He built up the military and industrial strength of the country at enormous human and economic cost. Leadership evaluation will therefore hinge on the magnitude of the costs associated with goal attainment. Leaders who achieve their goals at low cost to collateral values may be deemed more effective than those who impose a very high price for goal attainment.

It does not follow, however, that observers will dub such leaders "great." Such characterizations hinge more on the observer's values. If we deeply cherish the values sacrificed for the sake of goal attainment – such as the millions of human lives sacrificed by Stalin – then we may concede that Stalin was an effective but dastardly leader who attained his goals at an unacceptable price. Bringing this point closer to the present, one could concede that Boris Yeltsin was effective in sustaining the territorial unity of the Russian Federation yet condemn him for the price he was willing to pay toward this end in waging two wars in Chechnya. Or, with a similar logic, one could give Gorbachev high marks for attaining his goals of liberalization and democratization but condemn him (if one is so inclined) for his willingness to do so at the expense of the disintegration of the Soviet Union.

It is not surprising that those who condemn Yeltsin's leadership most vociferously also view the social and human costs of his policies as huge. They argue as well that those costs (e.g., the decline in the life-span of Russian men and women) were direct products of his policies – that is, costs that would not have been borne in the absence of his policies.[4] Similarly, those who most vociferously condemn Gorbachev's leadership tend to be those who most valued the Soviet system, the USSR, and/or the country's great-power status and who attribute direct causal responsibility to Gorbachev for the loss of those values.[5] Expressed in this way, the cost of goal attainment is acceptable or unacceptable according to the observer's scale of values. This is an appropriate standard for an evaluative exercise, which cannot escape some normative component. But it is not amenable to resolution through the marshaling of

---

[4] Jerry Hough, *The Logic of Economic Reform in Russia* (Washington, DC: Brookings Institution, 2001); Peter Reddaway and Dmitri Glinski, *The Tragedy of Russia's Reforms: Market Bolshevism against Democracy* (Washington, DC: U.S. Institute of Peace, 2000).

[5] This is a rare person in Western scholarship; it is common among Russian journalists of a revanchist persuasion.

evidence. Hence, a social-scientific approach to leadership evaluation will logically veer toward another set of issues: What was the alternative? How effective would alternative strategies have been for attaining the goals at a lower price?

THE INESCAPABILITY OF COUNTERFACTUAL REASONING

Leaders and their supporters often defend themselves against criticism of the costs of their policies by invoking an image of intractable constraints. The implication is that advancement or defense of cherished values could not have been accomplished by other means. That is a counterfactual claim. Thus, Viacheslav Molotov, a leading Politburo member under Stalin, referred to the human and economic cost of Stalinist policies as "regrettable necessities." Unrepentant Stalinists in many countries deflected criticism of the costs of Stalinism by arguing that "you cannot make an omelette without breaking eggs."[6] Gorbachev and his supporters tried to parry criticisms from Party conservatives by arguing that "there is no alternative" and that "there is no other way" (*inogo ne dano*). Defenders of Yeltsin's policies in Chechnya argued that even Abraham Lincoln had to wage a bloody civil war in order to hold the United States together. Defenders of Yeltsin's neoliberal macroeconomic policies frequently argued that alternatives to their preferred policies would not "work."

In all these cases, the counterfactual is usually buttressed by a theoretical claim. Stalin invoked a theory of state building, nation building, and economic development in a hostile international environment that seemed to narrow drastically the set of policies claimed to be effective in such a setting. Gorbachev's defenders suggested that only a policy that shattered the immunity of the Party–State elite could overcome the systemic stagnation that had beset the ancien régime. Yeltsin's defenders claimed that, even in democratic systems, force is required to prevent armed secession. Yeltsin's neoliberal advisers similarly argued that "shock therapy" constituted the only viable strategy for making the transition from a command economy to a market economy.

Both critics and defenders of Gorbachev and Yeltsin often join the argument not on theoretical grounds but on the basis of an empirical estimation of the intellectual availability, political feasibility, and practicability of

---

[6] Prompting Chalmers Johnson to ask: "How many eggs do you have to break to make a one-egg omelette?" (in "Foreword" of Alexander Dallin and George W. Breslauer, *Political Terror in Communist Systems* [Stanford, CA: Stanford University Press, 1970], p. vi).

alternative policies in the given historical context. Thus, when people criticize Gorbachev for not having pushed through a Chinese-style economic
reform and for not having adopted radical price reform early in his tenure,[7]
his defenders claim that he faced great uncertainty about whether the Chinese reforms would work in the Soviet context and about the compatibility
of price liberalization with political stability.[8] When Yeltsin is condemned
for adopting neoliberal policies in January 1992,[9] his defenders argue that, in
the concrete economic circumstances of the time, alternative policies would
have caused a financial and economic collapse with even more dire consequences.[10] And when Yeltsin is criticized for not being more accommodative
of the political opposition in the Supreme Soviet and Duma,[11] his defenders
argue or imply that the opposition was more powerful and more reactionary
in orientation than Yeltsin's critics allow. They argue that the opposition had
both the strength and the inclination to win power and to restore some variant
of the old regime – hence, the alternative (by this observer's scale of values)
would have been worse.[12]

In short, evaluation of a leader's effectiveness in attaining his goals at a pro-
portionate price hinges also on one's image of the strength of the constraints
facing the leader at the time. If the constraints were onerous, we would normally expect less accomplishment than if the constraints were loose. A leader
who manages to stretch (but not obliterate) the constraints in his environment, and thereby to initiate substantial movement at an acceptable cost, is
typically deemed both effective and impressive. By contrast, a leader who is
defeated by those constraints may be deemed ineffective but doomed to failure
if the constraints are perceived to have been immutable, or he may be judged
ineffective and incompetent if he failed to seize the opportunities available to
him. And if a leader accomplishes much but in a context wherein constraints

---

[7] Jerry Hough, *Revolution and Democratization in the USSR, 1985–1991* (Washington, DC:
Brookings Institution, 1998).

[8] George W. Breslauer, "Evaluating Gorbachev as leader," *Soviet Economy*, vol. 8, no. 4
(October–December 1989), pp. 299–340.

[9] Reddaway and Glinski, *The Tragedy of Russia's Reforms*.

[10] Anders Åslund, *How Russia Became a Market Economy* (Washington, DC: Brookings Institution, 1995); Andrei Shleifer and Daniel Treisman, *Without a Map: Political Tactics and
Economic Reform in Russia* (Cambridge, MA: MIT Press, 2000).

[11] This is a standard refrain by many scholars contributing to the Internet-based *Johnson's Russia List*.

[12] This is a major theme of Leon Aron, *Boris Yeltsin: A Revolutionary Life* (New York: Harper-
Collins, 2000); contrast this with Hough's depiction of the strength and orientations of the
opposition in *The Logic of Economic Reform*. Intermediate positions are struck by Lilia
Shevtsova, *Yeltsin's Russia: Myths and Realities* (Washington, DC: Carnegie Endowment,
1999) and Reddaway and Glinski, *The Tragedy of Russia's Reforms*.

were few and easily stretched, he may be judged to have been effective but unimpressive ("anybody could have done it").

Thus, leadership cannot be evaluated without some conception of its flip side: opportunity. If the challenge was so great as to be impossible to achieve, then (by definition) no amount of brilliance could have overcome the constraints. Under such circumstances, there was no opportunity to exploit. On the other hand, if the challenge was a simple one, or if existing social and political forces would have pushed through the changes we witnessed in any case, then the leader can hardly be credited with having "made history."

Notice that making these judgments requires us to think in counterfactual terms. We may gather a large amount of evidence regarding the nature of the constraints, the strength of social forces, and the like. But without trying to imagine how these constraints and forces would have evolved *in the absence of the leader in question,* or in the presence of either a stronger or weaker leader, we cannot estimate either the magnitude of the opportunity or the indispensability of a given leader for exploiting it. Since other leaders were not in power and since other approaches were not attempted, we cannot test with high confidence the size of the opportunity that was available. The difficulty in addressing the "might have beens" of history has led many historians to disparage counterfactual thought experiments as little more than fruitless speculation or parlor games.[13]

But without counterfactual reasoning there can be no evaluation of leadership. Methodologically, a convincing exercise in leadership evaluation must interweave counterfactual reasoning with traditional methods of analysis and explanation. It must combine disciplined speculation about available alternatives with analysis of the strength of constraints and efforts to specify the causes of outcomes. Thus, leadership evaluation must seek to determine how much causal responsibility to assign to the exercise of leadership for the outcomes observed; it must also ask whether hypothetical alternatives were indeed available. It must analyze the magnitude of the task, the magnitude and mutability of the constraints on change, and the magnitude of the divergence from the traditional (and currently available) skills and mentality required to carry out the task in the face of those constraints. Ultimately, it must address such questions as: To what extent was the individual's repertoire of

---

[13] Historians tend to reject counterfactual analysis as a scholarly exercise, whereas social scientists often embrace it. Such historians include E. H. Carr, A. J. P. Taylor, and E. P. Thompson. For a book by social scientists that is devoted to the methodology and application of counterfactual reasoning in the study of international affairs, see Philip Tetlock and Aaron Belkin (Eds.), *Counterfactual Thought Experiments in World Politics* (Princeton, NJ: Princeton University Press, 1996).

leadership skills, and the leadership strategy he adopted, a necessary (albeit not sufficient) condition for achieving the results observable during his years in power? How different would things have been had he not been in power? Could other individuals who were available at the time have accomplished as much as, or more than, he did? How powerful were the political constraints on his choices? Could he have succeeded in even more than he dared to attempt? Or would he have been forced from power – or at least frustrated – had he tried?

Given all these uncertainties, we might be tempted to abandon the task of leadership evaluation or to consign it to journalistic exercises in special issues of popular magazines.[14] That would be unwise. Historians and social scientists do not abandon their craft because the evidence is inconclusive; they seek to make the best of what they have and then to present their conclusions as always subject to future revision. The same goes for counterfactual speculation, which is not as different from historical explanation, methodologically or epistemologically, as many historians assume.[15] Moreover, no matter how indeterminate the exercise, people will go on evaluating leaders, for better or for worse, and their evaluations of leaders in power will sometimes feed back into the political process. How scholars, politicians, and journalists evaluate current or historical leaders can influence present-day politics. Indeed, with respect to current leaders being evaluated while in office, it can become part of the social constraints they face and can influence the opportunities they enjoy – and thereby affect their prospects of eventually succeeding or failing! Hence, to abandon leadership evaluation because of its inconclusiveness or indeterminacy is to abandon scholarship. And eschewing it because of its normative components and possible political impact is an unnecessary act of scholarly abdication.

Gorbachev and Yeltsin were unmistakably "event-making men."[16] Both of them began as reformers of the system and then sought to transform or replace it, though they chose very different strategies for achieving their goals. Both of them faced huge constraints at home and abroad. Both of them were unique figures within elite circles. It is difficult to imagine other leaders at the time who would have made an analogous degree of difference. In evaluating

---

[14] See, for example, the special issue of *Time* magazine (April 13, 1998) devoted to evaluation of twentieth-century leaders.

[15] See George Breslauer and Richard Ned Lebow, "Gorbachev, Reagan, and the end of the Cold War," in Richard K. Herrmann and Richard Ned Lebow (Eds.), *Learning from the Cold War* (forthcoming).

[16] The concept of "event-making man" is from Sidney Hook, *The Hero in History* (Boston: Beacon, 1943), p. 154.

Gorbachev's and Yeltsin's effectiveness as leaders, then, we must address the extent to which they achieved their stated goals and the price they proved willing to pay toward that end.

AUTHORITY BUILDING AND LEADERSHIP EVALUATION

Transformational leadership is a process, not an event. Such leaders must attend to many issues and dilemmas that unfold unevenly over a period of time. Throughout this process, they must attend as well to the condition of their personal authority. Are they building their authority in ways that will leave them positioned to sponsor a thrust – a breakthrough – that will overcome the constraints on fundamental change? Having accomplished that, they must attend to the challenge of authority maintenance. Have they justified their breakthrough to audiences that may have the capacity to unravel the changes? And, equally important, do they retain the credibility to engage in the follow-up required to elaborate on the changes?

A breakthrough may be required to undo the old structures and delegitimize the old culture. But numerous and repeated follow-up initiatives are required to put new structures in place and to build legitimacy for the new order. A leader's capacity to engage in such follow-up hinges on the condition of his power and authority. Did he squander them in the course of pushing through his breakthrough policies? Or did he position himself to retain the *power* for follow-up and explain himself sufficiently to retain the *authority* for follow-up? As we shall see, both Gorbachev and Yeltsin had mixed records on these scores.

13

Evaluating Gorbachev as Leader

Among observers who shared his goal of transforming the communist system, those who most approve of Gorbachev's record as leader emphasize the extent to which he broke down the ancien régime. Among the same set of observers, those who most disparage Gorbachev's record focus instead on the extent to which he fell short of building the new system he envisaged. Neither of these approaches is wholly satisfying; nor is a combination of the two. They are both linear and rote comparisons of outcomes with baselines. But they are useful starting points toward a more complex analysis.

If the past is our baseline, and if we postpone the problem of determining Gorbachev's distinctive contribution to the outcome, it is easy to sum up what changed under Gorbachev. We witnessed:

- desacralization of the Brezhnevite political–economic order in the eyes of the mass public, including the official principles and mind-set that underpinned it – the leading role of the Party, the "community of peoples," the planned economy, pride in the system's achievements, optimism about state socialism's potential, commitment to "class struggle" abroad, and a national-security phobia that justified a repressive, militarized regime;
- a sharp reduction in the power of constituencies that were pillars of the Brezhnevite political order – in particular, Party officials, ministers, and the military;
- legitimation in principle of movement in the direction of a market-driven economic order, a multiparty system, and the transformation of a unitary state into a democratic federal state;
- changes in politics and structure that (a) greatly decentralized political initiative, (b) created more open and competitive public political arenas –

including parliaments based on competitive, secret-ballot elections, (c) all but disenfranchised the *nomenklatura,* and (d) swept radical majorities into power in the governmental councils of major cities;
- dismantling of much of the command economy and the emergence of a nascent private sector ("cooperatives");
- introduction of civil liberties with respect to dissent, emigration, the media, travel, religion, and association;
- a vast opening of the country to Western political, cultural, and economic influences;
- elimination of Soviet control over Eastern Europe, reduction of Soviet military capabilities, retrenchment in Third World policy, and withdrawal of Soviet troops from Afghanistan; and
- changes in foreign policy that brought an end to the Cold War.

Historically, only revolutions from below have accomplished more in a shorter period of time. And revolutions from below have rarely been marked by the scant violence that Gorbachev's revolution entailed.

Using the same methodology, however, one could specify either how much had *not* changed during the Gorbachev era or had changed for the worse (by a short-term humanitarian standard):

- a doleful consumer situation that, in 1990–1991, was worse than it had been in 1985;
- an economy that was experiencing accelerating negative growth of national income, was ridden by a huge budgetary deficit and monetary overhang, and was suffering from potentially explosive repressed inflation;
- economic disorganization, lack of coordination, and massive corruption resulting from destruction of the institutions of a command economy without the construction of institutions of a market economy;
- widespread intercommunal violence in the southern republics of the USSR;
- disintegration of the unitary state as well as centrifugal pressures that left the country on the verge of separatism by half the republics in the union;
- a sharp increase in the incidence of violent crime throughout the country; and
- failure to induce the rich democracies to underwrite the Soviet economic transition.

Were the changes between 1985 and 1991 on balance positive or negative? This is a normative judgment. The answer depends on the relative weights placed on the values in question. Clearly, one glance at these lists indicates that things worsened with respect to the economic situation and the cohesion of the USSR as an entity; things improved in the areas of political freedom, cultural openness, and East–West relations, where "improvement" is measured according to Gorbachev's professed scale of values.[1]

Another approach would take as its baseline not the past but the vision of a future new order. The easy variant of this approach is simply to measure the shortfall between Soviet reality in mid-1991 and Gorbachev's vision of a stable social(ist)-democratic polity that was integrated into Western institutions and treated internationally as a great power, a tolerable federation or confederation, and a prospectively flourishing mixed economy based on a combination of private, collective, and state ownership.[2] By this standard, Gorbachev surely fell short as a transformational leader. He did not succeed in steering an evolutionary transition from the Soviet system to a system based on these ordering principles. Instead, the house collapsed upon him and he was ousted from office.

GORBACHEV: AN EVENT-MAKING MAN?

If we treat the list of positive changes between 1985 and 1991 as the basis for a positive evaluation of Gorbachev as leader, then we presume that he himself was causally responsible for the changes. That would be too generous a judgment, for we know that many outcomes after 1989 were products of forces over which he had little control. But we can still ask whether, on balance, Gorbachev was an "event-making man" whose uncommon personal traits led to outcomes that would not have taken place in the absence of the leadership he provided. In this exercise, the issue is not normative but causal. It does not matter whether we approve or disapprove of the outcomes, only whether we believe that Gorbachev was responsible for bringing them about. By this standard, Gorbachev was indeed an event-making man.

Changes in social structure during the post-Stalin decades are insufficient to explain the changes that took place during 1985–1989, though a focus on societal initiatives probably does explain much of what happened in 1990–1991. The social forces supportive of *perestroika, glasnost'*, democratization, and "new thinking" in foreign policy encouraged and facilitated Gorbachev's changes. Indeed, they were probably necessary conditions for the changes in

---

[1] Observers who mourn Soviet loss of superpower status and control over Eastern Europe would not place the "end of the Cold War" in the "improvements" category.

[2] For present purposes, I will treat the period of March 1985 to late August 1991 (i.e., through the coup attempt) as the "Gorbachev era." Thereafter, disintegrative trends accelerated sharply and Gorbachev's political authority had all but evaporated.

policy to be enacted, implemented, and sustained. It is difficult, for example, to imagine Gorbachev having accomplished as much as he did had he been leading the Soviet Union in 1955 rather than 1985. But the changes that had taken place in Soviet society, while providing a support base for Gorbachev to activate, were not sufficient to force policymakers to enact the policies Gorbachev sponsored. The relationship between social forces and sociopolitical change was heavily dependent on political leadership.

Gorbachev exercised active, determined leadership in the years following his consolidation of power. He intervened repeatedly to let the *glasnost'* genie out of the bottle, to encourage the public to criticize the bureaucrats, to hold off the forces of backlash, to recall Andrei Sakharov from exile, to release political prisoners, and to force through a democratization program that began the process of transferring power from the Party to the soviets. Gorbachev made the decisions that led to steadily expanding civil liberties of all sorts. Gorbachev made the doctrinal pronouncements that encouraged or tolerated *public* desacralization of the Brezhnevite order. This desacralization induced societal activists to believe that fundamental change was not only desirable and necessary (which many of them probably believed already) but possible as well. And Gorbachev's pronouncements had the simultaneous effect of discouraging recalcitrant bureaucrats from thinking that they could hold back the tide. He did all this at a stage of his administration when predecessors (Khrushchev and Brezhnev) had engaged in selective reincorporation – during their stages of ascendancy (see Chapter 11).

In similar fashion, Gorbachev took the lead on matters of foreign policy, often surprising his domestic political audiences with announcements of Soviet concessions on nuclear and conventional arms control, making the fundamental decision to cut losses in Afghanistan, and pulling the rug from under conservative East European elites by withdrawing the Soviet guarantee of protection against revolutionary forces. Gorbachev articulated a vision of a post–Cold War world, Soviet integration into the European cultural, political, and economic orders, and demilitarization of foreign policy that became the basis for both planning and legitimizing his turnabouts in both domestic and foreign policy. Gorbachev decided to turn on the faucet of emigration once again, allowing Soviet citizens to travel to the West more freely.

To be sure, once sufficiently emboldened and organized, social forces pushed to radicalize Gorbachev's policies more quickly and more fully than he was comfortable with at the time. In the face of this society-driven radicalization, Gorbachev still had a choice: he could have allied with conservatives to "draw the line" and enforce strict limits. Instead – until his course correction of late 1990 and with the exception of his response to intercommunal violence in the south – he typically made a virtue of necessity. He resisted the temptation to use force, often allying with more radical forces, using tactical surprise to further consolidate his power at the top, and purging or holding at bay those who would have preferred to use such radicalization as justification for reversing or halting the reform process. Thus, in 1989–1990, Gorbachev was more reactive than initiatory, but he was still event-making in his ability to prevent the use of state-directed violence against the radicalizing tide. (A tragic exception occurred in Tbilisi in April 1989.[3]) When he lost his nerve in fall 1990, he was no longer event-making at all and had actually though inadvertently created the conditions for both the bloodshed in Vilnius and Riga and the coup of August 1991.

The event-making man not only makes a difference but does so because of his exceptional personal qualities. On this score, the evidence seems to be conclusive. Even those who criticize Gorbachev for the limits of his flexibility in his last years in power acknowledge that he was an unusual member of the Chernenko-led Politburo. No member of that Politburo has been portrayed as capable of seizing the initiative on sociopolitical and international issues the way Gorbachev eventually did. Gorbachev's intellectual capacity and flexibility, his powers of argumentation, his serenity in the midst of social turmoil and faith that turbulence will "smooth out" in the long run,[4] his "sustained, single-minded motivation ... an irrepressible optimism,"[5] his energy, determination, and tactical political skill,[6] and his capacity for learning on the job[7] have been noted by observers and interlocutors alike. By previous Soviet standards, as well as by comparative international standards, he stands

---

3 A commission of inquiry, which included people closer to Yeltsin than to Gorbachev, exonerated Gorbachev from charges of having ordered the use of force (Archie Brown, *The Gorbachev Factor* [Oxford & New York: Oxford University Press, 1996], pp. 264–7); but it remains the case that he failed to prevent it.

4 Ronald Tiersky, "Perestroika and beyond," *Problems of Communism*, vol. 39, no. 2 (March–April 1990), p. 114; *Time* magazine, June 4, 1990, pp. 27–34.

5 Doig and Hargrove find this characteristic to be typical of successful leaders of the public bureaucracies they studied (Jameson W. Doig and Erwin C. Hargrove [Eds.], *Leadership and Innovation* [Baltimore: Johns Hopkins University Press, 1967], p. 19).

6 See Dusko Doder and Louise Branson, *Gorbachev: Heretic in the Kremlin* (New York: Viking, 1990), pp. 31, 304, and passim.

7 Ibid., pp. 31, 75, 106, 126–8, 157, 163, 218–19, and 374–6 for examples. See also Brown, *The Gorbachev Factor*, chs. 4 and 7, and Robert D. English, *Russia and the Idea of the West: Gorbachev, Intellectuals and the End of the Cold War* (New York: Columbia University Press, 2000), chs. 5 and 6. Henry Kissinger (*White House Years* [Boston: Little, Brown, 1979], p. 54) has argued that "it is an illusion to believe that leaders gain in profundity while they gain experience .... The convictions that leaders have formed before reaching high office are the intellectual capital they will consume as long as they continue in office." The evolution of Gorbachev's thinking during his first five years in office challenges the applicability to his

out as a man of unusual leadership capacity. Had Gorbachev not been chosen general secretary after Chernenko's death, destruction of the Brezhnevite
political order, the creation and nurturing of new democratic institutions and
practices, and the radical concessionary turn in Soviet foreign policy would
not have taken place as they did – or even at all – in the 1980s.

GORBACHEV'S STRATEGY OF "CULTURE AND POLITICS FIRST"

Gorbachev moved more quickly on political liberalization (*glasnost'*), political democratization, and ending the Cold War than he did on economic reform
and federalizing the union. Thus, he treated cultural and political transformation, at home and abroad, as preconditions for sustained improvements
in economic performance and inter-ethnic relations. Indeed, Gorbachev was
quite explicit about his conclusion that cultural change ("the human factor")
was a prerequisite for economic reform: "We have to begin, first of all, with
changes in our attitudes and psychology, with the style and method of work,"
he declared in April 1986. "I have to tell you frankly that, if we do not change
ourselves, I am deeply convinced there will be no changes in the economy and
our social life."[8] Some of Gorbachev's earliest boosters were quick to notice,
and to approve, this theory of transition.[9]

Gorbachev used the resources of his offices to delegitimize the old order –
both its institutional framework and the social values it allegedly protected.
He simultaneously created new public arenas within which the awakened society could exercise initiative for the political and economic good of the country.
He launched *perestroika* by defining the situation of the USSR in the world as
one that demanded emergency surgery lest the country descend into second-
class status. He reacted to unpleasant surprises (the Chernobyl disaster of
April 1986; a young German's landing of a Cessna airplane in Red Square in
May 1987) by purging members of the Old Guard and by arguing that those
surprises demonstrated the urgent need for cultural and institutional change.

---

leadership of Kissinger's generalization. If that challenge is sustainable, it would strengthen a
positive evaluation of Gorbachev's leadership skills. Alternatively, one could argue that Gorbachev's "convictions" were fixed before he came to power and that his learning was largely
"tactical" within the bounds of his earlier convictions. Part of the problem in deciding this
question is purely definitional. Does "conviction" refer to values alone or also to one's under-
standings about cause–effect relations within the domestic system, society, and international
environment?

[8] Gorbachev speech of April 8, 1986, as quoted in Doder and Branson, *Gorbachev*, p. 137.
[9] Robert C. Tucker, *Political Culture and Leadership in Soviet Russia: From Lenin to Gorbachev* (New York: Norton, 1987), ch. 7; Thomas Naylor, *The Gorbachev Strategy* (Lexington,
MA: Lexington, 1988).

He defined a tight connection between his foreign and domestic policies, harnessing forces in the international arena to further the cause of political and cultural change within the Soviet Union. In each case this served organizational and technical ends, but in each case it also served the more important goals of transforming politics, identities, and culture. Gorbachev sought to transform culture by simultaneously altering the ideology and the organization of Soviet politics.

Thus, by opening the Soviet economy to global competition, Gorbachev was trying not only to increase pressure on Soviet managers and draw in foreign capital but also to force elites and masses alike to define progress relative to the achievements of advanced capitalist countries, rather than relative to the Russian or Soviet past. By encouraging McDonald's to open an outlet in Moscow, by televising images of Western living standards, and by encouraging televised discussions of the progress of Chinese economic reforms, he not only whetted consumer appetites but undercut traditional images of "capitalist hell" through which the ruling elite had justified maintenance of a low-opportunity system. By opening the country to cultural Westernization, Gorbachev did more than reduce the political, scientific, and international costs of trying to insulate the country from the information revolution; he also challenged the idea of Russian or Soviet "originality" (*samobytnost'*) that had justified both the Brezhnevite order and the xenophobia of Russian ethno-nationalists. By working to reduce international threats to the USSR, he created preconditions for lowering the defense budget and diluted the national-security phobia that had been used to justify domination of the economy by the military–industrial complex. By repudiating class struggle abroad and by emphasizing the priority of "all-human values," he not only defused regional crises and paved the way for arms control (and other forms of superpower cooperation) but also undermined the rationale for the CPSU's continued monopoly on power and truth. Indeed, the extraordinary importance of ideas and doctrines in Leninist systems made it all the more imperative that transformational leaders in such regimes first delegitimize relevant aspects of traditional elite ideology – and its impact on mass perceptions of what is feasible – as a precondition for creating the political space for new patterns of behavior and organization.

As successful transformational leaders must, Gorbachev recognized that a precondition for fundamental change is the destruction of old identities and tolerance of the social conflict that inevitably accompanies such a passage. He used social and political conflict as occasions for educating citizenry and polity alike to the idea that there is no change without pain and no democracy without conflict. He reacted to unanticipated levels of conflict (except for intercommunal violence and the use of violence against state organs) by claiming them as proof that the old way of doing things was intolerable and, more importantly, was now capable of being changed. He articulated a vision of the USSR as a "normal" modern country on the model of the social democratic European welfare state, even as he fudged the question of whether a market-based pluralist democracy is consistent with "socialism." He spoke the language of evolution, defining change (both at home and abroad) as a long-term process that requires acclimatization to continuous change. Although he did not transform the welfare-state mentality of most of the population, he did foster a widespread belief in (socialist) pluralism and (socialist) markets as the desirable and feasible alternatives to political oppression and economic stagnation.

Gorbachev also tried to legitimize creation of a legal culture that would depersonalize legal institutions of the state and thereby provide a foundation of stable expectations for the protection of person and property. He called for a new legal code, a more independent judiciary, transfer of power from Party organs to soviets at all levels, and transformation of soviets into parliamentary institutions that generate legislation binding on all people. These were some of the components of his professed commitment to a "law-based state" (*pravovoe gosudarstvo*) to replace the previous order's arbitrary rule by Party officials. Of course, building a rule of law and instilling legal consciousness in the citizenry are long-term processes. But Gorbachev started the journey by legitimizing the search for a procedurally predictable alternative to arbitrary, personalistic governance and by disrupting the ability of Party organs to dominate the legal realm.

In like manner, Gorbachev sought to transform the culture of international relations. The targets of his attack were the dominant "realist" paradigm that emphasized the balancing of military power; the "enemy image" that fed worst-case planning and weapons procurement; and the "two camps" mentality that defined superpower competition as a confrontational, zero-sum game. Instead, he justified his concessionary foreign policy by propounding an idealist vision of international politics that sought to transform the image of the USSR into that of a partner in solving all-human problems. His conviction appears to have been that such a transformation in assumptions about the enemy was a prerequisite for ending the Cold War, and that ending the Cold War was a precondition for the kind of international climate needed to support Soviet internal transformation. The "new thinking," then, was aimed at both domestic and foreign audiences. In both cases, the purpose was ideational change; in both cases, the goal was to destroy an old way of thinking and to inculcate a new one.

On his own terms, then, Gorbachev was successful in delegitimizing the inherited approach to political life at home and abroad and its hostility to a democratic political order and a post–Cold War international order. Indeed, such change may be his principal claim to fame as a transformational leader.

Now I turn from Gorbachev's strategy of transformation to the political tactics he employed to make this a *peaceful* and *evolutionary* transformation. One place to look for guidance in this regard is the burgeoning literature on transitions to democracy. The prescriptions in that literature may not be entirely applicable to the case of a Leninist multi-ethnic empire, but they do remain suggestive of tactics for a peaceful political transition. Gorbachev's leadership can then be judged against those standards. If he failed in spite of using such tactics, then this may be more of a reflection on the inapplicability of his overall strategy in the Soviet context than on the appropriateness of his political tactics. Moreover, since Gorbachev's highest-priority domestic task was political reform and transformation, it is appropriate to treat him as a leader who tried to effect a transition to democracy and to judge him against the standards for leadership described in that literature.

GORBACHEV'S TACTICS AND TRANSITIONS TO DEMOCRACY

The Western literature on transitions to democracy has gone through several stages. The first generation of that literature treated democratization as a process that depended for its success on social, cultural, and economic preconditions. Little or no attention was devoted to leadership, which implicitly was treated as a hopeless exercise in the absence of the socioeconomic and cultural prerequisites. The more recent literature, in contrast, is much less deterministic and pessimistic. Its optimism and (some would say excessive) voluntarism are based on a reexamination of the West European historical experience and on observation of the recent successful transitions in Southern Europe, Latin America, and East Asia.[10]

This body of literature takes many confining conditions as mutable and not as decisive obstacles to democratic breakthroughs and democratic consolidation, even though it does acknowledge that some conditions may frustrate even the most skillful leadership strategy. It focuses on coalition-building strategies within the elites and on strategies for creating "political space" for new publics being mobilized into politics by the collapse of authoritarian regimes. Hence, it is primarily interested in leadership as a factor that

---

[10] The most voluntaristic and optimistic of these recent works is Giuseppe di Palma, *To Craft Democracies* (Berkeley: University of California Press, 1991).

not only facilitates the democratic breakthrough and consolidation but also guards against the ever-present threat of military coup and other forms of regression. Since this is precisely what Gorbachev was trying to do – although under socioeconomic and ethnic conditions that were less propitious than those facing traditional authoritarian regimes – a number of prescriptions for successful leadership tactics can be gleaned from this literature and applied as tests to Gorbachev.

Tactic No. 1: *Attempt to discredit alternatives to the democratic path in order to keep them less legitimate in the public and elite consciousness than is the prospective democratic outcome.* As Przeworski puts it: "what matters for the stability of any regime is not the legitimacy of this particular system of domination but the presence or absence of preferable alternatives."[11] From this standpoint, Gorbachev's strategy of initially desacralizing the old order made good sense; his tactic of arguing that "there is no alternative" to continuing along the reformist path likewise constituted good politics. His arguments that Soviet national security and competitiveness in the twenty-first century would be threatened by a failure to join the "modern" world, to become a "normal" country," and to "learn democracy" powerfully advanced the message that hypothetical alternatives to *perestroika* simply were not workable and that they were unpalatable from both liveability and national-security standpoints.

Tactic No. 2: *Mobilize new social forces into politics that will ally with reformist forces within the establishment.* This is precisely what *glasnost'* and democratization accomplished until 1989–1990, when those social forces broke with the establishment. When Gorbachev unveiled his transformational strategy in 1987–1988, he probably did not anticipate how far it would go. But when faced with the consequences in the subsequent two years, he did not lead a backlash. Rather, he accommodated himself to the tide, legitimized its "extremism" (thus making a virtue of necessity), moved himself to the "left" (toward radicalism) on the elite political spectrum, and sought to create new political institutions that would regulate the conflicts now made manifest. This was an important move. It sent out early signals of an attractive democratic game in order to avoid the early disillusion so common during failed transitions.

---

[11] Adam Przeworski, "Some problems in the study of the transition to democracy," in Guillermo O'Donnell, Philippe C. Schmitter, and Laurence Whitehead (Eds.), *Transitions from Authoritarian Rule: Comparative Perspectives* (Baltimore: Johns Hopkins University Press, 1986), pp. 51–2.

From this perspective, it was fortunate that Gorbachev's speech at the January 1987 plenum of the Central Committee called for multicandidate secret elections and general pluralization of the political order. It was also fortunate that the June 1988 Party Conference, and the first meetings of the Congress of People's Deputies and the Supreme Soviet, could be viewed on national television. The combination of pluralization and publicity managed to demystify politics and allowed people to believe that political involvement might be rewarding. Gorbachev was simultaneously mobilizing new social forces, discrediting the old political order, and creating new political institutions to regulate conflict between new social forces and the Old Guard. This also created new political space within which democratic oppositions could develop ties with moderates within the regime.

Tactic No. 3: *Create opportunities for the co-optation of leaders and activists of opposition groups into new political arenas in which they, and reformist members of the establishment, can pursue and learn the pragmatic and accommodative tactics of a democratic process.* In the most general sense, Gorbachev's creation of new political institutions sought to maintain stability by expanding the opportunities for authentic political participation at a rate equal to or exceeding the rate of political mobilization triggered by *glasnost'*.[12] But at the specific level of inter-elite interaction, these institutions proved to be arenas in which general issues of proceduralism, rule of law, parliamentary practice, and the like came to the fore. Although the path was a rocky one and littered with conflict, that is unsurprising in any democratic transition. What is significant is that the slow process of institutionalization got off the ground and gained momentum. Early studies of that process showed that respect for proceduralism had grown not only among reformists but also among fence-sitters and conservatives.[13] As di Palma argued, when moderate conservatives conclude that democratization is the only game in town, they can sometimes become very fast learners.[14]

Tactic No. 4: *Strip the privileged corporate interests of the old regime of their political immunity, but give them enough protection against dispossession that they do not exit en masse and seek allies who would help them to violently reverse the democratization process.* People whose immunity was

---

[12]   According to Samuel Huntington (*Political Order in Changing Societies* [New Haven, CT: Yale University Press, 1968]), maintaining a balance between the level of political participation and the level of institutionalization is key to maintaining political stability during times of change.

[13]   Victor M. Sergeyev and Nikolai Biryukov, *Russia's Road to Democracy: Parliament, Communism and Traditional Culture* (Aldershot, U.K.: Edward Elgar, 1993).

[14]   Giuseppe di Palma, *To Craft Democracies*, ch. IV.

guaranteed under the old regime had to be stripped of that immunity *and* given a sufficient stake in the new order so that they would not resort to "breakdown games."[15] The imperative is to "make institutionalized uncertainty palatable"[16] enough that significant segments of the Old Guard are more willing to play along than to defect. The idea is that they will not only play the game but will also come to learn and (eventually) value the new rules. It is imperative to frighten the conservatives into believing that there is no choice but to join the new democratic game as well as to reassure them that they have a place, protected by the leader, in that game.[17]

From these perspectives, Gorbachev's political tactics look wise. His reforms destroyed the political immunity of the Old Guard and reduced the influence of the military on domestic and foreign policymaking. At the same time, he distanced himself from the radical abolitionist forces and thereby maintained for a time his ties with conservative establishment forces. This strategy manifested itself in: (1) his unwillingness to endorse calls for confiscation of the elite's socioeconomic privileges; (2) his *honorable* retirement of many Politburo and Central Committee members; (3) his willingness to allow many conservative and reactionary forces to speak at televised meetings of the Central Committee and Congress of People's Deputies; (4) his introduction of an electoral system that initially reserved significant proportions of seats to elitist designation by Party, trade union, communist youth league, and Academy of Sciences executive committees; (5) the gap between his proposals at the 19th Party Conference (June 1988) and the proposals offered at that forum by Boris Yeltsin; (6) his approach to economic reform, which allowed many officials to find a stake in the private sector through a process of "spontaneous" or "*nomenklatura*" privatization (which other analysts might refer to as massive insider theft of assets); and (7) his gingerly treatment of the KGB.

To many radicals in the Soviet Union and abroad, these concessions appeared to be unacceptable conservatism and evidence of Gorbachev's upbringing as a believing communist and *apparatchik*. However, from the standpoint of people steeped in the comparative literature on transitions, it made sense.

---

[15] I take this concept from di Palma (ibid., p. 110–11).

[16] Ibid., p. 32.

[17] This power tactic is applicable to pluralist leadership more generally. Thus, writing about presidential power, Richard Neustadt advises the leader "to induce as much uncertainty as possible about the consequences of ignoring what he wants. If he cannot make men think him bound to win, his need is to keep them from thinking they can cross him without risk, or that they can be sure what risks they run. At the same time (no mean feat), he needs to keep them from fearing lest he leave them in the lurch if they support him" (Richard Neustadt, *Presidential Power* [New York: Wiley, 1960], p. 64).

At the same time, Gorbachev's deft use of crises – some manufactured, some not – to purge or marginalize conservatives in the leadership both disarmed forces of backlash and encouraged bandwagoning tendencies among the fence-sitters by maintaining high uncertainty about the chances of success if they bucked him.[18] Instead of being discredited by crises, Gorbachev used them in ways that allowed him to seize the political initiative and further radicalize his programs.

Tactic No. 5: *When stalemates arise, up the ante in order to increase the perceived costs of regression.* This prescription is based on Robert Dahl's famous dictum that democratic breakthroughs hinge on keeping the perceived price of repression higher than the perceived price of toleration.[19] The issue is not whether the current price of toleration is desirable or enjoyable; the issue is whether it is perceived to be more tolerable than the price of a violent backlash.[20]

On this score, Gorbachev pursued a consistently successful strategy during his first five years in power (until mid-1990). He was a "radical centrist," seeking to keep the process moving to the "left" while he himself dominated (but protected) the floating center of the political spectrum. By encouraging the activation of social forces pushing for more radical change, or by joining with those social forces when they surprised him, Gorbachev could more easily argue that the price of restoring the former status quo had become prohibitive. And by encouraging the public expression of popular views that were so impatient for change and so enraged by the privilege and corruption of the old order, Gorbachev could more credibly argue that any effort to restore the former status quo – even if successful in the short run – would only postpone the day of reckoning. At the same time, Gorbachev's selective protection of

---

[18] On the importance of creating incentives for bandwagoning by fence-sitters, see Avery Goldstein, *From Bandwagon to Balance-of-Power Politics: Structural Constraints and Politics in China, 1949–1978* (Stanford, CA: Stanford University Press, 1991); on the importance of using power in ways that simultaneously increase one's legitimacy as leader, see Neustadt, *Presidential Power.*

[19] Robert A. Dahl, *Polyarchy: Participation and Opposition* (New Haven, CT: Yale University Press, 1971), p. 15.

[20] Note here the parallel with Przeworski's ("Some problems in the study ...") theory of relativity regarding legitimacy. In each case – mass legitimacy or elite toleration – the issue is not whether the situation is perceived to be "the best" or even "desirable" but whether it is perceived to be the "least bad" among the alternatives defined at the time to be realistically possible. Note also that, in each case, we are dealing with an assumption of reasonably rational calculation on the part of the actors involved. For a critique that emphasizes the passion and rage in the Soviet Union that made such rational calculation unlikely, see Corbin Lyday, "From coup to constitution: Dilemmas of nation-building in Russia's first republic" (Ph.D. dissertation, Department of Political Science, University of California at Berkeley, 1994).

moderate and conservative interests allowed him to dominate the center of the political spectrum by encouraging the perception of him among middle-of-the-roaders as their protector against radical disenfranchisement.

Finally, by creating avenues of authentic political participation for released social forces, Gorbachev helped to disarm the forces of reactionary backlash during 1985–1990 by robbing them of an excuse to "crush counterrevolution." Rather than allowing the development of a situation in which social forces might have engaged in anomic outbursts or acts of revolutionary violence, Gorbachev pursued policies that at once raised the price of repression *and* lowered the price of toleration. In the process, he dominated the center-left of the political spectrum by increasing the level of felt political dependence upon him by many radical reformers, moderate leftists, and middle-of-the-roaders alike. This accounts for the fact that many reformists criticized Gorbachev's "conservatism" in 1989–1990 yet feared the prospect of his replacement.

Tactic No. 6: Harness forces in the international environment that will help to maintain the momentum of reform while also helping to raise the costs of retrogression. This was precisely the aim of Gorbachev's "new political thinking" in foreign policy, his approach to foreign economic relations, and his process of cultural Westernization. By opening the country to Western economic and cultural influences, including travel abroad, he raised dramatically the price in popular tolerance of efforts to reestablish a closed society while raising the actual and prospective benefits of openness. By defusing conflicts with wealthy adversaries, he increased the chances of receiving economic assistance for his program while reducing the prospective burden of defense spending. Furthermore, his concessionary foreign policies sought both to cut losses and to transform the international system so that foreign countries, companies, and publics would develop a perceived interest in adopting policies that favored a continuation of *perestroika*.

By simultaneously adopting radical reform in both domestic and foreign policies, Gorbachev expanded the number of issue areas within which he could seize the initiative, maintain the momentum of his leadership, and keep prospective challengers off balance. By developing such popularity abroad, he was able to build his authority as a statesman and so compensate for lack of economic progress at home. By delivering on his promise to reduce tensions abroad, he carved out a realm in which would-be challengers found it difficult to claim that they could do better than he.[21] Thus, just as his foreign

---

[21] This is how Doder and Branson (*Gorbachev*, p. 210) insightfully interpreted Gorbachev's calculations in convoking a three-day meeting of international intellectual and social elites in Moscow in February 1987: "The occasion, as he fully realized, offered an opportunity to

policies were central to his strategy of domestic cultural and political transformation, so were they crucial to his tactics for simultaneously expanding his political authority and making *perestroika* increasingly difficult to reverse.

In sum, Gorbachev went far to fulfill (whether he knew it or not) many of the prescriptions of those scholars who have examined the lessons of evolutionary strategies for transforming regimes in non-Leninist settings. His strategy and tactics came close to meeting Weiner's pithy summary: "For those who seek democratization, the lessons are these: mobilize large-scale nonviolent opposition to the regime, seek support from the center and, if necessary, from the conservative right, restrain the left..., woo sections of the military, seek sympathetic coverage from the Western media, and press the United States for support."[22]

MISSED OPPORTUNITIES AND THEORIES OF TRANSITION

Of course, Gorbachev must also take partial responsibility for what was *not* achieved during these years. In particular, the two areas of failure (relative to his goals) were economic transformation and negotiation of a federal or confederal alternative to the Soviet unitary state.[23]

Missed Opportunities on the Economic Front

Because the pace of economic reform lagged far behind the pace of change in other realms of policy, those who evaluate Gorbachev's leadership of the economy tend to arrive at conclusions that are, on balance, negative.[24] The argument is straightforward: If Gorbachev had launched a real and forceful

enhance his authority, not just in foreign politics but on the domestic front. His enemies, he knew, were lying in wait, ready to turn on him the moment he blundered on security moves or some other issue. But he was becoming increasingly confident in his diplomatic skills.... He demonstrated to the bureaucracy that he was the day-to-day captain of Soviet foreign policy.... His mastery of detail and the quality of his reflections on display before a glittering audience in the Grand Kremlin Palace proved that the Soviet leader was a forceful figure, commanding the respect of the outside world and thus deserving respect at home."

[22] Myron Weiner, "Empirical democratic theory and the transition from authoritarianism to democracy," *PS*, vol. 10, no. 3 (1987), p. 866.

[23] Brown (*The Gorbachev Factor*) is highly laudatory of Gorbachev's leadership in general. But when discussing the balance of the ledger, he concedes that Gorbachev failed in economic policy and nationalities policy. When set against successes in political reform and foreign relations, however, Brown concludes that, given the circumstances, two out of four is a good batting average.

[24] See, for example, Marshall I. Goldman, *What Went Wrong with Perestroika?* (New York: Norton, 1992).

economic reform in 1985–1986, or if he had chosen to reform agriculture first, or if he had followed the Chinese model of reforming the economy before reforming the political system, then the economy would have been in better shape than it was in 1990–1991.[25] This counterfactual assertion may be correct (though it is not uncontroversial), but linking it to leadership evaluation involves a further logical step: one must argue not only for the practicality and likely effectiveness of alternative strategies in Soviet conditions but also for their intellectual availability and political feasibility at the time they might have been adopted. To what extent were Soviet leaders aware in earlier years of the need for such immediate and radical economic surgery? If they were aware, to what extent did the Party leader have the political capacity in 1985–1987 to force its enactment and implementation?

The evidence is ambiguous, but it suggests that Gorbachev was a convinced radical on matters of economic reform when he came to power even though he was not yet aware of the specifics of a radical program that might work. During 1985, reform economists who were directors of several research institutes – and whom Gorbachev had consulted regularly as secretary of the Central Committee – forwarded to the Politburo programs of radical economic reform. Moreover, the Chinese economic reform was by then seven years old and was showing remarkable results. Hence, even allowing for the inconclusiveness of the historical record, it seems more than likely that radical economic reform of one type or another was intellectually available to the Politburo and Gorbachev already in 1985.

How politically feasible was it at the time – and if it was feasible, at what price? Although Gorbachev consolidated his power faster than any leader in Soviet history, he still had to deal with a challenge that faced any new Soviet leader: to enlarge his political base before radicalizing his program. In the meantime, he had to live with many powerful holdovers from the old regime. Even among the Andropovites who replaced Brezhnevites during 1985–1986, the dominant orientations were more technocratic and anti-corruption than radical reformist. It is entirely conceivable that Gorbachev did not push harder for economic reform in 1985–1986 because he was building his political base.

Yet this would not explain why, even when he began to push for economic reform in 1987, the measures were modest compared to the greater radicalism of proposals advanced by institute directors or compared to the scope of Chinese economic reforms. New laws on joint ventures, cooperatives, "individual labor activity," and the Law on the State Enterprise were radical departures

---

[25] This argument is made forcefully in Jerry F. Hough, *Democratization and Revolution in the USSR, 1985–1991* (Washington, DC: Brookings Institution, 1997), chs. 4 and 11.

compared to the Soviet past, but they constituted a "foot in the door" approach: delegitimizing old values and justifying *in principle* entirely new approaches to economic organization and the world economy. These policies were revised and (in most cases) made more radical in 1988–1989, but the crucial issues of price reform, agricultural reform, land reform, privatization of property ownership, and de-monopolization of the state sector were not tackled and hence constituted fatal drags on the effectiveness of many of the measures actually taken. One could argue, therefore, that the economy might have been more effectively reformed had Gorbachev opted for a much more radical approach in 1987–1988 – and that he bears responsibility for the failure to do so.

Gorbachev may have feared that urban unrest would result from liberalization of prices; price increases had set off deadly rioting in Novocherkassk in 1962. He may also have feared that too sudden a transition to the insecurities and risks of a market economy would have been intolerable to a population that had lived for sixty years without a market economy and for thirty years with a low-opportunity (but also low-risk) welfare state. He may have concluded that political reforms – including competitive elections, civil liberties, and authentic forms of political participation – were a *pre*condition for economic reform (the reverse of the Chinese model) because they would provide people with political safety valves for expression of their frustrations and thereby prevent economic reform from delegitimizing the political system. Of course, a dispassionate assessment of Gorbachev's leadership cannot take his fears as the measure of reality. He may have been too timid, indeed wrong, about the likely popular reaction.[26]

Gorbachev also may have been intimidated by the forceful objections to economic decentralization by some members of the Politburo.[27] Although Gorbachev had reached his stage of ascendancy within the leadership by 1987–1988, he was not an unconstrained leader. He had more power and authority than he had enjoyed two years earlier, just as Khrushchev and Brezhnev had more latitude for policy initiation and innovation during their stages of ascendancy. But he still had to live with political constraints. Would the

---

[26] Hough (ibid., pp. 19, 137–8, 345) is incredulous that Gorbachev did not take Ryzhkov's advice on price reform; Brown (*The Gorbachev Factor,* ch. 5) ignores the matter. In his memoirs (Mikhail Gorbachev, *Zhizn' i reformy,* vol. 1 [Moscow: Novosti, 1996], pp. 361–2), Gorbachev himself admits that his government missed a timely opportunity for necessary price reform in 1987–1988. He blames journalists and bureaucrats for inciting public opposition to the prospect, but he does not address any of his own fears at that time of the possible consequences of price liberalization.

[27] Personal communication to the author by former Politburo member Aleksandr Yakovlev.

leadership have tolerated an across-the-board radicalism that encompassed simultaneous transformation in the political, economic, and foreign-policy realms? We know that the leadership was sharply divided at the time on matters of both economic and political reform.[28] It is entirely conceivable that, in exchange for greater radicalism in economic policy, Gorbachev would have had to "trade off" some of his radicalism in foreign policy, defense policy, or policy toward cultural and political reform. This, in turn, could have compromised his efforts to transform the image of the USSR in the eyes of the Western world, which had been the basis of his efforts to undermine xenophobic forces resisting reform at home.

In any case, Gorbachev during 1987–1988 either chose or was forced to go slow on economic reform in exchange for a faster pace in other areas. If he chose to do so and had the power to do otherwise, then one could retrospectively blame him for lacking the vision, understanding, and strategy required by the economic conditions of the time. Alternatively, if one believes that radical economic reform was impractical in the Soviet Union in the absence of prior political, cultural, and international changes, then one could praise Gorbachev for understanding the need for preparatory changes in those realms.

Suppose that Gorbachev had been free to promulgate policy as he wished. Was he privy to a theory of transition that specified the relationship among political, economic, and cultural change in a Soviet-type system? Had there been a consensus within the specialist community as to what would "work," then Gorbachev could be criticized for ignoring it, but such was not the case. No consensus existed among either Soviet or Western specialists on the nature of the relationship between political and economic reform. Analysts and politicians disagreed about the proper sequencing of marketization and democratization. Some specialists argued that the two must proceed simultaneously in order to help break bureaucratic monopolies (thus preventing the development of a racket economy) and to build popular support and consensus during a period of disruption and privation.[29] Others argued that radical economic reform requires an authoritarian regime and that simultaneous political democratization will only undermine economic marketization.[30]

---

[28] On economic reform, see Anders Åslund, *Gorbachev's Struggle for Economic Reform* [updated and expanded edition] (Ithaca, NY: Cornell University Press, 1991); other evidence of discord within the Politburo can be found in previous chapters of the present book, citing memoir sources.

[29] See, for example, Janos Kornai, *The Road to a Free Economy* (New York: Norton, 1990), ch. 3.

[30] See A. Migranian, "Dolgii put' k evropeiskomu domu [The long road to the European home]," *Novii Mir*, no. 7 (1989), pp. 166–84; this was also the perspective that informed the Chinese approach to reform.

Specialists also differed about the workability of the Chinese strategy in Soviet conditions.[31] They disagreed with each other about the workability *and*
desirability of varying mixes of equity and efficiency considerations in the
setting of economic policy,[32] about the form and degree of political democratization that might best accompany economic reform, and about the forms
of economic marketization that might best (i.e., most workably) accompany
political democratization.[33] Still others argued that the decisive component
of a successful strategy must be international: opening up the economy to
world market forces.[34]

None of these theories was correct or incorrect on its face. Each simply
pointed to discord among the voices Gorbachev might have heard, directly or
indirectly, as he pondered his options. Options that he spurned were indeed
intellectually available, but there was no consensus as to their likely consequences. In a confusing and confused intellectual context, Gorbachev made
his choices. They did not work.

Lack of theoretical consensus is no excuse for leadership that is ineffective, though it is a mitigating circumstance. But we expect good leaders to
have a special ability to sense what will work. Hence, in the realm of economics, Gorbachev's handling of the situation was unimpressive even if we
make allowances for the uncertainties and constraints. True, he introduced
novel market elements into the economy. However, in this realm he was event-
making principally in a negative sense: in his ability to delegitimize values that
underpinned the old economic order and to undermine organs of the command economy. Since the rate of disorganization of the (industrial) command
economy exceeded by far the rate at which market relations were being introduced, the result was disintegration, not reconstruction. In this realm, it is
fair to say that Gorbachev was better at destruction than at creation.

---

[31] The argument against the transferability of the Chinese reform to the Soviet context ran as
follows. China's Cultural Revolution (1966–1976) had only recently wreaked havoc on the
cohesion of the Communist Party and had greatly weakened local Party control of agriculture. Moreover, in 1978 the Chinese leaders were facing spontaneous decollectivization of
agriculture. By contrast, the CPSU and the collective farms were entrenched in the Soviet
countryside, and the cadres had not been targets of a campaign of mass terror since the 1930s.

[32] See Ed A. Hewett, *Reforming the Soviet Economy* (Washington, DC: Brookings Institution,
1988).

[33] See Elemer Hankiss, *East European Alternatives* (New York: Oxford University Press, 1990);
Alexander Yanov, *Détente after Brezhnev* (Berkeley: Institute of International Studies, University of California at Berkeley, 1977); Boris Kagarlitsky, *The Dialectic of Change* (London:
Verso, 1990); Adam Przeworski, *Democracy and the Market* (Cambridge University Press,
1991).

[34] Jerry F. Hough, *Opening Up the Soviet Economy* (Washington, DC: Brookings Institution,
1988); Richard Parker, "Inside the 'collapsing' Soviet economy," *Atlantic Monthly*, no. 4 (June
1990), pp. 68–80.

Missed Opportunities and the Problem of Ethnic Nationalism

Similar counterfactual and theoretical arguments can be made regarding Gorbachev's handling of the ethnic crisis. Gorbachev may have been aware that (what Soviets called) "the nationalities question" was one of the most intractable issues on the agenda of Soviet politics,[35] but he was obviously not aware of the depth of ethno-nationalism, inter-ethnic hatred, and secessionist sentiment lying just below the surface.[36] Nor did he anticipate how quickly or fully his policies of *glasnost'* and democratization would release that potential.[37] Finally, he did not understand that the specific political reforms he chose – making regional Party officials suddenly subject to popular election and having republican parliamentary elections follow (not precede) all-union parliamentary elections – would accelerate the loss of central control.

One could argue that, had Gorbachev called a constitutional convention and offered the opportunity of a democratic federation in 1988, rather than begrudgingly and reactively in 1989–1990, he might have slowed the centrifugal forces and avoided the ultimate collapse of the union. Similarly, had he accepted the secession of the Baltic states in 1989 – assuming he had the power to do so – while defining them as a "special case," then he might have eased the path toward a negotiated federation among the remaining twelve republics. Alternatively, had he used force consistently to police the limits of acceptable protest and defiance of Moscow's writ, then he might by this means have kept the union from fragmenting.[38]

On this score, there was little theory to guide Gorbachev. Some people at home and abroad were urging him at the time to use determined shows of force to rein in centrifugal forces in the republics on the assumption that this would not have had the contrary effect. (State-directed violence sometimes deters escalation, but it sometimes creates rage and heightens defiance.) Other voices at home and abroad urged the negotiation of broader degrees of autonomy for the republics and moves toward a negotiated federation. Gorbachev heeded these voices, but his timing was bad (it proved to be too late) and his offerings tended to be outpaced by rising demands. The critical unknown is whether anything he did, coercive or concessionary, could have averted the centrifugal spiral of 1990–1991.

---

[35] As argued at the time by Jerry F. Hough, "Gorbachev's politics," *Foreign Affairs,* vol. 68, no. 5 (Winter 1989–1990), pp. 26–41.

[36] As argued at the time in Gail W. Lapidus, "Gorbachev and the 'national question': Restructuring the Soviet federation," *Soviet Economy,* vol. 5, no. 3 (July–September, 1989), pp. 201–50.

[37] See Brown, *The Gorbachev Factor,* ch. 8.

[38] As advocated in Hough, *Democratization and Revolution,* chs. 7, 12, 15.

We do not know how the Politburo and Central Committee would have reacted had Gorbachev suggested the nonviolent alternatives.[39] The point may be moot, for both his political strategy and his vision for the USSR left Gorbachev unwilling to consider those alternatives seriously. It is not even clear that, intellectually, he was aware of their availability and practicality. His image of a "third way" between socialism and capitalism was based on a mix of social welfare and democratic politics that had a place in the Marxist heritage, but his thinking shared with that heritage an assumption that economics – not ethnicity – is the primary motivator of human behavior.

To the extent that one views the radicalizing behavior of Boris Yeltsin (and of the government of the RSFSR) as primary causes of the collapse of the Soviet Union, one could argue that one of Gorbachev's key mistakes was allowing Boris Yeltsin back into politics. Gorbachev tried to prevent Yeltsin's victories in the elections of 1989–1991 but to no avail. The more the establishment tried to undercut Yeltsin, the higher his popularity rose in the eyes of the mobilized electorate. Perhaps Gorbachev would have had to bury Yeltsin politically in early 1988, rather than giving him a high position in the Construction Ministry that allowed him to remain involved in the arenas of power. Surely, the fact that he begrudgingly allowed Yeltsin to speak at the June 1988 Party Conference – on national television – gave Yeltsin a platform for mounting a populist comeback.

Perhaps nothing that Gorbachev did, short of aborting his political reforms, could have prevented the disintegration of the USSR. If that is true, then one can still criticize Gorbachev as being quixotic in failing to appreciate the strength of the centrifugal ethnic forces he was facing and unleashing. When we compare the results with his goals, Gorbachev's nationalities policy (like his economic policy) was unimpressive. He did an outstanding job of destroying the Soviet unitary state and of introducing democratic elections in the republics, thereby setting the stage for attempts to negotiate a federal or confederal alternative. But he never succeeded in finalizing those negotiations. Again as in economic policy, he was better at destruction than at creation.

THE BALANCE OF THE LEDGER

Viewed from the perspective of (say) early 1990, the first five years of Gorbachev's time in power looked like a qualified success story. His performance

---

[39] Gorbachev himself has argued (in retrospect, in personal conversation with the former U.S. ambassador) that, had he pushed for a confederation in 1989, the Central Committee would have voted immediately for his ouster as general secretary (Jack Matlock, *Autopsy on an Empire: The American Ambassador's Account of the Collapse of the Soviet Union* [New York: Random House, 1995], p. 659).

in creating a new economic and inter-republican order was unimpressive, but his performance in breaking the hold of the ancien régime in all realms – and in navigating a peaceful transition toward new political and international orders – was path-breaking. In the latter respects, he was an event-making man who exercised unique leadership skills. His policy programs and authority-building strategy were all appropriate to the challenge of forcing an obsolete system onto a new track.

From the perspective of 1990, Gorbachev's political tactics also appeared to be working. By selectively appeasing or allying with conservative forces while simultaneously raising the price of backlash, Gorbachev had been able to maintain the political initiative without inducing a conservative or reactionary coup. By releasing radical social forces but providing them with democratic avenues of political participation, he was able to keep up the momentum of reform while reducing incentives for nihilism on the left and repression on the right. By fashioning a foreign policy that mobilized international forces in support of *perestroika,* he increased the attractiveness of staying the course while raising higher the price to be paid for a backlash.

From the perspective of 1992, however, Gorbachev's leadership strategy appears much less effective. The shortcomings of his ethnic and economic policies came back to haunt him. They interacted with his political reforms such that rising levels of social and political polarization undercut his evolutionary strategy of transformation, destroyed the centrist base required for his political tactics to be effective, and stripped him of both power and authority. Most tragically from the standpoint of Gorbachev's preferences, they led to the dissolution of the country he was trying to transform but certainly not destroy.

Any rendering of Gorbachev's tactical political mistakes in reaction (after 1989) to sliding toward a period of political decline must include two things: (1) the reluctance of his efforts, such as they were, to make political peace with Boris Yeltsin; and (2) his course correction of fall 1990, which included firing several of his most liberal associates and replacing them with men who would eventually lead the coup against him in August 1991. Had Gorbachev had a better sense of the pace of societal polarization and a better appreciation that he could not arrest it without the use of massive force, he would have understood that Yeltsin and the radicals were the wave of the future. He would have kept moving to the "left" (i.e., in a radical direction) to keep pace with those social forces, though without necessarily capitulating to all their policy preferences.[40] Instead, by moving to the right but retaining his commitment not to employ widespread repression, he largely burned his bridges to the

---

[40] This is what I advocated in George W. Breslauer, "Evaluating Gorbachev as leader," *Soviet Economy,* vol. 8, no. 4 (October–December 1989), pp. 333–7. It remains an open question as

radical camp while divesting himself of the tools he would have needed to achieve the right wing's goals. The conservatives and reactionaries understood this better than he; they started preparing seriously for a coup d'etat shortly after Gorbachev rejoined negotiations for a union treaty in April 1991. His seven-month flirtation with conservative forces only increased the level of polarization within society and the political establishment without achieving anything substantive. Moreover, it helped to position the coup plotters for their subsequent adventure, which in turn destroyed all hopes that leaders of the Slavic republics would be willing to sign a new Union Treaty.

Gorbachev lost control of his political reforms and proved unable or unwilling to prevent things that he clearly hoped to avoid: the total collapse of communism in Eastern Europe; reunification of Germany within NATO; collapse of the USSR; and abolition of the Communist Party's right to exist. The balance of the ledger would be that Gorbachev made a great start (1985–1989) but was a poor finisher (1990–1991). This was especially the case in those realms (economics and ethnic policy) in which his performance is generally judged to have been unimpressive, but it was even the case in those realms of policy in which he is generally considered to have been successful. For the outcomes he most wanted to avoid (other than restoration of the ancien régime) were the very outcomes that circumstances forced upon him.

That would be the "harsh" evaluation of Gorbachev as a transformational leader. An alternative might be called the "generous" evaluation. Generous analysts would note that marketizing the economy and federalizing the union were the two most *intractable* problems facing the Soviet regime. The constraints on change and on building viable political coalitions for that purpose were much more formidable than in the areas of political reform and foreign policy. The generous evaluation would concede that perhaps nothing Gorbachev did would have averted the collapse of both the economy and the union – given the forces he had unleashed in 1987–1989, his willingness to allow Boris Yeltsin back into politics, and Yeltsin's political strategy. Moreover, the generous evaluation would emphasize that the realms in which he met with successes have yielded *lasting* change. The democratic political institutions that Gorbachev created (multicandidate secret elections, genuine legislatures, and wide-ranging civil liberties) have lasted beyond his years in power and in that respect qualify as among his greatest achievements as a *creator*. Similarly, even though Gorbachev did not aim for the breakup of the USSR, he did create the conditions that allowed the eventual breakup to be

to whether Yeltsin would have welcomed Gorbachev into the radical camp – or would have upped the ante again in an attempt to outflank Gorbachev. I will say more in Chapter 14 about Yeltsin's role in undermining Gorbachev's chances of success in achieving his goals.

relatively *peaceful* and to remain so in the years thereafter, when Gorbachev was in retirement. Finally, Gorbachev paved the way for a reevaluation of the place of the Soviet Union in the international system and thereby made possible a peaceful and (thus far) enduring end to the Cold War.

Both the harsh and the generous evaluations are based on judgments about Gorbachev's effectiveness in realizing his goals in the near term and long term. They are distinct from evaluations based solely on the observer's ranking of values. One can admire Gorbachev greatly – as I do – for the destruction and the creation he brought about, both intended and unintended (but tolerated); alternatively, one can condemn him for the same destruction and creation. But that is a superficial approach to leadership evaluation. Whether the harsh or the generous evaluation does greater justice to Gorbachev's record is bound to remain a matter of debate. The verdict will hinge principally on answers to the counterfactual question: Could anyone have done better in the circumstances without the benefit of hindsight?

14

Evaluating Yeltsin as Leader

Yeltsin, like Gorbachev, was both a system destroyer and a system builder. During the years that Gorbachev was endeavoring to transform the Marxist–Leninist system into a socialist democracy, Yeltsin evolved into a committed anti-communist revolutionary. His goal became to destroy the communist system along with all those features that Gorbachev hoped to preserve in the name of "socialism" and "Soviet civilization." Then, on the ruins of that system, Yeltsin promised to build on the territory of Russia a new system, which he depicted as a "market democracy." As in the case of Gorbachev, Yeltsin's effectiveness as a system destroyer can be evaluated separately from his effectiveness as a system builder.

YELTSIN AS SYSTEM-DESTROYER

During 1988–1991, Boris Yeltsin evolved into a hero of the anti-communist opposition to Soviet rule. After his overwhelming electoral victories of March 1989 and June 1991, followed by his facing down of the coup plotters in August 1991, his authority at home and abroad had become legendary. He had evolved into a charismatic leader of almost mythic proportions, especially among those who had assumed that the Soviet and communist control structures were unassailable. Thus, as an oppositional leader, Yeltsin is likely to go down in history as a uniquely courageous and effective figure who managed to prevail against seemingly overwhelming odds. His "resurrection" after being purged by the Communist Party apparatus in 1987 was a product of extraordinary political will, intuition, and an uncanny ability to sense and shape the mood of the masses. His success during 1990–1991 in decoupling the concept of "Russian" from that of "Soviet" was both intellectually and politically

inspired (given his goals), as was his insistence in March 1991 that Russia
choose a president by popular election for the first time in its thousand-year
history. Yeltsin was a revolutionary hero who achieved what he did through
his extraordinary personal traits. Controversy is likely to be based largely
on normative grounds. Those who approve of Yeltsin's role in destroying the
communist and Soviet systems will likely acclaim his leadership, and those
who disapprove of these ends will censure him accordingly. But neither side
would contest the observation, which is value-neutral, that Yeltsin was (in
this oppositional leadership role) an "event-making man."

Nothing that has happened since then is likely to alter this evaluation.
Yeltsin's oppositional role of the 1980s – like Churchill's wartime leadership
of Great Britain – can be judged independently of later events. It is an accomplished feat, capable of being assessed on its own terms.

When Yeltsin came to be president of independent Russia, communist
ideology and organization had largely been destroyed. The constraints on
progress were no longer products of the entrenchment of formal organizations and doctrines so much as their opposite: the fragmentation of governmental institutions; conflicting political jurisdictions within the inherited
polity; disorganization of the economy and impending collapse of government
finances; widespread disorientation and anxiety stemming from the collapse
of the USSR; and the absence of an accepted world view around which to
rally the population, now that Gorbachev's "socialist choice" had been discredited. Yeltsin's agenda therefore had to focus on tasks of *construction:*
state building; nation building; building a new economic system and a new
political order; forging a new international role for newly independent Russia; and defining an alternative world view to justify the new institutions and
policies. The tasks were both ideational and organizational, but in a context
quite the opposite of what Gorbachev had faced. Once Yeltsin had finished
administering the coup de grace to communist ideology and organization
during 1990–1991 – and to the USSR during 1991 – he was faced with the
challenge of creating new bases of order to put in their place.

How effective was he in building that alternative? As I did with Gorbachev
in Chapter 13, I will first outline the contours of Yeltsin's positive accomplishments. I will then examine the negative – in Yeltsin's case: (1) the rigidity of
the systems that Yeltsin built and their lack of adaptability to changing environmental requirements; (2) the exorbitant costs incurred in pursuing his
goals; and (3) the counterproductive impact of Yeltsin's operating style on the
achievement of his professed goal after 1993, which was to consolidate his
gains by "strengthening the Russian state." That said, I will then weigh the
balance of the ledger. I will conclude by comparing Gorbachev and Yeltsin
with respect to their effectiveness in building and maintaining authority.

YELTSIN AS SYSTEM BUILDER: THE FRUITS OF PERSONALISM

As we have seen in earlier chapters, Yeltsin approached his presidency with a self-conception as a personalistic leader. He was most comfortable exercising leadership that did not have to accommodate multiple institutional constraints. But he also believed that such leadership was necessary to achieve his primary goals.

Yeltsin's personalism need not be treated as a self-evident obstacle to progress. Indeed, given his concern to overturn the formal structures of communist power, to replace them with the formal organizations of a capitalist economy and a liberal democracy – integrated into Western organizations, within the territorial boundaries of the Russian Federation of December 1991, and resistant to both communist restoration and fascist reaction – one could argue that, in the near term, his personalistic approach to leadership went far to achieve those ends. He forced through changes that created the general framework for such a system.

Thus, he and his staff designed and won ratification of the Russian Constitution of 1993, which, however flawed, finally provided a consistent constitutional framework for the nascent Russian state. The parliamentary and presidential elections of 1993, 1995, 1996, and 1999 took place as scheduled and, while procedurally flawed in many respects, their general outcomes were probably not determined by fraud. Yeltsin resisted calls by many of his closest aides to postpone or cancel the gubernatorial elections of 1996–1998, even though these threatened to diminish his political leverage over regional elites. He also resisted the temptation to postpone the presidential election of 1996, even though in January his public approval rating had fallen to single digits and he was strongly tempted to cancel the election, abolish the Duma, and outlaw the Communist Party.[1] Likewise, he resisted calls to postpone or cancel the December 1999 parliamentary elections. Yeltsin also resisted the temptation to roll back the civil rights won by the Russian people under Gorbachev: freedoms to criticize, organize, worship, and travel. Books, newspapers, and television shows regularly roasted or ridiculed the president. They sharply criticized many of his policies, at times to the president's dismay and shock. These institutions survived notwithstanding Yeltsin's presumed distaste for the personal attacks.

Of course, we cannot give Yeltsin credit for declining to roll back progress that had already been made by his predecessor. Nor can we credit such resistance as an act of *creation*. Hence, this is more an indicator of his commitment

---

[1] Boris Yeltsin, *Midnight Diaries* (New York: Public Affairs, 2000), pp. 24–5.

to building a system based on some variant of liberalism than of his "success" as a state builder per se.

With respect to transformation of the economic system, Yeltsin – in the name of creating a class of property holders who would fight to prevent communist restoration – sponsored a program of privatization that allowed the rapid transfer of state property into private hands at a rate (and on a scale) that exceeded anything seen before in world history. Thus, Yeltsin was the "founder" of Russia's oligopolistic and kleptocratic yet nonetheless capitalist economy.

In his policies toward Russia's regions, Yeltsin sponsored a series of ad hoc treaties and agreements between Moscow and individual regions and republics that flexibly defined the respective obligations of the center and the periphery. The Constitution of 1993 tried to rein in centrifugal forces by prescribing a strong role for Moscow, but that document left many areas to joint jurisdiction and was vague on the mechanisms for resolving ambiguities and conflicts. This ambiguity – and the ad hoc treaties and agreements that followed – were consistent with Yeltsin's urge for personal flexibility in striking deals with the heads of different "subjects of the federation." [2] They were also consistent with the prevailing realities: the disparate resource bases of the regions, the varying resolve of their leaders, the lack of consensus among regional governors and republican presidents about constitutional principles, and the center's frequent incapacity to enforce its writ by other means. Only in the case of Chechnya did Yeltsin use the military to enforce the limits of his flexibility.

In the realm of nation building, Yeltsin consistently fought against those who would define the Russian Federation as an exclusionary ethnic-Russian entity. Instead, he sponsored and loudly argued for a civic and tolerant definition of citizenship in Russia, and he prevailed in the definition of policy on these matters.

At the international level, Yeltsin was one of the architects of the Commonwealth of Independent States, established to foster peaceful relations among the successor states to the Soviet Union. While he rhetorically defended the rights of "Russian speakers" resident in the successor states, he also insisted that such issues be resolved peacefully and rejected the arguments of those who would threaten or employ force. He proved to be a generous negotiator – giving far more than he got – with the leaders of Belarus, Ukraine, and Kazakhstan in the interests of maintaining good relations between Russia and those countries.

---

[2] See, for example, Yu. M. Baturin, A. L. Ilin, V. F. Kadatskii, V. V. Kostikov, M. A. Krasnov, A. Ya. Livshits, K. F. Nikiforov, L. G. Pikhoia, and G. A. Satarov, *Epokha Yel'tsina: Ocherki politicheskoi istorii* (Moscow: Vagrius, 2001), p. 397.

In relations with the Far Abroad, Yeltsin protested unsuccessfully against NATO's expansion eastward. But once this expansion became inevitable, he encouraged and monitored the negotiation of a NATO–Russian Charter in order to preserve good relations with Western partners and make NATO expansion tolerable to the Russian political elite. He successfully negotiated the expansion of the G-7 into the G-8. And he proved to be more interested in the "liberal internationalist" than the "statist" component of his policy toward East–West relations.

On the basis of this record, one could arrive at a positive evaluation of Yeltsin's effectiveness in realizing his primary goals: to found a new order, to guarantee that system against restorationist forces, and to integrate Russia into Western institutions. To reach such a positive evaluation, one would have to assume two things, one counterfactual and the other predictive: (1) that, absent Yeltsin as leader of Russia, the forces working for opposing goals would have prevailed in Russian policymaking; and (2) that Yeltsin's achievements have staying power – that they are likely to survive the years following Yeltsin's retirement. Indeed, these facts and assumptions are the bases for positive evaluations that are already in the record.

THE MACROSTRUCTURAL VULNERABILITIES

One could, however, also argue that Yeltsin's urge to found and guarantee a new order of things as quickly as possible – and to do so through personalistic leadership – planted the seeds of crisis that have been growing for several years and that finally came to a head in 1998–1999. In the political realm, Yeltsin's primary macroinstitutional accomplishment (the Constitution of 1993) established a framework that is so executive-heavy and so rigid that it may inhibit the system's adaptation to changing environmental requirements. It established a presidential system under which the powers of the president are enormous and include vast powers of decree, whereas the parliament and the constitutional court enjoy very limited powers. The Constitution was designed to ensure that the president would be (by far) the highest authority in the land, largely unaccountable to institutions and primarily answerable to the electorate at the subsequent presidential election.

Such discretion provides the president with strong incentives to ignore or infantilize the other branches of government. The courts, like parliament, are greatly underfinanced, while the presidency and the executive branch are hugely bloated with redundant personnel. The capacity of the president to bribe or intimidate members of parliament exceeds by far the capacity of parliamentarians to threaten the president. The executive branch serves almost entirely at the pleasure of the president, with little parliamentary control over the composition of the government. Hence, the overwhelming power of the presidency vis-à-vis other central institutions ensures that the general direction of policy is likely to reflect the president's preferences. But this also means that policy development and elaboration will depend largely on the wisdom and foresight emanating from the office of the president.

Yeltsin's "super-presidentialist"[3] constitution also eliminated the office of vice-president, so that no future VP could turn against the president the way Yeltsin's vice-president, Aleksandr Rutskoi, had done during 1992–1993. The lack of a vice-presidency in a system in which the president has such extraordinary powers means that any sign of presidential ill health – or the anticipation of such – sets off a chain of political maneuvering and demagogic rhetoric in anticipation of a new election. The legal ambiguity about the definition of "incapacitation" becomes magnified. Efforts to alter the constitution to establish a vice-presidency, or even to mandate that the prime minister serve out the former president's full term before a new election is held, are impeded by the nearly impossible terms for amendment. Moreover, the constitution provides an incentive for those most hopeful of winning the next election to oppose its amendment. Why reduce the powers of an office that you have reason to believe you can capture?

In the economic realm, Yeltsin's privatization program amounted to the greatest case of insider trading in history. It was consistent with Yeltsin's urge to build an economic elite as quickly as possible that would both support him politically and serve as a powerful bulwark against communist restoration. But the extraordinary concentration of wealth and conspicuous consumption that it allowed – along with the illicit (often criminal) means by which that wealth was acquired, the "crony capitalism" that resulted, and the intertwining of economic and corrupt political power – nurtured a widespread sense of social injustice that could explode in rage or generate anomic social protest at any time. Moreover, the mass impoverishment resulting from the chosen strategy of macroeconomic stabilization adds a powerful economic motivation for protest to the sense of injustice generated by perceived inequality. Even if ideological and organizational obstacles to the mobilization of mass protest prove insurmountable,[4] the situation could still lead to the eventual victory in presidential and parliamentary elections of those who advocate a populist authoritarian alternative.

[3] Stephen Holmes, "Superpresidentialism and its problems," *East European Constitutional Review*, vols. 2–3, nos. 4–1 (Fall–Winter 1993–1994), pp. 123–6.
[4] Stephen E. Hanson and Jeffrey S. Kopstein, "The Weimar/Russia comparison," *Post-Soviet Affairs*, vol. 13, no. 3 (July–September 1997), pp. 252–83; Victoria Bonnell and George W. Breslauer, *Russia in the New Century: Stability or Disorder?* (Boulder, CO: Westview, 2000), ch. 1 and passim.

Similarly, Yeltsin's decision to wage war in Chechnya to defend the territorial integrity of the Russian Federation proved disastrous for all concerned. The human toll – among Chechens, Russian civilians in Chechnya, and soldiers of Russia's armed forces – was enormous. Prosecution of the war further shattered the morale and cohesion of the Russian armed forces. And yet, while territorial integrity was temporarily defended, nothing was decided. This led to the decision in fall 1999 to reconquer Chechnya – a war that continues as of this writing. The first war might conceivably have deterred other regional executives from contemplating secession, which would be Yeltsin's sole claim to having played a positive role in preserving Russia's territorial integrity by waging the war. But even he stopped making this claim and admitted the war to have been his biggest mistake. This did not prevent him from launching another war in 1999 whose long-term costs and side effects are yet to be determined.

Then, too, Yeltsin's determination to stand "above political parties" as "director of all of Russia" inhibited the development of political parties, which provide the organizational buttress for a stable representative democracy. In the fall of 1991 and again in the fall of 1993 and 1995, Yeltsin was presented with the opportunity to sponsor presidential parties among reformist forces that might have helped them to build muscular, nationwide Party organizations. These could have expanded the mobilizational capacity of anti-restorationist forces and strengthened the organizational bond between politicians in the center and those in the periphery. The Russian president certainly had control of enormous material resources to invest in such a venture as well as a popular mandate to reshape political organization as he wished. Instead, Yeltsin opted for the ad hoc and personalistic approach to leadership, one that would leave him formally beholden to no particular organization and relatively free to shift support bases as his political instincts dictated. While this was consistent with his self-image as a leader and with his conception of the kind of leadership Russia needed in order to found and guarantee a new order of things, it left the political system demonstrably underdeveloped and fragile.

Yeltsin's strategy of political self-protection also undercut whatever contribution he might have made to cultural transformation in Russia. He made an excellent start in 1990–1991 with his secular and tolerant rhetoric of Russian nationhood and statehood. But throughout 1989–1991, the absolutist rhetoric of anti-communism, based on binary oppositions, was the dominant and most salient feature of his rhetoric. The two rhetorics coexisted thereafter, and it was to Yeltsin's credit that he did not sacrifice the tolerant to the intolerant. Nonetheless, continuation of the absolutist rhetoric after the collapse of communism polluted political language and led to popular cynicism about the politics and policies of the Russian government. Thus, just as he had defined either the Communist Party or the Soviet center as the enemy in 1989–1991, so he continued with "us versus them" rhetoric after 1991. Those who supported Yeltsin's policies were deemed "reformers," "democrats," and "marketizers," even when his policies were authoritarian, corrupt, or plutocratic. All those who opposed his policies were dubbed conservatives, reactionaries, or "neo-Bolsheviks."[5] These were not the rhetorical conditions under which the Russian citizenry was likely to learn to appreciate either markets or democracy. For the negative side effects of Yeltsin's policies – including the sustained failure to pay wage arrears and pensions – fostered cynicism about both capitalism and democracy in the minds of many Russians.

Yeltsin had the opportunity in 1991 to play the role of "father of the nation," embodying its dignity. Indeed, after the coup attempt of August 1991, this was both his self-image and his image in the eyes of anti-communist publics in Russia. Yet he managed, during his years as president of independent Russia, to squander the good will he had accumulated. It is extraordinary to note the contrast between Yeltsin's popularity ratings and public demeanor in 1991 and the same indicators in 1994. In contrast to de Gaulle, who managed to mobilize French patriotism in support of his policies and leadership, Yeltsin could only neutralize or deter neo-imperial chauvinism. He proved incapable of articulating and broadcasting a positive, patriotic message to mobilize support for the kinds of popular sacrifices his policies demanded.

Yeltsin did a brilliant job of exploiting the public arenas created during Gorbachev's efforts to transform the Soviet system. During his stage of ascendancy, Yeltsin tried to use the public arena to maintain and enhance his stature as father of the nation and hero of the people. However, he found himself in a situation of "dual power." The parliament of 1992–1993 was an arena for competitive politics that played to sentiments among the voting publics. The prolonged confrontation with this parliament – and Yeltsin's military suppression of that body – left Yeltsin soured on the idea that public politics should be based on divided government. The parliamentary elections of December 1993 left him painfully aware that the populace no longer viewed him as a hero. The result was that, just as an autonomous public arena had been

---

[5] Jerry F. Hough, *The Logic of Economic Reform in Russia* (Washington, DC: Brookings Institution, 2001). Yeltsin's rhetoric thus reinforced the mentality of "binary oppositions" that Michael Urban ("The politics of identity in Russia's postcommunist transition: The Nation against itself," *Slavic Review*, vol. 53, no. 3 [Fall 1994], pp. 733–7) claims to be a key feature of Russian political culture.

Yeltsin's ticket to power during the Gorbachev years, that same public arena had become the source of political frustration during his stage of ascendancy. He reacted to the double disillusionment by drawing inward and allowing re-privatization of the state. He allowed electoral machinations to corrupt some of the legitimacy of democratic elections, grossly violated campaign finance laws, and restricted his opponents' access to the televised airwaves during election campaigns. It is one indicator of Yeltsin's shortcomings as a transformational leader that he failed to institutionalize a genuinely competitive public arena.

The net result of all these shortcomings is that the cultural and organizational infrastructures of the Russian system are extremely weak: like a skeleton without ligaments, they are prone to collapse of their own weight or when they meet countervailing force – such as the international economic downturn it met in August 1998. Transformational leaders and the systems they build are frequently able to weather such times if they have created sufficient popular consensus and good will. But Yeltsin managed to squander his charisma and good will and later to discredit political and economic liberalism in the popular mind. Having discredited socialism in his role as an oppositional revolutionary and liberalism more recently, Yeltsin opened the door to the one ideology that had not yet been discredited: Russian nationalism. Perhaps radical nationalism will not emerge ascendant owing to its weak resonance among the Russian people and to the widespread awareness among elites of the country's real weakness. If radical nationalism does seize the initiative, however, it could destroy Yeltsin's greatest ideational accomplishment – acceptance of a secular and tolerant definition of citizenship – along with the fragile organizational system he set up.[6]

MISSED OPPORTUNITIES AND EXORBITANT COSTS PAID

The collapse of the Russian financial system in August–September 1998 and the subsequent withdrawal of IMF assistance served to highlight the fragility of the political and economic systems created during Yeltsin's presidency. Some observers took the opportunity to argue that this financial collapse

---

[6] For a comprehensive study of Russian nationalism before the collapse of the USSR, see Yitzhak M. Brudny, *Reinventing Russia: Russian Nationalism and the Soviet State, 1953–1991* (Cambridge, MA: Harvard University Press, 1998); for a study of the evolution of Russian chauvinist ideologies and organizations since 1991, see Veljko Vujacic, "Serving Mother Russia: The communist left and nationalist right in the struggle for power, 1991–1998," in Bonnell and Breslauer, *Russia in the New Century*, pp. 290–325.

revealed Yeltsin's leadership of independent Russia to have been an unmitigated disaster.[7] Other observers instead debated more broadly on how it had come to this.

Some analysts argued that a collapse was all but inevitable, regardless of what Yeltsin had done during his years as Russia's president. Hence, they are less inclined to blame him personally for the collapse. There are four explanations that run along these lines, though they are not mutually exclusive. One is cultural, arguing that Russian culture had never developed orientations compatible with impersonal markets, rule of law, or representative democracy. A second is institutional, claiming that the administrative fragmentation, tacit privatization, and widespread criminalization of the Soviet state during the late-Gorbachev era – or, in some versions of the argument, already under Brezhnev – constituted a legacy that the Yeltsin regime could not possibly overcome in so short a period of time. A third argument for inevitability is circumstantial: that Gorbachev had made a mess of the Soviet economy, the Soviet Union, and Soviet foreign economic relations by 1991. The result was a rupturing of economic relationships and dire economic straits that the Yeltsin regime, again, could not have overcome. The fourth is international: the circumstances of international dependency in which Russia found itself at the time placed it at the mercy of demands by governments of the rich democracies for certain types of policies – policies that ultimately led to the ruin of Russia's economy. If we combine these explanations and treat them as mutually reinforcing features of the domestic and international legacies bequeathed to Yeltsin, then the image of futility and inevitability becomes that much more credible.

An alternative approach (which I endorse) to the question of historical causality treats the current situation as a product of contingent policy choices made by Boris Yeltsin and his governments during 1991–1998. Without denying that the foregoing constraints were real, this argument claims that the constraints were not determinant of the fullness of the outcomes. That is, opportunities were missed to relieve these constraints; to build a new system more democratic, humane, productive, and resilient than the one that Yeltsin built; and to do so at a much lower cost than was paid by the regime in power.

Thus, a corrupt and "weak" state might have been difficult to avoid, given the initial conditions. But the scope and depth of political corruption, the administrative fragmentation and criminalization, and the "virtual economy"

---

[7] See Stephen F. Cohen, "Russian studies without Russia," *Post-Soviet Affairs*, vol. 15, no. 1 (January–March 1999), pp. 37–55; Stephen F. Cohen, *Failed Crusade: America and the Tragedy of Post-Communist Russia* (New York: Norton, 2000).

of 1998[8] were products of policy choices made in 1992–1995. Those choices included the particular approach to macroeconomic stabilization adopted in January 1992; the "loans for shares" program of 1995; and the growing encouragement or toleration over time of large-scale embezzlement of state assets.

Similarly, the fragility of democratic institutions might have been a product of the "dual power" built into the constitution in force in 1991, and that fragility might have been exacerbated by the widespread disorientation and political conflict caused by Russia's loss of its empire and global role. Nonetheless, the ongoing gridlock in executive–legislative relations, the declining influence of democratic forces, and the entrenchment of an overbearing presidency were products of choices about party building and state building made in fall 1991 (and again in fall 1995) and choices about constitutional design made in 1993–1994.

Limited adherence to "rule of law" and spotty protection of the population from physical insecurity might have been inherent in the early stages of any transition following the collapse of a state, especially in a society in which both the supply and the demand for rule of law were so low.[9] But the minuscule progress in building legal and judicial institutions and the extent of police withdrawal from law enforcement were products of decisions made in 1992 and of a continuous lack of priority given to the development of legal institutions.

Persistent defiance of central authority by the government of Chechnya might have been the bane of any Kremlin leader. Even so, the costs and consequences of the war against Chechen secession were products of policy choices made by the Yeltsin leadership in 1994–1995 and again in fall 1999.

Dependence on international assistance would have been a condition faced by any Russian government. But willingness to accept the prescriptions of the International Monetary Fund was a decision made by Yeltsin and his cabinet, and the corrupt use of those funds was a product of internal circumstances over which they had some control. Given the fears in Western capitals of "losing Russia," it is implausible to claim that the rich democracies would have abandoned Russia to her fate had Moscow adopted a different strategy of economic stabilization, marketization, and privatization.

In all, given its bequeathed legacy, Russia probably would have been in difficult circumstances regardless of the policies chosen during 1992–1998. With

---

[8] Clifford G. Gaddy and Barry W. Ickes, "Russia's virtual economy," *Foreign Affairs,* vol. 77, no. 5 (September/October 1998), pp. 53–67.
[9] On the supply and demand for law in post-Soviet Russia, see Kathryn Hendley, *Trying to Make Law Matter* (Ann Arbor: University of Michigan Press, 1995).

different policies, however, Russia would not have been in such dire straits, and prospects for a sustainable recovery would have been stronger.[10] Had Yeltsin done things differently in many realms of policy, we would have been better positioned to assess the resilience or malleability of cultural, institutional, circumstantial, and international constraints on change. But Yeltsin's initiatives instead typically acquiesced in or exacerbated the legacy he inherited. Hence, we cannot say with confidence just *how much* would have been different had Yeltsin acted differently. It does seem safe to argue that many of his general goals could have been advanced at a lower cost – in some cases, perhaps a much lower cost. Put differently, Yeltsin was not simply a victim of circumstances; he had opportunities to do things differently, but he missed them.[11]

Indeed, it was Yeltsin himself who rendered precisely this verdict on his leadership of Russia. Announcing his resignation on December 31, 1999, he averred:

I want to ask you for forgiveness, because many of our hopes have not come true, because what we thought would be easy turned out to be painfully difficult. I ask you to forgive me for not fulfilling some hopes of those people who believed that we would be able to jump from the grey, stagnating, totalitarian past into a bright, rich and civilised future in one go.

I myself believed in this. But it could not be done in one fell swoop. In some respects I was too naive. Some of the problems were too complex. We struggled on through mistakes and failures.

The man who had helped to destroy Gorbachev politically by accusing him of "half-measures" and of trying to "leap across a chasm in two steps" left office admitting that one could not bridge that chasm "in one fell swoop" after all.

PERSONALISM AND ADMINISTRATIVE RATIONALIZATION, 1994–1999

During 1994–1999, Yeltsin claimed that his goals had evolved and that his main goal was now to "strengthen the Russian state" in order to deliver peace, order,

---

[10] The economic recovery of year 2000 was based on windfall oil prices and the near-term impact of ruble devaluation following the 1998 crash. Neither condition can be counted upon to last, and accumulated debt payments will soon come due. Hence, the present-day recovery may well prove to be a temporary boom. For an analysis of what needs to be done to sustain the recent rebound, see Jacques Sapir, "The Russian economy: From rebound to rebuilding," *Post-Soviet Affairs*, vol. 17, no. 1 (January–March 2001), pp. 1–22.

[11] For the argument that Yeltsin missed even more opportunities than the ones I have enumerated, see Peter Reddaway and Dmitri Glinski, *The Tragedy of Russia's Reforms: Market Bolshevism against Democracy* (Washington, DC: U.S. Institute of Peace, 2000), pp. 636–41.

and prosperity to the Russian people. We may therefore evaluate his effectiveness as a leader in those years relative to the advancement of these goals. The verdict is a negative one. Even if he was sincere about his promises, the tactics Yeltsin employed for maintaining his power and authority actually impeded realization of those goals. Instead, Yeltsin's operating style undermined administrative efficiency throughout his years in office. His organization of the presidential apparatus and manipulation of the executive branch went far to strengthen his grip on the formal reins of power and perhaps to make possible the defense of his system *building* goals, but they simultaneously strengthened the corrupt bureaucracy's capacity to avoid rationalization and thereby undermined the consolidation and sustainability of Yeltsin's achievements.

Consider his approach to both the organization of advice within the presidency and the articulation of interests within government. On both scores, Yeltsin's preferred approach was individualized, anti-procedural, and anti-institutional. Within his personal staff and advisory corps, Yeltsin resisted the crystallization of even informal constraints on his power over the "children." He did not treat the political organization of his staff as a rational distribution of formal powers (*polnomochia*). Rather, he wanted to maintain fluidity and redundancy of jurisdictions in order to maximize his capacity to play subordinates off against each other and to maximize their sense of dependence on him for protection against the others. According to a former high-level staff member,[12] Yeltsin wished to get advice from staff members on an individual, not a collective, basis. He did not want his staff to get together, work out a common viewpoint on an issue, and present it to him as a collective judgment. Nor did he care to meet with them as a collective. Instead, he wanted each of them to come to him individually with their ideas. When they defied this preference, he could be strict.

Yeltsin's approach to interest articulation and aggregation was also suffused by personalism. He was highly responsive to particularistic pleading for tax exemptions, licenses, and subsidies. He preferred to deal with governors, military commanders, and ministers on an ad hoc, individual basis rather than through their organizations. While there may have been a *political* rationality to some of these preferences, the effect was to undermine the development of organized collectivities on which modern public administration is based. As Huskey aptly observes, it was "a style of rule associated more with traditional monarchs than modern chief executives."[13]

---

[12] Interview, Moscow, June 1998. Published support for this characterization can also be found in Aleksandr Korzhakov, *Boris Yel'tsin: Ot rassveta do zakata* (Moscow: Izd-vo "Interbuk," 1997), p. 221, and Baturin et al., *Epokha*, p. 212.

[13] Eugene Huskey, *Presidential Power in Russia* (Armonk, NY: M.E. Sharpe, 1999), p. 50.

It is true that, in all public administration, there is an inherent tension between the requirements of political control and those of administrative efficiency. What distinguishes administrative leaders, however, is how they deal with this tension and whether their solutions strike a balance that is consistent with the realization *and consolidation* of their general policy goals. Leaders like Charles de Gaulle, Franklin Roosevelt, and Kemal Ataturk understood this. In Yeltsin's case, the sacrifice of administrative rationality to the requisites of political control was such as to threaten the sustainability of his program. Bureaucratic fragmentation, corruption, and unaccountability worsened as a result of his approach to administrative control.

Yeltsin's approach to administrative organization of the presidential and executive branches was reminiscent of Khrushchev's approach in the early 1960s during the analogous (third) stage of Khrushchev's administration: constant reorganization, high turnover of personnel, and the regular creation of new units with jurisdictions that duplicated those of existing units.[14] The presidential administration evolved into a huge bureaucracy – larger in size than the CPSU's Central Committee apparatus and with at least as many departments. But there was scant rationalization of jurisdictions within the apparatus and between the apparatus and the ministries. Officials of the apparatus were left with neither stable expectations nor the requisite information to perform their jobs.

In theory, one could view the blurring of jurisdictions and the inhibition of stable expectations as a sensible way to organize a presidential administration. Organization theorists have long known that formal organization charts are a poor guide to how organizations actually run – or ought to run. Franklin Roosevelt found it useful to establish redundant jurisdictions to ensure that he received multiple sources of information and a variety of viewpoints on a given situation.

This was not the way in which Yeltsin ran his presidential administration and cabinet. Instability of expectations concerned not so much the sequencing of tasks as the continued existence of the agency and thus the maintenance of perquisites and privileges that accompany employment in the president's administration. Blurring of jurisdictions was not so much a functional means of ensuring diverse viewpoints as a proliferation of redundancies that left units unclear as to who actually was responsible for task fulfillment. Instead of fostering healthy coverage on all issues, the exponential increase in the size

---

[14] Huskey refers to the last of these tendencies as "the politics of redundancy"; see Eugene Huskey, "The state–legal administration and the politics of redundancy," *Post-Soviet Affairs*, vol. 11, no. 2 (April–June 1995), pp. 115–43.

of the presidential administration fostered duplication of the governmental–ministerial structure, duplication of jurisidictions between the executive and presidential branches, and proliferation of decisional arenas to which bureaucrats and others could turn in order to subvert the implementation of presidential decrees or parliamentary legislation. The frequent creation and abolition of agencies left officials little time for programmatic thinking and focused their attention largely on personal political survival.

More generally, Yeltsin preferred to manipulate diversity in ways that played factions off against each other and thereby maintained or enhanced his leverage as the "ultimate arbiter." Within the presidential administration, Yeltsin included representatives of all political orientations save intransigent communists and radical nationalists. This is certainly a rational strategy for power maintenance. It can also be a rational strategy for eliciting a diversity of inputs and for building one's authority with a multitude of constituencies. But it works this way only if officeholders and advisors feel reasonably secure in their jobs. If, instead, the "ultimate arbiter" frequently shifts back and forth between preferred factions and then forces the losers to pay with their jobs, the result is more likely to be sycophancy, individualized efforts to curry favor with the president, or collective efforts to destroy the credibility and favor of the competing factions ("backstabbing"). Yeltsin's modus operandi was to fire leading officials and their deputies with great frequency and sometimes to "balance off" a dismissal with the arbitrary dismissal of an equivalent figure in the opposing faction.[15]

One result of such an operating style was that ideological or professional factions crystallized within the presidential administration for mutual protection against the insecurities of working under an unpredictable commander. Another result of the general atmosphere of profound uncertainty and insecurity was widespread and deep-seated corruption within the presidential administration and portions of the executive branch. Many officials simply found it too tempting to resist feathering their nests while the opportunity was there. And why not? They lived with persistent uncertainty as to what actions were likely to fulfill the tasks assigned to them. They were equally uncertain as to how long they would keep their jobs regardless of their performance. They

[15] According to Kostikov, when Yeltsin formally fired his vice-president, Aleksandr Rutskoi, he also fired cabinet member Shumeiko. The latter had done nothing wrong, but Yeltsin told Kostikov that Shumeiko had to be "sacrificed" in order to "balance off" the firing of Rutskoi (Viacheslav Kostikov, *Roman s prezidentom: zapiski press-sekretaria* [Moscow: Vagrius, 1997], p. 210); conversely, Baturin et al. (*Epokha*, p. 209) claim that Yeltsin appointed the "democrat" Sergei Filatov to head the presidential administration in order to balance out the recent appointment of Viktor Chernomyrdin as prime minister.

found themselves in a privileged position that afforded many opportunities for using public office for private material gain, and knew that they might not be able to gather such resources – or avoid criminal prosecution – outside of government. In sum, rather than engendering a healthy dose of competition and uncertainty, Yeltsin's approach to administration of the presidential and executive branches did a good job of protecting his personal power against challenge and a poor job of creating the institutional and political support for rational decisionmaking.[16]

Apparently, Yeltsin did not understand the contradictions between his operating style and the requirements of administrative reliability. Put differently, he did not understand that his personalism actually increased the opportunities for midlevel officials to undermine his policies. Vague presidential decrees that either circumvented parliament or violated the Constitution had the dual effect of leaving interpretation up to the bureaucrats and of undermining the credibility of parliament as a force for oversight or discipline of the bureaucracy. The result was that the bureaucrats had both the intellectual and political space to ignore or reinterpret decrees to their own benefit.[17]

Yeltsin understood the general direction in which he wanted to push the country. But when it came to elaborating complex programs that would consolidate his gains by strengthening the state, Yeltsin fell short. Some memoirists criticize Yeltsin for allegedly lacking a political strategy or philosophy of transformation, as does one of his foreign advisors;[18] some point to his personality as a source of regular depressions or ambivalence that caused him to

---

[16] Viktor Baranets argues that the bloated and impenetrable mechanism of Russian political decisionmaking allowed Yeltsin to exercise ultimate control over his bureaucracy, including military officialdom. Every minor decision had to be processed by a multitude of organizations and administrative departments and only then submitted to the president for final approval. When Yeltsin was incapacitated, the situation became even worse. Many of the most pressing problems of either strategic or tactical importance never got solved and kept accumulating; V. N. Baranets, *Yel'tsin i ego generaly: zapiski polkovnika genshtaba* (Moscow: "Sovershenno Sekretno," 1998), p. 50. See also Anatol Lieven, *Chechnya: Tombstone of Russian Power* (New Haven & London: Yale University Press, 1998), pp. 294–9, for a case study of the impact of this operating style on military reform in Russia.

[17] This point is made and documented in Victor M. Sergeyev, *The Wild East: Crime and Lawlessness in Post-Communist Russia* (Armonk, NY: M.E. Sharpe, 1998) pp. 84ff., and in Nikolai Biryukov and Victor M. Sergeyev, *Russian Politics in Transition* (Brookfield, VT: Aldershot, 1997), pp. 260–9. Alternatively, Yeltsin may have understood very well what he was doing (i.e., maintaining his political control) and did not regret the side effects; this is the view propounded in Hough, *The Logic of Economic Reform*.

[18] O. Poptsov, *Khronika vremyon "Tsaria Borisa"* (Moscow: "Sovershenno sekretno," 1997), p. 431; Kostikov, *Roman*, pp. 300–1, 323–4; Anders Åslund, *How Russia Became a Market Economy* (Washington, DC: Brookings Institution, 1995), p. 91.

squander his political assets.[19] Whatever the source of his policy choices, the implications for realization of his consolidative goals were negative ones.

THE BALANCE OF THE LEDGER: PLUSES, MINUSES, AND MITIGATING FACTORS

Yeltsin was most successful in combining creativity with destruction, in balancing transformation with identity and stability, and in neutralizing the forces of reaction in three realms: East–West relations, relations with the Near Abroad, and Russian nation building. In a difficult international context, he managed to defend a combination of liberal internationalism and *realpolitik* that flexed Russia's muscles while acknowledging its weakness and seeking new associations abroad to offset that weakness. In a difficult internal political context, Yeltsin advocated a combination of patriotism, ethnic pride, and liberal nationalism that rejected the extreme alternatives being offered by the "red-brown" coalition. In all these realms, he also helped to create institutions that could sustain a liberal orientation over the longer term. Thus, his successes were both organizational and cultural – and held promise of sustainability.

With respect to state building and economic transformation, however, Yeltsin was much less effective. In these realms Yeltsin proved least able: (1) to engage in *creative* destruction by initiating construction of the regulatory infrastructure of a market economy and representative democracy; (2) to transform cultural and political attitudes toward belief in the new order; and (3) to create a climate and processes for sustaining the transformation in the long term. Instead, by tolerating the de facto creation of a corrupt state and re-monopolized market that bore much resemblance to the Soviet system they had replaced, Yeltsin put at risk his entire transformative project. By the time of his retirement, the market democratic project was treated skeptically, if not with hostility, by the majority of the population, and nationalistic attitudes were on the rise that could lead eventually to a reversal of the liberal successes in nation building, relations with the Near Abroad, and East–West international relations.

In evaluating leaders, it is insufficient to point to their successes and failures. One must also consider the magnitude of the constraints and obstacles they faced in each realm. Easy successes, or failures in "no-win" situations, are not appropriate indicators of an individual's leadership capacity.

---

[19] Yegor T. Gaidar, *Dni porazhenii i pobed* (Moscow: Vagrius, 1996), pp. 106–7, 310–14; Kostikov, *Roman*, pp. 141–2, 168–9, 174; Korzhakov, *Boris Yel'tsin*, p. 315.

Evaluation of Yeltsin's failures in the areas of economic transformation and state building must consider important mitigating factors. Scholars dispute the alternatives available to Yeltsin in 1991–1993; we cannot resolve those disputes with the evidence drawn in this book. Yet if one believes that few alternative strategies were practical in late 1991, then one would credit Yeltsin with making the best of an unraveling economic situation at that time.[20] Similarly, if one believes that the only politically feasible alternatives in 1993 were reaction or gridlock, then one would credit Yeltsin with sustaining democratic processes and instituting a new constitutional framework through the sheer force of his will.[21] Moreover, Yeltsin's failure to construct a robust organizational infrastructure happened to concern the most difficult problems for a president to overcome in a short period of time. Some presidents – notably, FDR and Charles de Gaulle – were up to the challenge, building organizations that would ultimately become the sinews of the U.S. and French regulatory states. Yeltsin was not up to this challenge, but he was also starting (his mandate notwithstanding) from a considerably more dire set of circumstances than either Roosevelt or de Gaulle faced.

The challenges of state building and economic transformation also required Yeltsin to overcome obstacles and constraints that were far more resilient than those he dealt with in the realms of foreign policy and nation building. It is much easier to strike a deal with a foreign leader than to effect

---

[20] Yeltsin has been roundly condemned for his "shock therapy" approach to economic reform in 1992. But little attention has been given to the counterfactual: what would have been the consequences of an alternative strategy for dealing with the dire economic circumstances – both macroeconomic and microeconomic – at the time? Critics speak vaguely of "gradualism" or an "evolutionary" approach without specifying how such a "policy" would have checked the economic crisis of late 1991. Strategies recommended by reformist Soviet economists for the stable conditions of 1986–1987 were not necessarily workable in the conditions of 1992. Hence, it is far from clear whether credible, alternative strategies were intellectually available and practicable when Yeltsin made his choice on behalf of shock therapy. Indeed, comparative analyses of post-communist economic reform suggest that Yeltsin's mistake may have been the opposite: to back off from shock therapy after April 1992 in favor of a broader coalition among economic elites, thus miring Russia in a condition of partial reform that encouraged massive corruption. See Joel Hellman, "Winners take all: The politics of partial reform in postcommunist transitions," *World Politics*, vol. 50, no. 2 (January 1998). Recently, some severe critics of Yeltsin's economic policies have proposed alternatives that might have been appropriate to the circumstances of 1992; see Reddaway and Glinski, *The Tragedy of Russia's Reforms*, pp. 252–5, 286–8, and Hough, *The Logic of Economic Reform in Russia*, pp. 127–9. See especially the impressive discussions of alternatives in Lawrence R. Klein and Marshall Pomer (Eds.), *The New Russia: Transition Gone Awry* (Stanford, CA: Stanford University Press, 1991).

[21] The link between this counterfactual conclusion and a positive evaluation of Yeltsin's leadership is exemplified by Leon Aron, *Boris Yeltsin: A Revolutionary Life* (New York: HarperCollins, 2000), pp. 540ff.

a durable change in the culture and process of public administration. It is easier to speak publicly about the need for tolerance in inter-ethnic relations than to deliver material satisfaction to the populace. It is also easier to withdraw troops from the Baltic States than to design and build the operating institutions of a regulatory state. Proper functioning of the "rule of law" requires organizational and cultural change, both of which require a good deal of time and effort. Moreover, in these domestic realms, Yeltsin faced more political and administrative constraints than in foreign policy. Unlike Gorbachev, he did not have a large apparatus of officials to process information and to whom he could delegate subtasks. He had to construct a "presidential administration" on the fly in 1991–1992 and was rapidly overloaded with decisionmaking responsibility. Given the constitutional ambiguities he inherited, the opposition he faced from the Supreme Soviet in 1992–1993 would have impeded ambitious efforts to construct a rule of law in Russia regardless of who was in power. In short, any leader put in Yeltsin's situation at the end of 1991 would have faced a daunting array of constraints on implementing a coherent, effective, and far-reaching strategy of state building and economic transformation. Yeltsin's successes were easier to attain than his failures were to avoid.

Comparison with Gorbachev helps to avoid double standards in evaluations of their leadership. Like Yeltsin, Gorbachev's greatest successes lay in destroying the old system and in preventing its restoration. Thereafter, like Yeltsin, Gorbachev was most successful in two realms of policy: Gorbachev in foreign policy and political democratization; Yeltsin in foreign policy and in constructing a new political and national order. Like Gorbachev's, Yeltsin's leadership was singularly unimpressive in two realms: consolidation of the new state and construction of a market economy. And like Yeltsin, given the constraints he faced, Gorbachev's successes were probably easier to attain (though not "easy" in an absolute sense) than his failures were to avoid.

These observations could be the basis for an evaluation of the two leaders that treats their accomplishments as essentially equivalent. The argument would go as follows. Both men were hugely successful in bringing down the political order they sought to supersede or destroy. Both men receive mixed grades for effectiveness in their system-building efforts. The areas in which they experienced success and failure were analogous, suggesting that they were frustrated by analogous constraints and helped by analogous opportunities.

Hence (the argument would continue), if we credit Gorbachev for "successfully" following a concessionary foreign policy, then we should credit Yeltsin for having done much the same vis-à-vis both the rich democracies and many states in the Near Abroad at a time of rising *realpolitik* sentiment within the

Russian elite. Similarly, if we praise Gorbachev for breaking the political and psychological bonds of Leninist doctrine, then we should praise Yeltsin for defending a secular and tolerant definition of Russian citizenship and nationhood at a time of rising revanchist sentiment among parliamentarians. If we laud Gorbachev for liberalizing and democratizing the system at the risk of bringing down both communist rule and the Soviet Union itself, then we may praise Yeltsin for tackling the issue of economic reform in 1992 – something Gorbachev never managed to do and that was becoming a dire necessity by the end of 1991 – even at the risk of impoverishing large numbers of citizens. If we praise Gorbachev for trying to negotiate democratic federalism as an alternative to the Soviet unitary state, then we may credit Yeltsin for negotiating treaties with the major regions of Russia as an alternative to the regional fragmentation and feudalization that was rampant at the time. If we praise Gorbachev for resisting the temptation to "restore order" in the face of political challenges, then we should give Yeltsin some credit for retaining the civil liberties enacted under Gorbachev and for resisting the temptation to impose the kind of one-man dictatorship found in so many successor states of the former Soviet Union.

Gorbachev looks better than Yeltsin, however, when we consider the *magnitude* and not just the nature of the constraints they faced. The domestic opposition to "new thinking" in foreign relations in 1986–1989 was much stronger than the domestic opposition to continuing an essentially pro-Western tilt after 1991. Support for a solidary conception of "the Soviet people" was stronger within the political establishment under Gorbachev than was support for Russian chauvinism and imperial revanchism under Yeltsin. Gorbachev's democratization program entailed the risky *diffusion* of power to unpredictable social actors, whereas Yeltsin's economic and political programs of 1992–1993 entailed the *reconcentration* of power after a subsiding revolutionary wave. Gorbachev's agonies of 1990–1991 were products of trying simultaneously to resist accelerating disintegration, to avoid a reactionary crackdown, and to negotiate an intermediate federal equilibrium. By contrast, Yeltsin's "asymmetrical federalism" came after the reconcentration of power and resulted in separate deals that avoided the challenge of institutionalizing either a federal or a unitary order. In this realm, Gorbachev was seeking to institutionalize a long-term solution; Yeltsin was seeking only to cope with near-term threats and pressures. Gorbachev plowed forward with his program in 1987 and 1989, resisting the political temptation to compromise his basic goals, whereas Yeltsin sought a centrist compromise at his stages of ascendancy and decline.

Then, too, Yeltsin and Gorbachev were interdependent political actors in ways that must be factored into an evaluation of their records. That is, Yeltsin himself was a conscious and powerful impediment to Gorbachev's success in negotiating an equilibrium to slow the disintegration of the political system. Put differently: Gorbachev's policies initiated a process of disintegration and political polarization, but Yeltsin served as a focal point for social forces seeking to accelerate the rate of both; absent Yeltsin, Gorbachev might have been more successful in renegotiating an equilibrium. In a similar vein, the magnitude of the constraints facing Yeltsin in 1991–1992 was in part a product of his own actions in 1989–1991. By consciously accelerating the polarization and disintegration, he ensured that, if he emerged ascendant, he would face a situation of collapse that might leave him few options. To the extent that a positive evaluation of Yeltsin's leadership hinges on the claim that he was forced to cope with dire circumstances in 1991–1992, such an evaluation must also attend to the fact that Yeltsin helped to create those very circumstances.

Furthermore, Yeltsin's strategies for founding and guaranteeing a new order of things were – more so than Gorbachev's – insensitive to the human costs of those strategies. If we take both men at their word (based on their public rhetoric), Gorbachev was committed to a peaceful management of the transformation process at home and abroad. He remained true to that goal, even at the cost of failure to prevent the collapse of communism in Eastern Europe and of the USSR itself. Gorbachev also rejected both "unbridled" capitalism and abolition of the Communist Party; even at the expense of his political power, he fought to the end to avoid these costs. Yeltsin built his authority championing greater equality, opposing privilege and corruption, opposing the use of military force against secessionist forces, and calling for the creation of a market democracy. What he tolerated when in charge, however, looked quite different: the creation and indulgence of a plutocratic elite; growing corruption within the political elite; inattention to widespread social misery; infantilizaton of political parties, judicial institutions, and parliament; and the wanton use of violence in Chechnya.

Only if one argues that Gorbachev missed many opportunities to do better – and that Yeltsin enjoyed many *fewer* opportunities to do better – can one make the case that Yeltsin was the more impressive transformational leader. Similarly, one can reach that conclusion only if one argues that Yeltsin faced constraints that were significantly more formidable than those facing Gorbachev. I find it hard to make that case.

AUTHORITY BUILDING AND AUTHORITY MAINTENANCE

Still another way to evaluate leaders is to ask: How good were they at exercising power in ways that built and maintained their credibility, stature, and legitimacy as leaders? It is noteworthy that Khrushchev, Brezhnev, Gorbachev, and Yeltsin all proved adept at building their authority initially, when they fashioned images for themselves that facilitated seizing the initiative and out-flanking political rivals. Subsequently, they all "rode high" with comprehensive programs that appealed to a range of political audiences. Were we to conduct leadership evaluations after the first 4–5 years of each man's rise, we would arrive at strikingly similar conclusions: all four leaders did excellent jobs of building their power and authority among relevant audiences and of achieving a position of political ascendancy within the establishment.[22]

Yet it is equally noteworthy that all four leaders ended their political lives on notes of failure or repudiation. Khrushchev and Gorbachev were forced from office. Brezhnev died in office with his domestic and foreign policy programs in shambles. Yeltsin ended his presidency with approval ratings in single digits and with many of his programs discredited.

What went wrong in the relatively short period between the successful consolidation of power and the radical decline of these leaders' authority and effectiveness? Answering this question requires a broad perspective on both leadership in general and leadership in the Soviet and post-Soviet systems. Globally, it is often the case that leaders who are successful at one stage of their political careers, or in grappling with one historical challenge, prove unsuccessful at later stages of their careers or in grappling with other historical challenges. Hence, the experiences of these four leaders are hardly exceptional; rather, they are indicative of the intrinsic difficulties of sustaining good performance and maintaining the authority one has built. Authority cannot be hoarded; one must use it or lose it. But frequently, in the process of using accumulated authority, one encounters obstacles that are more difficult to overcome than those met earlier. Or one proves to have a repertoire of skills that are better suited to resolving some problems than others, or one runs out of gas and makes mistakes that squander accumulated authority. Once one's reputation for success is damaged, those on whom one relied for political support begin to hedge their bets.[23] The result can be a cascading loss of authority.

Similarly, the process of initially building one's authority often takes place in a context in which competitors make promises but are not yet required to take responsibility for delivering the goods. Sometimes, one can accumulate

---

[22] Of course, they do not deserve equal praise for this achievement, since they each faced different degrees of challenge in accomplishing the feat. Brezhnev's challenge was clearly the easiest. Gorbachev's and Yeltsin's challenges were the hardest.

[23] This last observation was a theme of Neustadt's (Richard E. Neustadt, *Presidential Power: The Politics of Leadership* [New York: Wiley, 1960], ch. 4), though he generalized it only to the American presidency in normal (i.e., noncrisis) times.

authority simply by criticizing the proposals or past performance of political rivals in lieu of presenting a platform of one's own. To the extent that leaders succeed in building authority by these means, they are bound to experience a deflation. For once they emerge ascendant, they are expected to sponsor a comprehensive program for progress in many realms of policy. That is their function as leader. Once they do so, however, they are bound to experience some diminution of their authority as they take responsibility for policy performance, as results prove to be a mix of successes and failures, and as the costs of their comprehensive programs are felt.

These are universals of competitive politics in modern times. But the Soviet and post-Soviet contexts accelerated the transition from political ascendancy to political decline. In retrospect, we can see that Soviet and post-Soviet leaders could not avoid being dogged by manifold contradictions as they sought to deliver the goods. They could not avoid the basic contradiction between ideological aspirations and systemic capacity. Those contradictions ensured that leaders who had built their authority by promising to cure many of the country's ills would face mounting frustrations and that their authority would decline as a result.

Ironically, operating in a post-Soviet context, Yeltsin inherited some features of the Soviet mind-set that perpetuated this problem. He – like Khrushchev, Brezhnev, and Gorbachev – promised far more than he could possibly deliver. Yeltsin, like his predecessors in the Kremlin, embraced a campaignist approach to solving problems. He, like the others, believed that answers to contradictions lay in some combination of popular mobilization, cadre selection and motivation, money, and technology. He, like the others, failed to understand or appreciate the *institutional* requirements for coordination of economic exchange within a decentralized system. And some of the political constituencies on which he relied shared with him many of these features of the Soviet-era mind-set.

Some people argue that the Soviet system was doomed to collapse at some point, given its leaders' incapacity to conceive and "sell" programs that could transform it peacefully into a marketized and democratized system or (in Yeltsin's case) that could build such a system in Russia on the ruins of communism. If one believes that fragmentation and collapse of the Soviet system were inevitable and that Russia would follow a similar path because of the cultural and institutional legacy of communism, then all four leaders would come across as historically tragic, quixotic, or myopic figures.

I noted in Chapter 13 that Gorbachev got off to a great start but proved a disappointing finisher on many counts. The same can be said for Yeltsin; on their own terms, it can also be said of Khrushchev and Brezhnev. Perhaps that common outcome was less a product of their personal failings than of the intrinsic dilemmas they faced in the Soviet and post-Soviet contexts.

Such a conclusion lends broader perspective to the task of evaluating these leaders by expanding our appreciation of the constraints facing Soviet and Russian leaders during the past fifty years. But it is not entirely satisfying. It is difficult to believe that nothing they did could have averted the deflation of authority they all experienced. One can, of course, avoid a complex evaluation of leaders' performance in office by embracing a philosophy of history that leads to the deterministic conclusion. But if one rejects such an approach without going to the opposite extreme of assuming that "anything was possible," then one is back in the game of evaluating leaders on their own terms and of asking whether they could have done a better job in light of the constraints and opportunities they faced.

For example, had Gorbachev subjected himself to a competitive election for president of the USSR in 1989 – which he stood an excellent chance of winning – then he might have revalidated his popular authority and increased his leverage within the political arena, thereby heading off (or at least postponing) the radical deflation of authority he experienced in 1990–1991. At a minimum, it would have advantaged him in the political competition with Boris Yeltsin. Maximally, it might have positioned him better to propose a real federation or confederation without having to worry about his being deposed by the Central Committee. To take another example: had he not given Yeltsin a high position in the government after purging him from the Party apparatus, Gorbachev might have avoided the public political competition with Yeltsin that went so far to destroy Gorbachev's political base.

As for Yeltsin, he did an impressive job of building his authority in 1989–1991. Thereafter, he was successful in some policy areas and unsuccessful in others. He squandered his accumulated authority but proved to be exceptionally skilled at keeping would-be opponents off-balance and at maintaining his grip on power. If things improve in Russia, he may yet be credited with greater accomplishment than he currently is. If things go haywire, he is likely to be condemned for having created a fragile and unsustainable system at exorbitant cost. Either way, future archival research may permit a deeper understanding of the magnitude of the constraints he faced. As Dean Acheson put it: "Sometimes it is only in retrospect and in the light of how things work out that you can distinguish stubbornness from determination."[24]

---

[24] As quoted in Marshall D. Shulman in *The New York Review of Books* (June 17, 1990), p. 5.

Index

ACKNOWLEDGMENTS

First, I would like to thank all those involved with the Times Square redevelopment and everyone in the Clinton/Hell's Kitchen neighborhood who tolerated my questions and offered me the opportunity to spend time with them, including: everyone from the Hell's Kitchen Neighborhood Association; Joe Restuccia from the Clinton Housing Development Company; Bob Davis from the Midtown North Precinct Community Council; Mary Dorman from the Community Board Five Quality-of-Life Committee; Diane O'Connor from the New York Police Department; Estelle Stryker from the office of the New York City District Attorney; everyone from the NYPD Citizens' Police Academy; Rebecca Buzansky, Julius Lang, John Megaw, Scott Brown, and Dave Connally from the Midtown Community Court; Jasmine Hopper, Jared Delancy, and all the trainees from Times Square Ink.; Michelle Sviridoff, Eric Lee, Rob Weidner, and John Feinblatt from the Center for Court Innovation; Gretchen Dykstra, Frank Colarusso, Christine Krisch, and Suany Chough from the Times Square Business Improvement District (now known as the Times Square Alliance); Rebecca Robertson from the Forty-second Street Development Association; Pete Kozo from the Guardian Angels; Thomas Lueck from the *New York Times;* Cora Cahan from the New 42; Patrick Too from the

New York City Department of City Planning; Arthur Rosenblatt; Dan Rose; Barbara Feldt; Tom Lisa; Paula Jaslow; Amanda Burden; Stephen Wilder; Ken Philmus from the Port Authority of New York and New Jersey; and Anne Pasternak from Creative Time.

I would also like to thank all my friends, family, and advisors who provided support and guidance throughout this project, including: Steven Feld, Susan Harding, Donald Brenneis, Kathleen Stewart, Hayden White, James Brow, and Anna Tsing; Laura Kunreuther, Susan Lepselter, Stephanie Brown, and Ayala Fader; Greg Falkin, Bruce Johnson, Steven Lankenau, Bill Gottdiener, all the participants in the NDRI/MHRA fellowship program; James Carnelia, Sam Duffy, Karen Duffy, Jeff Morris, Amy Staats, Amy Pearl, Timothy Dennison, Martin Azevedo, Aaron Elstein, Isen Robbins, and Laura Stucin; and Kristi Long, Adi Hovav, and the staff of Rutgers University Press.

I owe special thanks to Maggie Hopp, for her wonderful photographs, and to Drew Phillips and Holly Lau, for the map. Rick Delaney's copy-editing of the manuscript pushed me to weigh my words. Laura Moss Gottlieb's brilliant index made me see the book in a new light. I thank both of them for their careful reading and thoughtful comments.

I am grateful to my parents, Penny and David Chesluk, for their support throughout this project.

I would not have been able to complete this book without the help of Henry Goldschmidt and David Valentine. Over many years of writing together, these true friends helped me find the story I had to tell.

Susannah Staats stood by my side and shared her encouragement and love. To her, I owe the greatest thanks of all.

Portions of chapters four, five, and six were previously published in *Cultural Anthropology* and *disClosure*.

Partial funding for the research and writing of this book was provided by NIDA under grant number 5 T32 DA07233–16. The views expressed herein are solely those of the author.

ABOUT THE PHOTOGRAPHS

Maggie Hopp has been making photographs in and around Times Square since the mid-1970s. Her images document the incremental process of the area's redevelopment, as the signs, stores, and theaters of previous eras were shut down, dismantled, renovated, or replaced. Hopp's photographs serve as a parallel visual accompaniment to the stories in the text. They are frozen glimpses of the transformation of the life of the streets in the Times Square area.

The photographs included in this book are drawn from two series by Hopp. The photographs of theater exteriors and street scenes are drawn from a portfolio entitled "Theaters under Siege," begun in 1989, which documented the interiors, exteriors, and details of theaters slated for demolition or restoration as part of the redevelopment of Forty-second Street. She writes about this work, "Inspired by the remnants of grandeur and commissioned to document work being done to stabilize and rescue the nine famous theaters on Forty-second Street, I was able to create an interpretive photographic portfolio of images including not only façades and streetscapes, but also images of interior spaces and vintage architectural details not accessible to the public."

The images of the 42nd Street Art Project, including Tibor Kalman's "Everybody" mural and the marquees with haikus and aphorisms, are

taken from a series of photographs commissioned by Creative Time in 1993–94 to document the site-specific art installations that constituted the project. Hopp used this commission to capture not only the artists' installations themselves, but also how they framed the changing streetlife of Forty-second Street.

MONEY *Jungle*

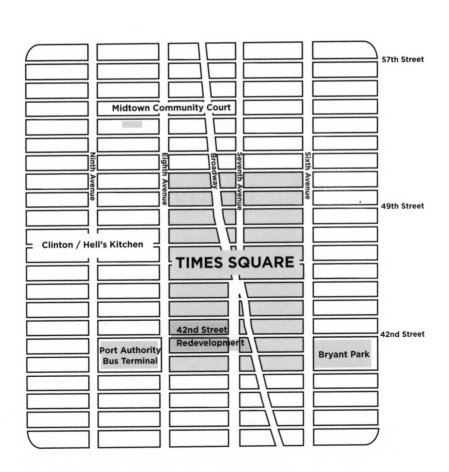

57th Street

Midtown Community Court

Ninth Avenue

Eighth Avenue

Broadway

Seventh Avenue

Sixth Avenue

49th Street

Clinton / Hell's Kitchen

TIMES SQUARE

42nd Street
Redevelopment

42nd Street

Port Authority
Bus Terminal

Bryant Park

Brilliant Corners

The Redevelopment of Times Square

In the late nineteenth century, real estate speculators and theater entrepreneurs remade what was then Longacre Square, an unfashionably rough area of tenements, bars, brothels, factories, and slaughterhouses, into a glamorous center for upscale nightlife and mass spectacle. Since then, Times Square has been, and still is, many things. It has been a center for all kinds of performance, including music, theater, movies, vaudeville, and burlesque. It has been a district of boarding houses and residential hotels, some cheap and some expensive. It has been an intersection for pedestrians, subways, and automobiles. It has been a place where millions gather to celebrate the New Year and to revel in the idea that their images are being broadcast via television to hundreds of millions more people around the world. It has been a center for commercialized sex, including prostitution, sex shops, pornographic movies, and strip shows. It has been an office district, with a growing population of law firms and multinational media corporations. It has been a tourist center, both lowbrow and upscale, filled with cheap camera shops and seedy entertainments as well as global theme restaurants

1

and chain stores. It has been a family-entertainment destination for poorer families from the outer boroughs of Brooklyn, Queens, and the Bronx, as well as a mecca for runaway youths, especially from these same families. It has been a center of nightlife for gay men. It has been a gathering place for patriotic crowds, political demonstrations, and public revelry. It has been a center for signs—specifically, the famous "supersigns," enormous billboard advertisements that deck the buildings facing the triangles of Times Square proper. It has been a place to read the latest news wrap around a skyscraper on electronic billboards and to see television programs displayed on huge outdoor screens. It has been a place to watch other people, and to be watched. And last, but certainly not least, it has been an image of colorful urban chaos, serving as the background for countless photo shoots, films, and TV shows.

Strictly speaking, the name "Times Square" refers to the southern of the two triangles (not squares) in the bow-tie of relatively open space formed by the intersection of Seventh Avenue, which runs from south to north, and Broadway, which angles from southeast to northwest. However, most people use the name more broadly. Times Square has come to refer to the northern triangle, formally known as Father Duffy Square, as well; the block of Forty-second Street between Seventh and Eighth Avenues; and the surrounding area as a whole, from about Thirty-eighth Street up to about Fiftieth Street and from Sixth Avenue to Eighth Avenue.

Starting in the late 1960s, private developers and state and city agencies began a program to comprehensively redevelop the area of Times Square and Forty-second Street in New York City. This was only the latest, but by far the most successful, of the many plans to remake the area that began to crop up even before Times Square gained its theaters in the late 1890s and its name in 1906. This latest Times Square redevelopment was a grand, collaborative socioeconomic engineering project. It brought together not just urban planners and real estate developers, but also architects, police officers, community groups, social workers, job trainers, and others. These numerous organizations shared a common goal: to radically reshape the built, legal, social, and economic environment of what the redevelopers like to call the New Times Square.

The redevelopers were remarkably successful in meeting many of their goals. The changes they wrought in Times Square are hugely visible, even viscerally felt as one walks through the neighborhood. The redevelopment has produced enormous shifts, both in the makeup and

in the scale of the business, architecture, and social life of the area. Nobody could portray the current Times Square with the images of abjection, degradation, and sexual squalor seen in films such as *Midnight Cowboy* or *Taxi Driver*. Times Square is now chockablock with enormous new corporate office towers, blazing commercial advertisements, and slick national and global business franchises. Along Forty-second Street, until recently filled with cheap movie theaters, sex shops, souvenir stands, and walk-up tenement buildings, new Broadway theaters and multiplex cinemas fill the streetscape, with more opening soon and four frankly gigantic skyscrapers looming overhead. The area's former booming market in pornography and other kinds of sexually explicit entertainment has been almost completely displaced. Instead, the new office towers of Times Square and Forty-second Street house tenants including global brand names in finance, such as Morgan Stanley Dean Witter, and mass media, including Reuters, Condé Nast, MTV, and, most controversially, the Walt Disney Company.[1]

Anthropology in Times Square

The redevelopment of Times Square might seem like a counterintuitive subject for a cultural anthropologist to study. Traditionally, cultural anthropologists study and document the lifeways and worldviews of particular groups of people through *participant observation*, or close personal engagement with them in their context. We call this work "ethnography." It is still most common for anthropologists to do their ethnographic fieldwork with a defined cultural group in a single geographic locale—a bounded group in a bounded place, usually someplace socially and geographically very far away from the anthropologist's own community, and also usually a group that is under threat from local elites, missionaries, Western imperialism, well-meaning but misguided development initiatives, or the spread and evolution of global capitalism more generally.

But cultural anthropologists are beginning to direct their attention to the missionaries, development workers, and local elites whose practices impact the "out-of-the-way" cultural groups on whose behalf we traditionally speak.[2] At the same time, anthropologists are more often doing ethnographic research on dispersed groups and on cultural realities that are not restricted to a single group in a single place, but are, rather, "multi-sited." When anthropologists do multi-sited research, we

attempt to apply our theoretical and methodological perspective, with its emphasis on understanding others' points of view through direct personal contact, on social forms that can best be understood by following the connections between different people doing different things in different places.[3]

This is how I did my research for this book. This is a multi-sited ethnography of the redevelopment project, which focuses on the cultural perspectives and practices of those in positions of power. While I carried out my research mostly within a relatively small geographic area—the square mile or so encompassing Times Square and Hell's Kitchen, with forays to other sites around the island of Manhattan—I divided my research among many different groups involved with the redevelopment project.

In my year of fieldwork in and around the organizations engaged in reshaping the people and places of Times Square, I conducted formal and informal interviews with a wide range of people, such as real estate developers, city planners, representatives of arts organizations, and officials from local pseudo-governmental organizations like the Times Square Business Improvement District. I observed numerous public discussions of the redevelopment and its impact on the social and economic life of the area and of the city as a whole. I watched the everyday goings-on in the new built spaces of the Times Square area, including the redesigned Bryant Park, Forty-second Street, and the Port Authority bus terminal. I sat in on many meetings between the NYPD and residents of the adjoining neighborhood of Clinton/Hell's Kitchen, and I attended the Citizens' Police Academy, where NYPD instructors put members of the community through a three-month simulation of police training. Finally, I studied the Midtown Community Court's experimental courtroom/treatment center, first as an observer, then as a volunteer with Times Square Ink., a job- and life-skills training center where ex-criminals learn how to live and work in Times Square's new corporate milieu. And, of course, I huddled, freezing, in the middle of Times Square on December 31, 1997.

December 31, 1997

In the eight years that I lived in New York City, I met only a handful of people who would say that they had ever been to Times Square on New Year's Eve, to watch in person as the globally telecast Ball drops to

signal the turn of a new year. By some fluke, before I moved to New York I had managed to ring in all of my New Years without ever seeing Dick Clark or even a television replay of the famous event. So I had almost no idea what to expect when I walked down Broadway into Times Square that night in 1997. I had tried to make it to Times Square on a trip to New York the previous year, but I fell so ill on that visit that I spent the evening mostly unconscious in a friend's apartment in Brooklyn, barely aware of the muffled thudding sounds of the distant fireworks. I felt that I had to be there this year.

On my initial pass through the area in the middle of the afternoon, I immediately sensed that I was entering a version of Times Square that was very different from the one I had begun to get to know in the preceding months residing in the city. The sidewalks, normally crowded, seemed almost empty, yet also charged with an unpredictable whooshing gravity. I felt yanked down Broadway into Times Square, whirled alongside knots of tourists toting coolers and beach chairs. (They came prepared.) The NYPD had already put up blue wooden barricades in the gutters, blocking off the street from the sidewalk, and I could see stacks of more barricades, unassembled, ready for use later in the evening. There was almost no car traffic. The air was gray and very cold.

I moved south on Broadway, into the open, irregular rectangle of Times Square itself. There, I saw even more groups of people I took to be tourists: standing in bunches, looking up at the buildings and the neon supersigns, talking to each other very loudly. Nobody seemed to mention the bitter cold, or even to feel particularly uncomfortable—many of the beefier groups of young men wore only sweatshirts and baseball caps. For my part, I felt the cold acutely, even through the wool army-surplus coat I had bought at a yard sale one summer in Los Angeles (an excellent time and place for bargains on winter wear). The groups of families and young men and women set up camp on the sidewalks, snapped photos, and called out to each other, watched over by a surprisingly large number of uniformed NYPD officers. Many of the businesses in Times Square, including all the movie theaters, were already closed, but the ones that were open seemed to be doing a brisk trade. The fast-food restaurants were packed, and the street vendors were out in full force, selling not only their usual wares—counterfeit designer sunglasses and watches—but also party hats, horns, and "glasses" made out of twisted white plastic that spelled out "1998" across the wearer's face. I heard a few horns tooting nearby. The Square had become visibly fuller in the few minutes I had been standing there, but despite the

growing crowd, the area still felt almost deserted. At the same time, I could feel an undercurrent of pressure, movement, and anticipation.

I walked down the sidewalk through the middle of Times Square and turned right, onto Forty-second Street. The entire block was eerily empty, with almost no pedestrians and only a single police car parked in the middle of the street at mid-block. Having spent so much time in the previous few months walking up and down this same block, watching the street scene, taking pictures, and making notes, it seemed outright bizarre to me that Forty-second Street could be so open and quiet in the middle of the afternoon. Turning back up into Times Square, I passed several news crews busily scurrying around, setting up their positions, and interviewing passersby. Far above me, atop the tower at One Times Square, silhouetted against the dim sun, I could see the famous flagpole with the Ball installed at its tip, still unlit, and the sign spelling out "1998" at its base. I had attended a press conference two days earlier, where I got the chance to see the Ball up close. It was at least six feet in diameter and very impressive, all chrome and strobe lights—it looked like a rhinestone-encrusted VW. From where I stood now, though, hundreds of feet away, the Ball looked like a tiny sparkling marble. I could blot it from view with my outstretched thumb.

I noticed that other things around the Square seemed different than normal as well. Food vendors were stocking their carts with case after case of bottled water and drinks to sell later. A few of the newsstands bore small signs advertising hot rolls and coffee. New vinyl banners hung from the streetlights, announcing "Times Square 2000." And the construction crew working on the new tower on Broadway between Forty-second and Forty-third Street had hung a hand-painted sign from the girders: "Happy New Year."

When I returned a few hours later, around 5:30 P.M., dressed in all the warm clothes I owned and stocked with whatever "research supplies" I guessed I might need that night (notebook, pens, camera, film, tape recorder, cassettes, sandwiches), I found the sidewalks absolutely packed, the barriers already crowded with people who had staked out their places. Night had fallen, and the sky was as dark as it ever gets in Times Square—a kind of deep, distant blue, held far away by the dome of light blazing out from the gigantic signs. It was even colder out than it had been earlier in the afternoon, and the chilly winds made the temperature feel well below freezing. I chose to stand at the corner of Forty-fifth Street and Seventh Avenue, close enough to watch the Ball drop and far enough back to have a good view of the crowd (the area

at the base of One Times Square was already completely jammed with people). The spot I chose was also strategically near the entrance to a fast-food restaurant, just in case I had to duck inside to get something to eat or just to warm up.

Automobile traffic was thinning, and groups of people strutted down the asphalt between the few cars and taxis. I heard conversations in many different languages in the growing throng, as well as seemingly random bursts of yelling and cheering from the group packed in at the base of One Times Square—it took me a good while to realize that they were cheering for the television cameras that periodically turned in their direction. Searchlights waved high over our heads, and the supersigns seemed even brighter than usual, enhanced by the absolutely clear and freezing air and also by the brilliant white lights posted around the camera platforms atop the armed forces recruiting post in the middle of the Square. The steam from the big cups on the signs advertising Cup o' Noodles and Chock Full o' Nuts Coffee poured out unusually thick and white, glowing in the reflected light of the TV platforms as the chilly breeze whipped it away.

At about six P.M., the Ball, the 1998 sign, and the screen below them on One Times Square lit up and went through their paces. The lights on the Ball strobed, the numbers lit up one by one and in unison, and the screen flashed a multicolor countdown ("10! 9! 8!"). The crowd cheered for each test. For the rest of the night, up until the last few minutes before midnight, the lights on the Ball blinked on and off in a pattern that made it look as though the Ball were rotating atop its pole. At this point, there was still enough room on the sidewalk for people to walk freely, and, while most stayed in their places, a few paced up and down, including a disheveled street preacher. I was pleasantly surprised to see that he carried, along with a boombox proclaiming a prerecorded message of salvation, a sign that read "The End Is Nigh." Following him came a salesman hawking fluorescent bracelets and more plastic horns, who chanted, over and over, "Lights an' horns! Lights an' horns!" The streets in the Square had been closed to traffic, and people were starting to duck under the barricades and stand out in the middle of Broadway. We could still hear those apparently random surges of cheering from the crowd at the base of the Square; it still wasn't clear who was yelling, or why, and everyone around me would perk up and look around to try and find the source of the sound.

The police now began to put up their blue wooden barriers. They swiftly partitioned the Square, setting up irregular pens in which spec-

tators were to stand, leaving a narrow lane on the sidewalk for pedestrians and forming broad, open aisles in the street for official vehicles to move through the crowd. People began to jockey around these new structures, ducking under and climbing over them, shoving them aside to move from place to place. One police officer approached me on the sidewalk where I stood. He asked, "Are you standing there to view?" When I said that I was, he told me to move into one of the pens.

I ducked under the barricade and found a place to stand near my original spot—still strategically near the restaurant, just in case. As soon as we were hemmed in by the barricades, I noticed people frantically bargaining with the police, asking to be let through the barriers to buy something to eat or drink, or so that they could cross to the other side of Times Square to make it to a play. The police near me demanded to see their theater tickets before they let them through. One man near me saw this and started jovially waving a dollar bill over his head, yelling, "Here's my ticket!" Still, we quickly saw that we were more or less stuck where we stood for the rest of the evening. Standing in the middle of the street, away from the buildings, I could feel the cold much more sharply, despite the crowd filling in around me. One large, older man at my side began jogging and dancing in place to stay warm; I heard him scatting "In the Mood" under his breath, over and over. A horn salesman prowled along the edge of the barricade among the police, who seemed to ignore him as he urged us, "C'mon, you gotta make some noise, it's New Year's—they're gonna chase me outta here!" Then he ducked away. Many of those around me stood drinking out of wineskins or cans or bottles of beer. One higher-ranking NYPD officer, who was angrily directing the other police to keep the sidewalk clear of loiterers, snatched a beer can out of a spectator's hand and threw it into the street; this was the only time I saw anyone confiscate anything from the crowd all night.

And then . . . we waited, the hours before midnight suddenly stretching out before us. It was so cold. The families around me bundled into each other for warmth, making encouraging remarks like, "This is a once in a lifetime event!" I found that I could track the evening's progress by the tenor of the remarks made by one couple standing just to my right: from "This is great, it's like Mardi Gras!," to, after a few hours had passed, "If we can just make it until ten o'clock, we'll be fine," and finally, much later, "I swear to god, honey, let's just make it through this and we'll never have to come back again." Time seemed to slow down as the minutes crawled and the temperature dropped. Occasionally,

an especially chilly wind would sweep through the Square. When this happened, everyone would hunch down and in on themselves, like the bent-legged dogs I'd seen taking their winter walks earlier in the day. By this time, my hands were truly numb with cold. This made it impossible for me to write notes or take photos; I kept my hands jammed in my pockets and chatted about nothing with the people near me. We kept this up for a few hours, until about 9:30 P.M. or so, when all our chatter was used up. Then I just shuffled and walked in place, stepping on my own toes to keep some feeling in them as we all waited blankly for the time to pass.

All we could really do was watch the signs. I could see the screen on the British Airways sign behind One Times Square showing ads for the Gap that featured musicians like Aerosmith and LL Cool J, along with occasional promotional spots for Times Square itself, announcing "The Ball!" and "This Is Where It Really Happens!" The screen at the top of One Times Square displayed similar messages, including "Times Square: Have a Ball!" and "Times Square: Feel the Heat!" (This was accompanied by an image of flickering flames, which seemed both ludicrous and, somehow, comforting.) The NBC television screen hanging halfway down the tower had long since stopped showing the closed-caption news programs that we had so enjoyed, switching instead to an endless, horrible loop of advertisements for NBC programs. We all complained to one another about the ads and voiced our wish that they would turn back to the news.

We also tried to keep ourselves occupied by cheering. For example, we would cheer whenever some dignitary or other would buzz past riding a golf cart through one of the open lanes nearby, or when the red-uniformed sanitation workers from the Times Square Business Improvement District walked past in formation, rolling their trash cans on wheeled carts. Two women off to my left joked about spotting celebrities in the crowd; they would yell "It's Ginger Spice!" whenever the crowd began cheering for anyone at all. But the excitement was most intense, and the cold most forgotten, when the television cameras would sweep over our sector of the crowd, bathing us in clear white light and throwing images of people nearby up onto the screen atop One Times Square. One man who stood some distance off to my right in the crowd kept ripping his shirt off, yelling and jumping up and down as he tried to attract the cameras his way. Others waved handmade signs over their heads. At about 8 P.M., we heard the crowd down at the base of Times Square chanting an old beer commercial slogan: "Less filling! Tastes

great!" We got especially excited whenever we saw the fast-food restaurant's sign on the big screen; it was a signal that the camera was focused near us, and might come closer.

More and more people began to push their way into our holding pen. I had no idea where they were coming from, or how many more could be crammed in. The police were getting much stricter about letting anyone out from under the barricades to escape temporarily into the restaurant. We had already heard a rumor that they were asking for receipts at the bathroom door inside, to keep out anyone who wasn't a paying customer. Now, the police were guarding the door, strictly enforcing the legal occupancy limit of 150. It wasn't just the police who were getting stricter, though; whenever someone would try to make their way through our crowded pen, saying they were looking for their friends or family, we would push back, surly, defensive, not wanting to let them through. I suppose we felt that we had already suffered to stake out our tiny, freezing corner of this pen in the middle of Times Square—now they would have to suffer, too. We did make one exception, though, edging aside for a young man, obviously drunk, who moved through the crowd in a serene, boneless lope. Once he reached the blue barricade, he leaned far out into the street, bent double, and puked copiously. We tried to call the police over to help him out—mostly to get him away from us, I think—but there was no response. Eventually, he straightened up, apologized in a quiet mumble, and shove-shuffled his way back into the depths of the crowd.

The emotional pitch of the crowd seemed to shift once we reached ten P.M. Somehow, it felt as though we had turned a corner, and were now heading into a sort of tedious home stretch. Perhaps the people I had overheard earlier encouraging each other to make it to this point had been right; I, for one, suddenly felt that I could stand there, waiting, forever. (Later, I wondered if this was a product of a life of watching lousy movies or television programs—we all knew that we could make it through two hours of *anything*.) And there was a new buzz of activity around us, as well. We could see a party come to life behind the windows of the studios of MTV. The people waved down at us as they danced; we looked back hungrily.

It was also at this point that the police and the sanitation workers began to hand out the pom-poms, tinsel leis, and long, brightly colored balloons that the Business Improvement District had created to turn the packed Times Square into a more telegenic spectacle. Finally, after the hours of freezing boredom, here was something to do! The ever-

growing crowd surged forward, everyone pushing each other out of the way to reach for the trinkets. Many in the crowd began to weave the balloons into multicolored hoops and bouquets As soon as the police had moved on, a group of young men shoved their way through the crowd, snatching the balloons out of their owners' hands, whapping people over the head with them, or teasingly stroking them from behind against the ears of people who stood stock-still, mortified but unmoving. Right beside me, one man lunged forward and clonked a young woman in the head with a short flashlight, yelling, "Gimme that balloon, bitch!" She let go of the balloon, stunned, and he and his friends moved away. I just stood there, feeling paralyzed, glad they were leaving.

All of Times Square seemed to be turning ugly, and desperate. Now we were less than one hour away from midnight! All night, I had kept myself from looking at my watch or craning my head around too often to check the time on the big clock overhead. Now, I couldn't help it. It was around this time that I heard the man beside me promise someone that they would never come back to Times Square again. When I heard this, it suddenly occurred to me that, as uncomfortable as I was, I had an advantage over my fellow revelers. There was no question in my mind that I had to stay where I was until the bitter end. How could I call myself an anthropologist if I couldn't last through this singular event? In other words, at least I knew I *had* to be there; everyone else had to keep pretending that they *wanted* to be there. I looked up at the screen on One Times Square. The television showed a sea of waving tinsel and balloons, cheering faces framed by the swirl of light from the signs above. It looked like fun, and I glanced around, trying to spot the area of the Square where people were actually enjoying themselves, until I remembered that I was already there, right in the middle of it. I also began to plan my exit, remembering a remark from an officer that I had overheard earlier, that by 12:15 A.M. Times Square would be empty.

The clocks read 11:50. Spotlights waved over our heads as we entered the final ten minutes, and green laser beams shot out from the top of One Times Square. All of Times Square cheered as one when the screen at the top of the tower stopped showing ridiculous ads and started counting down the remaining time until midnight. I felt strangely distant from the whole thing, too cold and uncomfortable to get very excited. I found myself feeling distracted, peering around aimlessly, losing track of the time and why I was even there in the first place. The countdown read 11:59. On the screen, it looked liked Mayor Rudolph Giuliani was doing something. I looked around for the laser I

had read about that was supposed to strike the Ball and set it in motion, but I couldn't see anything. The Ball began to descend. I watched it, or tried to, but what was there to look at? From this distance, it was nearly impossible to focus on the tiny disk of light as it crawled down the pole. The crowd roared, waving their balloons at the cameras, and the enormous numbers on the digitized screen blurred past in a buzz of tenths-of-a-second. Only in the last few seconds did I actually look straight up at the Ball. I watched as it slowly dropped down behind the sign reading "1998," which lit up and burst with pink flares. That seemed to be the end of it. There may have been fireworks overhead, but it was impossible to hear above the noise from the crowd. I didn't even notice that they had launched the confetti until it started to trickle down around me like snow a minute or two later. We all cheered briefly. Then, with everyone around me, I ducked under the barrier to my left and let myself be carried by the surge of people up to Forty-fifth Street and east away from Times Square. I looked back to watch the confetti drifting through the bright night sky, and saw enormous balloons slowly tumbling from the roof above MTV down into the street. Someone beside me complained that she'd forgotten to watch the Ball.

I quickly walked east to Grand Central Station. I was struck by the sense of freedom, of being liberated from the event now that it was over. I was able to stretch and walk and swing my arms for the first time in hours. My body felt as though it were coming back to life, muscles working, my skin warming. Descending into the subway station, I immediately stepped onto a southbound train that rolled up like magic. I rode away, to connect with the train that would take me to my friends in Brooklyn. What I felt in that subway car—the feeling of freedom, warmth, comfort, and command upon leaving Times Square a few minutes into the New Year—was more than I could capture in words, then or now.

I didn't realize it at the time, but in hindsight, my New Year's Eve in Times Square seemed to be a fractal image—a crystallization in miniature—of my entire experience as an ethnographer of the redevelopment project. Months later, I saw an aerial photograph of a crowded Times Square on New Year's Eve reproduced on the cover of a magazine published by the NYPD. This was a vision of Times Square as an archetype of safely controlled urban craziness—a picture of hundreds of thousands of people filling the nighttime Square, yet hemmed in, carved up into solid wedges of humanity, geometric shapes with clear aisles for police, ambulances, and dignitaries to move among them.

This was a beautiful and compelling image: individuals transformed into a unified, organized mass, gathered together in celebration and safely organized by a controlling authority. Yet this image was so radically different from my experience. One could only represent the New Year's Eve celebration in this way through such a photograph: a split second of time, captured from high above; instead of hours spent at ground level within the barricades.

The New Year's celebration represented one of the ways in which the redevelopment of Times Square transcended abstract ideology or policy changes to become a material, visceral experience. Everyone in the celebration was recruited as part of a grand televised spectacle advertising the brand-image and the real estate of Times Square itself. We in the assembled mass were cloistered there as part of the production of a symbol, a brand: the nationally and globally circulating mass-cultural spectacle of "Times Square" itself. Getting caught up in this spectacle, we were deeply invested in playing our part, in cheering and waving and freaking out when the cameras swept over us. At the same time, we were deeply alienated from the image of Times Square that we were helping to make, and we lived this out on the most visceral level: frozen, claustrophobic, immobile, bored beyond tedium. We loved being "Where It Really Happens," though we were only too painfully aware that, in many ways, absolutely nothing was happening in Times Square, and that we were there to help make something else happen, on television screens at parties far away.[4]

The Infinite Game of Urban Life

The focus of my research was on what the redevelopment meant, at the level of everyday life and experience, to the different people and organizations involved with it. In particular, I wanted to understand the ideas and practices of those responsible for creating the changes in Times Square. I carried out my research in the places where people *feel* these changes on a visceral level—where the redevelopment becomes real, both to those who make it and to those who pass through it.

New York City, like all cities, is saturated with human intention. The city is drenched with the will to advertise and the imagination of profit. Every space, every surface, is a potential venue for commercial announcement. Every thoroughfare, every gap, is measured for flow and efficiency and potential for use.[5] Every building, every structure,

even those not yet built, heralds its own potential transformation or destruction. Picture the spaces and places of the city the way planners and developers do, as a multitude of units of potential energy—unfathomable amounts of money waiting to be made. Picture the city the way they see it: not just as somewhere you live or work or pass through, not simply as your world or your context, but also as a game board, where, even if you don't know it, you are one of the players. Picture the corps of people who are consciously playing that game, strategizing how best to maneuver and expand their holdings and reap their dreams of windfall. No single overlord or authority wholly determines the shape of the city. Instead, dozens of city and state authorities, hundreds of real estate developers, thousands of property owners, and millions of city dwellers all work in their various ways, consciously or unconsciously, both to play the game and also to shape its rules.[6]

This is a complicated game. Like all speculation, it is played by partial knowledge, prognostication, and guesswork—"omens and prophecy."[7] Times Square was first created at the turn of the twentieth century as a gamble by real estate speculators—an attempt to make a highly profitable theater district out of a neighborhood of saloons and brothels. The current, ongoing redevelopment of Times Square can be seen as a similar speculative leap—an attempt to turn a heterogeneous district of entertainment and vice establishments into a part of the city's corporate business core; to appropriate the area as a space for elite work and mainstream tourist consumption.

The game of the city shapes human life within it, but this game is not played to human scale.[8] Places and spaces appear and disappear almost without warning; structures tower overhead or move underground according to plans and rules that the sidewalker never hears about and perhaps cannot fathom. It matters not at all that you have grown accustomed to the store on the corner, that you have come to feel at home in the neighborhood around your office, that you are fond of the basically drab view from your window, that you feel that you depend on the businesses along your block. In the city, everything is always-already on sale: "Everything Must Go."[9] Tomorrow, blue construction facades will go up, the sounds of demolition and rebuilding will be heard, and two months from now everything will be different again, at least if you live or work somewhere that developers or city authorities care enough about to transform. In the modern urban world, people live their lives and work to find a sense of meaning and agency in the spaces opened up in someone else's economic game.

The Cultural Logic of Neoliberalism

In some ways, the redevelopment of Times Square was only a recent, highly visible example of people trying to "solve" some of these problems of the modern city—problems that are intrinsic to its nature.[10] The city collects and crams together people who are very different from one another; not in spite of their being different but, rather, because they are different, and thus useful to one another.[11] To some, this is not a problem at all. They see the density, heterogeneity, and anonymity of urban life as embodying the highest ideals of market-based democratic society.[12] In this view, dense and crowded modern urban centers, with all their spectacular advertisements and grand department stores, are, literally, monuments to democracy. They therefore feel that these spaces must be kept free and open to all, as symbols and guarantors of democratic ideals. Others, however, see city spaces as "criminogenic," fomenting crime, fear, and uncertainty.[13] From this perspective, crowded streets, subways, and apartment buildings look and feel unnatural and oppressive, designed to bring out the worst in humanity.

The people involved with the redevelopment of Times Square and Forty-second Street confronted these age-old quandaries of urban space and social life in an era of urban economic crisis and uncertainty, brought on in part by economic globalization and the decline of U.S. urban industrial economies. Their response was to transform both the spaces of the city and what it meant to inhabit those spaces. They redefined the zoning codes and physical spaces of the city—the built environment and the rules by which new spaces are made. In this way, the Times Square redevelopment represented a new way of making urban spaces. But, beyond this, the redevelopers also worked to reshape what it means to have "the right to the city"—the ability to inhabit, and participate in, the urban social world.[14] The redevelopers transformed urban life, or at least this one section of it, into a commodified spectacle—a brand-image—and citizenship into playing one's part in that image. The ultimate commodity in this spectacle was, of course, the real estate of Times Square itself. The redevelopers successfully defined Times Square as a marketable brand name in New York City's version of what geographer Mike Davis calls the "infinite game" of real estate development.[15] In doing so, they gave the right to inhabit this place only to those who fit the brand image they hoped to cultivate. Everyone was invited, but only as long as they helped to sell the space of the city around them. In order to control the brand image of Times

Square, the redevelopers had to *reframe* this complicated space and the ways in which people were used to using it. They defined the professions and leisure activities, even the very physical presence, of many denizens of the area as impersonal, pernicious "blight."

The transformations in and around Times Square took place on both a local and a global stage. Every aspect of the redevelopment called attention to itself as a product tailored to Times Square and New York City, but also packaged for global consumption. The many different organizations involved in the redevelopment presented their work as examples of a new paradigm in shaping the socioeconomic life of the city, a paradigm for creating fun, profitable, historically "authentic" and "genuine" urban centers that could supposedly be applied to cities across the globe.

New York City has always been a place where the simultaneously creative and destructive powers of capitalism are highly visible.[16] Nineteenth-century writers marveled at the willful demolition of stores, houses, and entire neighborhoods to make way for something new seemingly just because they had been standing for a few years.[17] More recently, since the 1960s city communities have been forced to deal with the fallout of two linked phenomena: the decline of the city's industrial base and the city's shift to developing a postindustrial "finance, insurance, and real estate" (FIRE) economy. The city's name for this new development policy was "planned shrinkage." According to the policy of planned shrinkage, the city focused its efforts on developing its Manhattan-centered information economy, while writing off the industrial sections of the other boroughs, and the working-class neighborhoods around them, as relics of a past era. City budgets during New York's fiscal crisis in the 1970s began to withdraw basic services, including police, fire, health, sanitation, and transportation, from poor neighborhoods, rendering them unlivable.[18] Planned shrinkage was meant to restructure the city not just economically but, in a much larger sense, socially—to redefine New York as first and foremost a center for information and service industries rather than for manufacturing; for upper-middle-class, white-collar workers rather than for the blue-collar working class. This was only the latest moment in New York City's long history of elitist planning, in which economic interests, social prejudices, and aesthetic tastes of the wealthy and powerful have been written into city law and development strategies, and thus have become inscribed in the built environment and social life of the city as a whole.

Anthropologists working in New York have documented the ways in which the marginal communities of the city have struggled to deal with

planned shrinkage and with the city's larger legacy of elitist and exploitative planning and development. From the economic collapse of the Brooklyn industrial neighborhood of Greenpoint-Williamsburg in the 1970s and early 1980s, to the long history of political activism in the African American community of Corona–East Elmhurst in the borough of Queens, they portray the vicious competition that arises between marginalized racial and ethnic groups when pitted against each other for shrinking public resources, exacerbated by the city's overall focus on developing Manhattan's corporate core and luxury enclaves.[19]

Planned shrinkage and its socioeconomic effects were not unique to New York City, though they were extremely visible there. Instead, they were part of a larger social shift. The spaces of the city where residents live and work have always been defined by the money and status games of an interconnected network of city officials, powerful developers, and landowners, but their work in places like the redeveloped Times Square took a new form, in accordance with a new social and economic ideology. This was the ideology of neoliberalism, which is characterized by governmental handover of the public realm to private capital and the application of the model of markets and competition to all aspects of social life. Since the 1970s, neoliberalism has created a climate of intense, zero-sum competition among cities over scarce economic and political resources. This competition takes the form of a desperate "urban entrepreneurialism," in which city governments must increasingly rely on "elite partnerships, mega-events, and corporate seduction" to survive.[20]

While neoliberalism as an ideology and an economic model has restructured urban economic relationships in the United States and elsewhere, it has also fundamentally transformed our definitions of citizenship and personhood. Neoliberalism is not just a model for economists, developers, and politicians. It is also something much larger and more general: a moral framework for understanding our own actions and those of others in the world around us. In short, neoliberalism is a structure of feeling.[21] This new structure of feeling carries with it its own logical paths of action and moral imperatives—its own cultural logic. The cultural logic of neoliberalism is breaking down traditional barriers between public and private economics and cultural spheres. In their place, it brings "the resurgence of the private"—"public-private partnership," free markets, competition, and advertising merging with the public sector. In new kinds of public/private spaces, such as gated communities, barricaded streets, and privatized parks and beaches,

"the private realm is not so much pushing back the public as overlaying it," creating a "vast new territory . . . where fragments of the private mix with shards of the public in novel configurations."[22]

During my background research for this project, I became fascinated with the history of modern urban planning. I was especially intrigued by the genre of high-modernist "master plans," the Cities of Tomorrow, the Garden Cities, the Radiant Cities, with their austere towers, broad plazas, wide swaths of empty lawns, looping superhighways, and the total lack of any social improvisation, clutter, or grime—in some ways, the lack of anything really human at all. This was the planning ideology that informed U.S. government–sponsored urban renewal programs from the 1940s through the 1970s; programs that demolished city centers and carved freeways through poorer residential neighborhoods, as New York City's own master planner Robert Moses put it, "with a meat ax."[23] These plans seemed to me so grandiose, so simultaneously wonderful and horrible. They were such blatant expressions of the utopian dreams and raw biases of their makers—their dream of escape from the city's history into a new world, cleansed of conflict.[24] For urban renewal planners in the post–World War II era, "There was no reason to conform to the urban context. That context was the very thing they were trying to destroy."[25]

As I studied the history of modern urban planning and urban renewal before I came to New York City, I imagined that the people involved with the redevelopment project would have similarly grand and pure visions of Times Square. I assumed that my fieldwork in Times Square would be a process of recording similarly all-encompassing and crystalline cultural constructions. But things didn't turn out this way. As soon as I began my fieldwork, I discovered firsthand just how differently architecture and urban planning work in this era of frenetic competition for scarce resources than they did in the era of government-sponsored modern master plans. The people I met did not speak in the voice of the Master Planner. The planners and architects with whom I spoke did not seem to understand or care about my questions regarding their "vision for Times Square." In my fieldnotes from this period, in October 1997, I wrote: "I see that I keep asking people in [these] interviews about their vision for the area or for the city, and nobody is really responding. . . . I reflect that maybe I'm waiting to hear about a 'floating city in the sky.'" Instead, they were eager to mock the very idea of a single, comprehensive plan that could govern any part of New York City.

Indeed, I came to see that, for some people, the history of the Times Square redevelopment project itself signaled the end of modern urban planning and the start of something new, with a whole new economic and aesthetic outlook. As *New York Times* reporter Thomas Lueck explained to me, "The [original] plan for . . . Times Square was the last great attempt to do [modern urban renewal], because it involved all the elements: that the government buy the land for the developers; they move in the bulldozers; they clear it; you build anew at a very prominent intersection of the city. And just the whole character of the Square, this was all intended back then . . . to become something totally different. . . . Lo and behold, [Times Square] becomes even more garish in some respects than it ever was." In other words, over the course of the years since the redevelopment's inception in the 1970s, the project came to exemplify, even epitomize, a way of attempting to plan and design urban space and social life that was, at least on the surface, quite different than the modern era of government-sponsored clearance and rebuilding.

In this new approach, planners and developers emphasize what Lueck called the local "character" of a place. They see the "garish" commercial hubbub of places like Times Square not as a problem, but as a positive value, something to intensify, clarify, and market. In this way, the Times Square redevelopment is part of a much larger trend in the United States and elsewhere; a trend in creating "cultural spectacles, enterprise zones [and] waterfront developments" as the heart of urban socioeconomic revitalization strategies.[26] Geographers have called this new style of development "postmodern urbanism"; architects call it "New Urbanism."[27]

Where modernist planners sought to impose an artificial, but hopefully ultimately liberating, framework of order and control on developing industrial-age urban landscapes, neoliberalism's New Urbanists see themselves as celebrating "natural" urban socioeconomic mixture and competition. However, these seemingly open and diverse spaces are, at the same time, highly controlled. New Urbanist planners and architects work to suffuse their new built spaces with the principles of "defensible space" and "crime prevention through environmental design," in which the very layout of the built environment is designed to exclude people or activities the designers define as "undesirable."[28]

Just as the physical spaces of the city are reshaped by the cultural logic of neoliberalism, so, too, are policing, city services, and the laws governing public social space. These urban redevelopment projects go

hand-in-hand with the rise of "privatized forms of local governance."[29] The "deregulation" rhetoric of neoliberalism is paired with massive re-regulation, as local property owners exert new forms of control over city spaces by forming public-private hybrid governmental associations to better control their local area. The Times Square redevelopment is full of such groups: the Times Square Business Improvement District, the Friends of Bryant Park, the Forty-second Street Development Corporation, and the Midtown Community Court, to mention just a few that figure prominently in this book.

The redevelopment of Times Square and Forty-second Street is unfolding at the same time as numerous other development projects around New York City, including the creation of the pseudo-historical Battery Park City neighborhood and the South Street Seaport waterfront mall in lower Manhattan,[30] the transformation of Grand Central Station and Union Square into upscale shopping districts,[31] and the redevelopment of 125th Street in Harlem.[32] These projects all share many similar features: the creation of public-private hybrid governmental organizations and the use of public art and nostalgic historical references as a real estate mechanism to open up "underdeveloped" space for more profitable or respectable tenants.[33]

This trend is not restricted to New York City, of course. Since the mid-1970s, city governments around the United States have teamed with real estate developers to create "festival marketplaces" and have redeveloped upscale shopping districts in old ports, disused industrial areas, or city centers abandoned by white flight to the suburbs.[34] Smaller towns are also following this trend, "revitalizing" their downtown areas with nostalgic facades and prefab "loft-style" housing.[35] The most extreme example of this may be the town of Celebration in Florida, wholly owned and carefully designed by the Walt Disney Company.[36] In all of these cases, critics worry that local communities and historical legacies are being plowed under to make way for "the nonplace urban realm"—a new, corporate-friendly, generic urban landscape.[37]

Governments and developers outside the United States are picking up on this new style of transforming urban spaces as well. Emanuela Guano's study of Argentina shows how, in the face of growing economic polarization, the elite of Buenos Aires are transforming that city into a stratified and exclusionary network of shopping malls, gentrified waterfront arcades, and tourist historical-based spectacles.[38] Similarly, as shown in Teresa Caldeira's study of São Paulo, Brazil, members of the upper economic strata retreat in the face of the growing democrati-

zation of Brazilian society into ultra-secured private apartment towers and gated communities far from São Paulo's diverse city center.[39] Both of these examples from outside the United States highlight the powerfully antidemocratic and exclusionary aspects of neoliberal urban redevelopment. Urban density and heterogeneity, the experience of mingling closely with people unlike oneself, become theme-park experiences, something to indulge in only on special occasions, and only in safe, controlled spaces designed to present the city as a fun, historically rich, visually dazzling spectacle.

Imagination, Ethics, Creativity, and Power

The way we imagine the world to be affects how we act toward others, and toward ourselves. Imagination is not an abstract, private mental phenomenon. Imaginations exist in history. They have their own genealogy. Imaginations also have a physical dimension, to the extent that they inform conscious and unconscious behavior and to the extent that people have the power to turn them into reality. This is why there is a politics of the imagination. Powerful people, rather than wielding power only in concrete, direct ways, are also always engaged in theorizing their power and how to use it according to complex, culturally specific frameworks. It is through such imaginative structures of creativity that ideologies have material effects and become taken-for-granted, not in some abstract way, but as they are literally inscribed into the physical, legal, and social structures of everyday life.[40]

For this reason, *Money Jungle* focuses on the active, creative minds of the people involved with implementing the redevelopment of Times Square and Forty-second Street, and the practices by which they enframed and reshaped this complicated place.[41] I am interested in the ways in which people involved with the redevelopment imagined and constructed new forms of urban social and economic relationships. What were the imaginative practices by which people constructed images of city life? What were the genealogies of the images they created? What were the processes by which they worked to make those images real?

It can be tempting for anthropologists and others to view "the powerful" as a homogeneous block, driven by shared, rational economic interests to deform the lives of those we study, and with whom we sympathize. And there are good reasons for this. Cultural anthropology

has a proud legacy of speaking about and for those on the margins of political power. We tend to study those deemed "unimportant"; people who are subjected to the intentions and stereotypes of others very far away. However, this should not lead us to cast the cultural complexity and value of those we study against a blank backdrop of "the powerful." This simply reverses the distortion we wish to address. We risk putting ourselves in the position of advocating on behalf of those we traditionally study, the excluded, without fully understanding how those who do the work of excluding understand themselves.

What is potentially worse, especially for anthropologists, is that this lack of focus on the culture of power can fail to see how our own perspectives on social justice, difference, or liberation may be entangled with the work of those we think we oppose. Instead, we need to consider the cultural imagination of the powerful—to study them as members of a diverse group of creative people working with specific tools and assumptions to engage with the world as they see it; in other words, to look at their culture. When we attempt to "study up," we must do so with as much attention to nuance, complexity, texture, and experience as when we study the lives and works of those on the margins of power.

This is why this book focuses on the *ethical imagination of the powerful*— the ways in which people directly involved in the redevelopment understood the nature of Times Square in particular, urban space in general, and their role in transforming these. By "ethical imagination," I mean the ways in which powerful people and institutions in the Times Square redevelopment created a sense of themselves as ethical subjects, engaged with what they defined as particular social problems.[42]

The redevelopment of Times Square shows how power can be repressive, political, productive, and creative, all at once. The redevelopment project tells a story about control, prejudice, and profit at the same time that it tells a story about freedom, openness, and art. It shows how all these aspects of power, destruction and creation, discipline and play, articulate together; a web of power and significance that entangles everyone, at all levels of the infinite game of urban life.

Magnificent Spectacle
Real Estate, Theater, Advertising, and the History of Times Square

"No city ever got built on faith, hope, and charity."

—Ada Louise Huxtable

"A Testing Ground of Limits"

Times Square is a peculiar place, and has been for more than a hundred years: a troubling and exciting symbol of the ambiguities and apparent paradoxes of modern urban life; a monument to the possibilities and contradictions of consumer society and of modernity itself. This place is both a symbol and a product of the power of the speculative market in real estate that created New York City. It has always been a monument to inauthenticity, to commercialism, to the power of symbols over substance—"a testing ground of limits."[1] Times Square is a testament to the radical undermining of any and all social values under

the pressure of profit; to the radical transformations and destructive creativity indigenous to the real estate economy of New York City.

Times Square has been the battlefield for a century-long struggle for dominance between three industries: real estate, the performing arts, and sex.[2] At the same time, over the course of this battle, these three seemingly opposed groups collaborated and often merged with each other. Theater owners and impresarios were often one and the same; the performing arts industry's products often drew from or blended with those of the sex industry, and vice versa; and theater owners and real estate developers were happy to lease space to sex shops and porn entrepreneurs during lean economic times. Times Square was a world in which legitimate and illegitimate businesspeople, products, and consumers worked together, but not always in harmony, to define a new, hybrid form of secular-sexual-spectacular public space.

From its settlement by whites, the island of Manhattan has been an object of, as well as a center for, commodity speculation.[3] The primary commodity for this market has always been the spaces of the island itself. In 1811, the city government of New York formed a commission to develop a plan for the island, in order to steer the growth of the city and its real estate market.[4] The commission was charged with mapping the miles of "undeveloped" hills, farms, and swamps to the north of the tiny and crowded settlement on Manhattan's southern tip. The commissioners mapped the island as a grid—a series of parallel streets and avenues bounding identical rectangular city blocks, with each block waiting to be filled in by actual construction and settlement. By breaking the city up in advance into relatively small, predetermined blocks, the grid transformed the unbuilt spaces of the city into a commodity for development and speculation. Every lot was already enframed and ready to buy, sell, or trade for other land or for anything else that could be bought, sold, or traded. The act of enframing Manhattan in the image of the grid—the notion of the island as a series of spaces for sale— effectively made that image a reality.[5]

The 1811 commissioners' map allowed—even encouraged—the subsequent century's progressive segregation of land uses and social groups in what had been a dense and mixed city. By creating a speculative real estate market and encouraging the rapid development of the island of Manhattan, the grid permitted for the eventual concentration of governmental and financial institutions on the island's southern tip, the site of the original settlement, to the exclusion of housing and manufacturing. But the grid also ensured that such segregation would be

strictly temporary. Because each individual block or sub-block lot could be bought, sold, or traded, independent of its neighbors, the grid made it impossible for anyone to permanently distance their property from people or uses they found distasteful.

In effect, the grid pitted two groups against one another in a series of contests over space in New York. On one side of the conflict were those who wished to segregate types of institutions and types of people from one another, in the name of protecting land values and/or the social order. On the other side were those who were willing to flaunt such assertions of order in the name of potentially turning a profit. Histories of this period in New York City signal the conflicts at play in the progressive filling-out of the grid. Residential estate developers strove to produce "respectable" neighborhoods. These, they claimed, were places of solid morality separated from commercial life and from industrial production. At the same time, other speculators undercut those plans to segregate kinds of buildings and kinds of people. The drive to maximize profit, to give in to unrestrained clamor for attention and audience, worked against the drive to secure social and commercial "order."

Sometimes these drives wound around each other within the same endeavor. During the nineteenth century, speculators bought up parcels of land for development farther and farther north on the island of Manhattan. Meanwhile, the theater district, called the "Rialto," made a successive series of leaps northward from lower Manhattan, along the diagonal traverse of Broadway.[6] Facing competition from residential and commercial development, theater entrepreneurs stayed in business by moving their enterprises uptown, to newer and larger buildings in areas that were less well established and less prestigious, and thus cheaper. As the owners moved their theaters northward, however, commercial interests quickly followed, eager to take advantage of areas made newly "respectable" by the Rialto's stamp of profit and tenuous legitimacy. When offices, shops, and residences opened around the theaters, land prices and taxes in the area would rise. The theaters would become less and less profitable for their owners, impelling another move. Thus, Manhattan's department stores, newspaper headquarters, and so forth moved with the theater district and, in turn, kept it moving. The Rialto jumped from intersection to intersection along Broadway, moving first from the junction of Fifth Avenue and Twenty-sixth Street to Herald Square, at Sixth Avenue and Thirty-fourth Street (named after the *New York Herald* newspaper). Finally, in 1895, the Rialto came to

Longacre Square, at the intersection of Broadway, Seventh Avenue, and Forty-second Street.

When the entrepreneur T. Henry French opened the first theater on Forty-second Street off of Longacre Square in the mid-1890s, the area was already a socially and politically suspect place; a red-light district, known for saloons and brothels, as well as the center of a street prostitution market.[7] The area's bars and prostitutes catered to the working men who lived in the rooming houses of Sixth Avenue and the cheap tenements of Hell's Kitchen, as well as to New York City's male population as a whole. For years, Longacre Square had been the site of numerous official crackdowns on prostitution and alcohol. Churches lobbied against sin, while real estate speculators tried to create an air of respectability in the area in order to set the stage for profitable developments of middle-class housing. The coming of the theater industry would lend Longacre Square a twenty- or thirty-year window of official respectability and highbrow glamour. After this, the area would become a district for illicit entertainment once more.

French's American Theater was rapidly followed by others, including Oscar Hammerstein's theaters on Forty-second and Forty-third Streets, as well as other entrepreneurs opening theaters, restaurants, and bars. These coexisted fairly harmoniously with Longacre Square's sexual commerce. Theaters at that time depended for profit on after-hours cabarets, with their liquor sales and racy shows. The area's burgeoning reputation as a hyped-up consumer center and entertainment district also made it a center for mass public displays, such as electric billboards, which were then coming into prominence in urban centers around the world.[8] Adolph S. Ochs, who had just purchased the foundering *New York Times* newspaper, saw Longacre Square as a chance to improve the value of his holdings. He opened a glamorous new office tower headquarters in the center of the Square in 1904. Ochs convinced the city administration to steer the subway lines, then under construction, through the basement of the Times building in order to subsidize his distribution costs. The city went so far as to rename the area after Ochs's newspaper, and the publisher held a public New Year's Eve celebration to commemorate the renaming of Longacre Square as "Times Square."[9]

But the story of the Rialto and the renaming of Longacre Square is only part of the story of Times Square. The turn of the twentieth century saw an often violent jockeying for position within Manhattan's rapidly developing urban spaces between a number of groups, including

Manhattan's governmental and financial market district; the developers of housing for the wealthy; the shops catering to those wealthy residents; and the light manufacturing industries—especially the garment industry—that supplied those shops.[10] The well-to-do moved into residential districts farther and farther up the East Side of Manhattan, pushed northward up the quickly changing island by their desire to segregate themselves from their workplaces around Wall Street. They were closely followed by the dry goods emporia that sought their patronage. However, these same commercial interests, in turn, were pursued northward by their suppliers, the garment industries. Squeezed out of lower Manhattan by the higher rents of the burgeoning governmental and financial market district, garment manufacturers followed the wealthy and their shops northward. They did this for two reasons: first, for need of space to expand their operations, and second, in order to remain closer to the fashionable population to whose whims they sought to cater. These sweatshops brought with them not only the environmental effects of the garment industry (noise, pollution, etc.), but also, and more importantly, they brought crowds of ethnically diverse workers, and they in turn attracted a multitude of cheaper stores and eating establishments that opened to serve those workers. Wealthy store-owners saw the garment district strictly as a liability—a threat to the value of their commercial property. Would the wealthy of the city and the world come to shop on streets crowded with factories, industrial workers, and lowbrow establishments? After decades of legal battles, the owners of commercial property along Fifth and Madison Avenues and the proprietors of the loft factories of the garment district came to an informal agreement to concentrate the garment district in the loft buildings to the west of the upscale shopping strips. The new, official garment district would intrude no further eastward than Fifth Avenue and no higher north than Forty-second Street—in other words, just off Times Square, at the hub of the emergent transportation nexus defined by Grand Central Station and the important subway junction built into the New York Times building in Times Square.[11]

This agreement between the garment industry and the East Side commercial interests was set in stone in 1916, when New York City became the first city in the nation to adopt a comprehensive set of zoning ordinances. The agreement was bolstered in 1922, when the Municipal Arts Society banned the use of attention-getting, crowd-attracting electric signs on Fifth Avenue.[12] The agreement was further elaborated in 1929 by the New York Regional Plan, which sought to ameliorate the

effects of the skyscraper construction boom that the 1916 zoning laws had helped to shape. The designers of the Regional Plan addressed this new architectural crowding of lower and midtown Manhattan by carving the city up into land use districts, imposing legal and exclusive definitions on areas judged to be "industrial," "residential," and so forth. These zoning plans furthered the development of midtown Manhattan as an area strictly devoted to certain kinds of commerce. They did so to the detriment of other interests, as well as to the exclusion of nineteenth-century concepts of "respectability" in real estate development.[13] As real estate entrepreneurs sought to develop Longacre Square in the 1890s, they abandoned their historical emphasis on the production and marketing of "respectable" neighborhoods, where fragile middle-class subjects could thrive far from industry and unrestrained commerce. Instead, they began to change their "cultural [and] economic definitions of need."[14] Specifically, when speculators began to take an interest in the area that would come to be known as Times Square, they sought to maximize their own investments without giving much thought to guaranteeing "respectability," according to previous definitions of the term. Instead, they promoted commerce and display as values in themselves, a concept that ran contrary to old ideas of respectability.[15] However, the technical languages of zoning laws and land-use guidelines did not wholly abandon the discourse of respectability. They aimed to produce a new vision of social heterogeneity, an image of density and mixture that they could keep within limits—that would stay respectable.

Landholders sought to protect their property from the perceived degrading effects of labor (and laborers), just as middle-class families sought to distance the supposedly fragile subjectivities of women and children from the depredations of public life.[16] New York's city planners found themselves in a highly contradictory position of steering and encouraging commercial development, while, at the same time, voicing shock at the boundaries they were helping to break down themselves. The heat of the rhetorical voice they found in this contradictory position rings through this passage from the 1929 Regional Plan:

> Some of the poorest people live in conveniently located slums on high-priced land. On patrician Fifth Avenue, Tiffany and Woolworth, cheek by jowl, offer jewels and jimcracks from substantially identical sites. Child's restaurants [a low-priced chain] thrive and multiply where Delmonico's [a luxury restaurant] withered and died. A stone's throw from the stock exchange the air is filled

with the aroma of roasting coffee; a few hundred feet from Times Square with the stench of slaughter houses. In the very heart of this "commercial" city, on Manhattan Island south of 59th street, the inspectors in 1922 found nearly 420,000 workers employed in factories. Such a situation outrages one's sense of order. Everything seems misplaced. One yearns to rearrange things to put things where they belong.[17]

The language of the plan assumed a de-personalized, objective viewpoint that was, at the same time, deeply personal. The question of determining land use was linked to "one's sense of order"; one's "yearn[ing] . . . to put things where they belong." The new zoning laws that the city planners created to "put things where they belonged" reproduced the class prejudices of the nineteenth century. Working men and women were allowed to enter public life in Manhattan, but only in Times Square, and only as consumers.[18]

In this way, Times Square was the site where apparent contradictions in the planning and selling of space in New York City fought with one another and produced a new kind of urban space. Times Square's excessive spectacles of desire and fetishism (commodity and otherwise) beckoned to the tourists and workers upon whom the wealthy merchants and landlords of New York depended. At the same time, its concentration of spectacle kept the more obnoxious signs of these lower-class people's presence, and of the economy they supported, segregated from the elite spaces of the city.

The Spectaculars

Many observers at the time looked at Times Square as the material expression of new social contradictions: between the sacred and the secular; between the artistic and the banal; and between the tyrannical and the democratic. Their reactions were both enthralled and suspicious. They saw these contradictions vividly embodied in Times Square's "spectaculars": its huge neon billboards. Composed of curved and molded tubes of glass, filled with neon gas and shot full of an electric charge, these glowing signs dominated the sides of Times Square's buildings. Indeed, they towered over them, attached to enormous metal scaffolds. These electric signs featured extremely suggestive images of beautiful, scantily clad women, some with animated, billowing skirts or

petticoats.[19] In addition to advertisements for cars, cigarettes, coffee, chewing gum, and ginger ale (to name only a few of the most famous), every theater building in Times Square, from the early live theaters to the later movie palaces and amusement arcades, was decked with ever-more-fantastic arrays of moving, flashing light bulbs and neon tubes. The supersigns prompted Ezra Pound to ask, "Is not New York the most beautiful city in the world? It is not far from it. . . . Electricity has made for the seeing of visions superfluous. . . . Squares upon squares of flames, set and cut into one another. Here is our poetry, for we have pulled down the stars to our will."[20] But others saw the advertisements as signs of alienation and exploitation, calling them symptoms of "spiritual failure . . . the aesthetic appeals of the show windows stand for elements that are left out of the drab perspectives of the industrial city."[21]

The British cultural writer G. K. Chesterton captured the ambivalent reaction of the era's intellectuals to Times Square's panoply of signs when, after visiting it in 1922, he wrote, "What a magnificent spectacle . . . for a man who cannot read."[22] For Chesterton the supersigns symbolized what he saw as "new inequalities" in society. In his words, "The reality of modern capitalism is menacing the [democratic] ideal with terrors and even splendors that might well stagger the wavering and impressionable modern spirit. . . . These modern and mercantile legends are imposed on us by a mercantile minority and we are merely passive to the suggestion. The hypnotist of high finance or big business merely writes his commands in heaven with a finger of fire. We are only the victims of his pyrotechnic violence; and it is he who hits us in the eye."[23]

Did these spectaculars denote a new culture, and, if so, what was its nature? Did the signs effectively free the people and the spaces of the city, by hooking them up to what were seen as the innate creativity and power of private capital? Or did the new culture corrupt the city and its citizens, by inappropriately subjecting what should be popular decisions and public spaces to private whims and to the drive for corporate profits and control? These were the questions that arose at the founding of Times Square, and they remain in place. They continue to be some of the fundamental questions of the nature of life in capitalist society. We repress social contradictions such as these by redefining them as problems we can solve. One way that people have found to displace these questions about social life, exploitation, alienation, and freedom—in effect, to

attempt to forget about them—has been to project them onto concerns with the built environment and the "respectability" of urban space.

These same questions obsessed the early urban sociologists of the late nineteenth and early twentieth centuries. They were concerned with the compressed physical and social spaces of the metropolitan centers of power. They saw these cities, with their overwhelming diversity and their dependence on the rapidly growing "money economy," as sources of anomie, "nervous overstimulation," a blasé disregard for the condition of others, combined with a heightened regard for one's own, alienated, overstimulated, and fragmenting self.[24] In this world, people must struggle to reassert the power, indeed the relevance, of ways of measuring value other than by money—to find more "human"-seeming stories in the world; stories of meaning, of history. This was the period of a grand social shift toward mass consumption; a time when all sorts of social roles were cast up for grabs as production left the home, when love and excitement came to be located in department stores and urban shopping districts, when advertising and commerce were put at the center of city life.

Thanks to advances in production and to economic circumstance toward the end of the nineteenth century, the owners of manufacturing and marketing empires found themselves with huge surpluses of luxury goods. These business leaders sought to engender, among the middle- and working classes, the desire for goods like ready-made clothing and household appliances—commodities that formerly only the wealthy could afford. This represented a radical shift away from older systems of social distinction based on class and consumption. It was also a shift away from longstanding religious and ethical injunctions against desire, greed, and theatrical display.[25]

Times Square was just one of the new urban commercial centers created across the United States in the late nineteenth and early twentieth centuries. Like these other centers, Times Square was fashioned as a kind of theme park for this new consumer culture, with its attendant novelties of social mixture and commercial spectacle. These urban centers were not concentrated around traditional urban institutions of church or government. Instead, they were geared to "courting impulse, inviting people to spend their time and money freely, to indulge themselves, and to condone the indulgences of others."[26] In other words, Times Square was the embodiment of new ways of thinking about money, space, display, and the self. This was a new commercial culture

of desire; a culture organized around dreams, money, and freedom—
the freedom to gaze, to want, and to spend.

In this emergent consumer culture, planners and developers created
and promoted urban centers as fantasylands of commodity display—
"the dream world of mass consumption."[27] At the same time, the processes of producing these commodities and bringing them to market
were hidden from view. The new department stores were designed so
that loading docks, accounting departments, and such were hidden
from view of the customers, who would only see racks and counters full
of goods for sale.[28] Similarly, the goods advertised on Times Square's
billboards were never made there, nor were they necessarily even available for purchase there. Later, in the 1970s, when companies from
Japan and other Asian countries would begin to rent space for signs in
Times Square, the supersigns trumpeted brands of liquor or pharma-
ceuticals that were not even for sale in the United States.[29]

In this way, Times Square was made as a site for *desire and display*.
People and things were put on display in Times Square for the delight
both of those in the immediate area—those who worked in the factories and offices nearby, the growing millions who came to New York as
tourists, those who lived in New York and came there for purposes of
amusement—as well as for national and global consumption publics.
Times Square was the gathering place for an imagined community that
would be brought together by fantasy, desire, and money. As such, it was
the national showcase for a new urban landscape—a landscape structured around publicity and privacy, secrecy and display. This new urban
landscape carried with it a new form of citizenship, organized around
consuming spectacles and making oneself a spectacle for others to consume. According to this new model of citizenship, the freedom to want
and to make oneself the object of wanting was paramount.

The Changing Face of Entertainment

During the fifteen-year period between the naming of Times Square
and the declaration of Prohibition, the Square served as the nexus of
the urban commercial imagination, both for the United States and for
the world. Times Square was the center where the grand department
stores of Fifth Avenue could advertise their wares, even as the stores
kept themselves aloof, geographically isolated from their own billboard
spectaculars. This was the place where mass commodities were given

a mythical origin story. Times Square also was (and still is) the center of national and global theater syndicates. Vaudeville acts, plays, songs, and movies were given grand openings in Times Square theaters before being circulated across the country and around the world—films in their octagonal metal cans and plays via multiple touring companies controlled by a central production office.[30]

From the beginning, live theater in Times Square was forced to compete against the new cinematic forms of entertainment. But the early moving pictures failed to capture a mass audience. Nor did they soon achieve the "highbrow" societal respectability that theater had won in the latter half of the nineteenth century.[31] Despite this, Times Square's entrepreneurs were quick to see film's overwhelming commercial advantages over live theater. Producing a film involved comparatively huge initial costs relative to producing a play. However, after production, films did not have to be recreated in front of an audience by paid actors and technicians. Instead, theater owners could rent films from the central studio and show them again and again. Projecting light through a moving strip of celluloid onto a screen a single time cost more or less the same as showing the same film a hundred times. What's more, thanks to the Volstead Act of 1919, which proscribed alcohol as an illegal drug, theater owners could no longer rely on the profitable bars and cabarets attached to their "legitimate" theaters to boost their profits. These adult-entertainment venues had served the same function as contemporary movie theater snack bars—they were the real source of profits for the producers of the show.[32] Faced with tanking receipts, the landlords of Broadway and Forty-second Street converted most of their theaters into cinemas or burlesque houses. As long as it had been a center for legitimate theater, Times Square had also been a center to which wealthy men could go for risqué entertainment. Now, with the coming of burlesque, women were put on display for working-class men as well.[33] In addition, the proliferation of speakeasies throughout the area during Prohibition confirmed Times Square's role as a site for the purchase and consumption of illicit intoxicants. The Square would serve this function in the 1930s as a site for cheap marijuana cigarettes, for heroin in the 1940s, and for other proscribed and addictive substances in later decades as well.[34]

During the Depression that followed the stock market crash of 1929, new construction froze in Times Square, the demand for movies took off like never before, but live theater dove further into the red. More and more, the area's entrepreneurs catered their spectacles to a poorer,

more strictly male crowd. Burlesque stage shows and action movies competed for space with more upscale entertainment. In some ways, this was a return to Times Square's former identity as a site for masculine sociability and sexual commerce. Now, however, these existed side-by-side with Times Square's new, global cinematic/theatrical nexus. Unlike previous such junctures, the theater district could not preserve or reinvent itself by relocating to cheaper lands uptown. The island of Manhattan had filled in around the theater district during two boom decades of rapid development. There was simply no territory left for the theater owners to exploit. The fact that the Broadway theaters could be easily converted to movie houses is, perhaps, the only thing that kept these buildings intact during the decades after Prohibition, when property values remained sky-high but the live theater industry had to be radically curtailed. Only one new building—a movie theater—was built on Forty-second Street between Seventh and Eighth Avenues from 1920 until 1937, and none from 1937 to the late 1970s.[35] Instead, theater owners and real estate developers turned to a game of "milking" small lots, by leasing and subleasing to low-rent, high-turnover businesses, such as pornography and prostitution, which could afford to pay sometimes twice as much as other stores.[36]

Meanwhile, Times Square had become a key site for the denizens of many of New York's "alternative public spheres"—gay men, jazz musicians, prostitutes and their clients, and others.[37] Of these, some were hidden, some flamboyantly visible. The area provided a haven for those who sought the safety of anonymous or sheltered gathering places, as well as a space for those who wished to glorify themselves in public for dazzled tourists and theatergoers. All drew both materially and symbolically on Times Square's nexus of spectacle, travel, anonymity, and liminal license; the unique values of a place "only for [display and] consumption and nothing else."

At precisely the time when burlesque and action movies began to predominate somewhat over live theater on Broadway and Forty-second Street, Times Square was the center for gay public life in New York City.[38] Bryant Park, Forty-second Street, and, somewhat later, the Port Authority bus terminal all became sites for men to meet and cruise one another. Local bars opened their doors to this clientele to a greater or lesser degree. In fact, Times Square provided public social space for two highly gendered gay male publics, one more flamboyant and working-class, the other more genteel and middle-class. The latter, middle-class group disapproved somewhat of the former, claiming its high visibility

tarnished the public image of gay men in general. This was also a time of continual crackdowns by the police, public morals commissions, and local businesspeople on unrestrained gay male life in Times Square.[39] The police and other city authorities practiced a kind of capricious regulation of gay publicity. They sometimes permitted men to gather on corners or bars understood to be "gay areas." At other times, they stepped in to violently roust those whom local property owners claimed to find offensively demonstrative.

For the entrepreneurs and corporations that owned property in Times Square, these new marginal publics represented a threat to the speculative exchange value of their holdings. Times Square's shift away from its temporary upscale respectability had succeeded in panicking the theatrical corporations and others (notably, the publishers of the *New York Times*) that had invested in property in the area. During this time, planners and businessmen cooked up multiple plans to somehow connect Times Square with Grand Central Station, a few blocks east, and to the river, a few blocks west. They envisioned a "grand horizontal thoroughfare," a glamorous, and profitable, parade of office buildings and shops running from east to west. New York had none of these "horizontal thoroughfares" at the time and hasn't since. Nonetheless, they continue to delight the real estate imaginary, as they have from the formative moment when the original nineteenth century grid-map gestured at their future possibility.

Times Square remained a huge tourist site, even while the *New York Times* worried that its eponymous Square was declining. Also during this period, the "slum" of Broadway and Forty-second Street was increasingly memorialized by the same California film studios that were supposedly responsible, at least in part, for what was widely seen as the "decline" of Times Square. In movies like *42nd Street*, in 1933, and *Stage Door*, in 1937, Hollywood filmmakers depicted Times Square as a nexus for ambitious youth filled with lust for fame and fortune.[40] In the mythical geography of cinema, as well as in the dreams of theater owners and real estate speculators, Times Square remained a special place; what advertising pioneer Edward Bernays dubbed "the center of the universe."

Successive crackdowns on prostitution served to push sex off of the streets of Times Square and onto its stages, in the form of burlesque in the 1930s, strip shows in later decades, all the way to the live sex shows of the 1970s. New York's city government, along with various local coalitions of religious leaders, property developers, and theater owners,

made various attempts throughout this period to stamp out overtly sexual entertainment in Times Square. In these contests over the spaces of Times Square, the streetscape became a metaphor, a discursive image through which to talk about the health of the Social Body. "Respectability" of behavior was conflated with "respectability" of architecture, and vice versa.[41] In talk about Times Square, buildings and people could change places or stand in for one another. Developers imagined that a better class of buildings would attract a more lucrative class of tenants and customers, just as they imagined that a better clientele would constitute a market for a more lucrative class of buildings.[42]

For example, in 1931–32 a group called the Forty-second Street Property Owners and Merchants Association attempted to have the burlesque theaters and strip shows run by the Minsky organization declared immoral and made illegal.[43] Proprietor Morton Minsky and others brought forth "respectable" women employees who had worked backstage in their theaters. Their aim was to prove that long association with these supposedly corrupting forms of theater had not hurt these women's morals. As it turned out, though, the Forty-second Street Property Owners were not concerned with the moral state of the business's interiors, whether of the buildings or of the employees' souls. Rather, they wanted to change the area's architectural image; specifically, the run-down exteriors of the burlesque theaters themselves. The *New York Times* noted, in an editorial supporting the group, "[t]he alleged obscenity of the burlesque shows is exceeded by their external frowziness. The neighborhood of such theaters takes on the character of a slum."[44]

The area's sexual commerce was somewhat dampened for a few decades by the successful attack on burlesque in 1937. In this campaign, the Forty-second Street Property Owners and Merchants Association attacked the burlesque houses as "breeders of vice" and "loitering places for men who trade on the shady side of night life," and called Forty-second Street as a whole "a cesspool of filth and obscenity." Mayor Fiorello La Guardia supported these attacks, condemning burlesque as "organized filth." But the attempted banning of lewd displays did nothing to change the area's reputation.[45]

Next to come under panicky scrutiny from area landlords and the city government was the overall sexual tourism scene in Times Square. The area had become widely known, especially during and after World War II, as a center for sexual cruising by and for enlisted men, straight and gay alike. As one observer reminisced, "[t]he excitement, the sense of revelry, the sex in the air, were palpable. It was a mecca, especially for

singles and college students."[46] There followed a series of attempts to shut down Times Square's general atmosphere of public sexual license, especially its gay cruising scene, through the assertion of different kinds of controls over public space. The police conducted violent raids on gay bars and in Bryant Park, to roust the men who went to the park to sleep together (or, during and after the Depression, just to sleep). In 1944, the city mandated that Bryant Park be closed after dark. Similarly, in an attempt to remove the street peddlers and novelty vendors who hawked racy wares to tourists and servicemen along Forty-second Street, New York city planners revised the area's zoning codes in 1947, and again in 1954. The new zoning laws prohibited organized street vending in the area. However, these efforts backfired. Unable to sell on the street, the merchants moved indoors. Specifically, they outbid the bookstores and other businesses that had occupied retail space on Forty-second Street, and reopened sex shops in their place.[47]

These pornographic bookstores and peepshows received a boost toward the end of the 1960s, in the form of new Supreme Court decisions legalizing the sale of pornography. Now that they could sell openly, these "adult" stores boomed along Forty-second Street and throughout the Times Square area. Developers and others bemoaned the area's sex industry in this era for supposedly corrupting whatever legitimate culture was left. However, as numerous sociological surveys of the Times Square sex trade at the time observed, people shopping for pornography are remarkably circumspect and commit few crimes. "Ironically, and despite the plaints of reformers, the new sex industry eventually upgraded the neighborhood."[48]

Images of Blight

Times Square as a whole and Forty-second Street in particular were at this time highly gendered spaces. Many of my female informants and acquaintances in New York City—mostly, but not all, white and middle-class—told me that they would simply "never go" to Times Square and Forty-second Street in this time period: because their parents had ordered them not to, because it made them too uncomfortable, or because they felt there was nothing there for them. Where some middle-class women had formerly seen Times Square as a place where they could be free to take part in the city's otherwise gender-segregated public life, they now perceived the area as "a direct assault"

on them—a former haven, now occupied by the hostile forces of the male-dominated sex trade.[49]

However, during this same time period, Times Square was still an important public gathering place for individuals and groups that otherwise felt excluded from the important public and commercial spaces of the city. This was a place that was open to gay men and to black and Latino teens and families.[50] As an official from the administration of Mayor David Dinkins put it, "A lot of Black and Puerto Rican people still felt, perhaps rightly so, that [Forty-second Street] was one of the few blocks outside of Harlem they could more or less call their own. Going down to Forty-second Street, going to the movies and getting a bite to eat had been a tradition among their people for decades."[51]

It was at this point in the history of Times Square and Forty-second Street that the redevelopment project began to take shape. The redevelopers represented the period from the late 1960s through the 1970s and the early 1980s as a time of social and economic "blight" in Times Square. Supposedly, the area's decrepit architecture, downscale sexual entertainment, and street commerce in drugs and prostitution left Times Square and Forty-second Street in need of massive change—"a real rain to come and wash all the scum off the streets," in the words of Travis Bickle, the eponymous protagonist of *Taxi Driver*.

The redevelopers used the imagery of blight in order to "problemize" this place.[52] But, in using this imagery, they drew on highly class- and race-specific assumptions and prejudices that radically simplified the complicated and contradictory history and culture of Times Square and Forty-second Street. The imagery of blight transformed the area's legacy of urban heterogeneity, public spectacle, and contact across race and class lines into a problem—pure negativity, providing nothing to the city other than the need for immediate, drastic solutions.[53] Planning experts, the police, and local businesspeople formed images of Times Square and Forty-second Street during this period as "blighted" spaces of socioeconomic depravity; corrupt and corrupting. They envisioned Times Square as the domain of an entrenched criminal subculture, one that threatened all their potential efforts at redevelopment.[54]

At this time, Times Square was a thriving and profitable entertainment center, if a seedy, disreputable, and sexually exploitative one, with Forty-second Street as its heart, crowded day and night with commuters, sightseers, and moviegoers. The area had souvenir shops and newsstands, cheap action and second-run movie theaters, martial-arts supply stores, video arcades, and inexpensive restaurants.[55] This is not to

mention Forty-second Street's then-vast array of walk-up offices, art studios, and single-room occupancy hotels. All these existed side-by-side with its porn theaters, massage parlors, and sex shops. Real estate developers saw Times Square and Forty-second Street as a place to make a killing, in the traditional mode of real estate speculation, by radically transforming the area. Specifically, they could incorporate it into the midtown Manhattan office and upscale retail district located to the east of Sixth Avenue. The early plans were to do just this: to demolish many of the buildings along Forty-second Street, to build huge new office towers at the base of Times Square, and to put in new structures such as a huge "fashion mart" and an indoor amusement park. Needless to say, these plans met with much derision and outright resistance, not least from those who owned property on Forty-second Street and who did not want to capitulate to the developers' plans.

However, the nascent redevelopment project had to find a way to justify removing the already-existing low-budget and sexual entertainment economy of the area. To this end, developers and state officials made a concerted effort to portray Times Square as a "blighted" area. They claimed that the "blight" of Times Square and Forty-second Street threatened social and economic values, both for the surrounding area and for the city as a whole. Developers' plans for Times Square as an object of potentially lucrative development were based in this image of a blighted Times Square—of an area almost beyond hope, and therefore in need of massive official intervention. According to this image, Times Square needed socioeconomic transformation on a grand scale, but at too great a risk for conventional economic development without the legal authority of the state to back it up.

The developers, in the corporate form of a public-private hybrid called the Forty-second Street Development Corporation, had to argue in court that the very presence of the entertainment economy of Forty-second Street constituted a social and economic blight, preventing any development of the street itself and threatening any efforts to improve the area around it. But the task of differentiating Forty-second Street's supposedly bad present from its supposedly good past and its hopefully good future proved to require some effort. The Forty-second Street Development Organization commissioned social-science surveys of the demography of the area in order to lend credence to their claims that the street was hopelessly blighted. The crux of their claim was that Forty-second Street's concentration of "adult" uses, "loiterers," cheap movies, hustlers, prostitutes, panhandlers, and drunks constituted a single,

entrenched "subculture." They further argued that this subculture would cripple any attempt to attract desired tenants and visitors to Forty-second Street—as opposed to the people who were already there—because of the fear its members' communal presence struck into the hearts of "legitimate" passersby.

For example, in their Environmental Impact Statement, the developers claimed, "[Due to the] absence of office workers and other positive users having a territorial stake [in the area,] sidewalks are left free and available to loiterers and over time Forty-second Street has become their turf. . . . In a real sense, Forty-second Street is their territory, and others venturing through it perceive that they do so at their own risk."[56] This language of "territory" and fear similarly pervaded the survey commissioned by the developers in the late 1970s from the sociology department of the Graduate Center of the City University of New York (CUNY). On the surface, the findings in this document, known as "The Bright Lights Plan," seemed to do little to support any stereotype of Forty-second Street as a particularly violent, blighted, or "ghetto" street, nor that its sexual commerce catered only to "undesirables." Instead, the CUNY study demonstrated precisely the opposite. It showed that a great number (at least 25 percent) of the New York upper-middle-class white "tastemakers" surveyed claimed to have visited an adult bookstore or sex shop in Times Square within the previous year. The ethnographic portion of the study further observed that Forty-second Street's sexual entertainments attracted an especially well-behaved clientele, simply by dint of their not wanting to attract attention to themselves. Finally, the analysis of police statistics in the CUNY study showed that the crime rates in the area were relatively low considering its dense population. Indeed, the survey hinted that the high arrest rates reported on Forty-second Street might be primarily a product of the area's saturation with NYPD officers, rather than a result of the presence of a "criminal subculture." In sum, the CUNY survey linked the sexual entertainments of Times Square to a largely white, upscale audience; precisely the demographic the developers claimed were loath to tread on "blighted" Forty-second Street.

Most important, though, were the findings in the CUNY study regarding the racial and ethnic makeup of Forty-second Street. The study reported that, pretty much throughout the day, the population on the street constituted a more-or-less even balance among blacks, whites, and Latinos. Rather than a "ghetto street," Forty-second Street was more accurately a street where no one racial or ethnic group was clearly

dominant—a rarity in diverse but segregated New York City. However, the CUNY street demographers saw a connection between their findings and the developers' fearful and "blighted" stereotypes of Times Square and Forty-second Street. To quote the CUNY survey itself: "Thus, a large (over 30% on the weekend) group of like people were on the street. Most of these came for legitimate purposes; however, the distinction between legitimate and illegitimate users of the street is not easily made and, in the ebb and flow of the 42nd Street crowds, those standing around or congregating in front of a movie often appear as the pushers, solicitors and others 'doing business' on the street."[57] The implicit conclusion of the study was that racial and ethnic groups could not share the same entertainment district, not because of crime per se, but because of white people's fears of criminals hidden among crowds of blacks and Latinos.[58]

The survey's bland language, like "over 30% on the weekend," worked to make white racism seem like a self-evident fact, to which the developers are simply obliged to respond. In other words, the study "problemized" Times Square and Forty-second Street in terms of race, fear, and the perception of danger. It turned what could be seen as socioeconomic diversity and mixture into a social problem.[59]

The Discourse of Nostalgia

In contrast to this imagery of blight, the redevelopers selected fragmentary, sanitized images from Times Square's past to imply that their plans would return the area to what they framed as its past glories at the turn of the twentieth century. In doing so, they drew on Times Square's free-floating "discourse of nostalgia."[60] The redevelopers spoke this discourse of nostalgia, claiming that their work was both in line with the history of Times Square and amenable to this new style of privatized development. They portrayed a vision of order in Times Square—a framework that took idealized moments from the past and grafted them onto the potential future. In other words, they attempted to make the past conform to their desired "brand image" of Times Square as a place good for investors and tourists, but not fundamentally risky or unsettling in any way.

Times Square's complicated legacy of spectacular, transgressive commerce and social mixture might have suggested that it would be difficult for the redevelopers to find "authentic" images of the area that

would appeal to their desired clientele of corporate tenants and main-stream tourists. But in fact the reverse was the case. The people involved with the redevelopment were, in fact, quite fascinated with images of the area's history, and with demonstrating their connections to that history.

For example, take the most vivid icon of the changes in Times Square: the Disney Store that opened on Forty-second Street in 1995. The Disney Store in Times Square was much like the other Disney Stores of the world, if a bit smaller. However, the store was distinguished by its location at the corner of Seventh Avenue and Forty-second Street; this was one of the prime sites for the redevelopment. Architecturally speaking, almost the only notable thing about the Disney Store on Times Square was the enormous sign that decked its facade. Unlike most of the billboards in Times Square, this sign did not depict a single image, but, rather, a jumble of images. The huge rectangular billboard was cluttered with multiple, smaller advertisements. These signs-within-the-sign trumpeted wares like credit cards, movies, television shows, and so forth; they seemed to crowd in and around one another as they clamored for attention. The form of the Disney sign alluded to the redevelopers' nostalgic images of the Times Square area's supposed heyday. This was the time, at the turn of the twentieth century, when Times Square became a national and global center for theatrical and advertising spectacles. Photos of Times Square from that period show a streetscape crammed with numerous billboards. Tiny by today's measures, these advertisements crowded each other like the Disney Store's signs-within-the-sign.

When I spoke to the architect who designed the sign for the Walt Disney Company, he demonstrated how the sign intentionally played on this romanticized image of Times Square's early years. He showed me copies of the sketches he and his partners had made for Disney in the mid-1990s, when the company was first considering a move into the Development Corporation's anchor space at the corner of Forty-second Street and Times Square. The architect and his colleagues had envisioned a billboard that would integrate many smaller images into one. The signs-within-the-sign would seem to compete with one another, but together they would form a single, harmonious whole. Furthermore, the sketches showed that the individual sub-advertisements could be rearranged and replaced from time to time. Because the designers hadn't known what products Disney would want to advertise, they invented some on their own; the ads in the sketch featured suitably generic

logos for these fictional products. The implication was that any products could fit within this frame.

In this way, the Disney sign embodied a dream of urban commercial order. The sign enframed multiple, apparently competing social elements, creating a space for a kind of harmonious combat. The signs-within-the-sign seemed to crowd one another, but the authoritative oversight of a single entity—Disney—worked to ensure that this competition would always be doubly framed: both for proper brand "synergy" and for a pleasing aesthetic effect. The individual elements within the sign all accepted the authority of the owner of their shared frame.[61]

Times Square's redevelopers loved the old images of early-1990s commercial frenzy. They used them in slide shows and in publicity brochures throughout the 1980s and 1990s to demonstrate the image of Times Square they wanted to "recapture." For example, at a panel discussion on the redevelopment held on a local university campus, I saw a presentation by Rebecca Robertson, a former official from the Forty-second Street Development Corporation. Robertson showed slides of Times Square and Forty-second Street as they were when the Broadway theater district was in its early heyday, at the turn of the twentieth century, and claimed that the goal of the development effort on Forty-second Street, which she spearheaded, had been "to make Times Square more of what it had been, and to make it more open to more people." Robertson talked about the history of Times Square, its role as a center for mass-marketing campaigns and billboard spectaculars long before the theaters and the *New York Times* newspaper were located there. "Before there were buildings, there were signs."

She then showed slides of Forty-second Street as it was in the 1970s, reading the marquees of the porn theaters in a sarcastic tone:

Models working their way through college
Super Fly Boutique
Friksy [*sic*] Sexmates

She contrasted these ramshackle misspellings with the sleek and bright multicolored explosion of signs clinging to the outside of the newly opened Disney Store. Robertson's presentation construed the signs on Forty-second Street's sex shops as an anomaly in its history of signage. By extension, the sex shops themselves were presented as historical accidents or deviates from an assumed, essential Forty-second Street—

bold, bright, and classy, in the way that its 1870s commercial signage and 1910s theater marquees and 1990s Disney Store were bold, bright, and classy. It was not cheap and dumb in the way that the misspelled, weird slogans on the 1970s porn theater marquees were cheap and dumb. Indeed, the slideshow portrayed a history of Times Square and Forty-second Street as a history of advertising images. ("Before there were buildings . . . ") The audience was asked to fill in the implicit social narrative, deciding which signs were better or worse; but the presentation overall represented Forty-second Street strictly as a place to look at, not somewhere to live, work, eat, shop, or have any kinds of social interactions at all except those between spectators and signs.

In one of my conversations with Robertson about her role in transforming Forty-second Street, she described her criteria for whether the redevelopment had been successful. She said, "The test . . . is stories and fables. I can't tell you how many stories I know about Forty-second Street, so now I hope there will be more stories. There are no *stories* about Disney World, right? Folklore is the whole issue, right? It's about *meaning*, what big old cities still have that new cities don't, they have a lot of meaning! . . . You want those experiences that you think are genuine—to have a genuine wellspring for our project." Here, she paused and made a smiling comment on her use of the word "genuine" to refer to Forty-second Street, and specifically to the atmosphere of spectacular artifice she hoped to create. It is important, though, that she cited a Disney theme park as a way to define by contrast her vision for the area. Citing Disney World in this dismissive way distances the redevelopment and her involvement with it from the popular image of the "Disneyfication" of Times Square and Forty-second Street.[62]

These images of Times Square's turn-of-the-twentieth-century aesthetic also permeate the interiors of the redevelopers' own offices, as in the former Visitors' Center on Forty-second Street run by the Times Square Business Improvement District, or BID (see chapter three). Here, in a disused Broadway theater, tourists could find information on local plays, restaurants, and hotels, ask for directions, sign up for guided tours, and otherwise learn how to see the New Times Square from the BID-approved perspective.[63] The space of the Visitors' Center itself was a text on how to "read" Times Square. The walls were covered with hugely enlarged black-and-white photos of Times Square's advertising spectaculars, drawing almost totally from the early years of the twentieth century and with next to no pictures of the "blighted" sexual entertainments of the 1970s and 1980s.[64]

A similar array of images dominated the public reception area of "The New 42," Forty-second Street's nonprofit theater management subsidiary. A brain-shattering collage of old photos of Times Square covers an entire wall of the New 42's waiting room. Composed of what seemed like thousands of cut-up photographs, this collage was at least twelve feet high by twenty feet wide. As I sat in this room, waiting to interview one of the executives of the New 42, I felt caught in a sepia-toned nostalgia tornado.

The sign above the Disney Store reveled in the nostalgic intensity of these old images. Like the old photos of Times Square collaged on the walls of the Visitors' Center and the New 42 offices, the Disney sign's display of commercial competition formed a pleasing aesthetic whole. The redevelopment of Times Square hearkens back to hundred-year-old images of companies fighting for consumers' attention from rented billboards. Looking at static photographs of anachronistic advertisements, we do not see social turmoil or cutthroat competition. Rather, we see what looks like an inclusive space of democracy and dialogue. In this way, the nostalgia for images of the old Times Square blends into nostalgia for a certain image of public space as an embodiment of democracy, where everyone is free to compete with one another as supposed equals.[65] This is deeply ironic, considering that Times Square's spectaculars were seen by observers at the turn of the twentieth century as symbolizing the undermining of democracy by the power of big business to colonize the urban landscape. The redevelopment's discourse of nostalgia packaged these images of the past in a way that hides the controversies and conflicts that were so apparent when the photos were taken. At the same time, the redevelopers used these images to define a certain image of Times Square and Forty-second Street: a place where everyone was free to meet and compete for attention, but only within predetermined guidelines set by an overall owner.

The redevelopers made an effort to take control of the history of Times Square. But this history was not easily controlled. Instead, it was a history of how control and chaos worked together in the production of New York City's built environment. This was a dialectical story, tacking back and forth between order and disorder, spectacle and respectability. The redevelopers attempted to resolve this dialectic in the traditional way of development-minded social reformers, by identifying types of buildings and commercial uses with types of people. The association of sexual commerce with architectural "blight" and personal immorality became an important part of the argument to justify redevelopment.

This association, in turn, came to structure the present face of the built environment of Times Square, as in the nostalgized images and the Disney sign discussed above. The iconography of "blight" was appropriated and carefully restyled into a new, more respectable brand image.

This was perhaps most vividly illustrated by the new Warner Bros. Studio Store that rented the bottom stories of the tower at One Times Square shortly after the opening of the Disney Store in the late 1990s. Outside the Warner Bros. store stood statues of Daffy Duck and Bugs Bunny, posing, respectively, as a sleazy dealer in counterfeit watches and as a raffish sailor on shore leave. The very groups and stereotypes most demonized by the redevelopment are thus included in it, but only as cartoon figures that tourists can use for posed snapshots. Of course, these statues were up only as long as the Warner Bros. store was open—when the store closed, they disappeared.

Redefining the Disney Sign

In any event, some of the people specifically targeted for removal by the redevelopment found other ways to use the developers' images of nostalgia and urban freedom. During my research I learned that, after the redevelopment closed Times Square's porn theaters and attempted to shut down the gay cruising scene in the Port Authority bus terminal (see chapter three), some young men began to use voicemail networks or internet chatrooms to meet each other for sex—using electronic "spaces" as replacements for the old cruising scenes that the redevelopers had purposefully destroyed. Once these men had made electronic contact with one another, though, they would have to choose a New York City landmark at which to meet before they found somewhere to have sex together. They most often chose to meet at one particular landmark. They arranged to meet in Times Square; specifically, yes, under the sign on the Disney Store.

The appropriation of the Disney Store as a landmark for anonymous male sexual liaisons continued the area's long history as a place of public intimacy and social license. At the same time, the shift from men physically cruising one another in and around Times Square to electronic media for contact was certainly a significant one. Voicemail and the Internet are, in many ways, far less open and heterogeneous than were Times Square's old spaces of public intimacy. And yet the Disney Store itself, the most obvious and, to some, the most egregious symbol

of the redevelopment, could still be used as a landmark for all sorts of cognitive mapping projects, not just those consciously approved by the redevelopers.

Even the visible presence of Disney itself was far from permanent. An entry in my fieldnotes written in the spring of 2000 reads:

> The Disney Store in Times Square has been boarded up for a number of weeks and is being dismantled. The store seemed to vanish overnight—on a stroll through Times Square, a friend pointed out to me that the windows were completely blacked out. When I went back a few days later to investigate, the building itself was almost gone. I suspect that a new corporate supertower is going to go up in the Disney Store's place, but no one knows for sure; there has been nothing in the press about the building's sudden disappearance. In a matter of days, the Disney Store went from being a wide-open business to a dark and empty box, and finally to a trashed shell. However, the sign remains, perched on its scaffold above the wrecked site. No one can be certain what will be there tomorrow.

In the years since I wrote those notes, the new office towers have indeed risen up, again with little or no press attention. Looking at them from street level, or as part of the skyline as seen from the roof of my old apartment building, it was impossible to discern how they got there, or who created them, or why. To those who will see them now, for the first time, they will simply seem to be part of the city; just "there." They will seem to be precisely that which they are not: anonymous; innocent; eternal.

The New Spaces of Times Square
Commerce, Social Control, and the Built Environment

Like anyone involved in creating or transforming urban spaces, Times Square's redevelopers were faced with two seemingly incompatible ideas of the purpose of public space in the city. On the one hand, there was the ideology of democratic access and enjoyment. Part of the ideology of "public" space is that it must embody inclusive democracy. These spaces must seem open to all, without prejudice. The redevelopers could not openly select people for inclusion or exclusion. On the other hand, there was the impulse toward imposing respectability and control, in order to guarantee profit. To make the real estate of Times Square appeal to high-profile corporate tenants and mainstream tourists, the redevelopers felt that they needed to impose a new public face on the area, one that kept the brand identity of Times Square as a space of heterogeneity and excess intact, but under control enough to appease conservative sentiments and to guarantee safe investments. This was a difficult dichotomy to reconcile.

To deal with this contradiction, the redevelopers found ways to use the built environment as a technology of social order. They made

order and social control radiate from the makeup of urban space itself. In some ways, their new spaces resembled Jeremy Bentham's plan for a Panopticon prison, in which convicts would police their own behavior, by dint of the power of the prison's architecture to suggest that its inhabitants were under constant surveillance.[1]

The redesigned spaces of Times Square were meant to accomplish a concrete goal: to achieve a vision of urban social order, marketable diversity, and free-floating desire, all within the limits imposed by corporate aesthetics. The people who built and oversaw the new public spaces of the revitalized Times Square—planners, developers, managers, architects—imagined themselves to be fighting a war against crime and fear. By strategically opening and closing lines of sight, and by saturating these public spaces with icons of legitimate desire, the redevelopers sought to block what they saw as the intrinsically criminogenic properties of urban space and (some) urban denizens.[2]

To accomplish this, the redevelopers deployed brilliant, elaborate aesthetic tactics of the street—a strategic, selective deployment of color, art, beauty, comfort, and fun. By means of these aesthetic tactics, the redevelopers sought to transform the Times Square area as a whole into a space that was, in the words of one real-estate developer, "more open to more people." But if it was "more open" to some users and uses, it was also inherently "more closed" to others. Specifically, the redevelopers meant to make Times Square a place where specific, individual identities and experiences of consumer desire and spectacle would be possible, but where specific other forms of community and experience that had formerly found a place in Times Square would be impossible to sustain.

The redevelopers' aesthetic tactics of redefining the built and social environment of Times Square and Forty-second Street were part of a much larger social shift—a rethinking of the very concept of "order" in urban space, one that follows the cultural logic of neoliberal ideology. Traditional criminological approaches to issues of social control in urban space focused on identifying evil or maladjusted individuals, or "deviant" social groups. By contrast, this new perspective on space and order rarely makes explicit references to individual criminals or "undesirables." Instead, it replaces these with talk about the production and management of civil social space; specifically, spaces that do or do not foster criminality.[3] This is a discourse of environmental censorship. It mobilizes expert knowledge in the service of socioenvironmental censorship, to block crime before the fact.

This project of creating spaces that advertise a friendly sense of order and control is a curious one in a city like New York, where, as one reporter for the *New York Times* told me, breaking laws and stretching rules is "the basic planning principle." The city has always relied on granting exemptions from zoning codes and letting developers break the law in order to keep the development economy moving and growing. This project is even more problematic in a place like Times Square, which has always been seen as "a testing ground of limits."[4] As seen in the previous chapter, the history of Times Square is the history of consumer capitalism itself. This was one of the first places where society (or, more specifically, powerful political and economic interests in society) tentatively, ambivalently embraced the new values of crowding, mixture, spectacle, desire, and consumption. These were values that had formerly been seen as antithetical to the interests of social decency and personal morality. The redevelopers attempted to shape and control the excesses of this symbol of amoral consumerism and exploitation in order to fit the perceived desires of their hoped-for clientele of real estate investors, multinational corporations, and middle-class tourists. The spaces of the New Times Square testify to their contradictory success.

The Times Square Business Improvement District

The first example of the redevelopers' ideas in practice is the space of Times Square itself; specifically, the area under the rubric of an organization called the Times Square Business Improvement District (recently renamed the Times Square Alliance). The Times Square Business Improvement District was part of a larger movement of Business Improvement Districts, or BIDs, a movement that is most visible in Manhattan but that has spread to the other four boroughs of New York City and around the country as a whole. In a BID, local property owners form a voluntary association and raise money to supplement or take over services in their area traditionally handled by city governments, such as sanitation or business development.[5]

The Times Square BID was active in trying to rewrite commercial zoning regulations in Times Square, with the aim of reducing or eliminating sex shops in the area. The BID did other things, too: improving streetlights in the area; hiring a team of private sanitation workers to collect trash, sweep the streets, and steam-clean the sidewalks daily; hanging all manner of signs and banners in shop windows and from

lampposts throughout the area; and helping to stage-manage events like the New Year's Eve celebration.

More generally, the BID was concerned with shaping and disseminating a particular image of Times Square. The message they sought to convey was simple: There is a tourist- and business-friendly authority controlling this space. The most public manifestation of the Times Square BID was their private force of security guards that oversaw the streets of Times Square and the surrounding area. Though their uniforms were distinctive and imposing, the guards were unarmed—they carried a radio to contact the police if need be. I found the BID guards as a whole to be friendly and highly approachable. I spent a morning on patrol with one of these security guards. She told me that she avoids direct contact with the street peddlers and drunks upon whom she keeps a watchful eye. She explained that she sees her job as showing "them" that the BID is aware of their presence. As we walked around, she exuded the sense of someone walking through an area she was fascinated with and knew intimately; yet she was in it as a symbol of authority, making herself visible, and by extension making her presence known. She told me that she "gets into people's heads" while she's working, trying to suss out who is important to talk to, who she should radio the cops about, and the like. I remember her easy rapport with the drunks on the street. The strange thing was that they seemed much more scared of me than of her. She explained that this was because I looked "like a cop"—a young white guy with short hair in a leather jacket, standing off to one side behind her, not saying much. Overall, her demeanor and practices on patrol fit the image of order the BID worked to create: remote and aloof, yet vivid. Paradoxically, by keeping her distance, she advertised the BID's power. At the same time, she never needed to put that power to the test. Similarly, the colorful banners the BID displayed from streetlights in Times Square, with slogans like "Cleaner! Brighter! Safer! The New Times Square!," hung far out of reach. Passersby could not touch them, only observe their eye-catching repetition from lamppost to lamppost, one after the other.

The streetlight signs and the security patrols were both examples of the "official graffiti"[6] with which the BID sought to create an image of order in Times Square. Sometimes, these signs were meant to be invisible to one group, yet highly visible to others. For example, a security guard working for a local construction company showed me that the BID had provided scanning devices to his employers to electronically supervise him and his colleagues. These scanners were mounted in

unobtrusive plastic brackets, mounted every few yards along the construction facades surrounding the sites for buildings under development. The BID also gave the guard and his colleagues handheld personal signaling devices, which they would plug into the brackets as they patrolled the sites. This way, he explained, his supervisors could keep track of him from a distance. "They can see that I'm out here on patrol. I'm not at home or out shopping or whatever." The tiny scanning brackets were almost invisible to anyone not already aware of their presence. Nobody other than the security guards and their supervisors would know that the BID had programmed the developing real estate of Times Square to keep track of the people hired to guard it.

In the same vein, during my research, the BID collaborated with the city's Department of Tourism on a pilot project (later abandoned) to help make Times Square easier to navigate for first-time tourists. This project took the form of large square stickers, which were plastered on the backs of the walk/don't walk signal boxes at intersections throughout the area. Each sticker featured large arrows to orient tourists along the cardinal directions, as well as directions pointing them to likely destinations within walking distance but outside the immediate area, such as Central Park or the Intrepid Battleship Museum on the Hell's Kitchen waterfront to the west. An official from the Department of Tourism who was involved with the project explained to me that the stickers were meant to help novice tourists who were struggling with maps or who were confused upon emerging from the subway (something I could sympathize with, as it took me several months to get over feeling totally disoriented when I came up to the sidewalk from a trip underground). The information on the stickers was based on a list compiled by the BID of the twenty questions most frequently asked by tourists. Each sticker carried the BID and Department of Tourism logos, as well as "Welcome to New York" translated into one of twenty languages. The official specified that the stickers did not point tourists to private businesses, though he also mentioned that the project called for them to be "sponsored" by private companies, which would then have their logos printed on the stickers as well.

The BID and the Department of Tourism designed these stickers to be invisible to locals, yet highly noticeable to confused tourists. In a clever play on the popular stereotype that New Yorkers never look up at the vertical architecture of the city, placing the stickers on the backs of walk/don't walk signal boxes meant that they would rarely be noticed by locals walking quickly and with their heads down. Instead,

they would be directly in the sightlines of confused tourists looking around for streetsigns or otherwise trying to orient themselves. Not coincidentally, this project was initiated at a moment when the city and a privatized authority were proposing to place maps and directional signs throughout Central Park. The private organization, Friends of Central Park, argued that these signs would help first-time tourists make their way through the park's hills and winding paths. Some New Yorkers took issue with this plan, saying that making the park immediately navigable to novices would undermine a fundamental aspect of its nature, and of the nature of New York City as a whole—specifically, that it *should* be a confusing and complex environment, into which visitors would need to invest time and effort in order to feel at home. With the sticker project, the BID and the Department of Tourism were attempting to finesse this question, by making Times Square easy to navigate for tourists, but in a way that would not signal to native New Yorkers that this place was being redefined with non-natives in mind. Though, of course, natives felt this about the New Times Square in any case. An employee of a company based near Times Square told me that she and her colleagues referred to the area as "The Mousetrap," in a play on the image of the redevelopment as "Disneyfying" Times Square. They saw the New Times Square as a place designed to gather and contain the tourists they would otherwise resent for crowding the sidewalks and filling the restaurants in other parts of the city. For this, they were, ironically, grateful to the redevelopers.

A board member of the Times Square BID once remarked to me that, contra his organization's official antipornography position, he felt that it would be all right to have sex shops in the area if there were only a few. Specifically, he wanted just enough pornography to fit the brand image of Times Square that his organization was trying to mold—but no more. As he said, "You don't want to eliminate it totally, because it's that *spiciness* that . . . really is Times Square." In other words, while his organization was working as hard as it could to limit the pornography trade in Times Square, he also saw that a fragmentary, visible remnant of the area's sex trade was fundamental to the brand image of Times Square that his organization was trying to mold as an exciting, "spicy" place. He wanted just enough sexual commerce to play into the nostalgic image of what "really is Times Square"—but not enough to risk having that image become an uncontrolled reality.

In Times Square as elsewhere, those who played the neoliberal version of the infinite game of urban redevelopment had to walk this fine

line. They created development-friendly structures of control; at the same time, they tapped into nostalgic, brand-friendly images of spontaneity and urban license. Their creative solutions to this complex problem shaped the redeveloped Times Square as a space.

Strategies of Zoning and Design

Another example of how planners and developers approached urban space in terms of desire and control could be found in the new set of zoning guidelines that governed Times Square itself; specifically, the laws regarding commercial signage. Historically, zoning laws have focused on governing the uses to which buildings can be put, their maximum allowable bulk, and so forth. When zoning has addressed the issue of commercial signs in New York City, the laws have been concerned to limit the perceived ambient obnoxiousness of advertising. In the words of one New York real estate figure, "Nobody ever made money in the billboard business by worrying about what the neighbors might think."[7] The zoning laws have traditionally restricted the size and brightness of signs overall, and limited such signs to certain spaces throughout the city—specifically, to Times Square and certain other commercial centers.[8]

These limits and restrictions have, in turn, played a part in the intensifying debates over the proliferation of advertising throughout the island of Manhattan. I spoke with a former graffiti writer who angrily described the way advertising executives and art directors have "borrowed" from graffiti the insight that any surface can become a medium for advertising images and logos. The result has been a proliferation of stencils, signs, and stickers on sidewalks and other public surfaces around New York City. City residents and activists for historical preservation turn to the zoning codes as a resource in the fight to limit the presence of advertising in the built environment of the city—to prevent its spread and to mitigate what are seen as its deleterious effects on the urban social environment. These legal limits on signage have also featured in recent debates over the proliferation of advertising throughout the island of Manhattan, where corporations are experimenting with ways to work ads and logos into the skyline: the Travelers' insurance company's red neon umbrella, the Yahoo! billboard at Broadway and Houston, the stories-tall plastic sheets that have turned entire buildings on well-trafficked lower Manhattan streets into towering ads, and

Verizon's desire to install a giant, illuminated version of their logo high up on their building at the foot of the Brooklyn Bridge.

However, in a radical twist on zoning's legacy of anti-advertising activism, the 1987 "Times Square Urban Design Controls" took precisely the opposite tack. Rather than limiting signage, they mandated that all new buildings *must* deck the first ten or twenty stories of their facades with spectacular billboard advertisements. The text in a brochure printed by the City Planning Department explained that the goal of these codes is "to preserve, protect and enhance the scale and character of Times Square, and in particular its unique ambiance, lighting and large electric signs."[9] With this aim, the codes rewarded developers with less restrictive setbacks—effectively letting them build bulkier and thus potentially more profitable buildings—if these were accompanied by "illuminated 'super-signs,'" meeting specific minimum requirements for area and lighting. The Urban Design Controls also sought to preserve what they describe as the Times Square area's "active, visually stimulating, late-hour uses on street frontages."[10] They provided similar rewards for builders who create structures that maintain active businesses (or, at least, the *appearance* of activity) along the building's streetfront—anything other than a blank façade.

It used to be that developers could get permission from city regulatory authorities to add bulk to their office or apartment towers by creating plazas and public spaces. This was the "Plaza Bonus" program, the end result of which can be seen one block east of Times Square along Manhattan's Sixth Avenue—a parade of austere towers, each with its own set of similarly austere plazas and fountains. Many people I talked to during my fieldwork echoed the critiques of Sixth Avenue and the Plaza Bonus program articulated by urbanist William Whyte: that the plazas were inhospitable, unattractive, and unsuitable for what the Times Square Urban Design Controls call "the special character of Times Square."[11] The new zoning codes and development bonuses in Times Square granted real estate developers the right to create substantially bigger and bulkier buildings, as long as they ensured that they feature scenes (or simulations) of commerce and advertising adornment, instead of the forbidding glass fronts and blank streetwalls favored by modern corporate architecture.

In some ways, the Times Square Urban Design Controls represented a familiar aspect of the interaction of zoning codes and the New York real estate market. They proposed new guidelines, accompanied by bonuses that allowed developers to push legal restrictions, in an attempt

to shape the market and the built environment the market helps to produce. But in other ways, these new codes transformed the way commercial development and advertising were regulated. Historically, as discussed in chapter two, critics have cast a wary eye on Times Square's supersigns, regarding them ambivalently as symbols of freedom and/or alienation. In the early years of the redevelopment, developers and corporate tenants were initially strongly opposed to these signage requirements, seeing them as tainting the respectable image they wished to project. As one developer put it at the time these zoning codes were being debated, "Investment bankers and lawyers don't want to work in an environment surrounded by flashing lights. They want trees and clean streets . . . museums and sidewalk cafes."[12] This is a lyrical set of images of status and distinction, symbols of a class doing work far from any visible signs of industry and mass consumption. As shown in chapter two's discussion of the history of zoning in New York City in general, the sentiments of an upper class that wants to live and work far from any trace of its middle- or working-class employees or customers have always played a central role in shaping the built environment of this city. The planners in charge of the new Urban Design Controls had to grapple with this legacy.

The new controls did not define Times Square's signs as déclassé visual trash, symbols of alienation, or vehicles for exploitation. Rather, they sought to preserve and even increase the presence of the signs; to saturate Times Square with particular forms of light, activity, and intention. Similarly, by requiring that new corporate tenants in Times Square deck their buildings with ads, they broke down the traditional polar opposition of advertising and respectability in the New York real estate market. In effect, the zoning regulations transformed the historic image of Times Square as a center for commercial display into an official city landmark. They ensured that this image was preserved, not only in photos, movies, or memories, but also in law. In doing so, they enframed aggressive advertising itself as a marketable commodity, something of value to the area and to the city as a whole. They made advertising into a social good. Last, but not least, the additional light the signs projected on the street was valued as an anti-crime measure—saturating the streets with light to wipe out any dark corners.[13]

The zoning regulations in the Times Square area were still a hot topic during my year of fieldwork, the subject of angry newspaper editorials and of numerous debates at community meetings (see chapter seven). It was at one of these meetings that I met Patrick Too, a planner

from the City Planning Department who had been centrally involved in writing the pro-supersign zoning for Times Square. In an interview a few weeks later, I asked Too why he felt it was so important to encourage developers to build signs and active streetfronts in areas like Times Square. He replied:

> [R]ight now, every building in some way is telling the place, "Here I am; I am part of you," or, "Here I am; I am better than you," or that kind of thing. If a building is just an institutional building and [it has] a blank wall on the street . . . you'll see that the building doesn't care about the street. However, there are other people that care about the street; they will stand out on the sidewalk and sell things. So what does that tell me? It tells me that the building needs to relate to the street. Even if the building doesn't want to, somebody is going to make it relate to the street. . . . People take different attitudes. Police go on and say, "Get out get out get out." And if a bank is there, they don't want people selling things out there—"They're hurting my image." And then other stores, they say, "Well, you're selling things in front of my store, you're hurting my business," and so on and so forth. But to me, this is organic; this is organically linked. If you have no expression to the street, somebody's going to make an expression to the street. I want us to see that, yes, this building has to have meaning to the street. It *sits*. We have to [ensure that] there is a door, alright, and there is a *window;* there is an expression.

Too's words captured something of the underlying logic inherent in the new design codes for Times Square. As he described the relation of architecture to street life, every built structure presents a particular rhetorical image to the street: of inclusion, of domination, of "caring" or "not caring." He continued by pointing out that this rhetorical image was not under the sole control of the building itself. The space where a building presented a blank wall to pedestrians was also the space where a street vendor could set up shop. This is a telling example, one that conveys a great deal by what it does not say. Specifically, Too chose the street vendor, someone that "will stand out on the sidewalk and sell things," as his example of how people could appropriate urban space for their own uses. He did not mention prostitutes, panhandlers, drug dealers, or graffiti writers, all of whom also illicitly appropriate urban space to market illicit goods or images. Instead, he described the street

vendor simply as part of a group of "other people that care about the street." Too's account invited his listener to sympathize with the unlicensed peddler, and against the architect who designed the building that "doesn't care about the street." He implied that the landlords or storeowners who tried to keep control of the sidewalk space in front of their buildings were focusing on the wrong problem. Instead of attacking the vendors—"Get out get out get out" or "They're hurting my image" or "You're hurting my business"—he proposed that the owners' problem was, literally, structural; built right into their edifices. "The building needs to relate to the street. . . . To me, this is organic. . . . This building has to have meaning to the street." And as examples of the ways in which a building could express "caring" and "meaning" to the street, Too proposed doors and windows, pathways for vision and access.

Seen from the perspective that Too outlined, the entire operation of attempting to maintain control of commercial built environments appears *risky*. He invited me to think of buildings as structures for the flow of socioeconomic energy—for the movement of people and money along the sidewalk and into and out of the building. However, this energy was also a vector of potential crime. The energy that maintained commerce seemed to be identical to the energy that sparked criminality. Planners must steer the interaction between building and environs toward commerce and away from crime by using up all the available energy of "expression." Without structures such as doors and windows to channel the flow of crimino-social energy, "someone's going to make an expression to the street." According to this perspective, illicit entrepreneurs would inevitably crop up where planners and architects failed to create the proper mechanisms to shape what he called the "organi[c] link" between edifice and sidewalk. People who create buildings must attend to this energy flow; not to minimize it, but, rather, to create *enough* channels, *enough* doors and windows, that there is no social energy left over for anyone else. They must preemptively absorb and channel the energy of the street.

The Politics of Publicity in Bryant Park

Another example of how planners and architects worked with these same concepts of energy, access, and flow could be found in Bryant Park, which sits adjacent to the famous New York Public Library build-

ing on Fifth Avenue and Forty-second Street. The park occupies two city blocks, from Fortieth Street to Forty-second Street between Fifth and Sixth Avenues. As discussed in the previous chapter, Bryant Park has been subject to the same moral panics and official opprobrium as Times Square and Forty-second Street. From the 1930s through the 1970s, novels and newspaper accounts characterized the park as a skuzzy and isolated place. The urban planner Robert Moses had laid out Bryant Park in 1934 as part of a Depression-era public works project. The design Moses used elevated Bryant Park above street level and put into place tall fences and hedgerows around the park's perimeter.[14] This was in keeping with the urban design logic of the period, in which parks were thought of as vital, distinct shelters from the "intensification of nervous stimulation" of urban density and commerce.[15] City parks were meant to serve as quiet enclaves for those who wished to cultivate their sensitive subjectivities away from the hurly-burly of the street. However, the effect of this design was also to make the park a shelter for less socially respectable uses. Its elevation off the street, stone fences, shady trees, and overgrown hedgerows provided shelter indeed—somewhere one could hide in public, to sleep, or to buy or sell drugs or sex.

In the early 1980s, however, in a move that foreshadowed the redevelopment of Forty-second Street and Times Square as a whole, the city government turned the administration of Bryant Park over to a private consortium of local property owners, the Bryant Park Restoration Project. In a bid to improve the image of the park, and by extension the image of the Public Library and the office buildings on the land surrounding it, the Restoration Project radically redesigned the park. In 1979, the New York Public Library had asked urbanist William Whyte to study Bryant Park and to recommend how it could be rid of what was then a thriving open-air drug market. In his report to the library, Whyte stated that, "the problem is underuse. . . . Access is the nub of the solution."[16] Whyte advocated radically leveling the park's multilevel stairways, hedges, and terraces, all with the aim of opening the park to the street and thus to the attentive eyes of passersby and police.

The Bryant Park Restoration Project hired architect Laurie Olin to carry out Whyte's recommendations. Olin described his project in the following terms: "[Bryant Park] had to become more civic. We didn't care whether or not it was genteel, but we wanted people to be there in greater numbers and to mind their manners."[17] He agreed with Whyte that the original design of the park actively fostered fear and crime through its cultivation of public shelter. In the margins of his sketches

for the proposed redesign, he noted, "It seems that the terraces and balustrades, the railways and plantings [that] were meant to make life more gracious and somehow more European . . . have made it sinister. They allow for private turf to develop in a public place—an us and them phenomenon. It isn't open, accessible—one public place—but rather—levels, cul-de-sacs, etc. removed from [the] immediate and uniform access, surveillance, and social contract [that] even a Horn and Hardart's [a budget restaurant] . . . has."[18] As a result of Olin's redesign, Bryant Park was transformed into a beautifully manicured central lawn surrounded by stone benches and iron chairs. Whatever it was before, the redeveloped park was now a beautiful place, often crowded in good weather with tourists and officeworkers. As the director of the New York Public Library noted in regard to the redesign of Bryant Park, "Bad people need darkness to do nefarious acts. They just don't like to do them in public."[19] To drive this point home, the entrances to the new Bryant Park were chained off at dusk. But the park was never dark, even in the middle of the night. Rather, powerful spotlights located atop an adjacent office tower beamed artificial moonlight down onto the park. Filtered through the pruned tree branches, the spotlights suffused Bryant Park with a beautiful glow, ensuring that "bad people [who] need darkness to do nefarious acts" never found a cranny there.

It is interesting to note that, in the above quote, Olin compared Bryant Park's apparent failure as a public space with a Horn and Hardart's cafeteria, a private business, which, he implies, succeeds at being "open" and "accessible" in a way that the park did not. This telling comparison highlighted a controversial shift in the park's role as public space. The redevelopment of Bryant Park involved not only removing hedges and pruning trees, but also incorporating into the park several private businesses. Bryant Park now featured new cafés and games kiosks, as well as a luxury restaurant, backed up against the library building on the park's east side. Similarly, Bryant Park's new central lawn is often used for film screenings and for noontime concerts to promote Broadway shows. The Restoration Project also shuts down the entire park from time to time, leasing the lawn as a space for fashion shows or circuses. In the act of making the park more "open" and "accessible," the Bryant Park Restoration Project has also made it a good deal *less* open and accessible to certain uses and at certain times. As a result of its physical redesign and of its being put under the domain of a private authority, Bryant Park is now much less easily appropriated for illicit or unofficial uses. At the same time, it is much *more* easily appropriated for new,

officially approved uses—those sanctioned by the organizations that own property in the surrounding area.[20]

The Transformation of Forty-second Street

In the mid-1980s, the Forty-second Street Development Corporation announced their plan to declare the street's thriving strip of cheap action and pornographic movie houses, restaurants, martial arts supply stores, clothing boutiques, souvenir stands, sex shops, and other small businesses a "blighted" area, in order to take ownership of nearly all the buildings therein. The plans to redevelop Times Square and Forty-second Street took shape in the late 1960s, 1970s, and early 1980s—a time when the area was supposedly at its social and economic nadir. In many ways, the conditions then were the same as in previous eras in the history of Times Square. Crowded streets and darkened theaters provided anonymity, invisibility, and license; they opened up possibilities for forms of social life and commerce that were prohibited elsewhere. This new project aimed to radically transform these conditions in ways that previous incremental efforts had not even contemplated.

The Development Corporation was promptly faced with dozens of lawsuits levied by Forty-second Street's current tenants and landlords, from relatively poor owner-operated businesses at one end of the spectrum to the powerful Brandt theater organization/family at the other. At the same time, the city put in place a parallel development initiative to encourage the development of skyscraper towers in the upper regions of Times Square. By the time the Forty-second Street Development Corporation worked through their lawsuits and took possession of the block in 1990, the Times Square area was already facing a glut in new office space. This was a potential disaster for the Development Corporation. Their goal had been to transform the block, from a low budget, "underdeveloped" entertainment and sex business district into a prime investment opportunity for potential corporate tenants. The developers had been betting on their ability to sell new space in a booming market for office real estate, but this market had since collapsed.[21] The four new supertowers the Development Corporation had planned to build at the junction of Forty-second Street and Times Square were in jeopardy. The Forty-second Street Development Corporation now owned an empty city block lined with blank storefronts, with no tenants and few prospects. They were faced with a thorny problem: How to manage this

newly emptied-out space in such a way that it would invite and be ready for the eventual influx of investment and construction upon which their plans rested?

This brings us back to Rebecca Robertson, a real estate developer who was prominent in the Development Corporation in the late 1980s and early 1990s, who we first met in the previous chapter. Robertson explained to me, as we talked over breakfast at the Howard Johnson's restaurant in Times Square, that she and her colleagues did not consider it enough simply to go about finding new tenants for the newly vacant buildings they now possessed. In addition to this, the Development Corporation had to carefully, tactically manage the appearance of the block, for two reasons. First, they had to craft the streetscape of Forty-second Street, to prevent it from seeming as empty as it was. Second, and simultaneously, they had to call attention to its emptiness, both as a sign of imminent change and as an investment opportunity. They wanted to convey the impression that, far from being an empty commercial block in a dead market, Forty-second Street was actually on the verge of being transformed into something different and much more profitable.

As Robertson recounted, they felt that they had to choose a tactical aesthetics, a street-level artistic strategy that would speak to three distinct audiences. The first of these audiences was the thousands of subway and bus commuters who happened to pass up and down the block on their way to work every day. They had to experience the street as a comfortable place. At the very least, the street had to seem no *more* threatening than it had before to anyone walking along it on the way to somewhere else. The second audience consisted of the potential investors the Development Corporation hoped to bring to the site. This audience needed to perceive the block as an inviting opportunity to invest—as a good bet. Third, the development project needed to create an environment that would address the "audience" of graffiti writers, street vendors, panhandlers, prostitutes, drug dealers, and so forth—the people that planners homogenize under the term "undesirables." They felt that they had to keep these "undesirables" from interpreting the total lack of street-level economic activity on Forty-second Street as an opportunity to make their own mark on the area. In other words, the development project agreed with Patrick Too, the city planner quoted earlier, that "If you have no expression to the street, somebody's going to make an expression to the street." They needed to find the right expression, one that would speak to all audiences simultaneously. Specifically, they needed a way to mark the space of Forty-second Street that would stifle the "unde-

sirables" while at the same time not stifling the overall sense of opportunity and excitement they thought so crucial to attracting new investment. Furthermore, they had to do so using the only medium open to them: the surfaces of the stores and theaters that the State of New York had just helped them to empty. They could shape a mask, behind which the face of the street they hoped later to create could grow.[22]

To this end, as Robertson explained to me, they created a proposal for Forty-second Street, the "Interim Plan." The Interim Plan called for the Development Corporation to lease space on Forty-second Street to a variety of commercial tenants, rather than to single, massive projects as proposed in the original plans for Forty-second Street. The Interim Plan included projects such as multiplex movie theaters; a luxury hotel on the corner of Forty-second Street and Eighth Avenue, across from the Port Authority bus terminal (see later in this chapter); and new and refurbished Broadway theater houses. As of this writing, all of these projects have come or are coming to fruition. Most famously, in 1995, one of the vacant theaters on the block, the New Amsterdam, was leased to the Walt Disney Company, bringing national and international publicity to the redevelopment of Forty-second Street and to Times Square as a whole. According to the Interim Plan, these new tenants would occupy the vacant spaces of the block and make the area appear lively, even as the Development Corporation sought developers and capital to more permanently transform the street. Robertson noted that even the name of the Interim Plan was a tactical move—a step to building the sense of the street as undergoing rapid change, on the way to becoming something much greater.

Robertson told me that the original plans for the block had been approved for two reasons: because they drew heavily on the private sector for funding, and because they proposed a radical redesign for Forty-second Street's long-hated strip of frowzy theaters, souvenir stands, and sex shops. The Interim Plan would have to have the same key elements: total aesthetic transformation, to be accomplished with private funds. At the same time, the Interim Plan would have to be even less structured than the first had been—more open to whatever the Development Corporation could come up with once the local real estate market shifted. She said that she was inspired to create this new plan by the task with which she had been occupied throughout the end of the 1980s. This was the job of evicting and relocating all the previous businesses and tenants that had originally rented space along Forty-second Street. These included not just the sex shops and movie theaters,

but also a host of small businesses and memorable individuals. Robertson smiled as she listed them for me: a local cable television talk show host, a hairdresser, a pimp, a schizophrenic woman with an apartment full of cats. . . . She said that spending so much time in the area, getting to know all the old tenants in their homes and businesses gave her ideas; ironically, she was inspired in the very process of helping to permanently remove these people from the area. She told me that her goal was to create a set of aesthetic "anti-guidelines"—a legal structure that would ensure a particular "look" for Forty-second Street. The Development Corporation called this approach "unplanning."[23] The Interim Plan was not so much the creation of a certain visual experience, but the creation of a legal and economic environment where others would shape the street:

> I had a general idea that it should be . . . honkytonk and razzmatazz and all that. . . . You had to create a legal system where there were a lot of players fighting with each other, competing with each other for ad [space] and audience and notoriety. . . . [T]he visual experience [would] get really interesting, and *deep*. . . . I mean, just look at those Philip Johnson buildings [that were part of the original plan]—that's not a very rich cultural experience. The idea was to create the understructure, so that when this thing went totally market-free it would have its own momentum, and everybody would be fighting with everybody else to be sort of *out there*. So it meant that you had to have different developers, and you had to give a lot of power to the tenants to express themselves, and you had to really mix the old architecture with the new architecture. . . . The design guidelines had to be "anti-guidelines" in a sense. . . . They really needed to force people into taking the visual stuff seriously, but then not to force them into any particular look. If there was a look building by building—if there was a theme—it would be horrible!

However, before the Interim Plan could be put into effect, the Forty-second Street Development Corporation had to lay the groundwork for this hypothetical image of creative competition. Specifically, they had to manage the empty space of the street—to ensure that its pre-construction emptiness presaged only their approved possibilities for appropriation and commerce. The image that Robertson gave of creating "anti-guidelines"—that is, rules for complexity, spectacle, and fabulousness, all within the defined constraints laid down by the

corporation—is a powerful one. It was prefigured in the steps that she and the Forty-second Street Development Corporation took in preparing the street for the implementation of the Interim Plan.

First, she said, the Development Corporation lined the street-level façades of Forty-second Street with blue construction fencing, creating a blank, blue wall along the entire block. She told me that she meant this blue wall as an economical way to give to people who traveled Forty-second Street a visual and visceral shock, to reinforce the total disappearance of the sex shops, theaters, and other businesses that had until recently filled the block. The uniform blue fences also let her organization quickly notice and paint over any graffiti that people might be tempted to write on such an invitingly blank surface. This was a "zero-tolerance" technique borrowed from then-subway security chief William Bratton's anti-graffiti campaign.[24] The Development Corporation also cleared all the street vendors from Forty-second Street—all, that is, except for the Black Muslim incense vendors. Robertson explained that their hope was that the devoutly religious incense and perfume merchants would keep out vendors looking to sell other, more problematic goods, such as drugs, counterfeit watches, and so forth.[25]

In 1993, the Development Corporation followed the blue wall with another initiative, the 42nd Street Art Project, a series of installations curated by the Creative Time public arts agency. A brochure from Creative Time described the Art Project in the following terms: "Forty-second Street at Times Square—the world's busiest, bawdiest, and most visually raucous intersection, traversed by hundreds of thousands of tourists, shoppers, and commuters every day. When artists come here to develop site-specific projects, they create on America's most public canvas of all. . . . Times Square—America's Ground Zero and the hot spot under the melting pot." The blue façades were torn down, and the empty storefronts and metal-shuttered windows of the vacated businesses were painted in rainbow hues, chosen to match those in a standard box of crayons. (Again, the uniform color palette made for easy cleanup of unwanted graffiti.) The shop windows and vacant theater displays were turned over to artists, for work ranging from Karen Finley's homage to the street's former sex industry to a giant mural of children's book author Dr. Seuss's "Cat in the Hat" character (which I assumed was an advertisement for a Seuss-themed Broadway show when I first saw it in 1996).

Along with the various street-level art installations constituting the 42nd Street Art Project, including a huge, much-photographed mural

by Tibor Kalman that spelled out the word "Everybody" in stark black letters against a yellow background, below which were built in to the mural several chairs at which shoeshiners could set up shop, the Art Project also filled the empty movie theater marquees with texts. In 1993, the marquees showed "truisms" by the renowned postmodern artist Jenny Holzer. The Creative Time staff had selected Holzer's truisms for the exhibition because, in their textual compactness and alienated whimsy, they seemed suited both for the marquees specifically and for the image of "edge" the Forty-second Street Development Corporation wanted in general.[26] Indeed, Robertson chuckled as she described for me her glee when she imagined conservative, besuited commuters confronted on their daily walk down Forty-second Street from the Port Authority bus terminal to the financial institutions of Sixth Avenue with overhead marquees bearing unsettling legends such as:

lack of charisma
can be fatal

slipping into madness
is good for the sake
of comparison

most professionals
are crackpots

Later, in the summer of 1994, they replaced the Holzer truisms with short poems chosen by the Haiku Association of North America, in an installation called "Haiku on 42nd Street."

with a flourish
the waitress leaves behind
rearranged smears

her bifocaled eyes
magnetized to the hem
of my too-short skirt

Orion
has he put
on weight?

By all accounts, the "Haiku on 42nd Street" installation resonated with many as in some way exemplary of the character of the Times Square area and of the redevelopment of Times Square and Forty-second Street. Like the "Everbody" mural, which was featured in television ads for Pepsi-Cola and for the montage of New York City street scenes in the opening of *Saturday Night Live,* the "Haiku on 42nd Street" proliferated far beyond the immediate context of the poems and the marquees themselves.[27] When I spoke with Anne Pasternak from Creative Time, who had worked on the Art Project, she told me that, out of all the artworks that constituted the two years of the 42nd Street Art Project, the agency received fan mail only about the "Haiku on 42nd Street." As she described the mail to me, commuters found the poems "inspiring." Later, an urban planner, formerly of the New York City Planning Department, summed up all of his reservations and misgivings about the redevelopment of Times Square to me with one phrase: "Too haiku" (which I took to mean, "Too precious, too self-consciously arty for Forty-second Street").

Pasternak said that the Forty-second Street Development Corporation had wanted the artworks "to show to potential developers and tenants the great *promise* Forty-second Street has, and its once-great history." She went on to explain her agency's ambivalent relationship with the state's development project: she spelled out for me her questions about whether or not the redevelopment of Forty-second Street constitutes a suppression of deviancy, censorship, the destruction of New York City's diversity, and she recognized that, as part of the state's taking right of eminent domain over the block, a number of artists were displaced from their studios on Forty-second Street. But Pasternak concluded: "That redevelopment was going to happen anyway—and this was a unique opportunity" for artists to "reach millions and millions of people—to bring *content* and *ideas* to Forty-second Street."

Similarly, Robertson said that the Art Project was intended "to give an edge to the street." In other words, the Art Project was an aesthetic strategy. The powerful but elusive concept of "edge" refers directly to how *clearing* the street of life paradoxically opens up the possibility for a new kind of artistic play—a play of images that reference certain aspects of the street's history, while at the same time making way for an entirely new scale of real estate speculation. A street that was once the center of a complex, organic socioeconomic formation is resituated in the geography of real estate on the profitable-but-risky "edge" of terrain open for development.

The Development Corporation made Forty-second Street the site of a highly visible and publicized art installation in an attempt to stamp their own marketing image on the street, their own brand—"the world's busiest, bawdiest, and most visually raucous intersection . . . America's Ground Zero . . . the hot spot under the melting pot"; a street with "an edge." (This, just after they had fought dozens of court battles to evict all the "edgy" people and businesses who had occupied the street in the first place.) The 42nd Street Art Project was an active effort on the part of the Development Corporation to manage, in complex ways, not only the actual street, but also stories about the street circulating in various forms of mass media. Saturating the space of Forty-second Street with images full of high-art cachet and pop culture glitz, the Art Project left no room for unauthorized uses or images of the street to take hold. And, while many protested the Development Corporation's plans to turn Forty-second Street into a corporate office district, it is hard to imagine anyone registering a similar protest against the Art Project— another example of the ways in which, according to critic Rosalyn Deutsche, public art works as the handmaiden to urban development.[28]

Simultaneously, the 42nd Street Art Project was meant to produce a new, visceral sense of Forty-second Street for the many commuters who traversed the block every day. The Art Project was intended to have a direct effect on how people walked down the street—how they experienced the space on the level of the body and the unconscious. In a 1993 television news story on the Art Project, Robertson put it this way: "A lot of people have seen this as a place that they're afraid to walk on, and if they do walk, they keep their eyes straight ahead and they don't look to the right or to the left. The idea with this art show is to show them that it's safe." Turning the street into a kind of art gallery, the Development Corporation asked passersby to engage with Forty-second in a different way. Instead of walking with "their eyes straight ahead," the Art Project invited them to slow their pace, to enter a space of relaxed, aesthetic contemplation—window-shopping on a street where there was now nothing to buy, except for the street itself.

The 42nd Street Art Project ran through the summers of 1993 and 1994. Around this time, the Walt Disney Company and others began to express an active interest in renting space on the street. The art had served its purpose, and the installations were removed to make way for new construction, leaving Forty-second Street little more than a block of candy-colored empty storefronts, with a few businesses—a theater, a café, and a few souvenir stores—open at the intersection of Forty-

second Street and Seventh Avenue, just off of Times Square. Later in the decade, the Development Corporation finally found tenants and financing to build the huge office towers they had hoped for. As demolition and new construction got underway, new green façades went up to cover the crayon-hued storefronts, which by the end of my fieldwork in the area had begun to look pretty dingy. (Once the market for corporate development on Forty-second Street picked up momentum, the Development Corporation had much less incentive to keep repainting them.) However, unlike the Development Corporation's original "blue wall," these new façades were not blank. Rather, they were decked with an exhibition of photographs, titled "The People of Forty-second Street." There were about 250 of these photos when the exhibit went up in mid-1998, though the number varied, as exhibit space depended on the pace of building on the new office towers. Each photo showed an enlarged head-and-shoulders portrait against a white background— men and women of all ages and races. An accompanying caption in the lower corner of the photo gave the subject's stated reasons for visiting Forty-second Street; these ranged from "Hanging around" to "Meeting blind date" to "Documenting the changes in Times Square."[29]

The "People of Forty-second Street" exhibit seemed to come from nowhere. In this way, it was like all graffiti, official and otherwise—one day, it appears. A few years afterwards, on the event of the photos being published as a book, I heard a radio interview with the exhibit's photographer; he explained that he and his assistants had simply set up a white backdrop in an old theater entrance and taken a picture of everyone who passed by and felt like stopping in (with a few celebrity "ringers" thrown in, like rapper DMC, writer Tama Janowitz, and the Blue Man Group performance troupe).[30] But nothing of this process was apparent when these signs went up. There was no way of knowing how these faces had been selected as "The People of Forty-second Street." When I first saw the photos, what most struck me was that the people to whom I paid attention when I hung around Forty-second Street seemed totally absent from the exhibit. There were no police officers (at least none in uniform). There were no "flyer guys" passing out handbills for strip clubs. There were no street preachers of any denomination, neither Scientologists nor evangelical Christians; not even the black supremacists from the Israeli Church of Universal Practical Knowledge, who often set up their loudspeakers at the corner of Forty-second Street and Eighth Avenue. There were no members of the security guards and street cleaners who worked for the Times Square

Business Improvement District. There were no crews from the nearby Midtown Community Court, sweating out their sentences painting fire hydrants or erasing graffiti. (There *was* one portrait of a uniformed member of the Guardian Angels vigilante organization, a burly Asian man wearing the Guardian Angels' distinctive red beret, who was quoted in his caption as saying that he was "On patrol." I wasn't sure, but I thought I recognized him from the afternoons I had spent chatting with the Angels at their base in a donated walkup office in a seedy Eighth Avenue tenement. When I returned later with my camera, to take a picture of his picture, the poster had been removed.)

In other words, nobody in "The People of Forty-second Street" fit the definition of "urban characters" that I had been carrying around in my head during my fieldwork. In my attention to the people who *had* to be on Forty-second Street or in Times Square, I had more or less ignored these photographed people: tourists, average folks, passersby. And yet, here they were, their pictures smiling cordially at everyone who, like them, happened to pass down Forty-second Street—a public exhibition by the Forty-second Street Development Corporation of the sorts of people they wanted to attract to the block. I found the overall aesthetic effect of the exhibit to be enormously pleasing. It felt tremendously inviting to pass by one flatteringly photographed average person after another, each with their own individual reason for having come to the area, each smiling benevolently back at the viewer. The pictures impressed generosity, inclusion, and life on what was, at that time, a fairly wretched street; a strip of construction sites, fenced off from the sidewalk and hanging over it with dark, claustrophobic scaffolding.

This sense of friendly, watchful habitation in an uninhabited place fit perfectly with the Development Corporation's overall aesthetic strategy in managing the experience of Forty-second Street. Looking at the photos, I was reminded of something Robertson told me during our conversation: "I used to think of our project as *good housekeeping*. . . . You know, you do your house, you think about what it's going to look like, you do it differently at different seasons and different times, and you treat it in a personal way. . . . Buildings . . . get infused with personality." Like all the art exhibits described above, the faces of "The People of Forty-second Street" worked to saturate the street, erasing all potential gaps or dark spaces in which, it was feared, sex, crime, or other unapproved uses might find a niche. (It is perhaps a sign of their success that the pictures presented an inviting target for vandals, who drew devils' horns and obscene comments on the faces or scratched out their eyes,

but the damaged photos were always replaced in a matter of days with fresh, unmarked copies.) Furthermore, the faces modeled for potential commercial developers and tenants the demographic they might hope to reach if they were to lease space on Forty-second Street. They presented a vision of the street as fully inhabited by a desirable mass of individuals; a potential target audience. In doing so, like the earlier deployments of public art on Forty-second Street, the photos packaged the space of the street itself, holding it open and keeping it fresh and new. They "infused with personality" Forty-second Street, a space whose personality (if we can say it had one) was never more uncertain, never more at risk, than in the years when the Development Corporation took control over it.

Niches and Corners: The Port Authority Bus Terminal

This same form of aesthetic tactics was applied to another famous site in the Times Square area—not to an outdoor streetscape or a public park, but to the interior of a privately owned space: the Port Authority bus terminal, located at the corner of Forty-second Street and Eighth Avenue, one block west of Times Square. Managed by the Port Authority of New York and New Jersey, the terminal building was constructed in the 1950s, in conjunction with what was then the new Lincoln Tunnel, which ran under the Hudson River, connecting the island of Manhattan to neighboring New Jersey. The building itself dominates two entire city blocks, from Fortieth Street to Forty-second Street between Eighth and Ninth Avenues, with a maze of ramps overshadowing what is left of the old residential neighborhood to the west of the terminal.

As centers catering to, and frequented by, new arrivals, people passing through, or those seeking anonymity, bus terminals and transportation hubs in general form the locus of "the stranger's path" in any city.[31] Until recently, the Port Authority terminal was, perhaps, the most extreme example of this. As the western gateway to Forty-second Street and Times Square, the terminal had acquired a reputation as something of a social free-for-all.[32] In the press of the twenty-four-hour-a-day swirl of commuters, tourists, and travelers, people found spaces to engage in practices officially foresworn in public: taking or proffering drugs, pandering, hooking up for sex, or sleeping. Panhandlers, drug dealers, prostitutes, pimps, and other street hustlers worked the crowds. They were aided by the terminal building's warren of corridors

connecting hundreds of bus gates. Men cruised each other from the terminal floor or from the vantage of the balconies overlooking the main entranceway, scanning for sexual contacts, commercial or otherwise. People found a myriad of out-of-the-way corners in which to sleep, or counted on the terminal's air of liminality to shield them when they lay down with their belongings in public. Religious proselytizers, social services outreach workers, and sociologists all came to the Port Authority bus terminal in search of those who found shelter there.[33] Folklore has it that pimps came to the Port Authority terminal to nab unsuspecting would-be stars and starlets fresh off the bus from some farmyard; thus the nickname NYPD officers gave to the stretch of Eighth Avenue near the terminal: the Minnesota Strip.

But by the mid-1990s, the Port Authority had invested a great deal of time, thought, and money to change all that. I met Ken Philmus, the Port Authority manager who had overseen the cleanup of the terminal building, at a local community meeting, where, to an uninterested crowd of local functionaries, he had enthusiastically announced the Port Authority's plans to transform the outside of the terminal. Philmus said that the Port Authority wanted to deck the terminal with giant advertisements, similar to those in Times Square; to provide lights below the ramps that swooped out of the terminal, both in order to serve as an anticrime measure by lighting the streets below and to further "landmark" the building, giving it a more distinctive architectural profile; to build a new office tower above the terminal; and to install a golf driving range at the base of this new tower, to make the bus terminal a destination for lunchtime business meetings. Nobody else at the meeting seemed to pay much attention to his presentation, but I was fascinated, and I approached him after the meeting to tell him that I wanted to learn more about the changes that had already taken place inside the building. A few weeks later, I interviewed him in his office on the second floor of the terminal building. Throughout our conversation, the room rumbled with the heavy bass vibrations of busses leaving from the gates around us. Once I got used to the sound and sensation, it formed a pleasant background for our talk.

The first thing Philmus did was to play me a series of television advertisements the Port Authority had commissioned to publicize the changes they had made. In these ads, each lasting about thirty seconds, actors playing commuters stand as though waiting for a bus. The ad situates these commuters in empty space; they stand in a white void. They gaze absently about them with an attitude of studied indifference, as

bus terminal sound effects, such as revving engines, loudspeakers, and clanging doors, echo around them. The first ad shows a white man and an African American woman, both well-dressed, as they attempt to ignore a booming, metallic male voice that recites, "Now arriving at New York's Port Authority bus terminal. . . ." Instead of listing bus arrivals, the voice recites various improvements to the terminal building: "Brighter entrances, new information booths, convenient shops, attended bathrooms. . . ." As the voice rolls through this list, the two "commuters" begin to listen more and more closely. Then the voice reaches the last item on its list: "A new sense of protection and service." Suddenly, everything changes. Brash, power-chord-heavy rock music surges on the soundtrack.[34] The actors yell joyfully and grab hold of each other. The ad closes with a montage of them dancing wildly together, as a female voice reads a slogan that comes whizzing out at the viewer on the screen, word by word: "The Port Authority—you should see what we've done!"

The second advertisement begins with much the same scenario: two actor-commuters, one man, one woman, stand together in an implied bus terminal. (This time, their races are reversed.) Again, the voice booms through a list of improvements to the building: "Sparkling corridors, trendy cafés, late-night departure areas, bank machines. . . ." Again, the two people on the screen slowly come out of their shells, the man looking up from his paper, the woman removing her headphones. Again, when the voice announces, "A new sense of protection and service," music blares; this time, it is the Hallelujah Chorus. And again, the two cheer and embrace. But the music cuts off suddenly, and they back away from each other. The ad ends as the chastened commuters attempt to straighten their clothes while, pointedly, not looking at each other.

In the last of the three ads, we see a lone white male commuter wearing a shabby coat. He stands, reading the paper, bags under his eyes and a bag at his feet. As in the previous ads, the voice from above begins to speak. "Now arriving at New York's Port Authority bus terminal. . . ." Unlike the commuters in the previous two ads, the man talks back; we see a close-up of his face as he rolls his eyes and mutters, "Heeere we go. . . ." The voice recites, "Clearer signs, vandal-proof phones. . . ." He scoffs, "Yeah, right." When he hears "Great new shops," the man laughs out loud, saying, "You gotta be kidding me!" The voice replies to him, insisting, "No, sir, we're not kidding you." The man looks up and around, startled and dumbfounded. The voice finishes its list with, "And a new sense of protection and service, for peace of mind." "Peace of mind!" the man yells, and he throws his paper aside and drops to

his knees, clasping his hands and raising them in a posture of devout gratitude as the music of a church organ rises on the soundtrack. "Oh, thank you!" But the voice speaks to him again, saying, "Please, sir, pull yourself together." As the commercial ends, we see the man collecting his composure and trying to whistle with forced nonchalance.

The Port Authority bus terminal is largely absent in these advertisements. It is shown only as an empty white space, sparsely populated and ringing with the sounds of busses and a single, booming voice. Instead of showing us the terminal building, the ads tell us about it, as a list of conveniences and improvements. The voice does not mention what the terminal was like before the improvements. Similarly, the ad relies on familiarity or imagination to fill in an image of the terminal in the blank whiteness shown on the screen. In other words, the ad plays with a viewer's presumed negative experience with, or stereotype of, the bus terminal. The ad plays with the stereotypical reality of the terminal in other ways. The booming voice reads its list of improvements as though it was making a routine announcement of bus arrivals and departures. However, the Port Authority has no such public address system; schedules are posted on signs and in brochures, not announced. In other words, the ad asks us to *imagine* a terminal in which the Port Authority speaks with a single, public voice, even though viewers on local cable television, where the ads were shown, would presumably know that there was no such voice at the actual terminal.

This voice holds all the power in the ads. The actors play jaded commuters who have heard optimistic claims about improved city services in the past; they feel they know better than to believe the claims the Port Authority makes, at least at first. They sigh and do their best to ignore the voice, but to no avail. Their casual skepticism crumbles when they hear the last item on the voice's list, "A new sense of protection and service." As they believe the voice, so, too, they lose their defensive anonymity toward one another—the "blasé attitude" long pegged as the hallmark of modern urban life.[35] They dance, they embrace; in the last ad, the scoffing man swoons to his knees, overcome and helpless with thanks. But the voice of the Port Authority insists on decorum, saying to him, "Pull yourself together." Similarly, the sudden cut in the music in the second ad stifles the commuters' spontaneous celebration, forcing them back into themselves.

When the ads were finished, Philmus popped the tape out of the VCR, and we began to talk at length about the efforts to transform the Port Authority building that the ads were meant to publicize. He

told me that, as he saw it, the problem with the terminal had been that commuters and others who passed through to use the busses were intimidated by those who used the building as the wrong kind of shelter: "People were scared, and rightly so. Because, I mean, the guy who's lying around and sleeping on the floor is the same guy who robbed somebody yesterday. They're a crack addict, or whatever they may be or have been. . . . [Y]ou came in here five or six years ago and there were people laying on the floor, people doing all sorts of things that were breaking rules and regulations, they may not have necessarily been fully criminal things, but they were homeless people." At the same time, he acknowledged that the law prohibited the Port Authority from simply removing those they regarded as "undesirables" from the terminal. Several well-publicized court cases had determined that transportation terminals were to be legally regarded as public spaces, and people using them couldn't be removed arbitrarily. "They were human beings and they had every right to be in the building just like you or I. . . . [We didn't] just want to throw people out." The Port Authority was faced with a dilemma similar to the ones described in the sections earlier on Bryant Park and Forty-second Street: How to control a public space without resorting to a straightforward policy of exclusion?

As Philmus described it to me, one of the ways he addressed this dilemma was to resort to aesthetic tactics of saturation and surveillance, quite similar to the tactics already discussed in this chapter. He showed me how he could access the building's closed-circuit security system via the control panel at his desk; the image on the monitor flickered as he switched between the dozens of cameras situated throughout and around the building. But I had noticed the Port Authority bus terminal surveillance system before. In fact, it was impossible to miss the guards sitting at the huge bank of monitors that perched between the balcony and the main floor of the terminal building in its south wing. He explained that, previously, the security monitors had been hidden away in private offices like his, but that the Port Authority had taken the strategic step of making it a prominent, public part of the building. This served two functions. First, the control center interrupted the circuits of eye contact that had formerly passed between men cruising each other from the various levels of the terminal building. Second, and more generally, the pod of desks, monitors, and office chairs was part of an overall architectural rhetoric of control: "[W]e don't want to hide it, we want them to know that we're watching, that we're in control. . . . If you were here five or six years ago . . . there was a sense

that the building was out of control. There's clearly a sense now that the building is in total control. That's the image that we want to have. Not that it's a dictatorship or a despot, but that we have control of this building. And the commuter and the traveler can say, 'They know what they're doing.'" In other words, the newly public control center served a dual purpose. Not only did it allow the Port Authority to block people from sending unwanted messages to each other by filling up the empty space between levels, but it was also a message in itself—part of a larger circuit of communication that connected the management, the building, and desirable and undesirable users alike.

Philmus referred to this principle of the architecture and aesthetics of control again when he described the layout of one of the upscale cafés in the terminal building:

> [G]o out and look at the back of [a café in the terminal building]. It's a trapezoid . . . and there's a stair out to Forty-first Street. [He sketches the layout on a piece of paper as he explains this to me.] This was a nightmare, this stair. People were sleeping there, drugs were sold, drug addicts, prostitution, you name it. . . . I insisted that this back wall be glass. [Points with his pencil] Because now everybody in [the café] is going to see out to the stairs, and these people don't want to be seen. And their customers don't want to see it, so management will turn around and call the police and say, "Hey, there's somebody on the stairs." [Snaps fingers] Like that. It's gone. Problem is over.

He called this style of design "defensive architecture." Putting the security center in public view and opening up lines of sight to hidden nooks were both part of making the Port Authority terminal building architecturally "defensive." The last part of this defensive strategy was to remove all hidden spaces, a program the manager called his "Niches and Corners" survey. He told me that he interviewed everyone who worked in and around the building: security guards, janitors, ticket agents, bus drivers, etc. He asked each one about the places in the building where people could hide to sleep. "I said, 'Where are they? Where are the problems, where are the people, where are they hiding?' And we made a catalog, and one by one, we fixed them—took [the hiding places] away." He described how he and his team had bricked over corners, closed heating ducts, and sealed off overhangs at the gate areas, all to remove the places that made it possible to use the building in unwanted ways.

But the cleanup of the Port Authority terminal went beyond these architectural and aesthetic strategies. Along with these, Philmus told me that he had invited Urban Pathways, a social-services agency, to open an office in the terminal building itself, as part of a program that he had named "Operation Alternative." "[W]e have the alternative of saying to somebody, 'Either you get help, and we have it for you . . . if you won't take help, get out of my building. . . . You're breaking a rule or regulation, you're lying on the floor, you're spitting, you're urinating, whatever it might be—either take help or we'll ask you to leave, or give you a summons, or arrest you.' . . . And that's what the purpose of Urban Pathways is." The Port Authority cannot remove people from the building just for sleeping there. However, they *can* insist that someone sleeping in the building move to the offices of Urban Pathways. "If you won't take help, get out of my building." In other words, the Port Authority could not legally construe the presence of sleeping people in the terminal as a threat to commuters, but they could take it as a sign of threat to the sleeping people themselves.

I interviewed the woman in charge of the Urban Pathways office in the terminal building. Based on my conversation with her, and also on what others in the area told me about her agency, there is no question in my mind that Urban Pathways provides meaningful assistance in a thoughtful way to people who genuinely need their help. My point here is to highlight the ways in which the Port Authority's inclusion of Urban Pathways in the redeveloped terminal constitutes part of a larger strategy, that of finding tactics other than outright exclusion to control public spaces. Under "Operation Alternative," providing social services, such as referral to a shelter, becomes just such an option: an offer to help someone for their own good and for your good as well; an offer they cannot refuse.

This move on the part of the Port Authority to offer therapy, shelter, or other forms of "crisis intervention" to those they wish to clear from the terminal has a strong rhetorical component. They do not treat those they seek to remove as breaking the law. Rather, they treat them as though they were violating supposedly natural rules of behavior in public places.[36] As Philmus explained to me, "[The terminal]'s not a desirable place for someone to be for a reason other than to take a bus. There's no reason for them to be here." With this in mind, he said, "We made it a little uncomfortable—they couldn't be in here, they couldn't hide, they had to be in the open." But, to a great extent, the cleanup of the Port Authority bus terminal also needed to make it a place that

was *very* desirable for all sorts of reasons other than catching a bus. Remember the list of new amenities that the voice of the Authority recites in the television advertisements: "convenient shops, trendy cafes . . . " (not to mention the terminal's popular bowling alley). And remember the community meeting where I first heard the manager speak; he described the plans to make the terminal building a fun place for business meetings by installing a golf driving range on the roof.

I asked Philmus whether it ever became difficult to balance these two goals—to make the terminal building "a little uncomfortable" for some, but still comfortable enough to please travelers or people spending money at the new shops and cafés. He replied, "They're different needs. It is a balance, but they're different needs. It's definitely comfortable for people to travel through. That doesn't mean it's comfortable for someone to live in. Yeah, the temperature is fine, it's warm. . . . [I]f they want to come in, they have to keep walking, they have to keep moving. . . . [T]hat's not the comfort they're looking for, they're looking for a place where they can lie down and go to sleep. And we don't have those places."

Thus, according to this example, one can police a space like the Port Authority bus terminal according to a political economy of comfort. The space itself must be imbued with a low-level unease; a tension that impels motion, pushing people around and through the building without letting them find too much shelter there. The Forty-second Street Development Corporation wanted passersby to slow their pace and turn their heads when they walked down Forty-second Street from the terminal to Times Square; the Bryant Park Restoration Project redesigned the park in order to make it more inviting for people to enter and stay there. By contrast, in the Port Authority bus terminal, the *absence* of bodies at rest is precisely the image that drove the cleanup effort. This image rings loud and clear through all the areas described above: in the architecture of the building; in the new policies that govern its use; and, poetically, in the tellingly blank void that represents the terminal in the television advertisements.

It is also symbolized in one of the Port Authority bus terminal's pieces of public art, a kinetic sculpture by artist George Rhoads, entitled "Forty-second Street Ballroom," which has sat just inside one of the entrances of the terminal's north wing since the mid-1980s. Encased inside a transparent eight-foot cube, the sculpture is composed of a twisting labyrinth of brightly colored metal tracks, along which a number of billiard balls roll, spin, hop, bounce, and fly in an endless, complex

dance. Like many other visitors to the Port Authority building, I have stood rooted in front of "Forty-second Street Ballroom," hypnotized; it seems possible to watch for hours as the balls move through their maze. The effect is one of constant, flowing motion, combined with sharp anticipation: Look, one of the balls is finally going to bounce into that swinging cup! This ball looks like it's going to fall off the track—wait, it dropped into that spiral shape! When will another ball come along and dislodge the one caught in this tight angle over here? In this way, "Forty-second Street Ballroom" hearkens powerfully to the experience of watching from a distance as people move through complex public spaces like Times Square or the Port Authority terminal itself; it captures the same fascinating sense of abstraction and pure motion.[37]

At the same time, if the sculpture presents a vision of how crowds of people move through complex, open urban spaces, it is also a vision of these crowds that is highly structured, even choreographed. The balls are moving by gravity along pathways choreographed and constructed by a single intelligence. The flow of constant movement that the "Ballroom" sculpture represents is precisely the vision of urban public space that the Port Authority attempts to enforce in its cleaned-up terminal building: entertaining, continuously flowing, visually coherent, under control.

Architects, planners, developers, and others sought to create lucrative self-policing spaces in Times Square by building a certain form of intimacy into the very material structure of the city itself. The redevelopers used built space in the New Times Square as a technology for social engineering; shaping space, and bodies in space, in order to create idealized, highly marketable images of public places that are civil, yet exciting—places of "safe danger."[38] These places of safe danger were meant as advertisements to sell "Times Square" as a brand name. The new and transformed built spaces described in this chapter presented a catalog of idealized images of urban life: the dancing commuters, framed against a white void, overjoyed at the liberation of the Port Authority bus terminal; the broad green rectangle of the lawn in Bryant Park, filled with picnickers by day and glowing under artificial moonlight by night; the blaze of more, newer, bigger signs in Times Square; Forty-second Street, the Deuce turned into an art gallery.

The combination of money, creativity, political power, and good timing (and fortuitous delays) made it possible for the redevelopers of Times Square and Forty-second Street to make these images a reality, and the places they have created and transformed do offer tremendous

pleasures. They sought to create urban spaces that harnessed and intensified the power of Times Square's spectacular advertising, theaters, and crowds as social control mechanisms that would help maintain the area's new overall image of respectability. These social control mechanisms were meant to help drive out all the diverse phenomena the redevelopers homogenize into the category of "blight": prostitution, drugs, pornography, homelessness and visible poverty, gay cruising scenes, landlords not investing heavily in their properties . . . as though these represented an attack on Times Square by alien forces, rather than inherent aspects and products of its very existence.

The redevelopers redefined Times Square by editing all these people and practices right out of the built environment, giving them no room. Instead, they created a place that is saturated more than ever before by light, color, powerful images of desire. In other words, they invested massively in precisely the same things that observers early in Times Square's history saw as causing, or even constituting, social blight. Out of this problematic mixture of crowds, money, and spectacle, they created a fantasy image of the city as a space of controlled disorder—a space of pleasure and excitement, but within a context in which the spaces of the city, and the lives its inhabitants make, are always-already for sale.

The Midtown Community Court
Intimacy and Power in an Experimental Courtroom

One thing that made the redevelopment of Times Square so strikingly different from typical urban renewal projects was its collection of self-conscious, highly publicized efforts to "reach out" to marginal groups and include them in its transformation, rather than just exclude them from the area. These efforts represented a new strategy in the redevelopers' toolkit—a way to lessen negative publicity while still cleansing their new built spaces and surfaces of the public presence of poverty and filth. They also shed light on the redevelopment's transformation of the meanings of urban citizenship.

Urban planning and architecture have always drawn connections, implicit or explicit, between "city making and citizen making."[1] The built spaces of the city are always shaped around particular definitions of what sorts of people are going to inhabit them and what those people are and are not going to do there. Similarly, we shape our legal and social definitions of what it means to be a citizen around images of people acting and interacting in particular social spaces.

One form this took was a strong connection between the redevelopers and social service agencies and programs for the homeless, as in the ties between the Port Authority and Urban Pathways (as described in chapter three), or in the Times Square BID recruiting their sanitation crews from a local homeless service center. The BID's own publicity materials described an interestingly intimate relationship between the BID's own outreach workers and Times Square's homeless population; the BID knew (and probably still knows) every individual person who was reluctant to accept the offer of services.

These public-private partnerships actively incorporated social services outreach as a strategy for creating and maintaining a "cleaned-up" and thus more marketable streetscape. But this was far more than just a crass real estate tactic. These efforts represented the redevelopment's fundamental redefinition of the rules and meanings of citizenship in the spaces of Times Square. Redeveloping Times Square meant rewriting the definitions of criminality, community, and the rule of law. Nowhere was this more apparent than in the experimental courtroom–slash–social services and outreach center called the Midtown Community Court.

The Midtown Community Court

Affiliated with the city court system but funded by Broadway theater owners and private foundations, the Community Court was opened in 1993, in part as a result of efforts by local property owners to protect the Broadway theater industry and the rest of the New Times Square from prostitutes, petty drug dealers, illegal street vendors, and the homeless.[2] Real estate entrepreneurs and developers felt that these "undesirables" threatened the attractiveness of Times Square real estate by their very presence in the area.[3] These developers, in turn, provided the financial and political capital for the Community Court's core group of dedicated legal activists and social services experts. John Feinblatt, who was intimately involved with the creation of the court (and who is now serving as New York City's criminal justice coordinator) told this story:

> The court was born out of frustration. There was frustration within the court system about quality-of-life crimes. Judges felt they didn't have the tools to do their job. When it came to sentencing, they had to choose between "band-aids or brain surgery." But there was also frustration within the community. The residential

community of Clinton felt that their neighborhood had been inundated with street-corner drug sales and with prostitution, and there was certainly frustration a bit further east in the Times Square area, which was terribly frustrated by its inability to create the economic development boom it had hoped would occur. In Times Square, there was a deeply held sense that crime had just taken a very serious toll on economic development and economic activity, which I think it had. . . . I was deputy director of [a social services agency] at the time. And a mentor and a good friend of mine, Herb Sturz [who had worked in city government] and was at that time a real estate developer, was having breakfast with a friend of his, Gerald Schoenfeld [the head of the Shubert Organization, which owns a majority of Broadway theaters in New York City]. Gerry was rightfully bemoaning over bagels the toll crime had taken on Times Square and on Broadway theater ticket sales specifically. My friend Herb said that maybe the thing to do was to try an experiment, which was to have a community-based court right in the middle of Times Square. And [Schoenfeld] didn't miss a beat, and offered up [what was called] at that time the Longacre Theater, which had been dark for a couple of years. The funny story about the Longacre is that the first play produced there was the play, *It Takes a Thief,* and the last play to be produced there was *Ain't Misbehavin.'* So it seemed like the right theater, even though close by there was a theater called the Cort Theater, which would have been even better. So with real estate in hand, suddenly the words "community court" had some currency.

This group's goal was to test what was then a highly experimental approach to dealing with misdemeanor crimes: to create an integrated, rehabilitation-oriented institution that would address local residents' and property owners' concerns while providing meaningful services and treatment to the offenders. The origin story told above captures the ways in which social programs and real estate development are profoundly enmeshed with each other. Social programs need real estate to gather political and financial capital and real estate needs social programs to create the public image they seek.

Under this new program, the police took anyone they arrest for misdemeanor crimes like shoplifting, hopping subway turnstiles, or drinking in public in the Times Square area to the Midtown Community Court instead of to the centralized courtroom in Lower Manhattan. If the

defendant pled guilty at the Community Court, the judge there can sentence him or her to community service—to be carried out immediately and in the immediate area—as well as to a mix of counseling and medical treatment, some of which was available in the court building itself.

The court was able to do this in part because of its sophisticated computer system, which drew together the defendant's complete record and makes it available to the judge, the prosecuting and defense attorneys, and to the multiple social service providers based in the building itself. Not only did the computer system inform the arraignment process in the courtroom, but it allowed the judge and other parties to see at a glance how well someone was holding to their assigned sentence and course of treatment. As Eric Lee, the designer of the court's computer system, explained to me, "There's this graphic that has dots, that gives you a quick graphic summary of whether the person is in treatment doing what they're supposed to be doing, and whether their urine tests are what they're supposed to be or not. And it allows the judge in a second to look at what the picture is, and either congratulate or reprimand or impose a sanction on someone who's in long-term drug treatment."

Along with the computer tracking system, the court also created a new position within the social system of the courtroom itself, that of "resource coordinator." The resource coordinator was charged with examining the records in every case, discussing the case with both attorneys, making a recommendation to the judge, then following up with any outside agencies involved. As Eric Lee described the position to me,

The idea is that there are a broad range of alternatives, a far greater range of sanctions than are available in most courtrooms. Because the judge has a substantial case load, the resource coordinator makes recommendations that are thoughtful and which address the specific problems of a particular case. For most low-level cases, the recommendations are fairly consistent—for example several days of community service or short-term drug treatment. But on a significant minority of cases, there are specific kinds of problems, mental illness, homelessness, drug addiction, that require a tailored recommendation. And so the question is, "How can the court constructively address this problem?" The resource coordinator is the person who works to answer that question and calculates a sentencing recommendation. The other thing that the resource coordinator does, which is terribly important, is to serve as a bridge between the court and programs running the

nontraditional sanctions, like community service, drug treatment, prostitution groups, education groups, and so forth. The resource coordinator ensures the credibility of these programs in the courtroom. If there's ever a contested issue—"Did the person show up or did they not? Was the group cancelled, and the person showed up but got marked as a 'no'?"—the resource coordinator can get accurate, detailed information and ensure that the courtroom knows exactly what happened, so that their confidence in the programs remains high.

In other words, through this combination of the computer tracking system and the intermediary position of the resource coordinator, the Midtown Community Court effectively chipped away at traditional rigid lines separating prosecution, defense, and judgment. Here in the court, to a much greater extent than in a traditional courtroom, all the parties were talking to each other and working together to craft a sentence that suited the particular misdemeanor case before them.

"Thank You for Sending Your Prisoners"

The Community Court went out of its way to make itself known to the people in the area around it. Those assigned to carry out community service sentences, planting trees, cleaning graffiti, or painting fire hydrants, wore distinctive bright orange mesh vests while they work. Even critics of the court I spoke with mentioned these work crews, citing the impact they had on the aesthetics of the neighborhood: "They get their fire hydrants painted—how nice is that!" In the larger scope of New York City's seemingly permanent fiscal crisis, even during the relative boom times of the late 1990s, basic upkeep on municipal amenities like fire hydrants or lampposts could be deferred, apparently, forever. For a poorer neighborhood to have a steady source of free upkeep was no small benefit.

Community Court staff visited community meetings around Hell's Kitchen during my fieldwork in the area, describing the court and asking residents what sorts of services they might need from the community service work crews. Even when court staff were not present, people discussed the court and its impact on the neighborhood. At one meeting of the Forty-sixth Street Block Association I attended in the fall of 1997, the head of the association reported that a community service

crew from the Community Court had cleaned the tree pits on the block between Ninth and Tenth Avenues. This led to a joking discussion of whether, and how, to thank the Midtown Community Court for sending its arraignees to clean up the area. Someone asked, "How do you word that?" People jokingly tossed out several ideas: "'Thank you for sending your prisoners'?" "'Thank you for committing crimes in the area'?"

These outreach efforts to local groups were not seen as trivial by the court. Rather, they were part of what court employees characterized to me as its larger mission of redefining the meanings of criminality, victimhood, punishment, and rehabilitation. Just as the computer system and the resource coordinator served to connect the normally largely separate and oppositional prosecution and defense in the arraignment hearings, so the court worked to redefine the concept of victimhood and the impacts of "victimless crimes." As John Feinblatt told me,

Our breakthrough notion . . . was this very simple phrase: not only are individuals victims, but neighborhoods and blocks and communities are victims, too. When we first articulated that, we started to understand a lot of the power behind the Community Court. . . . Just as victims of crime felt left out, so did communities. And not only did communities feel shut out but so did social-service providers who had a powerful nexus to crime, because of the strong association between drug addiction and criminal activity. Service providers were like stepchildren to the criminal justice process—sort of an appendage, at best, to court systems, rather than inside players. One of our interests was to answer, "How do you integrate the criminal justice service delivery system with the health care delivery system and the treatment delivery system?" You know, traditionally, courts deal with "the case." The "case" at Midtown is not a terribly complicated case, certainly not from a legal perspective. But the crimes at Midtown are committed by people with very complicated lives, and they have a very complicated impact on the fabric of the community. It's those latter two things that we decided were worth focusing on. Certainly one didn't need to raise lots of money and get lots of federal research dollars to think about how to prosecute a jumping-the-turnstile case or a prostitution case. But you do need [support] if you want to think about why that case occurred, and how to deal with them in a more *problem-solving* way, and involve various stakeholders in fashioning the response.

This vision of the court's "stakeholders" extended not only into the surrounding neighborhood, but also across another traditional line of separation: between the courtroom and the police station. As Eric Lee explained to me, they specifically worked to include the NYPD and its individual officers in their network of information and "accountability":

> Generally, a police officer does not know what the outcome in court is when they make a misdemeanor arrest. We wanted the police to understand that what happens at Midtown Community Court is different and that the results are better. So we started giving the police paper reports which list every arrest, arranged by arresting officer, and which spell out the outcome in court—they pled guilty, they received a sentence of community service, did two days of community service, and so forth. We started that in our first year, doing these reports on a monthly basis. The officers loved it—it was very well received—and so we automated it. Now at Midtown North, in the precinct next to the court, there's a PC in the warrant squad-room where the officers can go and they can check on the status of any case that has come to the Midtown Community Court. They can look and see what happened on a particular case, they can look up their own arrests, they can look and see if someone has a warrant. They can get a really quick answer on what the outcomes are that are achieved in the Midtown Community Court. This is an important experiment in getting information to a partner, the police, who are often ignored or overlooked.

In this way, the Community Court redefined the formal relationships that otherwise might separate or oppose prosecution, defense, judge, social services, community organizations, and the police. All were included together as part of a single "problem-solving" unit, bringing to bear tremendous attention and resources to deal with cases that in most other courts would be seen as trivial at best.

An Intimate Court

Manhattan's huge central downtown courtroom struck me as rundown and impersonal during my visits to it. By contrast, the Midtown Community Court building seemed both intimate and sparklingly clean. The Community Court shared its space on West Fifty-fourth Street with

a number of small theater companies. When one first entered the court building, one saw a long, bright hallway lined with colorful maps and theatrical posters; the metal detectors through which all who enter the court must pass were not located at the front door, but just to the side of the building's main entrance. The holding cells were lined with clear Plexiglas instead of metal bars. Arraignment hearings at the court were held in a brightly lit, heavy-timbered room filled with wooden benches. The room felt more like a small chapel than the dark and lofty courtrooms downtown. The sixth floor of the Midtown Community Court building held the offices where defendants who pled guilty were sent to receive their community service sentences, counseling, drug tests, or acupuncture (for withdrawal symptoms). There was also a drop-in center, stocked with soup, bread, and pamphlets. Several employees of the court proudly told me that people who had completed their sentences sometimes returned to this center on their own: for food, to talk with a counselor, or for referrals to shelters or drug treatment programs.

The Midtown Community Court consciously cultivated this sense of itself as an intimate and inclusive space, conveniently housing resources that, in New York City, were ordinarily distributed among several organizations, located far from one another throughout the city. I asked John Megaw, the court's "treatment coordinator," about this experiment in courtroom design. He explained that, as he saw it, having everything together in one building was important for the sake of fostering, in drug users and other petty criminals, a desire to enter and stay in therapeutic treatment programs. He said, "[D]esire wanes as soon as you walk out of the building. . . . When you open the door and say, 'You need to go down the street,' you know, the *street,* we see it over and over again. . . . There's no question that we lose a lot of folks from here to the subway to the treatment program." Megaw went on to speculate about how beneficial it would be if an employee of the Midtown Community Court could personally accompany those in drug treatment from the court building to their treatment programs, to "help keep them focused on what it is they need to do." When I asked him to elaborate on why he thought traveling between the court and outside treatment programs presented a problem for drug users, he said:

> There are thousands of people out there that would be more than willing to . . . sell them crack. . . . [E]very time you go back into that environment, you have these pleasurable experiences, you know, "Thirty-eighth Street" or "Forty-eighth Street." Over time,

your brain remembers all these good experiences. . . . And the problem is that they don't have a whole lot of pleasurable experiences [of] clean time in their life because they just haven't experienced them. You have to sort of retrain people about, "You can have good experiences, get good associations about being clean."

His words mapped the drug user's body as contested ground, the site of a turf war between two competing desires. The first is a desire for drugs, engrained into the user's body by a history of experiential engagement with Midtown Manhattan's drug markets. This desire lured the user away from treatment the moment he or she left the rubric of the court. The second desire, which the court hopes to impart to its subjects, is a rational and well-meaning desire to improve oneself by ceasing to use drugs. But this second desire is often more fragile than the first. It has to be protected from the predations of the first in order to flourish.[4]

Thus, the Community Court's spatial totality—its enfolding of multiple institutions, normally bureaucratically distributed into separate buildings—was designed in part as a strategy against the undesirable's own mechanisms of desire. The physical layout of the court building sought to open up a space for public-minded subjects to take shape by denying access to public spaces, which the court saw as filled with possibilities for antisocial desire. The court created an "in here" to combat the dangers "out there." The court "helped keep [the users] focused" by creating a space that would work to replace one set of memories and desires with another. This turning-away from one desire in favor of another was constructed as a choice to be free—to free oneself from the effects of a drug habit, for instance. However, this was a choice that could not be made freely. In other words, one could be free to choose not to use drugs only when one was freed from the world that surrounded the court—the world of the streets of Times Square.

In this way, the Midtown Community Court presented itself as a place to which "quality-of-life offenders," even while being processed through the system, could retreat, to recover their true selves and leave behind bad desires. And the court certainly served this function for many, many people. But this work of freeing "quality-of-life" offenders from their untoward desires also benefited those who stood to profit from the redevelopment of Times Square. The Midtown Community Court was proposed and funded by the *New York Times* newspaper, the Broadway theater magnates, and others who own property in the area, in order to guarantee the success of their enormous investments in the

area's speculative real estate market. The court had the resources it brought to bear on those bad desires only because its backers feared the impact those desires, and the people acting on them, might have on the highly stylized and controlled image that the corporate real estate market demands. The intensity of the court's effort to rescue "undesirables" from their own bad habits was the result, not just of altruistic concern for their well-being, but of the lucky confluence of some skilled and concerned social service professionals with a huge and risky real estate gamble in Times Square. Simply put, if the redevelopers of Times Square were not so focused on erasing the public presence of these people, the Midtown Community Court would not exist to "help keep them focused" on rehabilitating themselves.

At a Community Court open house I attended, Megaw described the court to the assembled journalists and social service agency workers as "the mall of social services." "People walk in off the street" and get "same-day service," he said; service that helps to connect them, as the court itself is connected, to "the world of business." The presentations at this open house emphasized the court's novel computer system. One person who spoke was the special coordinator who manages this information system in the courtroom itself. He said that the computer system allows his staff to look at every individual's "composite pattern" of behaviors, in order to reveal what he called the "needs that underlie [the arraignee's] criminal behavior." Megaw remarked that this system often takes defendants by surprise. "The defendant feels like Big Brother is watching," he said, mentioning that they often ask him, "'How did the judge know all that about me?'"

This presentation reminded me of one of my original conversations with one of the Midtown Community Court's directors. She told me that part of working in the court's offices was everyday contact between court staff and defendants working off their community service assignments. She said that she might see the same cleaning crews over the course of the week, and that she and others in her staff occasionally befriended individuals on these crews, getting to know them and perhaps connecting them with social services or with a job. She mentioned one court worker who had arranged for the members of one such crew to get jobs with a local messenger service. Such unexpected personal contacts are probably part of any courtroom's functioning. The difference is that the Midtown Community Court, due to its small scale, flexibility, and heavy funding, made these normally informal connections—what she called "the funny little unexpected pathways"—part of its official, formal business.

Arraignment

The actual hearings at the Midtown Community Court presented something quite different from this image of organized informality. By contrast, the Community Court hearings I observed were highly formal and structured, albeit in complex ways. Sitting in the cozy courtroom, one could simultaneously see both the public face and the private machinery of the Court—what Erving Goffman, in his studies of how people organize their public faces, would have called both "front stage" and "back stage."[5] Specifically, "front stage" encompassed everything that happened in direct verbal contact with the judge; almost everything else was treated as invisible, inaudible, and unimportant. There was always a swirl of activity and actors between the wooden spectators' benches and the judge herself—lawyers, assistants, and technicians, running to and fro and consulting the large computer monitors placed throughout the courtroom; security officers moving defendants from their seats to stand before the judge's bench and back; the court coordinator and his staff talking together and looking over sheaves of documents; and so forth. The judge herself always moved calmly, and spoke only in measured, even tones. Others did their best to copy her intonations when they spoke with her. This official register of courtroom speech seemed to cut through the swirl of chatter and rustling papers that otherwise filled the room, and when the judge spoke, everyone dropped whatever they were doing and listened.

Her entrances and exits were always announced by the security officers, whose abrupt bursts of formulaic speech served to punctuate the hearings as a whole. They made their announcements—usually unintelligible but obviously somehow important—at the judge's arrival and before and after each individual hearing, dealing with the public formalities of the law in a memorized rush of words. When the defendants were called, they rose from the undifferentiated lines of pews where they sat alongside the spectators and went to stand before the judge, standing on the same level as the audience but separated from them by a low wooden barrier. After their hearings, they were sent to sit in the benches to the front of the lefthand side of the room; the guards led them out as a group whenever that section filled up.

The hearings themselves tended to be quick, impersonal affairs. Summoned to the bench by the guards, the defendants mostly assumed an automatic, deferential pose, standing with their hands clasped behind their backs, their twisting fingers invisible to the judge but

exposed to the spectators' eyes. They tended to stand frozen, saying little to their lawyers and next to nothing to the judge. The attorneys for the defense—mostly court-appointed lawyers from the Legal Aid Society—had a necessarily generic way of speaking about the people they represented. "My client instructs me . . ." "My client would like me to ask you . . ." (Once, on my way out of the courtroom, I heard a defendant ask one of the lawyers, "Can I ask you a question?" To which the attorney responded, "Were you my client?")

Despite this quick formality, there was also an air of intimacy to these hearings at times. When defendants came before the judge to report on whether they had complied with a previous sentence, Midtown Community Court social services staff occasionally came in to recount how well they had done in counseling or in a drug treatment program. Once, one staff member called for, and got, a round of applause for such a defendant. And the judge said, "This is the best part of my job. . . . Our support staff is here for you. I don't want to see you [again] as a defendant, but I do want to know how you're doing."

But sometimes, of course, this informality was a little less warm. Once, a man who was before the judge, charged with several counts of disorderly conduct, had his case dismissed because, in the words of his attorney, "There's no indication that the disorder was intentional." (I remember wondering what "disorder," that most flexible of charges, was a euphemism for in this particular case.) As usual, the security officers instructed the man to step away from the bench. He took a step or two as if to leave, then stopped and turned back to face the judge, asking, "Could I say one word?" There was a brief pause among all those ringed around the judge's bench—the judge, the prosecutors, the coordinator's staff—and his attorney quickly said, "I'd advise against it." On his way out of the room, the man turned back awkwardly and waved, saying, "Thank you, judge."

In another case, I saw a tense dialogue between a defense attorney and his scraggly bearded defendant, who had just been sentenced to five days in jail for criminal trespass. Instead of staying frozen and compliant like most defendants, he became visibly upset at his sentence. The man haggled and hassled with his lawyer, his body language palpably tense and hurt. I couldn't hear his exact words, but he spoke with a hostile and confrontational tone, despite his attorney's pleading that the judge had spoken and that was that. After a minute or two of this, a security guard called for some NYPD officers in attendance to "take charge." They stepped in and firmly led the man out of the room.

Despite these occasional interruptions, the atmosphere of the court was highly regulated and restrained. Each person had their prescribed posture: the court officers, relaxed and alert; the judge, personable but reserved and enigmatic in her robes and her elevated seat; the attorneys on both sides, earnest and officious; the busy support staff, typing and filing away. For their part, the glum defendants did their best to disappear when they faced the judge, standing silent but also trying to look alert, focused, and responsible, their hands awkwardly switching between their pockets to behind their backs.

This same regulated framework extended from the immediate area around the judge to encompass the pews where the spectators sat. Along with myself, the onlookers included journalists, groups of college students sitting with their professors, and occasionally someone like the man who sat in front of me one day, stinking of piss, his gray hair lank beneath a cowboy hat, with two gym bags lying at his feet. During one of the hearings, he turned to me and whispered an urgent story about how expensive it was to pay for rent and insurance in New York City, the details of his father's medical plan, how unfair it had been for him growing up poor in New Jersey, rejected by the elitist country club types and unfairly given the boot from his high school basketball team. . . . I nodded along, smiling uneasily, until a court officer told him to be quiet. The security guards often policed the etiquette of the spectators in the pews: "Take your hands out of your pockets!" "Take your hat off!" "Quiet down, people!" After becoming more familiar with the court, having spent many mornings watching the hearings, I began to see the metal detectors and the guards who stood outside the door, ready to confiscate my tape recorder, as yet another extension of this formal frame. The role of an observer in these hearings was a limited one, like all the roles there, including that of the judge; and this security infrastructure was merely one, highly formalized part of the apparatus that maintained the precise limits to which these roles had to conform.

The Center for Court Innovation

A few years after its inception, the Midtown Community Court spun off a separate policy consulting organization, the Center for Court Innovation (CCI). The CCI now runs the court, as well as similar courts and mediation centers in Harlem, the Bronx, and in the Brooklyn neighborhoods of Crown Heights and Red Hook. The CCI also consults with

related institutions nationally and worldwide and generally serves to publicize the community court concept.[6] CCI officials who helped start the Community Court and now worked in this policy think tank saw nothing unusual about a local initiative becoming the basis for a global consulting organization. In fact, they said, the concept of the Community Court as a model for national or global practice was there at its beginning. And it was only enhanced by its symbolic and physical proximity to Times Square and the redevelopment. As Feinblatt put it:

> The extraordinary thing about Midtown is that it was set up to be reflective, and that it was set up as an experiment. . . . We were having a conversation with a community that was reverberating beyond us. As we progressed, we certainly realized that the principles we were starting to articulate were really resonating with policy makers and researchers and practitioners across the country. . . . You know, the saying goes that if you can do it in Times Square you can do it anywhere, and I think that had an impact on people in two respects. One was, everyone thought that crime and quality of life problems in Times Square were age-old and intractable. At the same time, they knew that Times Square is the image-maker of New York, and that New York is really the image capital, in many ways, of the world. And there was a great curiosity about [the Community Court] because of those two elements. Could we make a dent in quality-of-life crimes in the quality-of-life crime capital of New York City—and if we could, would it change the image of New York around the world? Two pretty interesting questions.

Times Square's redevelopers always represented themselves as working, not just to transform Times Square itself, but also to create a new form of urban development. This was a new development program for preserving and intensifying the appearance of dynamic city life, and for turning this appearance of urban life into a new way of marketing urban space itself. The story of the Midtown Community Court and the Center for Court Innovation shows how the redevelopment sparked another such local/global confluence. Here, the needs of real estate developers to find new, politically palatable and controlled urban spaces combined with the interests of a dynamic group of individuals focused on reconceptualizing the nature and practice of an urban court of law. This combination of the real estate market fueling innovative social

policy produced a self-consciously national and global model court-room. The Midtown Community Court made itself an intimate space for judgment and rehabilitation. It helped to shape Times Square and New York City, "the image maker of the world," while drawing power from the socioeconomic energies at the city's heart.

Times Square Ink.
Redevelopment of the Self

The Midtown Community Court drew on the real estate capital and interests of the Times Square redevelopment to reorganize the rules by which an urban court judges, punishes, and rehabilitates. The Community Court reorganized the formal institution of the courtroom; it set out to redefine the relationships within the courtroom between defendant, judge, prosecution, defense, police, and community. At the same time, the Community Court also set out to redefine the very identity of the people charged there. The place where this mission was made most explicit in everyday practice was in what was perhaps the court's most personalized and innovative program—a job- and life-skills training program called Times Square Ink.

Times Square Ink. was a place where those being trained, and their instructors, experienced the changes in Times Square, not just on the macro-level of architecture, policy, and public space, but also on the micro-level of the self. Just as zoning laws, public architecture, and policing practice in Times Square were shifted to accommodate the imagined imperatives of corporate culture, so, too, the participants in the

Times Square Ink. program learned how to reshape and redefine their presentation and imagination of self in accordance with the norms and desires of the corporate world.

At Times Square Ink., a small number of ex–misdemeanor offenders worked in a nonprofit copy center while learning to conform to the Times Square area's new corporate culture. Appropriately, the Times Square Ink. program involved training these people to operate sophisticated photocopying machines—hence, the "Ink." pun in the name of the program. In a kind of urban renewal for the soul, Times Square Ink. functioned as a site where Times Square's redevelopers reached out to a small number of the people it targeted as "undesirables." Rather than evicting them from the area, it offered them the chance for cleaned-up and reorganized selves to fit this cleaned-up and reorganized space.

The Times Square Ink. program was aimed at a select group of the most marginalized citizens of New York City—those who formerly found in Times Square a space of anonymity and safety. These marginal citizens included the people most strenuously demonized and rejected by the redevelopers: people who had no jobs, who were homeless, who worked as prostitutes, who had drug habits, who were unavoidably and (to some) threateningly different. The two dozen or so trainees I met during my year of ethnographic fieldwork at the program were mostly young, nearly all black or Latino, and all poor. For these people, Times Square before the redevelopment—when it was supposedly in its most "blighted" state—represented a space of social possibility, if only because certain forms of surveillance seemed to be suspended there, as discussed in the historical survey in chapter two. From the perspective of the crime-prevention perspectives outlined in chapter three, of course, this social possibility represented precisely the wrong kind of freedom. Specifically, it presented too many opportunities for wrongdoing, to (presumably lower-class) individuals who could not be counted on to resist their baser, short-term impulses with long-term rational planning. This is how the redevelopment conceived of Times Square's "undesirables"—as victims of their own lack of judgment and of society's failure to design sufficiently controlled public spaces, but also as highly visible symbols of disorder and urban malaise, haplessly threatening the social and economic viability of celebratory new commercial-corporate spaces like Times Square and, by extension, the life of the city itself.

Like the other people involved in redeveloping Times Square, the Times Square Ink. trainees developed expert knowledge in how to

interact with the needs and tastes of the corporate world. However, unlike the other people involved with the redevelopment I studied during
my year of fieldwork in the area, what was at stake for Times Square
Ink.'s trainees was their very "right to the city"—their ability to live
and participate in the world around them.[1] Furthermore, rather than
working to shape laws, zoning codes, or architecture, the only material
upon which these marginal citizens could work any transformation was
themselves.

Times Square Ink.

Everyone who passed through the Midtown Community Court, whether
for an arraignment hearing, a community service assignment, a counseling appointment, or a bowl of soup, was made to sit through a video
presentation on Times Square Ink. If they applied to the program and
were admitted, they entered together in small groups—about two to
six trainees every month. The Times Square Ink. program itself consisted of three "Modules," or distinct units of training, each lasting a
month. Module One met in a small classroom in the basement of the
court building. Trainees worked on vocabulary lists, ran through public speaking drills, wrote autobiographical essays, and so forth. After
Module One, they spent the next two months working in Times Square
Ink.'s nonprofit copy center, located in the third floor of the court
building. During Module Two, the first month in the copy center, trainees learned to use various document copying and binding machines.
Module Three was much the same, except that, during this month, they
also prepared their résumés. They also began to look for outside employment, usually through one of the "outsource" centers, like IKON,
that provided technical support staff, such as mailroom clerks and
document handlers, to law firms and corporate offices in Times Square
and throughout New York City.

The program held small ceremonies as the trainees moved from
module to module, with a final graduation ceremony at the end of
Module Three. After they graduated from the program and, hopefully,
found work, their contact with the program did not necessarily end.
The Times Square Ink. instructors and Midtown Community Court
counselors tried to keep in touch with graduates by phone. In addition,
many graduates of Times Square Ink. returned to the copy center for
weekly meetings of the "Job Club." During these meetings, people who

had been through the program and who now worked for IKON or other such companies could share stories and advice with each other, as well as with those who had not yet graduated.

One of the directors of Times Square Ink. told me that they chose to have the program focus on copy center training because they saw it as a "growth industry" in the current Manhattan business climate. She said that the three-month period of training was like "playing at having a job" for the people in the program—a chance to rehearse for real experiences and challenges that might come later. When I asked her about the lengthy application process for the program, she said that Times Square Ink. aimed to accept only the cream of the crop of potential trainees. They selected only those who showed the skills and determination necessary to persist through multiple rounds of phone calls, interviews, standardized tests, and screening for drugs. The director situated Times Square Ink. as one part of what she described as an unusual "convergence" of groups and programs focusing on one urban space: "It's interesting, simultaneously, in many different directions, things came together to change the midtown area. So between the Times Square Business Improvement District . . . Disney coming in, for better or for worse, Giuliani and community policing, the Midtown Community Court—I think there are a lot of different forces that just came together . . . a multi-pronged attack."

Times Square Ink. offered extensive training in "job skills." Trainees learned how to run bulk postage meters and relatively high-tech copy machines. But the training the program offered went beyond these somewhat prosaic job skills. The program trained students, not just in how to operate a machine, but also in how to manage their presentation of self in the workplace. Trainees learned how to dress, how to carry their bodies, how to write résumés, how to speak in job interviews, and how to deal amicably with bosses and coworkers. The program further connected these concrete tactics of representing the self with more nebulous talents, which Times Square Ink., like other such programs, called "life skills." Trainees learned such life skills as how to narrate their own history and how to conceive of their ambitions or dreams as concrete "five-year plans."

The program implicitly taught its trainees, almost exclusively young black and Latino men and women, to navigate racial and ethnic prejudice in the workplace. It did so by implicitly showing them ways in which they could try to downplay or modify any of their own signs of racial or ethnic difference. Trainees learned to accommodate the aesthetic

desires of (presumably white) corporate managers, and thus to portray themselves as good potential workers. However, the trainees did not learn to think of their citizenship in the New Times Square in terms of serving corporations. Rather, the program trained them to think in terms of serving themselves. Times Square Ink. taught the trainees to use their labor in the corporate world in order to serve a particular framing of their own best interests. Just as Forty-second Street was turned into a frictionless outdoor art gallery in order to protect the transforming real estate market behind its scaffolding and façades, similarly, Times Square Ink. sought to impart to its trainees a new, fear-free exterior. It did this so that their newly discovered private selves could make a go of it in the world of work.

Codes of Publicity and Privacy

On the morning that I sat in the basement of the Midtown Community Court with a group of trainees for their first day of class, the instructor began by saying to the group, "Every aspect of this class is used to train you for something." She then told a story about two imaginary characters, "Buffy" and "Leroy"—the first a spoiled Ivy League graduate, the second a street hustler. The instructor described Buffy's blithe sense of entitlement (after college Buffy got a job from a family friend), in contrast with Leroy's day-to-day struggle. She asked the group, "Who has more common sense?" Everyone agreed that Leroy did. The instructor then asked the trainees which character they most resembled; they all decided that they had more in common with Leroy than Buffy. (She didn't explicitly say that one was white and the other wasn't, but the names and descriptions certainly gave that impression.) "That's right," the instructor said, "but even with that common sense, you still couldn't find a job!" She told them that the Times Square Ink. program would take the place of Buffy's well-connected family. But the program would go one better than this. It would teach them to handle difficult situations in which Buffy would be helpless. After all, the instructor wondered, what will Buffy do in the workplace, without her family to shield her?

I was somewhat taken aback by this story. To me, the story of Buffy and Leroy started out sounding like a structural critique of class privilege and the unequal distribution of opportunity among social groups. I heard it as a story about racial entitlement; about how some people

are born with more or less social capital, regardless of personal initiative. In fact, I had already heard a different version of the Buffy and Leroy story, on a visit to STRIVE, a Harlem-based job-training program with ties to Times Square Ink. In the STRIVE version of the story, Buffy succeeded by using her common sense; she knew to exploit her family connections to get a job. Leroy's street-hustling skills turned out not to count as "common sense" at all. The Times Square Ink. instructor turned this into another kind of story—a parable about the existence of something personal, beyond social capital or common sense. According to this version of the fable, neither social connections nor street instincts would suffice for the trainees to succeed. They needed to develop something else, something deeper inside themselves.

The instructor then asked the trainees to describe their previous experiences with work. The students shared common experiences, things I heard nearly all the trainees talk about at one time or another: having trouble finding a job; getting fired for what they thought were unfair reasons; hoping that Times Square Ink. would help their chances. As the trainees went around the table in turn, the instructor made comments that began to give a new shape to their stories. Specifically, she diverted the students' stories about their work histories away from overtly structural issues, such as employers' racism, and toward the students' own emotions and behavior patterns. One young man in particular, loquacious and stylishly dressed, made repeated mention of the "racist" and unreasonable bosses who, he said, had forced him to quit first one job and then another. The instructor cut his story off with a quick, "We'll get to all that later." She mentioned that he might want to concentrate on his own behavior, rather than that of his employers. As she put it in a general comment to the group, "We all know the rules, but sometimes we choose not to follow them."

After going over the program's dress and grooming code from a large sheet of paper taped to the wall, the instructor handed the trainees the week's list of "Power Words." This was the list of words that they would be asked to define and use in an essay at the end of the week: Assertive, Aggressive, Feedback, Responsibility, Detachment, Evaluative, Synergy, Intolerance, Tact, and Imperative. The class spent the rest of the morning filling out a questionnaire entitled "Who Am I?"

From the first, then, Times Square Ink. presented its trainees with a challenge. This was a call to attend to the world and to themselves in a mode of heightened scrutiny. As the instructor put it, "every aspect" of the class purported to carry instructive content. Similarly, the program

taught that "every aspect" of one's self communicated messages to the world. The trainees had to learn to understand the messages they were sending, in order to control them. The first day's exercises brought up three of the fields that the trainees would be required to master: their speech; their physical appearance; and their ability to narrate their own identity and history.

This fit with the Midtown Community Court's larger framework of assumptions about public and private realms. The court defined drug dependency as partially a matter of the drug user's mismanagement of the boundaries between the realms of publicity and privacy. According to this perspective, drug users had become too entangled with the public sphere; they needed to be removed from their former contacts, perhaps by force. Similarly, the Times Square Ink. program presumed that its trainees needed to be taught to manage the boundaries between public and private. It based this presumption simply on the fact of the trainees' having signed up for job- and life-skills training in the first place. A constant theme in the Times Square Ink. program was that, as the trainees learn to operate new photocopying technologies, they were also learning new ways of perceiving their own identities, their presentation of self. Throughout their course of training, the program's instructors taught the trainees how to keep things about themselves *private* in order to construct a viable *public* persona for the workplace. They did this by engendering new forms of observing and attending to the *self*.[2]

Times Square Ink. told trainees to cut or standardize ostentatiously braided, styled, or colored hair, to pare back elaborate nails and jewelry, and to wear dark, solid colors in place of bright patterns. These were all highly class- and race-specific identity markers in New York City, tokens of black and Latino "ghetto" fashions. The concern with clothing operated continuously throughout the three months of training. It started with stern warnings that the trainees must always dress appropriately during their time at the program. In a poetic twist, during graduation ceremonies at the end of the third month, officials from the Community Court gave the graduates gifts of clothing: ties, scarves, or button-down shirts. More generally, I often saw the Times Square Ink. instructors formally or informally critique the trainees' overall social behavior. I was present once at the copy center when two instructors jokingly admonished one trainee, who had nicknamed himself "Ghostface" in reference to his unsmiling demeanor. They told him that he should make an effort to smile more, in order to put prospective employers at ease. Another time, I saw one instructor strongly correct a trainee who

answered the phone, "Times Square Ink., what do you want?" The instructor waited until the trainee was off the phone. Then he pulled him aside and said, with an urgent voice, "What was that?! 'Times Square Ink., *how can I help you?*' That could be *jobs,* that could be *work!*"

On one occasion, I sat in on a visit to the Times Square Ink. copy center by a representative from the Fortune Society, an organization dedicated to helping ex-prisoners enter legitimate employment. The speaker from the Fortune Society addressed the group of a half-dozen trainees on how to navigate a job interview. He told them to always keep in mind what he called their "game plan." "The employer has a plan, and so should you," he said. He then defined what their "game plan" should be: "Bury the application." The speaker told the trainees to walk into a job interview armed with documents to back up every line on their résumé, every question on the application. They should be prepared to pass these papers to the interviewer unasked. He gave an example: "Yes, I graduated from such-and-such high school, and here's a copy of my diploma [voice rising for emphasis]. Yes, I learned a great deal from my time at Times Square Ink., and here's a letter of reference from the program." He stressed that, throughout the interview, "Part of yourself is listening, and part of yourself is thinking." The "thinking" part of the self, he said, should be strategizing how best to counter the interviewer's forays. He told them, "Answer every question with a question. He asks, 'What salary do you expect?' You answer with a question. 'Well, what do people who work in this position usually make?'"

The Fortune Society speaker warned the trainees that they would need to keep these tactics in mind especially when answering questions about their criminal record, since nearly all of them had learned about Times Square Ink. while being held at the Midtown Community Court after an arrest. He advised them to rush past any mention of conflicts with the law. Instead, they should reassure their interviewer that they had learned from their past. "Yes, I made some mistakes, and that's how I found out about the Times Square Ink. program. . . ." The speaker also warned the trainees to always dress conservatively for interviews, in dark colors and with little or no jewelry. He cautioned, "Don't take the focus off of *you.*" He told the trainees to be most careful when it came to answering the standard job-interview question, "Tell me about yourself." As he put it, "He doesn't want to hear about your family, he doesn't want to hear about your hobbies, he wants to hear about *you.*" He advised them to respond to the standard question with a standard answer; something like, "I'm a good worker, I learn quickly, I'm a

self-starter. . . ." In closing, he made a point of warning the trainees about being "drawn into informality." He advised them to be wary of casual or friendly seeming employers who might, in fact, be trying to trap them in over-familiarity.

The Fortune Society speaker's presentation framed the job interview as a situation in which the trainees would be required to put on a particular kind of performance. They needed to show that they could listen and respond both deferentially and strategically at all times. This sense of the strategizing self, placing in the forefront the trainees' crafted interview persona, was encapsulated in the speaker's dictum, "Part of yourself is listening, and part of yourself is thinking." His advice on how to answer questions about one's criminal record further laid out the contours of this deliberate split in the self. The trainees should reassure their interlocutors by referring to an internal sense of distance from the old self that had committed those crimes.

The Fortune Society presentation reminded me of an earlier conversation I had with the Times Square Ink. instructor who managed the copy center. He laughed when he told me that he deliberately acted the part of a difficult boss when he deals with the trainees at work. He did this, he said, in order to "test" them. He told them jokes, and then yelled at them for no real reason. He acted like a friend and then harshly reprimanded them for small slip-ups. In other words, he modeled the role that the speaker from the Fortune Society claimed that many employers take on in job interviews.

Times Square Ink.'s rules of self-presentation had to do with what was or wasn't to be made public at work. Trainees were taught to dress and hold themselves in a manner both style-free and highly stylized. In other words, they worked to become *unmarked* according to the cultural codes of the corporate world. Their clothes, hair, and so forth did not deny their identity as part of a group so much as they denied the salience of "identity" itself. Instead, the trainees learned to dress, speak, and act in ways that hinted at the presence of a hidden individuality; a private self that strategically masked itself in order to thrive in public. All that one was supposed to show at work was one's desire to work with all possible speed, skill, and initiative. Everything other than the desire to work was to be relegated to the private realm.

With this in mind, Times Square Ink. taught its trainees to approach the interview situation laden both with heavily coded presences and absences. These presences and absences were structured within New York City's supercharged political economy of racialized glances, momentary

impressions, and radical self-stylization. In this system, a black or La-tino interviewee's *lack* of chunky gold chains, elaborate fingernail pros-thetics, or braided hair spoke eloquently about their desire and ability to neutralize their own appearance according to corporate aesthetics.

The dark and austere clothing mandated by the program conveyed a similarity, a sameness. To wear the kind of clothing to a job interview that Times Square Ink. advocated was, in effect, to sign a social contract with strong class-based and racial overtones. The interviewee pledged to re-frain from stylizing their appearance, speech, and/or demeanor in a way that would complicate the employer's acceptance of them. Here, adorn-ments that called attention to themselves were lumped in with marked class-, race-, or ethnicity-based speech patterns or body habits. They were seen as unnecessary add-ons to the self, needing to be stripped away.

Just as Times Square's redevelopers worked to redefine the appear-ance and meaning of the area's public spaces—to change both how Times Square *looked* and what Times Square *meant*—so Times Square Ink. worked to redefine the trainees' own appearances and meanings. Redefining what was public and what was private was both the first step and also the master theme in Times Square Ink.'s program to redevelop these marginal citizens for the New Times Square.

The Private Self

Times Square Ink. was connected to a similar, larger-scale program called STRIVE. The offices of STRIVE are located in East Harlem, just a few blocks north of Manhattan's elite Upper East Side, but seemingly on another planet.[3] STRIVE received national and international public-ity for its attempts to train the young residents of this extremely margin-alized neighborhood in the self-presentation skills necessary for office work. I accompanied a trainee and an instructor from Times Square Ink. on a visit to STRIVE, to watch how STRIVE introduced itself to people entering the program on the first day of a training cycle. We sat in the back of the room, behind a hundred-strong crowd of prospective students, all clad in button-down shirts and ties, and listened for hours as a series of instructors paced up and down before the group, yelling, sermonizing, telling raucous jokes. Later, as we were walking out of the STRIVE classroom, I asked the Times Square Ink. trainee what he thought of the presentation. He told me that it reminded him too much of his time in the navy; it seemed, he said, "too much like boot camp."

I had heard remarks like this before. Nearly all of the administrators and instructors at Times Square Ink. used the comparison with military training to describe the program; they all commented to me, at one time or another, that Times Square Ink. was "not boot camp." Their comments served to differentiate Times Square Ink., not just from the armed forces, but from STRIVE and other programs like it. Instead of huge classes of dozens or hundreds of trainees, Times Square Ink. had small classes, which totaled, at most, about twelve or thirteen at any one time. Similarly, where STRIVE accepted all who applied and then weeded out those who could not meet their criteria, Times Square Ink. selected only a few students to enter the program, then worked exceptionally hard to help those people graduate and find jobs. By defining Times Square Ink. negatively—"not boot camp"—these comments also served to define it positively. The "not boot camp" image implied that this was a place relatively intimate and familiar. Times Square Ink. instructors did not roar or preach. Rather, they spoke quietly and casually. Students did not enter en masse, but in small units, and they were encouraged, even mandated, to "get to know each other." More broadly, the program demanded that trainees make public the potentially embarrassing or otherwise secret aspects of their lives. In this way, they could master these secret aspects, in order to more effectively hide them later. Times Square Ink. thus constituted itself as a kind of inside-out secrecy zone—a place where inward thoughts could, and must, circulate through particular networks of public speech and knowledge. It was a place of public secrets.[4]

Times Square Ink. taught its trainees that their emotions had contributed to their presumed lack of success in the mainstream economy. The trainees spent part of the first month in the program learning about "anger management." One handout they received, "What Is Anger?," demonstrated the proper method of managing one's angry or frustrated emotions in public. The handout showed two figures in the throes of anger. The first figure stood at a desk or table, pounding its fist and knocking over a vase. Lightning bolts of anger leapt from its mouth toward the person who sat across the table, mouth open in shock. By contrast, the second figure blew off steam by lifting weights, making the "OK" sign with thumb and finger while it smiled at its own raging reflection in a mirror. The two illustrations demonstrated how to manage the risks of letting anger affect one's social behavior. In the first illustration, the figure violently expressing itself in public put itself in danger by making others feel threatened. In the second illustration,

42nd Street, 1989.

Selwyn Theater, 1989.

Selwyn Theater (lights on), 1990.

Liberty Theater sign removal, 1990.

Lyric Theater and Victory Theater, 1989.

Harris Theater, 1989.

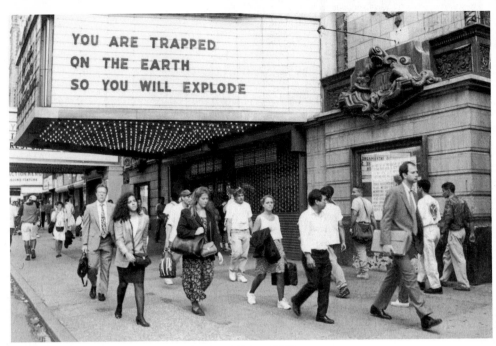

"You Are Trapped," marquee "truism" by Jenny Holzer, 1993.

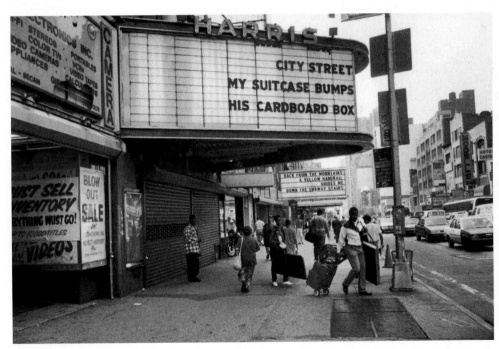

"City Street," marquee poem by Minna Lerman, 1994.

Restoration of the Victory Theater entrance (in background, marquee poem by Adele Kenny), 1994.

"Everybody," mural by Tibor Kalman, M & Co., 1993.

Apollo Theater, Times Square Theater, and Lyric Theater, 1989.

the figure safely recuperated its anger as productive energy in private, alone in front of the mirror, presumably at home. But anger was not the only dangerous emotion. I heard one instructor speak critically about a Times Square Ink. graduate who, he feared, was putting herself in jeopardy at work by flirting excessively with her fellow employees. Anything that might introduce untoward instability into the formalized relationships at work had to be regarded with suspicion and handled with care. This echoed the advice given by the speaker from the Fortune Society, when he urged trainees to rhetorically displace their own criminal past by referring to a new, more reflexive sense of self and purpose. ("Yes, I made some mistakes . . . ")

In much the same way that the larger redevelopment of Times Square had radically curtailed the area's former, highly public market in sexual commerce, so the Times Square Ink. instructors told the trainees that they must learn to displace potentially self-jeopardizing feelings. They had to remove them from the public sphere and relegate them to the private world of the self. Trainees learned to manage this displacement through a self-disciplining internal dialogue. I once heard a graduate from the program ask an instructor for advice on how to handle interpersonal conflicts with a coworker, someone who seemed to have a grudge against them and who went out of their way to aggravate them at every turn. The instructor's advice was blunt: "Fake it." Endure the conflict to keep the job. The self that was reacting adversely to such conflicts must be hidden somewhere inside, somewhere private. The program's rationale—the common sense it projected—was simple. Times Square Ink. taught that one must both know the self and hide the self.

The program defined aspects of the trainees' selves as particular kinds of objects, called "issues" or "attitudes." There were various formal contexts in which these "issues" or "attitudes" were tested, including in the entrance exams or final interviews that opened and closed the trainees' time at Times Square Ink., as well as the mandatory drug tests that they underwent throughout the program. This demarcation of the self also happened in more informal ways, as instructors asked or lectured trainees about aspects of themselves in the context of discussing their "issues." I cringed inwardly when I heard one instructor ask a trainee, "So, how about those drug issues? Are you still smoking pot?" I was standing right beside the trainee at the moment. I distinctly recall feeling outraged and embarrassed for him. I thought to myself, "How can she be asking him about something so private right in front of me?" My own definitions of appropriate public/private distinctions were

threatened by her demand that the trainee make public anything that would threaten his success, in the program or elsewhere. Similarly, on another occasion, when a trainee was sitting quietly, sullenly even, during an exercise requiring group speaking, the instructor, then the other trainees as a group, began to hector him for just sitting in his chair and not participating. They finally gave up on him. The instructor turned to me and said, exasperatedly, "He has some issues with his attitude."

The repeated demarcation of "issues" or "attitudes" as something separate from, but also connected to, the self, defined them as something like personal possessions. They were spoken of as potentially threatening *things*. The trainees needed to learn to pack this baggage when in public. But the process of learning how to hide one's "issues" and to protect one's public persona from their effects was precisely a process of making them enormously, vividly public: talking about them in detail, and being talked to about them in even greater detail. Times Square Ink. thus made a distinction between aspects of the private or interior self. There was the self of "issues"—the self that willfully sabotaged a person's chances to find and keep work. There was also the self that the instructor referred to in her comment, "We all know the rules, but sometimes we choose not to follow them." Repeated talk about "issues" served to reinforce the distinction between the two, in a form of battle-testing the disciplined self for work.

However, it was not always easy to produce these kinds of distinctions within the self. On that same first day in class when the instructor told the story about Buffy and Leroy, I watched as one trainee struggled with the "Who Am I?" questionnaire, which asked the students to describe themselves in great detail. Most of the people in the class seemed to have no trouble responding to the tasks demanded, such as listing their three best and worst attributes or imagining what words their friends would use to describe them. By contrast, this young woman anxiously chewed her pencil while trying to fill out the form. Then, when the instructor called on her to stand up and read her responses to the rest of the class, she burst into tears and nearly fled the room. The instructor asked why she was so upset. Tearfully, she blurted that my sitting there at the table with my notepad out made her nervous. I felt terrible for her, and offered to leave, but the instructor told me that I should stay put. She insisted that, however nervous and uncomfortable the trainee felt, she would have to "learn to deal with those issues."

Just as the planners and architects sought to keep Times Square "authentic" and "true to itself" while radically transforming the neighbor-

hood's place in New York's real estate economy, so Times Square Ink. emphasized this theme of being "true to oneself." The new dress styles and behavior codes were meant to connect to a true self deep within, and to index a fundamental transformation in that true self. In this way, the program turned the question of urban redevelopment—the question of making a place desirable *both* for real estate developers *and* for its current inhabitants—on its head and made it fundamentally personal. Times Square Ink. asked the trainees to consider the following question: What were the contradictions, if any, between working to find one's "true self" while at the same time working to make oneself a desirable commodity on the job market? In other words, who was the "self" Times Square Ink. worked to produce *for*?

Situating the Self in Time

This was why the talk about the trainees' selves became folded into the program's ongoing testing of their abilities to package themselves for work. Times Square Ink. taught its trainees to re-envision themselves as individual selves possessing a personal history. The program enframed this history as a personal and individual trajectory through time, based in individual decisions and discipline (or lack thereof). The trainees learned that they had to discipline their own sense of themselves as agents in history.

The program placed a heavy emphasis on practices of time management and making good use of time in the present, as well as on devices that rationalize time, like calendars, alarm clocks, watches, and personal planners. On one of my first visits to Times Square Ink., I overheard an instructor admonish two students for being late by pointedly asking whether they owned alarm clocks. The image of a population so cut off from New York City's corporate economy that they don't own clocks or calendars continues to crop up repeatedly in neoconservative discourses on "the underclass."[5] In fact, this was one of the issues that Midtown Community Court administrators were most curious about when I asked them for permission to do research at Times Square Ink. They told me how puzzled they were by so many of their clients' apparent lack of rational planning ability—how difficult it was for the program to keep in touch with prospective trainees once recruited, and how many of these recruits failed the drug test, even when they knew the date of the test in advance.

But Times Square Ink. did not solely teach trainees to manage time according to external parameters of rationality and efficiency. The program also taught them to locate themselves in time. Trainees learned to see themselves as situated, not just in the immediacy of the present, but also in the past, looking forward, as well as in the future, looking back. Early on in the program, the trainees began to work on their "life maps," a project that occupied them on-and-off for their month of training in Module One. These life maps were colorful posters, in which the trainees depicted the course of their lives in terms of a road winding from place to place. As the trainees worked on their life maps, they were asked to contemplate the bad choices they had made in their past. The life map was constructed as diagramming the harmful cultural patterns and bad personal decisions that had brought them to need the Times Square Ink. program in the first place. Through the map, the program taught the trainees to see themselves critically in the past; to imagine their past selves making thoughtless choices due to lack of self-discipline and perspective—just as the redevelopers portrayed Times Square and Forty-second Street as having been blighted by neglect and lack of proper social control.

When I first began to visit Times Square Ink., I was struck by the similarity among the many life maps taped up on the walls around the room. My first impression was that they all looked exactly the same—they showed an S-shaped road that passed through the Community Court and into the Times Square Ink. classroom, just before blurring into an uncertain but upbeat future. Various important junctures in the trainees' lives were marked along the way: "Came to the US from Trinidad"; "Graduated from high school"; "Started to use drugs." I saw one reason for this similarity when I sat in with a group of trainees who were starting to work on their life maps. Their initial sketches all followed a handout that the instructor passed around at the beginning of class, which showed the same S-curved road used on nearly all the maps posted in the classroom. In time, however, I began to notice differences among the various curving life paths. For example, one young woman's life map was literally dominated by her mother—pictures of her mother cropped up along the road more frequently than those of the subject herself. Meanwhile, the trainees who entered the program during my months of fieldwork began to take liberties with the form of the map, adapting or ignoring the outline on the handout. One trainee constructed an impressionistic collage of charged-up images clipped from magazine advertisements. This was not so much a "map" of linear

progress as a decentered, evocative snapshot of moments of desire and epiphany. Another trainee pasted personal snapshots and mementos of his unruly youth onto the surface of the map itself, including a condom in its wrapper that he stapled next to the words "High School."

As they cast their mind back into the past, so, too, the trainees looked forward into the future. The program encouraged them to construct a mental image of themselves in a bright future life, and then to imagine the connections between that future and the present in which they lived. One form that this took was when the instructors pushed the trainees to construct "five-year plans" for themselves. I occasionally heard the instructors ask the trainees rhetorical questions about these plans: "Where do you see yourself in five years? What is it going to take for you to get there?" The copy center manager liked to question trainees about their five-year plans during moments when the trainees showed self-doubt, or when they got into conflict with him or with their fellows. I saw him do so on several occasions when someone commented that they were unhappy working at the copy center, or that they were otherwise dissatisfied, either with Times Square Ink. or with their chances of finding a job once they graduated.

One such occasion came when I happened to drop by the copy center when several of the trainees were working late. As they were chatting casually with each other, several of the trainees began to tell to one of their number, a young man who was about to graduate from the program and start to look for work, that he should cut his hair, which was thickly braided against his scalp in an Afro-Caribbean style. They told him that the braids looked, in their words, "too ghetto," and that they would hurt his chances in job interviews. He tried to duck their advice, brushing it off with the casually defiant remark, "Nobody's going to make me cut my braids."

As soon as he said this, the instructor appeared in the doorway of his office. The trainees and I turned to listen to him as he began a rambling monologue about "choices." "You make your own choices," he said. "You deal with the consequences." I was mildly surprised. Was he approving of the trainee's reluctance to cut his braids? I saw the other trainees watching the manager uncertainly, wondering where he was going with this. He then began to address the young man directly. "So, where do you see yourself in five years? Where do you want to be? Do you have a plan?"

The trainee fumbled for a moment, then replied, "I want to have my own trucking company." The instructor nodded avuncularly, then

reeled off a list of questions. "A trucking company? All right. How are you going to get there? How are you going to raise the money? How are you going to get people to want to lend you the money to get started? How are you going to get the experience you need?" Haltingly, the trainee began to answer, but the instructor cut him off. "You have to make the right choices for yourself to get where you want to be," he said, then turned back into his office. A week or so later, the next time I stopped in at the copy center, I saw that the trainee had cut off his braids and shaved his head clean.

As this example suggests, the trainees knew that they were supposed to have these five-year plans, and the instructors asked them about their plans in public. However, the trainees and the instructors both kept the specific details of the plans mostly private. The trainees did not objectify their five-year plans in the way that they did other things in Times Square Ink., such as the public personae that the trainees rehearsed in mock job interviews, or the autobiographical essays that they wrote and posted on the walls. I never heard the instructors tell the trainees to write the plans down, nor did they ask them to verbally spell them out in any depth. In other words, *having* the plan counted at Times Square Ink., but the program remained largely agnostic regarding the plan itself. Like anger and sex, these plans were kept private. These five-year plans symbolized the sense of self-discipline and direction that the program encouraged.

In another future-oriented exercise, trainees drew two cemetery headstones, each with a different epitaph. On the first headstone, they wrote the epitaph they imagined they would receive if they didn't successfully graduate from Times Square Ink. On the second stone, more optimistically, they wrote the epitaph they hoped to receive once they had lived a full life after graduating from the program. When I talked about the headstone exercise with the Times Square Ink. instructor who gave the assignment, she told me that she adapted it from a standard job-skills training curriculum, in which people are asked to "write their own epitaph" in order to produce an ominous self-directed warning to stay on track. She said that she found this concept useful, but a little depressing, so she modified the exercise by adding the second, more upbeat headstone—with its more successful epitaph—in order to make the exercise "less downbeat."

What struck me upon looking over the drawings the trainees had produced was the intensity of the contrast between the two grave markers they drew for themselves. I was especially surprised by the vitriol the

trainees seemed ready to heap upon the self they imagined not finishing Times Square Ink. On these headstones, they wrote things like: "Never finished high school or got GED. . . . On welfare teenage pregnancy lazy move[d] from apartment to apartment lived off her son['s] check. Taught her son bad habits let her son do what ever he wants. Never stand up for her self. Just don't know how to change her life around."

Other trainees seemed to turn the headstone exercise into a "before and after" autobiographical essay, reflecting on their lives before the program from a position within it. Instead of two alternative fates for themselves, they wrote a single story, breaking off at the bottom of the first headstone and picking right up at the top of the second. In these, too, the decision to enter Times Square Ink. was inscribed as a definitive break, a turn from one alternative life (and death) to another. In the headstone exercise, the open-ended optimism of the life maps and the private genre of hoping encapsulated by the five-year plan took on the weight of, literally, life-and-death decisions. The question marks at the end of the life maps were replaced by the force of a self-chosen destiny.

These projects of mapping the past and the future mirrored the ways that Times Square's redevelopers framed Times Square and Forty-second Street's past in terms of wrong choices and governmental neglect; their present in terms of simultaneous "blight" and hazy potential; and their future in terms of grand public benefit. The life maps and five-year plans were exercises in which trainees mapped simultaneously their futures and their pasts in terms of wrong choices. In all of these exercises, the trainees objectified their sense of themselves as a subject in time. The past and future perspectives articulated in these exercises served to pull the trainees out of the potentially problematic experiences of the present moment. In this way, the exercises helped them to deal with the frustrations of going through Times Square Ink. in the first place, as well as with the difficulties they could expect to face in their hoped-for corporate jobs. As trainees prepared for full-time work running photocopy machines in the law firms and financial institutions of Midtown Manhattan, the past self and the future self were constructed simultaneously as havens *from* the present, as critical perspectives *on* the present, and as motivation to endure *in* the present. They were learning to see themselves as the redevelopers saw Times Square—the past was problematic (but interesting), the present was a critical turning point, and the future held infinite potential.

This managing of emotion through the objectification of time, desire, and imagination was made even more explicit when, as often

happened, the realities of working, or finding a job, or even just the program's own training, seemed too much to bear for the trainees. At one meeting I attended, numerous former trainees told stories about their difficult experiences after having left the program. One graduate told about a moment in a job interview when he panicked and lied about already having completed his GED. What was he to do? Should he call the interviewer, admit to his lie, and jeopardize his chances at this much-needed job? Or should he hope to bluff it out when—if—he was hired? Other graduates spoke about the difficulty of finding jobs that offered insurance benefits. (I found it interesting that they spoke only of life insurance, not health benefits.) They described bargaining with their bosses to get enough hours every week to meet their upcoming Christmas bills. One told a story about being arbitrarily fired after being tested unfairly on a broken copier.

Finally, one trainee panicked. She fairly yelled that she had lost hope. She said that she had already been worried about whether Times Square Ink. would lead her to a good job. Now, she feared that even if she got a job, work would be too fraught with problems. Immediately, the entire group turned to her. The instructor who was leading the Job Club discussion leaned forward in his chair. "Have faith," he urged her. He told her that her worries were, in effect, the product of trying to anticipate too far in the future. He advised her to "Slow down." At this point, the manager of the copy center, who had been leaning casually in the doorway on and off throughout the discussion, stepped forward. He suggested that she not plan five years in the future right now; that was too far ahead. Perhaps she should limit herself to making a "one-year plan." He told her to remember that she could "make it happen" for herself. The clincher came when one of her fellow trainees spoke up. This was a woman who, I was told by one of the instructors, had been homeless and working as a prostitute in the years before joining Times Square Ink. She told her panicky classmate not to worry about the future at all. Instead, she urged her to look back a year into her past—to picture herself and think about what it was that had pushed her to apply to Times Square Ink. in the first place. She offered an image of herself sleeping on a bench in Central Park, implying that the perils of finding and keeping a job in the corporate world had to be better than that.

Incidents like this posed a difficult problem for the trainees: How to stay hopeful in the face of finding work? How to keep a job once you found one? And how to endure the tedious pressures of the copying

and mailroom work for which Times Square Ink. was preparing them? In response to this multifaceted problem, the program offered a two-fold answer. First, one had to define one's work, not as an end in itself, but as a tool that one used to achieve a private plan. Second, one had to imagine oneself as multiply situated in time, commenting upon the present from strategically chosen points in the selectively remembered past and the desired future.

The IKON Trade Show

Times Square Ink. aimed to give its trainees the tools they need to survive in the corporate world. One of the first times I visited the program, I accompanied a group of trainees and one of the instructors on a sort of field trip into the corporate sector—a visit to a trade show put on by IKON, the document services provider where many graduates of the program found work. The group rode the subway together from Columbus Circle, near the court building, down to the office tower at Penn Station, where we took an elevator to the forty-fifth floor, disembarked, and signed in.

It was immediately apparent that we had arrived at a very different event than the instructor had envisioned. From what she had told me before the trip, I had imagined that we would be looking around a large convention center or arena, milling with people, where the trainees might meet prospective employers, try their hand on the sorts of machines they'd been training on, and so forth. Instead, the elevator let our group out into a quiet, sparsely populated suite of offices, where a few older male executives were participating in a lavishly catered session targeted at upper management. This was a trade show for the people who buy photocopiers, not the people who are contracted to run them.

The receptionist ushered our group into a large room full of very sophisticated-looking copy machines: a huge matte steel cabinet equipped to run off hundreds of thousands of copies on its own; a copier with a built-in computer that would edit documents as it printed them; a large color printer slowly churning out glossy photo-quality posters. Each machine was manned by its own suited attendant, explaining its features to those who walked by. I stopped with a few of the trainees in front of one machine to hear the man's sales pitch. His talk was oriented precisely away from the Times Square Ink. trainees; he showed off several features that allowed the machine to run independently,

without a human operator. "You can come in, make your copies, get back to work or have a cup of coffee." I wondered how the group would react to this—after all, they were being trained to handle other people's copies, and machines like this one could put them out of a job. But watching them move through the room, I mostly saw them testing out the interpersonal self-marketing and communication skills they'd been learning. True, some floated through the presentations, looking bored. Others made a concerted effort to look and act interested. They asked questions, nodded along with the answers, and picked up copies of the brochures laid out beside every machine. This was not something they did haphazardly. I saw them talking over strategy among themselves, pointing out opportunities to pick up papers and business cards, egging each other to ask questions. The instructor moved around the group, nudging them along in subtle ways; not confronting the bored ones or ordering them to look interested, but asking questions such as, "Why are you sitting here?" with a surprised, "I assumed you'd know better" tone in her voice.

Of course, not all the interactions between the trainees and the men talking up the photocopiers' features went seamlessly. I stood with two trainees as they watched the color printer turn out a glossy poster-size reproduction of a photorealistic still-life painting. This was an impressive machine. One of the trainees spoke up, to engage with the presenter as I assumed he'd been coached to. But his question was awkward, something like, "Hey, you could print up movie posters on that, couldn't you?" The man running the machine looked a little confused, but replied graciously, "Well, I think they'd use a printing press for a big job like that, but I guess you *could* . . . "

After looking over the copy machines, we were sent along with the other attendees into a small adjoining auditorium, to hear a series of presentations about IKON. Again, like the spiels about the copy machines, these presentations were definitely not targeted at the Times Square Ink. audience. One IKON executive after another got up to talk about their company, and how, in their words, it could work for "you, the executive" as an outsource service provider. The Times Square Ink. trainees stuck out in the room—after all, they were there as prospective outsource labor, not as executives deciding whether a contract with IKON would make their company "more productive." And I think some of the trainees were quite attuned to this. I heard one trainee whisper to another, "I thought standing there running the copier *was* being productive, but now I see that's not true!" Times Square Ink. was teaching

these trainees that being "productive" meant sorting mail or working at a photocopy machine instead of staying at home or getting locked up. Here, at the IKON trade show, they were hearing a different standard of productivity—intellectual work done away from the manual labor of running off copies. In some ways, this trade show was showing the trainees the limits, even the end, of the trade they were learning. The self-sufficient superphotocopiers on display will probably never become a routine feature of every office in New York City. But the clear implication of all the presentations at the trade show was that the vocation for which they were training at Times Square Ink. was not a stable, dependable niche. Rather, their "productive" future was an unstable, shifting piece of ground, one subject to erosion by forces and decisions completely out of their control. Mastering their own selves and skills might not be enough, not when IKON was working to show executives how human beings might not be required to run these machines at all.

After the presentations from IKON, the Times Square Ink. group went back out into the main room for lunch, a buffet very nattily spread out by a gourmet deli service. This lunch was the source of more cross-class cultural misunderstanding, and some humor. The instructor and I were the only two people in the group who knew what many of the items in the steam-table trays were. One trainee pointed down at a tray of marinated portobello mushroom slices, laughing, "Those look like someone's *tongue*, yo!" Two steps further down the buffet line, I joked with that same trainee about the calamari I was scooping onto my plate. "What *is* that?" she asked. "It's squid," I said. To which her reply was, "*What??* Eeew . . . " When I joined the group of trainees sitting off to the side of the room together to eat, she was repeating our exchange to the rest of the group. I encouraged her to try some for herself, and I made a comment about calamari and portobellos being gourmet fare. Another of the trainees, who had been bragging to the group all day about his new "pimp hat," heard me and drawled, "Yeah, where's the *fine wines* and the *cheeses*, you know what I'm saying, the *caviar* . . . " His lavish hip-hop lifestyle fantasies were well-rehearsed in terms of language, but he stuck with a plain roast beef sandwich for lunch. The reality of the glamorous life his words conjured up was both more prosaic and more alien in practice.

It was during this lunch break, with our group huddled off to the side of the room, that the Times Square Ink. instructor asked me, perhaps for the benefit of the trainees, exactly what was my profession. "Well, I'm an anthropologist," I said. One of the trainees muttered under his

breath, "Anthropologist, yo, what's that? . . . " The instructor immediately turned to him and said, brightly but forcefully, "Informational interview time!" The trainee sighed, looked inward for a moment as though gathering his concentration, then turned to me with an entirely different look on his face, earnest and serious. "So," he said, loud and clear and sounding very curious, "what exactly do you *do?*" I explained that anthropology was the study of culture, what people do in their everyday lives, and that I wanted to study Times Square Ink. and the rest of Times Square instead of working abroad as most anthropologists do. He nodded, "Oh, you study people's culture." I was impressed at the way in which he had taken up the instructor's challenge, to turn idle curiosity into a "productive" engagement with others—a crucial part of the Times Square Ink. program, to be sure.

After lunch, we ditched our plates and stepped into yet another small classroom to hear another presentation—this one, a speech from a college basketball coach, there to talk about basketball and about his charity work for "Coaches Against Cancer." Unlike the other presentations and demonstrations we had seen before, which had been sparsely populated, this room was packed with executives. They all came ready with questions about college basketball. (Nobody seemed interested in Coaches Against Cancer.) One of the Times Square Ink. trainees also had a question for the coach. She asked him, "How do you motivate your players every day?" He responded by listing all the different kinds of pep talks he had at his disposal, depending on the situation. He said that sometimes he gave his players long inspirational speeches; sometimes brief comments; and sometimes nothing. Later in his talk, he described his work motivating his players as "brainwashing." He explained, "I'm trying to get them to think like I do." At this point, the Times Square Ink. instructor leaned over and whispered to me, "I guess that's what *I* do, too." When the coach's presentation ended, so did the IKON trade show, and the instructor recruited me to help round the trainees up and get them ready to take the subway back up to the Midtown Community Court.

Throughout the IKON trade show, the Times Square Ink. trainees seemed to represent everything IKON was trying to *eliminate* from the workplace with its new machines. They were would-be copy machine operators, walking through the world of the people who were trying to phase out their niche in the workplace—to make them obsolete, at the exact moment that their instructors were coaching them to imagine handling documents as the path to a life that was more organized,

more productive, and ultimately more *meaningful*. To a limited extent, the trainees seemed to recognize the incongruity of their presence at the trade show, even to revel in it a little. When we first arrived and signed in, there was a bit of a debate among the group over who would get the red polyester canvas totebag IKON was giving away as a promotional gift. Everybody wanted one for themselves, but the receptionist only gave us one, which the instructor took without comment on her part. Later that morning, as the event progressed, I gradually saw first one trainee, then another, walking around with totebags slung over their shoulders. By the end of the trade show, pretty much everyone had their own. Where did they find them? Why did they want them so much? I never found out, but there was some humor in the way that the trainees turned their attendance at the trade show into an event based around navigating and outwitting the system that the organizers had set up to distribute these goodies.

Despite the fact that the Times Square Ink. group didn't really fit in, neither the IKON organizers nor the other attendees commented on our presence there. Nobody seemed much flustered by the trainees, their questions, or their hunt for the red totebags. Perhaps this indicated that they weren't quite as out of place as I imagined. More likely, it was a token of the extreme professionalism and good graces of all involved. But, of course, the trainees weren't there at the trade show to confront or subvert the event. For them, it was an "informational field trip," a window into their hoped-for future jobs and lives and a test of the skills they had been practicing at the court. Despite the game of finding the totebags, they and their instructor did their best to maintain this framework.

I tried to talk with some of the trainees about the trade show afterward. They all seemed pretty blasé about the experience as a whole. Still, I wondered whether the event might have had some kind of lingering negative impact for the attendees—some kind of unconscious recognition of the tenuous nature of the roles for which Times Square Ink. was training them. The instructor certainly thought it did, but for different reasons. She told me a few days later that she was worried that the IKON trade show might have given the trainees too much exposure to the wrong parts of the corporate sector. She thought that the trade show might have made the corporate world seem too distant, too foreign, too unattainable to the trainees. I thought about the besuited executives around us; the super-high-tech copy equipment; the foods that the trainees had found so disgusting and weird. The instructor

said that she was concerned the trainees might lose their motivation as a result of their experience, or otherwise "act out" their frustration. In fact, I found out later that two of the trainees had left the presentation and gone straight to Macy's department store instead of back to the Community Court. There, in an apparent instance of "acting out," they had gotten themselves arrested for shoplifting. Among other things, this resulted in their being expelled from Times Square Ink. Nobody at the program mentioned anything about the incident, at least not to me, which was a bit unusual, given the program's emphasis on discussing "issues" openly and in great detail. I never heard anyone comment on the trainees' absence, why they were gone, or what had become of them later. I never saw them again.

In this case, perhaps, the personal redevelopment offered by Times Square Ink. was aiming to overcome personal or social obstacles that were too challenging, at least for these trainees. It was one thing for the redevelopment of Times Square to reshape a complex and disreputable place and make it suitable for corporate tenants and real estate speculators. It was quite another to offer something like the same transformation to individual human beings. Buildings can be knocked down, rebuilt, or rehabilitated to suit anyone's tastes. People are harder to change.

Reorganizing the Self

During my fieldwork at Times Square Ink., I saw this process of ordering and rationalization enacted in a parallel form: in the physical environment of the program's classroom and copy center. Over the course of the year I was doing research there, the Midtown Community Court management decided to move the copy center from its first location, in a donated second floor in an office building just south of Times Square at the corner of Broadway and Fortieth Street, to an unused room in the Community Court building itself. This made their operation much more efficient, as trainees with business in both the court and the copy center during the same day no longer had to leave the building and walk through Times Square to meet their obligations.

Even more pronounced, though, was the transformation of the Times Square Ink. classroom in the basement of the Community Court building. When I first visited the program, this was a shabby and undefined room. Its walls were decked with a palimpsest of taped-up pieces of paper, including inspirational sayings, essays, and artwork left by previous

groups of trainees, a poster explaining the dress code, and so forth. Books were stacked up in all corners, along with reams of paper, boxes of envelopes, and other materials for the mailroom next door, where Community Court arraignees worked off their community service assignments mailing fliers for local nonprofit organizations. The chatter of people carrying out their sentences in the mailroom would filter into the trainees' classwork, and vice versa—a constant reminder of the lack of clear spatial separation between the mailroom and the Times Square Ink. classroom. On successive visits throughout the year, I watched as Times Square Ink. and the mailroom came to occupy ever-more-separate spaces. The classroom received a fresh coat of white paint; the papers that were taken off the walls during the painting never went back up. This made the room feel both sparser and more organized. Further, Community Court employees put up a wall with a locking door between the Times Square Ink. classroom and the adjacent mailroom. They also installed a separate heating and air-conditioning unit to give the newly defined classroom its own ventilation system. In short, both the Times Square Ink. classroom and the copy center underwent something like the same process of cleaning, tidying, and reordering that the program applies to its trainees.

Similarly, when faced with visits from important outside entities, the entire Times Square Ink. program went into a frenzy of preparation and activity. These whirlwind cleanups mirrored the kinds of anticipatory defensive procedures that the program teaches as part of getting ready for job interviews. On the two days I was present before a dignitary came to visit—one day it was then–Attorney General Janet Reno, the other some officials from a business school that was considering giving Times Square Ink. a substantial grant—I found the place in a tizzy. Before the attorney general's visit, the trainees had all been sent to the copy center, so I gave the instructor a hand; I helped with neatening up the papers on the walls, rearranging the clutter, cleaning the blackboard, and so forth. (This was before the classroom's minimalist makeover.)

A few months later, when the potential grantors were on their way, I sat and watched the instructor rehearse the trainees in the classroom over and over about how they would introduce themselves to their visitors. When she had to leave the room for a few minutes, they continued to drill each other. Occasionally, one of the trainees would use speech patterns that they had been taught to avoid. Specifically, he would nervously pepper his sentences with "knowutimsayin" or "nahmean."[6]

Another of the trainees corrected him whenever he did so. In a dead-on impersonation of their instructor's meticulously "correct" speech, she would primly shoot back, "Watch how you're speaking!" While the instructor was out of the room, the trainees also hotly debated among themselves the issue of whether to remove the condom one had stapled to his life map, which was on display on the wall. Throughout these drills and discussions, they hectored one of their fellows who sat quietly, refusing to talk at all, let alone to practice what he might say if one of the visitors were to ask him a question. "You've got to say something, man!" they said. "What are you going to say when they get here? Come on—don't mess this up for us!"

With all this rushing around to clean up the classroom and rehearsing student presentations, Times Square Ink. was, in effect, striving to communicate to its powerful visitors its own ability to put on a certain kind of performance—to show that this was a functional, agreeable, and well-organized place. This was, of course, the very performance the trainees were being taught to put on during job interviews. Also like their job interviews, the trainees later recounted to me how perfunctory these visits were, each lasting only a few minutes. This mode of performance, as much as anything, was what the program taught. The fact that the organization acted it out so intensely before these visits only points to how absolutely central this mode of performance was to the program's version of corporate culture.[7]

The vagaries of the "real" working world, in turn, could and did double back and attack the Times Square Ink. program itself. The difficulties of running a self-supporting, nonprofit copy center imposed a constant sense of unpredictability on the program. The need for personnel at the copy center always threatened to drag beginning trainees out of the classroom, and the entire group of trainees and managers were often kept working late to meet big orders. The actual economic pressures that drove the copy center's capricious demands on people's time contrasted vividly with the stable, intimate, and regulated atmosphere that the Times Square Ink. classroom tried to foster.

Another such unpredictable (but, in the world of work, eminently typical) turn of events changed my involvement with Times Square Ink. A few months into my research, the administrators from the Community Court who oversaw the program decided that they needed to make it more financially efficient. Therefore, they fired ("downsized") the Times Square Ink. "job developer." This was the instructor who was in charge of making contacts with area businesses in order to find jobs

for trainees once they graduated. In his place, they assigned job development duties to the instructor who ran the program's Module One classroom.

This shook things up a bit at Times Square Ink., to say the least. The classroom instructor was now under a double load; she was faced both with teaching and with finding jobs for the trainees. Seeing this, I volunteered to take over the part of her job I felt I could cover—I would help the program's advanced Module Three trainees to write their résumés. Meanwhile, I stayed in contact with the now-jobless job developer, with whom I had become friendly during my fieldwork. I was literally stunned the first time we met outside the copy center. While working at the program, he had always been clean-shaven, in full corporate regalia: pinstriped shirt, tie, suspenders—the works. Now, he was rumpled and unshaven, wearing a T-shirt and sweatpants. For a moment, it was as though I was watching a series of "before" and "after" images, such as Times Square Ink. so often offered its trainees, but this time with their sequence reversed. I remembered the words of the Fortune Society speaker, who had warned the trainees against being "drawn into informality." You couldn't get more deeply drawn into informality than he had.

If something similar had happened to a Times Square Ink. trainee or graduate, the instructors would have encouraged them to talk about it at a Job Club meeting. After all, one of the main tenets of the program was that work is unpredictable. Jobs are hard to find and uncertain once found. Employers and managers can be unfair or capricious. I have described some of the ways in which the program's instructors modeled the role of the employers, when they tested how the trainees would respond to their incitements to informality or emotion. They constructed the Times Square Ink. training environment, and, by extension, the workplace, as an ongoing *test* of emotional self-discipline.

In some ways, the trainees' hands-on work in the copy center was secondary to their emotional work of managing the distance between their interior and exterior selves. They were learning that the secondary task of marketing oneself to one's superiors was inextricable from the everyday duties of a job. Just as, in the new and redeveloped spaces in and around Times Square, the redevelopers aimed to construct an image of lively, theatrical street culture that was deeply imbued with themes of control and marketability, so too, in Times Square Ink., trainees were asked to construct an interior "true self" that was simultaneously disciplined enough to hide itself in public. The private interior

self was discovered and elaborated simultaneous with its hiding away inside, just as the "authentic," "honky-tonk" Times Square was represented and celebrated, over and over again, simultaneous with the radical upscaling and transformation of the area.

Testing the Self

The Times Square Ink. program extended the metaphoric model of the test over all aspects of work and life. I overheard several conversations between angry trainees and the classroom instructor, in which the instructor used the image of the test to displace conflict from the interpersonal level to the intrapersonal. On one such occasion, the instructor was annoyed with a trainee for asking her to change an appointment for a job interview she had arranged for him. The trainee had found a temporary job for himself setting up chairs for an event on the afternoon of the interview; for his part, he was angry at the instructor for refusing to call the interviewer with an alibi for missing the appointment. He railed at her for not understanding his situation, his inability to live on the pittance Times Square Ink. provides as a stipend. (The program paid its trainees very little—a few dollars a day and subway fare to and from the program.) She cut the argument short, telling the trainee that she saw the situation as an "honesty test" for him. Where the trainee tried to define the interaction as a conflict between their two interests, the instructor defined it as a test. The instructor seemed to vanish in her own construction, leaving the trainee alone to navigate his own, self-imposed dilemma.

This conversation exemplified the tension that Times Square Ink.'s testing frame created between the public and the private self. Both public and private selves took shape in relation to one another. Both were tested against each another. Did one's public persona serve one's private interests? Were one's private desires properly restrained, according to the need to present a public face? The conversation also illustrated the uses to which this same public/private tension could be put. In order to navigate the tension of deciding what must be made public or private, the trainees had to internalize it. The program portrayed this as a process of growing knowledge of, and control over, oneself.

I have discussed some of the ways in which the Times Square Ink. program focused on teaching its trainees how to craft their public personae so that they could get and keep a job—to successfully navi-

gate Times Square's redeveloped public sphere. The trainees learned to hide things about themselves. At the same time, they learned to be curious about themselves in terms of wondering what it is about themselves they must hide. Just as they learned to craft affable personae for work, the program also demanded that the trainees delve deeply into their feelings, memories, and wishes. They elaborated personal and interior selves to go along with their public personae. In order to learn to hide their pasts, their memories, their feelings of unease, their hopes or dreams, they had to make these private things totally public. While in the program, they talked about their family lives; their personal histories; their sexualities; their styles of dress and speech; their involvements with crime or drugs; their fears and uncertainties; their extravagant hopes; their anger; their boredom. At Times Square Ink., the trainees publicized everything about themselves that they would, presumably, later repress in the world of work.

The program gave a view of the working world as an elaborately structured performance, a game of strategies and deceptions. The program's instructors referred, over and over, to a set of standardized conventions that supposedly governed *everyone's* performances of self in the public sphere. This was exemplified in the instructor's observation, "We all know the rules, but sometimes we choose not to follow them." Trainees struggled through the challenging and frustrating work the program offered as a preparation for the challenges and frustrations of their hoped-for future jobs. As they did so, they learned a particular way of looking critically on their lives before the program—to see themselves as having failed to keep the right things private.

This was how Times Square Ink. both did and did not address the difficulties its trainees had to face. As mentioned above, nearly all the trainees I met while studying the program were black or Latino. One way of looking at the instructors' emphasis on controlling the boundaries between public and private selves would be to see all this as their attempt to teach the trainees how to navigate pervasive white prejudice in the workplace. The program did this by showing the trainees some ways in which they could try to downplay their own signs of racial or ethnic difference. Trainees learned to anticipate and accommodate the desires of corporate managers, and thus to portray themselves as good potential workers.

At the same time, the program attempted to contain the seeming impossibility of this assignment. After all, who can really control the fantasies others produce about them? It did so by explicitly telling the

trainees that they were *not* learning a set of tactics to deal with racial or ethnic prejudice. Instead, the program presented this training as the rescue of the trainee's "real self" from the mess of personal history. For example, at one graduation ceremony, a trainee thanked the program's instructors for teaching him to "listen to the man inside me." He then said that he hoped they would help him to continue to "listen" to this hitherto unrecognized part of himself. The program insisted that the students locate their narratives of success or failure *inside*. The focus was on whether the trainees had the ability to keep their selves properly divided into appropriate public and private sectors. However, the program was structured such that the trainees were put in the position of never knowing *exactly* what it was about themselves they were meant to hide. Was it their criminal record, if any? Was it their ethnic identity, as constituted through marked speech patterns, posture, demeanor, clothing, or jewelry? Was it their skin color—and how would someone hide this? Or was it a personal and essential interior—their "real self?"

Editing Résumés

This was a question that the Times Square Ink. staff seemed to have thought about a great deal. The question became even more complicated in the light of two factors. The first of these was the seeming mismatch between, on the one hand, Times Square Ink.'s rituals of imagining and performing a rigidly ordered corporate world, and, on the other hand, the experiences that people who had graduated from the program recounted to me. Many of the Times Square Ink. graduates with whom I spoke assured me that their job interviews were nothing like the relentlessly high-intensity mock interviews they had run through in the program, nor like the tests for which the speaker from the Fortune Society had attempted to prepare them. They told me that there were no probing questions, no conversational feints, and no chances for them to deploy their documents or scripted answers. Instead, the interviews they described were mostly perfunctory, "How soon can you start?" affairs, indicating as much as anything the booming Manhattan FIRE (finance, insurance, and real estate) economy's hunger for bottom-rung clerical support.

Furthermore, these same graduates told me that, in retrospect, they felt that the program placed too great an emphasis on emotional self-discipline and public formality. They said that this aspect of their train-

ing had little to do with actual everyday life in their workplaces. True, they were ostensibly working in high-toned legal and corporate offices, sorting mail, photocopying documents, and doing other such clerical work. However, their actual employers were outsource companies, contracting with those law firms and corporations. As contract employees of an outside firm, they were so thoroughly segregated from the day-to-day social life of their place of work that they felt they had little need to worry about looking or acting, as the trainee with the braided hair was warned, "too ghetto." Of course, their (exaggeratedly?) casual dismissals of Times Square Ink.'s simulacrum of corporate culture might simply indicate that the training the program offers worked perfectly. Did the program over-prepare them for a formalized and challenging world that, in practice, failed to materialize? Did they enter the workplace confused and relieved at how socially easygoing and informal their jobs were? The instructors would probably have regarded this as a sign of their success in readying the trainees for work.

As mentioned earlier, my role at Times Square Ink. changed from researcher to volunteer approximately halfway through my fieldwork, when I offered to help the Module Three trainees edit their résumés. Once a week, I would arrive at the Community Court building, walk through the metal detectors, sign the registration book, and go downstairs to the Times Square Ink. classroom. Often, a trainee would already be waiting when I arrived, on leave from the copy center upstairs. I would introduce myself and explain that I was a researcher doing volunteer work at the program. Then, we would sit at the instructor's desk. I would use the padded desk chair at the computer; the trainees always sat off to one side, pulling one of the hard classroom chairs around so that they, too, could see the screen. After they showed me the handwritten rough draft they had brought with them, we would get to work.

For me, this was by far the most satisfying part of my year of fieldwork. I was always happy to help the trainees create a good-looking résumé. I wasn't sure whether or not I was learning anything, but I felt much more secure than when I was wandering around Times Square or interviewing harried public officials. Working on the résumés put me in a position of authority. I was doing the one thing I felt confident that my graduate training in anthropology had prepared me for—editing a mass of somewhat haphazard data into a coherent story. It reminded me of working as a teaching assistant, helping students with their papers. What's more, I felt included in the everyday life of the Community Court, even though the guards upstairs never seemed to recognize me.

(They always searched my backpack and confiscated my tape recorder and my Swiss Army knife whenever I entered the building.) Even more important, I knew that the Times Square Ink. administrators, instructors, and trainees were grateful for my presence.

As we sat together, I would take the trainee's drafts and begin to fit them into the format I had adapted from the old résumés already stored on the instructor's computer. This meant that I had to ask them detailed questions about their past: "Where did you go to high school? Do you remember the address? Did you graduate?" Invariably, they would run into gaps—missing facts that they would have to fill in later, such as the ZIP code of their high school. As quickly as possible, I would get to the part I enjoyed most—their employment history. Their drafts might say something minimal, such as, "Worked in family bakery," or, "Maintenance man—two years." For me, the less information they had with them, the better (from a researcher's perspective, at least). Less detail on their drafts meant more time for me to talk with them.

Over the months I volunteered there, I developed a standard list of questions I would ask everybody. I always asked the trainees if they ever had people working below them; if they had to answer phones or otherwise deal with the public; if they were in charge of hiring, firing, or disciplining other employees; if they made their own schedules, or if they had to keep to a set timetable; and so forth. As I interviewed them, I rewrote their answers on the fly. I remember asking one trainee, whose resume said that he had worked as a maintenance man in an apartment building, "You say that the tenants in the building would complain to you about the heat in their apartments? Well, maybe I can put down, 'Responsible for recording tenant requests for service and relaying these to management.' Does that sound OK?" My goal was to break each job down into its constituent tasks. I wanted to describe the job of "security guard" in a way that would make its component skills and duties add up to a dense and thoughtful little paragraph. I narrated the trainees' past jobs in a way that would make them sound qualified to manage an entire Manhattan law firm, let alone to work in its copy center or mailroom. I enjoyed watching them smile as their one-line entries— "Assistant Manager, McDonald's, South Bronx, One year"—unfolded like an origami trick into densely edited mini-essays extolling their enormous competence, reliability, and initiative. They would laugh and nod, saying, "That's it, that's just like it was."

I began to treat the enterprise as somewhat of a game. Of course, I wanted them to have a well-written and accurate résumé. But I also

felt that I was making a point (at least to myself) about the ways in which the Times Square Ink. program enframed the trainees' histories. I felt that I was showing that these people had complex and meaningful lives before they were arrested and taken to the Community Court—before they started Times Square Ink.—and that these lives weren't just a wasteland of bad personal decisions. For me, the résumés became concrete evidence of the talents and abilities the trainees had accrued on their own. I meant to show that they were already well-suited to work in a buttoned-down office or anywhere else, no matter how demanding. Often, this process was gratifyingly easy. I would ask questions; the trainees would answer. "We" (really, I alone) would then edit the résumé, either reducing or expanding it to fill one side of a single sheet of paper, and then sit back to enjoy the result when it emerged from the printer.

Sometimes, though, the process was much more difficult. One such moment of frustration came when I was working with a friendly but somewhat sad-seeming middle-aged man, who appeared to fit in surprisingly well among the much younger group of trainees in his class at Times Square Ink. (Most of the trainees I met during my fieldwork were in their twenties, though the groups entering the program seemed more and more diverse as the year went on.) The other trainees treated him with real affection, calling him by the nickname "Preach." The draft of his résumé he brought with him said that, for a period of a year, he had owned and operated a laundromat in a town in South Carolina. However, this was all it said—the résumé had no information about what he did there, no details about why he had closed the business and returned to New York City, not even a street address for the business. When I asked him about this, he said that the town was so small that he didn't think the laundromat ever really had an address.

I tried to run through my usual list of questions. "What kinds of jobs did you do there on a typical day? Did you have anyone working under you? Did you deal with the public?" He looked down at the desk, mumbling vaguely. His responses gave me the impression that my questions made him uncomfortable. I said, "Well, it looks kind of strange to leave this laundromat in South Carolina here in the middle of your résumé like this. Maybe we should put something about why you closed it and came back to New York?" He kept looking away and said something about, "It just didn't work out." After this, he wouldn't say anything more about the issue; we went on to talk about the complexities of another job he once had, stocking the shelves in a New York City supermarket. When we were done, the line describing the laundromat job

did, indeed, look kind of strange. The single, enigmatic line muddled my efforts to make his work as a security guard and as a stock clerk seem like prime experience for someone who wanted to jump into the corporate labor pool. I saw no way I could use the information to enhance my account of his future potential, so I was tempted to delete the entry entirely, but I felt torn. It seemed dishonest for me to delete a year's experience running a business out of someone else's résumé. In the end, I left it in.

On another occasion, I helped to write the résumé of another older man. He was a relatively recent immigrant, who had worked for a number of years on construction sites in Mexico. The rough draft of his résumé was surprisingly organized and complete; there was little for me to do other than to enter it into the computer. But I felt that his descriptions of his work in Mexico included far too little detail about his workplace social interactions. Instead, he had carefully listed the types of construction equipment he knew how to use. The list specified cranes, backhoes, and so forth, down to the specific model numbers of the heavy truck engines he could operate and repair. He seemed annoyed when I suggested that this might seem like "too much detail." His annoyance grew when I began to edit out his lists of model numbers and ask my usual questions instead. "Were you in charge of making your own schedules? Did you supervise other workers or make their schedules?" Glowering, he answered mostly with, "I don't remember," or, "Well, I really don't know," or, "It was just construction work." His answers seemed to imply that my questions had nothing to do with what he remembered as being important about that work. At the time, I felt frustrated with him for not realizing what seemed like common sense to me—that the minutiae of truck engine maintenance had little to do with the copying and mailroom work the trainees were learning at Times Square Ink. Didn't he understand this? Didn't he want to tell the right kind of story about himself on his résumé? The information about construction equipment looked glaringly out of place to me, just as the enigmatic laundromat had looked out of place on the résumé I had made for Preach.

At first, I resented these frustrating incidents. I blamed them on the trainees' lack of willingness to go along with their own best interests. Later, I began to question my own feelings of frustration and blame in these moments. As I mentioned earlier, it was easy for me to see my work with the trainees on their résumés as a kind of game. I could poke a little fun at Times Square Ink., at least in my own mind, while at the

same time helping the program and the trainees. I thought that I was demonstrating that these trainees were already prepared for work—that all they needed was someone to point out the most strategic way to reveal this about themselves. However, this was exactly how Times Square Ink. enframed its relation to the trainees' lives as a whole. By helping the trainees to strategically reveal what I imagined as their hidden, work-ready selves, I was enacting much the same social drama as the Times Square Ink. program. After all, the instructors often portrayed their classes as a conduit for social knowledge the trainees *already knew*—as in, "We all know the rules, but sometimes we choose not to follow them." The program constructed the act of "choosing to follow the rules" as a tactical move in an ongoing life-game. This was how I understood my own role as résumé editor. I was there to help the trainees "choose to follow" what I took to be the obvious conventions of narrating oneself in this curious textual genre. When their judgments diverged from mine, I was annoyed at the way they seemed to willfully ignore these rules of the game.

My work at Times Square Ink. forced me to realize that I was far more deeply embroiled in the hierarchical culture of the redevelopment of Times Square than I had previously cared to admit. I started to see that the redevelopment of Times Square was not something that I simply could look at from the outside and pick apart, with all the theoretical tools and critical perspectives I could muster. Rather, this was something in which I could not help but be deeply involved and implicated myself.

The truth was that I felt perfectly at ease sitting in the Times Square Ink. instructor's comfortably padded chair, using the computer the trainees were forbidden to touch, as I helped to bring out what I saw as the most important aspects of their past. Rather than an outsider on the margins of the redevelopment, "speaking the truth to power," as we graduate students told ourselves was our mission as anthropologists, here I was, sitting in the seat of power, editing people's lives according to my vision of the truth. If the story of the redevelopment of Times Square was one of super-empowered individuals turning their big-business-friendly vision of urban life into material reality, then I was playing my own small part in the transformation, turning my own business-friendly vision of individual lives into paper documents.

For the past hundred years, Times Square has served as a site where New York City's marginal citizens could hide in plain sight, due to the area's

overall crowded anonymity and spectacular license. It has also served as the site where city administrators, real estate developers, moral reformers, and others have imagined the social benefits and financial profits to be reaped from excluding these marginal citizens from this, their refuge and their place in the spotlight. The formal and informal everyday interactions at Times Square Ink. echoed this conflict over public space and public life in New York City. The Times Square Ink. program sought to give a few of these "undesirables," targeted for exclusion, the sociocultural tools to make a place for themselves in the area's new corporate economy and sanitized street culture. Just as the people involved in the redevelopment targeted the spaces of Times Square as being infected with "blight" and in need of complete redefinition, Times Square Ink. asked its trainees to look on their former lives as having been "blighted" and in need of increasing respectability.

The anti-blight planning and policing concepts of the redevelopment viewed prostitutes, the homeless, drug users, and black and Latino youth as a homogeneous mass of threatening difference. Times Square Ink. aimed to incorporate these supposedly "illegitimate" subjects as citizens of the newly "legitimate" Times Square economy. It did so by teaching them to understand work, life, and the self as a test, or a game. What is more, the program taught its trainees that one of the rules of this game is that one should never fully recognize the nature of the game itself. This is why the program rushed past acknowledging anything *structural*, anything outside of one individual's ability to control, that might prevent any of the trainees from getting or keeping a job.

The picture Times Square Ink. painted of the corporate world was a harsh one. Throughout the program, trainees prepared for the verbal gamesmanship of job interviews. They learned to control the anger or frustration they might feel when treated unfairly at work by those in positions of authority. They practiced the proper etiquette, speech style, and body language appropriate to the corporate environment. In effect, Times Square Ink. made the world for which it was preparing its trainees sound culturally alien and rigidly formal. The image of the corporate world that the program constructed was one of strange hierarchies and verbal games. In this world, the techniques of distancing and disciplining the self that the program taught were crucial to surviving day-to-day working reality. How could one live in such a world, fraught with power and danger, without carefully watching one's words in order to navigate through office society? How could one make it

through a day of running a copy machine and enduring one's superiors without constant coaching from one's future self? "I'm not here in this office; I'm five years in the future thanking the 'present me' for putting in so much time here."

Obviously, this image of the working world as a cruel and inflexible machine of discipline and prejudice was somewhat exaggerated. As mentioned above, graduates from Times Square Ink. often commented to me that their actual job interviews were much easier than the rigorous mock interviews through which they had suffered while in the program. Similarly, they described their actual working environments as substantially more flexible and less formal than Times Square Ink.'s nonprofit copy center. This exaggerated quality was not accidental. Times Square Ink. asked the trainees to imagine a rigidly ordered world that they must enter. This was the corporate world, or rather a simulacrum thereof. By constructing representations of the corporate world, the program then taught them to construct selves that were rigidly ordered enough to inhabit it. Times Square Ink. worked to instill discipline in its trainees in the classic martial-arts mode, testing them for challenging situations that would probably never materialize. In doing so, the program presented something of a snapshot of the redevelopment's own self-image; a picture of what the redevelopers thought were the ground-rules for citizenship in the New Times Square.

"Visible Signs of a City Out of Control"
Images of Order and Disorder
in Police-Community Dialogue

How did everyday citizens relate to the redevelopment of Times Square and the larger socioeconomic shifts it represented? One place I began to answer this question was in the new institutions aimed at fostering community-police dialogue in the adjacent neighborhood known as Clinton or Hell's Kitchen. These were places where community groups gathered to communicate directly with the NYPD or other representatives of city government. These dialogues showed the complicated dynamics of building an image of "order" to fit the radical transformation of the area, catalyzed by the Times Square redevelopment.

The New York Police Department had long played a central role in the redevelopment of Times Square. By the mid-1970s, when the plans for the redevelopment project were announced and work was underway, the NYPD had already condensed the numerous small precinct commands covering Midtown Manhattan into two "superprecincts,"

Midtown North and Midtown South, in order to better manage their control over the area. The Koch administration's 1978 "Times Square Action Plan" announced a new NYPD program, called "Operation Crossroads"—an enormous increase in the number of uniformed and undercover officers on patrol along Forty-second Street and throughout Times Square. Operation Crossroads' focus on dispersing "loiterers" and deterring petty street crime was meant to help lay the groundwork for the state's eventual redevelopment of the area. Even the naming of the new precincts was connected to the redevelopment, helping to consolidate the brand name of Midtown as a single office district rather than as a cluster of smaller individual neighborhoods.

Later, in the 1990s, Mayor Rudolph Giuliani shifted the community policing programs developed by his predecessor, Mayor David Dinkins, to a much publicized "zero tolerance" strategy that involved, among other things, a crackdown on what were termed "quality-of-life offenses."[1] The Giuliani administration's policing strategy was only one aspect of the mayor's "quest for order."[2] Giuliani was very popular during his tenure as mayor, but also much vilified for what some saw as his betrayal of the city's liberal legacy.[3]

Perhaps the most controversial aspects of Giuliani's administration were the incidents of extreme police violence against African American residents of the city. My fieldwork was bookended by some of the most notorious of these cases. I came to New York in the fall of 1997, on the day that the Abner Louima police torture case hit the front pages; I stopped doing research around the time Amadou Diallo was shot by four members of the NYPD street crimes unit in the Bronx; and I was immersed in writing about the relationship between police and real estate development in Times Square when Patrick Dorismond, a Haitian American security guard, was shot in a scuffle with undercover officers posing as drug buyers near the Port Authority bus terminal, just west of Times Square. All three of these incidents led to an outpouring of criticism against what many saw as the excesses of then-Mayor Rudolph Giuliani's "order maintenance" strategies, and their disdainful, even violent, attitude toward nonwhite New Yorkers.[4]

When I carried out my fieldwork in the late 1990s, the Clinton/Hell's Kitchen area was already undergoing rapid gentrification, largely as a result of the redevelopment's buildup of "Midtown Manhattan" as an office and residential district for the city's white-collar economy. There was no single "community" in Hell's Kitchen, but, rather, numerous interconnected neighborhood groups and block associations, each with

its own history of engaging with the Times Square redevelopment in particular and with the growing pressures of the real estate development economy in general. These groups represented themselves as residents of Times Square in an attempt to mitigate the effects of the redevelopment and the pressures it placed on their neighborhood— the rapid rise of developers' interest in local real estate with its attendant rent increases, evictions, etc., and also the displacement of prostitution and drug dealing from Times Square and Forty-second Street into the side streets of Hell's Kitchen just to the west. Part of their work involved demands for increased police attention.

These meetings between police and community groups were a key site where ordinary citizens engaged with the redevelopment project and its representations of its ordering effect on the city. The ways in which these meetings framed urban social problems in terms of fear and crime, and how this framing played out in practice, revealed how people perceived and narrated their experience of urban socioeconomic restructuring under neoliberalism. In New York City, this entailed privatizing public spaces as well as other programs aimed at fostering a climate conducive to real estate speculation and development, often at the expense of residents. These encounters between police and community groups were a microcosm of the ideological struggles between neoliberalism and its discontents. These meetings acted out battles over this new political-economic order: its attempts to achieve hegemonic status; the efforts of individuals and groups to accommodate themselves to its harsh ideology; and the struggles of those who cannot comfortably find a place in the world neoliberalism makes.

Broken Windows Stories

People in and around the Times Square redevelopment project often explained their work and experiences to me in little parables of urban life. After hearing a half-dozen of these parables I came to think of them as a genre: "broken windows stories." I heard these broken windows stories from security guards, community activists, and real estate developers alike during my fieldwork. People told broken windows stories when they wanted to explain why they thought it was important to control even relatively innocuous disorderly behavior. For example, one board member of the Times Square BID used a version of the story to

explain why his organization had instituted its own trash collection services in Times Square:

> There's a philosophy of keeping things clean called the "broken windows syndrome." An empty building, if somebody breaks a window in it, a lot of people will break other windows in it. If you put graffiti on a wall, [and] people don't scrub the graffiti off promptly, pretty soon there'll be more graffiti, more and more. But keep the wall clean, it tends to stay clean. If the street's clean, it tends to stay clean. If there's trash flowing around the street, why should you not drop your gum wrapper or cigarette wrapper? I mean, somebody else does it. But if it's really nice and neat and clean, you are more apt to wait 'til you get to a wastebasket.

He laughed as he went on to give another example of what he considered a broken window: On the way to meet me at the coffee shop on Ninth Avenue where we spoke, he had spotted what he took to be the police commissioner's limousine, illegally parked half up on the sidewalk.

These broken windows stories all seemed to draw both their form and their content from a single, paradigmatic source. This was a famous 1982 article by the criminologists George Kelling and James Wilson entitled, "Broken Windows: The Police and Neighborhood Safety."[5] The title alluded to a story that the authors tell in the first pages of the article—the archetypical broken windows story:

> A stable neighborhood of families who care for their homes, mind each other's children, and confidently frown on unwanted intruders can change in a few years, or even a few months, to an inhospitable and frightening jungle. A piece of property is abandoned, weeds grow up, a window is smashed. Adults stop scolding rowdy children; the children, emboldened, become more rowdy. Families move out, unmarried adults move in. Teenagers gather in front of the corner store. The merchant asks them to move; they refuse. Fights occur. Litter accumulates. People start drinking in front of the grocery store; in time, an inebriate slumps to the sidewalk and is allowed to sleep it off. Pedestrians are approached by panhandlers.
>
> At this point it is not inevitable that serious crime will flourish or violent attacks on strangers will occur. But many residents will

think that crime is on the rise, and they will modify their behavior accordingly. They will use the streets less often, and when on the streets will stay apart from their fellows, moving with averted eyes, silent lips, and hurried steps. "Don't get involved." [. . .] Such an area is vulnerable to criminal invasion. Though it is not inevitable, it is more likely that here, rather than in places where people are confident they can regulate public behavior by informal controls, drugs will change hands, prostitutes will solicit, and cars will be stripped. Drunks will be robbed by boys who do it as a lark, and the prostitutes' customers will be robbed by men who do it purposefully and perhaps violently. Muggings will occur.[6]

Wilson and Kelling's story tacitly referenced numerous images of anonymity and social distance in urban life, as well as a plethora of sociological studies of city dwellers' attitudes of "reserve," self-concern, and unwillingness to help others.[7] But their story turned these classic images of urban life on their head. Wilson and Kelling characterized these, not as inherent characteristics of urban public space, but, rather, as signs of a pathological lack of urban community; not the default urban social order, but symptoms of the *failure* of social order. The authors used this story to call for the police to attend to what they call the "folk wisdom" of cracking down on "disorderly" acts like drinking or panhandling: "The citizen who fears the ill-smelling drunk, the rowdy teenager, or the importuning beggar is not merely expressing his distaste for unseemly behavior, he is also giving voice to a bit of folk wisdom that happens to be a correct generalization—namely, that serious street crime flourishes in areas in which disorderly behavior goes unchecked. The unchecked panhandler is, in effect, the first broken window."[8]

Wilson and Kelling concluded their article by calling for the police to go beyond the letter of the law to crack down on "disorderly" acts like drinking in public or sleeping outdoors. Instead, they say that the police should recognize the potentially troubling effects that are latent in every inappropriate public act: "Arresting a single drunk or a single vagrant who has harmed no identifiable person seems unjust, and in a sense it is. But failing to do anything about a score of drunks or a hundred vagrants may destroy an entire community. . . . [I]t fails to take into account the connection between one broken window and a thousand broken windows."[9] In this analysis, any rule that might protect a "disorderly" person—"a single drunk or a single vagrant"—from the actions of the police is trumped by the image of "a hundred vagrants,"

"a thousand broken windows." This is an image of ambient criminality, the potential for disorder and lawlessness latent everywhere in the urban landscape. The authors suppose that following the principle of zero tolerance will stifle these bad latent tendencies and bring about a general social good: "order." [10]

"Broken Windows" continues to circulate widely since its publication more than twenty years ago. Wilson and Kelling turned the image of the broken window into a powerful political symbol; a trope, a story encased in a single image, for a narrative of a struggle between order and disorder fought in the arena of everyday life and the taken-for-granted. "Broken Windows" has traveled throughout police and urban development circles and beyond, in the form of anecdotes, favorable media coverage, and Kelling's coauthored follow-up book, *Fixing Broken Windows*,[11] as well as being reprinted in collections of "classic readings" on policing and community-police relations.[12] In 1994, Mayor Giuliani and his police commissioner, William Bratton, brought "Broken Windows" into the heart of NYPD practice, as indicated in their inaugural manifesto, *Police Strategy No. Five:* "New Yorkers have for years felt that the quality of life in their city has been in decline, that their city is moving away from, rather than toward, the reality of a decent society. The overall growth of violent crime during the past several decades has enlarged this perception. But so has an increase in the signs of disorder in the public spaces of the city. . . . Mayor Rudolph W. Giuliani has called these types of behavior 'visible signs of a city out of control, a city that can't protect its space or its children.'" [13] *Police Strategy No. Five* went on to announce the NYPD's more general interest in controlling both crime as well as the *fear* of crime. In order to justify its crackdown on quality-of-life offenses, as well as its interest in understanding and controlling fear, the document expressed concern for New York City's "embattled communities," which it imagined as the terrified victim of these offenses.

Quality-of-Life and Community Policing, Zero-Tolerance Style

The Broken Windows image imagined a particular vision of "community policing." The story framed the community as an embattled victim, threatened both by outsiders and by neglect and complacency from within. But the story also referred to the community as possessing an intuitive and accurate perspective on how to combat the forces that

impact it. These threats to community solidarity were quantified under the concept of "quality of life." People used the phrase "quality-of-life offenses" to refer to those misdemeanors formerly known as "victimless crimes:" soliciting for prostitution, petty drug sales, drinking in public. At one such community-police meeting, I heard a New York City judge define "quality-of-life offenses" as "annoying, very annoying, *very* annoying misdemeanors that upset people as much as felonies—sometimes *more* than felonies." I also heard people use "quality-of-life" to signal a host of "disorderly" but noncriminal behaviors, as well as to talk about general perceived decay in the built environment around them.

This discourse on Broken Windows, quality-of-life, and community policing emphasized the importance of spaces for dialogue, where the community and the police meet to work out effective strategies for social control.[14] The image of community-police dialogue served as a "black box"; a nebulous place where important processes of empathy and information-sharing would "naturally" take place. However, in practice, the meetings I attended were often a good deal more contentious and fraught than the relatively cheery and straightforward image that "community-police dialogue" implies. One reason for this was that, as in all such meetings, Clinton/Hell's Kitchen residents and police brought their own agendas, which were neither entirely consistent within themselves nor congruent with one another. Another reason was that these meetings, and the larger discourse of which they were one institutional manifestation, incited people to reflect on and talk about their everyday experiences of urban life in ways that highlighted, even produced, moments of conflict and open-ended speculation. These were common group dynamics, but they were particularly intense and relevant in these dialogues, and they sometimes seemed to cut against the very premise of the dialogues—to help strengthen and enforce *order*.

The result was what I came to think of as a particular kind of cross-talk—a spiral of questioning and curiosity running at cross-purposes to the official aim of the meeting. Once those in attendance at such community-police meetings were asked to discuss their everyday fears and confusions, they rarely ran out of material. This was especially true when the police were present in the room, telling the residents that the NYPD might be able to make those fears and confusions go away. Members of the community would begin to think of more and more things that had bothered them as they walked down the street. They would call these out, asking whether or not the police could do anything about them. While their concerns regarding what the police

should and shouldn't do on their behalf were not always clear, what *was* clear was that the police often responded to these requests with suspicion, or even with anger. It was as though they were both inciting the community to speak about signs of disorder, à la the discourse of Broken Windows, then interpreting the results as though the community itself was a source of disorder.

The Hell's Kitchen Neighborhood Association

For example, take the February 1998 meeting of the Hell's Kitchen Neighborhood Association. The Neighborhood Association, which covered the area just southwest of Times Square, drew its members from the people who live in the lofts and tenements south of the Port Authority bus terminal, from Forty-first Street down to around Thirty-fourth Street, and from Eighth Avenue all the way to the West Side Highway. This was a deeply unglamorous mixed-use area, full of factories, storage facilities, and parking lots. I had seen the black-and-white posters in the area announcing a series of themed Neighborhood Association meetings; the theme of this meeting was "Safer." (The themes of the meetings to come included "Cleaner" and "Greener," reflecting the Neighborhood Association's unusually sophisticated contingent of lay city planners and housing activists.) The posters advertised the meeting as a chance for area residents to "share their quality-of-life concerns" with officers from the Midtown South Precinct. When I arrived at the tiny community center just off of Tenth Avenue where the Neighborhood Association met, the room was already packed. A large delegation of ten or so uniformed police officers, including the Midtown South commanding officer (C.O.), sat or stood at the front of the room, facing the eager crowd.

The meeting started slowly. A board member of the Neighborhood Association made some opening remarks, then threw the floor open to questions from the audience. But before anyone could begin, there was a disturbance in the back of the room. Someone poked their head in the door and said something in Spanish; at this, a group of ten or so Latino-looking people, who had been standing together in a group and looking around uncertainly before the meeting started, filed out. (I found out later that a tenants' rights meeting for Spanish speakers was being held that night in a building down the street.) The people around me had been swiveling their heads over their shoulders to look at the group even

before the interruption. Now, they exchanged glances with each other. The group seemed hesitant to speak at first, until one woman from the audience spoke up, identifying herself as "someone who lives on 'the border;'"—in other words, near the corner of Thirty-ninth Street and Ninth Avenue, close to the boundary between the Midtown North and South Precincts. She said that there was a group of men who would call out lewd remarks to her as she walked through the area. She thought the men, who she called "the harassers," crossed from precinct to precinct in order to avoid police attention, "like the border between the U.S. and Mexico." The woman went on to describe these men as "drunken people from these little *haciendas*—or whatever they are. . . . They're also getting *grabby*. It's like they set up *camp* on Thirty-ninth and Ninth with their chairs and their bottles of beer—in broad daylight!"

I was relieved for their sake that the Spanish-speaking group had left at the beginning of the meeting. What would they have made of these remarks? As it was, nobody present seemed to take offense. Rather, the woman's story about "the harassers" on "the border" catalyzed an outpouring of related stories from those in attendance. The tiny room was suddenly filled with a clamor of voices relating stories: of people calling out threats from the corner of Thirty-ninth Street and Ninth Avenue; of petty crimes like purse snatchings; or of "quality-of-life offenses" like seeing men drink in public or urinate against the wall of a building in plain view. Someone speculated that these men congregated around Mexican grocery stores and restaurants in that area. This remark, in turn, prompted a laughing wave of admonitions to the police not to close a favorite cheap Mexican restaurant on that corner.

Throughout these successive waves of stories—people sitting up in their seats and interrupting each other and laughing or looking serious as they told of their shared feelings of discomfort or danger—the men whose uniforms made a solid blue wall at the head of the room stood impassively. Their faces were studies in blank composure. When the riot of stories died down, the officers simply replied to those who had spoken that they would investigate if there were a serious crime to report. However, they added that the men gathered on the corner of Thirty-ninth and Ninth did not present "a police problem." The attendees looked stunned. Someone spoke up with a rhetorical challenge for the police: "So, what *do* you do if three guys say something really filthy?" One officer replied, "It's called freedom of speech."

It seemed that the police were largely and surprisingly dismissive of both the challenge and the complaints as a whole. But they followed

this by asking the audience to tell them more about what they called "other bad corners" and "trouble spots." People immediately spoke up, mentioning particular street corners; complaining about seeing someone selling drugs on the sidewalk outside what they called "a bad restaurant;" naming a bar on Eighth Avenue, saying, "It's a real trouble spot, and the building that it's in, I see lots of—kids—that I would describe as male prostitutes." Others talked about areas near the Port Authority bus terminal where manual workers would hang out and party loudly after quitting time, or of a "circus atmosphere" around the loading dock of a paper depot in the neighborhood.

I could see that the delegation from the Midtown South Precinct was having trouble maintaining their looks of calm attention. They were losing their patience, fidgeting and looking annoyed. Several times, either the Neighborhood Association board member who had opened the meeting or the C.O. from the police delegation attempted to cut the discussion short. However, each time they tried to move on to another topic, someone else from the audience would speak up about another "hot spot." It seemed that, once the attendees began to catalog their everyday experiences in the neighborhood in terms of "trouble corners," or areas where they felt uncomfortable or in danger, they tapped into a veritable geyser of stories. This was a well of narratives about gut feelings and fleeting impressions; it would never run dry.

One intense-looking man, who had been sitting silently behind me during the entire meeting up to this point, shot his thin arm into the air and began to talk about what he called a "potential hot spot" on his block. He said that construction workers had set up a great deal of scaffolding near his building. The trucks parked on the street alongside the scaffolding made him feel hemmed in and endangered; he said that he felt as though he was "in a trap." One officer asked if it was legal for the trucks to park there. The man replied that he thought it was, but that he wasn't sure, as the flimsy streetposts bearing the parking signs had all been knocked over by errant workers. The police officers were visibly appalled. One cut the man short, angrily demanding to know why "all you people weren't coming to your Precinct Community Council meetings [see below] with these little petty concerns?!" (As it happens, when I attended one of the meetings of the Midtown South Precinct Community Council, I was the only one present, aside from a few police officers and a representative of the Fashion Center Business Improvement District. He said that he was there to "respond to community concerns.")

There was a short, stunned silence following the officer's outburst. With this, it seemed that the police were ready for the Hell's Kitchen Neighborhood Association meeting to come to an end. Someone from the audience spoke up again with another "hot spot" story, but the officers simply ignored him. Instead, they quickly filed out of the room, leaving us in our seats, some with hands still in the air and more stories to tell. I wondered why the officers had attended, and what they made of the meeting.

The Midtown North Precinct Community Council

The Midtown North Precinct Community Council represented another part of the neighborhood, the shopping and residential district north of the Port Authority bus terminal. This area was gentrifying quite differently than the south, and much more rapidly, with older bars and shops on Ninth Avenue being converted into upscale lounges and restaurants catering to the burgeoning population of young professionals living in new high-rise apartment towers.

The Precinct Community Councils were created by the NYPD to mediate between the police and the residents of their territory—in this case, between the Midtown North Precinct and the residents of the area west of Times Square but north of the neighborhood covered by the Hell's Kitchen Neighborhood Association. Unlike the Hell's Kitchen Neighborhood Association, the meetings of the Midtown North Precinct Community Council were kept in relatively strict order by the officials of the group, especially the president, Bob Davis. Davis was an urbane man, who worked as a producer for a national network news program. When I interviewed Davis, he explained to me that he understood his role in the Community Council to be simply that of a mediator, helping to put stories and listeners into their proper alignment. However, his actual role in these meetings was somewhat more complex than this. He was charged with producing the orderly community subject that the Precinct Community Council claims to represent. Davis did this by presenting a "community" that was both friendly to, and intelligible by, the NYPD.

The council met monthly in the dining hall of a halfway house and residential treatment center for the mentally ill. This was interstitial space in the crammed built environment of midtown Manhattan—a rare space for "community" to gather in a densely packed neighbor-

hood with almost no indoor public spaces. The spacious dining hall was sparsely populated at the meetings I attended. Most of the large round tables scattered around the room held only two or three people. We would all sit facing the long table that dominated the front of the room, drinking tea and eating the stale chocolate-chip cookies the staff of the treatment center would lay out for us. At the long table sat the four or five officials of the Midtown North Precinct Community Council and the C.O. from the Midtown North Precinct. The two or three police officers he brought with him to every meeting would either sit at the long table or stand beside it, expressionless.

The meetings would begin with a standing salute to the U.S. flag. Then, when we were all sitting again, the officials of the Precinct Community Council would go over any questions left from the previous month's meeting. We would swiftly move to presentations from local groups, followed by questions for the police from the audience. The meetings were, for the most part, calm, unhurried and efficient; a study in easy back-and-forth dialogue. Someone would raise their hand with a question—for example, wondering what they should do about someone they suspected to be a drug dealer working out of a building on their block. The president of the Precinct Community Council would carefully rephrase the question for the commanding officer. The C.O., looking thoughtful, would reply, saying that citizens needed to know how to inform the police about suspicious activity without getting themselves directly involved. And we would move on to the next question.

In our interview, Davis explained that, as he saw it, the purpose of the meetings was to immerse the police in the everyday experiences of the Hell's Kitchen community: "The more [the police] know about a problem, the more likely [they] are to come up with a solution. . . . You hear a little old lady say that [she's afraid of restaurant deliverymen riding bicycles on the sidewalk], suddenly it puts a different spin on that particular problem." But the police can't or won't pay attention to everything about which people complain. Sometimes, the Community Council meetings produced stories about matters that ranged beyond the role of the police, as well as stories that didn't seem to open up clear demands for action at all. Davis said, "I would never tell people, 'You're wasting our time. Why'd you come to us with that?' You know, you try to be polite, but . . . [an older woman] always brings up health care. 'Health insurance for old people in this country is a problem.' That's true, but it's not a problem that the police department can solve. So she gets the floor to talk about whatever issue she wants, and then we

just go on. Because some of these things are just not anything that the police department is charged to do anything about."

During the meetings, Davis would lean forward intently when these seemingly aberrant stories would start to unfurl. It was as though he was physically straining to find the kernel of police business within their wide-ranging content. Only rarely would he ever interrupt anyone, and he never cut anyone off outright. Instead, once the questioner had finished, he would often distill and repeat their questions, or try to find the gist of their rambling stories. When I asked him about these editorial practices, he maintained that he was just "the 'flow control' person." He said that the question of finding the relevant issue was simply one of determining whether or not the complaints matched up to violations of the criminal code: "[I]t's a question of, 'Is this something that the police should be doing?' If you have problems because you live in an apartment building with a [broken] vending machine in the laundry room . . . that's not the police department's problem to deal with. If you have prostitutes sitting on your front step, that *is* a police department problem. . . . [I]t's not arbitrary, it's pretty obvious what the police should and shouldn't do."

The "obviousness" of "what the police should and shouldn't do," and the community's acceptance of this, was, in part, what Davis was at pains to craft, and enforce, during the meetings. He was not only facilitating a dialogue between the two groups, but also marketing each to the other. This entailed a power dynamic firmly tilted toward the police. For example, Davis told me that he would give each community member who rose with a question only three minutes in which to speak, to ensure that no single speaker dominated the proceedings. At the same time, he mentioned that he would give the commanding officer from the Midtown North Precinct as much time to speak as he liked. In fact, he faulted his predecessor, who, he said, used to cut the C.O. off in mid-sentence in a way that he thought was not only rude but, in a larger way, harmful to the esteem in which he wanted the police to hold the community.

Davis also mentioned that he would call likely attendees about a week before every meeting to ask them if they had any questions they wanted the police to address. He would then forward these questions to the C.O. He explained that he did this so that the police would not be taken by surprise by any community members' requests for help or information; the advance notice was to let the police draft a complete answer to the questions. In the meetings I attended, this practice had the

effect of making the police appear extremely professional and quick to respond to community concerns, with little confusion or fumbling for words, let alone to the outright hostility of the Hell's Kitchen Neighborhood Association meeting. It also ensured that the police would seem to maintain a good opinion of the community; specifically, that they would not visibly scoff at anyone, or feel that they were being blindsided by hostile requests.

However, the Community Council president's efforts, while largely successful in this regard, were necessarily limited by the formal structure and setting of the meetings themselves. Sometimes, residents of the treatment center where the meetings were held, who were always sitting around the room eating cookies and watching the proceedings, would speak up. Then, the orderly exchange of information between "community" and "police" would begin to slip into what I thought of as a narrative miasma; a deepening quicksand of tactile imagery or endless tangents.

On one such occasion, an old woman began a long and rambling diatribe about busses. This seemed to be related to other discussions we had heard at these meetings about obnoxious tour busses in the neighborhood. However, her words were both vague and urgent, thrusting around in various directions without ever pointing at a clear question for the C.O. Then, a fat middle-aged man sprawled in his seat at the side of the room spoke up in a gruff, drawling, drunk-sounding voice. He said that he had something to add: "So there I am walking down the street this morning, and I see this bus. And it's eight A.M. and I'm thinking, what is this bus doing there? So I'm looking at this bus and I'm looking around, and I don't see anybody on the street, so I'm wondering about this bus and I'm thinking, what's going on? So OK—" At this, one of the Precinct Community Council officials cut him off. Bob Davis tried to encourage him to get to the point. He asked him to articulate what was "important" about this bus. Was the man asking a question about the annoying tour busses that idle for hours on the side streets off of Tenth Avenue? Was he concerned for the safety of the bus driver? Rather than narrow down his story, the man replied by reiterating the fact of the bus at eight in the morning on an otherwise deserted street. The narrative miasma began to open once more.

The C.O. sat impassively through the bus story, as he did through every question or comment from the sparse audience. Around the room, however, the various block association presidents and community garden volunteers shared uneasy glances with one another and

with the board of the council, seated in front of the room behind their long table. These glances seemed to ask two questions, which I must admit rang insistently in my own mind as I listened to the man wax on endlessly about his eight o'clock encounter with the bus: "What is his point?" and, "What does the C.O. think of this?" The man's story seemed to gesture toward the logic of the Broken Windows story: I saw this inexplicable and disturbing thing, please explain and/or remedy it. However, the form of this Broken Windows story recapitulated its content—it became a Broken Window itself. The story served to open up a disorderly spiral of its own within the meeting, in the form of the wary glances flickering around the room.

When I asked Davis whether he ever noticed this dynamic at play in the meetings, he laughingly answered in the affirmative. He then told me the following story:

> [W]e have that young lady, she's always there. . . . It was a few months ago. . . . I called on her—her hand was up in the back, frantically [waves his hand in the air]—I called on her and she said [he adopts a slow, emphatic voice], "I want to know—*what* is the New York City Police Department—going to *do*—" (We're all listening intently, like, "This woman's right on target!") "—going to do about *all*—of these *space aliens* walking around among us?? There are more and more of them showing up every day; they're walking down the streets with us. What *are* the police going to do about this?" . . . I didn't want to insult her with, "What are you, a nutcase or something?" All I could think of was, "Space aliens are a *federal* problem. You'll have to call Senator D'Amato's office—let me get you the number.". . . I could just see Senator D'Amato's office the next day calling, "Did you tell her to call us?"

We both laughed at the fact that he was able to recover so smoothly in the face of the woman's question about space aliens. Much of the humor came from the response that he chose, which was to play at taking her question seriously. Rather than dismiss her as a "nutcase," he simply referred her to the Senate, not the police. He was able to play with knowledge about "what the police should and shouldn't do" in order to keep the meeting "working"; to avoid the miasmic potential of questions that seemed crazy, unintelligible, or simply overly challenging.

The distinction that Davis cited between "what the police should and shouldn't do" was not always so obvious in the context of the Com-

munity Council meetings. There was a sizable, poor Latin American enclave in the tenements and apartment towers along Tenth Avenue. (Thus the "anomalous" group looking for the Spanish-language tenants' rights meeting at the Hell's Kitchen Neighborhood Association.) I never saw anyone from this area of the neighborhood at the Precinct Community Council. When I asked Davis about this, he told me that they had held a few meetings in Spanish, parallel to the regular Community Council sessions. However, the people who came to those meetings never had anything to say about "police department problems." They wanted to talk about feeling unsafe in the laundry room of their building, or about why their elevators didn't work.

The president's role was to effectively limit debate within the council by constraining "irrelevant" questions, not just about space aliens, but about social and economic issues in general. He kept the conversation focused on "order" in the terms the police want to hear and speak about. In doing so, he subtly seduced the two parties, police and community, together, building conversational common ground and rapport between them. In order to keep the police interested in the community, he ensured that the meetings produced not just order, but a larger sense that the community exists as a coherent and reasonable body, one that shares a common definition of order and that is taken seriously by police and city government as a whole.

The Quality-of-Life Committee

There was, in fact, a body set up to address some of the nebulous questions that the Midtown North chairperson worked to exclude or reframe. This was the Community Board Four Quality-of-Life Committee, which met in the offices of Community Board Four, on Forty-second Street adjacent to the Port Authority bus terminal. The monthly meetings of the Quality-of-Life Committee provided a forum for area residents to air complaints about things like bar patrons zooming around on motorcycles late at night; noisy garbage workers picking up trash at three in the morning; or, as in the Precinct Community Council, idling tour busses saturating the air with diesel fumes. Most of the complaints at the Quality-of-Life Committee were cast in terms of businesses lacking in consideration for the people who lived in their vicinity. Sometimes a representative of the business in question would be present. With the urging of the heads of the committee, they would

invariably promise to immediately address all the complaints about noise, or trash, or whatever.

Sometimes only the complainants were present. Then, we would sit around the table, with the two chairpeople of the Quality-of-Life Committee at one end and the rest of us ringed around in folding chairs. We listened to carefully composed "community" members struggle to articulate their concerns. This was not always an easy task. Both the subject and the form of their complaints pushed at the envelope of the codes of propriety that seemed to obtain in these meetings. People told stories about sleepless nights; about the outrage of being woken up early in the morning by inconsiderate sanitation workers; about roadies for rock concerts loudly drinking, working, and socializing after late night shows at a local concert venue. They talked about their fruitless and repeated attempts to plead their case directly to bar owners or to tour bus company managers. They enumerated countless telephone calls to the Department of Environmental Protection to document noise levels they were *sure* were inexcusably and illegally high. Often, they brought with them binders of photos, or notebooks carefully detailing every phone call. As they spoke of all these offenses to their "quality-of-life," the complainants had trouble keeping their voices level. Anger crept into their speech. They would swerve from an impassive voice to an impassioned one, from reason to outrage. At those times, one of the two chairpeople would gently interrupt. They would not cut people off, so much as lead them back to what they considered the heart of the complaint. They did so by asking questions of fact, such as, "Did you call the police?"

Sometimes, the complaints that people brought in were not so easy to define. Complainants spoke of dangerous pit bulls at large in area parks and plazas. Their stories of feeling threatened by the dogs merged into speculations about the dogs' owners. "Who raised these people? Where are their parents? I worry about society." The chairpeople would gently step in to shut down abstract debates about "homelessness" or overly emotional rhetoric about the insensitivity of pit bull owners. They would refer to the agenda for the meeting, reminding us of the need to "move on" or "stay productive." Similarly, they would mediate between complainants and the objects of their anger, calling on each to speak and respond in turn.

At the Quality-of-Life Committee, the raw matter of "community" consisted of the voices of individuals speaking of troubled sleep or dirty air and asking for the state to intervene on their behalf. Part of the production of community in these meetings lay in the committee's ability to

generalize from the complainant's story to a kind of generic individual experience—to leap from one person's life to "quality-of-life." The term "quality-of-life" served to turn these stories into narrative commodities. "Quality-of-life" brought life experiences into public circulation. It enframed these experiences, allowing them to be quantified, generalized, and exchanged. It was up to the chairpeople to produce this enframing sense of interchangeability between the specific complaint and the "quality-of-life" of the community as a whole. They had to steer the stories told so that they were not overly specific to the individuals who recounted them. Rather, these stories had to be told as something that could have happened to anyone. At the same time, they had to weigh the specific exchange value of each story. What kind of official measure did this justify? Nothing? A stern letter from the Community Board? A visit from the Liquor Licensing Board? Additional NYPD officers to enforce traffic regulations?

When I interviewed Mary Dorman, one of the Quality-of-Life Committee chairpeople, a lawyer with a history of both engaging in and defending gay and lesbian civil protests, I began by asking her to define "quality-of-life." Dorman responded, "It's *all* 'quality-of-life' unless there's a hook, unless we can get a hook to send it somewhere else. For instance, if it's tenants being harassed by a landlord, that would be a housing issue. If it's elderly people involved, it might be a human resources issue. So unless we can get it out somewhere . . . it usually stays with us." To a certain extent, then, quality-of-life is defined by *negative* criteria. Unless a complaint fits into the rubric of another Community Board committee, the Quality-of-Life Committee must hear it. But Dorman also specified what she saw as a positive definition for a "quality-of-life offense." She defined a "quality-of-life offense" as an action that violates the "community" standards every New York City resident should know in their guts: "[W]e as New Yorkers and community members . . . we know exactly what *is* an acceptable noise level and what is *not* an acceptable noise level. It's not always gauged in a decibel measurement. . . . So we [in the Quality-of-Life Committee] do noise—noise is a big one of course—litter, trash, kind of visual littering, just things that are intrusive on people's lives." Thus, "community" is tight where "quality-of-life" is loose. "[W]e as New Yorkers and community members . . . we know exactly what is an acceptable noise level and what is not an acceptable noise level."

Sometimes, though, as in the Midtown North Precinct Community Council, people would raise larger, more ambiguous social issues in

the form of "quality-of-life" complaints. At one meeting I attended, the entire committee was swept up into a debate over whether or not to do something about "the homeless"—men sleeping on the sidewalks of Ninth Avenue. Ultimately, Dorman interrupted and closed the entire conversation. When I asked her about this, she said:

> There's a *huuuge* coalition of people trying to "get the homeless off Ninth Avenue," but what does that mean? Is that like sweeping garbage and taking it to a dump? What does that mean? Where are they going to go? Over to that Community Board on the East Side? What does that mean? I don't know! People say "Get them to move." Get them to move where? [. . .] I don't even understand the vocabulary. . . . Does it interfere with the businesses? Is there a crime threat? Is it a trespass? . . . [I]t gets very political because some people say, "I don't want to have to look at it." And then I say, "What do you mean, 'it?' You mean, at these people who are homeless? Is that what you are calling 'it'?"

She juxtaposed the sweeping and sometimes disturbing inclusivity of quality-of-life with her own editorial criteria as chairperson of the Quality-of-Life Committee: "Does it interfere with the businesses? Is there a crime threat? Is it a trespass?" As she put it, "[W]e had people come in, and the complaints were so amorphous, you couldn't tell how, who, or where—it was embarrassing."

As a lawyer, Dorman's embarrassment at these "amorphous" complaints points to the ways that quality-of-life stories often exceeded legal definitions of reason or proof. It was up to her to frame these complaints about "quality-of-life offenses" in a more "orderly" fashion. She said, "I insist upon proof in the first instance. I want the complainant, or a representative of the complainant if it's an elderly person or something, and a written complaint with names and numbers. . . . We don't function just by somebody calling in and saying, you know, 'The bar downstairs is making too much noise.' We really need verification of what they're complaining about." In this way, Dorman countered "amorphous" and "anonymous" complaints with "names and numbers." She demanded written documents and personal presence as part of the conversion of everyday trauma narratives into "quality-of-life" stories that justify official intervention. She did not see the anger that tore through complainants' voices as inexcusable or unreasonable: "People can exude emotion. Fine. And we know you're irritated and we know

you're upset and all of this—what's more important is, what *time* were you awakened by motorcycles? What alarm went off? Where were you, where was it, [where were] the cops?" Her task as chairperson of the Quality-of-Life Committee was to manage this precise transition, from, "we know you're upset and all of this," to, "what *time* were you awakened by motorcycles?"

Dorman had to ensure that the complainants were able to give voice to their feelings. At the same time, she had to ensure that the stories they told fell within two frameworks. The first of these was a legalistic framework: evidence, witnesses, testimony. The second was the framework of "community." The ideology of "community" demands a vision of the social body not torn by lingering hostilities and not subject to irrational forces or antagonistic conflicts. Dorman alluded to the theatrical element of this enactment of community when she noted how important it was for all complaints to end in a state of harmonious dialogue between offender and offended, produced by the mediating force of the committee. As she put it, "[W]hen people come in, [I] get the facts from them, and then, the most important thing to me, to show that we're doing a good job as nominated representatives of the community, is for me to be able to say, which I do say at the end of every complaint. . . . 'Is there anything else you want us to know? Is there anything else *you* want us to know, Mr. Respondent?' And if they say 'No' . . . then I think that we've done our job."

The Citizens' Police Academy

There was another site of police-community dialogue I was able to explore in my fieldwork, one in which the NYPD reached out to these same community groups to instruct them directly in the concepts of order and social life that the police use in their practice. This was the NYPD Citizens' Police Academy, an institution crafted by the police for the express purpose of interpellating key community members into the police perspective.[15]

I heard about the Citizens' Police Academy from several people I met during the early days of my fieldwork, including Mary Dorman and Bob Davis, as well as prominent members of block associations, tenants' rights organizations, and other community groups in the Hell's Kitchen area. What the Citizens' Police Academy offered to community members selected by their local precincts was an abbreviated simulation of

the year-long training course that NYPD cadets undergo in order to become police officers. The program was set up by the NYPD in the early 1990s as part of the Dinkins administration's community-policing initiative. The course was given every spring, held in the resolutely nondescript Police Academy building on East Twenty-first Street in Manhattan. There, for three hours one night per week for fourteen weeks, the hundred or so attendees were split into four "companies," based on the location of their home precinct. Grouped by company, they sat through classes taught by the police officers that work as instructors in the real NYPD Academy. These classes covered topics that ranged from constitutional law to firearms training to testifying in court. At the end of the fourteen weeks, there was a festive graduation ceremony; attendees received a diploma and had their picture taken with the police commissioner.

When my class gathered en masse in the academy auditorium on our first night, we heard a speech from the head of the Citizens' Police Academy alumni association. He told us that we were "all very special people, singled out by police folks" to become mediators between the police and "our communities." He said that, if we heard someone in a meeting complain about how the police treated them, we should now think, "Wait a minute, I was in the Citizens' Police Academy," and intercede. These sentiments were repeated throughout our course of training. As one Citizens' Police Academy instructor told us in class a few weeks later, "What we're trying to do is open the door a little and give you a little bit of insight." However, the "insights" that the academy instructors gave us were often ambiguous, if not outright frightening. The NYPD portrayed itself, in some ways, as an unpredictable and potentially dangerous organization, indigenous to a similarly unpredictable and dangerous world.

According to the image presented by the Citizen's Police Academy, the power of the police lay in their ability to gauge the world in terms of sources of potential threat. In the class devoted to gangs and juvenile offenders, we watched a video purporting to educate police officers (and, by extension, us) in the art of identifying gang members by their dress and behavior. The video began with a woozy, solarized tracking shot along a crowded school playground. The tracking shot of the playground recurred throughout the video, framing the video as a whole, as well as providing segues between talking-heads interview segments with people identified by subtitles as "gang experts." The slow, wary scan of the playground appeared to simulate the perspective of a

police officer, looking out the window of the patrol car as it rode past an after-school crowd. The video distorted the groups of children, making them distinctly hard to "read." The unintelligible video image gave the scene an alien, suspenseful quality. I was sure that the camera was going to pick out *something:* a fight, a mugging, a dead body. I found myself scrutinizing every hazy bunch of kids, looking for the crime I felt sure was there.

Later in the video, the camera did another drunken-style, distorted pan along a nighttime street scene. The narrator described how gang members identify themselves through "distinctive clothing." The video focused on a kid wearing a puffy jacket, zooming in until the label on the jacket filled the screen: "North Face." I was taken aback. What were the makers of the video trying to imply with this shot? Wasn't North Face just a regular brand name? Was there a gang that called itself "North Face," or whose members wore North Face garb? Whatever the message its makers intended, the gang video hinted at a world of mystery and menace to which prospective police officers had to learn to attune themselves. Nor was it clear whether or not this world of threat was confined to the spaces of the city outside of the Citizens' Police Academy. One instructor once asked our class, "You're a police officer and you come into this room; you see twenty-five people, and what do you think?" An older woman called out, "Trouble!" and the whole class laughed. The instructor went on. "We don't walk into the room and say, 'Twenty-five pretty people.' We walk into a room and say, 'Who doesn't belong here?'" In effect, the instructor was agreeing with the woman's joke.

This image of a world of crime and mystery came up again in a class devoted to "drugs and the occult." Here, we learned about "drugs" through a jumble of police lore, ominous-sounding statistics, and portentous, "urban legend"–type stories. We sat through a series of overheads describing rampant drug use:

Last year
Americans consumed
30 million pounds of
marijuana
120 thousand pounds of
cocaine
9 thousand pounds of
heroin

Around me, I heard members of the class whistling in surprise and loudly whispering to each other: "Ooh, wow. How do they know that?"

The instructor talked to us about the specific smell of crack cocaine; he said that it was something all police officers had to learn to recognize. He told us stories about dealers secretly adding LSD to temporary tattoos in Cracker Jack boxes. (Officer: "What happens is, the kids lick the stamps." Class: "Oooh.") He talked about the club scene in San Francisco. (Officer: "They have something out there these days called the *rave parties*. They put on psychedelic lights and dance around for eight or ten hours." Class: "Hmmm, mmmm." Officer: "That's what they do.") At the end of his talk, the instructor put up one more overhead about the massive amounts of drugs seized by police and the FBI in one year: 2,124 pounds of heroin; 233,094 pounds of cocaine. He then concluded with this remark: "If this is what they've seized, imagine how much is out there."

Throughout this presentation, the overheads and anecdotes whizzed by quickly in a seemingly haphazard manner, one on top of another. The instructor didn't convey much specific information about "drugs" at all. Rather, his lecture vividly evoked a pervasive world of criminal commerce and corrupting influences; the police, it seemed, could barely restrain the threat this drug world posed to the rules and boundaries of everyday social life. The instructor described the drug world by heaping together examples of what the authors of *Police Strategy No. Five* called "visible signs of a city out of control." Our education at the Citizens' Police Academy sometimes seemed to consist of immersion in these signs of "disorder." Our classes reveled in them, and our instructors told us to let these "signs" seep into our awareness of the city and its dangers.

After the unit on drugs, we heard from a man who introduced himself as the NYPD's specialist in the occult. (He told me after class that he had a doctorate in Religious Studies.) The class began with a succession of pictures: Charles Manson, David Koresh, Shoko Asahara (leader of the infamous Aum Shinrikyo religious group, which carried out a nerve-gas attack in the Tokyo subway in 1995), and a voodoo-practicing drug dealer the instructor called "Babyface." He proceeded to regale us with stories of fortune tellers, con artists, cult leaders, and a local occult bookstore about which he cautioned, "I do not think you should go there *alone*." Was he kidding? He seemed to be half-joking throughout his presentation, but I couldn't be sure. The members of the class seated around me whispered nervously and laughed as the instructor

switched between deadly earnest warnings of deranged would-be cult-ists and jokes about palm readers. He would reassure us that there was nothing to all this black magic, then hint that maybe there was some-thing to it, after all. . . .

These presentations gave the impression that the city was a strange and threatening place, on the verge of spiraling out of control. This was reinforced during our role-playing exercises, when we in the class would act out the part of officers responding to a call or playing the firearms training simulator video game. On the night we used the firearms training simulator, we sat in a darkened basement, the room lit only by the simulator's giant screen. Three class members stood in front of the screen, their bodies locked, stiff, and jerky. The rest of the class screamed and laughed in the dark as the simulator led the three through one scenario after another. A drunk man waved a machete over his head, a crying child strapped in a car seat hanging from his other hand. An angry woman in a suburban bedroom refused to put up her hands. Gunmen took hostages in an office building.

The simulator gave us a cop's-eye view, sidling warily around corners, looking for imminent danger. As the video progressed through its vari-ous nerve-wracking narratives, the instructor running the program ex-plained to us that we had to think like a police officer. He laid down some very explicit guidelines. We were to fire at the screen only in cases in which we later would have been able to explain to a judge, "At that moment, I feared my life was in danger." There were to be no warning shots. We shouldn't aim for an arm or a leg. We had to shoot for the "center mass"; in other words, the center of the torso. We watched as the volunteers from the class warily confronted the image of the machete- and baby-wielding drunk, or as they waited for the hostage-taker to leap out from behind the filing cabinets. And then BOOM BOOM the screen would freeze, and tiny red or green dots would flash to show the shooters whether they had hit or missed their targets. The videos ended the moment shots were fired. The entire scenario seemed to race up to that one moment; after that, time froze along with the video image. All that mattered, it seemed, was an officer's ability to explain a snap judgment. The consequences of that judgment—whatever happened after the program's story stopped—weighed far less than the explana-tion: "At that moment, I feared for my life." [16]

According to this perspective, the police must be constantly aware of the potential for violence around them. They must also be con-stantly poised to respond to threats with violence of their own. I began

to rethink the stereotypical image I had formed of the police during the community meetings described above. This was an image of the blasé cop wearing mirrored aviator sunglasses. No wonder they masked their eyes behind opaque lenses, I thought. Their parodically blank stares became, for me, an image of someone holding back spasmodic lethal force in the face of "a thousand broken windows"—a thousand potential threats.[17]

The question of the impassive gaze of the police officer came up several times in the Citizens' Police Academy. The first was when an instructor showed us a series of "crime spotting" videos. Some of these videos showed a crime in progress, such as a surreptitious pickpocketing in a city park. Others only portrayed a suspicious scene; for example, a darkened shopping mall with a door ajar. Our assignment was to watch these videos and imagine how we would explain what we saw and how we acted to a judge. Throughout the exercise, the instructor poked fun at the videos and their hokey cheaply-made-in-the-1970s anachronisms. Afterward, he turned to us and explained that, despite their dated qualities, the videos accurately demonstrated correct police procedure. He said, "You really do have to describe stuff like that all the time. . . . Having *cop eyes*—using your senses and your job together. There's no way to teach this, it's something that has to come with time." What's more, he said, the videos also illustrated why citizens often interpret the police as rude: "It's like part of your job to be nosy, if not almost suspicious. If you're on a foot patrol, everything that's happening potentially is your business. . . . Lots of people get offended—they say, 'Look at this cop, he's harassing me!' It's like a double-edged sword."

We heard this again from another instructor during the class on traffic stops. As we prepared to role-play the part of officers pulling a car over for speeding, he told us, "We'll try to give you an idea of what's going through the officer's mind while they're doing it [pulling you over]—why they're doing what they're doing. There *are* reasons." The reasons he gave all had to do with the dangers such a situation holds for the officer involved. The instructor described the officer's fear of the car, with its unknown occupants and its hiding places for weapons or attackers, not to mention the potentially lethal mass of the car itself.

This scanning for threat, for "visible signs of a city out of control," unfolds with an accompanying interior monologue. This is a narrative that the officer generates in order to explain his actions in the present to a skeptical authority in the future. As the instructor in the class on traffic stops told us, if an officer orders someone out of their car, "You'd

better believe they've already rehearsed their speech to the judge." This point was further brought home in the class on how to testify in court. We met, not in our usual classroom in the building on East Twenty-first Street, but at an NYPD building in Brooklyn, complete with a mocked-up courtroom. (We were told that officers came there to practice testifying before a judge and jury.) In the testimony workshop, the instructors taught us the fine points of converting our sense experience into narratives suited to authoritative scrutiny. We had heard this again and again in the Citizens' Police Academy—that police officers must constantly rationalize their decisions to question or search or arrest or shoot at the people in their ambit—but never so explicitly. Thus the blank gaze the police presented in public, in the face of social chaos. The blankness hid suspicion and ready violence. It also hid an ongoing private narrativization of the world, framing the jumble of it all in case of future judicial questioning.

The academy instructors sometimes made the NYPD seem as dangerous and mysterious as the world presented in the crime scenario video. On one such occasion, an instructor blithely informed us that NYPD officers (herself included) carried concealed handguns nearly all the time, even when off duty. An immediate sensation of shock and dismay ran through the room. I watched the class recoil. People were outraged. They began calling out confused and angry questions: "You're kidding!" "Is this true?" "Is this safe?" "This doesn't seem right. What if there's an accident?" "What if they get drunk?" The instructor didn't say anything in response. She just watched the questioners with an affably blank expression on her face until they quieted down, then moved on to another topic.

The social dynamic here was a strange one. My classmates seemed to take the instructor's words as revealing an implicit threat—that there were off-duty police officers going around heavily armed all around us all this time. They asked indignantly about the possibility of accidents, of officers getting drunk and behaving irresponsibly. Indirectly, their questions conjured up the image of NYPD officers as fallible, only human, prone to ordinary mishaps and personal downfalls . . . and perhaps maybe even a little more threatening than that. Why did the city allow these people to go about their lives carrying hidden weapons on their persons? But the instructor refused to engage with their anxieties. Instead, she turned her blank police face on the class—she might as well have been wearing mirrored sunglasses.

Meanwhile, the instructors worked to frame the Citizens' Police Academy in terms of a natural and egalitarian collective identity, a social contract that supposedly encompassed us ("the citizens"), the instructors, the police in general, and the law as a whole. As our first instructor put it, "Most of the time, the things you learn in my classroom, you already knew." (His words directly echoed the Community Council president and the chair of the Quality-of-Life Committee, both of whom stressed to me the "obvious," commonsense nature of the rules and definitions they worked to define and impose on their respective groups.) The form of the classes themselves reinforced this sense of a group that was always-already in consensus. The instructors would often speak with the class as a whole, in a staging of group consensus through a process of call-and-response dialogue. In one such discussion, in a class on law, the instructor began by asking, "What's our definition of law?" The class responded in unison, "Rules." The instructor followed, "And if we didn't have rules, how would we live?" The class answered, "Chaos."

The instructor then asked, "Why? Aren't we normal rational beings?" "No," the class said. The instructor continued, "We think we are, but we need structure. Other than that it would be—what?" But she answered her own question this time. "Survival of the fittest. What's wrong with that?" Someone from the back of the classroom called out, "Some people are stronger than others. They may have a bias." The instructor nodded. "The strong would prey on the weak. But isn't that how it is? So we have these laws that are designed to give everybody a fair shot."

The academy instructors were also fond of opposing the apparent informality of the Citizens' Police Academy with what they described as the rigid hierarchy of the real Police Academy, in whose classrooms we sat. They did this by making a show out of setting aside any kind of strict authority structure in the classroom. The instructors repeatedly told us to raise our hands and ask questions at any point. "If you have a particular incident, something that happened to you, that you want to share, just shout it out," they said. And they stressed how different this was, how much more natural, than the bureaucratic, authoritarian structure of the real NYPD Academy. They further highlighted this distinction by performatively slipping from one register of formality to another, as when one instructor mock-berated someone in our group for being poorly dressed and sitting in a slump. The instructor then turned to the class as a whole and commented, "If this was a *real* class, I would have cited *myself*, for not shaving right before I came in." Another

instructor, after having a long argument with various members of the class over whether racism was a problem in the NYPD, applauded that we could all disagree with each other "and still leave as friends."

In short, the instructors worked to reinforce the feeling that we were all there together, bound by a common purpose. However, what that common purpose might actually have been was never explicitly raised for discussion in class. Instead, the officer-instructors claimed that what they taught was organically linked to social knowledge we already possessed. The back-and-forth dialogue exercises enacted this supposed natural agreement: they spoke; we answered as one. The instructors sought to maintain a frame of orderly questions and answers, with some room for "reasonable" personal digressions.

And any disagreements we might have had were supposedly subsumed under our larger social enmeshedness. We could still "leave as friends." But, again like the meetings of the Community Council and the other groups described in the sections above, this straightforward framework of rational friendship and social contract was disrupted, time and again. The people in class didn't always act in a way that fit the instructors' frame. As in the police/community meetings described earlier, people would occasionally spill forth with endlessly detailed stories that seemed to wander far from whatever the topic of the moment might have been. For example, during the class on traffic stops, one older man began a long, rambling story about getting pulled over by the police. The instructor listened actively to his story, trying to find in it an apt subject for an explication of police procedure or the fine points of laws governing search and seizure. It was no use, though, and after a few minutes the instructor interrupted the man's story and simply went on with the lecture as before.

Most often, though, the class was pulled away from the instructors' orderly format by the intense presence of one particular woman. Always sitting alertly in the front row of the classroom, she leapt upon nearly every question the instructors asked, brandishing a lengthy reply. Her answers would begin as free associations on the instructors' topics, then quickly evolve into more rambling and digressive monologues, speeding faster and growing more and more vehement as she went on. When she wasn't speaking up in class, she didn't seem to be at all hostile toward the officers who were leading the class, or toward the NYPD as a whole. On the contrary, she was always the first to volunteer to pass out paperwork or readings for the next week's classes. However, in her diatribes, she often seemed to grow progressively angrier as she

stitched together topic after topic, as in this story that she told during a class discussion on "crime":

> When I was growing up, everything was sending the same message. School, music, parents, your churches, your synagogues, newspapers: stay a virgin, go to a trade school. Now you've got the left wing saying one thing, the right wing saying another, the academics think they know everything, nobody's on the side of the parents. We live in a greed-driven society. I don't believe in money, I believe in barter, but we have all these people who neglect their children because they need to fund their lifestyle. . . . The feminist movement has *lied* to women, telling them they're not worth anything unless they work. People have no shame, leaving their children to support their lifestyle, with their $190 Nike sneakers. . . . I'm a single mother. You can't just hand your children up to day care!

Whenever she began to speak, the rest of the class reacted visibly. Some sat forward to hear what she had to say, apparently fascinated. Others slumped back and muttered angrily to themselves or to their neighbors. For their part, the instructors simply watched her talk. Their faces were perfectly composed, without expression. The only time I ever saw one of them react to her in any visible way was when, after trying fruitlessly to cut her off, our instructor yelled, "Excuse me for a moment please!" and stormed out of the room. He came back in after a minute or two, quickly apologized to her, then resumed the class as though nothing had happened. Such moments served to illustrate the constant tensions that arose around the Citizens' Police Academy's attempts to enframe us as a community. The police tried to set the terms of the relationship, but theirs was never the only agenda at work.

In these institutions of police-community dialogue, the police worked to enframe a particular community subject, one that spoke with a unified voice on topics the police regarded as logistically and emotionally reasonable. The police struggled to maintain this framework around the dialogue that unfolded. In the process, they sometimes came to view the community suspiciously, as a potential source of disorder. At the same time, the community they attempted to enframe remained fragmented by a host of individual and group agendas. Some of these agendas worked to perpetuate or intensify the segregated status quo

of New York City, as, for example, in the Hell's Kitchen Neighborhood Association's wranglings over the Latinos present in the area and, initially, in the meeting itself. Others voiced implicit or explicit critiques of real or imagined social issues. These ranged from dangers facing the elderly to health insurance to commodity fetishism and the plight of single motherhood to extraterrestrial abductions.

All these diverse concerns shared something in common with each other and with the narrative quagmire and spiraling questions in the stories above. They showed how, in the institutions of police-community dialogue, the people hailed as "community" simultaneously accepted, extended, and challenged the police ideology of crime and crisis and its language of "broken windows," "hot spots," and "quality-of-life offenses." If they accepted the police perspective, they also extended it deeply into the experience of everyday life in the city; specifically, everyday life in a rapidly changing neighborhood on the margins of the massive Times Square redevelopment project, in a city that is infamously dense, confusing, anonymous, and annoying in the best of circumstances. They used the terms of the discourse of broken windows and quality-of-life to speak about, speculate on, and talk back to, the transforming cityscape around them, as represented most vividly by the changes in Times Square and the impact this has had on Hell's Kitchen. In other words, they spoke the language of order-maintenance policing to narrate their experience of how their part of New York City was changing under neoliberalism, with its pairing of sweeping privatization and the government's abandonment of public spaces and services. In doing so, they often challenged the police themselves, either implicitly, when they demanded that the police address health insurance or housing questions, or explicitly, as in the moment of visceral shock when the class at the academy heard that off-duty NYPD officers usually go about their off-duty lives armed.

All of these examples made the NYPD's use of the image of "visible signs of a city out of control" vividly, and ironically, appropriate. The people attending these meetings did their best to absorb the ideology of order-maintenance policing, to feel and speak on its terms. They took the police's image of "a city out of control" very seriously and worked with it as well as they could. But they were unable or unwilling to keep their talk about their "quality-of-life" within the bounds set by the police. Instead, they spoke about the changes they were witnessing in their neighborhoods and in the city around them—changes that broke all easy definitions of "order" and "disorder." They saw and experienced

a city around them that was indeed "out of control," or certainly out of their control, in all sorts of ways: loud or threatening strangers; car and burglar alarms going off seemingly at random and ringing incessantly; bikes on the crowded sidewalks (usually ridden by underpaid immigrants delivering food to them or their neighbors); haphazard construction work; cars, trucks, busses, and taxis jammed in the street; people sleeping on the sidewalks, in parks, or in vacant lots. They saw that they could not afford health insurance, that rents and all the other costs of living in the city were shooting up, that fancy new corporate skyscrapers and apartment towers were being built a block or two away from their hundred-year-old tenement buildings. And they saw the police themselves, with their blue uniforms and sunglasses and guns; their air of skeptical detachment from the city around them; their latent threat of deadly force.

The reality of life in Hell's Kitchen and similar neighborhoods far exceeded, and still exceeds, the moralistic, black-and-white fable of community solidarity under siege offered by "Broken Windows." As people do everywhere, the residents of Hell's Kitchen experienced multiple systems of order, and multiple agendas for organizing the city in their everyday lives. Needless to say, most of these operated on scales far beyond the individual or community-group level on which these dialogues with the police were staged. They responded to the police incitement to talk about these "visible signs of a city out of control" with stories of fear and disorder that unfolded into unruly spirals of questioning everything they saw around them, including things that the police would or could not do anything about. Above all, these were stories about the larger changes people felt were disrupting their neighborhood, their city, and their place in the world—changes that are always present, even when only half-perceived, like a new office tower whose shadow falls forty stories to darken the streets below.

"It Doesn't Exist, But They're Selling It"

The Debates over "Air Rights"

People in New York City and elsewhere didn't simply accept the new built environments of Times Square and Forty-second Street. They wondered over them, debated them, applauded them, critiqued them, or made a point of avoiding them completely. Dozens of New Yorkers I met during and after my fieldwork remarked to me, "Times Square? I never go there. Isn't it all, like, Disney now?" In general, there was a widespread feeling that the changes in Times Square reflected broader social changes, maybe for the better, more likely for the worse. The most poignant (and most problematic) of these critiques was the one that asked whether the New Times Square lacks "authenticity," or connection to local history and identity. Times Square's redevelopers claimed to have neatly "returned" Times Square to its imagined heyday. But others turned this official nostalgia on its head, by using references to history, identity, and authenticity to critique the redeveloped Times Square. I heard these critiques of the redeveloped Times Square articulated formally and informally, in all

sorts of situations where people had the chance to discuss the spaces of Times Square at the moment of their transformation.

The story of the redevelopment was a story of shifting conceptions of urban space and socioeconomic life—a story of changes in what elite real estate holders and others considered the meaning of owning and inhabiting urban space. But this was also a story of politics: negotiation, compromise, and, sometimes, daring confrontational stratagems, such as the series of lawsuits that temporarily stymied the plans to transform Forty-second Street, or the Municipal Arts Society organizing a blackout of the lights in Times Square to protest the original redevelopment's planned changes to the area. These were examples of very successful maneuvers. The lawsuits did slow, and, eventually, radically change the plans to redevelop Forty-second Street, and the Municipal Arts Society blackout contributed to the innovative zoning in Times Square that mandated more and brighter signs in the area.

Not all of these negotiations and protests were so successful. Protests against the demolition of historic theater buildings failed to stop the rise of the Marriott Marquee's black obelisk on Times Square. Nor were all of these protests so visible to the larger citywide or national public. Off to the side of Times Square, in the residential neighborhood of Hell's Kitchen, neighborhood preservation and tenants' rights groups worked from the beginnings of the redevelopment to challenge, or at least to mitigate, the social and economic impact they feared the planned changes would have on their neighborhood: economic disruption, displacement of crime westward from Times Square into the area, increased automobile traffic, intensifying pressure on long-term renters, etc.

These political actions against the redevelopment were, partly, direct confrontations with parts of the city's power structure, but also, more broadly, challenges to what people perceived the redevelopment to *mean*. These actions expressed local residents' suspicions that the New York City government viewed real estate development interests as paramount over other interests, such as those of renters or of long-term, lower-income property owners.

Within the meetings and protests I attended, two overall forms of political action took place. One was neighborhood activists' attempts to engage with the redevelopment on its own terms, speaking the redevelopment's language as it were, in order to negotiate with it. Those who took up this strategy sought to talk to the forces behind the redevelopment in order to blunt its most serious effects and, perhaps, win some good for the neighborhood out of the changes it would wreak.

The second, and more prevalent tactic (or, at least, the louder one) was local groups standing directly in opposition to the redevelopment, refusing to speak on its terms. Instead, they did everything they could to frustrate the redevelopers' attempts to describe and market their plans. Those who used this strategy spoke out as representatives of a set of values standing in contradiction to the redevelopment: neighborhood preservation and local identity versus elitist urban planners and corporate megalomania. The first group expressed a political interest. The second group expressed a worldview.

The contrast between these two strategies and those who used them was often quite stark. On the one side were those attempting to negotiate within the redevelopment; on the other side, those who sought to jam its frequencies and negate its very existence. At the same time, representatives of both groups often belonged to the same local political organizations and participated in the same strategic planning sessions. And while they each pursued a different path, both raised similar questions. These were fundamental questions of urban space and life: What is the city? What do the changes in Times Square and Forty-second Street *mean* for those who live in this city? What kinds of rights do people have to the city around them, and with what voice can and should they speak to the transformations they witness?

The Armed Forces Recruiting Post

For example, take the debate that occurred on December 5, 1997, in a church library above Fifty-third Street, on a night of freezing rain. A joint meeting of Community Board Five's "Land Use" and "Times Square" committees discussed the Armed Forces recruiting post that sits in a squat little structure at the center of Times Square. The members of the two committees had convened this meeting in advance of upcoming public hearings announced by a local city councilperson regarding the recruiting post and its presence in Times Square, leased rent-free by the city to the military.

The members of the Community Board committees raised a number of questions about the recruiting post: How did it affect foot traffic and "open space issues" in Times Square? Was it aesthetically pleasing—as one board member put it, "Does it 'work'?" And how many people did the post actually recruit into the military? These were technical questions, evaluating the building in terms of its effects. All three of these

questions were part of a larger debate: Should the committee recommend that the city remove the recruitment post in favor of a different kind of building or another use of the space entirely?

Regarding the first two questions—traffic flow and aesthetics—the committee members were in quick agreement. Several members mentioned recent newspaper reports of Times Square's crowded sidewalks, and they complained of their frustration at being forced to navigate through the dense crush of commuters and tourists when walking through the area. Everyone nodded at this. And all agreed that the recruitment post, situated as it was in the middle of a little-used concrete wedge in the middle of Times Square, probably had little direct effect on the issue of sidewalk crowding. The post probably wasn't in anyone's way, nor did many of the people crowding the Square come to visit the post itself. But they debated whether something could be done to the building itself—razing or redesigning it—to somehow open up that little-trafficked triangle, to help solve the general problem of overcrowding in Times Square as a whole. They were also unanimous in agreeing that the building—a one-story box that had been quickly thrown up in 1946 as a permanent home for Times Square's previous, temporary World War II recruitment post—looked ugly, and egregiously out of place in the middle of the Square's billboards, neon, and new office towers. The squat architecture and drab signage of the post failed to harmonize with Times Square's newly refurbished architectural image.

But when the committee began to discuss the issue of how many recruits actually join the armed forces at the Times Square post, someone from the small audience of which I was a part leapt up to interrupt them. He was a tall, dignified, middle-aged man, with gray temples and a long, dark coat. He introduced himself as a representative of a New York City veterans' association, and he took angry issue with the committee's debate. With a voice full of emotion, he lamented what he saw as the nation's crumbling appreciation for military veterans. He protested that the Times Square recruitment post was, as he put it, "the most visible one in the system," and that, even if it wasn't very productive in terms of actual recruits, it should be allowed to remain in Times Square as a "monument," a symbol of esteem. When he had finished speaking, he sat back down. Someone from the Community Board asked the veterans' representative, "Why is that particular location so important?" To which he replied with the rhetorical question, "Why not move the Iwo Jima statue?" Several committee members asked him more or less

the same question with slightly altered phrasing; each time, his answer was the same: "Why not move the Iwo Jima statue?" After going around with this exchange a few times, the committee tried to shift the debate over the recruitment post back to its original terms. "How many people does it recruit?" "Does it or does it not block foot traffic?" But the man from the audience rose again, saying, "The removal of that station is simply another nail in the coffin. We fought for you guys to have the freedom to make that decision. . . . That site *where it is* has value to many New Yorkers." A woman from the committee leaned forward and asked, in a sincere tone of voice, "Would a *beautiful plaque* serve the same purpose?" He replied, sternly, "*No.*"

At this point, another member of the audience stood up, a younger man, with a round face and body, wearing a baggy brown suit, who said that he worked as an attorney in the Times Square area. He began by paraphrasing the head of the Times Square Business Improvement District to the effect that, "The roots of the Times Square of the future are based in the roots of the Times Square of the past." The man began to speculate about the question of the post and the number of people it actually recruited into the armed forces: "How many people are brought in through that specific post? What about all the people who see the post in Times Square and decide to enlist later? What about the tourists who see it when they come to Times Square?" He went on, describing his own feelings as a member of the Army Reserves, seeing the recruitment post on his way to work: "I always thought it was *neat.* Like: there's the Army!" And he announced that he had an idea to make the post "fit in" with what he described as "the new Times Square, the digitalized Times Square, the glitzy Times Square." His idea, as he described it to the committee, was a big "digitalized" sign that would rotate atop the recruitment post. One side of the sign would depict the famous Eisenstadt photo of a sailor kissing a nurse during the frenzy of the celebrations in Times Square at the end of World War II. The other side of the sign would feature an enlarged image of the latest resident of New York to enlist in the armed forces.

The man concluded by talking about the role of the recruitment post in Times Square now that the redevelopment had closed nearly all of the businesses that catered to young people of color. He imagined the post as the last vestige of Times Square's history as a center for cheap entertainment: "They used to come through to play pinball, and you could get the fake IDs. Now they wander through the recruiting center, where they can get economically empowered."

There was a brief, somewhat stunned silence before the committee members began to speak again. When they did, none of them commented directly on any of the proposals, speculations, or personal narratives the man had put forth. Instead, they turned back to the veterans' representative. Again, the exchange of questions was repeated: "What is so sacred about that particular location?" followed by, "Why not move the Iwo Jima statue?" When the woman who had first asked about replacing the recruiting post with "a beautiful plaque" raised the possibility of removing the post entirely—"Because an open space in and of itself is a *fine thing*"—the veterans' representative protested, "Times Square is *it*, and they are *there*." She nodded in agreement, saying, "They're [the post] prominent—they're *ugly* prominent."

Someone else from the committee asked again, in a puzzled voice, why the man was so opposed to moving the post to an alternate location; for example, to the office tower at One Times Square. "Why is that particular spot sacrosanct?" The veterans' representative replied, "Simply by virtue of tradition. The station has been there for fifty-two years." The man in the baggy suit chimed in, pointing out what he saw as the irony of proposing to move the post to One Times Square, which, as he pointed out, "has recently been bought by a *German* insurance company." As with his previous comments, the committee appeared baffled. The veterans' representative added that some members of his organization had been offended by having the public celebrations in Times Square for the fiftieth anniversary of VJ Day overshadowed by the huge Trinitron screen mounted on One Times Square—a device, he said, built by Sony, a Japanese corporation.

There was no more discussion after this. The Community Board members passed a quick resolution to take up the matter at a later date. All of us, committee members and audience alike, stood, gathered our coats and umbrellas, and made our way down the narrow church stairs onto Fifty-third Street, out into the freezing rain. As I turned to walk away, I heard one man from the group gathered around the veterans' representative complain, apparently about the members of the Community Board, "They're all a bunch of 4-Fs and 5-Fs—they don't understand."

At the official hearings on the recruitment post held a few weeks later, the issues raised were entirely different—not whether or not the post "worked," practically or aesthetically, in Times Square, but whether or not New York City should rescind its donation of the space to the armed forces based on the prohibition in the city charter against doing business with organizations that discriminate against gays and lesbians.

The recruitment post was fenced off and hidden from view for a short time after the hearings. I wondered whether it was being removed. But while walking through Times Square more than a year after the hearings, I was startled to see that the construction façades had been taken down and that the post had indeed been modified to fit the hyped-up aesthetics of the area, much in the way that the Community Board Five members had recommended. Three of the small building's four walls were now clad in brushed, gleaming metal, according to the style of the moment. The wall that was left was covered by an American flag, composed of horizontal red, white, and blue neon tubes.

In this instance of debate over the redevelopment, the veterans' representative and others articulated a complaint that is often heard: the changes in Times Square have effaced important signs of public memory in the built environment, and that these changes represent a more general lack of proper respect for the past. For the veteran quoted above, it was a matter of the visibility and permanency of the station as a monument—an edifice that resisted commercial and city-management concerns for how the city should look. But others at the meeting also raised the concept that Times Square, in what the developers suppose to be its official nadir, was a haven; that it was an important place of socializing and gathering in public for various groups otherwise excluded from public life. The members of the Community Board more or less ignored this complaint, but it echoes back to the historic debates over Times Square and the conflict between respectability and spectacle. The debate over the recruitment post showed how different groups attempted to intervene in or talk back to the overwhelming theme of the redevelopment; namely, the redevelopers' quest to craft a specific brand image for the area, one that draws selectively on references to history while weeding out others in an effort to make Times Square seem "spicy" but, ultimately, safe for the most conservative real estate investors and developers.

"We Don't Want Money": Community Activists and the Air Rights Proposal

There was another proposal for changing the zoning and development policy for the area that was announced and debated throughout my fieldwork. This was the "Air Rights" initiative. It was far wider-reaching and more radical than the renovation of the Armed Forces recruiting

post. According to this plan, the owners of landmarked theater buildings in the larger Times Square area would be able to package and sell,
not their buildings, but, rather, the space that remained *unbuilt* above
their property. Specifically, they could sell space that could potentially
be built, but that remained unconstructed because, as the theaters were
landmarked properties, the theater owners had been restricted from
demolishing them and building the largest (and therefore, presumably,
most profitable) structure allowable by law on the lot. Not only would
the "air rights" to each theater be for sale, but theater owners would be
able to "float," or transfer, the unbuilt bulk, not just to another property next door or across the street (as had been allowable under city
zoning codes for decades), but all over the Midtown area—as far west as
Eighth Avenue.[1]

I first heard about the air rights plan from Joe Restuccia, a former
theater producer who had become active in tenants' rights and property development in Clinton/Hell's Kitchen. Restuccia explained the
basic concept of selling air rights to me in terms of "sugar cubes":

> They're talking about it in terms of FAR: Floor-Area Ratio. That's
> the number of "sugar cubes" you can put on a lot. You can put ten
> times the area of the lot, and those ten, if you've covered all that
> up, you have ten stories. Cover half the lot, go up twenty stories.
> You can do whatever you want with those same sugar cubes, but
> you've got a limit on the sugar cubes, right? What they want to do
> is give us more sugar cubes. [At the moment] people can go to
> ten, you can go to twelve with affordable housing—there's an af-
> fordable housing bonus.

Under the proposed changes, Restuccia said, this affordable housing
bonus would become economically unfeasible. It would simply be too
appealing for a developer to buy "unbuilt bulk" from a theater owner
instead:

> OK, fine, you want to go from 10 to 14.4—almost a 25 percent
> increase [over the FAR of 12 allowable with the affordable hous-
> ing bonus]—and you can choose what you want to do, either use
> development rights or build affordable housing. They'll just have
> a choice. Now if you are a developer, and you can make a deal with
> [a theater organization] to buy 200,000 square feet, a straight real
> estate deal for money, or go through the whole city process to

build forty units of affordable housing and involve seventeen community groups, boy, that's a real brainteaser there.

He explained to me that those active in the Hell's Kitchen neighborhood political organizations saw the Air Rights proposal as a threat for several reasons. First, the plan would substantially expand geographically the economic transformations and upscaling of the Times Square redevelopment, effectively bringing the redevelopment's new corporate office towers all the way to what had been seen as the border of Hell's Kitchen. Second, the City Planning Department had announced the proposal in a great hurry, and with what seemed like a great deal of secrecy. Even as community groups were given a short time in which to respond to the proposal, key aspects of it were left vague. What was not vague was the way the city planners and others were marketing the plan, as a way to save theater buildings that were supposedly under threat of being abandoned or demolished without the additional financial help the selling of air rights represented. The "unbuilt bulk" above the theater buildings would become the vehicle for those theaters' survival. As he put it, "It doesn't even exist, but we're selling it."

Restuccia was extremely cynical about the way the plan was being talked about as the "Broadway Initiative." He said,

> The way it's being pitched is that this is the way to save Broadway theater. Because .5 percent or .05 percent of every transfer is going to go to a new fund which people can fight over called the Broadway Initiative, which is going to renovate theaters, provide money for new productions, do costume work, provide seed money for artists—there was this whole presentation made to us at the Community Board, this guy from Actor's Equity. I just sat there and said, "Well, now that you've spent this money about forty-five times, are you for real?" It's such a shill.

He explained that the technical and abstract nature of the proposal made trying to organize on the community level extremely difficult. The highly conceptual plan to sell "air rights" and redefine "zoning envelopes" was simply too counterintuitive—too alien to most urban dwellers' experience of the built environment around them.

> We had a meeting in September of last year to plan for this Eighth Avenue stuff, but it didn't go anywhere because it was just stalled,

the actual change—it's hard to organize when there's no real thing. . . . It gets technical, and that's a problem, because when it gets technical people get lost—we try to focus the discussion on, "We don't want the bulk." I know for a fact we're going to get some bulk, because the pattern in the neighborhood is you negotiate for something to get something else. Well if we take some of it, we must mitigate it. What I said is, "*We don't want money.*" Because what got floated [by the developers] is, "Oh, we're going to build some housing in your renewal area." And I said, "*Fuck that . . .* that's money. No. I don't want any money."

When I asked Restuccia why he was so set against receiving money for the community to mitigate the Air Rights proposal, he described what had happened during the redevelopment of Forty-second Street in the mid-1980s, when he and others had negotiated with the developers for financial compensation. As he saw it, the money and its attendant pressures and bureaucratic requirements had threatened to destroy the community itself. He said, "It went from like this informal thing to this local bureaucracy, which we had no choice but to do—literally we had committees, we had deadlines—by the end it became highly politicized, and we almost killed ourselves. Easiest way to screw a community: give 'em money. They were really smart about that. We'll never take money again." Instead, he said, he and others would fight to reinforce zoning codes to "preserve the residential character" of the neighborhood. "There're other zoning changes that can strengthen, preserve, and protect the neighborhood. It's zoning for zoning. . . . You know, just very specific things that say, 'You're going to do this, then we get that.'" This was the epitome of the tactic he used in negotiating within the urban development process to secure some good for the neighborhood.

The Clinton Special District Council

My first direct experience of the issue Restuccia described—of organizing community groups against such an abstract and counterintuitive initiative—came at the meeting of a group called the Clinton Special District Council (CSDC) in early January 1998. I had attended meetings of this organization in the past, but they were nothing like this one. The big meeting room in the local community center was packed, and the people in attendance were buzzing with nervous energy. Local

media had begun to cover the Air Rights proposal, and the CSDC meeting was intended to provide an occasion for the community to develop its strategy for the upcoming series of public hearings on the plan.

The main order of business was announced early and often throughout the meeting—the need for everyone in attendance and more to appear at the next meeting of the Community Board. The CSDC leaders described this upcoming meeting as "the first step in this struggle. . . . They need to see the *community* behind the *board*." Their plan was for everyone from the neighborhood to stand up in unison when representatives from the CSDC rose to address the board—in other words, to directly manifest the image of a united community standing as one behind its delegates. Indeed, this was the other key dilemma of organizing the community around the Air Rights proposal. Not only was the proposal itself hard to visualize, but so was "the community." How to project an image of the community as a unified, oppositional force, especially in political contexts in which the opportunities for community groups to participate were so limited?

The CSDC's first step was to define the stakes. A council member spoke about the risk posed to the neighborhood by the plan's proposed development of Eighth Avenue. As property values rise, he said, "the businesses we know will go out of business and get replaced by some chi-chi restaurant." But he went on to explain why he thought it would be hard to mobilize public opinion against the proposal. First, he said, the city planners weren't framing the plan as a move to tear down and rebuild on Eighth Avenue, but rather, as a means to preserve supposedly endangered Broadway theater buildings. In other words, the proposal wasn't being marketed as a westward extension of the Times Square redevelopment, but rather as a countermeasure against the economic pressures the redevelopment had brought to bear on the area.

Second, and just as important, he said that Mayor Giuliani was simply too popular for Clintonites to demonize in the press. Unlike earlier popular fights against easily stereotyped absentee landlords or greedy developers, Giuliani and his city planners wouldn't make an apt target. And the group needed a target. The council member was quite explicit on this point. "There's got to be a political strategy—there's been some discussion over who to make the bogeyman! How do you define this evil character, then tear him down?" (As later events showed, they found an ideal "bogeyman" in the person of a highly visible city planning official, who returned the favor by playing the part of the snobbish, elitist bureaucrat to the hilt.)

The group turned to a discussion of possible ideas for public protests. The same council member who had spoken earlier described his idea for a rally, to be called something like "Hands Up Eighth Avenue" (an intentional pun?). His plan was for a long line of local residents to hold hands along the sidewalks of the avenue. He said that this "symbolic gesture" would show that "Clinton is a neighborhood that has value and identity. The impact will be tremendous, devastating." Someone else from the group stood to talk about their idea of producing buttons and flyers, which people could wear and display in windows throughout the neighborhood. They said, "You're going to be walking around the neighborhood, wondering why you keep seeing this same logo?" This plan seemed to borrow directly from the symbolic image of Broken Windows and from the legacy of the graffiti writers of the 1970s and 1980s—the image of uncannily repeated symbols cropping up throughout the area, making people feel uneasy, forcing them to wonder if some kind of drastic change is imminent.

Throughout the discussion of these and other tactical ideas, one attendee sitting behind me loudly cracked wise: "How about a plan to sell the mineral rights below the theaters to developers?" "How much access to Giuliani could the CSDC buy for the $20 fee to attend an upcoming public breakfast with the mayor?" While the group earnestly debated symbolic gestures, his jokes were his own symbolic protest, turning the meeting into his own theater of sarcasm.

After the meeting, I spoke with the president of the CSDC about his thoughts on the Air Rights proposal and why it was so important to organize against it. He spoke eloquently about what he saw as the special social character of the neighborhood, its mix of economic, ethnic, and social groups. He compared it to the village in Europe where he had grown up, where local merchants would give credit to people they knew if they were temporarily short of cash. Then, he spoke about sunlight. He was deeply concerned that the huge new buildings proposed for Eighth Avenue would recast the area into permanent shadow. He said, "I live between Eighth and Ninth [Avenue], and my window faces east. If this plan goes through, I will never see the sun again! I have plants, they need sun—I need sun to kill the microbes! These are *basic quality-of-life issues.* I hate to bring it down to a *microbe,* but . . . " Like the participants in the community-police dialogues described in the previous chapter, he turned the flexible and powerful rhetoric of "quality-of-life" back on itself, as a way to attack gentrification and high-profile real estate development planning.

A few days later, I attended the Community Board meeting for which the CSDC had been planning. While the group had wondered how to project a unified show of force, the Community Board helped their cause by calling all those from the neighborhood who had registered on the speakers' list up to the podium as a group. When the CSDC leadership walked to the front of the room, the rest of those in attendance from the CSDC stood up en masse, holding up yellow signs that showed a red slash through a picture of evil-looking bulldozers plowing through a cowering mass of buildings and people, with a slogan that read, "Don't let developers steamroll Clinton."

The president of the CSDC spoke. "You can imagine what this will do to our quality of life. This has been sugarcoated as a 'save-the-theater' deal. We see this as simply a real estate deal, a massive real estate deal. . . . Changes are already occurring in Clinton/Hell's Kitchen, within the character of our district. It's already happening within the zoning regulations. Why change anything?" The second speaker continued the theme: "I think it's very unfair to change something that works well. We're such a diverse community, with all kinds of restaurants, and I don't see how they can take it out from under us." The next speaker used a line I had heard him use before, in numerous CSDC meetings: "This allows developers to extend 150 feet into the blocks, and we're scared they'll ask for more. They'll ask for another 50 feet, and another 50 feet, and we'll be pushed into the Hudson River!" As in the CSDC meetings, the audience rippled and murmured at this image of developers' rapacious encroachment on the embattled neighborhood. These developers sounded greedy and evil; they didn't seem to be people with whom the community could negotiate. Instead, as with the yellow signs, the speakers' words portrayed a terrified and angry community, staring down the bulldozers as they moved in.

The City Planning Presentations

These strategy sessions and the Community Board forum were only the prelude to the main event: a series of three presentations, in which city planners presented the Air Rights proposal directly to various community groups. Watching these three almost identical presentations over the course of the two days in which they were held was, largely, an experience in hypnotic tedium. However, there were subtle, but important, differences between the three iterations of the city's plans.

The first presentation was grand and formal. It was held in a packed auditorium in a city building in Lower Manhattan. Most of the spectators who filled the rows were Clinton/Hell's Kitchen residents who had been in attendance at the earlier CSDC meeting and the Community Board session. They sat quietly, but tensely pressed forward, listening as hard as they could. Almost all wore signs pinned to their shirts, including the yellow "Don't let developers steamroll Clinton" signs. They also carried white sheets of paper laser-printed with block letters that spelled out a variety of slogans, including

Clinton is a neighborhood, not a spillover for Midtown expansion
Development rights short circuit public review
No single neighborhood should bear the cost of private subsidy
Don't sell Clinton to hungry developers
TOP SECRET: Why was the Clinton community kept out of the loop?

Throughout the meeting, people would shuffle through these signs and lean them against their chests or hold them up, not waving them, just keeping them propped up high. As the planners made their presentation, the community members would hold up the slogan most appropriate for the matter at hand, in a kind of silent, flexible picketing. The mass of recurring, recombining slogans was a way of projecting an angry and unified presence in the hushed and orderly surroundings of this official meeting.

The three city planners stood at the front of the room. Each spoke in turn on a different aspect of the Air Rights proposal. The first was a big man who, when he spoke, would quietly, patiently reel off volumes of city planning rules and regulations. He seemed to be the very personification of calm, bureaucratic rationality. In his quiet, bland voice, he discussed the unique concentration of large theaters in the area, and the district's centrality to New York's role as the cultural capital of the United States, maybe even of the entire world. Turning to the concept of FAR transfer, he described twenty-five theaters as having "available development rights." He emphasized that, presently, "they're preserved as buildings, not as theaters," and he listed former theaters that were now being used for other purposes. "The Mark Hellinger [Theater] is a church; Studio 54, believe it or not, is a legitimate theater. Maybe what used to go on there qualifies as theater. [silence] Bad joke. . . ." According to the city's proposal, if the owners of current theaters were to

transfer their development rights, the owners would make some sort of commitment to maintain the building as a theatrical venue. His portion of the presentation made it clear just how radically the theater industry had changed from the early days of Times Square. The city was asking us to see the Theater District, not as an opportune location for a group of socially marginal entrepreneurs in the business of mass spectacle, but, rather, as an important and imperiled public good—an endangered species whose natural habitat was threatened, maybe by those same angry bulldozers pictured on the CSDC signs?

The second planner was a younger woman, responsible for spelling out more of the technical aspects in detail. She listed "the problems we see on Eighth Avenue: different zoning on the east and west sides, each side can achieve different FARs, and, most important, there's no mandatory street walls, no mandatory urban design controls." The proposal, she said, would bring a much-needed (from a planner's perspective) coherence to the zoning of Eighth Avenue.

The third member of the group was an intense man who spoke about the aesthetic aspects of rezoning Eighth Avenue. He explained that the Air Rights proposal would create a new "Eighth Avenue subdistrict," one characterized by "retail continuity." He used the term "contemplate" to describe the new forms of street social and economic activity the zoning would encourage; for example, "this zoning contemplates retail." He stressed that the new zoning would both cap the height of new buildings as well as mandate continuous "streetwalls" (buildings facing the street in an unbroken "wall") of 50 to 150 feet, all to avoid what he called "tower-on-a-one-story-base" zoning.

Throughout the presentation, the chairman of the City Planning Department, who sat in the front row of seats, stood up repeatedly to make a steady series of interjections, spelling out some of the more technical details of the plan in less jargon-filled language. He gave the impression that he was deeply involved with this plan and was eager for everyone in the audience to understand how reasonable and well-thought-out it was. He also gave the impression of being utterly impatient and exasperated with any questions or critical comments from the community.

And there were critical comments. During the question-and-answer period after the presentation, one audience member stood to say that she thought the plan would both increase bulk and also cut the public approval process, not for the general good, but for the financial benefit of a few powerful property owners. The rest of the audience burst into applause several times during her remarks; she asked for them not to

clap so that she could keep her train of thought. As others in the audience raised questions, the chairman stepped in to answer as many questions as did the planners, or to interrupt them to field questions on their behalf. At one point, he referred to the way in which "some avenues have been developed as a hodgepodge." Someone behind me loudly muttered, "Unique!" Another audience member in front of me turned over one of their white signs and wrote out a new slogan: "We Want Hodge Podge!" Others in the audience similarly customized their signs and held them up to chip in to the Q & A period, with new slogans reading, "Where's the Environmental Impact Statement?" and "Actor's Equity wants a second look."

Throughout all this, the group at the front of the room fielded questions and comments from selected audience members—the chairman with visible irritation, the planners with quiet rationality, sometimes answering the questions and sometimes not. At one point, discussing some of the financial aspects of the proposal, the chairman looked out at the murmuring CSDC crowd and said that people could count up the numbers for themselves, then muttered under his breath (but still into the microphone), "If they can count. . . ."

After the afternoon meeting, I rode the subway back home with two of the CSDC organizers. They were hyper, bouncing up and down on their toes and talking excitedly about the presentation just completed, and the second one that would follow, scheduled for later that evening. "This is a war," one said. "We're really going to show them tonight!"

In another meeting that evening, the city planners made exactly the same presentation, but in a very different environment, in a stuffy auditorium in the basement of a local hospital, where they spoke before the Land Use and Zoning Committee of Community Board Four.

Throughout the presentation, the head of the Community Board committee stood up to mediate between the planners and the largely disgruntled and confused audience, many of whom began muttering loudly or cursing the planners under their breath almost before the presentation began. Meanwhile, two outside observers, one from the mayor's office and one connected to the theater industry, stalked the periphery of the room, seemingly concerned less with the information the planners were presenting than with the overall tenor of the crowd's response—how well the show was going.

When the planners came to the end of their presentation, the room literally exploded with noise, as masses of people from the audience

leapt to their feet, roaring, pointing fingers, screaming imprecations. The chair of the committee did her best to impose some kind of order, asking people from the audience to address "just aesthetic questions" rather than economic ones and trying to let committee members speak before members of the general public. This effort was mostly unsuccessful, as people from the audience continued to jump up and roar out speeches like the one given by a woman directly in front of me, who yelled, "FAR means Foul Air Rights," followed by an angry diatribe about the pollution and shadows that the new proposal would bring to the area.

The head of the CSDC accused the planners: "You're taking a large portion of Clinton and saying it's no longer Clinton—it's a land grab." He angrily jabbed at them with the repeated question, "Who have you met with?" The planners tried to dodge the question with evasive answers, then reluctantly started to list: Community Board Five, the Times Square BID, Broadway theater owners. . . . Someone from the audience jumped to her feet and shouted, "They don't represent our community!" Another audience member yelled, "We're going to have serious displacement and buildings falling down—it's going to happen!!" A third stood and spoke: "I happen to want to go to the Studio Coffee Shop for breakfast, I don't want to go to Starbucks—some new coffee shop that makes everything look *nice!*" Her voice rose with outrage as she continued, "This is called fascism, it is called totalitarianism, it is called corporate values that have nothing to do with humanity! It has nothing to do with humanity, with community, with family!" A fourth asked, "Who is going to be able to live anywhere anymore?" To which several in the audience called out, "Not us!"

Throughout all of these angry comments, Joe Restuccia, the local tenants' rights activist, kept insistently accusing the planners of having avoided meeting with community groups and of whitewashing the economic and environmental impact of their proposal by presenting it as a plan to preserve the Broadway theater district. When one of the planners tried to downplay his concerns, Restuccia angrily burst out, "You're redefining *who we are.*"

Nearly four hours later, after the end of the meeting, while the planners where tiredly taking down their blackboards and diagrams, the representative from the mayor's office who had been monitoring the presentation pulled me aside in the lobby to ask me who *I* represented. When I told him something about my research, he shook his head and confided that he wished that the planners had found better ways to

present their proposal to the general public. He said he wished they had "more of a sense of theater." I wondered whether more sense of theater would help get the proposal across to a group so dedicated to refusing to allow the planners to make their claims, as they believed, to rationally plan the space of the city for the good of all.

The third meeting of the series took place the next evening, in a large conference room high up in the offices of a design college located south of Hell's Kitchen, in Community Board Five. This space was different yet again from the previous two. Here, the room was tastefully, expensively lit, the air conditioning was on "high," the walls were hung with brightly dyed silk panels, and nearly all in attendance, presenters and audience alike, were formally, stylishly dressed. The planners propped their displays up on elegant wooden easels, rather than leaning them on folding office chairs as they had before.

The chair of the meeting, the head of the Community Board's Land Use committee, began his remarks by criticizing both the City Planning Department, for not including "the public" in the planning process for this proposal, as well as the people responsible for "ad hominem" attacks on the planners and their work that had been heard in the previous meetings. He told the group that, regardless of his problems with their proposal, he sincerely respected the planners as people and as professionals.

The planners began their presentation once again. By and large, their speeches were eerily similar to the ones I had heard twice before. The main difference was that the first speaker talked in a little more detail about the theater industry. He said that the theater was important to everyone in New York City, regardless of their social or economic level. "If we don't go to the theater, at least we know it's there, and it's something special."

After the presentation, the Community Board committee chair rose again. He told the planners that he was leery of how the plan would affect the "streetscapes" of the area; particularly, what would happen if a developer were to buy the air rights from several landmark theaters. They could, he said, raise the FAR of their buildings as high as 21.6, meaning that these new buildings could be extraordinary large, relative to the surrounding neighborhood . At this, the room buzzed. 21.6! I heard members of the audience loudly muttering and calling out for examples of comparable buildings in the neighborhood. I looked back and saw that a large block of chairs was filled by a group from the

CSDC. I also saw Rebecca Robertson (see chapter three) stalking the perimeter of the room, the way the man from the mayor's office had in the previous meeting. She looked annoyed at the audience's comments.

Here, though, instead of discussing FAR and its impact on local residents' homes, as in the previous meetings, the committee members steered the conversation to sidewalk crowding and the impact of the increased "streetwall" development in the Times Square area. The first planner defended the concept, saying that the new zoning "creates a wall, like the walls of a living room! It creates a *context*. It's an attempt to create a *streetscape environment*." But he faltered at elaborating why he felt this was so important.

As in the previous meetings, the event simply ended. There were no votes to tally, no consensus to gauge. The planners had presented their plan, the community groups had voiced their opinions, and that was that. I rode the subway home.

A few weeks later came the final presentation/confrontation, at a Clinton/Hell's Kitchen community forum held in a drafty church basement across from the Port Authority bus terminal. The CSDC was there in full force, holding up yellow "Don't let developers steamroll Clinton" banners and handing out new "vignette signs" with slogans such as, "Shadow! Shadow! Shadow! Shame!" (a reference to the light-blocking effects of the new buildings) and "Theater should not be in the real estate business." As the presentation began, I glanced back and noticed that the leaders of the CSDC were arrayed around the back of the room, standing with their arms folded, watching the crowd in the position of power that city politicians and developers had taken in the previous meetings.

The head of the City Planning Department rose to speak. Rather than beginning with the aesthetic and financial aspects of the proposal, he told a historical narrative, a story of the history of attempts to preserve and revitalize the Broadway theater district. He said that the success of the Times Square redevelopment would mean that major economic activity in the surrounding area was inevitable. "Eighth Avenue is going to be redeveloped in this business cycle!" The issue, he said, was for city planners to ensure that these inevitable new buildings would contribute to their surroundings. Again and again, he told the group that current Broadway theaters were under threat, and that they would be demolished if their owners were not allowed to "float" their unbuilt bulk to the developers interested in remaking Eighth Avenue.

He was interrupted mid-speech by a member of the audience, an older woman who rose from her seat in the front row and asked, in an angry, croaking voice, "Were you born here? Were you born in this area?"

"Yes I was, I was born in New York City, yes," he replied.

She went on: "Where was you born? Were you born in Hell's Kitchen?"

"No, I was not," he said.

"Well, that's why you want to destroy it!" she yelled triumphantly, and the crowd burst into applause.

When the noise died down, he looked a little flustered, but he collected himself and went on, turning to the list of questions that the Community Boards had submitted to the City Planning Department. However, instead of addressing each question, or even reading any of them out loud, he quickly scanned over the list and summed them up, in an unmistakably contemptuous tone. He glanced over the pages and described the questions, for example, "OK, what about the worries people have that this plan is going to cause all kinds of terrible problems for Clinton?" Someone from the Community Board Four Land Use Committee spoke up in protest, asking that he answer each question as written. He waved her off, casually defending his right to paraphrase at will. He also praised himself and his department for being willing to listen to the community reactions to their proposal, even the reactions of "people who don't understand the process at all." At this, the crowd buzzed with an angry murmur—it was obvious that he was talking both to and about the present audience.

The leader of the CSDC called out that the city was "changing the map," and that the group had the right to have their concerns taken into account. But the head of City Planning went on, reiterating that the Air Rights proposal was merely a way to steer an economic shift that was already under way. He said, "These theater buildings themselves are valuable instruments that must be preserved! When there's such a big disparity between what *is* built and what *can be* built, you're standing in the face of real estate development." Then, he abruptly walked out, leaving the three city planners to face the by now deeply annoyed crowd, which immediately burst forth with a torrent of accusations that the entire Air Rights proposal was a scheme to line the pockets of wealthy developers. The planners struggled to respond in their usual quiet, technocratic way, but the audience was having none of it.

The planners spoke of the need for symmetrical zoning on Eighth Avenue in order to turn the street into a Paris-style "boulevard." "We

experience *both sides* of the street," one of the planners said. "The *street itself* is a place." The people from the CSDC replied that, for them, Eighth Avenue needed to serve, not as an elegant boulevard, but as a barrier, clearly demarcating their neighborhood from Times Square and the Broadway Theater District. In other words, they insisted on framing the Air Rights proposal as a turf war over who owned the west side of Eighth Avenue. Was this a site for redevelopment, the next stage of the transformation that had begun in Times Square? Or was this part of Clinton/Hell's Kitchen, necessarily distinct from the economic boom to the east?

Someone from the Community Board reminded the audience, "We can't argue with City Planning." This meeting was for the sole purpose of letting the planners present their point of view and hear community complaints; actual, practical, contentious dialogue was not on the agenda. But when *would* be the right time for a resident of a Clinton tenement to argue with City Planning? Apparently, now, it seemed. A woman from the CSDC stood and spoke: "I have a question. I garden in Hell's Kitchen. I get sun only from 1:20 to 4:30 in the afternoon. Can you tell me how these changes will affect me?" The planners insisted that the new buildings allowed in their zoning proposal would not hurt her garden, but she continued: "These are basic human needs! This has nothing to do with theater. You go ahead and demolish Eighth Avenue and build a Disneyfied—If it works [to save the theater], I'll be the first one in the Disney parade!"

The talk shifted back to FAR, floor-area ratio. Representatives from Community Board Five asked about the bulkier new buildings the zoning would allow in the Times Square "bowtie," and about new pedestrians the plan would bring to the area, where the sidewalks were already "at capacity." Someone else from the CSDC constituency cut off this technical talk of FAR and pedestrian capacity: "All your mumbo-jumboing—just lower the ticket prices! We don't want to hear about block buildings, and dimensions, and what-not. We want human dimensions for our neighborhood!"

At this point, another Clinton resident tried to calm the debate. He observed that one reason the audience was so ready to voice strong complaints was that they perceived the planners as speaking on behalf of wealthy real estate developers. "It is about access to government," he said, access the CSDC and others in the neighborhood felt that they lacked. He then directly engaged the planners on their own terms, almost the only time anyone from this group ever did so. Hearkening

back to an earlier comment by one of the three that Eighth Avenue was his "favorite avenue," he asked them to discuss their views on "the great boulevards" of the world. "What's an example for you of great city planning and design?" The audience broke into laughing comments about putting the Champs Elysées on Eighth Avenue, and the planners smiled, but they did not answer his question. A few minutes later, the meeting ended abruptly, as the planners packed up their materials and left. As with the previous meetings, there was no attempt at any resolution, no group consensus about future actions to be taken or points to pursue in other such meetings. As the Community Board member had pointed out, these meetings were only meant for planners and local residents to hear each other's voices—not to actually understand each other.

Throughout all these presentations, the planners worked to describe the Air Rights proposal as a plan to better integrate, connect, and develop the spaces of the city. Just as diligently, the CSDC activists worked to portray the proposal as a plan to disrupt, isolate, and jeopardize their neighborhood. While some pursued a strategy of negotiation, debating with the planners and attempting to extract some good for the community (i.e., heightened zoning protections), others more aggressively stood against the planners' mere ability to articulate a plan. They did not argue about zoning or FAR; they condemned these notions as "mumbo-jumbo," obscuring the planners' real, evil intentions toward the less well-to-do of the city. In these situations, the planners faced a blizzard of contempt and skepticism, and either reacted with annoyance, or did not visibly react at all.

In many ways, the Air Rights proposal itself constituted a method of increasing the scale and volatility of redevelopment following the changes of Times Square. The residents of Clinton/Hell's Kitchen articulated their responses to this proposal in two ways. First, they spoke the language of "quality of life," referring to shadows, microbes, and other everyday annoyances as grounds to negate the plan. Second, they attacked the plan as representing another assault on their very existence. In the vision they presented, city authorities, private developers, and monolithic corporate entities like Disney and Starbucks stood united against the everyday life of the city's neighborhoods—one big line of evil bulldozers, ready to roll over any building or person in their way.

However, regardless of their stance toward the Air Rights proposal and the City Planning Department, the community activists faced the strict format limitations of the presentations in which they met. The

CSDC and other neighborhood residents took these presentations as meaningful, important occasions to meet with the city planners, either to attempt to engage with them or to shout them down. But even when the locals made a real attempt to speak with the planners on their own terms, there was no real dialogue. So why hold these presentations at all? For the city authorities, these sessions seemed to be an obligatory airing of plans that were being debated in offices very far away from the tenements of Hell's Kitchen.

Whatever the planners thought of the meetings, they showed neither the ability nor the patience to find any way to address the community members' stories of feeling under attack by redevelopment and, in many ways, by the planners themselves. These were the voices of people living on the stormfront of urban redevelopment, citizens of an unstable, booming city; renters, guessing fearfully at what moves the landlords might be contemplating. They argued or ranted back at signs of the shifting socioeconomic terrain, especially at the planners' happy acceptance of the imminent transformation of Eighth Avenue and the rest of the neighborhood. To the residents, these were Broken Windows stories, in which the threatening strangers occupying the street corners were Starbucks coffee shops and construction facades. These stories interpreted what the planners described as signs of prosperity and activity as threatening symbols foretelling the storytellers' imminent demise. They would be pinned behind a wall, crushed by bulldozers, herded into the river—washed away by the shift of the tide.

Conclusion

The Meanings of Times Square

The New Times Square was a place where people struggled to deal with the fundamental questions of modern urban life: How do we sustain ourselves and find meaning in an unstable world? How do we live in spaces of the modern city, the ever-redeveloping city, where every building is ready to be torn down and rebuilt, where everything we experience in our everyday lives feels as though it is about to change? How do we reconcile the human drive for roots, connections, memory, and meaning with an economic climate of change, competition, and transformation? How do we form a *sense of place*[1] when the same forces that shape our world are guaranteed to destroy and remake it before our very eyes?

Compared to many other such grand urban redevelopment projects, the Times Square redevelopment was a sophisticated, nuanced approach to these questions. The redevelopment was deeply tied to the images and legacies of the area's history; the organizations involved reached out directly to the socially marginalized people who inhabited the area; the new spaces of the redevelopment incorporated many

of the area's old uses, and remained open to new uses and appropriations by all sorts of people, much more even than the redevelopers had hoped for.

However, these aspects of the redevelopers' work were peripheral to the main purpose of the redevelopment, which was to create a payoff for the landlords and developers involved. The creative manipulation of the built, legal, economic and social environment of the area was not the end, but, rather, the means. The central goal of the redevelopment was to achieve a radical upscaling of the real estate market in Times Square. The redevelopers did this by creating "Times Square" as the brand name for a new corporate office district, one that was aesthetically somewhat different than other such areas in Manhattan, but not economically all that different. In this way, the redevelopment represented only a new set of strategies for achieving a very old goal—the continuation of what sociologists call the "growth ideology" of the U.S. urban political economy.[2] The city must grow and expand, and "underdeveloped" spaces, even the homes of longtime residents, must be turned into desirable commodities, in order to serve the needs of capital.

The redevelopers were a complicated and heterogeneous group of people and organizations, each with their own history, mission, and approach. Over the continuing history of the redevelopment project, they worked in shifting alliances and combinations, sometimes collaborating and sometimes competing with one another. But they did share some ideas and aims. The people involved with this project—local property owners and real estate developers, their prospective corporate tenants, city planners, community groups, the police—worked to remove the businesses and people they regarded as physical and social "blights" from the area. As they saw it, the most tenacious problem of the redevelopment of Times Square was to guarantee that the streetlife and aesthetic in the area would fit the profile that their hoped-for tenants and clients would demand. To this end, they redesigned many of the public spaces in the area; intensified police and private security patrols against both serious crimes and lesser "quality-of-life" offenses, such as prostitution, petty drug use, and public drunkenness; and even offered all manner of relatively lavishly funded social services, including housing, medical treatment, and job training, to the people that they and their clients regarded as "undesirables."

As we have seen, however, events during and after my fieldwork took Times Square in directions that the redevelopers did not always anticipate. The Disney Store is gone—it was only ever a placeholder for the

eventual development of the supertower that became the headquarters of the Reuters news agency. Andersen Consulting, the key tenant of another of the supertowers, no longer exists, having collapsed in the wake of the Enron scandals. Still, the redevelopment's re-creation of Times Square seems to live on, despite the radical shocks of 2001—the stock market collapse and the terrorist destruction of the World Trade Center. The events of September 11, 2001, shook the city's corporate economy to the core, and could well have heralded the death of the New Times Square. Immediately upon this unexpected and violent clearing of such a large tract of prime Manhattan real estate, developers and city authorities eagerly shifted their attention to the economic and social potential of the former site of the World Trade Center. But even in the wake of the 9/11 attacks and their aftermath, the Times Square redevelopment continues on, as more and more global brands (recently, Hershey's) open flagship stores in the area or add to the supersignage above street level.

The redevelopers conceived of urban spaces as brand names and commodities, open to radical transformations of identity and scale within the cultural world of contemporary real estate development practice. They understood themselves as players in the "infinite game" of urban development. They sensed the city as an open-ended, flexible gameboard of abstract spaces, always subject to better and more profitable uses, driven by dynamic competition within and between cities for scarce economic and cultural resources. They saw themselves as creative, ethical actors in the unfolding drama of capital and competition that is their city.

At the same time, they were well aware of the controversies surrounding their work in remaking Times Square and Forty-second Street. More broadly, they were, themselves, deeply engaged in the history and identity of the place. I was consistently struck throughout my fieldwork by the depth of their feeling for the area, and by their conviction that what they were doing was reconnecting Times Square to what they saw as its lost authentic history and identity. They explained to me that they felt Times Square had been left to decay for almost a hundred years by unscrupulous landlords and negligent city authorities. They meant to tap into the power and prestige of corporate players like Disney in order to brush away this century of neglect and resurrect the "real" Times Square.

However, this wasn't the way many people affected by the redevelopment experienced and conceptualized the city in general and Times

Square in particular in everyday life. The redevelopment was also a site of conflicts, sometimes tacit, sometimes explicit, as I found when I examined spaces where everyday citizens directly engaged with the redevelopment, either as participants or as critics. On the margins of the social world of the redevelopment, people responded to, and critiqued, the redevelopers' creative-destructive transformations of the city as though the spaces of the city were personal property, indeed inextricably bound with their sense of self and other sets of values of history, memory, and identity.

These were contradictory ways of perceiving the city: urban *space* as brand or commodity, versus urban *place* as an intimate network of pathways, landmarks, and identities. The cultural tension between these two was not a trivial or superfluous side-effect of the redevelopment. Rather, this cultural tension played out as a fundamental aspect of the redevelopment on every level, from the privileged cultural spaces of architects' offices and developers' plans to the social contexts where people outside the planning process were recruited into the redevelopment and asked to comment on it or participate in it in different ways. While the redevelopers worked to turn Times Square and Forty-second Street into new forms of commoditized space, others rejected their values, imposed their own frameworks, or attempted to get in on the development question themselves.

The redevelopers claimed that they were working to bring order to Times Square—clearing away the detritus of a century's mistakes and neglect in order to reveal the "real," more socially acceptable (and presumably more lucrative) Times Square beneath the grime. But they were playing the highly disorderly game of real estate speculation, the same inherently chaotic, creative/destructive process that had made Times Square in the first place. Because the redevelopment was based in the same phenomena that it claimed to oppose, it reproduced and intensified the same physical and social phenomena the redevelopers call "blight" or "undesirable." The conflicts over the redevelopment were conflicts over whether the redevelopment is *the* way, or only one of *many* ways of enframing the city; whether it represents order itself, or only *an* order, up for grabs and open to challenge from outside or from within.

Thus, looking closely at the redevelopment of Times Square gives us insight into how people from all levels of society struggle to deal with the tension between the human sense of place and the marketing of space as a commodity. These two contradictory ways of looking at the city are always present, and always in conflict with one another, sometimes

quite directly. The process that builds our world is always at war with our need to live in it. At the same time, people do not feel totally disconnected from the workings of capital; rather, they perceive themselves to be personally entangled with it, and feel invested in its success.

The tension between lived place and commodity space, between the value people find in using the city in their lives versus the value people find in exchanging pieces of the city on the market, is more acute in the United States than in many other places, because the power of the real estate market to shape urban politics is stronger here, even than in most other market societies.[3] This tension is extreme in New York City, due to its high density and heterogeneity. Within New York City, Times Square has always been a monument to market-driven excess, a place that was created by theater entrepreneurs, media barons, and real estate speculators in their drive to capitalize on their power to shape the urban landscape.[4]

And yet the spectacle of gigantic advertisements and theater billboards has functioned as something else, too. Times Square has been a place where people have found what feels like a particularly urban form of freedom, an exhilarating sensation of power as they walk in the light of the supersigns.[5] What on a theoretical level seems like precisely the most demoralizing and exploitative kind of place—a streetscape defined by powerful imagemakers imploring and ordering us to soak up their ads and desire their goods—is experienced as something quite different, a place where ordinary people are exalted by the light and motion that these corporations focus on our streets and our lives. We feel that Times Square is there for us—and, of course, it is. The advertisements and enticements reaching out to us tell us that we mean something, that we matter, for someone created all this for us to look at. In other words, while the spaces and signs of Times Square are commodities, their ridiculous commercial excess forms a space in which people—even (or especially) those usually denied a place in public life—can feel that they are empowered citizens of a world that is built to meet their needs. This is just one of the paradoxes of urban life— that our enjoyment of life can come from our entanglement in others' schemes for extracting profit from selling off the world around us.[6]

As we have seen, people at every level of the Times Square redevelopment had to find their way through this paradox, including the redevelopers themselves.

The planners, architects, and real estate developers involved in the project worked to create spaces filled with icons of local history and

designed to become, in Rebecca Robertson's words about the new Forty-second Street, places of "stories." One thing that the results of their efforts show is the difference between, on the one hand, places that people spontaneously and organically fill with stories and meanings over the course of years of use, and, on the other hand, places that have certain stories and meanings preselected and inscribed on them in advance, and in exclusion of other possibilities. The latter involves a great deal of editing and decision-making regarding precisely what kinds of stories people will and will not be encouraged to create in Times Square. After all, the place was famous as a space of exploitation and degradation at the same time that it was a place for freedom and spectacular public display—and the redevelopers were interested in projecting an image that reflected only part of this complicated legacy.

At the Midtown Community Court, and especially at Times Square Ink., workers and arraignees alike worked to create spaces and possibilities for socially marginalized people. The court and its programs were empowered by the same real estate players that demanded its programs. The court employees had to work to help the same people the redevelopers wanted to exclude from the New Times Square while serving the redevelopers' agenda. This was a delicate balancing act, as was made most vividly clear at Times Square Ink. There, the trainees worked to create and inhabit their own redevelopment, their own stories of personal transformation and uplift. However, they did so in the context of an unstable, rapidly changing social context that seemed stacked against them, and that certainly provided no firm ground upon which they could build their futures.

In the police-community dialogues and the Citizens' Police Academy, all the participants worked to build a sense that there was a strong, commonsense consensus between the NYPD and the neighborhood groups regarding the nature of social order and the threats facing it. As we have seen, building this consensus was never entirely straightforward. It involved the community groups overlooking some of the more alien or threatening aspects of police culture, as well as the community leaders editing out much of what their constituents had to say. It also involved looking past some of the incongruities of applying the "Broken Windows" story to a real urban situation like that of Clinton/Hell's Kitchen. This was a place where the local and state governments were working with local business leaders and multinational corporate elites to create more social disruption than any invading criminal "outsiders," drawn by a neglected broken window, ever could.

In the debates over the Air Rights proposal, neighborhood residents fought tooth and nail against even allowing the city development authorities the space to articulate what to the residents seemed a magical scheme for allowing theater owners to realize profits literally out of thin air. The neighborhood groups agitated to preserve their fragile place of residence, acutely aware of their vulnerability as inhabitants of an "underdeveloped," and suddenly desirable, sector of Manhattan real estate. From their perspective, the dramatic success of the city's growth agenda taking shape just a few blocks away represented a tremendous threat to their right to the city itself.

In all these spaces of the redevelopment, people struggled to reconcile the need to build their own sense of place in the New Times Square, and the larger neoliberal social order it represented, with the unavoidable knowledge that this place was shaped primarily by the interests of capital, not of everyday city dwellers. This place had to serve, first, as a commodity . . . just as Times Square had when it was first created as a distinct space. Indeed, this was a place where the idea of deliberately inhabiting a world of commodities was first made into a concrete reality.

The contradictory dilemma that faced everyone involved with the redevelopment was not unique to Times Square, to New York City, to the United States, or, indeed, to cities in general. Wherever we live in this world, we inhabit places that are shaped by people but, to a greater or lesser extent, for the benefit of capital. People everywhere who deal with the realities of capitalism struggle to live in a socioeconomic system that can be oblivious or even hostile to their existence. It is very difficult to reconcile this with our need to live and feel at home in the world.

Times Square has always been a place where the knowledge of the power of capital to shape the everyday was massively, exhilaratingly explicit and obvious. Here, people could go to thrill to spectacles of power that were primarily created in order to manipulate and extract profit from them. Paradoxically, perhaps due to Times Square's long-languishing real estate market throughout most of the twentieth century, as well as to the Theater District's unintentionally becoming permanently fixed there, Times Square became a place that represented, not just exploitation and helplessness, but also, simultaneously, power and freedom.

The ritual gathering on New Year's Eve continues to be the most obvious example of the way in which a throng of humanity can turn everything that is tedious, demeaning, and exploitative about Times

Square into the stage for their own exaltation, their sense of being at the very center of the world's attention. New Year's Eve is where people make Times Square theirs, though they do so in tandem with the ever-intensifying efforts of local property owners and city authorities to control the gathering and to "brand" the event as a unified, marketable TV image. Of course, what gets created out of all this is not really some idealized vision of a diverse urban carnival, but, rather, on the level of the street, a night of boredom and immobility, punctuated by cruelty. And yet people still fill the Square, every year, to be inside and part of the magnificent spectacle.

The redevelopers embraced the iconography of Times Square, not so much because of its pleasing aesthetics and light-emitting properties—in other words, not because of the ways in which this iconography has become codified in practice and in law—but because of what this imagery represented. Paradoxically, it is partly out of these old images of commercial spectacle and public license that we fashion our ideals of democracy, authenticity, and the public sphere. The public sphere that the redeveloped Times Square actually supports is, of course, one thoroughly shaped by the actions of highly empowered elite players, working for their own agenda and to further the market-driven ideology of growth. This is a public sphere that wholeheartedly embraces the values of spectacle and performance that seemed, to some, so antithetical to democracy and community when they first blazed to life above the junction of Broadway and Forty-second Street.

The supersigns shine down on us, exalting us in their light while they dwarf us with their size. And behind them tower new edifices that are designed to step back from the street and hide their true magnitude from those on the sidewalk. Is this to allow sunlight to the street, or to keep us from looking up and recognizing precisely how alien, how Other, is the power that brings such structures into existence? Such a recognition would provoke despair, or a riot. Or, at least, it would if we did not also feel a connection to these structures, a personal investment in the fortunes of those whose signs shine ever brighter and whose towers rise ever higher.

Our ability to cultivate this sense of connection to the growth ideology of the city around us is the source of so much of the everyday creativity that is the hallmark of urban life. The redevelopment was filled with this creativity. There was the practical creativity by which the redevelopers sought to destroy and rebuild the built and social environment of the city, working to create urban spaces that made

profit out of selectively controlling who can inhabit them. There was the rhetorical creativity by which the redevelopers claimed that they were not simply amplifying the same social dynamics that created the supposedly "blighted" Times Square they sought to replace. And there was the everyday creativity engendered by the efforts of everyone attempting to survive and find meaning in the places the redevelopment had transformed; their creative attempts both to challenge and to reproduce the social tensions inherent in the exhilarating beauty of the New Times Square.

NOTES

Chapter One. Brilliant Corners

1. The Walt Disney Company has played an enormous role in defining the public face of the transformation of Times Square and Forty-second Street. Disney held a huge parade through Times Square in June 1997 to publicize both its new movie, *Hercules,* and the opening of the Disney Store at the corner of Forty-second Street and Seventh Avenue. Disney also holds a long-term lease on the New Amsterdam Theater on Forty-second Street, where it has run a stage musical version of *The Lion King* since 1997. In addition, Disney has musical versions of some of its story properties, such as *Beauty and the Beast,* playing in theaters around Times Square, and several of its media subsidiaries have major streetfront operations in the area, such as the ESPN Zone sports bar at the corner of Broadway and Forty-second Street and the ABC television broadcast studios one block away at the corner of Forty-third Street. See Elizabeth L. Wollman, "The Economic Development of the 'New' Times Square and Its Impact on the Broadway Musical," *American Music* 20 (2002):447.

   The Walt Disney Company's very visible involvement in the redevelopment project, in all the apparent incongruity between Disney's sanitized and "family-friendly" corporate aesthetic and New York City's urban chaos, makes Disney the most vivid symbol of the redevelopment overall. See John Bell, "Times Square: Public Space Disneyfied," *The Drama Review* 42 (1998):25. Many native New Yorkers summed up their disdain for the redevelopment for me this way: "Isn't it all, like, *Disney* now?" The street preacher–cum–performance artist and activist Reverend Billy began his career holding forth on the sidewalks of Forty-second Street and leading invasions of the Disney Store. See Bill Talen,

What Should I Do if Reverend Billy Is in My Store? (New York: The New Press, 2003):55–79. But Disney's symbolic centrality can be deceptive: historical studies of the redevelopment of Times Square show that the company was, in fact, a latecomer to the project, and that they were courted to open their stores and shows on Forty-second Street only long after the basic structures of the redevelopment had been put in place. See Lynne B. Sagalyn, *Times Square Roulette: Remaking the City Icon* (Cambridge, MA: MIT Press, 2001):339–372, as well as Alexander J. Reichl, *Reconstructing Times Square: Politics and Culture in Urban Development* (Lawrence: University of Kansas Press, 1999):157–161.

2. For example, see Anna Lowenhaupt Tsing, *In the Realm of the Diamond Queen: Marginality in an Out-of-the-Way Place* (Princeton, NJ: Princeton University Press, 1993); Marilyn Ivy, *Discourses of the Vanishing: Modernity, Phantasm, Japan* (Chicago: University of Chicago, 1995); John Pemberton, *On the Subject of "Java"* (Ithaca, NY: Cornell University Press, 1994); James Ferguson, *The Anti-Politics Machine: "Development," Depoliticization, and Bureaucratic Power in Lesotho* (Minneapolis: University of Minnesota Press, 1994); Arturo Escobar, *Encountering Development: The Making and Unmaking of the Third World* (Princeton, NJ: Princeton University Press, 1995); and Kathleen Stewart, *A Space on the Side of the Road: Cultural Poetics in an "Other" America* (Princeton, NJ: Princeton University, 1996).

3. For a general discussion of the emergent trend of multi-sited cultural anthropology, see George Marcus, "Ethnography in/of the World System: The Emergence of Multi-Sited Ethnography," *Annual Review of Anthropology* 24 (1995):95–117. For examples of multi-sited ethnographic studies of the United States, see Ralph Cintron, *Angels' Town: Chero Ways, Gang Life, and Rhetorics of the Everyday* (Boston: Beacon Press, 1997), on conflicts between Mexicans and Mexican Americans and the White power structures of a declining Illinois industrial town; Steven Gregory, *Black Corona: Race and the Politics of Place in an Urban Neighborhood* (Princeton, NJ: Princeton University Press, 1998) on the emergence of African American political activists in dialogue with city authorities in and around a neighborhood in Queens, New York; and Emily Martin, *Flexible Bodies: The Role of Immunity in American Culture from the Days of Polio to the Age of AIDS* (Boston: Beacon Press, 1994) on the concept of "flexible specialization" as it develops in immunology and spreads to such areas as corporate training seminars and the lived experience of people living with AIDS.

4. Daniel Makagon experienced the New Year's Eve celebration from the opposite perspective, starting out in a party in a corporate office high above the Square, then descending to street level after the ball had dropped. See Daniel Makagon, *Where the Ball Drops: Days and Nights in Times Square* (Minneapolis: University of Minnesota Press, 2004):1–30.

5. "The competition for space [in the city] is great, so that each area generally tends to be put to the use which yields the greatest economic return." See Louis Wirth, "Urbanism as a Way of Life," in *Classic Essays in the Culture of Cities*, ed. Richard Sennett (New York: Appleton-Century-Crofts, 1969):155.

6. Logan and Molotch observe that "The legal creation and regulation of places have been primarily under the domination of those searching, albeit sometimes in the face of use value counter-demands, for exchange value gains." See John R. Logan and Harvey L. Molotch, *Urban Fortunes: The Political Economy of Place* (Berkeley: University of California Press, 1987):77. They point out that this is just one way of perceiving and inhabiting urban space, one that stands in contradiction to other, nonprofit-oriented modes: "The pursuit of

exchange values in the city does not *necessarily* result in the maximization of use values for others. Indeed, the simultaneous push for both goals is inherently contradictory and a continuing source of tension, conflict, and irrational settlements. . . . [T]his conflict closely determines the shape of the city, the distribution of people, and the way they live together" (Logan and Molotch, *Urban Fortunes,* 2).

7. See Elizabeth Blackmar, "Uptown Real Estate and the Creation of Times Square," in *Inventing Times Square: Commerce and Culture at the Crossroads of the World,* ed. William R. Taylor (Baltimore: Johns Hopkins University, 1996):151.

8. For more on the concept of "scaling" in urban life, including the difference between everyday lived scale and the scale of development, see Neil Smith, "Homeless/Global: Scaling Places," in *Mapping the Futures: Local Cultures, Global Change,* ed. Jon Bird, Barry Curtis, Tim Putnam, George Robertson and Lisa Tickner (New York: Routledge, 1993):87–119.

9. See Guy Trebay, *In the Place to Be: Guy Trebay's New York* (Philadelphia: Temple University Press, 1994).

10. According to David Perry, this has always been the fundamental contradiction of urban planning. Perry writes, "Planning embodies the contradictions of capitalism, both as a practice of corporate industrialism and a response to the chaos of the 'wild city' such relations of productions produce." See David C. Perry, "Making Space: Planning as a Mode of Thought," in *Spatial Practices,* ed. Helen Liggett and David C. Perry (London, Thousand Oaks, CA: Sage, 1995):215.

11. See Wirth, "Urbanism," 150.

12. In the words of urban anthropologist Teresa Caldeira, "At the core of the conception of [modern] urban public life are notions that city space is open to be used and enjoyed by anyone, and that the consumption society it houses may become accessible to all." See Teresa Caldeira, "Fortified Enclaves: The New Urban Segregation," in *Theorizing the City,* ed. Setha Low (New Brunswick, NJ: Rutgers University Press, 1999):94.

13. John Helmer and Neil A. Eddington, eds., *Urbanman: The Psychology of Urban Survival* (New York: Free Press, 1973).

14. Henri Lefebvre, *Writings on Cities* (Cambridge, MA: Blackwell, 1996):158.

15. Mike Davis, "The Infinite Game," in *Out of Site: A Social Criticism of Architecture,* ed. Diane Ghirardo (Seattle: Bay Press, 1991):77–113.

16. Max Page, *The Creative Destruction of Manhattan, 1900–1940* (Chicago: University of Chicago Press, 1999).

17. David Henkin, *City Reading: Written Words and Public Spaces in Antebellum New York* (New York: Columbia University Press, 1998):27–38.

18. See Mel Rosenthal, *In the South Bronx of America* (Willimantic, CT: Curbstone Press, 2000):37. See also Robert Fitch, *The Assassination of New York* (New York: Verso, 1993) and Ida Susser, *Norman Street: Poverty and Politics in an Urban Neighborhood* (New York: Oxford University Press, 1982):161, 180–181.

19. Gregory, *Black Corona;* Susser, *Norman Street.*

20. Jamie Peck and Adam Tickell, "Neoliberalizing Space," *Antipode* 34 (2002):393. See also M. Christine Boyer, *The City of Collective Memory: Its Historical Imagery and Architectural Entertainments* (Cambridge, MA: MIT Press, 1994):407–420, as well as William Sites, *Remaking New York: Primitive Globalization and the Politics of Urban Community* (Minneapolis: University of Minnesota Press, 2003):61–68, for a specific history of neoliberalism in New York City politics.

21. See David Harvey's discussion of time and space compression as aspects of the subjective experience of the neoliberal shift, which he conceptualizes in

terms of the move from Fordism to "flexible specialization," in *The Condition of Postmodernity: An Enquiry into the Conditions of Cultural Change* (Cambridge, MA: Blackwell Publishers, 1990):284–307.

22. See Andrew Stark, "America, the Gated?" *Wilson Quarterly* 22 (1998):64–65. See also Fainstein's discussion of the ways in which this new paradigm has reshaped the profession of urban planning, shifting its principles to a more open embrace of promoting private gain, "marketability," and public/private partnership, in Susan S. Fainstein, *The City Builders: Property, Politics, and Planning in London and New York* (Cambridge, MA: Blackwell, 1994):98, 100, 108–109.

23. See Peter Jukes, *A Shout in the Street: An Excursion into the Modern City* (New York: Farrar Strauss Giroux, 1990):205. For more on Robert Moses, see also Marshall Berman, *All That Is Solid Melts into Air: The Experience of Modernity* (New York: Penguin, 1982):290–312, 325–327; Robert Caro, *The Power Broker: Robert Moses and the Fall of New York* (New York: Vintage Books, 1974).

24. See Robert Goodman, *After the Planners* (New York: Simon and Schuster, 1971); Peter Hall, *Cities of Tomorrow: An Intellectual History of Urban Planning and Design in the Twentieth Century* (New York: Basil Blackwell, 1988).

25. Quoted in Sagalyn, *Times Square Roulette*, 21.

26. See Peck and Tickell, "Neoliberalizing Space," 393.

27. See Nan Ellin, *Postmodern Urbanism* (New York: Princeton Architectural Press, 1999); John Chase, Margaret Crawford, and John Kaliski, eds., *Everyday Urbanism* (New York: Monacelli, 1999).

28. See Mike Davis's discussion of the new trend of "militarized" architecture in Los Angeles in *City of Quartz: Excavating the Future in Los Angeles* (New York: Vintage, 1992):224–263, as well as Talmadge Wright's analysis of urban developers' "authoritative strategies" for keeping the poor away from their spaces, in *Out of Place: Homeless Mobilizations, Subcities, and Contested Landscapes* (Albany: State University of New York Press, 1997):179–224. See also Jeff Flusty's analysis of architects' technical strategies for designing hostile urban spaces, in *Building Paranoia: The Proliferation of Interdictory Space and the Erosion of Spatial Justice* (Los Angeles: LA Forum for Architecture and Urban Design, 1994), and art historian Rosalyn Deutsche's study of the theme of "exclusion" in supposedly inclusive redeveloped urban spaces in New York City and elsewhere, in *Evictions: Art and Spatial Politics* (Cambridge, MA: MIT Press, 1996).

29. Peck and Tickell, "Neoliberalizing Space," 393.

30. Boyer, *City of Collective Memory*, 421–476.

31. Deutsche, *Evictions*, 17–56.

32. Rosemary J. Coombe and Paul Stoller, "X Marks the Spot: The Ambiguities of African Trading in the Commerce of the Black Public Sphere," *Public Culture* 7 (1994):249–274.

33. See Deutsche, *Evictions*, as well as Neil Smith, "New City, New Frontier: The Lower East Side as Wild, Wild West," in *Variations on a Theme Park*, ed. Michael Sorkin (New York: Hill and Wang, 1992):61–93.

34. See Sorkin, ed., *Variations*, 1992; Martin, *Flexible Bodies*, 40–44; B. J. Frieden and Lynne B. Sagalyn, *Downtown, Inc.: How America Builds Cities* (Cambridge, MA: MIT Press, 1989).

35. See Cintron, *Angels' Town*, 48–50 and 204–209, as well as John Dorst, *The Written Suburb: An American Site, an Ethnographic Dilemma* (Philadelphia: University of Pennsylvania Press, 1989).

36. Douglas Frantz and Catherine Collins, *Celebration, U.S.A.: Living in Disney's Brave New Town* (New York: Henry Holt, 2000); Andrew Ross, *The Celebration*

Chronicles: Life, Liberty, and the Pursuit of Property Value in Disney's New Town (New York: Ballantine, 2000).

37. Charles Rutheiser, "Making Place in the Nonplace Urban Realm: Notes on the Revitalization of Downtown Atlanta," in *Theorizing the City: The New Urban Anthropology Reader,* ed. Setha Low (New Brunswick, NJ: Rutgers University Press, 1999):317.

38. Emanuela Guano, "Spectacles of Modernity: Transnational Imagination and Local Hegemonies in Neoliberal Buenos Aires," *Cultural Anthropology* 17 (2002):181–209.

39. Teresa P. R. Caldeira, *City of Walls: Crime, Segregation, and Citizenship in São Paulo* (Berkeley and Los Angeles: University of California Press, 2000).

40. This emphasis on the politics of imagination follows directly from Geertz's famous call for anthropologists to carry out "thick description," or the analysis of human social behavior and conflict from the perspective of culturally specific imaginative frameworks. See Clifford Geertz, "Thick Description: Toward an Interpretive Theory of Culture," *The Interpretation of Cultures* (New York: Basic Books, 1973). For the most important (in my opinion) contemporary ethnographic work on the politics of imagination, see Anna Tsing's ethnographies of development ideologies in highland Indonesia. Tsing herself points out that "efficiency and progress are always *projects of the imagination*" (Tsing, *Diamond Queen,* 287; emphasis added). Ralph Cintron creatively applies Tsing's framework to understanding urban social issues and development strategies in the United States (Cintron, *Angels' Town*). Here are some other examples of approaches to studying imagination, creativity, and power that have directly inspired this work: Geographer Mike Davis shows how wealthy and powerful people in Los Angeles build their fears and fantasies of the city's minorities and working class right into the physical environments of their homes (Davis, *City of Quartz*). Lauren Berlant explores the politics of American fantasies of national identity in *The Simpsons* and in other texts, in *The Queen of America Goes to Washington City: Essays on Sex and Citizenship* (Raleigh, NC: Duke University Press, 1997). Slavoj Žižek examines the politics of fantasy in Hollywood cinema, in *Looking Awry: An Introduction to Jacques Lacan through Popular Culture* (Cambridge, MA: MIT Press, 1991). Carol Clover does the same for more marginal horror films, in *Men, Women, and Chainsaws: Gender in the Modern Horror Film* (Princeton, NJ: Princeton University Press, 1992).

41. I am borrowing the concept of "enframing" from historian Timothy Mitchell's analysis of how British colonists and intellectuals "enframed" Egypt. "Enframing" makes space visible and intelligible as an object to a specific observer, and thus subject to commodification and exchange. Enframing is what makes it possible for space to "circulate" as a commodity. See Timothy Mitchell, *Colonizing Egypt* (Berkeley, Los Angeles: University of California Press, 1991):44.

42. I draw this theoretical framework of "ethics" and "problems" from a series of published interviews with the philosopher Michel Foucault. Foucault uses the concept of "ethics," or the ideas and practices "through which we constitute ourselves as moral agents," as a lens through which to track changing social views on subjects such as sex, social control, and self-governance; see Michel Foucault, "On the Genealogy of Ethics: An Overview of a Work in Progress," in *The Foucault Reader,* ed. Paul Rabinow (New York: Pantheon, 1984):351. If we compare what different groups regard as the means by which someone defines themselves as "ethical," we can come to understand a great deal about what that group regards as the underlying purpose of life—that group's ethos. At the same time,

Foucault analyzes the history of what he calls "problemization," or the ways in which social phenomena have been conceptualized as "problems" in different ways at different times. In Foucault's words, an analysis of "problemization" looks at "what has made possible the transformation of the difficulties and obstacles of a practice into a general problem for which one proposes diverse practical solutions"; see Foucault, "Polemics, Politics, and Problemizations: An Interview with Michel Foucault," in *The Foucault Reader,* 389. There is tremendous overlap between these two concepts. We can look at the connections between the ways in which people "problemize" aspects of the world and how these same people understand their responses to these problems as ethically in tune with what is best for themselves and for society. In the case of the redevelopment, I am interested in the redevelopers, the people who "problemized" Times Square and Forty-second Street and how they proposed to solve the problems they saw in these complicated places. At the same time, I am interested in the ways in which people involved at every level of the redevelopment analyzed themselves and their role in transforming Times Square as ethical—not just possible or practical, but also moral, good for themselves and for society as a whole.

Chapter Two. Magnificent Spectacle

1. Ada Louise Huxtable, "Re-Inventing Times Square: 1990," in *Inventing Times Square: Commerce and Culture at the Crossroads of the World,* ed. William R. Taylor (Baltimore: Johns Hopkins University Press, 1996):360.
2. Sagalyn, *Times Square Roulette,* 23.
3. See Rem Koolhaas, *Delirious New York: A Retroactive Manifesto for Manhattan* (New York: Monacelli, 1994).
4. Paul E. Cohen and Robert T. Augustyn, *Manhattan in Maps: 1527–1995* (New York: Rizzoli, 1997):100–105.
5. The gridding of Manhattan prefigured the mapping of the "unsettled" (by white people) portions of the midwestern and western United States as a vast system of interchangeable rectangular plots later in the nineteenth century. Debates over the history and politics of the island's grid greatly overlap with much broader debates over the relationship between capitalism, imperialism, and the establishment of the United States as a nation-state. Commentators agree that Manhattan's grid erased the geographic complexity of the island, as well as the twists and turns of local pathways and their history, in the name of fostering a more fluid development economy. However, they take different stances on what this meant. Peter G. Rowe celebrates the grid's democratic "transparency," in *Civic Realism* (Cambridge, MA: MIT Press, 1997):159. Taking the opposite perspective, Peter Marcuse deplores the way it blotted out Manhattan's precolonial native settlements, in "The Grid as City Plan: New York City and Laissez-Faire Planning in the Nineteenth Century," *Planning Perspectives* 2 (1987):287–310.
6. Marc Eliot, in *Down Forty-second Street: Sex, Money, Culture, and Politics at the Crossroads of the World* (New York: Warner Books, 2001):72–73, quotes historian Lloyd Morris's description of the Rialto as it appeared in the mid-nineteenth century:

> The [Rialto] was a city in itself, the domain of a society that flourished through the night . . . a city of beautiful nonsense. Here they all met on common ground—Wall Street financiers, industrial magnates, gilded fac-

tions of the Four Hundred, gaudy playboys, journalists, celebrities from Bohemia or the arts, the greatest stars of the theater, gamblers, jockeys, pugilists, professional beauties, chorus girls, kept women—notorious votaries of pleasure, the cynosures of a vast, prosperous public. Mingling with the crowds that surged up and down Broadway under the garish lights, you saw streetwalkers and confidence men . . . panhandlers, dope-fiends, male prostitutes, and detectives.

7. Timothy Gilfoyle, "From Soubrette Row to Show World: The Contested Sexualities of Times Square, 1880–1995," in *Policing Public Sex,* ed. Colter, et al. (Boston: South End Press, 1996).

8. Tama Starr and Edward Hayman, *Signs and Wonders: The Spectacular Marketing of America* (New York: Doubleday, 1998).

9. See Sagalyn, *Times Square Roulette,* 39. Sagalyn goes on to note that the *New York Times* insisted on claiming the name of Times Square in order to give the newspaper equal footing with its competitor, the *New York Herald,* which had already claimed the name of Herald Square, a few blocks to the south.

10. See David C. Hammack, "Developing for Commercial Culture," in *Inventing Times Square: Commerce and Culture at the Crossroads of the World,* ed. William R. Taylor (Baltimore: Johns Hopkins University Press, 1996):36–50.

11. Hammack, "Developing," 43–45.

12. Sagalyn, *Times Square Roulette,* 242.

13. See Blackmar, "Uptown Real Estate."

14. Blackmar, "Uptown Real Estate," 54.

15. "Profit . . . supplied an underlying motive for the economic and political cooperation that sustained midtown's commercial development. . . . Lest such self-serving motives [seem] too crude, business groups throughout the city joined in insisting that the true beneficiary of midtown's development was a broadly defined consuming 'public.' . . . In stressing the benefits of Times Square's development, promoters sought to establish the unproblematic commensurability of economic and cultural value." From Blackmar, "Uptown Real Estate," 52–53.

16. See also Peter Marcuse, "Housing Policy and City Planning: The Puzzling Split in the United States, 1893–1931," in *Shaping an Urban World,* ed. Cherry (New York: St. Martin's, 1980):45–47.

17. Quoted in Fitch, *Assassination,* 60 (emphasis added).

18. "[W]ageworkers were welcomed to Forty-second Street at night when they were prepared to spend money. This selective exclusion drew on the nineteenth century conviction that what made social spaces both attractive and valuable was the invisibility of 'productive labor.'" From Blackmar, "Uptown Real Estate," 63.

19. Eliot, *Down Forty-second Street,* 84.

20. Quoted in William Leach, *Land of Desire: Merchants, Power, and the Rise of a New American Culture* (New York: Vintage, 1993):344.

21. Lewis Mumford, quoted in Leach, *Land of Desire,* 346.

22. Leach, *Land of Desire,* 341.

23. Leach, *Land of Desire,* 347–348.

24. Circa 1900, the sociologist Georg Simmel examined what he characterized as the growing penetration of money into everyday life and social interactions. "Money—the universally interchangeable material code of commodity and exchange value—puts things in circulation. In doing so, money simultaneously

puts these same things at risk. Money . . . reduces all quality and individuality to the question: How much? . . . Money . . . hollows out the core of things, their individuality, their specific value, and their incomparability. All things float with equal specific gravity in the constantly moving stream of money." See Georg Simmel, *Simmel on Culture,* ed. David Frisby and Mike Featherstone (Thousand Oaks, CA: Sage, 1997):176–178. In other words, as a totem of the possibility that anything can be exchanged for anything else, money calls into question whatever uses or meanings might have formerly been imputed to the things themselves. Simmel's work charts the ways in which money increasingly became a mediator in social and economic relations at this time, spreading to permeate everyday urban experience. As he put it, money "becomes the center in which the most opposing, alien and distant things find what they have in common and touch each other" (Simmel, *Simmel on Culture,* 252). Simmel connected urban life and architecture to this new power and predominance of money. His work draws links between the conditions of life in crowded and anonymous urban centers, and the particular aesthetics of commercial display that he saw as endemic to metropolitan life at the beginning of the twentieth century. Simmel saw both of these as embodying what he called the "smooth[ing]" character of money" (Simmel, *Simmel on Culture,* 242). In his most famous essay, "The Metropolis and Mental Life," Simmel describes the experience of living in the urban milieu as loaded with deeply repressed currents of desire and hostility. Urban dwellers learn to mask these untoward emotions and impulses behind what Simmel called a "blasé" attitude—a heightened regard for one's individual self, combined with an exaggerated disregard for others. See Georg Simmel, "The Metropolis and Mental Life," in *Classic Essays in the Culture of Cities,* ed. Richard Sennet (New York: Appleton-Century-Crofts, 1969):47–60. For Simmel, as for others of his period (notably Walter Benjamin a few years later), money, the metropolis, and the delirious display of commodities formed a tripartite whole. This trinity was a metonym for what they saw as a new capitalist cultural paradigm rapidly taking shape: a shift away from an emphasis on production and toward an emphasis on consumption.

25. Leach describes this as a new consumer culture, one rooted in "[q]ualities once seen as subversive and immoral and as existing on the margins of American culture . . . [including] carnival color and light, wishing, desiring, dreaming, spending and speculation, theatricality, luxury, and unmitigated pursuit of personal pleasure and gain." See William Leach, "Brokers and the New Corporate, Industrial Order," in Taylor, ed., *Inventing Times Square,* 99–100.
26. Blackmar, "Uptown Real Estate," 63–64. In a similar vein, Sagalyn observes, "Commercial extravagance rather than aesthetic discipline set the prevailing tone for Times Square" (Sagalyn, *Times Square Roulette,* 36).
27. Rosalind Williams, "The Dream World of Mass Consumption," in *Rethinking Popular Culture: Contemporary Perspectives in Cultural Studies,* ed. Chandra Mukerji and Michael Schudson (Berkeley: University of California Press, 1991): 198–235.
28. Leach, *Land of Desire,* 147.
29. Starr and Hayman, *Signs and Wonders,* 230–233.
30. "Broadway" plays were not actually written or created in Broadway theaters. Rather, these were extensively market-tested elsewhere. Producers brought them to Times Square only when they were thought to be ready to be sold to

a global audience. The same system obtains today. See Elizabeth L. Wollman, "The Economic Development of the 'New' Times Square and Its Impact on the Broadway Musical," *American Music* 20 (2002):445–465. Similarly, the movies that showed there were never physically produced anywhere near Times Square, nor even very much in New York City after the rise of the Hollywood studios. Perhaps the only time that entertainment products for sale in the area were actually produced in Times Square was when organized crime families made pornographic films in the same Forty-second Street buildings that housed the sex shops and movie theaters in which they were shown. See Eliot, *Down Forty-second Street,* 109–113.

31. See Lawrence Levine, *Highbrow/Lowbrow: The Emergence of Cultural Hierarchy in America* (Cambridge, MA: Harvard University Press, 1988).

32. See Laurence Senelick, "Private Parts in Public Places," in Taylor, ed., *Inventing Times Square,* 331–332, as well as Douglas Gomery, "The Theater: If You've Seen One, You've Seen the Mall," in *Seeing Through Movies,* ed. Mark Crispin Miller (New York: Pantheon, 1990):62–63.

33. Senelick, "Private Parts," 335.

34. Reichl, *Reconstructing,* 57. See also Eliot, *Down Forty-second Street,* 40.

35. Sagalyn, *Times Square Roulette,* 45.

36. "Well positioned, erotica could [and still can] afford to pay high rents, rents sometimes as much as twice the front-foot rate prevailing for an ordinary store on West Forty-second Street." Sagalyn, *Times Square Roulette,* 47.

37. Marc Eliot describes the great diversity of cheap entertainment and commerce along Forty-second Street in this period:

> The street's row of once-legitimate theaters offered an endless supply of documentaries featuring pretty young girls playing volleyball in the nude, but also a fair share of westerns, horror films, foreign releases, and other genre-specific second, third, and fourth runs. . . . Each theater on the street had a specialty that attracted its own loyal following. . . . These films shared time and space on a street where, in 1960, forty cents bought an hour at John Fursa's Chess and Checker Club . . . where Huberts' Museum and Flea Circus operated . . . where tile-walled Nedick's sold a doughnut, fruit drink, and coffee for fifteen cents twenty-four hours a day. . . . (Eliot, *Down Forty-second Street,* 2001)

38. See George Chauncey, Jr., *Gay New York: Gender, Urban Culture, and the Making of the Gay Male World 1890–1940* (New York: Basic Books, 1994).

39. See George Chauncey, Jr., "The Policed: Gay Men's Strategies of Everyday Resistance," in Taylor, ed., *Inventing Times Square,* 315–328.

40. See Marshall Berman, "Signs of the Times," *Dissent* (Fall 1997):76–83.

41. Senelick, "Private Parts," 336.

42. Similarly, Sagalyn quotes sociologist Herbert Gans's critique of the later plans to redevelop Forty-second Street. Gans accuses the redevelopers of "an esthetic and an architectural determinism, by which land uses deemed esthetically and otherwise undesirable are thought to produce undesirable social effects." Quoted in Sagalyn, *Times Square Roulette,* 85.

43. See Peter Buckley, "Boundaries of Respectability," in Taylor, ed., *Inventing Times Square,* 286–296.

44. Quoted in Buckley, "Boundaries," 296.

45. All quotes are from Senelick, "Private Parts," 337. Marc Eliot connects Mayor La Guardia's support for the antiburlesque campaign with his overall authoritarian approach to enforcing public morality and order, which included banning trolleys (either after seeing a streetcar block a firetruck or blow up a woman's skirt, depending on which version of the legend you believe). La Guardia also instituted New York's infamous cabaret licensing laws, which control when, where, and by whom music can be played in the city (see Eliot, *Down Forty-second Street*, 35). See also Paul Chevigny's discussion in *Gigs: Jazz and the Cabaret Laws in New York City* (New York: Routledge, 1991) of the La Guardia cabaret laws and their negative impact, not just on the lives of musicians like Thelonious Monk and Billie Holiday, but more generally on art and commerce in New York City.

46. Quoted in Starr and Hayman, *Signs*, 144.

47. Senelick, "Private Parts," 338–339.

48. Senelick, "Private Parts," 340–341.

49. See Marshall Berman, "Women and the Metamorphoses of Times Square," *Dissent* (Fall 2001):75–79. One manifestation of the "rage" Berman describes was a series of public antipornography marches and demonstrations held in and around Times Square by feminist organizations. See also Josh Alan Friedman, *Tales of Times Square* (New York: Delacorte Press, 1986):164–166.

50. In *Times Square Red, Times Square Blue* (New York: New York University Press, 1999), Samuel Delany memorializes the area's bars and porn theaters in the late 1970s. Delany describes these spaces as the locus for gay life and male public sexuality for the pre-AIDS era. He waxes nostalgic over the anonymous sex between men for which the porn theaters provided a venue. For Delany, these bars and theaters, which some saw as a blight on the area and on the city as a whole, represented model institutions for the support of what he calls "contact" between people of different races and classes in a polarized city.

    Similarly, Kierna Mayo Dawsey describes Times Square in the 1980s as the locus for young black and Latino social life in Manhattan. Times Square was a place where they could congregate in public, to see and be seen, without also being seen and suspected by storeowners and by the police:

    > [F]or a welcome change, we Black and Latino youth weren't the primary target of suspicious white stares. The sideshow that was Times Square somehow shielded us from the piercing eyes that made browsing [elsewhere] uncomfortable, even impossible. Eyes that too often reminded you that you weren't exactly welcome in many parts of town. . . . Times Square was then . . . a place for carefree congregation, a place to be that [was] not where your parents sent you, a place that somehow at once allow[ed] for anonymity and attention. We did not know why we were at Times Square, so much as we understood why we weren't somewhere else. (Kierna Mayo Dawsey, "Forty Deuce," *City Limits* 21 [1996]:22)

    Both Delany and Dawsey call attention to the ways in which Times Square provided a combination of "anonymity and attention" that allowed for certain groups, otherwise pushed to the margins, to find a kind of intimate publicity at "the Center of the World." For the male sexual culture that Delany describes and the minority youth represented by Dawsey's account, the absence in Times Square of certain signs of state or private control over streetlife made it possible for them to socialize in public.

51. Quoted in Eliot, *Down Forty-second Street*, 232.

52. Foucault, "Polemics," 389.

53. See Kristine Miller's discussion of the use of "blight" rhetoric in the redevelopment of Forty-second Street as a prime example of the neoliberal appropriation of eminent domain law to serve private development interests, in "Condemning the Public: Design and New York's New 42nd Street," *GeoJournal* 58 (2002):140–142.

54. See Reichl, *Reconstructing*.

55. For a fascinating overview of the more offbeat and low-budget movies shown in the theaters of Forty-second Street from the late 1960s through the early 19980s, see Bill Landiss and Michelle Clifford, *Sleazoid Express: A Mind-Twisting Tour through the Grindhouse Cinema of Times Square* (New York: Simon and Schuster, 2002).

56. Quoted in Reichl, *Reconstructing*, 61.

57. Quoted in Reichl, *Reconstructing*, 63.

58. See Reichl, *Reconstructing*, 63.

59. See also Teresa Caldeira on the "riot realism" of architects in Los Angeles after the Rodney King riots in the 1990s, in *City of Walls: Crime, Segregation, and Citizenship in São Paulo* (Berkeley and Los Angeles: University of California Press, 2000):329–330. See also Gregory on the history of U.S. government mortgage agencies classifying neighborhoods with black residents as automatically "risky," in *Black Corona*, 61.

60. Berman, "Signs," 78.

61. The architect's sketches for the sign above the Disney Store are an apt metaphoric image of both the dream and the reality of contemporary corporate culture. The sign's designers had drawn on black-and-white images of Times Square's early role as an arena for cutthroat competition, bringing this image into line with the commercial environment at the turn of the twenty-first century—a time of brand diversification, multimedia partnerships, and cross-brand synergistic collaborations. In the sign above the Disney Store, as in real life, images heralding Disney films, television shows, the American Express card, and other products seem to compete for our attention. However, what looks from one perspective like competition sometimes turns out to be a choreographed dance. Corporations strike backstage alliances and partnership deals with one another; these deals synchronize the relations between the different entities, such as those that produced the advertisements within the Disney sign. Similarly, the smoothly hyperbolic aesthetics of brand management and environmental design work together to harmonize the relations between the advertisements themselves, not to mention the ads' relation to their prospective consumers.

62. When I looked over the transcript of my conversation with Robertson several months after our interview, it occurred to me that there are, in fact, *many* "stories about Disney World," and about the Walt Disney Company in general. There are "urban legends" claiming that Walt Disney himself was a closet fascist sympathizer; that his body is preserved, frozen, in Snow White's Castle at the center of Disneyland; that Disney films like *Aladdin* and *Snow White* contain hidden pornographic images. More generally, and specifically pertaining to the redevelopment of Times Square and Forty-second Street, there are rumors and sentiments regarding the Walt Disney Company as an evil force, working behind a façade of bland corporate warmth to colonize fairy tales and urban spaces alike. But I imagine that these are not the kinds of "stories about

Disney World" she was referring to; these are stories of evil conspiracies in the present, not of colorful individuals in a nostalgic past.

For an example of academic work on the Walt Disney Company, see Project on Disney, *Inside the Mouse: Work and Play at Disney World* (Durham, NC: Duke University Press, 1995). This collaborative work embodies all the paradoxes of academics studying Disney: outstanding ethnography and interview material, combined with free-floating paranoia and a sense that Disney embodies a coming world corporate order.

63. See also Roberto Rossi, "Times Square and Potsdamer Platz: Packaging Development as Tourism," *The Drama Review* 42 (1998):43–48. According to Rossi, the BID's Visitors' Center, with its photo exhibits and guided tours, addresses a public that "has had, for the most part, a negligible share in deciding the direction and shape of development. . . . [The center and its services] function as guides on how to appreciate, how to view, how to consume what the developers are preparing" (Rossi, "Times Square," 44).

64. The Visitors' Center was located on Forty-second Street until December 31, 1997, when the old theater building in which it was located collapsed. It was then moved to a new location, on Times Square itself. The new center is far more elaborate. Rather than just photographs, it features fragments of re-created theaters, and nightclubs representing eras of local history—of course, there are no re-creations of Forty-second Street's cheap movie houses or sex shops.

65. See Caldeira, "Fortified Enclaves," 94. See also Frank Roost, who criticizes the redevelopment's use, not just of these photos, but of a more general historical myth of the early-twentieth-century Broadway producer as "the individual entrepreneur," in "Recreating the City as Entertainment Center: The Media Industry's Role in Transforming Potsdamer Platz and Times Square," *Journal of Urban Technology* 5 (1998):16. Roost sees this myth of the lone intrepid entrepreneur as a way of glossing over the anonymous, global corporate character of Forty-second Street's new tenants.

Chapter Three. The New Spaces of Times Square

1. Michel Foucault famously used Bentham's Panopticon as a trope for modern society, in order to understand the nature of citizenship and subjectivity in a society based on preconditions, not of overt physical force, but of surveillance, law, and discipline. See Michel Foucault, *Discipline and Punish: The Birth of the Prison* (New York: Vintage, 1979):200–209.

2. In some ways, the spaces they created were similar to the kinds of spaces described by architect Oscar Newman in his widely cited monograph, *Defensible Space: Crime Prevention through Urban Design* (New York: Collier, 1973). Newman argues that builders must pay attention to things like sightlines, entryways, lighting, and stairwell design; all these must work to imbue the environments they construct with an inherent sense of what he calls "latent territoriality"; a built-in sense of ownership on the part of inhabitants, which excludes others who might seek to gain access: "All the different elements [that] combine to make a defensible space have a common goal—an environment in which latent territoriality and sense of community in the inhabitants can be translated into responsibility for ensuring a safe, productive, and well-maintained living space. The potential criminal perceives such a space as controlled by its resi-

dents, leaving him [sic] an intruder easily recognized and dealt with" (Newman, *Defensible Space*, 3–4).

However, Newman largely restricts *Defensible Space* to the design of successful apartment buildings and residential areas. It is trickier to apply Newman's discourse of "latent territoriality," "a sense of community," "residents," and "inhabitants" to places like Times Square and Forty-second Street. By all accounts, in the decades before the redevelopment, Times Square had sustained a variety of close-knit social scenes. This was, in short, a "community." But this was not a community the redevelopers wished to encourage, or even to allow to continue to exist. The redevelopment project was fueled by the desire to *erase* the image of Times Square and Forty-second Street as "a space . . . controlled by its residents." The redevelopment project had to find a way to apply Newman's principles of "defensibility" and "latent territoriality" in such a way as to make the area inhospitable to many of its previous denizens—to actively take away their "territoriality." At the same time, these spaces had to invite specific new groups of tenants and visitors to make it their own (literally, in the case of new tenants and developers).

3. See David Garland, "Governmentality and the Problem of Crime," in *Governable Spaces: Readings on Governmentality and Crime Control,* ed. Russell Smandych (Brookfield, VT: Ashgate):45–73; Heal and Laycock, eds., *Situational Crime Prevention: From Theory into Practice* (London: Her Majesty's Stationery Office, 1986); and Gerda R. Wekerle and Carolyn Whitzman, *Safe Cities: Guidelines for Planning, Design, and Management* (New York: Van Nostrand Reinhold, 1995).

4. Huxtable, "Re-inventing," 360.

5. For more on the Times Square BID, see Mark Sussman, "New York's Facelift," *The Drama Review* 42 (1998):34–36; as well as Doug Stewart, "Times Square Reborn," *Smithsonian* 28 (1998):34–45. See also Mitchell Duneier's discussion of the "space wars" between a BID in New York City's Greenwich Village and the poor sidewalk vendors working in the neighborhood, in *Sidewalk* (New York: Farrar Strauss and Giroux, 1999): 231–252.

6. See Joe Hermer and Alan Hunt, "Official Graffiti of the Everyday," *Law and Society Review* 30 (1996).

7. Quoted in Sagalyn, *Times Square Roulette,* 259.

8. See Blackmar, "Uptown Real Estate."

9. See City of New York, *Midtown Development Review* (July 1987):14.

10. Ibid.

11. City of New York, *Midtown;* see also William H. Whyte, *City: Rediscovering the Center* (New York: Anchor Books, 1988).

12. Quoted in Sagalyn, *Times Square Roulette,* 261.

13. See Sagalyn, *Times Square Roulette,* 252–262.

14. See J. W. Thompson, *The Rebirth of New York City's Bryant Park* (Cambridge, MA and Washington, DC: Spacemaker Press, 1997).

15. See Simmel, "Metropolis," 48.

16. Quoted in Thompson, *Rebirth,* 21.

17. Quoted in Thompson, *Rebirth,* 24.

18. Quoted in Thompson, *Rebirth,* 8.

19. Quoted in Thompson, *Rebirth,* 31. The Bryant Park Restoration Project's drive to make the park a "drug-free" space has been successful to such an extent that one graduate student friend told me he had to cross the street and hide in order to smoke a joint at an outdoor funk concert put on by the project in the mid-1990s.

20. Thanks to Doug Egberts for this insight.

21. See Fainstein, *City Builders*, 58–62, for a discussion of the New York City real estate slump of the late 1980s and its impact on the Forty-second Street redevelopment project.

22. See also Sagalyn's description of the Development Corporation's attempt to "consciously creat[e] an enticing visual image of what [Forty-second Street] could become," in *Times Square Roulette*, 277.

23. See Sagalyn, *Times Square Roulette*, 277. See also Roost, "Recreating," 16–17, where he discusses the way the redevelopers project images of "social diversity" on Times Square and Forty-second Street, but a highly managed diversity, where for example porn shops are banned.

24. See William J. Bratton, *Turnaround: How America's Top Cop Reversed the Crime Epidemic* (New York: Random House, 1998). For perspectives from graffiti writers, MTA officials, law enforcement officers, and others on the campaign to clean the graffiti in the New York subways during the late 1970s and early 1980s, see also Craig Castleman, *Getting Up: Subway Graffiti in New York City* (Cambridge, MA: MIT Press, 1982):133–157, as well as Joe Austin, *Taking the Train: How Graffiti Art Became an Urban Crisis in New York City* (New York: Columbia University Press, 2001).

25. See Stephen Duncombe, Stephen J. Sifaneck, and Andras Szanto, "The Incense Merchant on Times Square: The Black Muslim Ethic and the Spirit of Capitalism," in *Sex, Scams, and Streetlife: The Sociology of New York City's Times Square*, ed. Robert McNamara (Westport, CT: Praeger, 1995):43–55.

26. See also Makagon's discussion of the Holzer signs, in *Where the Ball Drops*, 144–148.

27. Photos of the haiku were featured in nearly every story on the Forty-second Street Art Project in the thick Creative Time clippings file. Richard Hunt, an amateur photographer who saw the "Haiku on 42nd St.," snapped a roll of film—one shot per poem—in order to preserve them, and in 1997, with the permission of the Haiku Association, turned the pictures into a poster. This poster was itself widely circulated around and beyond the immediate environs of Forty-second Street and New York City. It was displayed for sale in various New York bookstores (this was where I first saw it) and in a national poster catalog, and was itself the subject of newspaper and magazine stories. See Hunt, "Haiku to You, Too," *Hope* 11–12 (1997), as well as Carrie Steller, "Verse Case Scenario," *Star-Ledger* (June 4, 1997).

28. See Deutsche, *Evictions*.

29. Kristine Miller points out that many of these reasons were, apparently, quite different from the ones the subjects gave to the photographer. The poster of a woman who told the photographer that she was "Looking for chicks with dicks" states that she is "Being nice." A man who originally said that he was in Times Square "Looking for sex" is quoted on the poster as "Looking for love." The photographer was not consulted regarding these changes. See Miller, "Condemning," 143–145.

30. See the photographer's collected volume of these pictures in Neil Selkirk, *1000 on 42nd Street* (New York: Powerhouse, 2000).

31. See John Brinkerhoff Jackson, "The Stranger's Path," *Landscape in Sight: Looking at America* (New Haven, CT: Yale University Press, 1997).

32. Marc Eliot quotes someone who was involved in organized crime on Forty-second Street in the 1970s as saying, "You could kill your mother on that cor-

ner [in front of the Port Authority] and nobody would notice," in Eliot, *Down Forty-second Street*, 111.

33. For example, see Marcus Felson, et al., "Redesigning Hell: Preventing Crime and Disorder at the Port Authority Bus Terminal," in *Preventing Mass Transit Crime*, ed. R.V.G. Clarke (Monsey, NY: Criminal Justice Press, 1996):5–92.

34. The music in the ad sounds like a version of "Foxy Lady" by Jimi Hendrix—an ironic choice, in light of the Port Authority's efforts to end prostitution in and around the terminal building.

35. Simmel, "Metropolis," 51.

36. Rosalyn Deutsche refers to this process as "the functionalization of the city." The owners and managers of city spaces attribute their decisions to the space itself. By doing so, they position themselves as merely carrying out the will of the space they serve. See Deutsche, *Evictions*, 52.

37. Also, the sculpture provides a perfect match for the jittery, hypnotic time-lapse sequences of crowds moving through busy urban spaces found in films ranging all the way from *Koyaanisqatsi* to William Whyte's book and film *The Social Life of Small Urban Spaces*.

38. Thanks to Donald Brenneis for this turn of phrase.

Chapter Four. The Midtown Community Court

1. See M. Christine Boyer, *Dreaming the Rational City: The Myth of American City Planning* (Cambridge, MA: MIT Press, 1983):44. Similarly, James Donald writes that urban planners "who fantasize about turning the city into an efficient machine . . . want to render the city transparent, to get the city right, and so to produce the right citizens," in James Donald, *Imagining the Modern City* (Minneapolis: University of Minnesota Press, 1999):121.

2. See John Feinblatt and Michelle Sviridoff, "The Midtown Community Court Experiment," in McNamara, ed., *Sex, Scams, and Street Life*, 83–96.

3. See also Thompson, *Rebirth*, 1997.

4. D. Weinberg sees something similar in his ethnography of drug treatment centers in the United States, in "'Out There': The Ecology of Addiction in Drug Abuse Treatment Discourse," *Social Problems* 47 (2000):606–621. Weinberg notes the ways that the residents of these treatment centers, in talking about their former or current drug use and criminal activity, rhetorically construct a dangerous space outside the treatment center, which they call "out there." As Weinberg puts it, they "posit a space 'out there' marked by its degradation, dirtiness, solitude and savagery which commonly tempts those who must live there to also behave amorally, licentiously, and/or savagely" (Weinberg, "'Out There,'" 606).

5. Goffman (1959).

6. More information about the Center for Court Innovation and the Midtown Community Court is available at the CCI website, www.communitycourts.org.

Chapter Five. Times Square Ink.

Some of the material of this chapter was published in "Times Square Ink.: Marginal Citizenship and Corporate Culture in the New Times Square," *disClosure* 11 (2002):63–83.

1. Lefebvre, *Writings on Cities,* 158.
2. For theoretical perspective on the concept of the self as a technology of social discipline, see Michel Foucault, *The History of Sexuality, Volume One* (New York: Vintage, 1978), as well as Richard Sennett, *The Uses of Disorder: Personal Identity and City Life* (New York: Vintage, 1970).
3. Philippe Bourgois discusses the split between the Upper East Side and East Harlem as an example of New York City's "urban apartheid," in *In Search of Respect: Selling Crack in El Barrio* (Cambridge, MA: Cambridge University Press, 1995):19–47.
4. See Michael Taussig, *Defacement: Public Secrecy and the Labor of the Negative* (Stanford, CA: Stanford University Press, 1999).
5. In fact, this has become the focus of substantial debate in neoconservative circles: the mismatch between the demands for bottom-rung labor, especially in the service sector, demanded by the corporations of New York City, and the perceived lack of sociocultural and business skills possessed by the city's unemployed labor pool. For example, see Heather MacDonald, "Gotham's Workforce Woes," *City Journal* 7 (1997):41–49.
6. Here I borrow the ways in which writers for hip-hop magazines transcribe African American vernacular ways of pronouncing "You know what I'm saying" or "You know what I mean" as casual verbal interjections in everyday conversation.
7. If my experience and that of my friends who work in such environments is any guide, Times Square Ink.'s version of corporate culture is quite accurate, in this aspect at least.

Chapter Six. "Visible Signs of a City Out of Control"

Some of the material in this chapter was published in "Visible Signs of a City Out of Control: Community Policing, Quality-of-Life, and Broken Windows in New York City," *Cultural Anthropology* 19.2 (2004):250–275.

1. See Ralph Blumenthal, "Community Policing: A Case Study," *New York Times* (January 31, 1994):B1; see also Clifford Krauss, "Giuliani and Bratton Begin Push to Shift Police Aims and Leaders," *New York Times* (January 26, 1994):A1.
2. Sagalyn, *Times Square Roulette,* 475.
3. See Kevin Flynn, "Ex-Police Head Criticizes Strategies," *New York Times* (April 5, 2000):B3; see also Neil Smith, "Giuliani Time: The Revanchist 1990s," *Social Text* 16 (1998):1–20.
4. See Andrea McArdle and Tanya Erzen, eds., *Zero Tolerance: Quality of Life and the New Police Brutality in New York City* (New York: New York University Press, 2001).
5. James Q. Wilson and George L. Kelling, "Broken Windows: The Police and Neighborhood Safety," *Atlantic Monthly* (March 1982):29–32.
6. Wilson and Kelling "Broken Windows," 31–32.
7. For example, see Stanley Milgram, "The Experience of Living in Cities: A Psychological Analysis," in *Urbanman,* ed. Helmer and Eddington (New York: Free Press, 1973):1–22.
8. Wilson and Kelling, "Broken Windows," 34.
9. Wilson and Kelling, "Broken Windows," 34.
10. Critics of the Broken Windows theory have leveled a number of attacks at the concept. For example, see D. W. Miller, "Poking Holes in the Theory of 'Broken Windows,'" *Chronicle of Higher Education* 47 (2001):A14-A16. These critics

cite what they see as the article's binary opposition between "order" and "disorder." They claim that the Broken Windows theory's simplistic emphasis on "order" as an unquestioned good simplifies the social complexities of crime and disorder; that the theory works in the interests of property owners and business leaders to the exclusion of the interests of others; and that the theory provides the central rationale for extremely oppressive and intolerant policing. The authors of "Broken Windows" dispute these critiques, especially the last one; they point out that, in the original article, they call for the police merely to serve the interests of the community: "The essence of the police role in maintaining order is to reinforce the informal control mechanisms of the community itself" (Wilson and Kelling, "Broken Windows"). But, as Baird points out, this defense of Broken Windows remains problematic: "[The Broken Windows theory] seem[s] to draw substantially on a presupposition that 'community' is a universal term that encompasses naturally shared ideas of order and its proper expression—despite the fact that urban structures and harsh control measures are themselves contributing elements in community dissolution and dissent" (Ian Baird, "Fixing Broken Windows [Book Review]," *Canadian Journal of Criminology* 41 [1999]:97–104).

Looking specifically at New York City, Bernard E. Harcourt, in *Illusion of Order: The False Promise of Broken Windows Policing* (Cambridge, MA: Harvard University Press, 2001), questions the central premise of what the Giuliani administration called "order maintenance" policing—the goal of ensuring "order" by labeling and punishing "disorder." Harcourt argues that the false aggregation of diverse social practices (prostitution, public drinking, littering, graffiti) under the label "disorder" constitutes a highly effective rhetorical strategy for focusing hostile official attention on "the disorderly"—people deemed to be undesirable or unworthy. Through opposition, scapegoat categories like "the disorderly" help to constitute the equally constructed categories of "order" or "the community" that they are held to oppose. Harcourt critiques these processes of category and subject formation and maintenance as "unstable" and "self-deconstructing." (Bernard Harcourt, "Reflecting on the Subject: A Critique of the Social Influence Conception of Deterrence, the Broken Windows Theory, and Order-Maintenance Policing New York Style," *Michigan Law Review* 97 [1998]:346–347).

Further, Harcourt notes that the inception of the Giuliani administration's order maintenance policing policies saw substantial increases both in misdemeanor arrests and stop-and-frisk encounters between police and New Yorkers, as well as a significant rise in complaints by civilians of mistreatment at the hands of the police (Harcourt, *Illusion*, 167–171). He argues that the actual police practices that these approaches entail—preemptive arrests, sometimes violent, against even potential misdemeanor offenders—look awfully "disorderly" when considered as social behavior in the clear light of day. Harcourt suggests, too, that this rise in arrests and charges of misconduct weighs most heavily on poorer New Yorkers and on racial and ethnic minorities: "In effect, regularity on the street depends on irregularity in police practice—mixed, of course, with some regularity in the choice of suspects" (Harcourt, *Illusion*, 129).

11. George L. Kelling and Catherine M. Coles, *Fixing Broken Windows: Restoring Order and Reducing Crime in Our Communities* (New York: Touchstone, 1996).

12. For example, see Willard M. Oliver, ed., *Community Policing: Classic Readings* (Upper Saddle River, NJ: Prentice-Hall, 2000).

13. New York Police Department, *Police Strategy No. 5: Reclaiming the Public Spaces of New York* (New York: NYPD, 1994):4.

14. Police scientists and criminologists such as "Broken Windows" co-author Kelling claim that the police need to draw on citizens as a source of crime data: "The focus now is really on crime prevention. . . . And that implies getting closer to the community because the police know they can't do it alone" (Kelling, quoted in George James, "Involving the Community in Police Partnerships," *New York Times* [April 11, 1999]: Section 14NJ, Page 8). Similarly, commentators from a wide range of backgrounds argue that police departments need to build closer ties to the communities they serve to solve chronic problems of police practice, such as brutality, corruption, inefficiency, or anomie (for example, see Fox Butterfield, "Rethinking the Strong Arm of the Law," *New York Times* [April 4, 1999]:sec. 4, p. 1; Seth Faison, "Can Closer Links Deter Corruption?," *New York Times* [April 4, 1994]: sec. 4, p. 3; "Community Policing, Bratton Style [Editorial]," *New York Times* [January 31, 1994]:A16). A recent article by Kraska and Kappeler on "contemporary police reform" in the United States notes that, under the auspices of this movement, "reformers have asked the police to join in problem-solving teams, to design ways to take control of the streets, to take ownership of neighborhoods, to actively and visibly create a climate of order, and to improve communities' quality of life" (Peter B. Kraska and Victor E. Kappeler, "Militarizing American Police: The Rise and Normalization of Paramilitary Units," *Social Problems* 44 [1997]:13).

However, as the authors of this article go on to point out, "community policing" and "quality-of-life" mean many different things to different people. The terms encompass initiatives that range from foot patrols and neighborhood watch programs, at one end of the spectrum, to much more extreme measures, including the military-style police occupation of entire neighborhoods. For example, in New York City, this has entailed such diverse programs as: the ComStat statistical mapping of crime data, which catalogs the spaces of the city in terms of "hot spots" and "trouble corners" where crimes tend to occur; anti-drug measures up to the wholesale police occupation of entire blocks in poor black and Latino neighborhoods such as Washington Heights; and organizations meant to foster police-community dialogue.

Kraska and Kappeler go on to say the police themselves draw few distinctions between what seem like innocuous and extreme tactics; all are considered tools in the service of maintaining order and defending "quality-of-life." Moreover, the police and the communities with which they collaborate may not share the same definitions of what constitute matters worthy of police attention. For example, a newspaper article from 2002 on meetings between the NYPD and residents of New York's Greenwich Village quotes a skeptical police inspector: "After September 11 [2001], the quality-of-life issues started creeping back, but I don't think it's any worse than before. . . . I don't think it's as bad as people are saying. But that's what people are telling us. They are the voice." (Quoted in Denny Lee, "Street Fight," *New York Times* [March 31, 2002]: sec. 14, p. 9.) The community policing approach is also widely debated in policing and criminology circles. For example, see Jack R. Greene and Stephen D. Mastrofski, eds., *Community Policing: Rhetoric or Reality* (New York: Praeger, 1988). Aside from issues of implementation and effectiveness, critics question the very idea of "community" that underlies these initiatives. They point out that communities, like all social entities, are constructed, not naturally given, and that community policing initiatives may play a role in actually creating,

and limiting, the groups they purport merely to represent (Gregory, *Black Corona*).

15. See George James, "Police Academy, Too: What Citizens Can Learn From the Cop on the Beat," *New York Times* (January 12, 1997):Section 13NJ, Page 8.

16. The videos had all been shot by a company based in the suburbs of Sacramento, California. For me, this meant that the entire experience was a roller-coaster through the most weirdly mundane of all possible worlds—the land of my childhood. While the instructor joked about "La-La Land," I sat, dumbstruck, as the video transformed the bland Northern California landscapes and hairstyles I thought I knew so well into signs of a world of danger.

17. The experience of the firearms simulator came back to me in 1999, when a four-man NYPD Special Forces team fired forty-one shots at a man, Amadou Diallo. Diallo's death made headlines and sparked huge protests. The officers defended themselves by claiming that they thought Diallo was armed and acting suspiciously. He turned out to have been holding his wallet. Charged with murder, the four officers were acquitted in February 2000 at their trial in Albany, NY. Lawyers for the officers made repeated references to the NYPD's firearms training simulator during the trial.

Chapter Seven. "It Doesn't Exist, But They're Selling It"

1. See Logan and Molotch, *Growth Machine*, 77–78, for an analysis of how these "air rights" plans make the theater industry work as a "development tool" for urban redevelopment interests. As Logan and Molotch point out, plans like these "allow cultural institutions, in effect, to collect rents they otherwise could gain only by tearing down their structures" (Logan and Molotch, *Growth Machine*, 78).

Chapter Eight. Conclusion: The Meanings of Times Square

1. See Steven Feld and Keith Basso, eds., *Senses of Place* (Santa Fe, NM: School of American Research Press, 1996).

2. Logan and Molotch, *Growth Machine*, 77.

3. Logan and Molotch, *Growth Machine*, 2, 147–153.

4. For example, consider that Times Square itself was named after a private company, the New York Times, which deigned to build its headquarters there. Naming the area after a newspaper continued a trend that was begun a few decades earlier and a few blocks to the south in Herald Square, named after the *New York Herald*. This legacy of public commemoration of private power makes the protests against NASDAQ's demands that the city rename the corner outside its new Times Square headquarters "NASDAQ Plaza" seem a little naïve; or, at least, these protestors are fighting in a much longer-running battle than they probably knew.

5. Marshall Berman, in *On the Town: One Hundred Years of Spectacle in Times Square* (New York: Random House, 2006), his fascinating, touching account of Times Square's place in the historical psyche of his family, New York City, and the world at large, argues that the right to the city and the right to be part of the urban spectacle go hand in hand, and that we must fight for both. In the epilogue, Berman describes being ordered away by a security guard from the

front of the new Reuters building at the corner of Broadway and Seventh Avenue, in the heart of Times Square. The prospect of Times Square as the home to the headquarters of a powerful corporation that feels such ownership over the street that their private security force has no qualms about driving away bystanders is surely something impossible to imagine happening in any other era of Times Square's history.

The bulk of *On the Town* is Berman's thoughtful meditation on the role that Times Square served in the moral education of New Yorkers in the twentieth century. During that time, throughout the periods usually described as its rise to glory and slow downfall, Times Square was always a place where people aspired to become visible, to become famous, to grow up, to become sexual beings, to find love; to put themselves on display and become part of the spectacle of the city.

Berman pays special attention to the history of women and images of women in Times Square. The book is filled with lovingly lascivious descriptions of women on display in Times Square, in movies, plays, dances, billboards, and on the street—their faces, their clothes, their bodies. Both in his argument and in his style of writing, Berman makes plain what he sees as the historical connection between putting oneself on display in public and becoming part of urban public life, and how this has been so radically different for women than for men.

In fact, throughout much of the book, Berman struggles mightily with how Times Square has connected public life with the sexual objectification of women. His argument practically turns itself inside-out to assimilate the frank lewdness of the supersigns with his overall portrait of the area as an egalitarian, non-exploitative place for women and men alike. Berman goes so far as to argue that a Benetton billboard portraying naked youths actually has a progressive, even a feminist theme. He asserts that the billboard's secret purpose is to challenge the viewer to overcome (presumably) his desire for these nubile bodies—that the ad is urging us to rise above the images that it projects (Berman, *On the Town,* 15). In this way, Berman himself battles with the contradictory entanglement of spectacle, exploitation, freedom, and democracy that animates the culture of Times Square.

6. Historian Sam Bass Warner, Jr. points out that our ability to live in the streetscape created by skyscraper buildings depends on our willingness to accept the sheer concentration of capital and political power required to create such a building. Warner argues that one function of the concept of the "skyline" was to redefine skyscrapers for average urban citizens: not as a symbol of corporate power (which they certainly are for the people who build and occupy them), but as an aesthetic contribution to the public good. (See Sam Bass Warner, Jr., "Slums and Skyscrapers: Urban Images, Symbols, and Ideology," in *Cities of the Mind,* ed. Lloyd Rodwin and Robert M. Hollister [New York: Plenum, 1984]: 191–194)

INDEX

ABC Television, 197n1
advertisements: New York City as
    drenched in, 13–14, 54; regulat-
    ing, 54–55; as a social good, 56; on
    television, 67, 72–74, 78. *See also*
    consumerism; exploitation; signs
Aerosmith, 9
aesthetic tactics: of Bryant Park rede-
    sign, 59–61; against marginalized
    people, 99–105, 109, 111–112, 125;
    of Port Authority Bus Terminal
    redesign, 71–80; of Times Square
    redevelopment, 49, 62–71, 85–
    87, 105
African Americans: communities of,
    in New York City, 17; job- and
    life-training for, 96–133; police

violence against, 135, 213n10; on
    Times Square, 38, 39–40, 206n50.
    See also Harlem; racial prejudices
Ain't Misbehavin' (play), 83
Air Rights proposal, 171–174, 194
alcohol, 8, 26; drinking of, in public,
    83, 138, 140, 142, 189; prohibiting
    sales of, 32–34. *See also* drunks
alienation, 13; advertisements as signs
    of, 30–31, 56; of Times Square Ink.
    students from corporate style, 117,
    119, 132–133
American Theater (New York City), 26
Andersen Consulting, 190
anger. *See* emotions
anthropology (cultural), 3–4, 11–13,
    16–17, 21–22, 117–118, 127, 131

217

ABOUT THE AUTHOR

Benjamin Chesluk holds a Ph.D. in cultural anthropology from the University of California, Santa Cruz. He lives in Philadelphia.

CONTENTS

*Dedicated to Olive and Ezra
for the joy they bring to their own lives,
and to mine*

Library of Congress Cataloging-in-Publication Data
Chesluk, Benjamin Jacob.
  Money jungle : imagining the new Times Square / Benjamin Chesluk.
    p. cm.
  Includes bibliographical references and index.
  ISBN 978–0-8135–4179–2 (hardcover : alk. paper)
    1. Time Square (New York, N.Y.)—Social conditions—20th century.   2. City plan-
ning—New York (State)—New York—Political aspects.   3. Urban renewal—New York
(State)—New York—History—20th century.   4. Power (Social sciences) I. Title.
  HT168.N5C48 2007
  306.09747'1—dc22
                                                                    2007000030

A British Cataloging-in-Publication record for this book is available from
the British Library.

Visit our Web site: http://rutgerspress.rutgers.edu

Manufactured in the United States of America

Jungle

Imagining the New Times Square

Benjamin Chesluk

Photographs by Maggie Hopp

RUTGERS UNIVERSITY PRESS
NEW BRUNSWICK, NEW JERSEY, AND LONDON

MONEY

MONEY *Jungle*

PREFACE

It has been on my heart for many years to write a volume commending the Reformed faith. Not only have I found myself regularly questioned about the credibility of various aspects of Reformed theology (sometimes well represented, sometimes caricatured), but also students and leaders have asked for a reasoned presentation of this historic approach to the things of God. Although this book was intended to be much shorter, I found that most of the elements under consideration needed more than a brief paragraph in order to do them minimal justice. At the same time, this book is not an exhaustive theological text—far from it. I felt it important so to limit the volume that it would not alienate readers by its sheer size.

While it is impossible to predict where the book might find a readership, it is my hope that it may serve to introduce people to the broad contours of the Reformed position. Thus, it might be used more formally, for example in a study group, or an academic setting, or membership classes for the church. But I hope, too, that it can be used less formally, by friends who hope to introduce friends to this way of thinking.

It might be tempting to read one of the three sections without the others. While no great harm would be done, the sections are meant to hang together. The somewhat lengthy historical portion intends to give a background for the way Reformed theology developed and the way its fundamental characteristics may be found far outside the sixteenth century in Europe. The major doctrinal portion holds together as a unit but will be vastly enriched by looking at the historical background first. Similarly, the third, more practical portion makes sense on its own but is far more reasonable when coordinated with the two previous sections.

A book like this one is never written alone. I have been a follower of Christ for forty years now and have had extraordinary teachers. Some of them are quoted in the pages that follow. It is a special joy for me to dedicate the book to the Gathering of Friends, a group of men I meet with on a yearly basis, and their wives, without whom we would all be incomplete and ineffectual. They are

Bryan and Kathy Chapell
Ray and Diane Cortese
Barbara Edgar
Terry and Dorothy Gyger
Jim and Jan Hatch
John and Cynthia Hutchinson
Dick and Liz Kaufman
Tim and Kathy Keller
Al and Elaine LaCour
Joe and Barb Novenson
Randy and Carol Pope
Harry and Cindy Reeder
Skip and Barbara Ryan
Shelton and Anne Sanford
Scotty and Darlene Smith
Sandy and Allison Willson
John and Marianne Wood
John and Nina Yenchko

I would also like to thank the good folks at P&R Publishing, who have never been less than supportive and encouraging. My readers have often improved the text and spotted errors or infelicities needing redress. Special thanks to Peter Lillback, Carl Trueman, Dick Gaffin, and Sinclair Ferguson for their helpful contributions. My best editor, as always, is my wife, Barbara, without whose loving support I would accomplish very little. May this book serve in some small way for the advancement of the good purposes of the One who excels all loves.

INTRODUCTION

Reformed theology is a designation familiar to some, new to others. Those who know about it have different feelings about its merits. Some are zealous to defend it, possibly overzealous. Others are indifferent. Still others, perhaps a growing number, resent it and blame it for various problems in the church and in society. The present volume is an attempt to introduce the Reformed faith and to commend it.

So, then, what is the Reformed faith? It is a particular account of God and the world. Historically, as the name indicates, the Reformed faith was forged at the Protestant Reformation in the sixteenth century. Yet its central teachings are not meant to be innovative. The Reformers contended they were going back to the roots, representing not only the historic position of the church but also the contents of the Scriptures, as God's Word. At the same time, Reformed theology was not frozen in its sixteenth-century form but has been developed and expanded up to the present time. This book is a commendation of Reformed theology. A number of questions are raised at the outset.

Would it not seem that in our present world, especially within the Christian community, the call should rather be building bridges, being ecumenical, not controversial in matters of doctrine? Do not our times cry out for us to embrace, and not to exclude? Would we not be wise to worry less about articulating a version of the Christian faith that is precise, carefully defined, and systematic, and more about the spiritual and social needs of humanity? The answer is, yes and no! If one's goal is to set forth a theology whose main agenda is merely negative, one that inevitably considers many Christians from other persuasions to be outside the fold, that is misguided. It runs the danger of putting a stumbling block before brothers and sisters for whom Christ died. At times theologians have done just that. They have drawn lines in ways that are destructive, not constructive, falling back on self-assured conservatism rather than reaching out.

Many have been victims of rigid forms of theology and spiritual disciplines and are looking to open things up. Some invite us to become "new kinds of Christians," defining ourselves in fresh ways over against old formulations, though presumably without falling into the maelstrom of chaotic postmodernism. They rightly complain that religion is too easily shaped into cultural forms that steer it away from biblical norms or from a direct relationship to God. They suggest redrawing boundaries that will not resemble the older ones. Will Protestants always be divided against Roman Catholics or Eastern Orthodox believers? Will evangelicals and mainline liberals always clash? Should not all Christians unite against common enemies, closing ranks against persecution, hunger, racism, and the like? Put this way, without any qualifiers, we must answer in the affirmative: it is time to open doors, join forces, work toward that unity that the gospel prescribes (John 17:22; Eph. 4:13).

But things are not so simple. Theology need not be ossified to be sound. This book will argue that real theology, healthy theology, is not isolated from spiritual life, nor is it exclusive, but quite the opposite. One need only read some of the great, lively theologies of Augustine or Calvin or Bavinck to see that orthodoxy need not be cold. Further, by a strange and wonderful paradox, real unity is not achieved by uncritically widening boundary lines but by combining carefully wrought systematic theology and such a walk with the living God that communion among his people is authentic. Precision is not the enemy of universality but its friend. This goes to the heart of the gospel. The good news depends on the reality of the incarnation of Jesus Christ. That means the second person of the Trinity became not humanity in general, but a man, a unique person from a unique place. Jesus Christ and his teachings, as William Temple once put it, were a "scandal of particularity." In S. Mark Heim's felicitous expression, "If God were to be as human as we are, Jesus must have a fingerprint as unique as each one of ours."[1] Only from this extraordinary particularity can Jesus then be universal. He did not look down from heaven and proclaim timeless truths with no application to culture. Rather, he became a real human being, a particular Semitic male, at a particular time of history, because such concreteness is the only way to be human. Because Jesus is a particular man, his message is then truly applicable to all of humanity, to women and to men from every race and group.

And so, the message has a shape. It has contours. It is particular in order to be universal. Just as God brought about the redemption of every kind of person through the one man, the God-man Jesus Christ, so his revelation, though encapsulated in words from the Hebrew, Aramaic, and Greek languages, is universal, valid across all boundaries of time and space and culture. In the same way, we would argue, Reformed theology has a particular form and comes out of a particular history. But its reach is meant to be universally valid, applicable across all kinds of boundaries. Its success is no doubt less than perfect. But it is not certain that any other version has done quite as well.

True Confessions

Not that all of its advocates are winsome. The first time I heard the expression *Reformed theology*, I was not much attracted to it. I was a beginning student in a graduate school of theology, and the term *Reformed* was being used by certain colleagues who, it seemed to me, were feeling quite superior to the rest of us who were not especially conversant with it. They made it known that the "five points of Calvinism" were a nonnegotiable foundation for authentic doctrine and that the major ailments of worldwide evangelicalism boiled down to a rejection of this particular system of faith. Sometimes it was illustrated with the image of the *tulip*, which left me unamused.[2] It sounded cold and

---

1. S. Mark Heim, *Is Christ the Only Way?* (Valley Forge, Pa.: Judson, 1985), 63.

2. It is an acronym for the five heads of doctrine of the Canons of Dort: total depravity, unconditional election, limited atonement, irresistible grace, perseverance of the saints. Not only is the order wrong, but also the terms are not the most favorable rendering of the canons. We will take this up in chapter 3.

au fond deterministic. It had little to do with my warm experience as a recent convert to biblical faith. Its God seemed far away and somewhat foreboding.

At the time I also had a vague understanding that Reformed churches were the perpetrators of many cruelties, such as apartheid in South Africa and slavery fostered by the Dutch East India Company. In addition, on a subject I cared deeply about, African-American history, it appeared the Presbyterian role in dismantling slavery in America was less than illustrious. Baptists, Methodists, and Quakers did more than their Reformed peers. And for that matter, I had to wonder, at least from my vantage point, why so many Protestants kept the whole process of manumission painfully slow in North America. Was that connected with their system of faith? I was distressed to find out that for some Reformed divines race discrimination was given a theological warrant.

Of course, I was also deeply concerned about the role of Christians in the Second World War. My closest friends at university were Jewish, and so I had and still have a special sensitivity to Jewish–Christian relations. On one reading of the events, Christian Europe was at best uninformed and thus silent about the systematic persecution of the Jews by the Nazis, and at worst in complicity.

Other obstacles added to these initial feelings. Having grown up in the Episcopal church, but without a genuine faith, I was led by my spiritual odyssey to associate with Presbyterianism, which is one of the major groupings with a Reformed heritage in the Anglo-Saxon world.[3] I did love it but still found it to be, well, verbose and lacking in aesthetics. As a new Christian I went to "Bible-believing" churches, most of them Presbyterian, and was quite happy to do so. But I had a hard time with the pulpit-centered architecture and the lack of artwork and good music in the worship. I kept wondering, Was I in church? There exists a caricature of the austere, hardworking Protestant down through the ages. The image of the Reformed pastor in

---

3. Historic Anglicanism is Reformed in character. The Thirty-Nine Articles were strongly influenced by Calvin. While in the American province—the Protestant Episcopal Church—only a minority today embraces a Reformed persuasion, the Anglican communion worldwide does.

French literature is that of a somber, black-robed moralist. Sometimes the portrait was deserved.

My mind was changed over a period of time. During seminary I learned about the rich contours of the Reformed approach from some of the most godly professors on the planet. In their presentations, theology was anything but cold and deterministic. I sat under biblical scholars, systematicians, historians, and preaching coaches who were ardent about the best way to formulate the doctrinal nuances of the Christian faith but also deeply motivated to reach the unchurched. In addition, many of them were passionate for social justice and the training of ethnic minorities in places such as the world's cities.

Eventually I investigated the real and the imagined role of Reformed Christianity in South Africa, the Netherlands, and America. I learned a great deal. Certainly considerable damage was done in the name of Reformed theology here and there. But the story is not so negative, or at least so one-sided, as I had imagined. I began to learn that effective change cannot occur through revolution or through top-down coercion. Christian faith has been an extraordinary agent of change throughout the centuries, but not always instantaneously or precipitously. I discovered that there is a paradox at the heart of the social vision of biblical faith, especially in its Reformed version: it is conservative *and* progressive. The reasons for that are complex. The Bible teaches that real and effective transformation usually comes about gradually, through transformed awareness and courageous action across the social and cultural board, rather than through violent revolution. While a certain kind of conservatism can and does lead to inertia, there is another kind that learns to work within the structures, in order to undermine their evil aspects without turning everything to confusion. Most often, down through the ages, the best kinds of reforms in society occurred because a measure of stability allowed the truly radical character of Christian ethics to be unleashed. Reformed theology has great pride of place here.

The case of South Africa speaks eloquently to that point. There is no denying the devastating effects of racism and apartheid, which were often justified by Reformed Christians. One can feel the impact of it in the powerful writings of Alan Paton, who recorded the injustices being perpetrated for supposedly Christian reasons and the true reconciliation made possible through the gospel. While the injustices and cruelties of the system did enormous harm, there is another side. One sees the power of the gospel at work in the events that led to the dismantling of apartheid in the 1990s. Paton died in 1988 and never saw the most poignant transformation of his "beloved country," though he had hoped for it. Even secular sources, such as *Time*, described the outcome as miraculous.

Specifically religious factors were at work in public ways and behind the scenes. Among other players in the oft-told account of the events of April 1994, none had a more significant role than the wise Kenyan professor Washington A. J. Okumu. A devout Christian, he quietly but insistently brokered an agreement between Nelson Mandela of the ANC, Prince Mangosuthu Buthelezi of the IFP (Inkatha), and President Fredrik Willem de Klerk, a man who had just made one of the most powerful public apologies in the modern era. Repenting of the sin of apartheid, this Reformed believer paved the way for a bloodless transition to a more just society. Assuming the presidency in a free election, Mandela came to lead a coalition government. As we know, South Africa today is no paradise. Much was lost, and much is still to be regained. But throughout the process, and into the rebuilding of a country, there have been surprisingly few reprisals and a surprising quest for truth and reconciliation.

In order to examine the authenticity of Reformed theology I took another look at the history of slavery. Again, untold horrors were perpetrated, often in the name of God and sometimes in the name of the Reformed faith. And admittedly the journey to emancipation was slow and painful. Still, the true story is complex. A strong voice against slavery has been there since the beginning. What was interesting is the fact that quite often the merchants and colonizers vehemently opposed different Christian efforts to end the slave trade and the practice of slavery. Former slavers became fierce advocates for emancipation. Thanks to the popularity of the hymn "Amazing Grace," we have learned about the dramatic conversion of its author, John Newton. He was led to turn from the cruel life of a slave trader to being a powerful advocate for abolition through the influence of the great

Reformed preacher George Whitefield. One of the few evangelicals in the Anglican church of his day, he was befriended by the Parliamentarian William Wilberforce, whom he persuaded not to go into the ministry but to stay active as a legislator. Wilberforce, with the support of the Clapham Group, as well as that of Prime Minister William Pitt, made it his life's goal, in the name of the gospel, in the historic Reformed, Anglican tradition, to abolish slavery and reform British morals. He was attacked and ridiculed by politicians and plantation owners alike. Eventually, though, compelled by the love of Christ, Wilberforce and his colleagues ushered in the passage of the law abolishing slavery throughout the British empire.

In America, the story is less honorable. It is clear that some Reformed Christians, among them some of the ablest theologians, supported slavery or at least were reluctant to dismantle it. Certain enlightened Presbyterians did oppose the abuses wrought by human bondage. Eventually a bloody war decided the issue, at least in part. However, the gospel did effect a remarkable change. The most important way was not political at the outset but spiritual, in the best sense. When the Christian message was embraced by slaves, not only did it help them through the horrors of slavery, but by the time of emancipation, having a profoundly biblical consciousness became the most significant factor in the lives of black Americans. It provided for cultural identity and for an ideology of resistance against overt and covert oppressors. In time, the churches founded by and for Afro-Christians became the most important institutions for the training of leaders in the march to freedom. They gave the faith new vitality and reimagined its shape and emphases. Thus, in combating the evils of slavery and oppression, Protestant Christianity was not always a liberating force from the top down, and at times it was woefully slow to act, but there were many effective ways in which it was one of the most powerful agents of transformation toward a more just society.

In my quest, I also looked very closely into the role of the church during the Second World War. This is not the place to enumerate all my findings. But suffice it to say that while there is blood on Christian hands, the relation of the different churches to the Holocaust was not monolithic.[4] In the midst of the moral ambiguity one must at least recognize the remarkable accounts of courageous opposition to the deportations. A number of those episodes specifically involve Reformed Christians.[5]

The Roots of Persuasion

What eventually endeared me forever to the Reformed position, though, was not only its effect on social issues, important as that may be. It was two things. First was watching the way in which a Reformed world-and-life view was held by very real, very human advocates. Some of them were prominent figures. Many of them were humble servants, doing their work quietly and yet powerfully. In effect, they were tried and not found wanting. Along with the black-robed moralists, there is a far greater number of extraordinarily courageous and real Protestants.

Our family had the enormous privilege of living in France for many years, working mostly with the Protestants in that country. There we were steeped in the memory of the Huguenots, those persecuted Reformed Christians who had suffered so much for their testimony from the sixteenth through the eighteenth centuries. I read Calvin's *Institutes of the Christian Religion* in French and was greatly moved by its genius, its clarity, and its deep pastoral concerns. I read the Canons of Dort, which gave us the famous five points, and found that they were neither the trite phrases signified by the Dutch flower nor the reputed austere dogmas about a fatalistic God. They emerged to me as a rich, balanced account of the major issues surrounding God's plan of redemption, his loving power, along with a strong emphasis on human responsibility and the free offer of the gospel.

4. We are not likely soon to see a consensus emerge. Perhaps someday the heat generated by studies such as Daniel J. Golhagen's *Hitler's Willing Executioners* and *A Moral Reckoning: The Role of the Catholic Church in the Holocaust* . . . will turn to light. At any rate, many different stories have been told, and yet many remain to be told.

5. One of the most extraordinary occurred in Le Chambon-sur-Lignon, where the Huguenots managed to save some four thousand Jews, many of them children, from the death camps.

I also had the opportunity to work out some of the thornier issues of Reformed theology with my colleagues and mentors at the seminary in Aix-en-Provence where I taught. While interacting with them and with students from all over the world, more caricatures were shed. These Reformed Protestants from every walk of life exhibited the deep-rooted reality of a living faith, one that was able to see them through many of life's greatest difficulties.

Second, the formulations of Reformed theology fit what I was reading on the pages of Scripture and on the pages of God's general revelation. It made the most sense of the different aspects of revelation. It appeared to resolve the apparent contradictions while not steamrolling over the stubborn problems. Reformed theology helped me understand the relation of the Old Testament to the New. It illuminated areas of ethics I cared about. It presented a more credible account of God's power in relation to human significance.

Ultimately, I suppose, it does not matter very much how or why I came to believe this position. In the pages that follow, I would like simply to commend the Reformed faith for its biblical authenticity and its spiritual vitality. In the first part, we will briefly explore the origins of Reformed theology and trace some of its worldwide impact. In the second part, we will look at some of the major teachings of the Reformed interpretation of the Bible. Finally, in the third part, we will discover some of the implications of this view for the life of the church and our calling in the world.

Reformed Christianity has not yet reached its full potential for biblical maturity. Much needs to be corrected. I still think it tends toward intellectualism. It could use more aesthetics. It has much to learn from other branches of the worldwide communion of Christians. But still, it is profoundly biblical. It is arguably the most consistent expression of evangelical faith. It is surprisingly diverse. It begins and ends with the glory of God, placing him at the center of all things.

It is my sincere hope that this volume will help those who are naturally disposed to such a theology, as well as those who are not, to discover the fundamentals of the Reformed outlook and find them compelling. I have said nothing new here; at least I hope not. It would be gratifying if readers were inspired to look further into the great

Reformed classics. Recommendations are made in the appendix. This book is far too brief to qualify as a complete outline of Christian doctrine. It will have served its purpose, though, if some readers will become attracted enough to the Reformed faith to want to pursue it in greater depth. It is written with a profound sense of inadequacy but also with a profound sense of gratitude to all my teachers and guides, instruments of the Lord God, surely, in reforming me, to the small extent that it may have happened.

PART

1

FOUNDATIONS AND HISTORY

1

SALVATION BELONGS
TO THE LORD

~~~~~~~~

Our Greatest Good

The purpose of this first part is twofold: first, to explain the foundational idea of reformation, and second, to explore the historical manifestations of the Reformed outlook. Readers are free to go directly to the second and third parts, which set forth the basics of Reformed theology in a direct fashion. However, they would be missing something important. History is the arena for the display of the principles we are discussing. Having some idea of the place of the Reformed faith in the world enables us to appreciate and evaluate it with much better perspective.

Theology (from *Theo-logos*) means words about God and his truth. Why should we worry about words about God, especially words in human language? Is not all theology abstract and theological enterprise antiquated? Do the formulations of religious principles matter? Why should it make any difference which system of theology, if any, has it right?

One fundamental reason goes to the heart of God's relation to his people. First and foremost, God is honored by the way we speak about him. A dim analogy might be the way we are pleased when someone speaks well of us. Second, good theology means we understand who God is and what his view of the world is, because the claim of theology is that it comes from God, from his revelation to us. Good theology is what the New Testament calls a "stewardship from God that is by faith" rather than "speculations" (1 Tim. 1:4). Sound words are health-giving for us as well. Our words about God put us in right relationship to God. In this way, good theology is restorative.

The Bible affirms this in a thousand ways. For example, telling his people to return to him, the Lord, through the prophet Jeremiah, connects restoration to precious words: "If you return, I will restore you, and you shall stand before me. If you utter what is precious, and not what is worthless, you shall be as my mouth" (Jer. 15:19). In another example, the apostle Paul exhorts his young student Timothy to "follow the pattern of the sound words that you have heard from me, in the faith and love that are in Christ Jesus" (2 Tim. 1:13). Notice how trusting and loving the Lord is inseparable from sound words (literally, wholesome words). Speaking rightly about God and his world, which is what theology really means, is not a luxury. It issues from communion with God and brings health to our souls. It goes to the heart of who we are and nurtures our greatest good.

Reformed theology aims at nothing less than recounting the way things are. From the creation, to the fall of humankind, to the new creation in Christ, the story told by good theology is the right account of reality. It is at once sobering, convicting, and life-giving. Good theology speaks to the human person in order to diagnose his or her condition and call that person to be reconciled with God.

Human beings are creatures, rooted in the earth. Our feet are planted in the soil. As creatures, we share much with the animal world: we breathe, we see and smell, we reproduce, we hunger and thirst. At the same time, we are profoundly different from anything else in the world. Human beings need meaning. We need transcendence. We are made to commune with a higher being. When these are denied, alienation and aimlessness come to characterize us. Sometimes this is conscious, taking the form of a quest for meaning and value. Sometimes it is unconscious, in which case either we may be satisfied, more or less, with the way things are, with family and work and pleasures, or we may be despondent and depressed about the way things are. In any case, it is profoundly characteristic of human beings that we experience the desire for meaning and the frustration of that desire.

The great North African bishop Aurelius Augustine (354–430) begins his masterpiece of meditative theology, the *Confessions*, with the thought that our human instinct is to praise God. Despite the sad effects of the fall on the human creature, he still has that insistent, clamant desire to praise God: "You stir man to take pleasure in praising you, because you have made us for yourself, and our heart is restless until it rests in you," Augustine tells us.[1] Our desire to praise God is so deeply ingrained that it has led some skeptics to assert that all belief in a deity is merely a projection of our needs, the translation of human aspirations into the image of a heavenly father. Undoubtedly such wishful thinking is often involved in matters of religion. But Augustine adds a qualifier, the needed corrective to thinking religion might succeed as human projection. To complete the phrase, he says, "He bears about him the mark of death, the sign of his own sin, to remind him that you would 'thwart the proud.' " With him, then we realize that though we need to find God, there can be no successful humanistic construction that will arrive at the truth unaided.

The dark Book of Ecclesiastes puts it realistically: "[God] has made everything beautiful [appropriate] in its time. Also, he has put eternity into man's heart, yet so that he cannot find out what God has done from the beginning to the end" (Eccl. 3:11). Our search for meaning, the *desiderium aeternitatis*, is given to us by God, but our limitations and the vanity of the world in which we live prevent us from finding that meaning in any satisfactory manner. Thus, the author concludes, "However much man may toil in seeking, he will not find it out. Even though a wise man claims to know, he cannot find it out" (Eccl. 8:17).

The hunger for God takes many forms in our present world. It may be in the vague, New Age quest for spiritual reality. It may be in the fanatic guise of revolution or terror. In the West, we are discovering that all of our prosperity, all of the technology at our disposal, the

---

1. Augustine, *Confessions,* trans. Henry Chadwick (Oxford: Oxford University Press, 1991), 1.1.

travel, the communication, our extraordinary freedoms, all of these are as of nothing compared with happiness and a contented life. Yet we cannot seem to find them. Something has gone wrong. Things are not as they are meant to be.

This same double-edged truth is put in tragic terms by the apostle John in the prologue to his Gospel: "[The one true light] was in the world, and the world was made through him, yet the world did not know him" (John 1:10). Jesus Christ was the one through whom the creation came into being. His imprint is found on every part of it. There is not one realm of the physical world or of social life of which he was not a definitive interpreter, because he framed the universe. Yet the world did not know him. The text goes on to say he came to his own people, the people of Israel, and even they did not receive him (John 1:11). Stark words. Stark contrast.

But things do not end here. Hopeless in itself as our restless search may be, there is yet hope. This same God whom to know is life and joy, this same God who cannot be discovered by merely human religion, has made himself known in spite of it all. He has given his creatures the power to know him as a free and unconditional act of love. And so, John goes on: "But to all who did receive him, who believed in his name, he gave the right to become children of God, who were born, not of blood nor of the will of the flesh nor of the will of man, but of God" (John 1:12–13). We can receive God, we can know him, because he changes us profoundly. We are "born of God," that is, we become his children by the supernatural operation of his Spirit (see John 3:3, 5). Precisely because Jesus has come into the world, not only as the one true light but also as the Word made flesh, born himself to die and then to be raised from the dead, renewal of the most revolutionary kind has been effected. Christ loved his own, he "loved them to the end," by making them completely clean (John 13:1, 10). Christ, the "firstborn of all creation," and the "firstborn from the dead," is able to reconcile all things to himself and to translate all God's children from the kingdom of darkness to his own kingdom, filled with his real brothers and sisters (Col. 1:13–20).

The Reformed faith seeks to do full justice to these two sides of the quest for meaning. It knells the sober sound of humanity's spiritual death, its incapacity to lift itself up and bring meaning to life on its own. The Reformed diagnosis of the human condition is beyond pessimism, though more ultimately hopeful than any kind of optimism. The creation itself is made futile, placed under a bondage, and we are buried in its depths, as "flesh" that is hostile to God (Rom. 8:7, 20–21). But then the power of God's love is the power of resurrection, which triumphs over all this weakness. Having been slaves to sin, because of Christ's resurrection we can now be empowered by goodness, so that sin can no longer have dominion over us (Rom. 6). Not only God's people but also the entire creation is being saved, and one day there will be a new heaven and a new earth where everything in this tired, miserable world will pass away and be no more (Rev. 21:1).

Whatever else may be good, the world, family, culture, friends, the arts, all that human life possesses that has worth, our highest good is not in these things but in knowing God and being known by him. Any theology that impoverishes this calling, either by injecting false optimism into the assessment of our condition or by minimizing the power of God's love, is ultimately a poor rendering of the way things are. Any theology that gets the balance wrong, either by making God all too human or by making humanity all too divine, is short of the mark. And so, we can begin to see how critical it is to get it right.

The apostle Paul warns the Colossians against the delusions of "plausible arguments," because they remove from "the riches of full assurance of understanding and the knowledge of God's mystery, which is Christ, in whom are hidden all the treasures of wisdom and knowledge" (Col. 2:2–4). Good theology, then, is based on God's revelation. It wants to find wisdom and knowledge in Christ, not human groping. Reformed theology wants to recognize the full authority of its source, and then say it right.

Mere Reformed Faith

So, what is Reformed theology? What does it mean to adhere to the Reformed faith? Is there one all-encompassing summary of the

Reformed outlook? To make such a claim runs the danger of paring everything down to an abstraction and forgetting the riches and depth of our faith. Still, part of the task of ordering our theological ideas is to assign a center and then move toward the periphery. Think of a wheel, with its hub, and then the spokes, and finally the rim, which connects to the ground. Put in that way, we can venture a statement or two. There truly is a center to Reformed theology. The Bible proclaims a hub, from which the rest of the wheel is defined. It would be hard to say it better than the final words of Psalm 3:

> Salvation belongs to the LORD;
>   your blessing be on your people! (Ps. 3:8)

David no doubt made this statement at the end of a prayer when fleeing from his son Absalom, who had tragically turned against his father and become a political rival (see 2 Sam. 15:14–17). In his appeal, he also complains of the taunts of his many adversaries, who tell him God is not going to save him. We ought to understand salvation to mean, first of all, a rescue from enemies. But putting this in context and looking at its full meaning, salvation has to be understood as far more than deliverance. It is the comprehensive emancipation from every kind of oppression, including, more than anything else, the oppression of human sin and guilt. The main point of this verse, then, is that it is God who saves. Not only that, but he blesses his people, that is, he endows them with the peace and the joys of his presence.

The same thought is found in Jonah 2:9: "Salvation belongs to the LORD!" Indeed, this central theological and highly practical doctrine is spread throughout the pages of Scripture (e.g., Ps. 37:39; 62:7; Isa. 43:11; 45:21; Jer. 3:23; Hos. 13:14). Reformed theology has noted the strong connection between an utterly powerful God and the outworking of his loving, gracious purposes. Isaiah, just after the wonderful promise that death will be "swallowed up forever" and all tears will be wiped away from all faces, anticipates the declaration that God's people will make when that great day arrives:

It will be said on that day,
> "Behold, this is our God; we have waited for him, that he
>   might save us.
> This is the LORD; we have waited for him;
> let us be glad and rejoice in his salvation." (Isa. 25:9)

Here, God's perfect, sovereign presence, the surety of the God who is there, is juxtaposed with the rewarded faith of his people, who waited for him not in vain. Now, at this hour, they may be glad and celebrate because of the reality of salvation.

In the New Testament this language is sometimes repeated verbatim, as it is in the last book of the Bible (Rev. 7:10). Or, it may be conjoined with complementary notions: "Hallelujah! Salvation and glory and power belong to our God" (Rev. 19:1; see Rev. 4:11; 12:10). The heart of Reformed theology is to credit all good things, especially the comprehensive plan of redemption, to God and no one else. Paul tells Timothy not to be ashamed of the gospel message, despite the sufferings it will entail, but to recognize the power of God, "who saved us and called us to a holy calling, not because of our works but because of his own purpose and grace, which he gave us in Christ Jesus before the ages began" (2 Tim. 1:9).

In this sense, then, the central concern of Reformed theology is the sovereignty of God. But great caution is required here. This is often the place where most people struggle with the Reformed approach. Sovereignty appears to them to be cold and authoritarian. Perhaps we should find a better word. *Ascendancy? Supremacy? Dominion?* None of these quite captures it. In the end, the title *Lord* may say it as well as any. What we want to arrive at is a formulation that respects the all-powerful nature of God and the significance of human beings.

Put as a question, if salvation belongs to God alone, how is this not some kind of fatalism, the work of a God who coldly carries out his will and dangles people on a string? The clear answer from the vantage point of Reformed theology is that there is an enormous difference, one with life-and-death consequences. God is indeed fully in control. But being Lord means he establishes the world with its own significance, its freedom, and its responsibility. It is a measure of his greatness that he can be fully in control of all things yet at the same time create a world that is real and a humanity that has freedom (Phil. 2:12–13). Creator and creature do not relate by a kind of trade-off whereby God gives up some of his power in order to ensure freedom for the creature. So, in fact, his power is far greater than that of the determinist. In Islamic teaching, one learns that Allah is more a cold programmer than a truly powerful orchestrator of the universe. What appears to be sovereignty is only a mechanical ability, like someone running a machine. Reformed theology tries to honor a God so great, so powerful, that the creature is truly free. There is great mystery here, but it is crucial not to fall into the temptation to downplay either God's power or human significance.

What many people fear when confronted with such a view of power is the impersonal. They fear a God who is far off, who is difficult of access. But the best kind of Reformed thinking stresses that what lies behind the plan of redemption is nothing of the kind. There is a God moved by love. The reason he saves is not to initiate a mechanical plan in some self-serving manner but that he has a heart of compassion for lost persons. "I have loved you with an everlasting love; therefore I have continued my faithfulness to you," the prophet Jeremiah records (Jer. 31:3). It is the love of God that causes salvation to occur, a love so compelling that it will stop at nothing to save (1 John 4:8–12). "God so loved the world," begins the best known verse of the Bible, "that he gave his only Son, that whoever believes in him should not perish but have eternal life" (John 3:16). The point, again, is that God is not an impersonal force, but a person, an all-powerful person to be sure, but yet a person who loves. His love is powerful, and his power is loving.

Here, the reader may be asking, what is so unique about this point of view? It is not entirely unique. Reformed theology shares a great deal with other accounts of the Christian faith. It agrees with the historic synopses of the Christian faith. One of the most succinct is the triad of creation, fall, and redemption. God made the world and everything in it. Humankind, his image-bearer, turned away from the Creator and attempted to live without him, resulting in the curse of a fallen world. But then God saved his people from death, condemnation, and misery, through his only Son, Jesus Christ. There is nothing original about Reformed theology here, except that it wishes to draw the three themes out more powerfully and to give each its due weight, each in the right relation to the other.

Full Expression of the Historic Faith

Put this way, the Reformed faith means to give fullest expression to the basic statements in many of the creeds of the church. One of the best summaries of Christian belief is the Apostles' Creed, which many churches recite in the worship service. It was later enriched by other creeds but is remarkably full for such an early time in the church.[2]

I believe in God the Father Almighty, Maker of heaven and earth;

And in Jesus Christ his only Son our Lord; who was conceived by the Holy Ghost, born of the Virgin Mary, suffered under Pontius Pilate, was crucified, dead, and buried; he descended into hell; the third day he rose again from the dead; he ascended into heaven, and sitteth on the right hand of God the Father Almighty; from thence he shall come to judge the quick and the dead.

I believe in the Holy Ghost; the holy catholic Church; the communion of saints; the forgiveness of sins; the resurrection of the body; and the life everlasting. Amen.

This succinct yet integral summary of the fundamentals of the faith statement has withstood the test of time. Reformed theology wishes to build on this kind of creedal statement and work out the implications in depth.

The claim of Reformed theology is to be more consistent in the expression of these truths than other kinds of theology. It wants to give a fuller significance to each of these doctrines. It wants to avoid choos-

2. Not literally written by the apostles, it no doubt stems from the Old Roman Creed in the latter second century. It was used extensively in the early church.

ing some of them over others or stating one by diminishing another. True, there are constant themes running through the fabric of Reformed theology. The center, as we have seen, is the assured triumph of God's plan of redemption. In Paul's marvelous phrase, "The gifts and the calling of God are irrevocable" (Rom. 11:29). But this center should highlight all other doctrines, not favor one over another. For example, it will stress two things about humanity. First, as God's image-bearers we have nobility, dignity, beauty. But, second, because of the fall, a parallel theme is a profound distrust of human virtue, combined with an urgent call to lean on the Lord for any hope. Reformed Christians have sometimes been caricatured for their negative assessment of human capabilities. Perhaps this is deserved in some cases. In its best expression the idea is not to denigrate human beings as creatures but fully to recognize the tragic effects of evil. The fall into sin has not reduced humankind to animals, but the fall has rendered humanity incapable of pulling itself up on its own.

Thus, Reformed theology hopes to go into more depth as it reflects on the basics. It should not be static but always seek to improve, to reform. Just as for people, growing in grace is not a luxury but a certainty, so in theology we should always look to improve. A famous motto, whose origins no one is sure about, has it that the church should be *semper reformanda quia reformata* (always reforming because reformed). In a word, it seeks to improve God's people by itself being a truly improving theology, one that constantly refuses conformity to an evil world and constantly looks to improve in its formulations and its practice (Rom. 12:1–2). This means that while it stands on the solid foundations of the past, this theology always wants to look for ways to be more faithful. In this endeavor Reformed theology should be in constant relation to other expressions of faith. It has a great deal to learn from other traditions. But it is also aware of its claim.

Two dangers present themselves. The first is a stubborn conservatism that refuses to accept challenges and insights from different sources. For example, there is a tendency of certain Reformed people to idealize the sixteenth or seventeenth century. Some would restrict their focus to the insights of John Calvin. Others would hold that the Puritans were the high-water mark of the Reformed universe, as though little of real significance had been accomplished by anyone since. Without question, the theology and practical Christianity of the Puritans were astonishing, leaving to their distant heirs riches untold. But stopping the clock there is to deny the continuing work of God's grace down through the ages, including our own. In a certain way, we could not go back to the Puritan mentality, because the issues around us have changed. The Bible warns us against thinking that some former time was better (Eccl. 7:10).

The second danger is in a way the opposite. It is to be constantly looking for something new and original, like a branch trying to grow without a trunk. Some theologians are all too willing to abandon traditional formulations only because they are out of fashion. In the words of the apostle, this is from "itching ears," or, worse, "an unhealthy craving for controversy" (1 Tim. 6:4). It is without root or stability. The cult of the new is one of the chief plagues of our times. Even the exhausted mood of postmodernism is little more than a search for something different from the past. Theology that turns its back on the discoveries made by our predecessors for the sake of finding something new is simply foolish. The Holy Spirit continues to teach the church today but always builds on the shoulders of giants.

Living orthodoxy is the goal of Reformed theology. Of course, labels are not the most important thing. The best theology is not such because it has a label but because it agrees with "the sound words of our Lord Jesus Christ and the teaching that accords with godliness" (1 Tim. 6:3). No label or creedal list can guarantee either life or orthodoxy. Indeed, there is no human statement of doctrines, however correct and well-ordered, that in itself can safeguard our faithfulness. Only when the humility of true godliness is combined with obedience to the sound words can a theology emerge that may hope to be orthodox (1 Tim. 1:10; 2 Tim. 1:13; Titus 2:2).

So, with all of these conditions in mind, we still want to contend that there is something faithful and true, something beautiful, something of concord and congruence, in Reformed theology. It is a fulsome, harmonious expression of the great truths of biblical faith. At its core, it wants to be profoundly biblical. It seeks to love God with the heart and the mind. Because of that, we commend it with all our heart.

The Idea of Reformation

The actual term *reform[ed]* is rare in the Bible. If Reformed theology is so important, why do we not find the expression throughout the pages of the Bible? There are only two New Testament references that use the word. In the beginning of his prosecution of the apostle Paul before Marcus Antonius Felix, procurator of Judea, the accuser Tertullus expresses gratitude for Felix's administration. He notes his reforms on behalf of the Jewish people (Acts 24:2). In the context, it appears that Tertullus is thinking of various political benefits that accrued under this governor, which made the life of an occupied minority more tolerable. The second reference has a more religious connotation. The Book of Hebrews develops the contrast between the former age of symbols and the present age of fulfillment in Christ in some depth. In Hebrews 9:10 the author discusses the former "regulations for the body," which were regulatory "until the time of reformation." The Greek word behind the text is interesting. It means something like "making straight," either physically, as in the mending of a broken limb, or legally, as in amending a law or correcting an institutional deficit.

The fundamental idea of reformation, though, is spread throughout the pages of Scripture and is hardly dependent for its warrant on a particular word. What is that fundamental idea? It is, quite literally, the re-forming, the transformation that brings about change for the better. Reformation is not simply a matter of individual change, important though that may be. It is more intensive and more extensive than simply an improvement. The idea is expressed in Peter's proclamation from Solomon's Porch at the Jerusalem temple. After explaining why Christ is the true Savior, foretold by the prophets, he tells his listeners to get right with God: "Repent therefore, and turn again, that your sins may be blotted out, that times of refreshing may come from the presence of the Lord" (Acts 3:19–20). Change is at the heart of Peter's command, but it is not simply the change of moral improvement. Rather, it is a massive turnabout from a previous condition of liability before God to the cleansing from guilt. Notice the wonderful language used to describe this renewal: "times of refreshing [lit., cooling, as in cleansing waters] from the presence of the Lord."

Reformation, in the Bible, is the radical renewal of a people who will know the presence of their God in every aspect of their lives. It presupposes that something has gone seriously wrong and then that the favor of the Lord comes to make all things new (Rev. 21:5). One could speak of a de-formation whose merciful remedy is a re-formation. Seen in this way, reformation is the fundamental story told in Scripture. Within a few paragraphs in the first book of the Bible we have an account of the fall of humankind and the ensuing pain and guilt. Over and over again, the people of God fall from their place of honor and privilege. But over and over they are restored to grace. It is wearisome to read through the Old Testament and experience its litany of corrupt rulers, jealous and vengeful men and women, blasphemous nations. But it is exhilarating, if deeply humbling, to read of God's patience, of his extravagant, humanly impossible promises, and, finally, of his coming to us in the flesh, to bear our burdens, to suffer for our sins, and then to triumph over evil, so that we may become new creatures in Christ (2 Cor. 5:17).

One of the most moving accounts of reformation in the Bible is the story of the rebuilding of the wall of Jerusalem under the leadership of Nehemiah around 445 B.C. The people of Israel were in exile from their promised land. Their corruption had warranted the terrible judgment of banishment. Yet the Lord allowed them to return to their land and to its capital, the city of Jerusalem. Though the land was occupied, they had considerable freedom to worship God in traditional ways. The record describes three waves of returning exiles: under Zerubbabel, who saw to the rebuilding of the temple; under Ezra the great preacher; and finally under Nehemiah, who oversaw the rebuilding of the great walls of Jerusalem. In the book named for him, the text describes the way in which a weak and disheartened people were revived. The centerpiece of their reformation was responding to the book of the law. Not only were the five books of Moses read publicly (perhaps with other portions of the Old Testament), but also they were interpreted so that the people understood them clearly (Neh. 8:5–8). At first the people wept. So much had been lost. The Scriptures were a painful reminder of their unfaithfulness to God. But then they were told to stop weeping and to begin a feast, just like the old days: "And do not be grieved, for the joy of the LORD is your strength" (Neh. 8:10). In the days and weeks to come, this law was further studied and further applied, until the people renewed their covenant with the Lord. By learning to live for him despite being in occupied territory, they were able to rebuild an entire culture (Neh. 9:38). Truly, a reformation had occurred!

Moving from decadence to renewal is the heart of the biblical message. Real reformation is a transformation. Indeed, the successive transformations accorded by God are so great that we are told that John the seer beheld an unspeakably massive change, a cosmic reformation:

> Then I saw a new heaven and a new earth, for the first heaven and the first earth had passed away, and the sea was no more. And I saw the holy city, new Jerusalem, coming down out of heaven from God, prepared as a bride adorned for her husband. And I heard a loud voice from the throne saying, "Behold, the dwelling place of God is with man. He will dwell with them, and they will be his people, and God himself will be with them as their God. He will wipe away every tear from their eyes, and death shall be no more, neither shall there be mourning nor crying nor pain anymore, for the former things have passed away. (Rev. 21:1–4)

Any idea of reformation short of this glorious finale is inadequate to what God has for his people. Reformation, that is to say, is the process whereby God brings about the comprehensive, consummate change from the old to the new, from death to life, from enmity and alienation, to friendship and communion with God.

Reformation Today

It may go without saying that much of the world stands in need of reformation at the present time. Particularly in the Northern Hemi-

sphere, much of the Christian church is stagnant. As it faces globalization, shifting moral values, and all kinds of social and political realign-
ments, the northern church is truly in exile, like the Jews in the time of
Ezra. While there are many pockets of vitality, there has been considerable accommodation to the surrounding culture. We need to be brought
back to the roots. In the light of the Word of God, we need to mourn,
and then to rejoice at God's work of redemption, and then to rebuild,
to *re-form* our lives. Even in the Southern Hemisphere, where so much
amazing church growth is occurring, unless new believers are rooted
and grounded in a solid world-and-life view, walking with God in love
and integrity, it will not be long before decadence sets in. To watch the
church in Africa, in Latin America, and in Asia is to witness extraordinary life and impact because of the gospel's power on those continents.
But the growth will be on rocky soil, and birds are ready to scavenge the
newly sown seed, unless a robust theology is featured along with the
enthusiasm of new faith.

2

REMEMBER THIS
AND STAND FIRM

~~~~~~~~~~~~

A Firm Foundation

The parables of the kingdom of God in the New Testament impress on us that God's presence in history is radical yet gradual. It is radical because God is at work, not simply ordinary human factors. It is gradual because it does not occur all at once, or even dramatically. In Matthew 13 Jesus instructs his followers about the kingdom by using a series of images that convey both points. One set of metaphors portrays the brilliance, the power, the marvel of God's presence. The kingdom is like a treasure in the field, for which a man will sell everything he has to purchase it (v. 44). It is like the one pearl of great value (vv. 45–46). Another set of metaphors describes the gradual growth and fruition of the kingdom. From the seed sown, it grows on different soils (vv. 1–9, 18–23). Like good seed sown in the midst of evil weeds, there will be a gathering day when the weeds are burned off (vv. 24–30, 36–43). From the smallest of circumstances the kingdom grows into a visible, full, worldwide presence, much like small seeds producing large trees or a small clump of yeast yielding a rich loaf of bread (vv. 31–33).

The history of the Christian church is much like this process. It comes into the world gradually, yet when it appears fully mature, it is beautiful to behold. This follows from the way God relates to his creation. And it follows from the way he saved the world. The nations are saved through one man, Abraham (Gal. 3:8). Full redemption and adoption of all believers is accomplished by the God-man, Jesus, sent to be born in a particular time and place, a Son whose influence two millennia later is immeasurable (Gal. 4:4–5). Christ is now ascended and fills the whole church with his presence. In all things he is preeminent (Col. 1:18). It follows that the theology that is done for Christ's sake, like the kingdom, is universal and particular. It is universal because there is one Lord and one faith (Eph. 4:5). But it is particular because he equips the whole church, in every place, with the means to grow up in every way into him who is the head, into Christ (Eph. 4:15).

Historians today rightly call the presence of the kingdom of God down through the centuries the *world* Christian movement. Indeed, true religion did not begin in the first century any more than it did in the sixteenth. Biblical religion originated when the first human beings began to worship and reflect on God. In the most accurate sense, such worship bestirred itself at the moment human creatures were made as God's image-bearers, in the gladdened primeval times before the fall. It did not end there, though it could have. Early after the catastrophic events of the fall occurred, the Bible records that "at that time people began to call upon the name of the Lord" (Gen. 4:26). From then on there has always been a church, a community of believers who would seek to understand God's ways with his people and to praise him for them.

God's revelation came to his people in an especially concentrated way in Judaism. Then, later, all of the preparation of the Old Testament administration was accomplished in the person and work of Jesus Christ. The earliest manifestations of Christianity, following the end of the apostolic age, proved radical in their challenge against unjust local traditions and remarkably adaptable to the surrounding culture. The major theological issues to be faced were the defense of the integrity of Christian faith and practice (apologetics) and vigilance against heretical deviations from that faith (polemics). In addition, the gospel was a powerful social force. It liberated women, defended small children, and treated all believers as equals. Not that it was revolutionary, at least in the destructive sense. Change was effected deliberately, carefully, sometimes very slowly, but in the end, substantially.

From Conflict to Conviction

The church grew in love and in firmness of conviction. Part of its struggle was against persecution from without. Yet, as Tertullian put it, "the blood of the martyrs is the seed of the church." Part of its struggle was over dissension within. Heresies developed that needed to be addressed biblically. As the Christian faith spread into the world, there was some room for variation. In Syria, it kept a certain Semitic tone, particularly in its worship style. In Greece and Asia Minor, leaning against the prevailing elitism and social hierarchy, the equality of every church member was a notable characteristic. Contributing to this parity and to a dynamic, growing church were the outstanding leaders given to the fledgling community. Ignatius, Polycarp, and others governed with a firm hand, but always by the solidarity of love. Despite the lack of blood or ethnic commonality, and despite the temptations to fragmentation presented in that society, these residents of the pagan Roman Empire managed to express radical unity. Their theology reflected these values.

Down through the centuries, the church grew extensively and in depth. It spread from Asia Minor to numerous regions, especially throughout the Mediterranean. Significantly, the church reached the great city of Rome, the dominant center of the empire, and slowly acquired an episcopal structure, under which the bishop would later be known as *primus inter pares* (first among equals), eventually ushering in the papacy. However, other great centers, especially Constantinople, held their own. The church slowly formulated foundational doctrines. Based on the Scriptures and confirmed by various councils, these doctrines have continued to inform mainstream Christian faith. Most of the significant gains in doctrinal clarity were accomplished through reforms. The church advanced by wrestling with issues and settling disputes, not by sitting in a seminar room. We do not have to wait until the momentous events of the sixteenth century in Europe to find the true spirit of reformation at work. At least two cases stand out.

The Nicene Creed. A notable example from the fourth century is the way the Arian controversy was settled. Arius, an Egyptian presbyter, taught that Christ was something between God and a human. He was not absolutely God, yet he was more than a man, having come before the rest of creation. A lot was at stake here. Not the least was the doctrine of the Trinity. How does the Father relate to the Son and to the Holy Spirit? And this in turn was critical for the doctrine of redemption. If Christ were only a godlike man, could his work of death and resurrection have been effective?

Here is a rough account of the way things happened. According to Arius, Christ was given the title of Son of God only as a point of honor. While he did hang on the cross, his spirit somehow left him before the moment of death, and so in a way, it was only a man that died. It seemed almost indecent that God should be subject to death. At one point it looked as though Arius's views would carry the day in the church. At this point, a remarkable group of leaders was raised up. One of them was Athanasius (296–373), who became bishop of Alexandria and a fierce enemy of the Arian view. He contended strongly for monotheism, the one God, with the implication that each member of the Trinity is nothing other than God. Also, a group known as the Cappadocian Fathers (Basil the Great, Gregory of Nyssa, and Gregory of Nazianzus) were instrumental in showing that only if Christ were truly God could sinful creatures be reconciled to a righteous and holy Deity. As was true in those days, politics also played a part. The emperor Theodosius I helped pressure the church into arriving at a clear statement of full orthodoxy. In our day of the separation of church and state, it may appear misplaced for a magistrate to enter into theological disputes. But in the early centuries of the church the lines were less clear, and so it was common for governors to take a strong interest in doctrinal issues.

Eventually, the Arian controversy was settled in a series of statements meant to do justice to the complex data from the Scriptures. The First Council of Nicea (325) and the First Council of Constantinople (381) were milestones, in that they established the full deity of Christ and the Holy Spirit while not sacrificing their distinction. These two councils are often linked together, known as Nicea-Constantinople. The results were eventually represented in what we call the Nicene Creed. This statement went beyond the Apostles' Creed because it addressed more detailed questions raised by Arianism. Among other things, this wonderful statement of Christian faith affirms the unity of the Godhead and the true distinction between the divine persons. Here are the key phrases:

> We believe in one God. . . .
> And in one Lord Jesus Christ,
> the only-begotten Son of God,
> Begotten of the Father . . .
> God of God,
> Light of Light.
> . . . of one substance with the Father. . . .
> And in the Holy Ghost . . .
> Who proceedeth from the Father and the Son;
> Who with the Father and the Son together is worshiped
>   and glorified. . . .[1]

Such familiar words to us today, and yet, such hard-fought terminology! Christ is of the same "essence" (of one being) with the Father. The Greek term, all important, is *homoousios*. At the same time, the Son is not the Father, nor is the Spirit the Father or Son. Arius had thought that there was a time when the Son did not exist. But Nicea-Constantinople proved from the Scriptures that Christ is the Son of God, not from being honored, but simply because he is the second person of the Trinity. He is the Son, from all eternity. And, further, the Holy Spirit is the unique third person of the Godhead, also from all eternity. Son and Spirit are God in every respect. The term for this Christian doctrine is the Trinity.

The Creed of Chalcedon. One other major issue threatened the unity of the church in the early centuries. It was no doubt connected to the

---

1. *The Creeds of Christendom,* ed. Philip Schaff, rev. David S. Schaff, 3 vols. (reprint, Grand Rapids: Baker, 1998), 1:27–28.

first, but it focused more specifically on the nature of Jesus Christ (Christology). A certain Nestorius (c. 428–451) from the cities of Antioch and Constantinople held that Christ was two persons, divine and human, held together in a "voluntary" relationship within the incarnate Christ. He came to this view by the strange route of objecting to calling Mary *theotokos*, the bearer of God, a term that had been around for at least two centuries. The expression appeared to Nestorius to diminish the humanity of Christ and to underplay Mary's part in begetting Jesus the man. He ended up saying that Christ was two persons, somehow bundled together. His views were eventually condemned at the Council of Ephesus (431). Nevertheless, Nestorius continued to claim orthodoxy. Eventually a church was formed in his name, one that had great missionary zeal, taking the gospel to China, India, and Arabia.

More controversy followed, spearheaded by the views of Eutyches (c. 378–454), an anti-Nestorian monk, also from Constantinople. His view was that Christ had only one nature, a mingling of divine and human into a third kind: "the humanity being merged with the deity as a drop of honey mingled in the ocean." His view led to monophysitism, the view that Christ is only one (*mono*) nature (*physis*). How can this issue of persons and natures be resolved? In the end, a most significant council was called at Chalcedon in 451. In response to groups like the Nestorians, who believed Christ was two persons, and the Monophysites, who taught that he had only one nature, the bishops who sat at Chalcedon formulated Christology in a more biblical way, seeking to respect Christ's full deity and full humanity. They determined that he was *one person with two natures, divine and human.* Again, we may say, nothing short of reformation was at work here. What might seem to us rather abstract reasoning was a breath of oxygen, giving us a succinct formulation that has been our precious heritage ever since.

A Major Parting of Ways, East and West

These early councils and statements did not settle every question, of course. Controversies were not always so happily resolved by church councils. Increasing tensions developed between the Eastern branch and the Western branch of the church. They argued, among other things, over the specific relationship of the Holy Spirit to the Father within the Trinity and over the appropriate place for the veneration of icons. These arguments were never uniquely theological. Political and cultural tensions were strong. Institutional unity eventually was broken.

In 312 the Roman emperor Constantine prayed to God for victory against his enemy Maxentius at the battle of the Milvian Bridge. He won and then, in gratitude, declared the Christian religion to be legal throughout the empire, which it had not been for the first three centuries. The effect of this was far-reaching, for good and for evil. By the end of the century, Christian faith not only was legitimate but also had gradually become the dominant one throughout the empire. Constantine founded a new capital on the Bosphorus, to be known as Constantinople, or the new Rome. It was the hub of the great Byzantine civilization. Gradually, though, a separate outlook developed, the one centering in Constantinople and the East, and the other in Rome and the West.

The Eastern church developed its own culture. While previously the entire church had been called Catholic, meaning "worldwide," increasingly the Eastern branch preferred to be known as Orthodox, meaning "right belief" (lit., "right praise"). The Western church is known as Latin, because of the dominance of Roman culture and its language, while for a time the Eastern church was known as Greek. Invariably, doctrinal issues were mixed together with political issues and with strong personalities. The Eastern church rejected the claims of the bishop of Rome to be Peter's unique successor and the arbiter of official doctrine. Its government was vested in patriarchs, not in one pope. Clerics were allowed to marry, unlike the developing tradition of celibacy of priests in the West. Orthodoxy stressed the unity of doctrine with worship and missions. So it spread across the Greek world and the Russian world, developing rich and distinctive theological traditions in the process. Eventually the two would culminate into two different expressions of the same heritage, Greek Orthodoxy and Russian Orthodoxy.

While remaining close to the Western church in many of the essentials, Eastern Orthodoxy stressed certain distinctive beliefs. After the seventh official church council it no longer was considered Catholic. Many theological concerns were at issue. Orthodoxy made far more use of images, or icons, than the Western church thought was healthy, to guide believers in their worship. Further, the Eastern church contested the later addition of a clause to the Nicene Creed, known as the *filioque* clause, which says that the Holy Spirit "proceeds from the Father and the Son." What may appear an innocent formulation was believed by the Orthodox to deny the Father's nature as the unique fountainhead of divinity, which in turn denied the integrity and unity of the Trinity.[2] Orthodoxy also has a high view of the church, so high that tradition often rivals the Scripture as the infallible authority over human conscience. It also conceives of salvation as the lifting up of the soul into the Godhead, to the extent that human beings become absorbed into divinity, though never deified.

Gradually, tensions grew into schism, and in 1054 a writ of excommunication was signed by a Roman papal delegation against the Orthodox patriarch Kerularios and his associates. Attempts at patching things up led to refusals by the Orthodox to trust the Latins. This mutual mistrust came to a head when the Latin armies destroyed Constantinople in 1204 during the Fourth Crusade. This date represents the final blow, and thus the irreparable split between East and West. After the fall of Byzantium in 1453, Orthodoxy stood in a complex relation to the Western church, especially as the West split with the Protestant Reformation. Protestants as well as Catholics have made various overtures to Orthodoxy, and vice versa. Occasionally they came close to reuniting, as when Cyril Lucaris composed a confession that for all intents and purposes was Calvinistic. More often, they have remained distinct, even hostile.

2. The issue of procession is fraught with difficulties. The Eastern church has a point. One does not want to subordinate the Spirit to the Son and the Son to the Father. But the Western church was attempting to do justice to the way the Son sends the Spirit into the world. There may be a confusion of being and function in both camps.

Perhaps the most creative period within Orthodoxy began in the nineteenth century. A renaissance occurred in Russia, and on into the Soviet Union, in which Orthodox writers and theologians were widely read and widely influential. Calling it a reformation would be no exaggeration, although it met such obstacles along the way that no enduring social or cultural transformation resulted. The great Russian novelists and philosophers, disillusioned with the approach of realism and holding severe criticisms of the institutional church, began to look for spiritual answers to political, social, and psychological problems. The *startsy*, holy men from monasteries such as Optina Pustyn, became admired models for Leo Tolstoy, Nikolai Gogol, and Fedor Dostoyevsky, who not only portrayed them in their novels but also saw them as examples of integrity to emulate in an age of compromise. Dostoyevsky (1821–81) in particular wrestled in his novels with issues of sin, crime, patricide, redemption, liberty, and truth.

From the turn of the twentieth century, Russian culture was filled with challenges from a tyrannical government and a church that often shared in its authoritarian spirit. Increasingly, secular views like Marxism, atheism, and various theories of revolution were in the air. And yet, remarkably, something like a reformation occurred in this setting. A large number of intellectuals came to believe that the oppressive institutions of government and church threatened human freedom. What were the alternatives? These thinkers and writers looked afresh into Orthodox tradition but mixed it creatively with certain modern philosophies that could give traditional theology a more contemporary flavor. They believed that unless Russian culture moved away from its oppressive secularism, disaster would follow. Their views developed into a movement of reform within the church, as well as outside it. Many Russian intellectuals hoped for some kind of Christian society. Had things gone differently, these ideas could have led to a proper separation of church from state and even freed the Orthodox church to have a large influence on Russian culture, while at the same time experiencing more intercommunion with other denominations. An important manifesto at the time, known as the *Vekhi* (signposts), called Russia to repent and yield to the Spirit of Christ. However, in the years before the Russian revolution, a strong reaction, a sort of counter-reformation, took place. And then the Bolsheviks rendered void any real hopes for a Christian society.

Still, in the ensuing decades, a number of refreshing, creative thinkers kept alive the hope of a Christian answer to the basic dilemmas facing humanity.[3] It remains an open question, however, whether a true and lasting reformation will occur in the Orthodox church. It is hard to know, too, whether reunification with the other major branches of the Christian family could occur.[4] Orthodoxy has attracted renewed interest in the West. Many younger people, particularly evangelical Protestants, have fled from what they perceive to be their dry, unaesthetic home churches to the richer Eastern expression. Are the times ripe for a change? Will the West be reconciled with the East? On what conditions could either Roman Catholicism or Protestantism go along with such a reconciliation? For now, it is best to know that although we do not have a common institutional structure and although several crucial doctrines do divide us, we have real and true unity in Christ with all who confess him. At the same time we must continue to strive better to express that unity in doctrine and in discipline (Eph. 4:4–6, 11–16).

The Protestant Reformation

The present volume is about the Reformed faith. Its main contours were forged in a decisive way at the Protestant Reformation. As the word suggests, it was a movement to protest. That is, the movement was the assertion of certain truths, the protestation that these truths were fundamental. Two things ought to be remembered. First, the basic principles of Reformed thinking are not a sixteenth-century

3. This group includes men such as Vladimir Soloviev (1853–1900), Nikolai Berdyayev (1874–1948), Leo Chestov (1866–1938), and more recently, Georges Florovsky, Vladimir Lossky, and Olivier Clément. Their influence has been enormous and gives promise of fruitful discussions on numerous theological issues in the near future.

4. The Orthodox church belongs to the World Council of Churches, while the Roman Catholic Church does not. However, the WCC is not a merger of churches but rather a consultancy.

phenomenon. Too many Protestants forget that the Christian faith is older and wider than the particular expression of it developed in the Reformation. The great Protestant Reformers claimed strong links to the church fathers. This is as it should be, if the church really is a world Christian movement. Second, though, it is clearly the case that the Protestant Reformation, particularly in its Genevan expression, represents a defining moment for this theology we are portraying. Because of that, it is worth pausing for a brief historical foray.

Historical Background

It may be asked why the Reformation occurred when it did, in the beginning of the sixteenth century, and not earlier. There certainly was widespread corruption in the church during various portions of the late Middle Ages. Bishops collected revenues from their dioceses without ever visiting them. Pastors were uneducated, sometimes to the point of ignorance about the rudiments of salvation. At one point there were rival popes who excommunicated one another. A great barrier existed between the clergy and laity, exemplified in the rood screen, a latticed partition separating the priests from the populace. One orator in the fifteenth century spoke of "the long slumber of the church."

A good number of movements and institutions to redress the situation were generated. One could note the rise of the great universities of Europe, from Bologna (1190) to Oxford and Paris (1208), to Rome, Florence, Prague (1348), and so many others. All of them were founded to foster theological education. Many new orders were founded, from preachers, such as the Dominicans, to popular movements of piety, like the Brethren of the Common Life in the Netherlands.

Individuals emerged who stood for reform in powerful ways, well before the Protestant Reformation. The Englishman John Wycliffe (1329–84) stressed God's dominion over all of life, his forgiveness of sins, the primacy of Scripture over any other authority, and the preeminence of preaching in the function of the church. The great Czech reformer Jan Hus (1372–1415) also stood for the superiority of the Bible over tradition, advocating the Bible's translation into the current language of the people, and the centrality of "faith formed by love accompanied by the virtue of perseverance" rather than reliance on visible conformity with civil religion. Other great proto-reformers and other widespread movements of spiritual and social redress could be mentioned.

Why did none of these movements and activists have the tremendous impact of the Protestant Reformation of the sixteenth century? No single answer to this question can be given, and no single cause of the Reformation can be assigned that sets it off against its predecessors. There were special background developments in European social history that became important catalysts of the Reformation. Humanism, a new respect for humane letters, that is, the study of the great classical texts, put into question the authority of the medieval period and its pretensions. It fostered a critical examination of texts that helped dispel blind allegiance to tradition and promoted better access to the Bible. Furthermore, the development of Renaissance statecraft, as exhibited, for example, in the city-state of Florence, helped give reform-minded leaders more protection and freedom. This was the case in Germany, where Martin Luther found favor with the local prince, who protected him against the pope in Rome, and enabled the German people to embrace Protestant ideas.

While these factors have their crucial importance, they were not the central ones. The driving force of the Protestant Reformation was preeminently theological. The social and intellectual backgrounds were critical. But the heart of the Protestant Reformation was about conviction. No previous reforms had so articulately set forth such a combination of beliefs as had the Reformation. Its convictions were fresh, although not meant to be radically new. Indeed, none of the major views set forth by the Reformers were meant to replace the good foundation of tradition. In a famous exchange between Jeanne d'Albret, the Protestant queen of Navarre, and Cardinal Armagnac, she declared, "I am not planting a new religion but restoring an old one." The Reformer Bullinger once quipped that the Christian religion was the oldest and most established of all. Of course, these fresh views did challenge the bad part of tradition. Reading the Bible less symbolically, allowing clerics to marry, and organizing the church without hierarchy were new in one sense. But the Reformers came to these innovations by going back to the source.

What were these central convictions? Three of them stand out. First, God was placed in the center of life. The Reformers did enact great social ameliorations and fiercely attacked the corruption of the church and of society. But their originality was in their primary concern for God: God's revelation, God's views of the human condition, God's judgments. In a word, the Reformation was about God's authority. It is true that justification by faith is a central axis of Protestant doctrine, but that had meaning only within a total framework wherein God's authority reigned over life and death. Furthermore, and contrary to popular understanding, the Reformation was not primarily concerned with individual, human religious experience. It was about God's person and his standards and our relation to them. It is because of this recognition of divine authority that a high view of the Bible emerged. Not the church but the Scripture, the Old and the New Testaments, is the supreme authority in all of life. God spoke through it. In no way did this mean the Bible is a set of words on paper; it is the voice of God speaking to the conscience by means of the text.[5]

Second, the Reformation was about getting right with God. The Reformers stressed the gravity of sin and the impossibility of being reconciled to God without the death of Jesus Christ. Salvation is not simply a matter of straightening out or of showing greater fidelity to the church. Indeed, the church was often part of the problem, not the solution. Salvation is a free gift, to be received by simple trust in God's mercy. It means believing the Word of God, when it declares that righteousness is a present to a needy soul, and not a possible goal obtained by a long journey of human piety. This was the great liberating call that opened up the gates of heaven to laity and clergy alike.

5. It is often thought that several Latin slogans characterized the Reformation, one of them being *sola Scriptura*. In point of historical fact no such catchphrases occurred until at least the eighteenth century. When they did, a certain amount of confusion was caused since opponents worried that Protestants believed in an uninterpreted Bible, one that did not require the church. That thought is foreign to the true spirit of the Reformation, which had a strong doctrine of the teaching ministry of the church.

Third, the Reformation elevated Jesus Christ in a way that had not been done hitherto. The vision of Christ held by many in the late Middle Ages was that of a judge. One can feel this when gazing at the great cathedral portals or the altarpieces with Christ dividing the saints from the sinners, with awful images of the descent of sinners into hell. So austere and unapproachable was this Christ that by way of compensation the church developed traditions that made religion a bit more human: the Virgin Mary (a woman and a mother), the Mass (with automatic grace and an apparent re-sacrifice of Christ), and looking at all of life as a sacrament. The Reformers understood Christ as coming to us "clothed in the gospel," identifying with our humanity and our guilt. Christ is the entrance into heaven and the great dynamic of the Christian life. They saw Christ presented on every page of Scripture. The death of Christ on the cross meant the death of every human solution to life's conundrums. His resurrection was the triumph of God's rule and righteousness over the kingdoms of this world. Most of all, Christ was the guarantor of salvation.

The First Flowering

There were many leaders and many voices in the Protestant Reformation. Three of them in the early stages were monumental.

Martin Luther (1483–1546). The extraordinary German pioneer of the Reformation, Martin Luther, set the church on a course with tremendous implications for theology. At one level, his theology was deeply personal. He once said, "It is through living, indeed through dying and being damned that one becomes a theologian, not through understanding, reading, or speculation."[6] Luther tended to put things in dramatic ways. But his point is instructive. Theology is not so much a matter of conjecture. It is born of wrestling with God in the rough and tumble of everyday life. Luther's experience bears this out. Few of his treatises are without testimony to his personal struggles with good and evil. His theses were censured, his books were burned, and he was

---

6. Quoted in Carter Lindberg, ed., *The Reformation Theologians: An Introduction to Theology in the Early Modern Period* (Oxford: Blackwell, 2002), 1.

placed in the most precarious positions in relation to the power of the church. Yet, at another level, it should not be forgotten that his fundamental, pioneering contributions to the heritage of the Christian faith were centered in the bold proclamation of the reality of redemption in Jesus Christ. Echoing this, his doctrines were objective theological affirmations that have served God's people ever since he set them down.

Luther's grand rediscovery, which led to the Reformation, was that God's righteousness is not a standard to be reached by meritorious human achievement. It is a gift from God, a revelation through Jesus Christ (Rom. 3:21–22). How could God make such a gift? Because his Son had purchased it on the cross. How could the gift be received? Neither by an inward change nor by spiritual aptitude, but only by faith. Faith for Luther was a matter of believing God's Word. For modern evangelical Christians this would seem old hat, though it is regrettable to think of such a liberating truth as old hat. But for the sixteenth century this was nothing short of a Copernican turnaround. Hitherto, most of the teachings available on ways to reach God and be pious recommended some combination of spiritual self-discipline and faithfulness to the sacraments. For the most serious seekers, as was Luther, it often meant racking one's conscience to make sure nothing had been forgotten. Medieval Christians were often beset with doubts and anxiety about salvation.

Luther reckoned the official church was not only of no real help in these matters but harmful to the soul. He once named the Roman system a "veritable torture chamber of consciences" because it would never proclaim Christ without some kind of qualifier. His overriding concern, then, was to lift up Jesus Christ as the only hope of salvation and the only deliverer from what he called "the monster of uncertainty." Theology, in this view, is a science that puts Christ in first place. In the lectures on Galatians, he says that theology is secure when "it snatches us away from ourselves and places us outside ourselves, so that we do not depend on our own strength, conscience, experience, person, or works, but depend on that which is outside ourselves, that is, on the promise and truth of God, which cannot deceive."[7]

7. Martin Luther, *Luther's Works*, ed. Jaroslav Pelikan, 55 vols. (St. Louis: Concordia, 1963), 26:387.

While Luther occupied an important place in the Reformation, the Protestant movement was widespread and diverse. Germany was one of its major hubs, not only in the Rhinelands, under Luther's influence, but also in the south, especially in Strasbourg, under the leadership of Martin Bucer (1491–1551), whose reforms in liturgy and worship had a wide impact. The Reformation winds also blew across France. And while persecutions against the Protestants came in great waves from the sixteenth century through the eighteenth, significant advances were made on a number of fronts. Bible scholarship, preaching, apologetics, church government, and statecraft all flowered on French soil.

Ulrich Zwingli (1484–1531). Surely the most significant place for the consolidation of the Reformation was Switzerland. The great intellectual Ulrich Zwingli was based in Zürich. He helped to move Switzerland from its culture of militarism to one of democracy and refuge. He popularized preaching the *lectio continua*, that is, basing sermons on an entire book, from the first to the last chapter, however many Sundays this might take. The outstanding scholar John Oecolampadius (1482–1531) from Basel kept strong links with the church fathers while reforming the sacraments, especially the Lord's Supper. The visionary Guillaume Farel (1489–1565), from the French Alps, preached the Reformation message throughout the French-speaking portions of Switzerland.

John Calvin (1509–64). By any reckoning, the most important second-generation Reformer was John Calvin. If there is one figure whose approach more than anyone else's shaped the way Reformed theology is done, it has to be Calvin. Indeed, though he would have objected strongly, Reformed theology is often called Calvinism. Born in Noyon, north of Paris, he trained in theology and law. He came under the influence of Renaissance humanism and was drawn to the pioneers of what would soon be a movement that would challenge the prevailing way to understand religion. He soon was drawn to the Bible, and he began to articulate a theology based on the Word of God that could lead the church to deep, personal, humble knowledge of God.

Calvin became the clearest voice for the basic truths of the Reformed faith. He was a pastor in the city of Geneva for most of his career. He was deeply concerned for the message of the Bible to be rendered simply and clearly to everyone around. As a Frenchman he never lost his burden for the suffering church of his homeland. He spent untold amounts of time ministering to his suffering brethren through correspondence and by training ministers for them. The heart of his theology is the glory of God.

Calvin is no doubt one of the most controversial persons in history. Even today, the popular caricature of Calvin is that he centered his entire system on a fatalistic predestinarianism and that he ruled the city of Geneva with an iron hand. Calvin's theology is nothing of the kind. While he did teach the predestining grace of God, it was the furthest thing from fatalism, and the doctrine of predestination was only one element of a much larger vision, centered on the glory of God. Calvin did do most of his work in Geneva, but he hardly ruled the place. He came in response to strong requests from Farel and from the city. He had made no plans to work in Geneva, and he was banished shortly after he got there. When he came back, he did have great suasion over the city, but only as a pastor. He became a citizen five years from the end of his life and struggled with the ruling council of the city in matters of public policy much of the time. Still, Geneva was utterly transformed from a place of considerable decadence to one of health and moral strength. It was a center for learning and a model for thousands of refugees and visitors, including some of the major pioneers of the Reformation.

In his short life Calvin was almost never free from serious physical ailments or family tragedy. Yet he managed to produce an enormous body of written work and to leave a legacy that is still yielding its riches. He preached regularly. When things settled down in Geneva, Calvin's pattern was to mount the pulpit at St. Pierre twice on a Sunday, and then once a day every other week, and every week on Wednesday. He also lectured at the theological school. The magnitude of this task can be further appreciated when one realizes each sermon was an hour long and when one understands that preaching was only one of several pastoral activities. He visited the sick. He had a voluminous

correspondence with people from all over Europe, especially the persecuted Christians of his homeland. He wrote treatises and com-
mentaries. His masterpiece, one of the greatest classics of literature,
is the *Institutes of the Christian Religion*, which he began at age twenty-
six, and he finished the fifth and final edition in 1559. In its pages all
of the principal doctrines of the Christian faith are set forth and
explained. Beyond his great learning and his extraordinary knowledge
of Scripture, displayed in this volume and everywhere he wrote, it is
Calvin's humanity, his pastoral concerns, his utter disdain for the meritorious achievements of mortal creatures, his looking only to Christ
come to save his people, that emerge as predominant.

Once again, neither Luther nor Zwingli nor Calvin meant to break
away from the historic church in the West. The last thing they wanted
to do was start a new religion. This point has consistently been missed
by critics of the Reformation. But finding no sympathy for the gospel
of grace, each was forced to work in a fresh place. Eventually a new
church developed. New denominations grew out of the Reformation.
Grouped together, they represent the Protestant communion. While
sadly divided, they are not so separate as it might appear. They are one
in many ways. Their unity, not institutional but foundational, transcends their differences.

Extension and Opposition

In the ensuing generations, despite many obstacles and in the
face of heavy persecutions, the flames of reformation burned brightly
throughout Europe and even beyond.

France. The case of France represents one of the most bittersweet
episodes in the advance of the cause of evangelical religion. On the
positive side, the churches grew in numbers and in depth. The first
truly Reformed synod, or general assembly, as Presbyterians would
call it, occurred in 1559, in Paris. The meeting was significant, among
other reasons, because the confession of faith adopted there, known
eventually as the Confession of La Rochelle, outlined a system of

church government in which elders had absolute parity. That is, there was no hierarchy from a bishop down, but an equality of all presbyters. According to many scholars, this synod's structure is one of the foundation stones for modern democracy. By 1561, the date of the Colloquy of Poissy, there were more than two thousand congregations of Reformed believers. The colloquy was an attempt to establish a working relation between Protestants and Roman Catholics in France. The Huguenots, as they were known (probably because of the Swiss-German term *Eidgenossen*, or "federated ones"), had a tremendous influence in France and abroad. Their view of the honorable calling to labor made earning daily bread more than drudgery, advancing what is called the Protestant work ethic. Marriage was changed from a social arrangement to a relationship of love. Every class, from the simplest to the noblest, sang the psalms and read the Bible in the vernacular. Schools were founded. The arts were fostered.

On the negative side, Protestants never quite achieved acceptance in France. Indeed, during various terrifying episodes, they were bidden to give up their convictions or die. The Colloquy of Poissy failed to construct a way of tolerance, and thirty-five years of religious wars followed. The Saint Bartholomew's Day massacre of 1572 saw the mass murder of more than twenty thousand Protestants. Although a period of relative toleration was inaugurated in 1698, when the Protestant king Henri IV penned the Edict of Nantes, the peace lasted less than eighty years. The edict was revoked in 1685, and a period of untold persecution was unleashed. It became legal to be a Reformed Christian only toward the end of the eighteenth century. Hosts of Huguenots fled the country. By the nineteenth century, with Napoleon's laws in place, while Protestantism was reestablished, the numbers were down. Today, there is a small but struggling body of Reformed Christians in France.

England. The story of the Reformation in England involves the great irony that the ruling monarchs were often as much part of the problem as part of the solution. Henry VIII is well known for his ambition to forge alliances and produce at least one male heir, regardless of the fates of his wives or his acquaintanceships. His early sympathies with Protestantism allowed the voices of Lutherans and of French-Genevan Calvinism to become widely popular. Among other things, these views served as a corrective to the decadence of the British clergy. Cambridge University, with its White Horse Inn (nicknamed Little Germany), was the seat of a significant voice for Protestantism. It was a great seed bed for leaders of the English Reformation, which included Robert Barnes, Thomas Cranmer, Hugh Latimer, and Nicholas Ridley, all of whom would be martyred, but not before stirring up a powerful movement of Reformation.

Henry VIII broke with Rome in 1534, declaring himself to be the "only Supreme Head on earth of the Church of England." This move was motivated not only by the desire to divorce Catherine of Aragon, a desire that the pope opposed, but also by the growing conviction toward Erastianism, from the Swiss theologian Thomas Erastus, who argued that the state had temporal authority over the church. However, the Act of Supremacy, while it meant a break from Roman authority, did not mean the embrace of Protestantism. That came for theological and spiritual reasons. Henry's new wife, Anne Boleyn, whom he had married in secret, the mother of Elizabeth, had strong Protestant convictions. The Reformation was really established under Edward VI, Henry's son with Jane Seymour. While things regressed under his successor, Mary Tudor, eventually an accommodation was reached in the third generation, under Elizabeth Tudor (1558–1603).

Many heroes emerge from those turbulent times. William Tyndale (1494–1536) was the marvelous scholar whose zeal to translate the Bible into the vernacular paved the way for the King James Version of 1611. He made great use of the printing press, and beginning in 1525, and then in successive versions for years, his English translation of the New Testament spread widely throughout Britain. One can understand the anger of the Roman Catholic bishop of London, Cuthbert Tunstall, when discovering that Tyndale had translated the Greek word *metanoeō* as "repent" rather than "do penance," as it was in the Latin Vulgate. He further translated *presbyteros* as "elder" rather than "priest." These words were a crucial part of the Reformation movement, in that they placed the Word of God in the hands of the people. Bishop Edward Fox noted that the laypeople knew their Scriptures better than the clergy. Forced to do much of his work in exile, Tyndale was eventually betrayed and martyred.

Undoubtedly the chief architect of the Reformation in England was Thomas Cranmer (1489–1556). He became archbishop of Canterbury by appointment of Henry VIII, but his Protestantism came into its own under Edward. Among his many achievements was drafting the statement of faith that eventually became the Thirty-Nine Articles (established under Elizabeth in 1563), a balanced, biblical statement of Reformed theology. His most significant contribution is undoubtedly the Book of Common Prayer, begun in 1549 and revised in 1552. With services of worship and provisions for church officers, it follows the principle so crucial for this branch of Christian expression, *lex orandi, lex credendi* (the rule of prayer is the rule of belief). Some have argued it is the second great masterpiece of theological literature after Calvin's *Institutes*. Anglicanism was born.

Scotland. In Scotland things ended up far better for Protestants, though not without great struggles for recognition. The first voice for the Reformation in Scotland was Lutheran. Heroes such as Patrick Hamilton were burned at the stake for embracing Luther's ideas. But by the mid-1540s, the French and Swiss versions predominated, largely owing to the role of John Knox (1513–72), who had taken refuge in Geneva (calling it "the most perfect school of Christ"), and also to the many historic Scottish-French connections. The Scots Confession of 1560, though penned in some haste, showed Reformed sensitivities that would mark the church for generations thereafter. Presbyterianism was born from a largely Scottish heritage.

Knox came into Protestantism because of a series of encounters with individuals who carried ideas from Luther, Zwingli, and Calvin into Scotland. Because its archenemy, England, had embraced the Reformation, Scotland held on to Catholicism for some time. Knox had joined a revolutionary Protestant party in Saint Andrews. Victims of the French bombing of the great castle, the survivors were condemned to the galleys, chained to their oars as slaves. When liberated, Knox settled in England. There, as already mentioned, King Edward VI had begun to rule. Because his regents favored the Reformation,

England began seriously to embrace the Reformation. Many Protestants fled to England for refuge. The Book of Common Prayer replaced the Mass as the way to worship. Knox had an active role in shaping the church under Edward. Along with men such as John Hooper, he managed to enact numerous reforms. Unfortunately, Edward's successor, Mary Tudor (who arose after the failed attempt to place the Protestant Lady Jane Grey in power), was fiercely anti-Protestant, earning her the nickname "Bloody Mary." By 1555 some eight hundred Protestants fled to the continent, including John Knox.

Arriving in Geneva early in 1554, he developed theologically under Calvin's influence. However, he had his own mind and taught that revolution against idolaters, "be they kings or queens," was legitimate, a point almost all other Reformers disagreed with. Returning to Scotland the next year, Knox wrote against the "monstrous regimen of women," and urged both English and Scots to overthrow their rulers forcibly. Calvin disowned this view, arguing that in the Old Testament God approved the authority of such women as Huldah and Deborah. Elizabeth succeeded Mary and found Knox's position deeply offensive. It was only her fear of foreign presence that swayed Elizabeth to support the Scottish Reformation. In 1559 the French withdrew from the land, and the Scottish Parliament abolished Catholicism, establishing the country as officially Protestant. Nevertheless, it was ruled by the charming Roman Catholic Mary Stuart (Mary, Queen of Scots). Despite her diplomacy Knox preached against her to the point that she often broke down when listening to him. Her rule in fact ended in scandal, leaving the Reformation well established in Scotland.

Eight decades later, in 1639, war broke out between Scotland and the Stuart Charles I of England. Because he needed tax revenue to support the war, the Long Parliament, beginning in 1640, thought it opportune to ask him to agree, in the bargain, to legislation that would reform the church. In 1643 it called for a special assembly of "divines" (ministers) to revise the Thirty-Nine Articles of the Church of England. But then an alliance was brokered with Scotland, known as the Solemn League and Covenant, which included expanding the assembly to count the Scottish and the Irish delegates in their number. The work of the assembly continued until 1652 during the rule of Oliver Cromwell. The result was a truly ecumenical set of documents now known as the Westminster Standards. They included the Form of Church Government, the Confession of Faith, and the Larger and Shorter Catechisms. Though adopted officially only by the Church of Scotland, the Westminster Standards have had an impact far beyond Scotland. Modified in only a few details, they have become the major doctrinal statement for Presbyterians around the world. The Westminster Confession of Faith is unexcelled for its breadth, its balance, and its felicity of expression.

The Reformed faith owes so much to the people and events of these first generations. Despite a heavy burden of persecution and despite controversies and conflicts, the documents and traditions that emerged from this time have continued to be a most significant set of building blocks placed into the edifice of the church of Jesus Christ. Our debt to God for the men and women of these times is enormous. And yet, time moves on. History continues. New challenges and new opportunities face the church. Where will they take the Reformed faith?

3

YOU SHALL BE
CAREFUL THEREFORE

~~~~~~~~~~

Doctrine and Life: The Next Generations

Often in times of spiritual renewal, the first generation belongs to the innovators and the next one to the consolidators. In the case of the European Reformation this was generally the case, although it is easy to exaggerate such a distinction. There were plenty of systematicians in the first generation, and the next ones had a good number of reformers. The sixteenth century was one of extraordinary creative energy doctrinally and institutionally. The Reformed churches spread in a most dramatic fashion. Naturally, no single pattern of growth can be detected, because so much depended upon the character of the country in which expansion occurred. But it is generally the case that in the generations after the Reformation, two major trends can be detected. The first, stemming from the need carefully to define the further implications of Reformed doctrines, is the tendency to draw certain lines. The second is renewal and spiritual awakening. In the best cases, these two trends went together. At other times, there is tension between them.

It has become customary to label the seventeenth century as the time of confessional orthodoxy, in which a carefully elaborated Protestant approach to doctrine was developed and applied. Some scholars feel strongly that life and spontaneity were sapped during this time, because theologians were too concerned to explain the faith with precise formulations. They label the approach Protestant scholasticism. The name comes from the medieval method of the schoolmen but also carries with it a negative ring. Doctrinal precision at the expense of spiritual vitality is always a danger in the church. No doubt the temptation lurked during these decades after the initial flowering of the Reformation. Yet, things are not so simple. In most cases, Protestant orthodoxy was zealous not to lose the personal, spiritual warmth of first love, while at the same time seeking greater precision and order.

As was the pattern of the early church, controversies were resolved, and creeds were crafted. One of the prime motivations during the years following the Reformation was the desire to make the newly rediscovered biblical truth more accessible, more teachable. In keeping with that, various catechisms (from the Greek *katēcheō*, "instruct") were developed. Catechisms, which were meant to be memorized, go back to the earliest centuries of the church. At the Reformation, however, many such texts were developed that were meant to teach not only children but pastors and laypersons as well. Because of the influence of his *Small Catechism*, Luther could boast that fifteen-year-old people knew more doctrine than "all the theologians of the great universities." In various Protestant denominations the practice of confirmation was developed, whereby a young person declared the faith to be his or her own.

A favorite Reformed document is the Heidelberg Catechism (1563). Although it was born out of certain disputes, notably against Catholicism and even certain aspects of Lutheranism, it is remarkably irenic, devoid of the usual attacks on problematic doctrines (with some exceptions, such as question 80 in the third edition, which sets the Lord's Supper off against the "Papal Mass"). Its organization is distinctive. It has three sections of questions and answers, patterned after the Book of Romans: sin and misery (3–11), redemption (12–85), and gratitude, that is, the Christian life (86–129). These questions are further ordered into Lord's days, so that a church can cover the entire catechism in fifty-two Sunday services. Furthermore, it is deeply personal. The first question and answer are so beautifully put that many churches not necessarily in the Reformed tradition like to insert them into their liturgy:

Q. 1. What is your only comfort in life and in death?

A. That I belong—body and soul, in life and in death—not to myself but to my faithful Savior, Jesus Christ, who at the cost of his own blood has fully paid for all my sins and has completely freed me from the dominion of the devil; that he protects me so well that without the will of my Father in heaven not a hair can fall from my head; indeed, that everything must fit his purpose for my salvation. Therefore, by his Holy Spirit, he also assures me of eternal life, and makes me wholeheartedly willing and ready from now on to live for him.

While the Heidelberg Catechism is outstanding, many others were composed and widely used throughout Europe and North America. For the Church of England, Cranmer ensured that a Reformed catechism appear in the first edition of the Book of Common Prayer (1549). On the Continent, various creeds and catechisms were developed in order to consolidate the Reformed faith within the life of the church. One of them was the French Confession (1559), later known as La Rochelle.

The most complete and the most detailed Reformed creeds and catechisms came as the result of the Westminster Assembly. Although the articles of the Westminster Confession may appear strong and precise, they were often the result of compromise after significant debate. What emerged is nothing short of a masterpiece. The first chapter on the Bible is a magnificent summary about the attributes of Scripture. The chapters on divine sovereignty and human responsibility are even-handed. The emphasis on covenant and law is balanced by matters of personal piety, ethics, and assurance.

The Shorter and the Larger Catechisms were the fruit of the previous work of the assembly that produced the Westminster Confession of Faith. These catechisms eventually replaced most others, at least within the Presbyterian churches coming out of the British Isles.

Their doctrinal content is identical with that of the confession. While the Larger Catechism (1648) was meant to be used for expository preaching, the Shorter Catechism (1647) was considered easier and intended for the instruction of "new beginners" and children. Many Presbyterian churches around the world still practice the memorization of the catechism by its young people. These two texts admittedly lack some of the warmth and personal flavor of the Heidelberg Catechism, yet they make up for that in precision and balance. And some of the questions and answers are as powerful as any. The first, for example, may be one of the most often quoted summary statements of the Christian message of all times:

Q. 1. What is the chief end of man?

A. Man's chief end is to glorify God, and to enjoy him for ever.

Both catechisms are organized into two overarching parts: what we are to believe concerning God and thus concerning all of life; and what duties God requires of us, which leads to an exposition of the Ten Commandments, faith, and the sacraments. The exposition of the Decalogue by the Larger Catechism is a rich source for the application of the law to everyday life. Each commandment is treated in terms of duties and prohibitions. For example, the Sixth Commandment, "Thou shalt do no murder," includes, as duties, studying ways to preserve life, patience, the care of the body, diet, courteous speech, comforting the afflicted, and defending the innocent.

The Challenge of Rome

Besides the need to pass on the faith, another motivation governing Protestant orthodoxy was the need to respond to the renewal occurring in the Roman Catholic Church. During the sixteenth century, while the most notable events surrounded the birth of Protestantism, Rome hardly remained static. In part because of the challenge laid down by the Reformation and in part because of an internal push to reform, the Church of Rome made considerable efforts to establish its identity. It did so negatively by condemning various Protestant teachings and positively by redefining Catholic spirituality. Negatively, various texts were forbidden. The Index of Prohibited Books was developed from its modest beginnings in 1521 to its fuller version in 1559 and in successive editions. Protestant books were forbidden, but so were humanist texts, such as Boccaccio, and even works by the middle-of-the-road scholar Erasmus. The special congregation of the Holy Office responsible for such censorship was abolished in 1966, following Vatican II. Rightly or wrongly, Roman Catholicism gave many outsiders the impression of being a repressive religion. It did not help that the Inquisition, with roots back to the thirteenth century, continued to play on the fears of the people. The reality of its power over the centuries has been much debated. It was surely more effective in countries like Spain, where the church and the state were in an alliance, than in others where the power of the Catholic church was increasingly marginalized.

This defensive approach was not nearly as effective as the positive. Some scholars would argue that it is unfair to label the church's stance a Counter-Reformation, since that limits it to being merely reactive. To have a sense of the inner dynamics of the Catholic Reformation, as some would call it, consider its leading figure. Ignatius of Loyola (1491–1556) represents the essence of a non-Protestant seeking to reform the church. It is surely likely that even had there not been a Luther or a Calvin, there still would have been an Ignatius. He founded the Society of Jesus (the Jesuits) in large part in order to give some structure to the spiritual renewal he pioneered. A man who suffered much, he developed his famous *Spiritual Exercises*, published in 1548, as a guide for those seeking to obey the will of God. Using it correctly involves a four-part reflection, in the space of four weeks, that would lead the user to a better understanding of personal failure followed by greater holiness. Simply put, Ignatius's perception, unlike Luther's, is that the human will needs reforming, not the doctrines or structure of the church. And unlike some older monastic traditions, missions and education were valued far above contemplation. Indeed, loyalty to the church, however absurd its teachings may appear to rational minds, is never in question, according to Ignatius.

The teaching of the Society of Jesus is one of the principal inspirations behind the Council of Trent. This extraordinary gathering, which lasted from 1545 to 1563, is the epitome of the Catholic response to the needs of the day and articulates the two major concerns: the need to reform itself and the need to oppose Protestantism. Its ulterior hope was to restore unity to a now broken Christendom. In this it failed, but not without redefining a large part of the Western church as Roman Catholic. This had the effect of making this communion look like a denomination, much like Protestant denominations, rather than a truly universal church. Until Vatican II, the church would be known as Tridentine.

The Council of Trent did not officially condemn Luther, at least in a judicial sense. But its content was clearly a reaction against Protestant teachings. In response to the Reformation watchwords *sola scriptura* and *sola gratia* (Scripture alone, grace alone), Trent articulated what had been an unofficial but generally understood approach to the authority of the Bible and the work of grace. For example, it asserted that apostolic tradition must be revered with the same deference as Scripture. The rationale for this was to avoid the danger of private interpretation. Jerome's Vulgate version of the Bible, an old Latin translation, was decreed the only standard for resolving doctrinal issues. In response to *sola gratia* the council asserted that free human cooperation with grace is a necessary component of salvation. Despite the efforts of certain Augustinians to define justification in such a way that would ensure redemption to be all of grace, yet with the necessary addendum of human transformation ("double justification"), the Jesuits won the day. Justification was deemed an infusion of grace. Furthermore, transubstantiation during the Mass (Christ's substance being transferred to the bread and the wine) was strongly asserted.

All of this spelled the end of hopes for reconciliation between Protestants and Roman Catholics, at least for a time. The pope even decreed in 1564 that Trent was authoritative and that only he had the right to interpret its canons. From a Protestant point of view, Trent represents a considerable roadblock to reconciliation. Vatican II, called in the early 1960s by Pope John XXIII, did make numerous roadways into attuning the Roman Catholic Church to modern times. Many welcome changes were written in, though not to the liking of all Catholics. But in the end, one can question how fundamental to the system these changes were. For example, the Vatican II statement on the Bible (*Dei Verbum*) is remarkable. In places it even sounds Protestant. Still, it clearly affirms the dual authority of Scripture and tradition, even asserting that Scripture alone cannot suffice for certainty on all points of revelation (*Dei Verbum* 1.9). The way to interpret the Bible is "in the end subject to the judgment of the Church" (*Dei Verbum* 1.12).

In my view, the impasse is still there. Matters have not been made easier by fundamental changes in large portions of Protestant churches, particularly the move to liberalism over the last two centuries. Yet, until the Roman Catholic Church is willing to alter its authority structure, it will not be able to claim with a clear conscience, at least as an institution, that it can be fully instructed by biblical truth. To be sure, there is much life in this communion of faith, as we can testify from close associations with many of its leaders. Catholic laypersons are newly discovering the Bible. The church engages in extraordinary acts of mercy and often stands up for human rights, despite recent scandals and abuses. Historically, it is a fact that the papacy was a great force in the dismantling of Communism in the late twentieth century. But in spite of such vitality and despite laudable attempts to define its doctrines in a more cordial way toward Protestants, a significant barrier still exists because of the way authority is understood and practiced. It is sad for me to have to write these things. I am deeply aware of the great shortcomings in the Protestant communion. What may occur in the future is reconfigurations in both groups (even all three, including Orthodoxy) and new alignments formed across the borders, based on the true spirit of reformation.

Arminian Theology

Catholicism and Trent's decrees were not the only challenges to Protestants after the Reformation. Various schools of thought within the Reformed tradition emerged that attempted to make sense out of the difficult matter of God's omnipotence and human responsibility. If God predestines, then how may human beings be held accountable? Does God ordain the reprobation of the lost as well as the salvation of the redeemed? If not everyone receives Christ, then how does his death apply to all humankind? Is it possible to lose one's salvation despite having once possessed it? These questions were raised and debated during this time, and the terms of the discussion, as well as the conclusions of the various sides, have made their mark on the Protestant church in the ensuing generations. Nowhere was that debate more focused than in the Low Countries.

The Reformation came to the Netherlands amid great conflict. (That name is given to a host of small provinces and duchies, including Holland.) Because of the fierce determination of Charles V, the Holy Roman Emperor, to extirpate heresy from his hereditary realm, and because Protestants there did not at first have strong patrons to defend them, as they had in Germany, more martyrs for the cause of the Reformation can be counted in the Netherlands than in any other European country. Eventually things reversed, and Charles's successor, Philip II of Spain, had a revolt on his hands. Despite fierce reprisals from the Spanish Inquisition, Calvinism eventually made sufficient inroads so that the equation of national unity with allegiance to the papacy was not credible to the Netherlanders. Under the leadership of William of Orange, and then of his son, Maurice, Spanish domination was shaken off. Calvinism gained much ground. Its ethos was welcomed for many reasons. One of them, perhaps, was that it appeared somehow more compatible with the Dutch spirit of enterprise than a top-heavy, centralized Catholicism. An era of prosperity and creativity was ushered in from which those lands have benefited ever since.

So successful were the Reformation principles in the Netherlands that a special problem surfaced, the result of its new freedom. Ideally, religious pluralism is to be highly prized. The coexistence of multiple versions of Christian faith, even within a narrower expression, such as Calvinism, is a good thing. But freedom from oppression can breed a sort of discontent. To put it in the most positive light, in times of peace there is freedom to debate some of the outworkings of a theological position. There is time to debate matters that would previously have been considered finer points of doctrine. Thus, a significant number of theological controversies arose from within Calvinism. One of them was the conflict that issued in the Synod of Dort, which has given us what are called the five points of Calvinism.

A controversy over the relation of predestination to grace raged in the Netherlands and was tearing the churches apart. In 1589 Professor Jacob Arminius (1560–1609) was asked to refute the views of Dirk Coonrhert, particularly his objections to predestination. Instead, Arminius was drawn to them and ended up defending a mitigated view of divine sovereignty. Arminius was uncomfortable with the view that appeared to him to limit the free offer of grace and the responsibility of human beings to receive that grace. He did not accept the classical view of original sin, which seemed to him to make people incapable of choosing any good thing.

Arminius had been a student of Theodore Beza, Calvin's colleague and successor in Geneva. Using his great learning and his training in Aristotelian logic, Beza had developed a tightly woven theological system intended to be a synthesis of Calvin's ideas. The degree to which he may have modified the lively, pastoral approach of Calvin and locked things in to a rigid scaffold is an ongoing debate. With regard to predestination, it does seem that his system is neater and simpler, though not necessarily more biblical, than Calvin's. Beza argues that God's eternal decree functions in a virtually parallel manner in regard to the destiny of the saved and the lost. In a famous chart that first appeared in Beza's *Tabula preadestinationis*, God is at the head of the chart, as the predestining cause of all things. He decrees some to be saved in Christ and others to be condemned for their guilt. Then come the creation, the fall, and the unfolding of two different sequences. In the one on the left there is a chain of realities, beginning with God's love for and the effectual calling of his elect, their response in faith, and their passing into glory. On the right, the chain follows analogous steps but begins with God's just hatred of sinners, the lack of calling, a hardening of hearts, and finally, judgment and eternal death.

Arminius objected to Beza's double predestination, and particularly to the deterministic quality of the chart. Arminius was appointed a professor at Leiden University in 1603. There he entered into conflict with Francis Gomar (1565–1641), whose views were akin to Beza's. Arminius's death in 1609 did nothing to abate the conflict. The following year supporters of his position drafted a remonstrance in five articles (a remonstrance is a legal document used to state points of grievance). From thence this position would be known as Remonstrant Arminianism. At first blush, these five points do not seem radically at odds with the orthodox view. At issue was neither predestination nor the power of God's grace—only the way they worked in relation to human decision. But a closer look shows a considerable difference.

The Remonstrant Articles of 1610 state five positions: (1) God predestines those who, by the grace of the Holy Spirit, shall believe, whereas those who do not respond, he "leaves in sin." (2) Jesus Christ died for all and obtained redemption for all, yet only believers come to "enjoy this forgiveness." (3) We have neither saving grace in ourselves nor any ability to save ourselves, so that the new birth through the Holy Spirit of Christ is necessary in order to "will and effect what is truly good." (4) While good things can be accomplished only with assistance of grace, yet the mode of operation of that grace can be resisted. (5) Those who are in Christ have his full power to fight against temptation only if they are "ready for the conflict and desire his help," to which a phrase is added that raises the question and calls for further examination of Scripture to decide whether believers can fall away from grace.

The Synod of Dort

Virulent conflict over these articles arose. Very capable thinkers defended both sides. And true to form for such quarrels, politics and personalities were also involved. A number of meetings were called to try to settle matters, but without success. Eventually, a synod was called, which was to be fully international. It was less an open debate than a hearing for the Remonstrants, who were not recognized as orthodox. It opened November 14, 1618, and lasted six months, until May 6, 1619, when the Canons of Dort were accepted and promulgated. The Synod of Dort (meeting in the town of Dordrecht) was not called to restate all of orthodox doctrine for the Reformed churches but only to respond to the five points of the Remonstrants. Things were stormy in the room. The Remonstrants argued with such vehemence that they had to be thrown out in January 1619. They had tried to play on the differences within the orthodox over Beza's views. The discussion went on without them.

It has often been thought that the Canons of Dort are the essence of Calvinism. Taken strictly, that would be an anachronism, since Calvin died more than fifty years before the synod. However, one could plausibly argue that had he been alive, he would have sided with the orthodox in the controversy. These canons seek faithfully to extend the basics of Reformed theology and apply them to five important areas of discussion. However, they do not represent in themselves anything like a complete statement of faith. That is why those churches that adopt them as their confessional basis typically join two other, more extensive documents to their constitution, namely, the Belgic Confession and the Heidelberg Catechism. Together they are known as the three forms of unity.

Those unfamiliar with the canons, and especially people inclined to be hostile toward them, are sometimes prone to caricature what the canons say. For that matter, people who endorse the canons can in their enthusiasm also reduce them to a caricature. Both groups miss the subtle ways in which compromise was achieved all along. Though participants in the synod were unanimous in rejecting the five Remonstrant Articles, arriving at satisfactory, balanced statements on orthodox doctrine was not an easy matter. It took 154 sessions for the synod to accomplish its work, after which its position on the five points of Remonstrant Arminianism became the norm. A careful look at the statements reveals the rich fruit of much discussion.

Divine Predestination

The first head of doctrine is the subject of divine predestination. The Remonstrants affirmed that God's election of his saved people is grounded on the foresight of human faith, that is, God's knowledge that some would respond, not his eternal decree to save. To them this is the legitimate way to think of election. In response, the canons ground election in God's unchangeable purposes. This first point labors to defend God's sovereignty while avoiding any semblance of fatalism. The article does not begin with election but builds up to it, beginning with the premise of our sinfulness and deserved judgment, of the free offer of the gospel of Christ, of the need for human means (preaching) to proclaim this offer. It insists that the causality for unbelief resides in the guilty human being, whereas salvation comes as a free gift, given out of "mere grace." The immutability of God's election is based on the nature of God. How could it be otherwise? If God is truly all powerful and all wise, any other ultimate cause would diminish his being. So, all is of God. Yet, this article carefully differentiates between the processes of election and reprobation. The elect are chosen in love, whereas the reprobate are "passed by in the eternal decree." The elect are saved by God's mercy, whereas the reprobate are condemned by God's justice.

Admittedly, this view is the single most controverted doctrine of the Reformed faith. For many reasons, it seems rationally and emotionally difficult. While this first article of the Canons of Dort does not settle all the issues, it is concerned to explain things. It is remarkably sane and even pastoral. On the philosophical level, it presents both sides, that of God's sovereignty and that of human responsibility. Rather than explaining the apparent contradiction involved, it settles for mystery but not mystification. The article does not commit either to supralapsarianism (Beza's view whereby the decree to elect and to pass by is decided before the decree to create and permit the fall) or to infralapsarianism (whereby election is decreed after the decision to create and permit the fall). But it does stress the equation of election and mercy in Christ for fallen creatures. On the emotional side, the article radiates with God's attention to the needs of the soul. For example, it tells us that one reason for the importance of divine election is to guarantee salvation. God does not merely make salvation available; he saves. This is so certain that no human factor can enter as a condition. And for those whose reaction to such high and holy things is fear, it assures them that patience pays off. If we lack assurance today, then it is worthwhile to wait for "a season of richer grace," knowing that a merciful God will not "quench the smoking flax."

The Death of Christ and Human Redemption

The second head of doctrine responds to the question of the intent of the atonement. Did Christ's death intend to save all, only not all took advantage by their faith, as the Remonstrants believed, or was his death intended only for his people? Here again, the article is quite careful. It states two things clearly. First, because of who Christ is, his death is "of infinite worth and value," meaning it is sufficient to clear the sins of the whole world. Put somewhat awkwardly, if one more person were added to the number of the elect, Christ would not have had to suffer any more than he did. Second, the efficacy of Christ's death is sure for all his people, such that nothing can thwart their salvation. The intent matches the result. This article is sometimes known as the limited atonement. Some scholars refer to it as the particular atonement. Far better is to deem it the definite atonement, meaning that every one of God's elect will be saved. The article specifies that this includes people from every tribe, nation, and language.

This point is also controversial. Many people gladly embrace the other four points but stumble over this one. For one thing, various biblical passages seem directly to contradict its claims. John 3:16 proclaims that God so loved the world that whosoever believes will be saved. On the surface, this would appear to indicate that salvation is available to everyone. A closer look reveals, however, that what is in view is neither the number of those to be saved, be it large or small, nor the amount of love required to save a large number, but rather the quality of God's love, judging by its object and the price he paid. It is the world, that is, God's enemies, that is loved. So great is his love that he gave his only Son in sacrifice. A number of New Testament passages use the noun *all*, or its equivalent, to indicate the objects of the atonement. In 2 Corinthians 5:14 Paul specifically says that Christ "died for all, therefore all have died" (see also 1 Tim. 2:6). However, the intent of such passages is not to teach that Christ died for each and every person, some of whom took advantage of his gift, but rather that none of those for whom Christ died have any other status but union with him. Christ's death is so efficacious that every person for whom he died is also dead to sin and alive to Christ. It is unthinkable that he could have died for some who would never know this transformation.

Another passage that appears hard to reconcile with the definite atonement is 1 John 2:2: "He is the propitiation for our sins, and not for ours only but also for the sins of the whole world." Does this not specifically separate between the death of Christ for his people and for everyone else? Perhaps on the surface this is plausible. But in reality that is most unlikely. Put in context, it appears John is addressing a group that thought it would receive special treatment. They thought their redemption was essentially different from that of others, and they presented the church with the unacceptable notion that they were free from sin. He refutes them by insisting that such a claim is the height of deception (1 John 1:8). Sin is an equal-opportunity dysfunction, so that Christ needed to die not only for a special elite but for all kinds of people.

Finally, perhaps the most challenging passage is 1 Timothy 4:10, which states that God is "the Savior of all people, especially of those who believe." What can this mean? To begin with, it cannot mean that all people are saved, in the full, biblical sense, since this goes against clear and abundant biblical teaching against universalism. Furthermore, why would Paul have to add, "especially . . . those who believe"? Could it simply mean, as some interpreters have surmised, that God is the Savior of all people, that is, of those who believe? That is attractive, yet the Greek word *malista* clearly means "especially" or "most of all." More likely, to name God Savior of all does not in this case imply that the atonement is effectual for everyone but serves to identify the kind of God we have. He is the unique Savior. No one is saved other than by him. Jehovah God is the one who saves, and there is no other Savior. This is the one to whom we must come if we are to be saved. Not everyone is actually saved by the Savior. Israel knew God as the one who delivered them from Egypt, yet not all Israel entered the promised land with a new heart; so today, God is the only deliverer, yet not all are delivered.

Why labor to harmonize such verses with an article from an ancient canon of faith? Because the central point of the article flows out of the heart of the gospel as it is it clearly set forth on every page of the Scriptures: no power can prevent God from carrying out his loving purposes. His elect people will be drawn to him and saved. The death of Christ purchased their redemption in a way so definite that "there may never be wanting a Church composed of believers, the foundation of which is laid in the blood of Christ" (Canons of Dort 2.9).

Human Corruption and Conversion

The third and fourth heads of doctrine were combined in the synod's statement. Here the canons argue that human beings are completely incapable of their own salvation. What we sometimes call total depravity is set forth with great strength. The articles in these two heads tell us that we have forfeited God's excellent gifts and have become prone to evil. People are not willing to return to God "nor to dispose themselves to reformation." Being prone to evil does not mean that we are as bad as we could possibly be or that we are now demons. It means, rather, that nothing in us can lift us up to God's favor. Depravity is total in that every part of our being, from the body to the mind, is sinful. We are saved neither by the light of nature nor by the law of God but only because of the "glad tidings concerning the Messiah."

Again, Dort presents an excellent balance between the certainty of salvation for those whom God has called and the genuine free offer of the gospel even to those who will not respond. When they refuse, it is no fault of the gospel or of Jesus Christ who is offered to them. The blame rests on them, because they are accountable. Furthermore, the means of grace, the preaching of the Word, the right use of sacraments and church discipline are not played down but upheld. Indeed, free will, which belongs to human nature, is not removed from fallen creatures but required. Yet no credit can be ascribed to that free will when the gospel is embraced, for faith and repentance are a result of the gift of God. By God's grace human will is "activated" so that a person can repent and believe. The canons touchingly add that anyone who becomes the subject of God's grace "owes eternal gratitude to God, and gives him thanks forever."

The third point of the Remonstrants was not fundamentally erroneous: We have neither saving grace in ourselves nor any ability to save ourselves, so that the new birth through the Holy Spirit of Christ is necessary in order to "will and effect what is truly good." It did not state matters as strongly as they could have been stated. But taken together with the fourth point, which described grace as an "assistance" that could be resisted, the Remonstrants considerably weakened the effectual power of grace. In response, the canons resolutely affirm the efficacy of God's call. Everyone God desires to save will be saved.

Perseverance of the Saints

The fifth and last head of doctrine asserts two things about perseverance. First, those who are called into the fellowship of the gospel will not fall again or return to a state of condemnation. Left to our own strength and owing to indwelling sin that remains all too painfully in us, we would not continue in a state of grace. But because God has provided not only for our redemption but also for our perseverance, we can never fall away. Here the synod is realistic. It contemplates the insistent power of sin, which can grieve the Holy Spirit and even incur a "deadly guilt." It cites the case of the fall of David, of Peter, and of other saints. Yet, despite this, God's preserving grace can never be corrupted, and by his mercy, he will always restore us and lead us back to full fellowship with him. If not, then the work of Christ would be rendered ineffectual. We may not always fully feel the grace of God operating in us, and we may enter into serious doubts about our status before God. But the Lord will never leave us altogether without the comforting assurance of the Holy Spirit.

The second assertion is that not only will the saints persevere, but they must persevere. The canons contemplate the possibility of false assurance and a prideful sense of security. At the extreme such misguided confidence could lead to antinomianism, or the teaching that once saved, no obedience is ever required. In answer to that, the synod does not return to pure human effort, adding meritorious good works to our walk with God. Rather, it reminds us of the need to continue in the means of grace, particularly the hearing and reading of the Word and the enjoyment of the sacraments. Thus any human effort—required, to be sure—is still caused by God's grace. The whole balance between our perseverance and God's comes down to that same mystery of responsibility and grace that characterizes the synod's wise teaching. But that is not primarily a cause for theological speculation but for worship. The last statement of the canons is in praise of this glorious doctrine of perseverance, calling it an "inestimable treasure," because "God, against whom neither counsel nor strength can prevail, will dispose her to continue this conduct to the end."

More Than Doctrine

Why spend so much time on this one episode from the history of the church? First, it has become something of a lightning rod for those who are examining Reformed theology for themselves. Dort is often a stumbling block for those who are concerned about human freedom.

Second, while doctrinal concerns were at the heart of the synod's work, there was much more at stake. Many Dutch Calvinists still believed in so-called Erastianism, the view that the state should have considerable control over the church.[1] There was considerable danger for those out of line with the powerful ruler's views. Because Arminians were often in positions of prominence, they made life hard for the orthodox. A civil war was impending until the synod was called by the state. The Synod of Dort operated in response to that call but determined its views without pressure from the state, and thus it moved the church toward the separation of church and state. A reversal took place over what might have been expected. Afterward, although Arminians were eventually allowed to preach in their own churches in the Netherlands and elsewhere, the Canons of Dort were accepted

---

1. Thomas Erastus (1524–83), a Zwinglian living in Heidelberg, taught that the church had no right to discipline its members because only the civil magistrate was authorized to govern all the people of a country.

by mainstream Reformed churches in most European countries where they were known. Naturally, though, discussions went on, and still do, wherever the matter of God's rule over state and church is at issue.

Third, it is important to realize that these five points are only one piece of the larger theological fabric of Reformed theology. Admittedly, they are crucial. They argue that spiritual death makes us incapable of coming to God on our own, even though we are responsible for our condition. At the same time, God's love is so great that he will stop at nothing to save his people, nor will he violate their freedom in the process. Rarely has a group of human beings so carefully and thoughtfully arrived at theological statements that do justice to both sides of this fundamental gospel truth. Ultimately, one system was pitted against another. It should be remembered that besides the matters at stake, Arminians were not always sure about connected doctrines such as original sin, justification by faith alone, and even the full deity of Christ. Thus, truly, what was at stake was not simply smaller particulars such as predestination and the like. The gospel itself was at stake.

THOSE WHO HAVE NEVER
HEARD WILL UNDERSTAND

~~~~~~~~~~

The Quest for Consistent Living

Biblical religion is as old as the creation. Down through the ages one sees an hourglass pattern from the universal to the particular and then back to the universal. In the beginning the earth was full of the knowledge of God. But with the fall, divine interventions narrowed down the societies that possessed God's oracles. Biblical religion eventually narrowed down to the one faithful servant, Jesus Christ. Yet he is the Savior of the whole world. But even as his followers are gathered into the church, one witnesses to further narrowing down and further broadening out. This is why we have spent some time looking at developments in the West. Historically, though, the Christian faith was not a Western product. It was born in the Middle East. All along, the church has been alive and active outside the West. Furthermore, most of the expansion of the church in modern times has been truly global. The West still has an important role, but only in partnership with the worldwide Christian community.

From the narrower part of the hourglass, we begin to move out to the wider part. Thus, the work of consolidation and systematization continued into the late eighteenth century. In the British Isles, adherents of the basic tenets of the Reformed faith moved beyond the original Anglicanism of Thomas Cranmer as it affected England, Wales, and Ireland. While enjoying the closest ties with the Continental Reformation, Anglicanism developed distinctive features. In matters of church order, the local parish is the basic community of faith, led by the rector, or vicar. Several parishes and missions come together as a diocese, led by the bishop, who is the chief officer of the Anglican churches. These dioceses are in turn organized into provinces, and all entities of the worldwide Anglican communion are presided over by the archbishop of Canterbury. Every ten years the bishops from around the world gather at Lambeth, in London, to attempt consensus on the matters facing the church.

In the centuries following the Reformation, the Anglican church has centered on worship. According to the prayer book, the basic purpose of that worship is "when we assemble and meet together to render thanks for the great benefits that we have received at [God's] hands, to set forth his most worthy praise, to hear his most holy word, and to ask those things which are requisite and necessary, as well for the body as the soul."[1] From this central orientation, considerable diversity is found in practice around the world. Anglicanism spread far and wide during the rule of the British empire and has continued to expand in the postcolonial era. At the present time various parties have emerged, often diverging considerably one with the other. Evangelicalism, stressing a historic, gospel-driven faith, characterizes East Africa, Australia, and much of the Southern Hemisphere churches. The more sacramental Anglo-Catholic party is found in South Africa as well as in various parts of the Northern Hemisphere. Liberalism, which questions traditional doctrines such as the incarnation and the Trinity, is found in Great Britain and North America to a considerable degree. For the moment, these parties have coexisted in communion with the archbishop of Canterbury, but this coexistence is being severely tried in recent times.

1. *The Book of Common Prayer*, Protestant Episcopal Church (U.S.A.), 1789, Morning Prayer 6.

Historically, many adherents of one party were not able to remain inside the Anglican church. The Puritan movement developed from the Reformation in Great Britain but found itself in difficulty with some of the unreformed elements within the Anglican church, as it saw them. Initially a term of derision, *puritan*, as the name implies, signifies the desire to go further in reforming the church. The Puritans had two central concerns. First was purity in worship. The Puritans on the whole did not think the Anglican church went far enough in reforming public worship according to the Scriptures. They objected to robes and candles and even to set prayers. Second was an emphasis on living consistently under the rule of the Lord God. Puritans believed true religion should be "experimental," that is, practical, not limited to doctrine alone. Special emphasis was laid on recognizing one's sins and coming over and over again in honest repentance before God. Because of their strong commitment to predestination, the problem of assurance arose and was extensively treated. One scholar has described this concern as the "experimental predestinarian tradition." The Puritans were doctors of the soul, precursors to modern counselors and therapists. Yet the Puritans were also concerned to extend gospel principles to every area of life, from work to marriage to citizenship and even to the arts.

Great figures like William Perkins (1558–1602) worked out a Reformed theology that drew upon the magisterial Reformers but applied it to the transformation of British society under Elizabeth I. His writings were extensive and covered many different areas of life. His work on calling, knowing God's will, is particularly powerful. The Dutch theologian Gijsbert Voetius called Perkins "the Homer of practical Englishmen to this day." His student William Ames (1576–1633) wrote further on devoting every aspect of life to the glory of God.

Eventually tensions arose over the Puritan desire to reform the church further than English magistrates allowed. Richard Sibbes, Thomas Goodwin, and the remarkable John Owen represented a generation of Puritans who tended toward independency, that is, the separation of church from state, and the tendency toward congregational government, whereby each congregation is virtually autonomous rather than joined in diocese or presbyteries. Because of tensions and dangers, many Puritans fled north or to the Continent, and especially to

America, continuing the Puritan tradition in those places. In North America, Puritanism developed in continuity and in distinctiveness from its British roots. The Puritan influence is not the only dynamic behind American culture, but it is surely one of the most powerful. American Puritans were remarkable for their sense of duty, their commitment to God's law, and their willingness to sacrifice for the cause of righteousness and truth.

John Cotton (1584–1652), one of the architects of New England congregationalism, preached and wrote extensively on calling. Whereas the medieval church had relegated vocation to the clerics, the Puritans, following the Reformers, stressed the nobility of calling for every Christian. Yet they did not do so romantically, since they understood the hardship, the burdens, and the ultimately ephemeral nature of the world in which we do our work. Cotton, in *The Way of Life*, states that each person should be drawn to a "warrantable calling." But while Christians will need the skills and gifts necessary to fulfill that calling, yet they must look at the strength to work as "a dead work unless God breathe in him." Any worldly success must be held with a light hand: "Now faith is like a poise: it keeps the heart in an equal frame; whether matters fall out well or ill, faith takes them much what alike; faith moderates the frame of a man's spirit on both sides."[2]

One of the most powerful expressions of Puritan doctrine, one known the world over, is *The Pilgrim's Progress*, by John Bunyan (1628–88). Because of his strong Calvinism and his convictions about preaching outside the established church, Bunyan spent twelve years of his life in a damp county jail. Yet his work was widely influential. Next to the Bible, *The Pilgrim's Progress* was the most respected book among the middle and lower classes in England, and worldwide it became the best-selling book of the eighteenth century. Today it is still the most universally cherished work of piety found on every continent. It is an allegory of the Christian life, told as though it were a dream, using the two heroes, Christian and Faithful, to represent the believer on the journey from the City of Destruction to the Celestial City. Using

2. John Cotton, "The Life of Faith," in *The Way of Life* (London, 1641), 439, 441, 446.

simple but memorable images to represent the spiritual realities of sin (a burden on the back), conversion (passing through the wicket gate), a host of temptations (characters such as Obstinate, Pliable, Apollyon, and Formalist) as well as good guides (Evangelist, Prudence, and Hopeful), Bunyan takes the reader on a journey full of obstacles (Vanity Fair, the Slough of Despond), places of refuge (the Interpreter's House, the Pleasant Valley), and finally, across the deep river to the Celestial City.

Eventually this extraordinary Puritan vision gave way to more secular versions. Calling became "manifest destiny." Assurance of salvation was confused with confidence. Bunyan and the pilgrim theme were modeled by authors like Herman Melville, whose Moby Dick takes the aptly named Captain Ahab on an obsessive journey, narrated by the outsider Ishmael ("wanderer"), in search of a great white whale. The whale was a source of life in nineteenth-century New England, but also elusive and dangerous. Like Christian in *The Pilgrim's Progress*, there is a self-discovery here in the way the narrator recounts the events. But unlike his journey to heaven, Ahab's is a Promethean quest to violate an elusive beast that had once violated him. He dies in the process. As Melville puts it in one of his Civil War poems, "And death be busy with all who strive—Death with silent negative" ("The Conflict of Convictions"). We are a long way from the faith of the Puritans, and behind them, the Reformers.

Reason and Religion

Much in the years following this heyday of faith in action had become cold and moralistic. The decline from a strong, systematic religion to a rationalistic self-reliance can be illustrated by comparing François Turretini (known as Francis Turretin to English-speaking readers) with his son, Jean-Alphonse Turretini. The family was originally Italian but was forced to flee to Switzerland during the Reformation. François (1623–87) was the embodiment of Reformed orthodoxy. His father, Benedict, was a great advocate of the kind of theology formulated at the Synod of Dort. In 1679 through 1685, an extraordinary volume, the *Institutes of Elenctic Theology*, was published. It was to become the major theological textbook in Protestant seminaries, including Princeton. The term *elenctic* (from the Greek for "conviction") refers to the polemical character of the work, which is set in a fairly traditional scholastic form. We can read this work today to great profit.

However, within one generation, orthodoxy gave way to a much more rationalistic approach. Jean-Alphonse Turretini (1671–1737) engaged in a rather different approach. Still nominally orthodox, he nevertheless used human reason to complement revelation. For example, he explains miracles as God's modification of the normal natural patterns. Daniel in the fiery furnace was saved because God blew the flames in a different direction. Jesus walked on water because the element of water was changed in order to make it support a human body. Jean-Alphonse did accept mystery, but mostly for things that reason could not explain. This procedure may seem a harmless, practical kind of apologetic, but the overall effect was to make human reason far more authoritative than it had ever been.

A similar shift can be traced between the American Great Awakening, a movement of tremendous spiritual impact, and the succeeding generations. The undisputed leader of the Great Awakening was Jonathan Edwards (1703–58), who may well be America's ablest theologian. By his time many of the ideals of the Puritans for a godly New England had faded. Religion was perfunctory. Then, various manifestations of revival could be felt with the rise of itinerant evangelists, such as Theodore Jacob Frelinghuysen (1691–1748) and especially George Whitefield (1714–70). In 1734 Edwards preached a famous series of sermons on justification by faith in the Congregational church at Northampton, Massachusetts. People responded in great numbers. The town was changed to become, in Edwards's words, "never so full of love, nor so full of joy, nor yet so full of distress, as it was then."[3] He wrote profound volumes of theology, including his treatise on *The Religious Affections* (1746), which many scholars consider to be the greatest masterpiece of theology since Calvin's *Institutes*. It is a study

---

3. Quoted in Alexander Smellie, "Introduction" to *The Religious Affections* (Edinburgh: Banner of Truth, 1986), 10.

of the true and false manifestations of the work of God's grace in human beings. Edwards was dismissed in 1750 over a dispute involving qualifications for the Lord's Supper, and he went to Stockbridge as a missionary. There he preached some more, wrote a great deal, and promoted the cause of reaching the Native Americans with the gospel. He died prematurely just after arriving at Princeton as president, after receiving an inoculation against smallpox.

The technical word for what we are observing is *secularization*. Not long after the Great Awakening, America was confronted with the singular forces of rationalism and deism. Originating in Europe, these movements represented elevating human rationality to a place it never had for Edwards and Whitefield. According to this secularist way of thinking, God did create the world but was only distantly involved in it afterwards. Furthermore, the common bond of morality was much more central to religion than obscure doctrines, as it was thought, such as the substitutionary atonement, irresistible grace, and the like. Joseph Bellamy (1719–90) was in many ways Edwards's successor. Yet certain key modifications in his approach were portends of a different America from that of the Great Awakening. He believed God is a "moral governor," that is, the somewhat deist idea that God runs the world through supervision over human moral order rather than through his decrees. Wrong behavior results in severe consequences rather than God's judgment. God permits sin in order that some good may be achieved. In this view, the work of Jesus Christ, particularly his atonement, was not so much the satisfaction of God's justice but the best way to keep the world going. This was decidedly a more rationally acceptable religion than that found in the tenets of strict Calvinism.

Revival and Romanticism

Such a rationalist spirit could not last. Even if books such as John Locke's *The Reasonableness of Christianity* (1695) and John Toland's *Christianity Not Mysterious* (1696) attempted to marry the spirit of the Enlightenment with the legacy of the Reformation, a reaction was bound to set in. The French Revolution had attempted to provide humanity with a truly rational religion, including the worship of nature and the elimination of privileged classes by the clean atonement of the guillotine. But the hopes of the French Revolution, begun in 1789, ended in the Reign of Terror, signaling the dismal failure of the purely rational.

Already, countermovements had set in. On the Roman Catholic side, Jansenism attempted to steer the church away from human and rational religion toward a more Augustinian stress on the sovereignty of God. Blaise Pascal (1623–62), closely tied to the movement, was a scientist and a theologian who advocated an unpopular view of human submission to God's grandeur. On the Protestant side, on the Continent, Jean-Jacques Rousseau (1712–78) affirmed the natural goodness of humanity and the corrupting, though necessary, influence of civilization. A man full of contradictions, he spoke of religion as being rational, yet more than rational. True religion was one of conscience, emotional in the deepest sense. In the British Isles, John Wesley (1703–91), inspired by the German Pietists, rediscovered the reality of regeneration. He led a movement for the renewal of the church's spirituality. Neither he nor his brother Charles intended to leave the Church of England. Rather, they sought to warm the souls of believers through the knowledge of Christ. Yet eventually, after their death, a group separated out of the larger church to be called Methodists.

A widely influential though vaguely defined movement called Romanticism began to replace the reasonable, predictable world of the Enlightenment. Romanticism was at first a literary and artistic movement that stressed the imagination and the role of intuition. It held that we cannot arrive at truth merely by human measure. After a period full of skepticism and moralistic reductions of faith, a more transcendent religion returned, one that even courted mystery. Theology moved in the same direction. After a time of rather cold, rational theology, a religion of the heart was elucidated. As in the wider cultural trends, much was good and much was a problem. What was good?

A number of extraordinary revivals of Christian faith coincided with this shift toward Romanticism. In Great Britain a wide range of believers, including Methodists and many others, began to experience the reality of God, his love and forgiveness, but also the urgency of the need for missions and works of mercy. Broadly known as evangelicals, these believers stressed the gospel as a force that could change the world. They understood the world to be moving toward increasing turmoil. Numerous missions societies were formed, some independent, some interdenominational. Specific evils, such as slavery, were addressed. Indeed, social justice was high on the evangelical agenda. William Wilberforce (1759–1833), the converted parliamentarian, together with the Clapham Sect, as it was known, forcefully pleaded for the abolition of slavery and the reform of British morals. Other groups attacked white slavery, the abuse of laborers through the machine and the industrial system. The chapel culture saw the spread of satellite missions to the increasingly troubled cities of Great Britain. The Salvation Army, founded by William Booth in 1865, reached out with the gospel to the poor with impressive effectiveness. In Scotland, Thomas Chalmers (1780–1847) combined strong preaching with Christian education and, especially, missions. He believed foreign missions was good in itself but also good for the sending church. He not only devised new and creative ways for the local parish to meet the needs of the poor but also became in effect one of the founders of modern sociology. Numerous Bible societies were founded in order to get the Scriptures into the hands and hearts of as many as possible at home and abroad.

Flowing out of these movements of awakening was a new commitment to world missions. The nineteenth century has justly been called the century of missions. Christian religion in general, and the Reformed faith in particular, had been present around the world, down through the centuries, in various degrees of strength, well before the European missions outreach. As we saw, the historical origins of the Jewish and then Christian religion are Middle Eastern. The gospel spread far and wide into places throughout Africa and Asia as well as to the New World. But now a special impetus was given, fueled by the awakenings and revivals of the nineteenth century. William Carey (1761–1834), an English Baptist, argued that Christ's great commission (Matt. 28:18–20) still applied and had not ended with the apostles, as was widely held. After urging his parishioners to "expect great things from God" and to "attempt great things for God," he took his family to India under the Baptist Missionary Society. There he worked in a factory and studied the local languages in order to translate the Bible into the vernacular. He saw hundreds come to faith and encouraged new believers to spread the gospel to their fellow nationals.

Missions spread evangelical fervor far and wide. A number of societies, such as the Sudan Interior Mission and the China Inland Mission, believed that the gospel ought to penetrate deeper into each continent and not remain on the coastlines. In North America, important evangelistic movements reached out to the Native Americans and to Africans, many of them bound in slavery. The Second Great Awakening was the setting for great evangelistic campaigns led by preachers like Charles Finney and Dwight L. Moody. The theology of these groups was certainly a mixed bag. Some was decidedly not Reformed. Wesley had taught a sort of perfectionism, believing that truly sanctified Christians could achieve moments of complete freedom from sin. Charles Finney, known as a New School Calvinist, appealed to the human ability to repent and the perfectibility of the heart as well as society.

Yet the Reformed faith was a strong ingredient in these world revivals and missions, though far from predominant. In England, Charles Haddon Spurgeon (1834–92) combined Reformed doctrine with evangelistic passion. Baptist by conviction and largely untrained, Spurgeon became the most popular preacher of his time. His sermons were published around the world and could be found in libraries of kings and paupers.

In Holland *Het Reveil* was a revival of Christian faith that ultimately influenced Groen van Prinsterer and Abraham Kuyper, the spearheads of our contemporary Reformed, worldview thinking. In their vision, every sphere of life must come under the aegis of the Word of God. Kuyper (1837–1920) came to evangelical faith through two influences that bear mentioning. The first was reading the romantic English novel *The Heir of Redclyffe* by Charlotte Yonge and finding its view of the spirituality of the church deeply compelling. The second was the witness of one of his parishioners, Pietje Balthus, a cobbler's daughter, who courageously corrected the rationalist theology of his educational background. He wrote hundreds of books and articles. He founded a newspaper, in which world events were reported from a Christian point of view. He was active in politics, eventually becoming prime minister of Holland. He also founded the Free University of Amsterdam, whose curriculum reflected his worldview approach to all of life.

In Switzerland and France movements of awakening swept across the population. Pastors like Alexandre Vinet (1797–1847), the Swiss pastor, and scholars like Merle d'Aubigné (1794–1872), the French historian, both strong adherents to the Reformed outlook, wrote movingly about all of life beginning from the religion of the heart. Francophone missions societies were founded and sent missionaries to French colonies, including many African countries as well as various South Sea islands. Bible societies and works of social concern were also founded, similar to their British counterparts.

In America the Reformed faith gained new strength in church life and in academia. In the North and the South, the Presbyterian church had considerable strength. Princeton Theological Seminary was founded in 1812 and became one of the great citadels of learning from a Reformed orientation. At least two outstanding professors brought systematic and biblical scholarship to new heights. Charles Hodge (1797–1878) wrote a systematic theology that made him possibly the most influential theologian in American history. His successor and the great voice of the Princeton theology, Benjamin B. Warfield (1851–1921), was a most careful and prolific defender of an Augustinian and Calvinian approach. This tradition continued through the mid–twentieth century, when the fundamentalist-modernist controversies led to a reorganization of Princeton Seminary and the departure of key members of the faculty.

Stepping Outside of Orthodoxy

What was problematic? Alongside all of this religious revitalization was renewal of another kind. Also loosely related to Romanticism, a bold new trend began to develop. At the heart, it was a tendency so to relegate religion to the nonrational that first things and truth itself became ultimately mysterious. Furthermore, the authority of reason grew even stronger than in the works of Jean-Alphonse Turretini. Still restricted to its own areas of competency, reason expanded its claim until it became a critical judge, not a responsive servant. In philosophy, Immanuel Kant (1724–1804) set the tone. He professed to establish the rights of unaided reason and a place for religion. He did this by radically separating two fields, reason and religion. In his *Critique of Pure Reason* (1781), Kant set forth what would become a defining notion. As he put it in the introduction, the aim of the book is to "assure to reason its lawful claims, and dismiss all groundless pretensions, not by despotic decrees, but in accordance with its own eternal and unalterable laws." First, reason is autonomous though limited. Reason is what we need in order to do science and to understand the world around us. Second, however, religion and morals are given their full rights, as he understood them. But they became untouchable by ordinary means. Notions like goodness, the immortality of the soul, and the existence of God, indeed truth itself, were made "safe." That is, they were isolated from the possibility of examination: "truth is an island and we must not navigate on the surrounding waters thinking we may get beyond experience."[4]

In a way, then, religion was reduced to morals. This idea was far-reaching. Not that many people could read Kant and understand his dense prose. But the point of view he set forth was in the atmosphere, and many would breathe it in and arrive at approaches to religion that defined the age.

As a result, liberalism was born. For evangelicals, the word *liberalism* has come to mean anything bad or objectionable. That is not quite fair, since liberalism has a wide range of application. In economics, it signified a free market. In ethics, it meant toleration, respecting one's neighbor's rights. In the ecclesiastical realm, it often meant allowing the church freedom from state control. In extreme cases, especially in Roman Catholic countries, this meant anticleri-

4. Jean Brun, *L'Europe des philosophes* (Paris: Stock, 1988), 256.

calism. In theology, the central tenet of liberalism could be called free examination.

The father of theological liberalism is undoubtedly Friedrich Schleiermacher (1768–1834). From a Pietist background and drawn to Romanticism, Schleiermacher desired to make theology empirical rather than speculative. And so his massive book of dogmatics, *The Christian Faith*, relates all doctrines to the experience of the church. But for him Christian faith is not primarily conceptual. Concepts are only reflections on what is really central: religious experience. He famously redefined the heart of religion as the "feeling of absolute dependence." The self, he believed, could be conscious only if it was in touch with transcendence. The value of the Christian religion is that Jesus, its center, was perfect in his consciousness of dependence and so is able to mend the church's confused awareness. Not intended to be subjectivist, because this dependence is a response to God's revelation, Schleiermacher's views nevertheless consistently resisted understanding God objectively. He was perplexed by the traditional Reformed doctrines of the Trinity, the Chalcedonian Christology, the substitutionary atonement, miracles, and providence. Like Kant, and following the liberal idea of free examination, he believed science could judge in many areas without assailing the fundamental propriety of the Christian faith. In effect, he redefined the project of theology. Rational criticism was a good thing, but it could never assail the essence of religion, a feeling that gives life meaning and provides moral guidance.

Schleiermacher's successors would go much further. For a number of German scholars, free examination meant that the reliability of the biblical authors to report the events they were in touch with could be questioned. F. C. Bauer taught that several books of the New Testament were written so long after the actual events that they had little historical value. D. F. Strauss and the French scholar Ernest Renan wrote lives of Jesus that excised the miraculous and presented a very human Christ. Biblical criticism, combined with the new confidence in evolutionary theory, revamped the traditional approach to the Bible and its authority. Julius Wellhausen and others proposed that it was not reasonable to think of a man claiming to be Moses as possessing the kind of culture and high ethics of his time. The Pentateuch (the first five books of the Bible) was more likely patched together during Israel's exile, when the people needed to believe in a creator God who was also a deliverer from oppression. Anthropologists began to compare all religions and find in them far more commonality than hitherto suspected. Friedrich Nietzsche, admittedly an extremist, even argued that Christian morals were a product of the resentment of the weak for the strong.

None of this was meant to detract from the central meaning of the Christian religion, which liberal theologians thought they were protecting. The effect, though, was to raise a high wall between the divine and the human. At one extreme, this did have the effect of handing over the most important truths of religion to scientific disparagement. At the other extreme, the essence of religion was thought to be out of the reach of science, something so good and transcendent that discrediting eyewitnesses and accounts of miracles was irrelevant to what mattered most.

To Draw the Line

How would the Christian faith fare in this context? Many aspects of a so-called Christian society began to give way to more secular ones. More so in Europe, but increasingly in North America as well, church attendance decreased, laws became more permissive, and the knowledge of the Bible was diminished. Science, while not intrinsically opposed to faith, was regularly marshaled into the service of reducing religion to a human level. Early in the twentieth century, William James suggested that there were varieties of religious experience, some of them healthy but none of them true. Sigmund Freud flatly asserted that whether more primitive or more advanced, religions all were explicable in psychoanalytical terms as neurotic efforts to respond to a threatening world.

Many different attempts were made at responding to such secularization. One was to accommodate to it in some degree. For example, certain tenets of socialism were accepted as compatible with Christian views. Worker priests, Christian trade unions, boys' clubs, walking holidays, and the like were sponsored by churches. At the extreme, in the latter part of the twentieth century, secularism and even theories such as the death of God were merged into Christian theology. More often, the church revised some parts of its theology while working harder on issues of social justice and ethics. They tried to make the worship service more attractive to outsiders and young people. As was mentioned earlier, the great Second Vatican Council was called by Pope John XXIII. For three years (1962–65) it met and reformulated most of the traditional doctrines of the Roman Catholic Church in order to respond to modern issues such as poverty, world religions, and biblical criticism.

On the Protestant side, one significant response to the surrounding world was the ecumenical movement, with its various councils and groups. Unity, it was thought, should be a central witness to a fragmented world in relation to which the denominational divisions of Protestantism were ineffectual. To accomplish this, ecumenism should combine reconciliation with missions. Things began well. In 1910, under the leadership of John R. Mott, the International Missionary Conference was held in Edinburgh. Two of the groups to emerge from that first conference (Life and Work and Faith and Order) proposed the establishment of the World Council of Churches, which came together in 1948. A number of significant meetings were held in the ensuing decades. The slogan "doctrine divides, service unites" was promulgated, with the not unexpected weakness of definition and ultimately a lack of effectiveness. The Roman Catholic Church did not participate in these meetings, although at Vatican II it declared, for the first time, that Protestants were "separated brethren." In 1965 the Orthodox church and the Roman Catholic Church lifted their mutual excommunication, which had existed since the separation of East and West in 1054.

Other efforts at drawing lines were made. Karl Barth (1886–1968), the most influential Protestant theologian of the twentieth century, reaffirmed the sovereignty of God in Christ, using a dialectical model. That is, in strong reaction against the liberalism of mainstream theology, he heralded a wholly other God who became "wholly present" in Christ.[5] Barth, along with Martin Niemöller and others, opposed the Nazi program of government involvement with social causes and particularly restrictions of Jewish people from German life, which led to their extermination in huge numbers. His theological project is known as neo-orthodoxy, because it restates some of the central emphases of the Reformation. Yet it is different from traditional Reformed theology in important ways. The dialectical method prevents Barth from holding to the classical triad of creation, fall, and redemption.

Neo-orthodoxy, or dialectical theology, is not a single, unified movement. Emil Brunner in Germany, C. H. Dodd in Great Britain, and the Niebuhrs in America gave it their own flavor. For most of them, however, the creation order lacks concreteness and permanency. It is not certain that the transition from God's wrath to his grace occurred through Jesus Christ in history. Barth in particular objected to rational defenses of Christian faith. Some scholars have suggested he was weak on the Trinity as well. What is certain about most of the neo-orthodox theologians is their constant movement, revisiting one area after another, trying to balance one statement against another. But is this theology the long-needed answer to liberalism? Many people in the more conservative branches of the Reformed tradition would argue that it is not.

Liberalism not only survived the neo-orthodox turn but also developed further along its own trajectory. The best-known neo-liberal is Paul Tillich (1886–1965). He insightfully set forth a "method of correlation" that understood theology to be an answer to the major questions being raised in the surrounding culture, questions about meaning, alienation, psychological freedom, and the like. Eventually this approach made theology all too this-worldly, and seriously hushed objective, verbal revelation.

5. The term *dialectical* goes back at least to Socrates. The dialectical method questions and opposes opposites in order to arrive at truth. Barth was intrigued by Søren Kierkegaard, who believed paradox was at the heart of theology. In this view, creeds and propositions should be put in tension with existential anguish, so that only faith can resolve the tension.

After the Second World War, a strong concern for social justice developed within Catholic and Protestant traditions. Stemming from the oppression of the powerful against the disenfranchised in Latin America, liberation theology was generated. It asked the church to give a "preferential option" to the poor. When the church did not fully respond, lay-led base communities were formed as catalysts for liberation principles. Sometimes combining Marxist concepts with the impetus of Vatican II, liberation theology was echoed in Protestantism by black theology and feminist theology, similarly concerned to combat the oppression of African Americans and women in the name of the gospel.

Evangelicalism

Arguably the most significant movement in modern Christianity, one that is generally Protestant but not contained within denominational boundaries, is the gospel-centered movement known as evangelicalism (from the Greek word *euangelion*). That word means to believe and proclaim the good news, the message that Jesus Christ has come to die for the forgiveness of sins and to be raised up for victory over the forces of evil. As a movement, evangelicalism does not depart from the historic Christian faith. It does stress its central beliefs over some of the particulars, however, and it is especially oriented to heralding the good news at home and abroad, that is, to missions. Thus, evangelicalism tends to accentuate personal conversion more than other movements might.

Historically, evangelicalism in some form or another goes back to the beginning. Anyone who would preach the gospel, whether it be Ambrose of Milan, Bernard of Clairvaux, or Jan Hus, is an evangelical. At the Reformation the term took on a technical sense, in that Lutherans were called *Evangelische*, a name they still carry in today's Germany. But the modern form of the movement was born in the awakenings mentioned above. John Wesley, Jonathan Edwards, and George Whitefield owed much to Puritan preaching but moved beyond the Puritans by their stress on the new birth and the assurance of faith for individuals. Then in the late nineteenth and early twentieth centuries, evangelicalism became more self-conscious as a worldwide trend. It saw the birth of many parachurch organizations, such as the YMCA, the Salvation Army, and IFES (with its British and American chapters, Inter-Varsity Christian Fellowship).[6] In addition, numbers of missionary societies were formed that sought to bring the good news to nations around the world. One common feature of the evangelical missions groups was finding support either through deputation, that is, traveling around to churches and individuals who were asked to respond, or by a faith-based approach, whereby financial needs were mentioned to no one except to the Lord in prayer.

Two Twentieth-Century Movements

Two manifestations within, or alongside, evangelicalism are worthy of mention.

Fundamentalism. Part of the impetus for evangelicalism in the twentieth century was the need to respond to the forces of secularism and theological liberalism. One of the stronger parallel movements was fundamentalism. Perhaps the label is unfortunate, because it groups together so many strange bedfellows. At its most sophisticated, fundamentalism took its orders from the series *The Fundamentals,* published around 1912, in which authors like G. Campbell Morgan and B. B. Warfield restated the great first things of the Christian faith for the new century. In the 1920s, particularly in America, a controversy opposing fundamentalists to modernists arose. Fundamentalists generally stressed the reliability of Scripture, and above all the need to save sinners from worldliness. Not indifferent to social issues, they thought that the best way to address them was through the conversion of individuals first, followed by their influence as Christians in society. Generally, fundamentalists did not do well in their arguments with liberals, and as a result they tended to separate from the larger denominations and form their own institutions. While their views

---

6. In Britain today, Inter-Varsity is known as UCCF (Universities and Colleges Christian Fellowship). In France, it is the GBU (Groupes Bibliques Universitaires). Each country has its own IFES subgroup.

tended to coincide with traditional evangelicalism, they also could harden lines on issues and in so doing become more reactive than active. For example, in morals some fundamentalists added restrictions on the Christian liberties to the Ten Commandments. Abstinence from alcohol, dancing, moviegoing, and the like were considered part of one's testimony to the world.

Fundamentalist views of the Bible could slouch into a literalism that obscured the organic character of biblical writing. One example of this is the movement known as dispensationalism, so called because it distinguished between seven eras (dispensations) of history, one of them being the millennium, from Revelation 20, the time when Old Testament prophecies would have their literal fulfillment. Part of the appeal was the sense of the imminence of Christ's return, which would be much-needed relief in a troubled world. Another reason for its draw was fundamentalism's simple interpretation of Scripture. It did not force the text into symbolism or excise the miraculous, as liberalism was wont to do. Rather than spiritualizing, fundamentalists were anxious to reconcile the Bible with the clear findings of science. Some tended to look to the Bible for confirmation of scientific data. When such concordances were not forthcoming, an appeal was made to do science differently. For example, in order to respect what looked like the plain meaning of Genesis 1, indicating twenty-four-hour days, a version of geology and paleontology was developed (with precedents from the nineteenth century known as catastrophism) that confirmed the text. Because this view stressed the instantaneous over a process, it spoke of God creating "with the impression of age," and in some versions it included viewing the Genesis flood as a time of catastrophe in which fossils were formed suddenly but looked ancient.

Important exceptions to this approach, but still identified with fundamentalism, are represented by the work of scholars such as J. Gresham Machen (1881–1937). Machen strongly advocated the theology of Princeton yet believed that the institution had been so changed as to attenuate that theology. He eventually left to form West-minster Theological Seminary, which today is one of the strongholds of the old Princeton tradition. Machen's *Christianity and Liberalism* (1923) put him on the side of the fundamentalists in its critique of the liberal method. But it was neither anti-intellectual nor literalist in its view of Scripture. While forced to separate from the larger Presbyterian church in 1936 for refusing to support its missions board, Machen was a Presbyterian, and his convictions about the church were squarely Reformed though not characterized by the fierce independence or the anti-worldly attitude of many fundamentalists.

Fundamentalism was a populist movement. It often had an anti-intellectualist bias. Even its bright and capable leaders feared the control of academics and other elites. The more conservative exponents of the Reformed faith found themselves in a somewhat lonely place. They shared something with fundamentalism, especially its commitment to first things. But they could not endorse dispensationalism or some of the human-centered appeals to conversion in fundamentalist preaching. At the same time, it was not possible for Reformed people to endorse liberalism or even the Barthian corrective.

Neo-evangelicalism. The other group, developing after the Second World War, is loosely known as neo-evangelicalism. Like fundamentalism, much of it is white and American. Its chief voices were Carl F. H. Henry and Billy Graham. Its principal institutional supports were the National Association of Evangelicals (NAE), Fuller Theological Seminary, and *Christianity Today.* Neo-evangelicalism generally agreed with the great fundamentals of the faith but parted company with fundamentalists over the issue of fellowship. While fundamentalists tended to separate from those not sharing a strict view of doctrinal essentials, neo-evangelicals were willing to work with nonevangelicals. Scholars like E. J. Carnell thought fundamentalism was sectarian and anti-intellectual. He tried to build bridges between the sciences and a Christian worldview. Neo-evangelicalism is moving from its white, North American base into far more ethnically diverse manifestations. There is even an African-American chapter within the NAE. A major step toward opening out was taken at Lausanne in 1974, when the International Congress on World Evangelism gathered to assess the state of the evangelical movement. Under the leadership of John R. W. Stott, a declaration was penned, the Lausanne Covenant, repenting of evangelical indifference to social issues.

Committees were created whose consultations have ensured a truly global identity for evangelicalism. Entities such as the World Evangelical Fellowship (WEF) have helped shape evangelicalism into an ecumenical movement parallel to the World Council of Churches.

Where We Are Today

Today the Reformed faith is truly worldwide. In its different modes, the Reformed outlook has found its way into more cultures and places than any other expression of the Christian faith, including the Roman Catholic tradition. From the outset, the intention and deepest motive of Reformed thinking has been global. Since the Second World War, and now into the twenty-first century, Reformed theology has interacted with numerous world trends. One of them is the continuing process of independence from the West. No longer tied to the civilizing arm of colonial expansion, evangelism and missions have developed an independent character, with national leadership. Missions today are more a partnership than a one-way street.

Every indication points to the shifting center of gravity in the presence and life of the Christian church from the Northern to the Southern Hemisphere. The Reformed churches are no exception. In some cases extraordinary growth has characterized them on various continents, even as they decline in the West. Today, the Reformed churches in Africa, Asia, and Latin America far outnumber the churches of Europe, North America, South Africa, and Oceania. This growth is especially felt in the major cities of the world.

A number of examples prove the point. Brazil is predominantly Roman Catholic, with considerable syncretism with local religions. But the Reformed faith represents close to two million people spread over twenty denominations. Specifically Presbyterian seminaries are functioning well. The astonishing growth of the Reformed churches in Indonesia, Korea, and Nigeria is an outstanding example of this worldwide presence. Today, these three countries host the largest Reformed communities in the world. Presbyterian and Reformed churches in South Korea represent something of a modern miracle story. More than one quarter of the population is Protestant, and most of that number is specifically Reformed. During the Japanese occupation, despite heavy persecution, the Reformed churches showed special strength and courage, leading to rapid growth when peace came. Today these churches have one of the largest missions task forces in the Christian world. One can find their missionaries almost everywhere, including China and Japan. From parts of China, they are able to reach into North Korea, one of the most opaque countries of all.

The story is multiplied in many continents. Protestant and Reformed churches have expanded in extraordinary ways throughout sub-Saharan Africa. The story of South African Reformed churches is better known, but there is an increasing role in Nigeria, Uganda, and many other countries. Recently, the Anglican churches in places like Africa have been able to challenge some of the ethical and doctrinal laxness of the older churches in the North, spelling a new trend in church power. The South is now in a position to minister to the great needs of the North. New versions of theology and creedal statements are coming from the two-thirds world, and in the generations to come they ought to be guiding the rest of the world.

At the same time, while this growth in the South is noteworthy, much of it is so rapid that it lacks depth. Some historians have been predicting the rise of a new Christendom in the Southern Hemisphere, one that may well be unsympathetic to democracy. This is unlikely. But what may happen is that evangelicalism's famous volunteer approach and its focus on conversion may lead the South into considerable pluralism. This can be a good thing, preventing the creation of giant international bureaucracies. But it can be a weakness, as well, because it is individualistic and thus does not foster careful thinking about the transformation of culture. Here, the Reformed approach has a special calling.

Reformed theology has unique experience in formulating matters of faith in multiple contexts. The Western churches, having a certain longevity and having faced modernity, with more or less success, still have something to say to their non-Western partners. And while Reformed theology in the future should by no means be restricted to its Western formulations, even less to its sixteenth- or seventeenth-century documents, it would be absurd to neglect them and reinvent the wheel. Together, then, the churches around the world, particularly the Reformed churches, should address the perennial task of being in the world but not of it. They are to "grow up *in every way* into him who is the head, into Christ, from whom the whole body, joined and held together by every joint with which it is equipped, when each part is working properly, makes the body grow so that it builds itself up in love" (Eph. 4:15–16).

THE FABRIC
OF TRUTH

I AM THAT I AM

~~~~~~~~~~

God's Truth

History shows us how the Reformed faith was born and how it has become worldwide. Having looked at some of those developments, we can now turn our attention to the heart of the matter. What does Reformed theology believe? Where are its doctrines discovered? Here, we sense a great weight of responsibility. It has always been the task of teachers rightly to handle the word of truth. They follow the example of Ezra and his colleagues, who read from the Scripture and also rendered its meaning, so that God's people could understand what was read (Neh. 8:8). The sacred writings can make us wise for salvation through faith in Christ Jesus (2 Tim. 3:15). This means they are profitable for training in righteousness, so that we may be equipped to serve God (2 Tim. 3:16–17). But this is a daunting task. Teachers will be judged with more severity than others (James 3:1). Yet we are jars of clay, Paul reminds us (2 Cor. 4:7).

The task is also daunting because while the occasion for doing theology is the particular historical and cultural circumstance of those who are generating it, the aim of theology is to speak God's truth. The world in the Northern Hemisphere in the twenty-first century is no longer the world of the sixteenth-century Reformation. We are postcolonial, the Cold War is over, human rights are fully recognized by international organizations, we are laden with technology, we face the AIDS pandemic, third-world debt, terrorism. A theology that does not grapple with those realities may have virtue, but it will not be fully Reformed, in that it will not apply the eternal Word to the changing world. At the same time, a theology that does not construct a universal, normative account of God's revelation will be less than good theology. It will have no real authority, because it will ultimately begin from our circumstances and attempt to make sense of God's Word in their light, rather than beginning with God's Word and making sense of the circumstances in its light.

So, we are weak, jars of clay. But we are handling the truth. Our only comfort, then, in setting forth the basics of Reformed theology is that though our weakness is real, it cannot prevent God's light from shining through. Christian doctrine is life-giving because it comes from God. Our Lord promised that his Holy Spirit would guide us into all truth (John 16:13). He does it primarily by illuminating our understanding of the Scriptures, the word of truth that sanctifies us (John 17:17). Accordingly, what follows is an outline of the fundamentals of those truths that sanctify. Clarity, not originality, is the goal. Commendation, not truism, is the aim. This is not meant to be a weighty systematic theology. Yet, may these pages be a faithful rendering of what God has revealed to us. May we, like Timothy, heed Paul's charge to present the truth not as an abstraction but as the consequence of our covenant relation to the triune God: "Follow the pattern of the sound words that you have heard from me, in the faith and love that are in Christ Jesus. By the Holy Spirit who dwells within us, guard the good deposit entrusted to you" (2 Tim. 1:13–14). Much is at stake: nothing less than God's truth.

To Know God and Enjoy Him

"Do not come near; take your sandals off your feet, for the place on which you are standing is holy ground." As we come to consider the central reality of the Christian faith, it is well to remember these words spoken to Moses by the Lord, who appeared to him in a burning bush (Exod. 3:1–6). In ancient cultures, removing one's shoes was the sign of utmost respect for a high dignitary. Here we are in the pres-

ence of far more than a potentate. Indeed, Moses was afraid to show
his face, for fear of looking at God. We are in the presence of the Lord
God, who identified himself to Moses by these words: "I am the God
of your father, the God of Abraham, the God of Isaac, and the God
of Jacob" (v. 6). God is the great *I am*, the Creator of heaven and earth.
But he is also the great Redeemer of Israel, the God of the patriarchs
and of all who believe. In the New Testament times in which we live,
Jesus Christ is the Son of God, the second person of the Trinity, the
true *I am* for the ages, the Redeemer of all his people. And so, before
him, we should take our shoes off our feet, spiritually. The least we
owe to him is the proper fear of reverence.

What distinguishes a specifically Reformed understanding of God
from other versions? Reformed theology states the great principle
already alluded to and states it more fully than others:

> Salvation belongs to the LORD;
> your blessing be on your people! (Ps. 3:8)

The doctrine of God according to Reformed theology gives fullest
honor to his power, his love, and his sovereignty as Creator but especially as Redeemer. And so God's people are provoked to more personal humility and to the greater praise of his name. In discussing
God's nature, then, our aim should always be, less of me and more of
him. Several issues are at stake, the first being the knowledge of God.

Can we know God? Does our knowledge of him fit who he really
is, or is it only an approximation? The question and the answer are at
the core of the Reformed faith.

Can we prove the existence of God? The answer depends on what
is meant by the term *proof*. In a way, everything around us and everything inside us is compelling proof for the reality of God's person. As
Psalm 19:1 reminds us, "The heavens declare the glory of God, and
the sky proclaims his handiwork." As one French astronomer put it,
"The universe bristles with intelligence." Even the negative parts of
the world declare God. Romans 1–2 is a study of the way in which
something has gone terribly wrong with the world precisely because
there is a God whom we know but walk away from in a thousand ways.

It argues that evil is a confirmation that God is and that he holds us accountable. The most fundamental reason we can know God, though, is that we are his image-bearers, we are like him, and he does get through by his revelation (Gen. 1:26–27). The essence of being God's image is the knowledge of God, so that knowledge of anything is possible only because we know God.

This is not to say we can demonstrate the existence of God by a logical or even emotional or aesthetic necessity, starting from a neutral platform and moving inevitably upward, from this world to himself.[1] But, still, we know God. We know the God who is. We know him truly, without reservation or equivocation. We know him because everything around us and inside us speaks eloquently of him. We know him because by him we know all that we need to know about him! As Francis Schaeffer used to put it, "God is *there*." But that is something far richer and more meaningful than existence.

Even though we are darkened in our understanding, yet we still see God. The whole world bears his imprint. Everything proves him! We, as God's image-bearers, are uniquely endowed with the knowledge of God. Our knowledge of God is so true, so direct, that it is as though we had seen him. For unbelievers, this knowledge of God is not comfortable. Yet it is nevertheless real and full (Rom. 1:18–25).

God is, of course, invisible. He is not a creature that we should see him. Yet, by becoming a man, he made himself visible. To John, for

---

1. The typically medieval reasoning process, such as Thomas Aquinas's so-called cosmological argument, begins with a certain fact connected to this world, such as motion or cause and effect, and moves upward in a logical chain to an unmoved mover, or a first cause. In other words, the argument begins with a given, an observable set of data that everyone is meant to recognize without any special warrant; then it builds on that and arrives at God. The difficulty is fourfold. First, is this set of data truly self-evident? Is the world correctly understood as being in motion or as having cause and effect? Why could things not be simply held together in a steady state, without a causal relation? Causality turns out to be a most ambiguous and fragile idea. Second, why does there need to be a regression back to an unmoved mover or a first cause? Who is to say there could not simply be an infinite chain of motion or of causality? Third, the God one demonstrates from this kind of argument has little to do with the personal God of the Bible. There is an enormous difference between a principle, like an unmoved mover or a first cause, and Yahweh, the Lord who is Father, Son, and Holy Spirit. Finally, of what real interest is a god who merely exists?

example, he was so accessible that he has no problem explaining that he saw the glory of God: "And the Word became flesh and dwelt among us, and we have seen his glory, glory as of the only Son from the Father, full of grace and truth" (John 1:14). The reality of seeing God was confirmed by Jesus, who reminded his doubting apostles that "whoever has seen me has seen the Father" (John 14:9).

Today, we do not see God in Christ. Yet the essence of what the apostles had received is replicated by us, who know God. We can love him without needing to see him. "Though you have not seen him, you love him," the apostle Peter tells his believing readers (1 Peter 1:8). Such understanding is not achieved by unaided human reason but by God's gift. John explains, "And we know that the Son of God has come and has given us understanding, so that we may know him who is true" (1 John 5:20).

What an amazing thought! We can know God and love him, even though he is incomprehensible. His greatness is unsearchable (Ps. 145:3). His understanding is beyond our measure (Ps. 147:5). The knowledge God has of himself and of this world is so great that no one can fathom it (Ps. 139:6; Rom. 11:33–36). But, still, we can indeed know him truly. It would be false humility to claim otherwise, for he has experienced enormous suffering in order to make himself known. We know him truly but not exhaustively. Incomprehensibility is not an attribute of God. It is a limit to human knowledge of the Godhead. Surely that is what Paul means when he says, "[God] alone . . . dwells in unapproachable light, whom no one has ever seen or can see" (1 Tim. 6:16). It cannot mean that we have no knowledge of God or any sight of him, as we have just discussed. It means, rather, that he is so far removed from our ways that we cannot equate our ways with his, our knowledge with his; we cannot exhaust him.[2]

---

2. The best way to put this, then, is to say we know God by analogy: not by approximation but by thinking his thoughts after him, in the mode of the creature. We can know him by depending on him. We do not simply know about God, but we know God. But we know him as grateful servants. Sometimes what he tells us makes sense to our human rationality. Sometimes we cannot find the formula that would explain seemingly contradictory data. For example, he tells us to pray. But he also tells us he is utterly in control. On the surface, these do not compute. In human terms we have a contradiction. But in God's logic it makes perfect sense. So we live with his sover-

The Being of God

A second major concern for Reformed theology is about God's being. Debates about the existence of God are always a bit misleading. God is not some principle that exists. He is a person, with a name, a character, and a purpose. One of the dangers of ancient Greek philosophy was to make God into a sort of universal soul, a being higher and fuller than any other. For human beings this meant worshiping a being greater than any other. Following a theory known as imitation, artists and moralists tried to imitate the lofty principles of divine harmony and perfection connected to this being. What is wrong with this theory? The effect was to make the divine being somehow dependent on our own world. If he (or it) is merely the best, or the most, then he is still a part of the creation, or perhaps the creation is a part of him, which amounts to pantheism.

Instead, the Bible presents God as having characteristics not merely better or even opposite but ones that are utterly different, transcendent in relation to the creature. There are two kinds of being: God's being and created being. The author of the letter to the Hebrews puts it powerfully: "For whoever would draw near to God must believe that he exists [he is; the Greek word is *estin*] and that he rewards those who seek him" (Heb. 11:6).

Sometimes it is helpful to use the language of comparison, because that is the only language we have. So we call God infinite, eternal, immutable, immense, omnipotent, and so forth. To be infinite is to be not finite, to be eternal is to be not temporal, and so on. These are sometimes called God's incommunicable attributes, because no creature could possess them. Yet in a way, all of God's attributes are incommunicable, because none can really be shared with the creature. God is God. But now comes the amazing counterpart. While God is utterly removed from the creation and thus transcendent, he is nevertheless at the same time intimately connected to it and thus immanent. He is here with us, closer to the world than any part of the world. How can he be

---

eignty and our responsibility. It does make sense that we should not be able to reduce God to human proportions, even though we know him and love him.

transcendent and immanent at the same time? There is a great mystery here. God is God. His greatness is so great that he can condescend to the level of the creature without lessening his divinity. The Westminster Confession of Faith puts it this way: "He is the fountain of all being, of whom, through whom, and to whom, are all things" (2.2).

In the account of God's meeting with Moses in Exodus 3, Moses asks God by what name he should be known. The Lord instructs him to tell the people of Israel that "I am" has sent him on his mission to leave Egypt's land and its bondage. The Hebrew word here contains four letters, which we call the Tetragram: *JHWH*. When God gave this name, saying, "I AM WHO I AM" (Exod. 3:14), he was reminding them that they already knew him: I am what I have always been to you. But in later Judaism a tradition developed whereby it was forbidden to speak the divine name for fear of profaning a holy being. The written Hebrew language does not have vowels, and so pronunciation was a matter of oral tradition. But in the case of the Tetragram, the word could never be pronounced, and so we do not know what the appropriate vowels are. In English, we sometimes say Yahweh or Jehovah, but this is based on guesswork.

There is something appropriate about this tradition. We dare not become casually familiar with God or come to him in a cavalier way. Modern evangelical Christians sometimes talk of God as though he were a pal or a buddy. God is lofty, removed, far above the creation:

> Thus says the LORD, the King of Israel
>   and his Redeemer, the LORD of hosts:
> "I am the first and I am the last;
>   besides me there is no god.
> Who is like me? Let him proclaim it." (Isa. 44:6–7)

The Scripture abounds with such statements of God's otherness, his completeness.

Still, something important is lost in the Jewish tradition of fearing to pronounce his name. God is a person, and he does have a name. We do know him, and we even have personal communion with him at the deepest level. Not only would he not hide his name from us or make himself inaccessible, but also he has deliberately told us his name, so that we may know him personally. In Christ, he is fully revealed.

So God is wholly other, or transcendent, and wholly present, or immanent. If we forget his transcendence, we become either pantheistic or cavalier. If we forget his immanence, we become deists, and, in the manner of Islam, God becomes distant, fatalistic, and impersonal. Instead, according to biblical faith, he is both. He is, as the hymn puts it, our "Creator, redeemer and friend."

God's Moral Attributes

Third, Reformed theology wants to know who God is, what his qualities are. What can we say about God's character (for God and his character are one and the same)? How may we adequately speak of God and describe him intelligibly? No human system can possibly match the matchless greatness of God. Yet, we still may attempt to put God's attributes into some kind of order for clarity's sake. We shall begin with three, sometimes known as God's moral attributes. They are overlapping qualities presented directly in the Bible as the essential divine features. Their most succinct statement is from the apostle John, though proclaimed throughout.

God Is a Spirit

What does it mean to say that God is a Spirit (John 4:24)? For one thing, it means he has no body. He is incorporeal, without material parts. As the Westminster Confession puts it, God is "a most pure spirit, invisible, without body, parts, or passions" (2.1). That God is without a physical nature is fairly straightforward. But what does it mean to say he is without passions? It does not mean that God has no feelings, for he is a divine person. What it signifies is that nothing outside of him can induce fear or guilt or even regret in him, as though he were a human being.

There is much more. The Greek word used for "spirit" is *pneuma*. It has an onomatopoetic value (try saying the word, and it makes you force breath out of your mouth). It is the same for the Hebrew word *ruach*, the Old Testament equivalent. Often in the Bible, the word *ruach* is used to describe moving air, even a strong wind or a storm. If God is a Spirit in this sense, it means he is an active, powerful agent, one who accomplishes his purposes. At the opening of Genesis, the Spirit of God is active over the creation, hovering over it like an eagle, noisily hovering over its young (Gen. 1:2; Deut. 32:10–11). The Spirit is life-giving (Ps. 104:30; Job 33:4). He is, in the words of Sinclair B. Ferguson, a "governing presence."[3] God is present by and because of his Spirit in the life of Israel (Ezek. 39:29). The Spirit enables men and women to have wisdom, even to fashion works of art (Num. 11:25; Exod. 31:3–4; Eph. 1:17). The Spirit of God anoints his messengers to preach liberty to the oppressed and jubilation to the poor (Luke 4:18–19).

God Is Light

John proclaims as his message that "God is light" and adds, "and in him is no darkness at all" (1 John 1:5). The contrast is between God's light and human darkness, described as unrighteousness and not walking in the truth. God is necessarily and eternally righteous. He *is* truth. Often, the Bible uses parallel terms for these virtues. One of them is holiness. To be holy means two things. It means to be removed, or other. In God's case, it means to be utterly transcendent, in an altogether different mode of being from the creation (1 Tim. 6:16). But it also means to be pure, without evil. God's moral righteousness is more than simply a detached goodness. His holy righteousness is active, incapable of tolerating anything contrary to its demands. Ferguson captures it well: "God's holiness is the searing purity of his eternal and infinite being."[4]

God is called the "Father of lights" by the apostle James (James 1:17). James is describing the way God sends his good gifts upon his people. He wants them to stand firm during trials. The contrast is with those who claim that when they accomplish evil it is because God tempts them. But this is not possible, for God does not change,

---

3. Sinclair B. Ferguson, *The Holy Spirit* (Downers Grove, Ill.: InterVarsity, 1996), 21.
4. Ibid., 16.

and therefore he cannot go back on his good intentions. James adds, by way of explanation, that with God "there is no variation or shadow due to change." Perhaps quoting from Malachi 3:6, James is reinforcing the truth that God's good purposes for his people are as secure as his own unchangeable nature. When God promises redemption, he puts his character on the line. Such is his righteousness that, like the eternally pure light that he is, his salvation will be accomplished.

A point of clarification is in order. While God is necessarily pure and righteous, not everything he does is motivated by that necessity. For example, he did not plan redemption because his righteousness required it. That would be a denial of the amazing grace of the gospel, which is not driven by necessity but is sparked by the Lord's compassion. To be sure, the plan of salvation does exhibit God's holy righteousness. Indeed, it reveals new depths of his holiness that might not otherwise be revealed. But God's righteousness is simply who he is.

God Is Love

The third biblical statement about God's attributes takes us to the richest characteristic of all. "God is love," John tells us (1 John 4:8). The passage is a carefully wrought instruction about assurance and the authenticity of faith. John's definition of divine love depends on demonstrating God's great initiative in achieving the salvation of humankind through the sacrificial work of his Son, Jesus Christ, on the cross. The initiative is God's; hence our assurance that we know and believe this God-centered love. Because of that we too ought to love others. Yet, no more than the gift of his righteousness is God's saving love a necessity. God is love, it is true. But that love, which is a part of his being, great as it may be, does not make bestowing mercy on the human race an obligation for him. At the same time, his redemptive love does show us something of the depth of his capacity for love. And it tells us something about what love is.

God's love is free and it is sovereign. The best-known text in the Bible surely testifies to this extraordinary love: "For God so loved the world that he gave his only Son, that whoever believes in him should not perish but have eternal life" (John 3:16). In a way, we would be hard put to go any further than this. We have an ultimate. Yet, we can say a few things about this love of God that help to characterize it. First, it is a self-motivated love, originating in nothing or no one else than God. There is no other factor than God's good pleasure that motivates his love. Second, it is a particular love, though originating in eternity. Commenting on the great sovereignty of God's love, the apostle Paul praises his grace and joins love to election: "In love he predestined us for adoption through Jesus Christ, according to the purpose of his will" (Eph. 1:4–5). Third, the love of God for his people is a compassionate and selfless love, one that sets its heart on unlovely, rebellious creatures. And fourth, it is an extravagant love, a love that searches out its objects until they are found, a love that requires the sacrifice of himself on the cross, a love that adopts them into his family and gives them joy forever. Before such a God, one can only sing with amazement, "What wondrous love is this, oh my soul, oh my soul?"

God's Transcendental Attributes

The reason these basic three attributes are called moral ones is that they show some analogies with human moral attributes. We know something of what it means to be spiritual, to be pure and good, and to have love. Traditionally these moral attributes are distinguished from the rest, which are called transcendental, or metaphysical, because they refer to God's unique power and divinity. In the end, none of God's attributes are comparable to ours, because he is the holy Creator and we are creatures. But the transcendental attributes focus on those qualities that are particularly inimitable. What are they? The list is extensible, appropriately so, in that God cannot be reduced to a series of carefully enumerated traits. For convenience, though, one could list five metaphysical attributes.[5]

5. We follow, with some variation, Herman Bavinck's basic enumeration of the incommunicable attributes. See Herman Bavinck, *Our Reasonable Faith: A Survey of Christian Doctrine*, trans. Henry Zylstra (Grand Rapids: Eerdmans, 1956), 136.

God Is Independent

Nothing is behind God. Nothing determines how he will act or what he may think. By contrast, all creatures are dependent, no matter how powerful they may seem. God alone is independent.

Near Mars Hill, where the apostle Paul was urged to explain the Christian faith, were a series of altars to the gods, and even one to an "unknown god." One of Paul's arguments against the idolatry of his Athenian audience was this: "The God who made the world and everything in it, being Lord of heaven and earth, does not live in temples made by man, nor is he served by human hands, as though he needed anything, since he himself gives to all mankind life and breath and everything" (Acts 17:24–25). His logic is simple and compelling. Since God made everything, nothing in our ideas about him should give the impression that he has needs, as a creature might.

In another argument, in a different setting, the apostle reflects on God's control over history. After explaining how Jew and Gentile, despite the estrangement of each from God and each other, are included in the plan of salvation, Paul stops to thank God:

> Oh, the depth of the riches and wisdom and knowledge of God! How unsearchable are his judgments and how inscrutable his ways!

And then, to add tonality to his doxology, he quotes from Isaiah (Isa. 40:13), the prophet whose voice is woven into the fabric of the epistle:

> For "who has known the mind of the Lord
>   or who has been his counselor?"
> Or "who has given a gift to him that he might be repaid?"

Then Paul concludes his doxology with words that could serve as the hymn of Reformed theology:

> For from him and through him and to him are all things. To him be glory forever. Amen. (Rom. 11:36)

To put it far more prosaically, God is independent of all human design and purpose. The idea of giving God counsel is as foolish as supposing he were not self-sufficient. He has all the depth and riches in himself.

An adjunct to God's independency is his omnipotence. God is all-powerful. This is why the Apostles' Creed begins with the statement, "I believe in God, the Father almighty," and follows with, "Maker of heaven and earth." This great power of God is not always well understood. Children sometimes ask whether God could create a rock so heavy that he could not lift it! They imagine an insuperable conflict within the notion of omnipotence. But the answer is no. God is all-powerful, but not to achieve things contrary to his nature. The idea of a creature that could be stronger than he is an absurdity. To be created means precisely to be dependent. The wonder of his power is that he could create anything, make a world with real significance and meaning, and still be in total control of it.

We need to pause here over a delicate issue. If God is all-powerful, then must he not have created evil? According to certain deterministic philosophies, like Islam, God is the author of evil, because his omnipotence is a bare fact, without any conditions. Because evil exists, God must have made it, as he did everything else, so the argument goes. The problem with this view is that it defines power in a raw, mechanical way. A more biblical way is to think of God's power as emanating from his whole character, that is, his person, together with his total design for the world. Simply because of principle, God could never create an evil force that contradicted his light and his love. On every page of the Bible, God condemns evil. He is nothing if not unremittingly against it. Well, then, what about his omnipotence? True, if he is all-powerful, then evil must somehow have been purposed by him. It must fit his good purposes, though we cannot say how. He is not the author of evil. Evil can never be anything less than repugnant to God. There is mystery here. The way around it, though, cannot be to diminish God's omnipotence. It is best to say he is so powerful that he can include evil in his plan without in any way being guilty of it.

God Is Unchangeable

Seasons change. The tides rise and fall. Human beings go through life cycles; they learn and change their minds. But God is not subject to change. Psalm 102, which pleads for God's mercy in prayer, extols him as unchangeable in the face of a changing and unstable world:

> Of old you laid the foundation of the earth,
>   and the heavens are the work of your hands.
> They will perish, but you will remain;
>   they will all wear out like a garment.
> You will change them like a robe, and they will pass away,
>   but you are the same, and your years have no end.
>   (vv. 25–27)

From this certainty of God's immutability, the psalmist concludes with confidence:

> The children of your servants shall dwell secure;
>   their offspring shall be established before you. (v. 28)

Like every one of God's attributes, this one is not an abstract feature of a faraway deity but is meant to comfort God's people with the assurance that he will not go back on his promises or deny his faithfulness. In the lines from Lamentations, which have been metricized into a familiar hymn, Jeremiah renders the same truth:

> The steadfast love of the LORD never ceases;
>   his mercies never come to an end;
> they are new every morning;
>   great is your faithfulness. (Lam. 3:22–23)

Unlike the creature, then, who is subject to whims and fancies, God never changes (James 1:17).

Here is another delicate issue. What are we to make of the many places in Scripture that suggest God does change his mind? Passages such as Genesis 6:6 tell us that God saw human evil and was sorry he had made humankind, so he determined to blot out humanity in judgment. Other ones, such as Genesis 18:22–33, suggest that God is open to Abraham's pleading for the inhabitants of Sodom. God had told Abraham he would "go down and see," in terms that sound quite human, whether the rumor of their evil was true (Gen. 18:21). And then Abraham bargains for mercy, pleading that if there were only fifty righteous, on down to ten, could God not spare them? And God agrees. And what of places that describe God's patience, his desire that no one perish, his pleas with many people that they should return to him and be faithful? These texts make it sound as though God were somehow dependent on the world, on its history, on the choices of men and women, for his decisions.

How can such descriptions be reconciled with God's unchangeableness? Once again, we are faced with mystery. It is a mystery the advocates of so-called openness theology are not willing to concede. What they typically maintain is that God does change. He does not always accomplish everything according to his immutable plan. He waits to see what the creature will do. Thus, he is ignorant to some degree. Such notions begin with a good intention: refusing to believe in a God who is deterministic but affirming one who is compassionate, able to come alongside suffering believers because their trials are not programmed. Yet, this gives up too much. It is far better to continue to affirm that God does not change. At the same time, we can say, without fear of running into any final contradiction, that God's world is real, that his creatures are significant and make binding choices. When God is said to change his mind, it is real enough. But he does so in his covenant relationship to the creature, which is a true and meaningful relationship; yet he does this without any change in his attributes or in his decrees. His attributes converge so that he is at once immutable and also intimately and personally related to his creatures.

In this setting, prayer becomes truly meaningful. One could ask, why should we pray, when God knows what we are going to ask and has already determined what he will do about the request? Put in this way, the question is hard to answer. But consider another way of putting it. When our Lord commented on prayer, he used this doctrine in order to show us the depth of what human prayer could mean. In the Sermon on the Mount he tells his followers, "Your Father knows what you need before you ask him" (Matt. 6:8). He is not answering a question about why pray but about how to pray and with what attitude. Hypocrites pray with loud voices and empty phrases, because they have only a human audience (Matt. 6:5–7). But believers can and must pray sincerely, often in secret, not caring who hears the prayer, except for one: the Father. Why does the Father want to hear our prayers? Because they are of the essence of our relation to him. Because prayer really does change things, since through our friendship with the Lord, we are granted the true status of children. We then will know the privileges and blessings of sons and daughters of the living God, who loves to hear and honor our requests. And because he is unchangeable, he will accomplish these things for us.

God Is Simple

The doctrine that God is simple has been controversial. On the surface, it may sound as though God were some sort of pure essence, with no characteristics. This is unacceptable, given what we have already said about his many attributes. What is behind the idea, though, is that God is not a compound. He is not Spirit plus something else. He is not part Creator, part creature. Nor does his thought require any sort of process, the way ours does. God's reason and his will are one. He does not have to think something through, weighing the options, before acting. What he has, he also is. As Cornelius Van Til puts it, his being and knowledge are coterminous. One could say this of all his attributes: his being and attributes are the same. God is pure light, with no darkness (1 John 1:5). He has pure life, because he is life (John 5:26). He is the fountain of life necessarily, because of who he is (Ps. 36:9).

The doctrine of simplicity is meant to describe two truths. The first is that of God's noncomposite nature. The second is of his unity. There is one God, and only one. At the opening of the Ten Commandments, God's people are told, "You shall have no other gods before me" (Exod. 20:3; cf. Deut. 5:7). Literally, the Hebrew text reads, "You shall have no other gods before my face." There is no room for any but one God, since everything that occurs is subject to his gaze. The great appeal to Israel known as the Shema calls God's people to affirm his simplicity: "Hear, O Israel: the LORD our God, the LORD is one" (Deut. 6:4). This becomes interesting in discussions of the Trinity, for, according to a trinitarian understanding of God, there are three persons, three centers of consciousness, in the Godhead. What happens to the doctrine of simplicity in that case? There is no real conflict. Even though God is three, at the same time he is also one. Thus, even though in three persons, he is nevertheless still one person. His triunity does not contradict his simplicity.

God Is Eternal

These different attributes harmonize. To say that God is eternal means that in a particular way he is outside of time. The first verse of the Bible says it powerfully: "In the beginning, God" (Gen. 1:1). It goes on to say that God created the heavens and the earth. The Hebrew word for creating, *bara*, means to bring into existence. In traditional theological terms we sometimes hear the phrase "out of nothing." This may be a helpful way of saying that God did not make the world out of any preexisting stuff, whether spiritual or material. And he did not create from his own being. Yet, even the idea of nothing should not be construed to mean any particular reality. God is; and creation happened. There are two kinds of beings, God and creation. They are absolutely separate and different. Sometimes the term *universe* is used to describe all of reality, including God and the creation. That, too, can be useful, and yet the danger is present of thinking of the two as somehow one.

God is eternal, whereas the creation has time. Time is one of the features of the created world. Again, we do not quite know how a timeless God relates to a time-bound world. We can state both truths and find a mystery there. In more biblical terms, we might speak of the great attribution of God as "I am." The "I am" relates to his creatures, not by emptying itself of divinity but by stating the two realities together. As Jesus reminded his critics, "Truly, truly, I say to you, before Abraham was, I am" (John 8:58). By the same token we can derive great comfort from God's eternity. One of the most moving pieces of

Hebrew poetry is Psalm 90, attributed to Moses, leading the people wandering in the desert. While the people of Israel are suffering for their sins and are experiencing God's judgment, nevertheless Moses derives great comfort from the God of eternity. And so he begins his prayer with the strongest statement of God's timelessness:

> Lord, you have been our dwelling place
>   in all generations.
> Before the mountains were brought forth,
>   or ever you had formed the earth and the world,
>   from everlasting to everlasting you are God. (Ps. 90:1–2)

In rational terms, it boggles the mind to compare God's timelessness with the security of his person as a dwelling place in space and in time. Yet, that is exactly what we have here. God can be the most secure dwelling place for his people precisely because he is everlasting and not bound to the frailties of human time and history.

God Is Omnipresent

Finally, we may speak of God's omnipresence. God is there. But he is also here. God is transcendent, and yet he is immanent. "Where shall I go from your Spirit," asks the psalmist David, "or where shall I flee from your presence?" (Ps. 139:7). The entire psalm is a beautiful description of the knowledge of God, who by his presence in the world, even in its deepest parts, is immanent. God is closer to the smallest details of the creation, from its energy types to the theoretical strings that may hold things together, than those details are to themselves. This truth renders the idea of a search for God promising, if only we can know how to look. In his speech to the Athenians, Paul goes on to quote one of the familiar Greek poets to prove his point about God's omnipresence:

> In him we live and move and have our being.[6]

6. An excerpt from Aratus's poem "Phainomena."

The reality of God's presence is so evident that even the pagan poets of antiquity were well aware of it.

God's presence in the world is not an abstract idea of the relation of two beings. It is an active notion. Paul describes the second person of the Trinity in this way: "And he is before all things, and in him all things hold together" (Col. 1:17). God, in the person of his Son, so knits the world together that nothing has any meaning apart from him, because nothing subsists without his active power. Further, it is an intelligent power, full of purpose. The author of the Hebrews puts it this way: "[The Son] upholds the universe by the word of his power" (Heb. 1:3). Again, this doctrine is revealed for our benefit. Everything about the creation, from its beauty to its history to human significance, is assured because God is here.

The Trinity

The final consideration of God's nature takes us into the most precious of all Christian doctrines, the divine Trinity. Again, we should remember we are standing on holy ground. As Herman Bavinck so beautifully reminds us in the tenth chapter of *Our Reasonable Faith*, God reveals himself more richly and vitally in his Trinity than in the divine attributes. Before the trinitarian God we must remain childlike in a spirit of adoration and wonder. We do not have here a human construction, nor do we have the crafty systematics of the church. We have . . . God. The Apostles' Creed does not begin, "I conclude the following about God," but "I believe in God," a God who is Father, Son, and Holy Spirit.[7]

God is one. Yet he is not a characterless monad. He is three. From abundant biblical data, the church has come to name him the Trinity. Far from being an abstract solution to complex data, the Trinity is of the essence of who God is. It is in the Trinity that we understand the fullness of his attributes, for they express themselves in the Father, the Son, and the Holy Spirit. This is so much the case that we cannot

7. Bavinck, *Our Reasonable Faith*, 143–44.

rightly know God unless we know him in his triune essence. Reformed theology wants to do full justice to the presentation of what is an unfathomable mystery.

It is tempting to say that God revealed himself first as one and then, only in later times, as three. When confronting the pagan views of Near Eastern religions, the Old Testament needed to assert God's uniqueness. The term *monotheistic* is perfectly appropriate to set the biblical God apart from the polytheism of many religions. But even at the earliest stages of revelation we see important evidences of the Trinity. To be sure, a full understanding of the three persons does come progressively, and it comes fully only in the New Testament. Yet we have many indications of the Trinity from the earliest times.

From early times, the divine name *Elohim* is in the plural. Sometimes God speaks in a plural way, as he did when he created humankind in his own image: "Let us make man in our image, after our likeness" (Gen. 1:26). There is more than a hint of the Trinity in the call of Isaiah. When God addresses him, he asks, "Whom shall I send, and who will go for us?" (Isa. 6:8). But more significantly, the Lord revealed himself as covered by three pairs of angels, who sing out, "Holy, holy, holy is the LORD of hosts," a threefold song of adoration. Similarly, when God tells Aaron to bless the people of Israel, he shows him a threefold benediction:

> The LORD bless you and keep you;
> the LORD make his face to shine upon you and be gracious to
>   you;
> the LORD lift up his countenance upon you and give you peace.
>   (Num. 6:24–26)

Furthermore, he adds that such a blessing is a way to put God's own name on the people. One name—three words of blessing.

The angel of the Lord is often a prefiguration of the incarnate Son. When God calls Abraham out of the heavens and tells him to give up his son Isaac, while he goes willingly, there is a marvelous reversal of the story (Gen. 22:1–14). God then calls Abraham a second time, but as the angel of the Lord, who rewards Abraham's faith, saying, "because [he had] obeyed my voice" (Gen. 22:15–18). So there is God, and then there is the angel of the Lord, who speaks as God. The angel often accompanies Israel throughout its trials. He is a divine warrior, and he is a savior (Exod. 3:2; 13:21; 23:20; Num. 20:16; Pss. 34:7; 35:5). The second person of the Trinity has thus shown himself before the incarnation.

The Spirit of the Lord is also often revealed in the Old Testament in various tasks. For example, he hovers over the waters of the world at the dawn of creation (Gen. 1:2). The Spirit descends on the judges alongside Moses, giving them wisdom and understanding (Num. 11:17, 25). He leads his people in the ways of the Lord (Isa. 63:9–12). So characteristic of God's presence is the reality of his Spirit that David asks that he not be taken away from him (Ps. 51:11).

In the New Testament we have the full revelation of the Trinity. It could be argued that the crucial events of redemption are trinitarian: the plan of salvation from all eternity, the forgiveness of sins through the atonement, and the renewal of God's people through his good gifts. The Father conceived the plan of salvation by his love, the Son executed the plan by his faithfulness even unto death, and the Holy Spirit was poured out upon God's people as a gift. Throughout the work of Jesus Christ on earth, there is trinitarian activity. Christ's conception is a gift of the Father through the power of the Holy Spirit (Matt. 1:20; Luke 1:35). His baptism is attested by the voice of the Father from heaven and the descent of the dove-like Spirit (Matt. 3:16–17). His death is an offering to God in the Spirit (Heb. 9:14).

Apostolic theology makes a good deal of the way redemption is rooted in the Trinity. For example, John compares Christ with the Word. In the most famous opening words of his Gospel, he relates the Son's eternal status to his work of redemption on earth. First, he goes back into eternity:

> In the beginning was the Word, and the Word was with God, and the Word was God. He was in the beginning with God. All things were made through him, and without him was not anything made that was made. (John 1:1–2)

Then he completes the parallel in the temporal realm:

> And the Word became flesh and dwelt among us, and we have
> seen his glory, glory as of the only Son from the Father, full of
> grace and truth. (John 1:14)

Not only is the Son as Word eternally the Son, but also he is the Word
incarnate, come to speak truth and give life to men and women. John
favors this metaphor and uses it again in his first letter (1 John 1:1–2)
and again in the Book of the Revelation (Rev. 19:13). One reason for
its use is that Jesus Christ is the final revelation, thus, a word from
God, one that originates in the Godhead itself.

The apostle Paul also likes to draw the analogy between the Son
in the eternal Trinity and the Son in redemption. In Colossians 1, he
builds a powerful equivalency between Christ as the firstborn of creation in terms of his status and Christ as the firstborn of the dead in
the resurrection (Col. 1:15–20). Just as he is the one by whom and for
whom every facet of the world came into being, so he is the one through
whom all things are reconciled. The love and honor that exist between
the Father and the Son and that were exhibited in the work of salvation did not originate in human history but outside of time, in the way
things are.

It is the same with the Holy Spirit. He is a separate center of consciousness (1 Cor. 12:11). He has equal status with the Father and
the Son (Heb. 9:14; 1 Cor. 12:4–6; John 3:3). He is sent by the Father
and the Son into the world to teach it, to intercede for God's people,
and to endow the church with renewing gifts (Rev. 2:17; John 14:26;
Rom. 8:27; Eph. 1:13–14; Gal. 3:14; 5:5, 25). The eternal Trinity is
thus altogether involved in our redemption, each person with his own
calling. Aaron's blessing can now be translated into the trinitarian
blessing: "The grace of the Lord Jesus Christ and the love of God and
the fellowship of the Holy Spirit be with you all" (2 Cor. 13:14). And
just as God put his threefold name on his ancient people Israel (Num.
6:24–27), so now his people in the church are baptized into the Father,
the Son, and the Holy Spirit (Matt. 28:19). "In other words, just as

all things are *of* the Father and *through* the Son, they all exist and rest *in* the Spirit."[8]

The Christian church did not come to formulate the doctrine of the Trinity easily or rapidly. While the one God in three persons emerges from the pages of Scripture, as we have seen, arriving at a faithful articulation required serious prayer and serious debate. Put simply, the challenge was to avoid two equal and opposite temptations. The first is monism, that is, God's oneness trumps his threeness. His unity is thus prior to any diversity. Many forms of this distortion exist. One is called modalism, because it is held that there is one God with three faces, or modes. Islam is a sort of radical modalism, because it denies any real deity to the Son and the Spirit. The other error is the opposite. It holds that the three persons are separate entities, tied together only by a certain commonality. A common form of this view is known as tritheism. This view surfaces when one person is elevated at the expense of the other two. For example, in radical Pentecostalism, the Holy Spirit is isolated from the Son and the Father.

The people of God are called constantly to guard against these two errors and maintain both the unity and the diversity of the Godhead. As reflections on God's triunity progressed down through the centuries, language had to be found that could do justice to the biblical data. God's being was described as an essence, whereas his trinitarian nature was described as persons. The term *person* began to be understood as a substantial reality, a center of consciousness, not simply an aspect of the divine essence. Improving on the insight of the Cappadocian Fathers, the Reformers believed that the essence of God was not so important as the persons of the Godhead. The three persons, Father, Son, and Holy Spirit, are equal in every respect. While the Nicene Creed refers to the Son as "begotten, not made," no intention of lowering the Son (subordination) should be implied. Likewise, when the creed speaks of the Spirit as one "who proceeds from the Father and the Son," no idea of inferiority is implied. As B. B. Warfield

8. Ibid., 155.

puts it, each person in the Trinity is *autotheos*, that is, God in his own right, not merely by appointment.[9]

There are differences in the nature of the three persons, however: not differences in status but differences in function. The Father is the source for deity, the Son is "begotten" (whatever that might mean in eternity), and the Spirit is the bond of unity for the Godhead. These differences are sometimes known as the economical Trinity, because they represent different gifts, as we humans might display the stewardship (economics) of gifts. It contrasts with the ontological Trinity, which refers to God's being. The economical Trinity helps us understand the persons' different roles in the accomplishment of redemption. The Father sent the Son, not vice versa. The Son became a man, still one person but with a human nature added to his divine nature. Thus, the Son died on the cross, not the Father or the Spirit. The Holy Spirit brings the benefits of redemption to the people of God, he draws them to the Son, he causes the new birth, he dwells within his church. Having said all this, and to repeat, there is no hierarchy in the ontological Trinity. Each person is in a voluntary relation to the other. Each person is joined to the other by love. Not only that, but to see God is to see all three persons at once. Each person is a complete manifestation of God's being.[10]

It may well be that the Trinity, with its perfect unity and diversity, is a good model for certain issues confronting human life and life in the church. The unity of the Godhead reminds us of the essential equality among human beings. Women are neither less important nor lesser creatures made in God's image than are men. Children are not lower than adults. All were created from Adam, and so all are one. At the same time, the diversity of the Godhead reminds us that we are not a lowest-common-denominator blend. There are offices and ranks as well as gifts and privileges not shared across the board. Significantly, societies in which Christian faith has been a strong influence will tend

9. B. B. Warfield, "Calvin's Doctrine of the Trinity," in *Calvin and Augustine* (Philadelphia: Presbyterian and Reformed, 1956), 251, 272–74.

10. The technical term for the full equality of the persons is *perichoresis*, or *co-inherence*, meaning every attribute fully belongs to each of the persons: the Father is omnipotent, the Son is omnipotent, the Spirit is omnipotent (Col. 2:9).

to respect differing points of view and will separate religious institutions from other legitimate sectors of society with more liberty than do societies in which true diversity is not an ultimate.

Great caution must be exercised here. We are on holy ground. We will have to be careful not to make equations where they are not warranted. For example, to make an analogy between the human body, soul, and spirit and the Trinity is misguided at best. To derive an entire social program from the Trinity is dubious. To resolve fundamental philosophical problems by repairing to the Trinity can be speculative. Along with our caution, however, great freedom ought to characterize our love for the Trinity and our faith in the triune God. Above all, this amazing doctrine, which is at the heart of all of theology, ought to cause us to bow down and worship. God has put his triune name upon us, so that truly the grace of the Lord Jesus Christ and the love of God and the fellowship of the Holy Spirit constitute our deepest identity. In return, we glorify God and enjoy him forever.

THE FRUITFUL LAND
WAS A DESERT

~~~~~~~~~~

Divine Revelation

We have begun to know about our God, the holy Trinity, in his power and divinity. Everything begins with him. And everything is accomplished in him. As we explore the contours of Reformed theology, we may move from an understanding of who God is, to an understanding of how this God we have been describing relates to his creatures. A central concern of the Reformed outlook is to make sure our relationship with God is not based on speculation or human construction. If we want to know God and to be known by him, then we are dependent on his revelation if we want to get it right. What is revelation, and what does it tell us?

There is no single way to summarize it, no one formula that says it best. A most helpful way to summarize the information given to us by revelation, however, is the one suggested earlier, dear to the Reformed faith: the three-part synopsis, creation–fall–redemption. We appropriately call the triad a Christian worldview because it aims to be comprehensive, not fragmentary. Many believers today look at religion in piecemeal fashion. For many, religion is a particular experience, one that varies in intensity depending on the circumstances. In church or reading the Bible, they may feel especially spiritual. In other parts of life, the feeling may not be so strong. For example, at the workplace, there may be little connection with spiritual feelings. Some even speak of holding a secular job, by which they mean doing something not strictly connected to religion.

But according to the Reformed outlook, religion is not a feeling to be experienced more or less intensely. Rather, as the word implies (from *religare*, to "join together"), religion is a worldview, a way of life. "Life is religion," so the expression goes. The center of true religion is God. But moving out from the center, we may have an understanding of the world and of ourselves. Thus, revelation tells us about God and about the rest of reality from God's viewpoint, not exhaustively but truly and with clarity about how things fit together. Receiving this revelation requires humility. We do not have the final word on every realm. But if we receive revelation by the Spirit of God, we may humbly and tentatively but confidently arrive at the truth.

It could be fairly said that knowledge is one of the central problems of our time. Our age is one of great confusion in areas such as hermeneutics (the interpretation of reality) and science (finding models to explain the world). We are in a crisis of knowledge. This is not the first time in human experience, though. The prophet Hosea cryptically diagnosed the central problem of Israel in the eighth century B.C.: "My people are destroyed for lack of knowledge" (Hos. 4:6). He is not talking about lack of education or culture but specifically of the knowledge of God through the law that he had given the people. The Lord's accusation demonstrates that whatever we think and do begins with the knowledge of God. The summary statement, "There is no faithfulness or steadfast love, and no knowledge of God in the land," is followed by a list of crimes committed regularly in the land (Hos. 4:1). How can we know God and be reformed? Through words of truth, through revelation.

Our culture is full of verbiage. Words have become cheap and random. Ironically, we have a dearth of good words, pure and powerful words. We resemble the age of the prophet Amos, who proclaimed a famine worse than one of hunger, a famine of the word of God (Amos 8:11). Where can we go for wisdom? Where do we find life-giving truth?

Only one has the words of eternal life, the Lord God, Creator of heaven and earth. Only God is fully rational. Only he exhaustively understands all things, for only he is God. God is a God who speaks. We have no access to the eternal, divine intertrinitarian communication. But speech is surely an essential characteristic of his being. God is a rational, speaking person.

We cannot have any true knowledge, then, unless it comes from God. The good news is that he has graciously revealed his knowledge to us. It is important to underscore God's kindness in making his knowledge accessible to us. He does not owe it to us, particularly since we have been bent on rejecting him. But in his great love, he has reversed our famine and spoken to his undeserving image-bearers.

One God, Two Modes of Revelation

Revelation has several features worth mentioning. First, its source is God. While God uses a variety of modes, from words to events to the creation, the origin of all revelation is God. The apostle John describes the message he has heard as "that which was from the beginning, which we have heard" (1 John 1:1). Even the tragic condition of our present society, with its conflicts and perversions, is not just the way things are. It is a revelation from God in heaven (Rom. 1:18). Second, God's revelation is self-disclosure. That is to say, the content of God's revelation is his. "Your word is truth" is Jesus' warrant for his petition to the Father asking him to keep the disciples faithfully grounded (John 17:17). But God's truth also emanates from nonverbal revelation, such as the physical world and the events of human history. Third, revelation is for God's sake. It has God as its purpose. It is perfectly true that human beings are the special objects of God's truth. Yet, they are not the final purpose of revelation, which is to pass through them, as it were, and return praise to God. To summarize, God's revelation is from him, about him, and for him.

So, there is essential unity to revelation. God's self-disclosure coordinates perfectly with his plan. It fits the scheme of creation–fall–redemption. In this way, revelation shows us a philosophy of history. At the same time, there is also diversity. Traditionally a distinction is recognized between *general* revelation and *special* revelation. General revelation is mediated in the ordinary phenomena, such as the events of history, the physical world, and the promptings of conscience. Special revelation uses the more unusual phenomena, such as prophecy, miracles, the Bible, and God's appearances (theophanies), culminating in the incarnation of Jesus Christ.

One must not separate these two modes. Although different, they are complementary. Indeed, they require one another. Without general revelation we would not know how to interpret the commands of Scripture. We could not know how to avoid theft (special revelation in the Bible: the eighth commandment) if we did not know about possessions, property, human rights, and the like (general revelation). It works the other way as well. We could not rightly interpret the world around us if it were not for God's Word. For example, we might look at the world and conclude it got here by chance, unless we believe Scripture, which tells us the world was created by God.

General and special revelation coordinate with the different episodes of history. Before the fall, general revelation enabled our first parents to live in a garden that they were to dress and keep and to name (to understand) the animals they found in that environment (Gen. 2:20). But God's special revelation intervened to forbid the enjoyment of one of the trees, for a particular probationary purpose (Gen. 2:16–17). After the fall, general revelation makes known a world grown hostile to the dominion of the human race, producing thorns and thistles, together with difficulties in childbearing. But, again, God made special promises, beginning with an announcement of Satan's defeat (Gen. 3:15), progressing through the ages, with miracles, kings of Israel, and prophecies, and ending with the coming of his only Son, Jesus Christ, the Word of God. Today, through general revelation God proclaims his power and goodness in the world he has made (Ps. 19:1–2), and he increases the world population for the express purpose of seeking and finding him (Acts 17:26–27). But in the Bible, and when the Word is preached, he also specially announces the gospel, the good news that Christ came to save lost sinners (Rom. 3:16–17). General and special revelation harmonize perfectly. Both are authoritative, and both are necessary and sufficient for their purpose.[1]

The Bible as a Covenant Book

Within special revelation, the Bible stands out as the most precious of all of the church's possessions. What sort of book is it? For one thing, it is divinely inspired. More accurately, its words have been breathed out by God into the minds and the pens of its human authors (2 Tim. 3:16; 2 Peter 1:21). For another thing, it is a covenant document. That is, the Bible is a constitutional text, something like the founding documents of a modern country, though far more. When the people of God were gathered at the foot of Mount Sinai, right after the momentous events of their liberation from Egypt, their mediator, Moses, received what we call the Ten Commandments, engraved on a couple of stone tablets. It was a covenant text, containing more than simply a series of laws. The Hebrew word for "covenant," *berith*, means, literally, a bond or a fetter. It may go back to a term meaning "to cut." This would give special significance to the Ten Commandments, chiseled on those tablets. In any case, a covenant is an arrangement whereby God, out of his love, binds himself to redeem his people and requires of them a response in faith, proven by obedience. The entire Bible is based on this model. It is a constitutional document, rich in its diversity, centered on the covenant promise of God to save his people, and requiring a response of faith, evidenced through obedience.

We will have more to say about the nature of the covenant in the next chapter. Putting it like this is a good way to underscore the unity of the Bible. While it may appear somewhat cold and purely contractual, the Word of God is living and powerful. Like the sword, it is able to penetrate deep down into the recesses of the human soul (Heb. 4:12). But it is also a life-giving strength, a delightful wisdom (Ps. 19:7–11). A perusal of Psalm 119 will show that God's Word is worth meditating on over and over again, because it connects the believer

1. I owe the insight for putting it this way to Cornelius Van Til. See his "Nature and Scripture," in *The Infallible Word: A Symposium*, 2d ed., ed. N. B. Stonehouse and Paul Woolley (Philadelphia: Presbyterian and Reformed, 1967), 269–83.

with the Lord God, the one who reveals himself through the Word. The study of the Bible is indeed able to make us wise for salvation (Ps. 1:2; 2 Tim. 3:15).

Unity and Diversity in the Bible

Special revelation is one and many. The Bible has unity and diversity. Somewhat parallel to the Trinity, there is one truth, with many components, in the Scriptures. The unity derives from its primary author, the God of revelation, who is one God. Its unifying message is the central theme, the covenant of grace, whereby God deigns to save his people by the death and resurrection of Jesus Christ, sealed and applied by the Holy Spirit. But the diversity of Scripture is also a precious attribute. It is exhibited in the extraordinary differences in the personalities and purposes of its authors. There are numerous genres in biblical literature: history, poetry, letters, prophecies, apocalyptic writing, legislation. Besides, special revelation is progressive, coming in seasons and epochs that build upon one another. The writer of the Hebrews puts it succinctly: "Long ago, at many times and in many ways, God spoke to our fathers by the prophets" (Heb. 1:1).

We earlier mentioned in passing an influential movement in American Protestantism known as dispensationalism. It rightly recognized the epochal nature of biblical revelation. It divides the seasons of revelation into specific time periods, known as dispensations. These are administrations, each one revealing a particular purpose of God's provision. But then the system becomes awkward at best. The divisions become too rigid and perhaps even contradictory. Usually dispensationalists divide history into seven separate periods: innocency (Adam before the fall), conscience (Adam to Noah), promise (Abraham to Moses), Mosaic law (Moses to Christ), grace (Pentecost to the rapture), the millennium (Christ's earthly reign), and the eternal state (heaven and hell).

One of the most serious problems with this sort of scheme is uncovered when we consider that dispensationalism sharply separates Israel and the church. According to this view, all the Old Testament promises to Israel indicate an earthly kingdom in the future, with no fulfillment in the age of the church. Believing Jews may join the church individually, but as descendants of Abraham, Israel must wait for the thousand-year reign of Christ. The reality of this reign, known as the millennium, is based on a literal interpretation of Revelation 20:2–3, which appears to predict a temporary restraint of Satan's activities, from which dispensationalists extrapolate a return of the Jews to a promised land, the rebuilding of the temple, animal sacrifices, and so on. There are many difficulties with this view. For one thing, it tends to exaggerate the differences between the so-called dispensations. While known for its legislation, the revelation through Moses is not about approaching God through the law but about grace. Consider the way the psalmist, living in the Mosaic epoch, meditates on the law of God and finds a blessing in it, because God has by grace put him into right relation with that law. For another thing, the clear teaching of the New Testament is that the church is the final form for God's people in community. The church is the final temple, filled with the Holy Spirit. The church age is not a sort of waiting station until a more national kind of covenant could be established, in a particular thousand-year period. That would be a step backwards.

One of the major problems with the dispensational view is the rule of biblical interpretation used, which says, "literal where possible." On the surface, coming from authors who lived in the heyday of biblical criticism, this rule appeared to preserve the integrity of the text and guarded against reading into it. But in reality the rule tends to throw out the baby with the bathwater. A more faithful reading of the biblical texts must show respect for the genres. Some are historical, but others are more poetic. Prophecy, for example, is often metaphorical, using images that are meant to suggest far more than a literal meaning. When Zechariah predicts a new age, full of the glory of God, he says the very bells on Israel's horses shall have the inscription, "Holy to the LORD," and every pot in Jerusalem and Judah shall be holy to the Lord of hosts. Surely, much more is going on than animals, bells, and pots (Zech. 14:20–21). The key is in the New Testament, which tells us in the age of the church Christ will so fill his people with his presence that temporary, ceremonial rules will no longer be needed (Mark 7:19). It will be so glorious that nothing in the Old Testament is comparable. Previously, we had shadows; now, in Christ, we have the final reality: "But as it is, he has appeared once for all at the end of the ages to put away sin by the sacrifice of himself" (Heb. 9:26). No temple is now needed, nor any more animal sacrifices, which are mere shadows (Heb. 9:11–12; 10:1).

A further problem with the dispensationalist view is that it separates Christians from the world in a radical fashion. For example, believers will not suffer in what is called the great tribulation, apocalyptic troubles that are scheduled to occur before the millennium. Instead, they are raptured while others are left to suffer. This rapture is secret, that is, the Christians are taken up to heaven while unbelievers stay behind.[2] Again, such theories are based on a very literal interpretation of texts such as the Book of Revelation and Jesus' discourse about the end times, given on the Mount of Olives (Matt. 24:21, 40–41). While the words of such texts are not always easy to understand, they speak generally, not chronologically, about the character of the age of the church. Believers will not be exempt from suffering, though they will indeed be acquitted on the day of judgment. We are delivered from the present evil age (Gal. 1:4), but not by escaping its hardships in the short term (Rev. 2:9–10). The presence of God in the life of Israel was real enough, but Israel was also a model, a type for the last days, of which the church is the antitype. So connected are they that Paul can call the church "the Israel of God" (Gal. 6:16). Today, we have a temple; we do not have to wait. It is a real temple, to be sure, but it is the church, in which Christ dwells through his Holy Spirit (Eph. 2:20–22).

In any case, the Bible is diverse, but not in the way dispensationalists conceive of things. A better way, one developed with special care in Reformed theology, is to underscore the single covenant of grace while at the same time recognizing two major administrations, the Old and the New Testaments. The Bible reflects this diversity and unity at the same time. True enough, there are separate epochs and events. The present age is not yet the new heavens and new earth in

2. Many scenarios have been proposed by dispensationalists. The Book of Revelation has been a special target for predictions of events surrounding the second coming of Jesus. Today, one of the most popular versions of theories about a secret rapture is the *Left Behind* series.

their fullness. We await the visible return of our Lord to restore all things. And yet even the present time is already–not yet. That is, the present age is the end times (1 Cor. 10:11), and we are already living in the heavenly places in Christ (Eph. 1:3, 20; 2:6; 3:10). The kingdom of God is here (Mark 1:15; Matt. 10:7). That is because all the promises of God find their *yes* in Jesus Christ (2 Cor. 1:20; Rom. 15:8). What we call the second coming of Christ is the final unfolding of what we already have. That is why it is convenient to talk about our age as the already–not yet.

Preaching and Teaching the Bible

The basic purpose of the Bible, then, is to be our covenant book, a powerful, truthful, and practical Word for Christian living. Because of its God-breathed character, the Bible is able to make us "wise for salvation" and to equip us for every good work (2 Tim. 3:16–17). Every part of the Bible is not equally clear to us, and we will never be able to exhaust its meaning, but yet this Word is forever firmly fixed in the heavens (Ps. 119:89) and is a lamp for our feet, a light to our path (Ps. 119:105). If we read it expectantly, we will see God. If we hear it correctly explained and applied in the regular preaching of the church, then we will grow in grace until the day dawns and the morning star rises in our hearts (2 Peter 1:19).

The Bible is not a collection of virtues or a book about heroes. A good deal of preaching limits the meaning of Scripture texts to moralism. That is, a passage is read, an explanation given, and then marching orders are given for better living, with no reference to grace. While the Bible does contain a great deal for righteous living, that is not an end in itself. Rules and virtues become oppressive if they are not grounded in the grace of the Lord. We miss the central point of the Bible if we miss the message of Jesus Christ bristling on its pages. To the Pharisees, who did know that the Bible shows the way of life but who had turned religion into a set of morals without recognizing God's exclusive provision, Jesus said, "You search the Scriptures because you think that in them you have eternal life; and it is they that bear witness about me" (John 5:39). The Bible centers its message on Jesus Christ, because redemption is through the Son. But ultimately, the Bible is about the trinitarian God, who loves his people and comes to seek and to save them. On every page, one God as Father, Son, and Holy Spirit is displayed for our contemplation, our obedience, but most of all, our love. Once we understand that, we can enjoy exploring its pages, from the poetry to the history to laws and prophecies, and find the Lord God exhibited and honored throughout.

Creation

If God's revelation displays his trinitarian self, it does so, as we would expect, as a worldview. At the heart of our worldview is the larger setting of creation–fall–redemption. In this chapter, we examine the first two components, creation and fall.

The first reality in our threefold synopsis is creation. The Bible tells us about the creation on almost every page. It always relates the creation to God the Creator. He is a glorious God, and the creation is resplendent with his glorious beauty. He is a God of great power, and his creation is full of his mighty works. He is a God of life, and the world is plenteous with every kind of living being. He is a God of goodness, and his creation is good and delightful, through and through. In short, "his invisible attributes, namely, his eternal power and divine nature, have been clearly perceived, ever since the creation of the world, in the things that have been made" (Rom. 1:20). We cannot help but see him in the visible world, because every facet of it reflects his divine self. Just as the artist's personality is perceived through works of poetry or music or painting, so the person of the Creator is clearly manifest in the things he has made.

It is easy to get tangled up in schemes of reconciliation between the Genesis account of creation and various theories of origins prominent in our times, without first acknowledging the great wonder of God's handiwork. Since God is the Creator, there is undoubtedly a true way to harmonize the discoveries made in geology, paleontology, and other sciences with the great fact of the creation. But far more important than trying to discover such a harmony is the humble acknowledgment that this world as originally created was marvelous.

Nowhere was God's grandeur more gloriously displayed than at the creation.[3]

In no wise should such glory prohibit full and confident investigation of the world by means of the sciences. Rightly practiced, they tell us more about the glory of God, his handiwork, his ways, and the patterns he uses. The miscast battles between theology and science are ideological conflicts that have little connection with either true science or true theology. Ultimately there should be no real or final conflict between the words of the Bible and the "speech" of the universe, because God is the author of both (Ps. 19). To some extent, science and theology operate in two different realms. Yet they overlap. If both are done within the worldview of creation–fall–redemption, there may be all kinds of apparent contradictions and issues that may or may not be resolved, but none of them should put either enterprise into question.

The Bible tells us that God made every single portion of the universe. Genesis succinctly has it that he made "the heavens and the earth" (Gen. 1:1). In simple, elegant terms, the biblical writer is telling us that God made everything, everything down here and everything beyond. In our day the author might have talked about energy, subatomic materials, and galaxies.

Unlike the worldview of modernity, the Bible also describes two different realities within the creation, the visible portion and the invisible portion. The world in our ordinary experience is a vast foment of places, of life, and of nations (Matt. 24:14). At the same time, there is more. There are realities not ordinarily available to our measurement. One of these is angels. We are not told a great deal about these extraordinary creatures. We know that they, made by God, sang during the creation of the world (Job 38:7). They also sang at the birth of Jesus Christ (Luke 2:13–15). Thus, their primary purpose is to praise and worship God. They are also his servants, his messengers, doing his bidding (Ps. 104:4; Heb. 1:7). They are present during special occasions when God is at work to bring about his great purposes on earth (Mark 16:5; John 20:11–12; Dan. 7:9; Acts 1:10).[4]

3. Nowhere, that is, except in the coming of Jesus Christ into the world.
4. As we shall see, one portion of the angelic creation did not remain obedient to the will of God: the devil and his followers.

It Was Good

The entire creation is a witness to God's generosity. It is a testimony to his rightful rule over us according to his generous purposes. Over and over, Genesis tells us that after each major stroke God beheld what he had made and saw that it was good (Gen. 1:5, 10, 18, 21, 25). At the end of the creation week, the text tells us, God ceased from creating, and he saw everything that he had made, "and behold, it was very good" (Gen. 1:31). The sad accounting of the human condition by Paul in the beginning of Romans is that although God is known undeniably from the works of his hands, we fail to honor him and to thank him as Creator (Rom. 1:21). This is because we will not acknowledge God's goodness. John puts it differently in his Gospel account. Of the Son of God, he says, "He was in the world, and the world was made through him, yet the world did not know him" (John 1:10). The great tragedy is that his works exhibit his goodness, his majesty, his power, and his beauty, yet we would rather find some other meaning in them.

God's creation exhibits his goodness and beauty, but, related to that, it proclaims his justice. Our English word *fair* puts both concepts together. The creation is fair, because God made it. In Moses' parting words to the assembly of Israel, he invites them to proclaim God's greatness because he is "the Rock, [whose] work is perfect, for all his ways are justice" (Deut. 32:4). So it is only right, but it is also delightful, to honor him and give him thanks. Skeptical people might quip, "I didn't ask to be born," implying they are victims of circumstance. But life is a gift, and the world is God's theater, which constantly displays his goodness and grandeur for us to enjoy.

One of the most remarkable features of the biblical account of creation puts it in stark contrast to almost every other philosophy. God did not shape the world out of any preexisting material. The opening words of Genesis are clear about this: "In the beginning, God," not matter. So he did not create out of something that was already there. At the same time, the creation is not an extension of God's being. Many religions understand the world to be a part of God. They see the universe as one sort of being, perhaps rising from a lower type to the higher type, with God as somehow the highest. In pantheism God

is somehow the center of an amalgam that spreads out to lesser existence. But in the biblical religion no such relationship exists. There is
God, and there is creation. The universe and its rich glory came into
being out of nothing (*ex nihilo*). This expression does not occur in the
Scriptures, and strictly speaking, God did not make the world out of
anything, for nothing can only beget nothing. Yet an important point
is made by the expression. God did not make the world out of something that already existed.

In the language of Hebrews 11:3 we have it put cogently: "By
faith we understand that the universe was created by the word of God,
so that what is seen was not made out of things that are visible." This
tells us two important things. First, God made the world by his word.
He spoke and it was: "And God said, 'Let there be light,' and there
was light." God may well have used various processes to bring the
world into being, but fundamentally he did it by fiat. Second, all that
we can see and measure is temporal. At one point, it did not exist, for
only God existed.

Once again, the Christian faith stands or falls on this issue: Is the
creation good? In the biblical account, God created the world freely,
for no reason other than his good pleasure. He spoke, and it was. He
called the vast systems of galaxies into being, without effort. The world
is the work of God's counsel. His will is good and wonderful (Isa.
28:29; Jer. 32:19). In the Book of Revelation, describing the praise
that is spoken in the heavenly throne room, the living creatures bow
down to worship, saying,

> Worthy are you, our Lord and God,
>> to receive glory and honor and power,
> for you created all things,
>> and by your will they existed and were created. (Rev. 4:11)

God's will is the reason behind all of the creation. And as such it is
flawless, full of glory and honor and power. It is impossible to overstate the importance of beginning with a good creation, one that in
no manner impugns God's will.

If we cannot begin from a good creation, one that was willed by God for his excellent purposes, then all is lost. For one reason, the world would be meaningless. Without God's goodness, embedded in his good purposes, it has no purpose. For another reason, the presence of evil in the world would be a part of the way things are. At best, it is embedded in the fabric of creation. At worst, evil is somehow God's doing. We are victims of the way things are, not fallen from an original righteousness. Crucial to the Reformed way of thinking is the permanency and the original righteousness of the entire creation.

Humanity Was Created Upright

Original goodness is especially true of the human race. Our first parents were created upright, flawless. The Bible has little in common with Jean-Jacques Rousseau's doctrine of the state of nature. The beginnings of humanity are in a garden, but not because "nature" is elevated above "civilization." Biblical scholars inform us that Eden was a royal garden, befitting the ancient Near Eastern king, who was a city builder. As the race advances, it comfortably moves into cities and produces culture. Our first parents were royalty, for they were God's image-bearers. And so are we, their descendants.

It is worth noting that God paused during the creation week and took counsel. Within the divine majesty, a specific determination was made to create humankind after his image (Gen. 1:26–27). It is a special moment in the rich process of creation. A creature was to be made unlike all the others. This creature would have God-likeness. What can this mean?

We are religious creatures. Human beings are profoundly religious. Our first purpose is to bring honor and even pleasure to Almighty God, in communion and fellowship with the divine Trinity. This is why Augustine, reflecting on the most fundamental questions of life, can say, "You stir man to take pleasure in praising you, because you have made us for yourself, and our heart is restless until it rests in you."[5] In a world gone awry, that religious drive has been diverted, and it

5. Augustine, *Confessions*, trans. Henry Chadwick (Oxford: Oxford University Press, 1991), 1.1.

centers on objects other than the Creator God. But the religious drive will not go away.

We are moral agents. It does not take a great deal of insight to recognize that one of the basic differences between us and the animals is moral sensibility. We make decisions based on right and wrong. We make judgments based on ethical criteria. Today, even in a radically fallen world, there are norms recognized by nearly every race, in every geographical location. The flip side of the coin of moral agency is responsibility. We are accountable for our decisions, because as God's image-bearers, we owe a debt of allegiance to the Lord God. Paradoxically, this dependence on God is the guarantee of our freedom. Received wisdom would say it is a contradiction: to bow to God is to give up our liberty. Biblical wisdom says, with the Anglican prayer, "[his] service is perfect freedom." We can, and indeed we do, turn away from God by the use of our moral agency. However, the result is not real freedom but bondage.

We have a divine design. Our purpose as human beings is designed by our loving, righteous Creator. Genesis tells us about the marvelous calling we have had from the beginning: to worship God, to work, and to join together in families. It is of critical importance to recognize that men and women are fully the image of God. No suggestion of an oppressive hierarchy is made in Genesis. In later revelation a male leadership role is taught within marriage (1 Cor. 11:7–12; Eph. 5:22–33), but it is an office, not an essential difference between the sexes. Marriage is instituted at the beginning, when Adam recognizes his wife, Eve, and begins the long and wonderful tradition of children growing up and leaving their families in order to form their own (Gen. 1:24). Having children and continuing the multiplication and development of the human race is grounded in the institution of marriage (Gen. 5:1–3; Matt. 19:4–6).

We are one and many. Each of us is a unity with diversity. God created the person, a "living creature," out of the dust of the ground and the breath of life (Gen. 2:7). Sometimes the Bible describes the person as united in the heart, which is the center of one's being (Ps. 86:12). This is why the greatest commandment is to love the Lord your God with all your heart (Matt. 22:37; Prov. 3:5). At the same time, we have various complementary parts. The Bible does not give us a detailed and technical anthropology. Sometimes it speaks of the mind, sometimes of the soul. Sometimes it speaks of the flesh or the body. The only possible larger category into which these many attributes may fall is the duality of spirit and flesh, sometimes described as the soul and the body. We sometimes can note the difference. For example, when Jesus died, he yielded his spirit to the Father, while his body rested in the grave for three days (John 19:30). Paul feels the power of sin particularly in the light of the human body full of death (Rom. 7:24). But this duality should not compromise the essential unity of the human creature.

And it should caution us against the popular but wooden scheme of trichotomy. In this view our attributes exist in a hierarchy of body, soul, and spirit. This anthropology is more Platonic than scriptural.[6] More than a strictly technical problem, what is at stake in trichotomy is making one part of us to be somehow naturally closer to God than another. Usually the body is disdained as something lower, whereas in the Bible the entire human person, including the body, is God's image. Even the traditional view, not trichotomy, holds to the immortality of the soul. Sometimes the idea is that while the body dies, the soul always lives, though either in heaven or in hell. However, life in the Bible is to be with God. Not to have fellowship with God is therefore death, for body and soul. God alone is immortal.

We have a cultural mandate. The primary purpose of the human race is to praise and worship God. The secondary purpose is to fill the earth in order to understand it and to rule over it as God's servants. All of these tasks and functions are to redound to the glory of God,

6. Upon close examination the Scripture passages used to lend support to trichotomy are not teaching it. For example, Hebrews 4:12 is not about a division between soul and spirit but a penetration to the deepest level. Another example is 1 Thessalonians 5:23, where Paul is not detailing a precise set of categories but heaping up attributes that are complementary.

under his blessing (Gen. 1:28–30). This is sometimes called the cultural mandate, because it has to do with the way we cultivate the earth and engage in its development artistically, economically, scientifically, and in every way represented by the image of culture.

Today, having children, spreading out to all corners of the earth, and subduing it by hard work is very much under question. Many people see family and work as an earthly necessity, with no particular heavenly connection. Christians secretly feel they are not doing God's will if they are not in some kind of ministry. The Reformed faith does not accept the dichotomy between sacred and secular callings. All legitimate vocations—from family life to citizenship, to agriculture, business, the arts, or the holy ministry—are on equal footing before the Creator God. While today we tend to elevate some of the professions above others and to denigrate certain callings as being less than spiritual, the Bible does not support such a view. "You are a chosen race, a royal priesthood, a holy nation, a people for his own possession," the ancient text tells us, "that you may proclaim the excellencies of him who called you out of darkness into his marvelous light" (1 Peter 2:9).

We were made for eternity. The history of the human race was to extend far beyond the Garden of Eden. To speak technically, there was an eschatology to the purposes of creation in general and of humankind in particular.[7] Had there not been a fall, a wonderful future was in view. Generation after generation would have continued the primary purpose of worshiping God and the secondary purposes of having families and laboring to cultivate the earth. While the first creatures already had perfection, they were meant to have something even greater than perfection, something even greater than the happy conditions known by the first generation. Our race was meant to progress beyond the simple, though perfect, estate in the Garden, to the consummate bliss of eternal life. Adam and Eve were told about two trees. One was the forbidden tree of the knowledge of good and evil. The other was the tree of life. The latter tree symbolized more than perfection. Its

---

7. The word *eschatology* means "study of last things." It signifies a final purpose, the end in view.

fruit could not be tasted unless resisting the first tree was done. Had they respected this prohibition and confirmed their allegiance to God, the human race would have been in the running for eternal, consummate bliss.

We all know what happened. Our first parents refused to honor God's command and thus were barred from eternal life. Yet God was merciful. In his love he provided another access to the tree of life. It was the long, hard road of battle against evil, culminating in the death of his Son on a cross (Gen. 3:15). The path to eternal life for the human race still lies in allegiance to God. Jesus Christ, the "last Adam," obeyed in our place and won back the right to eternal life for the redeemed portion of humanity (1 Cor. 15:45).

Good Government

One of the distinctives of Reformed theology is to hold a high place for God's government of the world after the creation was finished. Specifically, it connects God's nature and the purposes of the creation to his subsequent care for the world. After the sixth day of creation, he would superintend all of the affairs of the world and of humankind by his good government. God's providence, by which he presides over all of the creation, is not, then, a continual process of creation. The creation is finished, but now God's care and oversight of that creation are in full function. God governs the world not by autonomous laws of nature, as deists and secularists might think, but by the Father's wise plan, through the Son and in the Holy Spirit.

John Calvin once made the point that the world is distinct and yet not separate from God. The world and its history are properly distinct from God, because they are not a part of his being. They have responsibility and worth. The world is even, tragically, capable of evil and of turning against the Creator. At the same time, the world and history are in no way independent or autonomous. God rules the world. Though we do not understand how, we recognize that God is somehow sovereign even over the coming of evil into the world. This is why the creeds often distinguish between the primary and the secondary causes of events. God is always the primary reason behind everything that takes place. He causes everything to come to pass, though in many different ways. Yet at the same time, the world, and human creatures in particular, are free; they are real secondary causes, not robots or puppets.

Creation! Providence! What matters for the praise of our Creator! Whenever things seem to have no explanation, God is there nevertheless. Whenever we are perplexed by the contradictions of life, we can affirm that God is neither distant nor uninvolved. We may not understand why this episode or that event occurred, but we can say with certainty, God willed it for his good purposes. During the worst circumstances imaginable, having stood over the painful judgment of the people of God in a stark desert, a people that had such a destiny, now dashed into oblivion, Moses, their leader, could still say:

> Lord, you have been our dwelling place
> > in all generations.
> Before the mountains were brought forth,
> > or ever you had formed the earth and the world,
> > from everlasting to everlasting you are God. (Ps. 90:1–2)

Without fully understanding all his purposes, we can still praise God in all circumstances. When we try to force the events of the world into a human scheme, as did poor dear Job, searching to explain the calamities that had befallen him, then God chides us and reminds us that he knows what he is doing. Just as the wonders of the creation were kept from us, so the wonder of his ways with our lives is not always accessible to our grasp.

> Where were you when I laid the foundation of the earth?
> > Tell me, if you have understanding.
> Who determined its measurements—surely you know!
> > Or who stretched the line upon it?
> On what were its bases sunk,
> > or who laid the cornerstone,
> when the morning stars sang together
> > and all the sons of God shouted for joy? (Job 38:4–7)

The marvels of the universe God has made, and the marvels of his providence, will forever be inexhaustible to us, because God cannot be exhausted. Praise God!

The Fall

Os Guinness, a wonderfully articulate spokesman for the Christian faith, advocates what he calls "bifocal" vision. That is to say, inasmuch as we love and respect the original goodness of the creation, we do at the same time recognize the sad reality of the fall. Both are true. Take away the first, and we are plunged into despair, with no way out. Take away the second, and we will find no credible way of accounting for the dreadful contradiction between the goodness of God and the reality of evil in the present life.

The fall has a historical beginning. There is a before and after. The account in Genesis explains that our first parents, while perfect, were given one restriction in their otherwise free reign over the creation. They were not to eat of the fruit of the tree of the knowledge of good and evil. This is sometimes called the probation. Its essential purpose was to show, by means of a simple test, that God could be trusted. Most of the time, there was such abundant evidence for his goodness that the decision to trust God should not have been particularly difficult. For reasons shrouded in mystery, Adam and Eve listened to the subversive voice of a serpent, and they succumbed.

A host of questions surrounds this primeval drama. At what point exactly did the suggestion of disobedience cross the line in the couple's hearts and move them from temptation to illicit desire? How could such a simple act as eating from a fruit tree be liable for capital punishment? How can it be that through this one act of disobedience the entire human race was brought down into disgrace? The answer is that a great deal was involved in God's command, far more than Adam and Eve could have known. Yet they did not need to know all of the implications in order to remain faithful. Honoring God is a dreadfully serious matter in itself. Not to do so is treasonable.

Why would God start everything off with a test? The reason goes back to the purpose of creation, its eschatology. This prohibition was a trial, one that would give our foreparents a deeper knowledge of what friendship with God entailed. The Lord would allow them to have a brush with evil, in order to grow in love and obedience for him and to become strong as persons. The great stories of pilgrimage in literature reflect this idea. The quest for the Holy Grail, the Masonic trial by fire, these are dim echoes of the primary trial from Genesis. Notice the tree is called the tree of the knowledge of good and evil. It is possible to know evil without giving in to it. Had Adam and Eve succeeded, proving their love for God for his own sake, they would have gained the right of access to the tree of life, and thus they would lead the human race not to destruction but to a state of consummate bliss, a state even better than perfection in the Garden. So this was not an isolated test but part of a larger plan to bring the creation from where it was, which was very good, to where it could be, which was eternal life. Hence, much was at stake.

To facilitate this test a strange, unwanted guest was introduced into the Garden. Why did a serpent speak? No doubt some angelic being, once in communion with God, and now himself in revolt against him, craftily used a low-lying animal as his mouthpiece. Today, the world is filled with devils ruled by the evil one (Eph. 2:2; John 12:31; 2 Cor. 4:4; 1 Peter 5:8). But in the Garden, it was one strange, lone voice. Why did the primeval couple listen to it? There was no good reason. They had everything they could need, and more. Indeed, they had fellowship with God. Still, for no good reason, they listened, and they changed allegiance. The lone voice suggested that God might not have the best intentions for them. Today, we hear such voices all of the time. Lots of arguments exist tempting us to distrust God's intentions. But our first parents were walking on beautiful, virgin territory. The voice was speaking nonsense. Yet, they believed the voice and doubted God. The rest, as they say, is history.

East of Eden

The simple, profound narrative from Genesis tells us the sequel. Some of it would be comical if it were not so deadly serious. When

God calls out for his traitorous creatures and asks why they are hiding, the man and the woman shift the blame. Adam tells God he succumbed because the woman "whom you gave to be with me" gave it to him (Gen. 3:12), and the woman blames the serpent (v. 13). God, the judge, does not accept these excuses but metes out serious consequences upon them and their progeny. Because of this decision the whole world would live under a curse. Death would reign over the human race. And just living would become a great hardship. Childbearing would no longer be a joy but painful. Work would no longer be easy but troublesome. Food would be scarce (vv. 16–19). Most critically, the tree of life was forbidden them, and they were banished from the garden of God (vv. 22–24).

Because of the fall, every relationship is distorted. Death, defined as separation, destruction, perversion, now gets the upper hand in all of them. Instead of that free, open communion with the Lord God we once enjoyed, we are alienated, attempting at once to hide from God but struggling to find him. Instead of a natural, affectionate relationship across the gender line, marriages and male-female friendships are stormy, full of conflict. Every social bond is threatened, and warfare rather than peace becomes the norm for human history. Relating to our selves has lost its original harmony, and we know psychological disorders and physical disabilities, disease and great suffering. Our reasoning process is no longer at the service of truth, but renders idolatry plausible. Finally, our relation to the earth is reversed. Whereas we were meant to have dominion over God's world, it ultimately reclaims us, and we return, by physical death, to the dust from which we were formed.

What is sin? At the root it is being against God. Specifically, this means moving out against what God has revealed to be true and right. The Westminster Shorter Catechism puts it soberly: "Sin is any want of conformity unto, or transgression of, the law of God" (A. 14). There is unity and diversity to sin. In one sense, when we transgress, we go against the whole law (Rom. 2:10). One sin is always related to all the others. To break one of the Ten Commandments is to break them all. If I steal, for example, I am having another god, making a graven image, lying, and coveting. The gospel of God's love would make no sense as an appeal to the whole world if it were not for the whole world of sin that had risen up to dishonor God. At the same time, there are differences within sins. Some are more heinous than others. Some develop more strongly in one person than another. Some are more pronounced in one culture than in another. Some are committed in ignorance, others with premeditation.

The Bible assesses our condition as sinful by nature. We do not have to learn all about sin or teach it to children. Nor does it come from the environment or from circumstances. While these may characterize the shape and intensity of sin, its origins are in the human heart. Sin is conceived in the heart and brought forth into the world as an evil thought or deed (James 1:14–15). It is when we are confronted with the pure will of God that we begin to see how intricate and tangled are our motives.

Sin is thus exposed and aggravated when heavenly matters come close to home. After watching him perform the great miracle of catching a large number of fish, Peter, on his knees, told Jesus: "Depart from me, for I am a sinful man, O Lord" (Luke 5:8). The more courageous may ask God to reveal their secret faults, but for most of us those faults will have to be uncovered despite our inertia (Job 34:32; Ps. 19:12; 90:8). God can, in judgment, exacerbate our sin by hardening the heart, but he never does this without a naturally disposed hard heart to begin with (Deut. 2:30; Josh. 11:20; cf. 1 Sam. 6:6; Matt. 13:15). And so, the presence of Jesus Christ is life and health to some but a stumbling block to others, because it reveals their true propensity (Luke 3:24; Matt. 21:44; 2 Cor. 2:16). When the Lord searches the heart, what is discovered is so ugly that it is a mystery to behold: "The heart is deceitful above all things, and desperately sick; who can understand it?" (Jer. 17:9).

Solidarity in Sin

One difficult question inserts itself and needs some attention. How is it that the one act of disobedience by the first couple, led by Adam, could plunge the entire human race into sin and misery? The doctrine is sometimes known as original sin. We may not be able to answer the question in every detail, but we can make several affirmations that put it in perspective.

There should be no doubt that the human condition is universally sinful. We can travel far and wide, we can observe the growth of each human being from birth to maturity, and we will find sin. Solomon, as he appeals to God for mercy on succeeding generations, acknowledges that no one is without sin (1 Kings 8:46; see 1 John 1:8–10). Perhaps each of us can remember a time when our sinful hearts were exposed. Alexandr Solzhenitsyn, imprisoned in the gulag, was appalled at the arbitrary cruelty of the guards who murdered his mentor, the good doctor Boris Kornfeld, until it dawned on him that he was basically no better in the way he had treated others. There is no escaping the universal reality of personal sinfulness.

We share this condition and its consequences. Only in the modern West are human beings regarded as atomistic, self-driven individuals, with little or no relation to others. In all other societies, and certainly in the biblical mind-set, humanity is regarded as one. There is an organic relation, a solidarity of the human race that makes it more than simply the composite of each individual. Physically, we come from, and have, as it were, one blood. This is not a chance fact but is by God's design (Acts 17:26). But then also, legally, one might say, we are one because the same law is given to all of us, to every group and age and culture. The individual is not lost in the network of human solidarity but rather further defined. In one way it would be unjust to be blamed for the sins of others. The prophet Ezekiel discusses the personal responsibility of fathers and sons and concludes, "The son shall not suffer for the iniquity of the father, nor the father suffer for the iniquity of the son" (Ezek. 18:20). At the same time, the iniquity of the fathers may be "visited" on children to the third and fourth generation of those who hate God (Exod. 20:5). Ultimately, then, each person does bear his or her own burden (Gal. 6:5), and yet we also belong to one another and so must accept the consequences of this social dimension of the human community.

In God's wisdom, we are led by a covenant head. This point is perhaps the most difficult for modern Westerners to understand. We recognize such governance in the political realm, even in a republic, where one person represents an entire constituency. We further recognize that we share the credit for the good decisions of our representatives but also share the blame for their bad ones. The stakes are far higher when it comes to Adam's representative headship over the entire human race. The Scripture tells us we are dead in Adam, even though we did not transgress with him. His one trespass led to universal condemnation (Rom. 5:18). Paul tells us, cryptically, that "in Adam all die" (1 Cor. 15:22).

Is this fair, we might ask? It would surely be unfair if our guilt from personal commitment to sin were not a reality. That we inherit a sinful nature from our covenant representative does not diminish the guilt of personal sin. It may be true that I am inclined to evil, so that by nature I cannot please God, and I did not "choose" my inclination (Rom. 8:8). But my sinfulness is not excused by my inclination, because I agree with it! We saw earlier how the Synod of Dort described total depravity as inclination and a choice. So, to put it one way, at the judgment day, when we appear before God to give an account of our lives, we will not be able to say, in effect, "Lord, I couldn't help it, since I am by nature a sinner." Being unable to resist sin does not make us innocent. It is not the ability or inability to sin that renders us accountable. Rather, it is knowing and agreeing that sin is liable, yet doing it anyway. Having said that, being in Adam is more than to have inherited a sinful nature. For we die in him, because of his transgression. There is an immediate imputation of guilt on his progeny, simply because of his position in relation to ours.

Before we call this arrangement unjust, we might also consider that our redemption is made possible because of a similar arrangement between us and another representative, for it is the case that Jesus Christ has become our new covenant head. He represents his people legally, by justifying them, and vitally, by giving them power and life. Paul argues before the Corinthians that since death came by a man, so resurrection has also come by a man (1 Cor. 15:21–22). He boldly calls Jesus the "last Adam" and the "second man" (vv. 45–47), adding that just as we have worn the image of the first, so we will wear the image of the second. Christ's person and work are far greater, and with far richer implications, than Adam's. But each is a covenant head, and we come under that arrangement for the fall and for redemption.

Sown in Dishonor, Raised in Glory

Altogether, then, we live, in this life, under the oppressive rule of sin. This state of affairs would be unbearable were it not for the grace of God, which mitigates the misery and hardship of it. Returning to the events recorded in the first chapters of Genesis, we see that hope was pronounced at the beginning. It is characteristic of our loving God that he did not dangle his children in their despair. In words spoken to the deceiver, the Lord inaugurated at the beginning a conflict between good and evil in which good would ultimately triumph:

> I will put enmity between you and the woman,
>   and between your offspring and her offspring;
> he shall bruise your head,
>   and you shall bruise his heel. (Gen. 3:15)

These startling words shine a ray of promise in the midst of trouble. They are said first, before the curse on Eve and Adam was pronounced. Human history will display a fundamental conflict between those who side with the serpent and those who side with the woman. Despite the transgression, Eve would be the mother of a redeemer who would atone for the sins of humankind and thus triumph over the evil one.

To extend Guinness's image, we now ought to have "trifocal" vision. First, the creation is still good, and its structures continue to function under God's care. Second, everything is distorted, fallen, so that the direction things should have taken is wrong, being diverted. But third, there is hope. As the seasons of revelation unfold, we find out more about all three, but especially about the nature of our hope, the gospel, the good news that in spite of sin, God has so loved us that sin will not have the last word. The promised redemption is for more than restoration, which would be blessing enough. It is for a new heaven and a new earth, where God is at the center, giving life eternally. The tree of life, once forbidden, is now available for the healing of the nations (Rev. 22:1–5). The original eschatology is kept, even enhanced. The garden of God will become a city where, finally, God will dwell with his people as their God, in an unbroken, eternal communion (Rev. 21:3).

7

THE PROMISE IS
FOR YOU

~~~~~~~~~~

Redemption Accomplished

We cannot redeem ourselves. No religion, however beautiful, however lofty, can move us out of the bondage of sin into the freedom of God's children. Many religions have engaging cultic practices, whereby God or the gods are appeased through ritual. Many affirm lofty ethical obligations that improve the believer by discipline and conformity to various laws. But in the end, the different systems, however noble in themselves, cannot open the doors of heaven, for no matter how elaborate the cult or rigorous the moral practices, nothing can fully satisfy the requirements of a truly righteous and holy God. The sober truth is that "none is righteous, no, not one" (Rom. 3:10). We are not so much missing basic information as we are unwilling to process the information we have correctly. To put it another way, the fall is not so much downward, in scale, but lateral, in ethical revolt. It is often said that even if someone may not know how to find God, at least his sincerity will be rewarded. Two problems refute this idea. First, how could sincerity ever atone for guilt? And second, who can honestly claim sincerity?

However, there is good news. God has left heaven and come to earth to find us and bring us back in, throwing the gates wide open.

Unlike the different religious systems of the world, which urge us to ascend to heaven through ritual or obedience, the God of the Bible descends to our level and pays an unspeakable price to purchase our redemption. We do not have to earn it; we cannot. "God shows his love for us in that while we were still sinners, Christ died for us" (Rom. 5:8). And so now, no one who is in Christ will be condemned (Rom. 8:1). Not only that, but we can now walk in newness of life (Rom. 6:4). What no religion or philosophy could do, God has done for us, by his Son Jesus Christ (Rom. 8:3). Here is grace, amazing grace. Reformed theology insists on the fullest possible statement of this wonderful truth: redemption is accomplished.

A Heart of Love

What reasons can we possibly recognize for this matchless plan of redemption? We do know the primary answer, although it puts us on the threshold of inexhaustible wonder: the love of God! The reason for the death and resurrection of Jesus Christ in view of our reconciliation with God is God's unalterable love. Once again, the best-known verse in the Bible puts it powerfully and simply: "For God so loved the world, that he gave his only Son, that whoever believes in him should not perish but have eternal life" (John 3:16). It is significant that this text comes on the heels of an interview between Jesus and Nicodemus, a well-placed Pharisee who struggled to understand the spiritual significance of Old Testament teaching in the light of Jesus' presence in the world. Nicodemus had a number of things right, but he could not quite see that the kingdom of God was at hand. Nor could he see that all of the ancient prophecies about judgment were being fulfilled, not by the expulsion of the Roman oppressors but by Jesus, the second person of the Trinity, come in human flesh, to expose the world and its guilt, in order to prompt many people to believe and be saved (John 3:17–21). And behind it all is the love of God.

God so loved the world . . . Why would God love a world gone horribly against him? We cannot say. Why would God love such an unlovely object? We cannot find any reason beyond the character of love. We have an ultimate here, and blessedly so. It is true and of great significance that God is love (1 John 4:8, 16). We saw earlier that his being love is as much a characteristic of God as his being spirit and light. God cannot choose to be anything else but love, for that is who he is. And yet, it is of the very essence of love not to be obligated to express it toward such undeserving objects as we. Here, we have a wonderful mystery: love is God's deepest characteristic, yet love is driven not by obligation but by the one who loves. John Murray puts it particularly beautifully:

> It was of the free and sovereign good pleasure of his will, a good pleasure that emanated from the depths of his own good- ness, that he chose a people to be heirs of God and joint-heirs with Christ. The reason resides wholly in himself and proceeds from determinations that are peculiarly his as the "I am that I am." The atonement does not win or constrain the love of God. The love of God constrains to the atonement as the means of accomplishing love's determinate purpose.[1]

To say it differently, in the way Blaise Pascal might have put it: God's love for his people in a fallen world is not awakened by anything else but reasons of his heart, which reason cannot fathom. He did not plan redemption because all along he knew that the fall would occur and that he would have to save us anyway. The death of Christ did not earn God's love. Nor did God love us because he saw great potential in us. There is no reason we can fathom for his redeeming love. How liberating, though, to be able to stop right there! If in a human relation we ought not to ask, "Why do you love me?" all the more should we not ask this of God.

Determined Love

If we cannot and should not go behind the love of God, that does not mean we can say no more about it. God's love is not vague

1. John Murray, *Redemption Accomplished and Applied* (Edinburgh: Banner of Truth, 1961), 10.

or ephemeral. It has shape and form. First, following Scripture, we can say that his love has its origins outside of time, in eternity. God's love is a predestining love, not simply an open invitation. Many biblical texts attest to this. The first chapter of Ephesians is almost a hymn about God's eternal, purposeful love. In it, Paul tells us, "In love he predestined us for adoption through Jesus Christ, according to the purpose of his will, to the praise of his glorious grace" (Eph. 1:4–6). The gospel is a mystery, once hidden but now revealed (v. 9). Our inheritance in Christ was ordained in accordance with God's great purposes: "In him we have obtained an inheritance, having been predestined according to the purpose of him who works all things according to the counsel of his will" (v. 11).

As we saw in our earlier discussions on the Synod of Dort, the subject of predestination is meant not to frighten us but to comfort us. To be sure, as the Westminster Confession of Faith puts it, "The doctrine of this high mystery of predestination is to be handled with special prudence and care." Yet this is in order that we may have assurance, leading to worship: "So shall this doctrine afford matter of praise, reverence, and admiration of God; and of humility, diligence, and abundant consolation to all that sincerely obey the gospel" (3.8). As Paul puts it to the Thessalonians, "But we ought always to give thanks to God for you, brothers beloved by the Lord, because God chose you as the firstfruits to be saved" (2 Thess. 2:13). Predestination should lead us to praise God. After all, it is most comforting to know that nothing can thwart God's purposes. Consider how Psalm 33 turns the sovereign purposes of God into a subject for gratitude in recognition of the ultimate blessedness of believers:

> The counsel of the LORD stands forever,
>   the plans of his heart to all generations.
> Blessed is the nation whose God is the LORD,
>   the people whom he has chosen as his heritage!
>   (Ps. 33:11–12)

Among other matters, this assures us that God's love is unconditional. His predestining love is not conditioned on his foreknowledge of what will take place. He could not have foreknowledge of events and people in the first place if he did not ordain them. Does Romans 8:29 contradict this? It appears to make a distinction and to base predestination on foreknowledge. A closer look reveals the two terms are complementary, using biblical parallelism. Foreknowledge, in this context, means personal communion, a love that emanates in eternity. Predestination is a further definition of such foreknowledge.

At the same time, wonderfully, mysteriously, there is no conflict between this sovereign love and human responsibility. If we worry that predestination erases our moral freedom, we are in good company. All kinds of schemes have been developed in the history of the church to work out the relation rationally. Usually, though, one side or another of the equation is lost or diminished in such schemes. Often, to ensure God's sovereignty, the significance of human agency is denied. We find such an approach in Islam and in hyper-Calvinism. Contrariwise, in order to ensure human freedom, God's power is diminished, as is the case in Pelagian and Arminian theologies. The problem is trying to reduce the terms to make them fit the criteria of autonomous human reason. They just will not fit.

Still, we cannot sit and wait for God to come through for us, regardless of our response to the gospel offer. Our job is not to figure out the intricacies of the relation but to turn and trust in the saving God. Thus, as we have seen, far from removing human freedom and significance, the doctrine of predestination secures them and requires them. Practically speaking, there is no point in waiting and wondering if you might be one of the elect. When the gospel is offered, we need do only one thing: respond in humble faith, asking God's mercy in Christ. Second, rather than puzzling over the mystery to the point of distraction, we ought to praise God for his predestining salvation. It means that nothing can separate us from the love of Christ (Rom. 8:35). It means that all things work together for good for his chosen people (Rom. 8:28). Praise God!

The Covenant of Grace

The plan of redemption is structured as a covenant, the covenant of grace. After the failure of our first parents to obey God's command in the Garden, and thus their banishment, and with them the condemnation of the entire human race to perdition, God, of his mere good pleasure, moved by love, promised his mercy upon his people. Reformed theology has been preeminent in recognizing this particular formulation of the promise. It is known as the covenant of grace, because it enacts an arrangement whereby God binds himself to redeem his people, with the stipulation that they turn from their ways and place their faith in him. From the Scripture, the heart of the covenant is summarized in the words, "I will take you to be my people, and I will be your God" (Exod. 6:7; Deut. 4:20; 29:13; Jer. 31:33; Hos. 2:23; Zech. 8:8; Rev. 21:7).

Though the term *covenant* is used of God's promise to Noah (Gen. 6:18; 9:9), the pattern for the covenant was first made clear in the promise to Abraham, God's blessing and his pledge that he would become the father of many nations.[2] We learn that sacrifice is needed to establish the covenant, through the symbolism of the fire on the animal carcass and the symbol of circumcision (Gen. 15:17–21; 17:9–14). The most important covenant in the Old Testament is at Mount Sinai, when the people of God are officially constituted. Here, the covenant is resumed in the Ten Commandments, written on tablets of stone (Deut. 4:13; 9:9). Marvelously, the great distinctive characteristic of Israel before the nations is reflected in the nearness of a God who could be called upon and in the glory of the law that he gives, a

---

2. Various Reformed approaches have argued that covenant is such a basic arrangement for the relation between God and humankind that it can well be applied to the pre-fallen state. The Westminster Standards refer to the "covenant of works" (Westminster Confession of Faith, 7.2). The idea is that life was promised to our first parents upon "condition" of their obedience. This is true, when stated this way, but it can give the unintended impression that there was an absence of God's gratuitous goodness before the fall, which is quite mistaken. For this reason certain theologians prefer terms such as "Adamic administration" to the traditional "covenant of works."

law "that will be your wisdom and your understanding in the sight of the peoples" (Deut. 4:6–8).

In the New Testament, the covenant comes into its own in Jesus Christ. Not only is he the object of all the promises of the Old Testament, but also his coming is so glorious that it is called the new covenant. Though the principles are the same with the Old Testament administration, so final, so momentous is it that the new covenant can be said to displace the old covenant (Heb. 8:10; 10:9). It is an eternal covenant (Heb. 13:20). At the same time, the heart of the covenant is the same, only heightened and deepened in Christ, through his sacrifice, a sacrifice far greater than the ordeals of the ceremonial law. God is our God in Jesus Christ, and we are his people, for the praise of his grace before the nations (2 Cor. 6:16–18; 2 Peter 2:9–12). The covenant is the gospel (2 Cor. 3:6)!

God's covenant of grace is unilateral in its establishment. That is, it originates in his love and is given unconditionally by election. God cannot fail to keep his covenant promises (Lev. 26:44–45; Deut. 4:31). It is one-sided because God operates it and determines the terms. At the same time the covenant of grace is two-sided in its application. A response in faith, followed by obedience, is required. Faith alone is the condition for coming to God in Christ, but true and authentic faith is never alone. This is why God commands his people to obey and keep the covenant, even though it is given by grace. So there is a condition to the covenant, even though it is given unconditionally. One way to express this is by noting that no one can merit salvation by grace, and so no causal condition can qualify the covenant. Yet faith proven by obedience is required in order that we be made beholden to God, and thus there is an instrumental condition to the covenant (Rom. 10:7). The Westminster Confession of Faith nicely defines the covenant of grace as that "whereby he freely offereth unto sinners life and salvation by Jesus Christ, requiring of them faith in him, that they may be saved." Then it adds, lest there be any doubt, "and promising to give unto all those that are ordained unto life his Holy Spirit, to make them willing and able to believe" (7.3).

Implications

A word about Israel's future. Most Reformed theologians believe Israel's general lack of faith and legalism in the time of Christ has disqualified the Jews from the old covenant promises. While this is true, several things should be noted. First, whether old or new covenant, the terms are the same. The covenant promises of the Old Testament were never automatic or bound up with ethnicity. What always mattered was faith from the heart, not good works, nor belonging to a particular people (Rom. 4:16). Second, the temporary hardening of the Jews became, in God's wisdom, a means to open the doors to the Gentiles, who enter into the covenant by faith. This is the chief burden of Romans 9–11. While it may appear that Paul's kin according to the flesh have renounced their privileges, that renunciation is neither definitive nor permanent. It spells a wonderful opportunity for the Gentiles. This accords with much of Jesus' teaching, whereby the kingdom is taken away from its rightful heirs and given to those who are not the children of the promise (Mark 7:26–30). Third, however, the Jews are still no more and no less the objects of God's love in the new covenant than the Gentiles, and so the promises to them are still valid, in Christ. They will see the response of the Gentiles and return (Rom. 9:4; 11:27–29; Eph. 2:12). There is legitimate debate as to whether the Jews will return en masse in the last days, or whether they will come into the covenant one by one, just as Gentiles do. My conviction is that they will come one by one.

A word about the place of children. Most Reformed people (with the exception of Reformed Baptists) argue that children are no less members of the covenant than they were in the Old Testament times (Isa. 59:21; Luke 18:15–17; 1 Cor. 7:14). The apostle Peter, in his great Pentecost sermon, proclaimed the gospel as a promise for "you and for your children" (Acts 2:39). Naturally, when children grow up they must fulfill the requirement of personal faith evidenced by obedience rather than presume they are saved without the need for personal engagement. We will address this question more fully under the rubric of baptism.

A pact from eternity. The covenant of grace is rooted in a prior arrangement, a compact between the Father and the Son. Some theologians call it the "covenant of redemption." Others call it an "intertrinitarian arrangement." Perhaps the best phrase is the "pact of salvation." Accordingly, the Father and the Son are of one mind regarding the plan to save a people. Yet their parts are different. In the first instance, the Father will represent God in the arrangement. The Son will represent his people. The Father will give the Son a people for his heritage. He promises to provide all that is necessary for the redemptive work of the Son. This includes the gift of the Holy Spirit, who will be the principal agent in applying the blessings of redemption to the people of God (John 16:7; Acts 2:33; Eph. 2:18). In the second instance, the Son in turn agrees to lay down his life and to take it up again (John 10:18). He will obey the Father, even to the point of death, in order to gain a people for the praise of God. Thus the Son can say of himself, citing the ancient words, "Behold, I have come to do your will, O God, as it is written of me in the scroll of the book" (Heb. 10:7, citing Ps. 40:7). Such technical language may make the plan of salvation sound cold and contractual. The reality is far more than one of a mere legally binding agreement. But it is at least that.

The price of atonement. If saving his people was motivated by God's love and thus anything but a necessity, once the decision was made to do so, the price to pay was atonement. "For it was fitting," says the writer of Hebrews, "that he, for whom and by whom all things exist, in bringing many sons to glory, should make the founder of their salvation perfect through suffering" (Heb. 2:10; see v. 17). Or, even more pointedly, the legislation of the Old Testament ceremonial law established that "without the shedding of blood there is no forgiveness of sins" (Heb. 9:22). Thus it was necessary, the text continues, for the sacrifice of Jesus to replace all the temporary ones provided by the ceremonial law (Heb. 9:23). If an easier way could have been found, surely God would have done so. This makes us appreciate all the more the extraordinary humility of Christ's incarnation and his suffering for our sakes.

The Person of Jesus Christ

The covenant of grace, as determined by God's sovereign, loving, eternal will, requires four participants: the Father, the originator; Jesus Christ, the mediator; the Holy Spirit, the validator; and God's people, the beneficiaries. Jesus Christ is the mediator of the new covenant (Heb. 9:15; 12:24). He is the "one mediator between God and men" (1 Tim. 2:5). By becoming a man, by suffering for his people, he guaranteed our redemption. He is the only high priest worthy of the name, because he shed his innocent blood in a single, costly offering of himself to the Father, one that perfects all who are being prepared to commune with God (Heb. 10:12–14). In order to grasp something of the wonder of this, we will consider, first, Christ's person, and second, his work.

"But who do you say that I am?" Jesus asked his followers (Matt. 16:15). On the answer to this question depends nothing less than the fate of the world. On the answer to this question hang life and death, salvation or perdition. Jesus Christ is not the founder of Christianity, as he is sometimes presented. There are two reasons, a minor one and a major one. The minor reason is that the term *Christianity* is a problem. Properly understood, the Christian faith is not a realm or a domain. The term *Christendom* is worse, since it refers specifically to a geographical area, and to an epoch when a strong tie between the church and the state led to confusion at best and distortion at worst. But "Christianity" too can be confusing. It is often offensive to outsiders, as though there were a well-defined cultural and theological system available only to insiders. The major reason is that Jesus Christ is not the founder of a religion that began in the first century. He is neither a great moral teacher (at least, not in any ordinary sense) nor the charismatic leader of a new group.

Rather, Jesus Christ is the second person of the Holy Trinity. As we saw earlier, the Son is equal in every way to the Father and to the Spirit. He is God, all-knowing, all-powerful, and worthy of worship. He is the Alpha and Omega (Rev. 1:8), the same yesterday, today, and forever (Heb. 13:8). Yet, moved by compassion and in accordance with the covenant of redemption, the second person humbled himself and became a human being (Phil. 2:6–8; Col. 2:15–20). J. S. Bach's setting of the phrase *incarnatus est* ("and he became incarnate") in his *Mass in B minor* expresses it powerfully in music. The notes contain a figurative rendering of descent, using various downward intervals, and a sober, quiet, yet joyful mood that captures the momentous miracle of God becoming flesh. The Gospel narratives of Matthew and Luke recount the wonder and joy of this central event in redemptive history: a virgin conception, the fulfillment of prophecy, Herod's thwarted jealousy, angelic praise, Mary's meditations, Simeon's departure in peace. John's Gospel proclaims the grand theological mystery signified by the event: the Word that was in the beginning, the mediator of creation, becomes flesh, and "tabernacles" among us, revealing a fullness of grace far beyond Moses and John the Baptist.

Peter answered his Lord's question correctly: "You are the Christ, the Son of the living God" (Matt. 16:16). Jesus blessed him for it and promised that the victorious church and the all-defining kingdom would be built on that confession. The names given to the incarnate second person are themselves pregnant with meaning. He is called Jesus, a Greek form of the Hebrew *Jehoshua* (see Josh. 1:1; Zech. 3:1), or, in its postexilic form, *Jeshua* (Ezra 2:2). The word means "to save" or "savior." He is also called the Christ, which is the equivalent of Messiah or the Anointed One found throughout the Old Testament. The kings and priests were anointed, and so was one prophet, Elisha (1 Kings 19:16), in a ceremony that confirmed their office and the power of God to accomplish their task (the oil symbolized the Spirit of God). Jesus' baptism was the ceremony of ordination to the three offices he held: prophet, priest, and king. In his case the Spirit of God came upon him directly, and the voice of the Father conferred the offices (Matt. 3:16–17). He is also called the Son of Man, his favorite self-designation, perhaps because it was fresh and rarely used otherwise. The title derives from the Book of Ezekiel, and especially from Daniel 7, where "one like a son of man" comes to the Ancient of Days, in order to be conferred dominion and glory before every nation (Dan. 7:13–14). He is also called, directly, the Son of God, in ways that refer to his being as well as his position. Jesus was frequently called Lord, a title appropriate for his person, showing respect for his office and the recognition that he is God.

Neither his friends nor his enemies missed the affirmations Jesus made about himself. He not only proclaimed the forgiveness of sins, but also forgave them. When he healed the paralytic and forgave his sins, some scribes in the audience immediately understood: "Why does this man speak like that? He is blaspheming! Who can forgive sins but God alone?" (Mark 2:6–7). Jesus often equated himself with God. He was fond of using comparisons preceded by the famous "I am" from Exodus: "I am the bread of life," "I am the good shepherd," "I am the light of the world." Once, the point was so clear and so unlike any ordinary moral teacher that the religious leaders attempted to stone him to death. He affirmed that Abraham rejoiced to see his day. When the group asked him how this could be, since he was not yet fifty years old, he replied, "Truly, truly, I say to you, before Abraham was, I am" (John 8:58).

Jesus is clearly God. He is also clearly a man. He ate, he slept, he wept, and in the end he died, though he would be raised from the dead. His humanity meant that he was conceived in a mother's womb. He was born and grew up. He had to learn, just as any other child did (Luke 2:46). Certain things were kept from his knowledge. For example, he did not know the day or the hour of the end of the world (Matt. 24:36). He knew the human emotions of joy, contentment, anger, and exasperation, and he could be tempted as a man, yet without succumbing to sin. To save us he had to be God. But he also had to be a man in order to represent the redeemed portion of the human race and be the last Adam.

The Heart of the Incarnation

How may we understand this profound mystery of the incarnation? And it *is* a mystery. Paul put it this way, using what may have been an early hymn of the church:

Great, indeed, we confess, is the mystery of godliness:

He was manifested in the flesh,
    vindicated by the Spirit, seen by angels,
proclaimed among the nations,
    believed on in the world, taken up in glory. (1 Tim. 3:16)

Is there any way to understand at least some of the most basic features of the incarnation? As we saw earlier, the ancient church wrestled with the problem of Christology, because distortions were easy to fall into. Some groups, such as the Ebionites, affirmed that Jesus was fully human but denied his full divinity. The Arians had a subtler scheme that depleted Jesus' deity, making him something like a demigod (modern Jehovah's Witnesses do the same). Other groups, such as the Monophysites, diminished Jesus' humanity while affirming his deity. Many other variants could be found. The Eutychians, as we mentioned, thought the human and divine were mingled into a third nature that was a little of both.

As we saw in part 1, the Council of Chalcedon (451) took a giant step forward. Taking the various data from the Scriptures and knowing that without full humanity and full deity Christ could not have saved his people from sin, the theologians at Chalcedon crafted a balanced formulation, using certain Greek concepts that have stood the test of time. They used the term *person*, mentioned earlier in reference to the Trinity, to understand Christ's unity. Christ is one person, but he has two natures. Sometimes the one person is characterized through the expression *hypostatic union* (from the Greek word for "person"). This formulation safeguards the point that the Son is the same person before and after the incarnation. He was God, the second person of the Trinity, but then he added humanity to himself, yet without abandoning that personhood. As the Council of Nicea had already said, he was consubstantial (*homoousias*), "being of one substance with the Father," because he was and remained God. At the same time, by adding humanity to himself he did not end up as a third entity, as the Eutychians would have it. He was in two natures, the one human and the other divine.

Thus, Christ, after the incarnation, is one person in two natures. Chalcedon specified that the two natures were without mixture, without change, without division, without separation, and with two wills. These qualifications are all meant to guard against the danger of seeing Christ as something other than God who is human. As Louis Berkhof puts it:

> The one divine person, who possessed a divine nature from
> eternity, assumed a human nature and now has both. After this
> assumption of a human nature the person of the Mediator is
> not divine only but divine-human; He is now the God-man.
> He is a single individual, but possesses the essential qualities
> of both the human and the divine nature. While He has but a
> single self-consciousness, He has both a divine and a human
> consciousness, as well as a divine and human will.[3]

Human formulations are limited, of course. But Chalcedon is a most
profound way to understand the different data from the New Testament. Thus, when we see Jesus weeping (John 11:35), or anxious and
agonizing (Luke 22:44), we can say these are possible with respect to
his humanity. When we observe him multiplying the loaves of bread
and the fishes (Matt. 16:36–39) or teaching that to fail to follow him
is to be condemned at the judgment (Mark 8:38), we can say these
are possible with respect to his deity. And finally, in all cases, they are
manifest in the one person.

All kinds of questions plunge us into the depths of the mystery.
Could Jesus the man really forgive sins? If he were only a man, it *would*
be blasphemy. But the person of Christ could forgive sins, because he
is God in the flesh. It was possible with respect to his deity. Does Jesus
have a human body and soul? Yes, and they are united in one person
to his deity, which has neither body nor soul. Was Jesus really tempted
by the devil in the desert (see Matt. 4:1–11; Mark 1:2–8; Luke 3:2–17)?
How can he have been if he is God, since "God cannot be tempted
with evil" (James 1:13)? If that were the case, then the temptation is
a piece of theater, and we could then never say, with the author of the
Hebrews, "because he himself has suffered when tempted, he is able
to help those who are being tempted" (Heb. 2:18). Even less could we
say that he is one "who in every respect has been tempted as we are,
yet without sin" (Heb. 4:15). The way to understand this is to agree
that the person was tempted, a temptation made possible with respect

3. Louis Berkhof, *Manual of Christian Doctrine* (Grand Rapids: Eerdmans, 1933),
184.

to his human nature. Did God weep? Did God die on the cross? We tremble to say such a thing, because God cannot die. But yet, Christ the person, the second person of the Trinity, died on the cross. He was liable to death with respect to his human nature.

The Work of Jesus Christ

If Jesus Christ was the God-man, how did that affect redemption? What work did he accomplish on our behalf?

Jesus' work as mediator. To begin with, it is customary to speak of Christ's two great states as mediator. First was his humiliation. Becoming a man truly meant a lowering of himself. For the purpose of becoming human, he laid aside the privileges of divine majesty. By the Holy Spirit he entered a virgin's womb as a tiny embryo. He was born into a cruel world. He who made the law became subject to the law. He who could have called down legions of angels submitted to a mock trial at the hands of a petty despot. "He suffered, died, and was buried," the creed tells us. He suffered the pangs of hell. During none of this did he lose or diminish his deity, nor did he give in to temptation and sin.

Next was his exaltation. "On the third day, he rose again from the dead," the creed goes on to say. The resurrection was not only coming to life again. It was the triumph over all the forces of evil. Christ is the firstfruit, "the firstborn from the dead, that in everything he might be preeminent" (Col. 1:18). After the victory, he sits at the right hand of the Father and rules the world, a world that has been given to him for redemption and for judgment. This Lion of the tribe of Judah, this Root of David who conquered, is alone worthy to open the book of history (Rev. 5:5). "All authority in heaven and on earth has been given to me," he tells his followers before sending them into the world to make disciples of the nations (Matt. 28:18). He is now the sympathetic high priest for his people, interceding for them from heaven. At the end, Jesus will come again in visible, personal form to judge the earth and usher the new heavens and new earth into final reality. Throughout his exaltation, he continues to be the God-man, one person in two natures. It is an awe-inspiring thought that he will forever be truly human, with a physical body, as well as truly divine.

Jesus' call as prophet, priest, and king. We may speak of the offices Christ held, and still holds, as Savior. They are the three great offices of prophet, priest, and king. Humankind's original purposes could rightly be subsumed under those categories. We were meant to be prophets, understanding and evaluating the world around us with clarity and precision. We were meant as priests to take the riches of the world and offer them to God in grateful sacrifice. And as kings we were meant to rule the world, subduing it with care and judging it with equity. We failed miserably in those tasks, turning prophetic gifts into ideologies, priestly gifts into idolatry, and kingly office into abuse. But God, out of his love for us, provided a Son who would restore those offices and give new and richer meaning to the calling of prophet, priest, and king.

We failed in the execution of these callings, and God could well have left us to perish in well-deserved judgment. But instead, moved with compassion, he went to the great extreme of atonement. The bloody sacrifice of the Son of God is the only remedy for the horror of the human condition. In it, God set forth his only Son to be the propitiation, that is, the covering of his own face from the dreadfulness of sin. Propitiation does not make a wrathful God into a loving God. Rather, it turns away the wrath of a most loving God and makes a way for redemption. Instead of meting out judgment on a particular people, because of propitiation he can forgive. "My little children," writes the tender John, "I am writing these things to you so that you may not sin. But if anyone does sin, we have an advocate with the Father, Jesus Christ the righteous. He is the propitiation for our sins, and not for ours only but also for the sins of the whole world" (1 John 2:1–2).

Christ's work of obedience. We can well summarize the work of Christ in terms of his obedience. In the great prophetic passage, Isaiah 53, Christ is foreseen as a suffering servant. In the Gospel of John, we learn over and over again that Jesus came to do the will of the Father and to lay down his life to follow the Father's command (John 6:38; 10:17–18). Paul puts it tersely: "He humbled himself by becoming obedient to the point of death, even death on a cross" (Phil. 2:8). And, as he compares the role of Adam to Christ, he labels the one disobedient and the other obedient (Rom. 5:19). Reformed theology often distinguishes between the active and the passive obedience of Christ. The former refers to his fulfilling all the positive demands of the law. The latter refers to his willingness to have all the penal sanctions of the law meted out upon him.

A perfect work. We must characterize Christ's work as perfect. It is perfect in many ways. First, it occurred in history. In the last two hundred years certain forms of liberal theology have maintained that the atonement and resurrection were constructs of the early church. Nothing could be further from the truth. God sent his Son "in the fullness of time," to redeem his people "while we were still sinners" (Gal. 4:4; Rom. 5:8). Second, the atonement was final, once and for all. In the history of the church the finality of Christ's work has been compromised by various theologies that affirm the continuation of his work through the church. In some accounts, the church is believed to be an extension of his incarnation and the Mass is understood to be a re-sacrifice of Christ.[4] But such teaching in effect denies everything central about the atonement. The Book of Hebrews forcefully defends the once-for-all finality of Christ's sacrifice (Heb. 1:3; 9:12, 25–28). When our Lord pronounced the words "It is finished" from the cross, this meant the work of atonement was done. Of course, the work of Christ was not done! He rose from the dead. He rose up to heaven and governs the affairs of humankind for his kingdom purposes. He is, most actively, our heavenly high priest, interceding for us at all times. But the intercession is possible only because the work of active and passive obedience is done. "But if anyone does sin, we have an advocate with the Father, Jesus Christ the righteous. He is the propitiation for our sins" (1 John 2:1–2).

4. We will look at this in more detail when we come to the sacraments.

Once again, putting matters this way may seem somewhat cold and abstract. When we read the Gospel accounts of Jesus' life, we see the power and meaning of his teaching, his miracles, his interactions with people, and his suffering. When we read the large sections at the end of the Gospels we are plunged in to a great tragedy, the passion of Christ. Crucifixion was one of the cruelest forms of punishment ever devised. It was meant to torture the victim physically by suffocation, but it also was meant to shame the person by stretching him out and exposing him to the public. What Jesus went through on our behalf was unspeakably awful. There is no human equivalent. He is God, and so the suffering was far beyond what anyone can imagine. The Son of God suffered physically and morally, qualitatively beyond what any mere human has ever gone through. He, the second person of the Trinity, was literally abandoned by the Father, given up by him, considered liable for rebellion. Though innocent, Jesus appealed to his God from the cross, but, unlike all the previous times when he had prayed, heaven was silent.

Blessedly, this tragic death was the end of Christ's humiliation but not the end of the story. Because he had done nothing wrong and because the whole purpose of his coming to earth was to secure a victory, the most amazing event in all of history occurred. He was raised up from the dead. Mary looked for him in the grave on Easter Sunday morning but could not find him there. Peter and John went inside to look for him and found only grave clothes, neatly folded up. Jesus was alive! He had been raised from the dead, by the glory of the Father (Rom. 6:4). Having been crucified in weakness, he now lives by the power of God and in the Spirit of holiness (2 Cor. 13:4; Rom. 1:4). Jesus is now the firstborn of the dead and the ruler of kings on earth (Rev. 1:5; 5:6; Matt. 28:18).

An effective work. The atonement is definite. This means that Christ's death was efficacious. He did not die to make redemption possible or to remove certain obstacles so that we would have to do the rest. He died to redeem. Earlier, we looked at the struggles surrounding the Remonstrant group, with its Arminian theology, and the Synod of Dort, over the question of the extent of the atonement. Based on texts such as 1 John 2:2 and others, the Remonstrants claimed that Christ died to make salvation available for everyone, whereas only believers took advantage of it. The part truth here is that his sufferings were sufficient. Should there be more believers than were first counted (something impossible in reality), he would not have had to suffer more. The other part truth here, the one John refers to, is that Christ's death avails for believers all over the world, not only for the small circle that first read his letter. John specifies that Jesus is the propitiation for the sins of the whole world, as well as for our sins. Further, all kinds of benefits come to humankind, short of redemption, because of the cross and Jesus' reign.

Having said this, it is impossible that Christ's death be effectual for every human being. He died for his people. Titus praises the God and Savior Jesus Christ because he "gave himself for us to redeem us from all lawlessness and to purify a people for himself a people for his own possession who are zealous for good works" (Titus 2:14). His work did not make us redeemable; it redeemed us. Or, to put it the other way, how could it ever be that someone for whom Christ died was never saved? In Romans 8 we are told in several ways that if God is for us, by the atoning work of his Son, then no one can oppose us (Rom. 8:34). If we are Christ's, then the same Spirit who raised him up lives in us (Rom. 8:11). If we are Christ's, we have been predestined to be called, justified, and glorified (Rom. 8:30). Not only that, but as many as Christ died to save are also dead in him. We have died in Christ, because he died for us (Rom. 6:3–11; 2 Cor. 5:14–15; Eph. 2:4–7; Col. 3:3). The wonder of it is that his people died with Christ, through the cross, so that they now live for him. The atonement is that definite.

The rule of Christ. Jesus rules in the present. He is the supreme governor of the world. All authority has been given to him (Matt. 28:18), and with that authority he directs the events of history (Rev. 5:5). He assures the world of his patience. His rule is not always visible, but yet he puts everything in subjection under his feet (Heb. 2:8). He gives earthly rulers a right to govern (Rom. 13:1; John 19:11). And he calls the world to come to him for life, in view of the coming judgment (Acts 17:30).

Jesus particularly rules his church. For forty days he remained on earth and appeared to many people. First, he appeared to Mary, the first to have recognized him. He then appeared to all the disciples, even to doubting Thomas, whose fatalism had rendered him incapable of believing the clear testimony of others. He showed himself to large crowds. During this brief period, before ascending to heaven, Jesus gave orders to the disciples. He told them to make disciples throughout the world (Matt. 28:19). He told them to shepherd his sheep and to use the power of the Word of God to build up the church (John 20:23).

He gave many directives to his people, but most of all he promised the great gift of the Holy Spirit (Acts 1:8). The long-awaited Spirit of God would be poured out and would graciously apply all of the virtues, all of the benefits gained by Jesus, because of his death and resurrection. Through this extraordinary gift, not only would the sins of his people be forgiven and the power for living before God be theirs, but also they would be granted authority to accomplish all of the high tasks they were assigned. The church would be fully equipped to live in the world, to remain citizens of heaven while in an earthly exile. Each of us is given a gift in order to build others up in the faith (Eph. 4:7–16).

Glorified life through his Spirit. Finally, this life-giving Spirit will raise each of us up in glory (1 Cor. 15:43–45). Though by faith already we behold the glory of the Lord, who is the Spirit, the day will come when, together, his people will be ushered in to the new heavens and the new earth by the Spirit, and they will live in his power and glory and life forever.

The coming of the Lord in glory is personal and visible. He comes to rescue and vindicate his people. The days of the end are carefully numbered, so that Jesus can save his people from the great distress that visits the world (Matt. 24:22, 31). We are warned specifically not to speculate on the time or the date of that rescue (v. 31). We are further told to understand that the entire time between Christ's first and second coming is characterized by two realities. First, there is a time of trouble. The biblical language speaks of tribulation and darkness, wars, and false religions (Matt. 24:4–12). Second, though, it is a time of the great success of world missions and of the testimony of God's kingdom throughout the world (v. 14).

There is also the coming of the Lord in judgment. In the words of the creed, "He is coming again to judge both the quick and the dead." This arcane language means that every human creature from every age and place will have to render an account to God, who will sit on the "great white throne" of judgment from which there is no escape (Rev. 20:11). In the end, there will be only two verdicts. The one will be the condemnation of those who have refused to honor God in their thoughts and lives. The other will be the acquittal, already in hand, of believers who have placed their faith in Christ's mercy. This has to be. The God of all righteousness must judge the world. For those who have known the light but have suppressed it in order to walk without God, there remains the dreadful prospect of eternal death (the "second death," or hell, as the New Testament puts it; Rev. 20:15). For the redeemed, who are in the book of life, it will be the bliss of the new Jerusalem. Redemption is accomplished. Glory be to God!

UNSEARCHABLE RICHES

~~~~~~~~~~

Redemption Applied

How definite is redemption? How complete is God's saving work? The Canons of Dort, reflecting the Scriptures, tell us that the value of Christ's death and resurrection is not vague and generalized. Their value is infinite. So great is the effectiveness of Christ's atonement that it seeks out and finds each one of God's precious people in order to save them, to embrace them into his bosom. The atonement is of such astonishing power that it takes each beloved sinner and turns him or her into God's daughter or son. Not only so, but whatever the nature of our alienation from God, whatever evils we may own, from the least visible, private sins, to the most public, heinous crimes, the sacrifice of Jesus Christ has dealt with them. Whether they are past, present, or future, our iniquities and corruptions have been conquered. Our guilt has been erased. Redemption is not only accomplished; it is applied.

Theological talk holds the advantage of clarity but also the danger of losing sight of the momentousness and the personal implications of what is at stake. To speak of the accomplishment, the application of redemption should never sound like a cold, textbook explanation for God's purposes. The accomplishment of redemption was for us. This great work of atonement having been completed, the work of application is ongoing, in us. The same love that motivated the Lord God to choose me from all eternity will tirelessly seek me out, will preserve me, will transform me and make me fit for eternal life. Not only so, but I am in the company of all God's people, a vast and countless number of former enemies for whom Christ died. And while what we possess is already amazing, what is to come is even more so. The blessings of redemption far exceed mere restoration to an original state.

It is extraordinary to think that God did not save us reluctantly, nor is redemption a minimal rescue. It is full and rich and good. God loves us not barely but extravagantly. He pursues us not grudgingly but relentlessly, until he has us in his loving grasp. It is unthinkable that he should provide the foundations of redemption but not its application. It is unthinkable that he should accomplish redemption without taking it to its ultimate purpose, the seeking and saving of the lost. As we've emphasized, Augustine once said we were restless until we could rest in God. But we could, with justice, turn the expression around. God's love is so great that he is restless until he can place that love on its object, his people, you and me! Jesus Christ accomplished redemption on the cross and at the resurrection. Now the Lord applies it to his people. He brings each one to himself. The application of redemption benefits even those believers in Old Testament times who trusted God before Christ's earthly ministry, in the fullness of times. The classical language of the Canons of Dort puts it this way:

> It was the will of God, that Christ by the blood of the cross, whereby he confirmed the new covenant, should effectually redeem out of every people, tribe, nation, and language, all those, and those only, who were from eternity chosen to salvation, and given to him by the Father; that he should confer upon them faith, which, together with all the other saving gifts of the Holy Spirit, he purchased for them by his death; should purge them from all sin, both original and actual, whether committed before or after believing; and having faithfully preserved them even to the end, should at last bring them free from every

spot and blemish to the enjoyment of glory in his own presence forever.[1]

The accomplishment of redemption can be considered in two general categories, known as already and not yet. We already live in the reality of the heavenly places, even though not yet in the full, consummate bliss of the heavenly Jerusalem. Reformed theology sometimes calls this the already–not yet of redemption. Formulating redemption as a two-part accomplishment helps us better understand where we are. While we are saved now, and while nothing can snatch us out of the hands of our Savior, yet we still live in a world full of evil. While we are made holy (literally, we are saints, holy ones), sin and guilt continue to plague us. God has won the warfare, but particular battles are still being fought. The D-Day of redemption has been accomplished, but now numerous conflicts remain until the last adversary is wiped out.

The double reality of already–not yet also helps us understand the New Testament language about ethics. If we are redeemed, then we ought to live more consistently with what we are, in view of what we are going to be. Christian ethics has a double focus. We do not have to strive for something alien: we become what we are. At the same time, until the new heaven and new earth we will always be far from the mark. We died with Christ and are alive in him already (Rom. 6:4, 11; Col. 3:1, 3). Therefore we ought to put away sin and yield ourselves to life, a life that we have not yet fully achieved but are assured of obtaining in the resurrection in glory (Rom. 6:5; Col. 3:1–2, 4).

The Central Gift: Union with Christ

Redemption is like a symphony of gifts. Its gifts are many, and its application is rich and varied. But there is one music, one unified sound. We are about to explore the many gifts God pours out on his people as he brings them into communion with himself. Yet there is one purpose, and therefore one central reality from which all the oth-

---

1. Canons of Dort, second head of doctrine, article 8.

ers flow. All of the blessings of redemption can be subsumed under the large heading of union with Christ. This is a marvelous truth. Consider how many times the New Testament speaks about being in Christ. Even our election from eternity is in Christ. Think of the way the Gospel of John portrays Jesus as the bread of life, of which we partake, and the light of the world, which gives us the "light of life," and the true vine, of which we are fruit-bearing branches. The church, God's people, is loved by Christ, who "gave himself up for her" (Eph. 5:25). Even death, or should we say, especially death, cannot separate us from Christ. The people of God do not die outside of Christ but fall asleep in him, as they wait for the final resurrection in glory (1 Thess. 4:14–15). In the final reign of heaven, we have his name on our foreheads (Rev. 22:4). We are glorified in him (1 Cor. 15:22; Rom. 8:17). Union with Christ is thus wide and all-encompassing. It begins with election, before the beginning, and ends with glorification, which will have no end.

This union with Christ is rightly called a mystical union. This expression has a specific definition. We sometimes use the word *mystery* to mean something strange or otherworldly. The biblical sense does not quite fit with that. Rather, it means something once hidden in the heart of God but now made known through Jesus Christ in the gospel (Col. 1:26–27). To be sure, this makes the mystery of union with Christ precious, intimate, and complex. At the highest level, our union with Christ is compared with the union of the Father and the Son in the divine Trinity (John 14:23; 17:21–23). This is astounding. Sometimes, at other levels, it is compared with the union of husband and wife (Eph. 5:32; John 3:29), of Adam to his children (Rom. 5:12–19; 1 Cor. 15:19–49), and of a building to the cornerstone (Eph. 2:19–22; 1 Peter 2:4–5).

Being a mystery, it must be understood by faith—not an irrational leap in the dark but intelligent trust in something true, though beyond our immediate grasp. This wonderful mystery gives us hope and meaning in a dark world. Without it, we can have nothing to lean upon. This is one of the reasons that other religions, other philosophies, can have no final meaning or be true, ultimately. They may and do contain much wisdom. But there is nothing even remotely like union with Christ, even in the most mystical and spiritual religions. The ideal of Buddhism is detachment, not personal union with the incarnate Son. The ideal of Taoism is harmony with the cosmic forces of yin and yang, not a relationship with Jesus. The ideal of Islam is slavish obedience, not grateful fellowship with God.

The primary agent of our joining to Christ is God the Holy Spirit. He it is who was promised to Jesus by the Father and who was poured out at Pentecost, to remain in and with the church for the duration of its earthly pilgrimage and on into the new Jerusalem (Acts 2:33). He it is who baptizes God's people into the one body of Christ (1 Cor. 12:13). It is by the Spirit we can confess that Christ is Lord (1 Cor. 12:3). The gifts and the offices of the church are from him (1 Cor. 12:4–11; Eph. 4:11–12). The Spirit who inspired the Word of God gives us the Word of God for our greatest good (Eph. 6:17). The Spirit transforms our poor prayers into acceptable ones before the face of God (Rom. 8:26–27). The Spirit gives us assurance that we belong to the Lord as children and heirs (Rom. 8:16–17). In Christ, we are being built together into a holy temple where God will dwell by the Spirit (Eph. 2:22).

While union with Christ began in eternity, we do not become actual partakers of the benefits of Christ until redemption is applied. Before we are actually redeemed, we are outside of Christ and have no hope. We may have been elected from eternity, but we are not saved until we come, effectually, into his fellowship. Unless the Spirit of God takes the things of Christ and applies them to us, we are not God's children. In a word, we are not Christ's until we are converted. Conversion occurs in history. It most often manifests itself in our awareness (although one could argue that infants dying in infancy and mentally challenged people can be converted without full consciousness of their position). For convenience, and because the Bible gives us warrant to do so, we may consider conversion under several distinct rubrics. They are not necessarily distinct in time, but they are nevertheless distinct. Implied, too, is a logical sequence, which will become important as we try to do justice to each one.

Gifts in the Order of Salvation

In Reformed theology it has become customary to understand the various components of the application of redemption within our union with Christ and to put the many different gifts of God in a certain order. The traditional term for the sequence is the Latin phrase *ordo salutis*, the order of salvation. This concept has often been a stumbling block for those considering the merits of Reformed theology. They worry about the danger of forgetting that what is at stake is not abstract taxonomy but the patterned way in which the different blessings are lavished on us.[2] Each of them is a grace from God. And while they may be separable, each one having a specific nature, they all come from the same generous heart of God the Father, because of the same efficacious work of Jesus Christ, and through the same liberal outpouring of the Holy Spirit. Like a beautiful symphony, none of the parts is so separate as to reduce the harmony of the whole. Nor are the terms and the order the only way to express the great riches of God's application of redemption to believers.

Accordingly, two dangers can occur if this order is not well understood. The first is to overstate the separation between each of the elements in such a way that it removes them from their essential grounding in the covenant relationship between God and his people. There is a certain fluidity to the different elements, and, besides, they are not always used in the same way in different contexts, whether in Scripture or by particular theologians. For example, John Calvin uses the term *regeneration* to mean something like the transformation of the believer from worldliness to holiness, whereas later evangelicals use it to mean the first entrance into the kingdom. Furthermore, too much can be invested in questions of logical and chronological order, when the Bible is not so precise. Reformed people have made a great deal

---

2. William Perkins's famous treatise, *A Golden Chain: Or, the Description of Theology* (1591), describes the *ordo salutis* from election to the final consummation in terms of four degrees of God's love: effectual calling, justification, sanctification, and glorification. Dependent on Beza and Zanchius, Perkins makes many different distinctions and uses complex, mechanical diagrams that may seem scholastic to the modern reader. The book is nevertheless a fascinating volume, particularly when understood in its historical setting.

out of the priority of regeneration over faith. There is a point to that, but expressed in the wrong way it can reduce the human responsibility of responding by faith to the gospel. They have also traditionally placed regeneration before justification. But, as Abraham Kuyper pointed out, this may diminish the biblical emphasis on the justification of the ungodly (Rom. 5:6–11).

The second danger is the opposite. If we ignore the order we risk the loss of crucial truths, many of them connected with Reformed distinctives and some involving the gospel. For example, if we do not properly distinguish the more legal or declarative gifts and the inward, transforming ones, we may diminish or even destroy the good news of God's grace. We earlier referred to the story of the Reformation. Recall that Martin Luther's struggles, in a way, were over the difference between justification and sanctification. It was only when he came to understand the objective nature of justification that comes as a once-for-all acquittal, not a process of improvement, that he was free. There is an order, a pattern, in God's ways with us, because he is a God of order. Even his love is expressed to us in harmonious parts.

These gifts, the different elements of God's bringing his chosen ones to himself, are not experienced only individually. They do come to individuals, but they also come to a people, God's people. Even the wonderful blessing of salvation is not to be experienced only for oneself. One of the most marvelous benefits of becoming believers is that we are immediately brought into the community of faith, the church. Our gifts are for others, not just ourselves. In this way, the gospel is countercultural against the prevailing individualism of the modern West. The application of redemption even has cosmic implications, since it is not finished until the new heavens and the new earth, inhabited by God's immortal people.

Effectual Calling

The first category in the application of redemption may be known as effectual calling. Although in the general sense "many are called, but few are chosen" (Matt. 22:14), in the effectual sense, that is, in an enabling way, only God's chosen people are called (Rom. 8:30). We can distinguish between two major levels of calling.

First, in the narrower sense, calling is a divine summons into his kingdom. The New Testament puts this in different ways. We are called by the gospel (2 Thess. 2:14), called out of darkness into light (1 Peter 2:9), and called into eternal life (1 Tim. 6:12; Heb. 9:15). We are called to repentance (Acts 2:28–29). We are called into fellowship with Jesus Christ (1 Cor. 1:9). We are even called into the body of Christ (Col. 3:15) and into his kingdom (1 Thess. 2:12). God is the author of this call. Paul invites Timothy to share with him in suffering for the gospel "by the power of God, who saved us and called us to a holy calling, not because of our works but because of his own purpose and grace" (2 Tim. 1:8–9).

Second, in the broader sense, each of us is called to specific tasks here on earth. Paul tells the Ephesians to "walk in a manner worthy of the calling to which you have been called" (Eph. 4:1). He goes on to show some of the areas of life this is meant to cover: church life, occupations, money matters, moral comportment, and family relations. Our calling should affect every area of life. One of the great breakthroughs of the Reformation was to challenge the medieval idea that calling, or vocation, was only for clerics and religious professionals. Every Christian is called, so that, as Luther put it, the work of the least householder is worth that of monks and nuns. In this way, he was recognizing the biblical emphasis on the cultural mandate. At the dawn of history God gave humankind a mandate to fill the earth and rule over it (Gen. 1:26–30). Today this command has not been abrogated because of sin or superseded in the missionary mandate, known as the Great Commission (Matt. 28:18–20). Rather, it has been given new meaning in Christ, who leads the redeemed in subduing the earth to his full kingdom purposes (Heb. 2:5–9).

Every Christian is expected to live in the church and in the world. In the church, we come together to worship God. We hear the Word preached, we help build each other up in Christ, and we reach out to the poor and to a needy world. In the world, we live in various spheres in order to transform it for God's glory, without accommodating the world's evils. This overlapping life, in the church and in the world, depends on a process that begins by the transformation of the mind and the refusal to be conformed to the patterns of this world (Rom. 12:1–2), and it ends in authenticating the good and perfect will of God in practice. Only in practice can that balance be achieved (Rom. 1:2; Heb. 5:14). Those who are effectually called must participate in church life, using their gifts for the praise of God and for edification and outreach.

Believing families must strive to enjoy the blessings of marriage and parenting as God intended, without idolizing the family or abusing its members. Redeemed citizens must submit to authority by recognizing the offices duly appointed under God's provision, without compromising their moral and religious convictions. The Christian musician must strive to recognize the wonderful world of sound in the creation and tell a story through music, without forgetting either the sadness of sin or the joy of God's healing. None of this is possible without the gifts and the power of the Holy Spirit, who works in us and through us, to shape and reform us. Thus, we become God's workmanship (literally, his poems), created in Christ Jesus for good works, which God prepared beforehand that we should walk in them (Eph. 2:10). In a world that has lost a sense of meaning, the doctrine of calling is desperately needed.

Regeneration

The second gift in the application of redemption is regeneration. The same God who calls us into the fellowship of his Son gives us the means to enjoy it. The expression *born again* has been misapplied and perhaps overused. Yet it has a great importance in our union with Christ. Being born into the family of human beings on this earth inevitably means sharing in the condemnation of Adam's offspring. And so, in order to have access to the enlivening power of Christ, we must be born into another family. We must be born anew, or born from above. This was the burden of Jesus' discussion with Nicodemus in John 3:1–8. "That which is born of the flesh is flesh, and that which is born of the Spirit is spirit," Jesus told this teacher in Israel. The allusion to water and the Spirit undoubtedly means the cleansing waters represented by the purification ceremonies of the Old Testament (Ezek. 36:25) and the Holy Spirit, who is the source and the means of new birth (1 John 3:9; 4:7). By regeneration we are made new creatures, cleansed from sin and given a new heart. In one way, regeneration is a lifelong process. If someone asks, "Are you regenerate?" it is correct to answer, "Yes, and I continue to be regenerated."

Understood in this way, by regeneration we are made capable of faith. The priority of regeneration over faith has sometimes caused difficulty. Sometimes the way Reformed theology defends the principle sounds quite deterministic. Everything depends on the meaning given to priority. What is not meant is that regenerate people do not have to believe. Also, what it does not mean is that we can have one without the other. We have to work on the tangible front, testing our faith, not on the intangible reality, wondering whether or not we may be regenerate. Our job is not to wonder what may be going on in the background, but to believe. Further, regeneration and faith may be separated in time. In the case of infants, for example, we cannot know exactly when regeneration has occurred.

What the priority of regeneration over faith signifies is not meant in any way to diminish our responsibility to believe. Rather, it means that we cannot believe without God turning us from incapable unbelievers (Rom. 8:8) into believers. This is the plain meaning of Jesus' words, "Truly, truly, I say to you, unless one is born again he cannot see the kingdom of God" (John 3:3). We cannot greet the kingdom of God with the eyes of faith, unless we are converted. Ephesians 2:1–10 is eloquent to this point. We were once dead, the apostle tells us, walking in the flesh. We were as dead as Lazarus in the tomb. Then God made us alive by grace. Salvation is by grace through faith, and faith is our activity, but the introduction into life is the gift of God (Eph. 2:8). God gives us the entire reality of salvation, including the power to believe, as a free gift.

Faith

Now we come to the third element in the application of redemption, which is faith. This is such a crucial part of the gospel that we must be careful to be clear about it. As we saw earlier, one of the great contributions of the Protestant Reformation was to define faith more biblically. We want to do the same. Faith has a warrant and a nature.

The Warrant of Faith

Why should we believe? How can we know that God will receive us and that our trust is not misplaced? God is trustworthy. Over and over again, he proves himself to be a God we can rely upon. Throughout the history of redemption, he showed himself faithful to his promises. Even when God's people wandered so far away from him that salvation seemed out of reach, God came back and forgave. It is worth meditating on Psalm 103 to grasp this amazing truth. In many ways it reminds us that God gives multiple benefits. He forgives iniquities, heals diseases, redeems us from the pit, and crowns us with love and mercy. "The LORD is merciful and gracious, slow to anger and abounding in steadfast love" (Ps. 103:8). He remembers our weakness. He puts our sins away from him as far as the east is from the west. How can God be this way? He is disposed to forgive and have mercy, but he cannot simply wave a wand and forget our sins. His justice requires that sins be paid for.

And so, he sent his only Son, not sparing him but giving him up (Rom. 8:32). Christ's death and resurrection are the warrant for trusting God. How can Jesus invite burdened people to be free of their load and promise that whoever comes to him will receive eternal life? Because of the perfection of his finished work and the virtues that reside in him forever. The appeal of the gospel is made to all sorts and conditions of humankind. It is not restricted to the elect. It is sincerely offered to "whosoever." We should not come to Christ because we think we are elect. Nor can we hesitate to believe because we fear we may not be elect. Trying to make any such connection is dangerous.

Rather, we must come to Christ with empty hands, pleading for mercy. Like the tax collector in the story, we must beat our breast, confess our unworthiness, and ask for mercy (Luke 18:9–14). The Pharisee in the same story commended himself to God based on his religious zeal and moral uprightness. But God was not impressed. God does, however, love to save. He does not desire sinners to perish but pleads with all of them to turn from their ways (Ezek. 33:11; 1 Tim. 2:4; 2 Peter 3:9). The fact that greater numbers do not turn is not a problem with the warrant or the sincerity of the offer but of the short-sightedness of unbelievers. It is true that in God's secret council, some are elect and some are not. God's plan will always prevail. And yet, in the mystery of that plan, human beings are significant. Their decisions are not programmed as one might program a computer. It is also true that unless we are regenerated, we will not believe. But the connection is never presented in the Scripture as diminishing human responsibility to believe. To believe is rightly to respond to the warrant. Not to believe is to invite deserved condemnation. On the last day, when we come face to face with God on his judgment seat, we will not be able to say, in effect, "Lord, I did not believe because you neither elected nor regenerated me." At the same time, no one who does believe will be denied God's grace. No one.

The Nature of Faith

If the warrant for faith is the love of God in Christ, what is the nature of faith? It is a human response to the divine offer. Faith is our activity, not God's. God does not believe through us; we believe because of him. Without faith we are not in proper relationship to God.[3] Faith, as Francis Schaeffer used to put it, is a nonhumanist value. Faith lifts up empty hands and receives God's gift. We do not believe because we have been saved; we believe in order to be saved. We do not believe in order to add some religion to our lives or to receive a few more presents from God. We believe because we are utterly lost without God's mercy.

In the Reformed tradition faith is usually divided into three components. They are complementary and need to be seen together.

Knowledge. It may sound contradictory to say that faith involves knowledge, since, at one level, if we know something we don't need to believe it. But at another level, it is crucial. Without knowledge, faith

---

3. The only possible exception to this rule might be infants, who do not yet have the full capacity for faith, and the mentally disabled, who cannot carry out the basic functions of faith.

is a mindless leap. The Bible underscores the factual, content-filled nature of true religion. Paul to the Corinthians makes the point that the resurrection of Christ was attested first by the Scriptures and then by the eyewitness accounts of hundreds of people, including himself (1 Cor. 15:3–9). While the resurrected Jesus gently chides Thomas for refusing to believe before he could touch his wounds and praises the faith of those who did not actually see him, he does not deny the need for proof (John 20:24–29). The very apostle who described the scene with doubting Thomas goes on to say that Jesus did many "signs," some recorded, some not. The ones he wrote about are meant to inspire us to believe (John 20:30–31). "So faith comes from hearing, and hearing through the word of Christ" (Rom. 10:17).

It is often assumed that faith is against reason, or at least somehow above it. Strictly speaking, this is not true. Reason can be a pretentious critic, an arrogant judge. We might call this autonomous reason (the Reformers referred to it as magisterial reason). This kind of reason is indeed incompatible with faith. But it can also be a marvelous servant (ministerial reason, in Reformation language), receptive and re-creative of divine revelation. In this sense, our faith is reasonable. God asks Israel to reason together with him (Isa. 1:18). James calls the wisdom from above open to reason (James 3:17). Our hope needs to have reasons, according to 1 Peter 3:15. Even worship should be reasonable (that is the root meaning of the word often translated as "spiritual" worship in Romans 12:1). It is true that the love of Christ surpasses knowledge (Eph. 3:19). But that does not make it irrational. Nor is it somehow accessible to faith any more than it is to reason. There is no part of us somehow naturally open to God. Faith is limited, as is reason. But we cannot do without either. Simply put, reason should be faithful, but faith should be reasonable.

Conviction. Sometimes known as assent, conviction is an aspect of faith different from simply knowing. It means believing a thing to be true. Conviction has many levels. It means receiving Christian teaching. It can mean believing Jesus to have existed and even to be what the Bible argues that he is. Further, conviction can mean that we believe what the gospel is corresponds exactly with our need. This is one reason we often speak of the conviction of sin. A person may be under conviction when one realizes that God has been offended and that he is just to condemn. By contrast, an unbeliever usually stumbles at this place. To be sure, an unbeliever may also lack knowledge. While no one is without some knowledge (Rom. 1:19; Ps. 19:1; Acts 14:17), that knowledge is suppressed and distorted, and it is incomplete. Fundamentally, though, an unbeliever lacks the conviction that the claims of the gospel are true.

Trust. Knowledge and belief are thus essential. But unless one has the third component, one does not have biblically defined faith. That component is trust. I can know a great deal about Jesus Christ as he is presented in the gospel. I can even believe that Christ is who he says he is and that the gospel is offered to me. But unless I place my trust in Christ, I am not a Christian. Unbelievers may know the gospel to be true. The demons believe—and shudder—James tells us (James 2:19), but they are not thereby saved. It is a frightening thought, but someone can be orthodox in theology, know the Bible to be true, realize he or she needs Christ, and yet not truly believe. This is sometimes referred to as cold orthodoxy, although we ought to be uncomfortable with the term. Real faith, true orthodoxy, is when I place my confidence in Christ and ask for his mercy. As John Murray beautifully puts it, faith is "direct personal contact with the Saviour himself, contact which is nothing less than that of self-commitment to him in all the glory of his person and perfection of his work as he is freely and fully offered in the gospel."[4]

Living Faith

True faith is not one bland trait without variation. In order to understand more about the nature of living faith, we ought to look at five more characteristics.

4. John Murray, *Redemption Accomplished and Applied* (Edinburgh: Banner of Truth, 1961), 112.

Faith is an instrument. It has no value in itself. Strictly speaking, we should not even speak of saving faith, since it is not faith that saves, but Jesus Christ who saves through faith. In this sense, only faith can put us into the right relationship with Christ. Paul tells the Romans that "one is justified by faith apart from works of the law" (Rom. 3:28). The Reformers insisted on this and raised the slogan *sola fide* to herald the truth that no human activity, whether in the love of God or of neighbor, can do anything to save us. However, faith, if it is true, living faith, will always be accompanied by good works. These good works cannot save us. Good works are evidence of true faith. We should take no comfort in claiming to believe when there is no evidence. James asks, rhetorically, "What good is it, my brothers, if someone says he has faith but does not have works?" (James 2:14). He even adds, ironically, that a person is justified by works and not faith alone (James 2:24). But a careful reading of the context tells us there is no contradiction with Paul's affirmation. James is making the point, using strong, provocative terminology, that faith without works is not only impossible but also hypocritical. If we hide behind such a façade, we cannot see how God is "compassionate and merciful" (James 5:11).

The flip side of faith is repentance. This old-fashioned word translates a spiritual necessity never out of date. We need to turn, with sorrow, from what we have been to what we may become by God's mercy. In this way, faith and repentance go together, since the heart of faith is to trust in Christ, which means to cease from trusting yourself or another god. This is such a basic truth that sometimes repentance replaces faith in the wording of the gospel offer. In Luke's version of the last commandment of Christ, the resurrection of Christ seals the mandate that "repentance and forgiveness of sins should be proclaimed in his name to all nations" (Luke 24:47). Peter tells the first group to hear the Pentecost message that they must "repent and be baptized every one of you in the name of Jesus Christ for the forgiveness of your sins" (Acts 2:38).

Repentance is very different from regret or remorse. We often are sorry that we have sinned, but more because we were discovered or the sin got us down than because we want to change. Nor is repentance to be confused with penance or other compensatory practices, although true repentance ought to have some evidence for it. The real spirit of repentance is well captured in the old Anglican prayer of confession:

> But thou, O Lord, have mercy upon us,
> spare thou those who confess their faults,
> restore thou those who are penitent [those who repent],
> according to thy promises declared unto mankind
> in Christ Jesus our Lord.

Two cautions may be introduced. The first is to be careful that repentance does not become a new way to introduce good works into the mix. In some preaching, repentance is proclaimed in such a way that it removes the freedom of faith. It casts unnecessary doubts on the simplicity of coming to Christ. It may lead to unhealthy introspection, where we wonder if we really are sincere, if we really have given up all our idols, if we really have changed. Faith by no means has to be burdened by such qualifications in order to be genuine. The second caution is the opposite. It is to reduce faith to easy believing. In some modern preaching there is a tendency to invite people to make cheap decisions, weighing neither the depth of our attachments to sins and idols nor the costly riches of divine pardon. We are asked to assent to certain truths, to accept Christ, almost as though he were fortunate that we give him some due. The doctrine of repentance reminds us that the stakes are high. We are terribly lost, full of guilt, justly condemned, unless we turn from our ways in shame and place our hopes in Jesus Christ as he is presented in the gospel.

Faith may be strong or weak. Faith may grow rapidly or slowly. Even a little faith, as small as a mustard seed, can move mountains (Matt. 17:20). And a great amount of faith without love, that is, without the fundamental Christian motivation behind faith, is empty (1 Cor. 13:2). No Christian believer has such faith that it coincides with sight. After all, the essence of faith is to believe things not seen (Heb. 11:1). We hope for what we do not yet see (Rom. 8:25). We walk by faith, not by sight (2 Cor. 5:7).

Faith is related to assurance. Is assurance of the essence of faith? Should we, as believers, always be sure we are saved? One of the great breakthroughs of the Reformation was to prove our free access to God, without the intermediary of penance or other church-based duties. John Calvin defined faith as the assurance of salvation: "Now we shall possess a right definition of faith if we call it a firm and certain knowledge of God's benevolence toward us, founded upon the truth of the freely given promise of Christ, both revealed to our minds and sealed upon our hearts through the Holy Spirit."[5] To which he adds, "[Faith] requires full and fixed certainty, such as men are wont to have from things experienced and proved."[6]

Later Reformed theology tended to separate assurance from faith. The Westminster Confession treats faith in chapter 14 and assurance in chapter 18, stating that assurance is not so tied to faith that believers may not go through prolonged periods of darkness and doubt before retrieving it (18.3). No doubt the authors were concerned for two things. The first is presumption. If we find ourselves deeply drawn to sin and are content to stay comfortable with ungodly patterns, then we must give up the right to assurance. We cannot lose our salvation or undo our election, but we may not claim them with assurance unless we begin to walk in the light. Never perfectly do we so walk; often it is with full awareness of our distance from God's requirements. But yet it is normal to keep short accounts with the Lord and fight against the sin that clings so easily. The second concern is surely the scriptural evidence that the men and women of faith recorded on its pages had many ups and downs. The psalmists regularly confess their doubts and darkness. "But as for me," states Asaph, as he contemplated the injustices of the world, "my feet had almost stumbled, my steps had nearly slipped" (Ps. 73:2). "Do not forsake me, O Lord!" cries David, as he watches enemies and friends abandon him (Ps. 38:21). Paul, as he wrestles with his ever-present sinfulness, implores, "Wretched man that I am! Who will deliver me from this body of death?" (Rom. 7:24).

5. John Calvin, *Institutes of the Christian Religion*, ed. John T. McNeill, trans. Ford Lewis Battles (Philadelphia: Westminster Press, 1960), 2.2.7.
6. Ibid., 3.2.15.

What is the answer? "Thanks be to God through Jesus Christ our Lord!" (Rom. 7:25). And that is the answer to the problem of assurance. Although we suffer and at times wonder where God is, although we go through periods of darkness and yield to temptation, nevertheless, Jesus Christ is there, at the other end of the tunnel and in the tunnel itself. The Good Shepherd's rod and staff comfort me even through the valley of the shadow of death, so that fear is banished, replaced by comfort (Ps. 23:4). "For I know that my Redeemer lives," Job defiantly tells his accusers, in the midst of his troubles (Job 19:25). The ground of our certainty is not our experience, however encouraging that may be at times, but the promises of God, guaranteed by the finished work of Christ, are the great warrant for our assurance. God is not only trustworthy by nature, so that when he promises a thing it will come true. He also accommodates our trembling souls by sealing his promise with an oath, "so that by two unchangeable things, in which it is impossible for God to lie, we who have fled for refuge might have strong encouragement to hold fast to the hope set before us" (Heb. 6:18).

In matters of assurance, the Bible has a special role. As we read its pages, we can have our doubts dispelled because of its clarity and authority. The Scriptures draw our attention over and over to the gospel and the sure promises of God. No one who comes to him will be cast out (John 6:37). Whoever believes in him will have eternal life (John 3:16). The gospel is God's power to save everyone who believes, because in it God's gift of righteousness is revealed for faith (Rom. 1:16). The story goes that Martin Luther was depressed and racked with a guilty conscience. He heard, as it were, the voice of the devil reminding him of his many sins. Awaking from his torpor, Luther shouted at the devil that he could add more to the list himself, and then Luther threw his inkwell at the devil, stating that all his accusations were empty, because God's Word said Luther was justified!

What about faith and works? We will have more to say about that relationship when we discuss sanctification. But for now, a few reminders are in order. The church throughout its history has struggled with the question of the relation of faith to good works. We are commanded to do good works. Indeed, the Book of James reminds us that faith without works is dead (James 2:14–26). At the same time, we are constantly tempted to turn the tables. Instead of good works being the fruit of our relationship to God, we want to introduce some degree of personal merit. In various expressions of the medieval church God's grace was placed alongside human effort. Grace and free will cooperate in order to produce the merits of good works, it was thought. The Council of Trent went so far as to say that Christ's passion enables us to merit recompense, so that "even a cup of cold water given in his name shall not be without its reward, and of satisfying for our sins."[7] The church systematized the doing of good works into such sacramental acts as penance, celibacy, and the repetition of various prayers.

We do well to remember Luther's struggles once more. He came to the realization that no good work could take away his guilt or bring him closer to God. He then saw that God's standard, though hopelessly high, was attained in Christ, imputed to his people as a free gift. When he understood this, as it were, the gates of heaven were opened to him. The apostle Paul puts it in the strongest terms: "Then what becomes of our boasting? It is excluded. By what kind of law? By a law of works? No, but by the law of faith. For we hold that one is justified by faith apart from the works of the law" (Rom. 3:27–28). This is true for entrance into God's presence and remains true in the daily experience of God's presence.

If that is so, how can we avoid *antinomianism*, the view that says because salvation is a gift, I may do as I please? And what about the hundreds of commandments to do good works, for believers to do them? Paul goes on in Romans to make a strong case against antinomianism. His basic argument is that justified people are also changed people, and changed people do not go back to what they were (Rom. 6). But note the *also* here. He does not confuse justification and sanctification, that is, he does not redefine the good news of God's acquittal with the evidence of transformation in the believer. Rather, he goes back to union with Christ: we have been united with him, which gave us our justification but also our changed nature. Therefore, we walk

7. Council of Trent, chapter 4, question 67.

in newness of life (Rom. 6:4). We cannot go back to our old ways. John makes the same point using slightly different language. If one is born of God, he or she will live in righteousness (1 John 3:9–10).

Good works are absolutely necessary. But they are the fruit of faith, not the cause of merit (Titus 2:14; Eph. 2:10). Everything hinges on this distinction. How then can we keep it straight? We puzzle over texts such as Matthew 25, where the sheep are taken but not the goats, because the sheep were kind to Jesus by being kind to his brethren. We puzzle even more over a text such as James 2:24, "You see that a person is justified by works and not by faith alone." But a close look at the context of such texts reveals just the principle we are defending. The purpose of the story of the sheep and the goats in Matthew is not to encourage merit but to warn against legalism. Many in our Lord's audience were prone to define religion as a series of preprogrammed duties rather than a heart of compassion. So Jesus challenges them to change their view. In so doing, he drives them to the grace of God, given to them by the cross and the resurrection, which immediately follow the teaching about judgment.

In the Book of James, something similar is being set forth. The second chapter addresses hypocrites who claim to have faith but whose lives exhibit no Christian fruit. If you say you have faith but show no good works, what does that say about your faith, James is asking. The correct way to put it together is this: "I will show you my faith by my works" (James 2:18). His point is that only faith saves, but it must be a living faith, one that issues forth in good works (James 2:26). The statement he makes in James 2:24 about being justified by works is no doubt meant to shock the readers, who may have been lulled by elevating one part of Paul's theology, that justification is by faith apart from the works of the law, to the neglect of the other part, that we must walk by the Spirit and produce good fruit (Gal. 5:22–26).

9

THE JOY OF THE LORD
IS YOUR STRENGTH

~~~~~~~~~~

Justification

Only one thing matters in life and in death. It is to know God. Rather, it is for God to know us in such a way that we enjoy him forever. Everything else comes afterwards. Knowledge, in the biblical sense, is more than intellectual. It is a relationship. We were made for knowledge, especially knowledge of God. As his image-bearers we have the capacity to know God at the deepest level. That is amazing. An even more amazing truth is that God created us in order that he may know us! He, the holy, living, all-powerful God, would enjoy communing with his dependent creatures.

However, something has gone terribly wrong. Meant for this high purpose, we have gone astray. We have become God's enemies. Even more sobering, God has become our enemy (Rom. 1:18; 5:10). There is no more grim news in the world than for God to reveal his anger against the children of disobedience (Eph. 5:6; Col. 3:6). God's anger is not the fitful rage of a jealous tyrant. It is the just indignation of the judge of the universe against his unjust creatures, who have deliberately walked away from what they know to be right and true and good. In a word, we are unrighteous before him and deserve nothing but condemnation.

God is a God of love. He is full of compassion. But this love does not stand in contradiction to his holiness. Love and high standards go together. Because of his holiness, God is outraged at the presence of evil. If God were not against evil with all of his being, then it would be vain to place any trust in him, for who could believe in a God who winks at evil? Justice may be delayed in this troubled world, but it will not be denied. "You are of purer eyes than to see evil," declares Habakkuk (Hab. 1:13). And so evildoers will be condemned (Ps. 5:5).

How Can We Be Justified?

The most fundamental question we could possibly ask is, How can we be right with God? Put another way, how can we become just before him? This is the right question to ask, since our alienation from God stems from our injustice, our unjust condition. Here is the extraordinary answer. God, out of his free grace, provided a way to declare us just. What is justification? It is God's pronouncement of acquittal. Justification is not to be made righteous. Our union with Christ will ensure transforming us. But that is not the nature of justification. If it were, we would be lost. How so? Any righteousness we may acquire, though it be conferred on us by God, is still far from adequate to meet his high standards. Even if we could become perfect today, a state reserved for us only in glory, this would not erase our sins of the past and our solidarity with the human race through Adam. No, justification is simply and powerfully God's declaration that we are just.

Justification is the opposite of condemnation. To condemn is not to turn someone into an evildoer but to find him or her guilty. Similarly, justification is not to turn someone into a good person but to declare that person innocent. Regeneration transforms us. Justification says something about us. Regeneration is life-changing. Justification is forensic. Why is this so important? If we confuse the two, or if we confuse any of the life-changing gifts of God with justification, we slip into works-based righteousness, and all is lost. This is what the Reformation was about. This is why Reformed theology has put so much emphasis on it. Today many Christians wish to downplay this forensic aspect of our relationship to God. They fear it will lead to cold individualism. They stress instead the warm, human aspect, the life-changing personal friendship we may have with God. While the two, the legal and the vital, should never be wrenched apart, there is every reason to put justification first in the order. No matter how beautifully changed we may become by the grace of God, we will remain lost if the guilt remains.

Is Justification a Legal Fiction?

So justification is a declaration. But it must be based on truth. How then can God forgive the unforgivable? Does he twist the truth? In a human court, we hold someone innocent or guilty based on the person's conduct in relation to the law. A verdict of not guilty means that according to the evidence, no crime was committed. But in the case of humans before God the judge of humankind, all the evidence points against us. God, the perfect judge, cannot but condemn us, at the peril of his own character. So, how can he acquit us? By causing our legal relationship to him and to his law to change. To put it technically, God constitutes us righteous before him.

How can he constitute us righteous? Because of the substitutionary work of Christ. Jesus Christ, the God-man, obeyed perfectly (his active obedience), thus fulfilling all of the law's demands, and he also took all of the consequences of our sinfulness on himself at the cross (his passive obedience), thus perfectly satisfying the demands of a just God. The New Testament puts this in hundreds of ways, so basic is the truth of it. Here is one: we receive "the free gift of righteousness . . . through the one man Jesus Christ" (Rom. 5:17).

Every truth of the Christian faith comes together here. The gospel is good news for us, because God has made a way to acquit us, while not lowering his standards one inch. The message of the Book of Romans centers not primarily on human justification but on God's! God remains just, but he still can justify the one who trusts in Christ (Rom. 3:26). How can he remain just? Because of the costly, perfect, sacrificial work of Christ. He did not have to save. But deciding to do so, he had to remain righteous. In fact, he reveals the full glory, the splendor of his righteousness, in the gospel.

God declares to be true what was not true to begin with but what now is true, because he has made it so. As Martin Luther once put it, we have been given an "alien righteousness." Christ's righteousness is imputed to us. Further, it is a God-righteousness, far beyond mere obedience to the law, and beyond even the righteousness of Adam and Eve before the fall (Rom. 1:17; 3:21; 10:3; Phil. 3:9). The good news is not that we are merely restored but that we have been given the gift of Christ's righteousness. The little saying "justification is *just as though* we had never sinned" is far short of the mark. First, justification is not just as though, but really so. Second, it is not only that we are considered innocent, but that we are actually constituted righteous.

When Does Justification Take Place?

What is the timing of justification? Justification is once and for all. A person is either righteous in Christ or not. But justification will have its final meaning at the judgment on the last day. It is in view of our ultimate acquittal that we are now declared just. And so, on the way to that day, we may encounter many trials and challenges. We may face different accusers. But nothing can undo the judgment of God. "There is therefore now no condemnation for those who are in Christ Jesus," the apostle forcefully puts it (Rom. 8:1). And there never will be. There is no double jeopardy with God's justice. "Who shall bring any charge against God's elect? It is God who justifies," Paul says again (v. 33). To assail his verdict would be to assail the death, the resurrection, and the ascension of Jesus Christ (v. 34). No earthly power, indeed, no power anywhere, can separate us from the love of God in Christ (vv. 35–39)!

How Do We Obtain Justification?

What access do we have to justification? Justification is by faith. This is why faith precedes justification in the order. We do not believe as a way to trigger justification. Rather, we believe in order to obtain justification. How else could it be? Nothing in us could lead to justification. No good work, no religious exercise, no amount of sincerity could provoke a just God to justify the ungodly. Only our knowledge, conviction, and trust in his mercy can receive the gift of justification. The moral life is a good thing. Justified people will progress toward moral improvement. This is commendable, but it will do nothing to save us. God's gift is generous and unique, which is why it must be exclusive. To use the old adage, "the gospel plus" is the gospel minus. This is why Paul and the other New Testament authors are so polemical about justification. No good work, no ceremony, nothing at all can give us access to God. Nothing, except the empty hands of faith, lifted up to receive his gift:

> For all have sinned and fall short of the glory of God, and are justified by his grace as a gift, through the redemption that is in Christ Jesus, whom God put forth as a propitiation by his blood, to be received by faith. (Rom. 3:23–25)

Faith is not a virtue but an instrument. We are justified through faith, not on account of faith. Strong faith is good. Weak faith is still admissible. But neither will save us. Only God's grace, by which he elected us, called us, regenerated us, and justified us, will save us. We receive it simply by humble, imploring faith. This is why the tax collector in the story, not the Pharisee, went away justified. Whoever comes to God with such faith will be justified.

Adoption

Justification is crucial. It is at the heart of the gospel. But it is not the only grace we receive. We have already considered several others. And we have stressed that all of them, including justification, center on our union with Christ. Our knowledge of God is deep and rich and full. It is made possible to guilty persons because of this great step of justification. But there is far more.

One of the most precious is our adoption as sons and daughters into God's care. We call him Father, because he has given us authority to become his children (John 1:12). Think of it! God the Father is uniquely the Father within the divine Trinity. He is particularly the Father of the second person. This is unique and a privilege no one else can share (John 20:17). Furthermore, there is a sense in which God is the Father of all the families on earth (Acts 17:28; Eph. 3:15). But in the gospel an extraordinary revelation is made. We are God's children. John loves to remind us of that in his letters. "See what kind of love the Father has given us, that we should be called children of God; and so we are" (1 John 3:1). Paul tells us we can call God "Abba, Father," from an Aramaic word meaning "Daddy" or "Papa" (Rom. 8:15). If we are children, he adds, then we are heirs, even fellow heirs with Christ (Rom. 8:16–17). We are Christ's brothers and sisters (Matt. 12:50; 25:40; Heb. 2:11). Christ is our true elder brother, who, unlike the uncompassionate son in the parable, went out to seek and to save the foolish prodigals who are now in his family, and of which he proudly says, "Behold, I and the children God has given me" (Heb. 2:13; Luke 15:11–32).

Children who have been adopted into human families, when things have been handled well, begin to understand that they were wanted children, as much as or more than biological children. God has wanted us to come into his family. Parents who have known the agony of childlessness and the joy of adoption may have some sense of God's joy in adopting us. Christian adoption is on the highest order. God takes desperate orphans and makes them children of the king.

Sanctification

Now we come to the term that more than any other stands for the Christian life. This timeworn word means "making holy." In medieval tradition only certain heroic Christians were considered saints. In the New Testament, all Christians are saints, because they are called into holiness. They are "called to be saints together with those who in every place call upon the name of our Lord Jesus Christ" (1 Cor. 1:2). Unlike justification, which is outward and forensic, sanctification is transformational. Like regeneration, it is effected by the work of the Holy Spirit, who indwells us and directs our steps. This is why Christians are often called spiritual in the New Testament (1 Cor. 2:14–15). The word *spirituality* in our times has come to mean a vague religious sensitivity, characterized by disciplines like prayer and meditation. In the New Testament it means something quite different. A spiritual person is indwelt and controlled by God's Holy Spirit, who applies the benefits of Christ's work to our lives.

A Twofold Concern

The overriding concern of sanctification is twofold: deliverance from the power of sin, and conformity to Jesus Christ. In answer to the question, "What is sanctification?" the Westminster Shorter Catechism puts it eloquently: "Sanctification is the work of God's free grace, whereby we are renewed in the whole man after the image of God, and are enabled more and more to die unto sin, and to live unto righteousness" (Q. & A. 35). Justification delivers us from the accusation of God against our sin, but it does not change us toward greater holiness. Justification and sanctification are works of God's free grace, but they have different purposes.

Individually and corporately, we are still sinful. Anyone who denies that not only is self-deceived but makes God a liar (1 John 1:8, 10). Sin clings to us so strongly that it is appropriate to say that we are "of the flesh, sold under sin" (Rom. 7:14). To be sure, surviving sin is not the same thing as reigning sin. Sin will never again get the upper hand or destroy us (Rom. 6:14). Yet remaining sin in us is still the great contradiction that plagues us until the day when we can be fully delivered, the day when our sanctification is complete (1 Cor. 15:53–57; 2 Cor. 5:4). This is one of the main reasons we long for the resurrection (Phil. 3:11). We want to have done with our sin and be so characterized by the Holy Spirit that we become spiritual bodies, clothed in immortality (1 Cor. 15:44, 53; 2 Cor. 5:2–5). This we have not yet attained (Phil. 3:12). When we consider the depth of our evil natures and compare that to the high demands of God for holiness, we would be foolish to claim any kind of perfection.

But change is what God is accomplishing in us. Sanctification is not a luxury. It is not possible to be justified but not sanctified. Here is a warning and a comfort. The warning is that we should not think we can claim to have faith or agree to the principles of salvation in Christ while having no measurable walk in holiness. The New Testament is full of admonitions not to boast that we have the light or that we love God, without evidence, such as loving our fellow believers or recoiling from the world's ways (1 John 2:7–11). We saw earlier the idea that I can do as I please because God's requirements no longer have a hold on me. The name for this error is antinomianism, which means "against the law." We saw also that Paul denounces antinomianism in the strongest terms: "Are we to continue in sin that grace may abound? By no means!" (Rom. 6:1). The comfort is that if we are believers, we will be sanctified. If we are justified, we also are sanctified. Further, he who began a good work in us will bring it to completion at the day of Jesus Christ (Phil. 1:6). God will do it, not us. Our sanctification is just as much a part of his plan for us as justification. That is comfort indeed.

When Are We Sanctified?

Sanctification has two related facets. The first is once and for all. The technical name for this is definitive sanctification.[1] If we are in Christ, we truly are new creatures. The old is gone, and the new has come (2 Cor. 5:17). This happens right away. We are definitively changed. We have departed the sphere of sin and death and entered the kingdom of God's love (Col. 1:13). Romans 6 tells us we are dead to sin and we are alive to God (v. 11). This is our condition. We have been set free from the slavish bondage of sin and have put on a yoke of righteousness (v. 18). This is not just the legal change of justification but also the actual change in us.

The truth of definitive sanctification is signified by baptism, a sign of our real death in Christ (Rom. 6:4). Not only did Christ rise for believers, but also believers are alive with Christ today. So real and effectual is this once-and-for-all aspect of sanctification that the apostle can say sin will have no dominion over us (v. 14). It may cling to us, it may drag us down, but it will never gain mastery over us. This is surely the meaning of John's constant reminders that if we "keep on sinning" and do not "practice righteousness" we cannot claim to be born of God (1 John 3:1–10). Neither he nor Paul

---

1. The term was coined by John Murray. See, for example, John Murray, "Definitive Sanctification," in *The Collected Writings of John Murray*, 4 vols. (Edinburgh: Banner of Truth, 1977), 2:277–84.

is suggesting any sort of perfection. But they are telling us about the grace of sanctification.

The second facet, then, is progressive and gradual. The two are related. We have another case of the already–not yet. To put it another way, sanctification is becoming what we are. It is because we are new creatures in Christ that we are expected to grow in his image. It is because sin will not have dominion over us that Paul can command us not to let it reign in our bodies (Rom. 6:12). It is a wonderful combination: "If then you have been raised with Christ, seek the things that are above, where Christ is." And, he adds, "For you have died. . . . Put to death therefore what is earthly in you" (Col. 3:1–5). One way to put this is that we must become what we are. Just as redemption is already–not yet, so sanctification is already–not yet.

Sanctification, understood this way, is the opposite of moralism. So much teaching on the Christian life today is moralistic, either expressly or by implication. Christians ought to do this, or they ought not to do that, because Christians ought to espouse virtue. But this is deadly. And it is depressing, since we are no more able to be good because we are told to be than we can be saved by good works. The New Testament never gives rules in isolation from who we are in Christ. Why should we be kind to one another and forgive one another? Because God has forgiven us in Christ (Eph. 4:32). How can we answer those who question the reasons for our hope? By lifting up Christ in our hearts (1 Peter 3:15). How can we run the race without growing weary? By looking to Jesus, the pioneer, and drawing on his strength (Heb. 12:2–3).

What Is Our Part in Sanctification?

Sanctification is no more deserved or of human origin than justification or any of the other graces of salvation. Like them, it flows from our union with Christ. It is a gift. Furthermore, we receive this grace by faith. "Consider yourselves dead to sin and alive to God," Paul tells the Romans (Rom. 6:11). Considering ourselves something means believing it is true. If we stop believing and try to roll up our sleeves, then we have forgotten the condition for our covenant relation to God.

Yet, unlike election, calling, regeneration, justification, and adoption, here human effort is required. We are justified by faith alone, but not by a faith that is alone. There is work to be done. The Christian life is often pictured as a fight or a foot race. In Ephesians, Paul tells us to "put on the whole armor of God" (Eph. 6:11). There is no room here for quietism or for the popular view that says, "Let go and let God." Paul uses the strongest language to incite us to hard work: "Work out your own salvation," he tells the Philippians (Phil. 2:12). How do we reconcile this with the grace of sanctification? How do we avoid moralism? The answer is in the full context of this passage from Philippians. First, Paul does not say that having begun by grace, we finish with works. His expression is telling: we are to work out, or work out of, our own salvation. That is, we are saved by the grace of God in union with Christ. Again, now, we must become what we are. Furthermore, this work is not in reliance on our own abilities. Rather, it is in "fear and trembling," an Old Testament expression meaning humble trust in God. As if to anticipate any remaining question, he adds, "for it is God who works in you, both to will and to work for his good pleasure" (Phil. 2:13). If we work, then it is God at work. If our work results in the conformity of our desire and our actions to God's pleasure, then all credit goes to God, out of whose salvation comes any good thing we may produce. Furthermore, knowing that God will be at work gives us great incentive to work. Why do it otherwise? Once more, the marvelous mystery of God's greatness and human significance is kept in balance.

Peter has a special way of requiring human effort in the process of sanctification. After telling his readers that God's divine power has granted to us all things that pertain to life and godliness despite the corruption of the world, he adds:

> For this very reason, make every effort to supplement your faith with virtue, and virtue with knowledge, and knowledge with self-control, and self-control with steadfastness, and steadfastness with godliness, and godliness with brotherly affection, and brotherly affection with love. (2 Peter 1:5–6)

He adds that if these things are ours, we will be effective and fruitful in the knowledge of Christ (v. 8). Faith is not alone. Our effort is required.

Furthermore, sanctification is God's work, but there are specified means to be honored. They are often called the means of grace. According to the emphases laid down in Reformed theology, there are four. The first is the Scripture. Because the main purpose of the Bible is to communicate grace to us, it has a special place in the Christian life (2 Tim. 3:15; John 20:31). The Bible must be preached (Rom. 10:11–15; 1 Cor. 1:17–18). It may also be ministered in different ways, such as informal teaching, personal reading, family devotions, and so forth. The second is prayer. In prayer we praise God and ask for his kingdom purposes to be done on earth, which includes my life and the life of the church. Prayer is a refuge and a struggle. Paul tells us to pray "at all times in the Spirit, with all prayer and supplication" (Eph. 6:18). The third means of grace is fellowship with the saints, that is, with fellow Christians. The most significant place for this is the service of worship. Neglecting this assembly is a serious fault, because we cannot benefit from mutual encouragement (Heb. 10:25). Other forms of fellowship are, of course, endorsed. Fourth, the regular participation in the sacraments is enjoined. Baptism and the Lord's Supper (known as Communion or the Eucharist) are the signs and seals of God's covenant work in our lives. Some Protestants, particularly in the Reformed tradition, tend to be so word-oriented that they neglect the crucial place for the sacraments.

Who Is the Primary Agent of Sanctification?

As we may see from all that has just been said, we do not sanctify ourselves, but God does. And he does so in keeping with his nature and his purposes, and thus in trinitarian fashion. The Father draws us to the Son. He hears our petition when we pray, "Thy will be done." In the Son we have all the blessings, all the virtues of redemption. None of his accomplishments was without benefit for his people. In him we are mystically united. But sanctification is quite specifically the domain of the Holy Spirit. He, one might say, is the primary agent of sanctification.

At Pentecost, the Spirit's role is singled out, though always in relation to the other two persons: "Being therefore exalted at the right hand of God, and having received from the Father the promise of the Holy Spirit, he has poured out this that you yourselves are seeing and hearing" (Acts 2:33). What was visible and audible on that day is more characteristically hidden in the experience of the church. But it is no less real. The work of the Spirit is generally hidden. We do not know his ways or the mode of his sanctification. Occasionally it may be given to us to get a glimpse of the Spirit at work. But the Spirit far surpasses our conscious, rational ability to track him.

The Holy Spirit has always occupied a prominent place in Reformed theology. John Calvin devotes all of book 4 of his *Institutes* to the work of the Spirit in the life of the church. More recently, particularly stemming from the discipline of biblical theology, the Holy Spirit has been recognized as the chief presence in our eschatological times. We are indeed end-times people, according to Paul (1 Cor. 10:11; Rom. 13:12). And these last days can also be characterized as the age of the Spirit. This is what so many Old Testament prophecies are about (Isa. 32:15; Ezek. 39:29; Joel 2:28–29). The defining presence of the Holy Spirit was inaugurated at Pentecost and then became the driving principle during all subsequent times. The Book of Acts, sometimes known as the Acts of the Apostles, might more properly be called the Acts of the Holy Spirit. To quench the Spirit is to stifle the work of the one who places us at the center of God's purposes for our times (1 Thess. 5:19). To grieve the Spirit is to sadden the one who seals us for the day of redemption (Eph. 4:30).

What does the Spirit do? He draws on the power of the risen Christ and continues to apply all his virtues to his people. The Spirit gives us life, the life of resurrection power (Rom. 8:11). It is particularly because of the Holy Spirit that we are not left as orphans. The Spirit helps us be assured of being God's children (Rom. 8:16). Even though Jesus has departed into heaven, he sent us his Spirit (John 14:18). For by means of the Spirit, the Father and the Son take up their home in us (John 14:23). Think of it! Almighty God resides in us, through the Holy Spirit. And from that secret place of indwelling we are in such communion with the Lord that we bear his fruit (John 15:1–17). And so we can do nothing without him. But by him, we can have the peace of Christ and the victory of this one who has overcome the world (John 16:33)! By a strange and wonderful economy, the Spirit of the Lord is sent to us by the Lord of the Spirit, who transforms us into the image of the glorious Lord. This Spirit, being the very opposite of a slave maker, gives us freedom.

Such freedom is concrete. How might we face a particular sin in our lives? Here is one example. In Galatians 5:26, Paul forbids three vices: "Let us not become conceited, provoking one another, envying one another." Simple enough. Or is it? These three vices are not always visible and rarely dramatic. They do not easily translate into testimonies of success, as an alcoholic might testify of beating the bottle. Rather, this unholy triad—pride, badgering, and jealousy—is a constant, hard-to-shed group. There are recovery groups for gamblers or the obese but not for the arrogant or for those who love to taunt. Envy is particularly pernicious, known in literature as a green-eyed monster. But look where the apostle places the triad. It is last in the paragraph; and it is contrasted to life in the Spirit. The three vices are deadly serious, because they gnaw at us. We invest so much secret energy in sorrow over someone else's success that it will destroy us like a cancer. But look at the remedy. Paul does not isolate the moral injunction from the status of the offender. Rather, he tells us that we have crucified the flesh with its passions and desires. And we do live by the Spirit. There is the already. There is what you are. Now comes the not-yet, the becoming what you are: *Let us not* . . . Struggle, yes. Discipline, certainly. But never merit. Never trying to become something out of reach. What a different slant this puts on the struggle against sin.

Finally, the Holy Spirit guides us through all of our suffering. The Christian life is one of hardship, and ultimately, for all but those who remain at Christ's coming in glory, it is one of death. Suffering is not the lot of a few chosen ones. It is the necessary condition of our fellowship with Jesus (Rom. 8:17; 2 Cor. 1:7; Col. 1:24; 2 Tim. 2:12). At Lystra, Paul and Barnabas build the reality of suffering into the message: ". . . encouraging [the disciples] to continue in the faith, and saying that through many tribulations we must enter the kingdom of God" (Acts 14:22). Yet it is precisely here that the Holy Spirit's assistance is particularly notable.

Romans 8 is a matchless account in all literature on the reality of suffering and the relief of God's power. And at every step Paul shows us how it is the Spirit of God who carries us through. It is the Spirit's law of life that sets us free (vv. 2, 11). Setting our minds on the Spirit gives us life and peace (v. 6). The Spirit of God dwells in us, so that to have him is to belong to Christ (v. 9). It is by the Spirit that we put to death the flesh and live (v. 13). Being led by the Spirit means we are God's children (v. 14). In the midst of our suffering, when we may be tempted to feel abandoned, the Spirit testifies to us that God is our Father (vv. 15–17). Though we groan with the entire creation in our misery, yet we have the firstfruits of the Spirit, and thus the patient certainty of the day of full adoption and full redemption, even for our bodies (v. 23). The Spirit of God helps us in all our weaknesses, even in praying, or we might say, especially in praying, since we do not know how to pray properly (v. 26). In the midst of our suffering, when we do not understand how our allotted circumstances can bring any good and our prayers are inarticulate, the Spirit intercedes according to God's will and thus assures us of our right relation to him, and, in the bargain, of God's good purposes for those who are his beloved, elect people (vv. 27–30).

Much more could be said about the grace of sanctification. Everything we think and do as Christians should be related to our spiritual walk. We live messy lives in a dirty world. But God has entered our world and our messiness to give us life and hope and to bring us fully from darkness into his marvelous light, the light of his presence.

Perseverance

Next in the chain of God's gifts is perseverance. This particular component is closely tied to sanctification, but it brings out a special aspect of our salvation, one that has caused a great deal of discussion.

We Will and Must Persevere

Reformed theology has always underscored the certainty of the perseverance of the saints, but not as a cheap eternal security. Believers will persevere, because nothing can separate them from God's love. At the same time, though, they must persevere. Many warnings are given to us about the dangers of being disqualified or falling away. So perseverance is never independent of human effort. But that effort is energized by God. We are kept through faith by the Lord, who cannot fail (1 Peter 1:4–5). Once again, we want to avoid two dangers. The first is double jeopardy, that is, that once having saved us, God would condemn us again. The Bible speaks in the strongest terms against this view, arguing that if we could be lost again, then the work of Christ would have been ineffective. Nothing can separate us from the love of God in Christ . . . nothing (Rom. 8:39). The second danger is antinomian security. It is deluded to think that our journey to the new heaven and new earth is without regard to our faithfulness and obedience. We will persevere, as we must persevere.

How do we keep the balance? Many non-Reformed types of theology claim that salvation once gained may be lost. They will point to passages such as Galatians 5:4 or Hebrews 4:1 and 12:15, which imply that one may fall from grace or fail to keep it to the end. Those views begin properly with a concern to avoid antinomianism, but they end up sacrificing the full effectiveness of God's grace for us. The passages are not saying that once saved you can become unsaved. Galatians 5:4 is a warning that relying on the law for justification disqualifies you from grace, because you are not relying on grace. You have "fallen away" from the whole principle of grace if you are trying to come to Christ by works. In verse 10, Paul expresses confidence that true believers will understand this and will confute those who teach otherwise. Similarly, Hebrews 4:1 and 12:15 are reminders to be careful not to miss the principle of standing in the gospel of grace, nor to listen to "bitter roots" who try to teach another principle. But, still, what do we make of those people who begin well but for various reasons never finish in the faith? The sobering truth is that the grace given to some is not effectual to begin with. There may be certain temporary signs of the work of the Spirit in a person's life, ones that may be remarkable. Still, that is far different from true regeneration.

The parable of the sower is insightful (Matt. 13:1–9). The same seed may fall on good ground or on rocky ground. It may be snatched up by the crows. Similarly, people may respond to the gospel with preliminary signs of the new birth. But they may not persevere, because the ground is not regenerate. Jonathan Edwards wrote powerfully of the different types of true and false religious experiences one may have but still not truly be awakened by God's saving work.[2] The list of signs of apparent Christian experience is extensive and includes many patterns good in themselves, like prayer, a forgiving spirit, church attendance, and theological correctness. But only true Christians will continue in the faith.

The possibility of such false manifestations is a warning, but it is not meant to scare us away from assurance. If anyone is in Christ, nothing can tear that person away. Very simply, all who come to Christ by faith will be kept by him. He will lose nothing that the Father has given him, but he will raise it on the last day (John 6:39). Otherwise, as we said, his work would be insufficient, ineffectual, incomplete. No, even though the mountains may depart and the hills be removed, God's steadfast love shall never depart from us. He has promised it and sealed it by covenant (Isa. 54:10).

How will we persevere? What is the guarantee? We persevere only because Jesus Christ, sitting at God's right hand, intercedes for us with the Father, who in turn gives us the Spirit for our perseverance. The Book of Hebrews has a particularly rich teaching on the heavenly high priesthood of Christ, as it is called. From his place, because he himself was tempted, he can help us in our temptations (Heb. 2:18). We must persevere (Heb. 3:14; 4:11), but we will persevere because of our high priest (Heb. 4:14). His prayer for us, his children, takes the form of advocacy. "If anyone does sin, we have an advocate with the Father, Jesus Christ the righteous" (1 John 2:1). He is the lawyer for the defense, as it were. His plea is not, "There he goes again; please forgive him yet one more time." Rather, his plea is, "He is forgiven

---

2. Jonathan Edwards, *The Religious Affections* (1746).

because of my finished work of propitiation; sanctify him now in your truth, until the day of glory." Jesus' high priestly prayer, recorded in John 17, is the proof for the unshakable argument of his advocacy: "I have glorified you on earth, now glorify me in my people, and keep them in your name." If Jesus had not glorified his Father on earth, then there would be cause to worry. But he did, so there is not.

If we find ourselves overcome by sinful patterns, the temptation is to short-circuit the process and wonder, are we elect, am I God's child? But while caught in sin's web we should not be distracting ourselves with speculation about our election; rather, we should be turning to God for forgiveness and restoration. If we are in Christ, no matter how dark the journey, no matter how deep the fall, we will be restored, because no true child of God can ever be orphaned. God will drive us back into the light.

Through Many Dangers, Toils, and Snares

As we mentioned under the topic of sanctification, it must be stressed that we who have been called to this great purpose of conformity to the image of Christ will for that reason also be called to suffer with Christ. If we want to know him and the power of his resurrection, then we will need to share in his sufferings, becoming like him in his death (Phil. 3:10). Not that our death in any way is redemptive. Only Christ's death can save. But yet, if anyone is in Christ, then that person has glory and hardship in store (Rom. 8:17). We are often caught off guard by our sufferings, as though we ought to be exempt. We reason that since we are not condemned, then why should we continue to pay any price?

We hardly have all the answers for the mystery of suffering, especially the suffering of Christians. Ultimately, only God can have reasons for the evil in this world and the pain inflicted on its inhabitants. We do know that the immediate responsibility for evil is ours, not God's. But we wonder why believers who are acquitted from this responsibility still must receive the consequences deserved by sinners. The Bible explains that suffering has a number of purposes connected with sanctification. One of them is the purification of our faith. As gold is refined by fire, Peter tells us, so our faith is perfected by hardship and trials, so that it will result in praise and glory and honor on the last day (1 Peter 1:7; Rev. 2:10; 3:10). Such an approach is corroborated in our experience. When we suffer we begin to know what matters and trust only the things that last. We make fewer investments in the transitory and ephemeral. Suffering helps us because it enables us to endure and gives us character (Rom. 5:4). Moreover, it strengthens our hope, the kind of hope that will never be shamed in the final outcome (Rom. 5:5). For this reason we can be glad for the pain that God allows us to endure. Not because there is anything good in itself about pain. Nothing could be further from Christian faith than the adages "Joy through pain" and "No pain, no gain."

The central reason for Christian suffering is to have fellowship with Christ. We should not be surprised at the trials that come our way but glad that they mean we are communing with Christ's sufferings (1 Peter 4:12). It can even be said that we fill up what is lacking in Christ's afflictions (Col. 1:24). It is easy to misunderstand such statements to mean we are somehow continuing the unfinished business of Christ's passion. The idea is blasphemous. Christ's suffering was once and for all (Col. 2:14; John 19:30; Heb. 9:26; 10:11–14). That is, the atoning value of his work on earth, culminating on the cross, is sufficient and accomplished. Flagellants and others who believe they are participating in the atonement by their self-inflicted pain are far off the mark. However, not all suffering is for atonement. The afflictions of Christ while on earth did not extend forward to include every hardship endured by his people. When we suffer, it is for his sake (Mark 13:13). When Christians are persecuted, it is Christ who is the object (Acts 9:4–5). Although attacks on Christ during his lifetime brought complete satisfaction to God, his enemies were not yet satisfied, and so they continue to attack him by attacking the church. His afflictions are now received by us.

The whole creation groans with pain, as we mentioned earlier (Rom. 8:22). This sorrowful, broken world was subjected to futility by the same God who cursed the human race for its disobedience. And we suffer and groan along with it (vv. 20–23). Romanticism about nature, nostalgic views, and utopian views about the beauty of the creation do not coincide with the reality of world history. But world history does not end with death and futility. It ends with the freedom of the glory of the children of God (v. 21). In fact, the whole creation will come to glory with us. The end is so unspeakably beautiful that our present sufferings are not worthy to compare with the glory to come (v. 18). Physical death no longer has that dreaded finality it once had. Death is now the gateway to full communion with the Lord. "For you have died, and your life is hidden with Christ in God. When Christ who is your life appears, then you also will appear with him in glory" (Col. 3:3–4).

Glorification

The last grace of God, the final element in the application of redemption, then, is glorification. While we already are in possession of our full blessings, we are not yet in the consummate bliss of the new heavens and the new earth. And while there is essential continuity between the first and second comings of the Lord, the events are separate, and we find ourselves in between the two. We are in the last days. Pentecost has ushered in the full equipping of the saints for their sanctification. And we already sit in the heavenly places in Christ (Eph. 2:6), but the glory has not yet fully transformed everything. The Holy Spirit has guaranteed our inheritance, but we have not yet acquired possession of it (Eph. 1:14).

And so we patiently await the consummation. The Bible talks a great deal about this goal at the end of history. Neither an escape nor the vague, Platonic heaven of popular art, glory will be the earth remade:

> For behold, I create new heavens
> and a new earth,
> and the former things shall not be remembered
> or come into mind.
> But be glad and rejoice forever
> in that which I create;
> for behold, I create Jerusalem to be a joy,
> and her people to be a gladness. (Isa. 65:17–18)

How will this place be characterized? Many of the details we will not know until we arrive there. But we do know the most salient points.

The first is that glory is overwhelmingly characterized by the presence of the Lord. The Book of Revelation reflects on this in many places. In his vision of the last things, after paraphrasing Isaiah 65, John adds the words of the covenant: "And I heard a loud voice from the throne saying, 'Behold, the dwelling place of God is with man. He will dwell with them, and they will be his people, and God himself will be with them as their God.'" And he adds, touchingly, "He will wipe away every tear from their eyes, and death shall be no more, neither shall there be mourning nor crying nor pain anymore, for the former things have passed away" (Rev. 21:3–4). No temple is needed in the new Jerusalem, for its temple is God and the Lamb, Jesus Christ, by whose light the nations walk (vv. 22–23).

In a way, that is all we need to know. What does glory mean for us? The full and uninterrupted presence of our Lord and our God. Everything in the world that today diminishes the experience of his presence will be gone. Then, he will fully turn our mourning into dancing (Ps. 30:11; Jer. 31:13). It will be a time for feasting, for celebration, and, most of all, for praising God for all his goodness toward us.

This is why we may call this state the resurrection. Glorification is not the happy occasion of our going to be with the Lord at death. We will be with him, and we will be made perfectly holy at that time, and it will be a happy occasion (2 Cor. 5:8; Heb. 12:23). But glorification is when death itself is destroyed (1 Cor. 15:54). Our bodies will be transformed so as to be like Christ's (Phil. 3:21). "Beloved," the apostle John tells his readers, "we are God's children now, and what we will be has not yet appeared; but we know that when he appears we will be like him, because we shall see him as he is" (1 John 3:2). If today we are without honor in our natural bodies, at the resurrection we will be raised in glory, and our bodies will become spiritual, in the image of the man from heaven (1 Cor. 15:42–49). We cannot fully imagine what this will be like. Glory means, literally, honor, joy, splendor, beauty, and such things. We get a tiny glimpse of it when we think about what Christ could do in his postresurrection appearances.

Our resurrection occurs because of Christ's. More than that, our resurrection coincides with the coming of Jesus Christ in glory. Our glorification will occur at the same moment that the Father's full glory is revealed through Christ. And it will be together with every believer. No one gets there first (1 Thess. 4:16–17). Here is no secret rapture, no partial resurrection for special saints. Here, rather, is the glorification, together, when the voice of a great multitude will sing "Hallelujah!" to the Lord our God forever (Rev. 19:1, 3, 6).

Far from the dull, static heaven of popular caricature, the real place will be endlessly fascinating, full of new revelations, a place to learn and to enjoy great treasures. The new heavens and new earth, far from being otherworldly and a-cultural, will be the very embodiment of what the world was meant to be. This is why it is said that the glory and honor of the nations will be brought in (Rev. 21:26). Again, we do not have many details, but we do know that what we have worked on here on earth will be blessed and multiplied in the new earth (2 Cor. 3:13–14).

The redeemed and unbelievers will be "raised," but the former to everlasting life and the others to everlasting contempt (Dan. 12:2). This is why, as we saw earlier, it is somewhat confusing to talk of the immortality of the soul. The soul is in itself not more naturally prone to life than the body. And the true meaning of life in the Bible is to be in fellowship with God as his image-bearers. When we walk away from him, we walk into death, not immortality. True enough, unbelievers will die and yet still have consciousness. They will have a resurrection of sorts. But it is hardly unto life. They are not immortal. Eternal life, God's gift, is not built on some natural immortality but is such a quality of life that our whole person is renewed into the image of Christ. It begins when we become converted and comes to its fullest expression when we are glorified.

Being justified by faith, there is no condemnation for believers. At the same time, there is an evaluation of accomplishments and misdeeds during earthly life (2 Cor. 5:10). Not much is said in Scripture about this evaluation. But surely two things are true. The first is that we have been acquitted because of Christ, and nothing can reverse that. No upsetting surprises, then. The second is that our lives have had different twists and turns. Some have been more diligent, others less. In accordance with the principles of fairness, God will reward some with major responsibilities in the new earth. Others will have fewer of them (Matt. 25:14–30). Never is the reward deserved, for it proceeds from the same grace of God that saved us. But it appears there will be different types of recompense for different people who, having exercised their work here on earth with different degrees of diligence, will have some recognition for that. The last thing we should do, though, is speculate about who is doing more and who is doing less. Appearances are deceptive. It is better to remain humble and not compare (Gal. 6:4–5).

So, for believers, nothing but the most wonderful hope is set before us. It is the hope of a new heaven and a new earth in which righteousness dwells (2 Peter 3:13). On God's chosen day, everything will change. A trumpet will sound. And then everything will be different. We will be changed from mortal into immortal. Every enemy will be overcome, as we are more than conquerors. Death itself, already defeated, will be scorned. God will be all in all (1 Cor. 15). His people will have an exodus far better than the one led by Moses. They will have a homecoming far better than the one led by Ezra. Nothing will separate us from the love of God in Christ. "For from him and through him and to him are all things. To him be the glory forever. Amen" (Rom. 11:36).

PART

LIVING
REFORMED
THEOLOGY

10

HEAD OVER ALL THINGS
TO THE CHURCH

~~~~~~~~~~~~~~

A Pillar and Buttress of Truth

Having summarized the principal doctrines of the Reformed faith connected with God's nature, his ways, and his work of redemption, we now turn our attention to some of the great implications of this faith in the life of God's people. We will focus, first, on the church, and second, on our calling in the wider world.

A central teaching of the Reformed faith is that we worship God in everything we think, say, or do. We do not need to go to church in order to worship God. Worship is not restricted to special, concentrated devotional activities such as prayer and Bible reading. In his discussion with the Corinthians about foods bought in the public market, Paul gives the memorable directive, "So, whether you eat or drink, or whatever you do, do all to the glory of God" (1 Cor. 10:31). From the trivial to the crucial, from the ordinary to the sublime, nothing is outside of our primary calling to love God. Pierre Courthial, dean emeritus of the Reformed Seminary in Aix-en-Provence, used to say, "There is no sacred-versus-secular dichotomy, for everything is sacred."

Having said this, there are distinctions in life. Not every endeavor is the same. We have six days to work and one to rest. We have general friendships and special friendships, including the most special of all, marriage. Not every institution is the same. We have the state, and we have family. And we have the church. The church is like no other gathering. Participating in the church is like no other activity. Worship in the context of the church is not altogether the same as worship in all of life.

Reformed theology has always stressed the central place of the church. This may come as a surprise to some people, for the Protestant Reformation resulted in separated denominations. The multiplicity of Protestant churches, including those with a Reformed character, is an embarrassment to many. To be sure, there is something wrong about a divided church. And Protestants appear more divided than any other branch. But perhaps a few reminders are in order. First, the Reformers never intended to leave the Roman Catholic Church. Their desire was to reform the church from within, as the name implies. However, in the attempt, many of them were forced out. Second, the church cannot be limited to its institutional structure, important as that may be. Protestants understood the church in such a way that its true identity transcended denominational or magisterial structures. The visible church, as they defined it, was marked by the faithful preaching of God's Word, the sacraments rightly administered, and a discipline that ensured the continuity of the church's ministries. Thus, in their thinking, the Reformation churches were more truly apostolic than the Roman church. Third, the magisterial Reformers, especially John Calvin, were far more ecumenical and far less individualistic than their successors in the centuries to come. They did not hesitate to call the church catholic, meaning general or worldwide.[1] Their view is beautifully reflected in the typical articles about the communion of the saints in the great Protestant confessions. The Westminster Confession devotes a separate chapter with three sections to it, proclaiming, among other things, that the church is to be in communion with everyone everywhere who calls on the name of the Lord Jesus (26.2).

1. The modern French creeds substitute the word *universal* for "catholic." It is an understandable reaction but not a happy one, for the two words do not convey the same meaning.

We have stressed that according to the Reformed faith, walking with the Lord is not only individual but also communal. The nature of the covenant with God is that the Lord, the holy Trinity, calls a people to himself: "I will take you to be my people, and I will be your God" (Exod. 6:7; Jer. 31:33). The new humanity, chosen in Christ before the foundation of the world, is gathered together for God's praise. The connection of this covenant to worship is evident in the Book of Revelation. The great multitude that no one could number, from every nation and tongue, gathers together before God's throne and serves him day and night, while he shelters them, through the Lamb, with his presence (Rev. 7:9, 15).

Accordingly, the church is the fellowship of all those who are called to live in covenant communion with the Lord. As such, the church did not begin in the New Testament but right after the fall. It is specifically said of Adam and Eve's immediate offspring, "At that time people began to call upon the name of the LORD," language implying worship in the gathered community (Gen. 4:26). Throughout the different ages of the history of redemption, the church has taken on varying forms. With Abraham it expressly became covenantal, coming into line with God's great promise of a numerous offspring and entering by way of the sacrament of circumcision. At the time of the exodus the church was constituted Israel, a nation treasured by God, a kingdom of priests and a holy nation with a body of law for itself. And then, particularly significant is the increasing local identity of the church, its worship eventually centering at the temple in Jerusalem. In the exile, when the temple and land were no longer Israel's possession, the church learned of its spiritual identity and deepened its sense of longing for the Messiah.

When Jesus came to earth, accomplishing his work, the church was transformed into the people of the new covenant (1 Cor. 11:25; Heb. 8:7–13). It became his church, built upon the foundation of apostolic confession, with access through the spiritual and declarative authority of its gatekeepers (Matt. 16:18–19). Indeed, Christ is now the true temple. The Holy Spirit was poured out at Pentecost sealing the reality of new covenant people for all times. The church became a household, built on the foundation of apostolic teaching and discipline, a place where the Holy Spirit dwells, with Christ as the chief cornerstone (Eph. 2:20–22). The church is open to the Gentiles, not only to historic Israel. And its locality is now the heavenly Jerusalem, with earthly expression in congregations around the world, who worship in the Holy Spirit and in the final truth of the New Testament revelation (Heb. 12:22; John 4:21–24).

One, Holy, Catholic, and Apostolic

The Greek word for "church" is *ekklēsia*, meaning "the called ones." God's people are called out of darkness to live in the light of his presence. Peter identifies the New Testament church, built upon Christ the cornerstone, with reference to several Old Testament concepts:

> But you are a chosen race, a royal priesthood, a holy nation, a people for his own possession, that you may proclaim the excellencies of him who called you out of darkness into his marvelous light. Once you were not a people, but now you are God's people; once you had not received mercy, but now you have received mercy. (1 Peter 2:9–10)

The church does not exist simply as a concession to our weakness, a convenient way to be reminded of first things. It is the chief object of God's love, the apple of his eye. True, we ought to *go* to church. It is the chief place where God ministers his gifts to us. We need to stir each other up by mutual encouragement (Heb. 10:24–25). But the church is far more than a local group that meets with an agenda. It is a new creation, the Israel of God (Gal. 6:15–16). It is the fellowship of the Holy Spirit, because of the grace of Christ and the love of the Father (2 Cor. 13:14).

Customarily, and following the creeds, we confess four attributes of the church: it is one, holy, catholic, and apostolic.

The church is truly *one*, despite the divisions in its earthly manifestations. Its unity is in Christ. We are one, together with the church in the past, the church triumphant, because it is now victorious and waiting for the rest, and the church present, the church militant, because it is still fighting the good fight. According to Ephesians 4:3–6 there is only one body, one Spirit, one baptism. As was the case in sanctification, what we already have is also what we strive for: becoming what we are. So in the same breath, Paul urges the Ephesians to maintain that unity and to strive for maturity and unity (vv. 3, 13–16).

The church is *holy* because it is consecrated by the holy God, called to sainthood. The church has been purified. While far from consistent in its earthly pilgrimage, the true church is rightly called holy. Sometimes the distinction is made between the visible church and the invisible church. The former has a membership that includes some who do not know Christ, while the latter is pure. The distinction has limited value. It obscures the fact that the visible church is really the church and not the distant manifestation of something more hidden.

The church is *catholic*, as we mentioned, because it is worldwide. That is, inasmuch as the church holds to the fullness of the faith it should know of no rivals.[2] Despite the existence of many denominations, the basic catholicity of the church remains valid.

The church, finally, is *apostolic*. This means it holds to the teaching of the apostles, who were the founders of the New Testament church. Thus, it is proper in one sense to speak of apostolic succession. What that means is that the true church is built on the foundation of apostolic confession. What it does not mean is that there must be the laying on of hands from the apostle Peter to the bishops of today. When our Lord responded to Peter's good confession by saying "on this rock I will build my church," he was not appointing Peter the first pope (Matt. 16:18). Peter went on to deny the need for the death of Christ in the next moment, earning him the name of Satan's spokesman (Matt. 16:21–23). Paul had to rebuke him for going back to the ceremonial law (Gal. 2:11–14). Peter did become the first preacher at the day of Pentecost, and he was undoubtedly a prominent leader in the church (Acts 2:14; 15:7). But James was more likely the convener of the first assemblies at Jerusalem. And Paul became the most prominent of the apostles. What mattered to all of the apos-

2. This is true, despite the sad divisions of the church into various branches.

tles and what came to be the united voice of the New Testament authors was to guard the great deposit of Christian truth throughout the generations (1 Tim. 6:20; 2 Tim. 1:14; 2:2).

Ardor and Order

The Reformed tradition has always stressed the great importance of having a church discipline that accords with the general rules of government advocated in its principles. The expression *church discipline* has a negative tone to some people. It can sound managerial and even exclusionary. Should not the church be a free, organic body whose purposes are so defined in relationship to Christ that discipline would be stifling? Certainly, but such freedom requires rules to ensure its survival. Like a fire in the hearth, the church preserves its warmth within certain boundaries.

Church discipline can become top-heavy and litigious. But in its best expression, it is anything but negative. Its basic purpose is to help strengthen God's people. The word *disciplina* in Latin means training, exercise, or instruction. In the church, discipline is far more than censure and judicial process, though there are times for those. When they do have to occur, they should be integrated into the whole purpose of discipline. Indeed, "Only where the personal disciplines of learning and devotion, worship and fellowship, righteousness and service are being steadily taught in a context of care and accountability (Matt. 28:20; John 21:15–17; 2 Tim. 2:14–26; Titus 2; Heb. 13:17) is there a meaningful place for judicial correctives."[3]

Discipline has characterized the people of God from the beginning. In the New Testament, it is connected to the proper government of the church. The central thrust of church government is that Jesus rules the church, by the Holy Spirit. That he does so through human instrumentality is a mystery and a privilege. He could have ruled directly, from heaven, but for reasons to do with his love for us and his desire that we grow into maturity and develop strength, he works

---

3. J. I. Packer, *Concise Theology: A Guide to Historic Christian Beliefs* (Wheaton, Ill.: Tyndale, 1993), 220–21.

through humans. He could have proclaimed the gospel to the world, as though by miracle, but instead he has chosen to use "jars of clay" in order to show, through our weakness, the power of the message (2 Cor. 4:7).

Jesus instituted church discipline in the strongest terms. Using images such as the "keys of the kingdom," he authorized the apostles to bind and to loose (Matt. 16:19; 18:18). His language refers to the apostolic authority to interpret the Bible for the purpose of formulating doctrine and setting the bounds of orthodoxy. He gave them and their successors the special authority to declare the forgiveness of sins (John 20:23). It should be noted that this power is ministerial and spiritual. That is, the authority to forgive sins rests not in the person or even in his office but in the Lord Jesus Christ, who rules the church by the Holy Spirit, through his servants, the officers. This power is real, but it is moral and declarative. At certain points the church has overstepped this boundary and confused its power with the temporal and the political. At other points, though, the church has forgotten to exercise any significant discipline, thus allowing unorthodox views and scandalous morals to creep into the body of Christ.

The procedures outlined in the New Testament for the proper exercise of church discipline are as gentle and firm as the Lord. They begin with always checking one's own motives, to be sure the discipline is well intentioned. In most cases a word of encouragement, or a word of admonition, is sufficient. When that does not succeed, discipline must escalate to the next stage, where another witness or two are brought in (Matt. 18:15–17). If the accused still does not respond, then the church must judge. In the Reformed tradition the elders sit to consider the case. If, in their view, after repeated attempts, the accused still will not heed the Scriptures, then they must declare the person "a Gentile and a tax collector," that is, the equivalent of the outsider in Jewish times. The technical term for this is excommunication. This is the proper use of the keys of the kingdom. Paul talks of handing over an obstinate person to Satan, the prince of this world (1 Cor. 5:1–5, 11; 1 Tim. 1:20). The basic principle here is that public sins, that is, those open to the view of the church, should be publicly dealt with, for the sake of the church's holiness and the sinner's health.

Again, it must be stressed that even the extreme measure of excommunication is for a positive end: "so that his spirit may be saved in the day of the Lord" (1 Cor. 5:5; see 2 Cor. 2:5–8; Gal. 6:1). The disciples misunderstood this when they wanted fire from heaven against a town in Samaria (Luke 9:49–56). Paul's discussions with the Corinthian church are revealing. He could come to them with a heavy hand but chooses to stay away, so that they could grow and be built up, not receive grief from him (2 Cor. 2:1–4).

Such proper exercise of discipline cannot occur if there is no proper governmental structure to ensure it. As mentioned, Christ rules his church by the Holy Spirit. But this rule is administered through human structures and channels. As Edmund P. Clowney felicitously puts it, the Holy Spirit brings ardor and order to the church.[4] Not only is there abundant life in the church, but also there should be good government. While the Bible outlines no one blueprint for church government, certain emphases can be discovered that should define the structure of the church.

The unity of the church is organic, not just structural. Each person contributes to the whole. There are many gifts. In the founding decades of the church, various gifts were recognized by attributing an office to their holder. By the time of the Pastoral Epistles (First and Second Timothy, and Titus), a more permanent structure begins to emerge, anticipating the ongoing church after the departure of the apostles. In the Reformed tradition, some variety exists in the number and the distinction of offices in church government.[5]

What are the permanent offices of the church? In many modern Reformed churches we usually find three.

---

4. Edmund P. Clowney, *Living in Christ's Church* (Philadelphia: Great Commission Publications, 1986), 99.

5. Calvin speaks of four permanent offices: the pastor, the teacher (doctor), the governor (elder), and the deacon. He takes apostles, prophets, and evangelists (Eph. 4:11) to be foundational offices that nevertheless can be raised up again in times of need (John Calvin, *Institutes of the Christian Religion*, ed. John T. McNeill, trans. Ford Lewis Battles [Philadelphia: Westminster Press, 1960], 4.3.4). In one place, for example, he calls Martin Luther an apostle.

The general office of the believer. Every church member is said to hold the general office of the believer. The general office is not some sort of concession to the need for identity or a day in the sun for those not called to leadership. Truly, to be a member of the church is to hold an office, a most privileged one at that.

The office of church elder. Elders are guardians and overseers.[6] They govern and teach. Some churches distinguish between teaching elders and ruling elders, with various degrees of difference between them. Different emphases characterize the office of elder, for some may be called into full-time service as ministers of the church, while others participate less intensely. Teaching elders may be called pastors. At the same time, there is meant to be equality among these officers. Sometimes Reformed churches forget this and elevate the pastor to an exalted position. The equality, or parity, of the eldership generally defines Reformed polity over against more hierarchical models. The Reformers rejected the Roman system of lower to higher offices, culminating in cardinals and the pope. In fairness, most churches with hierarchical government call their bishops "first among equals," but in practice there often is little such parity. According to Paul, the eldership is a desirable office but a daunting one, worthy of great respect, to be held only by leaders without reproach (1 Tim. 3:1–7; 5:17; Titus 1:5–9; Heb. 13:17). Thus, one ought to aspire to the office but not rush into it.

At the same time, Reformed polity is not congregationalist, that is, each congregation being essentially independent in relation to others. Instead, the Reformed approach wants to respect the local nature of the church and its unity, which unity has several levels of expression. Each local church has a congregation made up of believers, holding the general office, and elders (consistory or session) who govern and teach. Then, these local churches, because they are gathered in cities or other geographical units, meet in official presbyteries or classes (or dioceses, in the Anglican and Methodist tra-

6. The terms *elders* (*presbyteroi*) and *bishops* (*episkopoi*) are apparently interchangeable in the New Testament (Acts 20:17, 28). Some churches, including Anglican and Methodist, place bishops over several presbyters.

ditions), as the expression of the church in a particular locality. In Presbyterian government regular meetings of presbytery gather together the elders from each local church, who deliberate on matters of doctrine or life. The final level of expression is sometimes called the synod, or the general assembly. It is meant to include all elders from the entire church (modeled after Acts 15:6, where apostles and elders all came together to resolve a dispute). In practice this may mean appointing delegates, but the idea is to have the entire church represented.

The office of deacon. The task of deacons, as they are usually called in Reformed churches, is specifically related to various stewardship concerns in the church. The office recognizes gifts for service.[7] The office of deacon is distinct from that of eldership (1 Tim. 3:8–13; Phil. 1:1; Rom. 16:1). The work of the deacon is often traced to a group of seven men, called to help the widows of the Grecian Jews who were not being properly supported by the church (Acts 6:1–6). It is not entirely clear that the seven were the first to hold a separate office. Among them was Philip, who was an evangelist (Acts 21:8). Still, the recognition of this special task, summarized as "waiting on tables" (6:2), was a crucial step leading to the office of deacon. This office was devoted to the service of the whole church. It was for service to the saints (Luke 10:40; Acts 11:29; 12:25; 1 Cor. 16:15; esp. 2 Cor. 8:4, 19–20). It was a ministry of mercy (Rom. 12:8, 13; 1 Cor. 12:28–29). In any case, the ordained office of deacon is meant to recognize the perennial need in the church for relief for fellow Christians. Discernment is needed to distinguish between those in need and those who lean on the church when they could be providing for themselves (1 Tim. 5:5–6). A balance as well should be maintained between serving the saints and serving outsiders. Paul is clear about this when he tells the Galatians, "As we have opportunity, let us do good to everyone, and especially those who are of the household of faith" (Gal. 6:10).

7. The term *diakonos* is of unknown origin, though it always refers to service, doing the will of a master.

Leadership and Gender

A lively debate is present in many Reformed churches around the world about the ministry of women. The historic position generally has been to reserve the eldership for qualified men. Biblical texts in support of this tradition include 1 Corinthians 14:34–35 and 1 Timothy 2:11–12, where Paul enjoins learning in silence for women. In recent times using such texts to bar women from church office has been challenged. Careful attention to their content and context shows that conclusions may have been hastily drawn. We will not settle the issues here, but a few reminders are in order.

That the apostle does not have in mind gagging women is clear from the contexts and from rest of his writing, as well as the evidence in the historical portions of the New Testament. Earlier in the Corinthian letter he had explicitly outlined the protocol for women who prophesy or pray in church (1 Cor. 11:5, 13). It is even doubtful whether Paul is addressing the matter of church office in these passages, though they are not irrelevant to the issue. Paul is attending to local problems in the Corinthian church and in Timothy's charge. As always, he draws on important theological principles in order to correct whatever was off base. It may be that women in those churches were using their newfound Christian freedom to flout societal norms for them. Otherwise, references to clothing and veils would make little sense.

Possibly the strongest argument for reserving the eldership to qualified men is from the analogy between the church and the family. In Titus 1:5–9 the elder is specifically described as "the husband of one wife." In 1 Timothy 3:5, he must manage his own household well. These terms suggest the same sort of male leadership in the quite different context of Christian marriage, where the husband is told he is the "head" of his wife (Eph. 5:22–33).

Having said that, it is important to recognize that every argument has not been made. Further discussion of relevant biblical passages needs to occur. Also, because eldership is only one avenue for service, women's ministry, whether ordained or not, needs much more development in many Reformed churches. Even discussion about what ordination means is in order. Another area of discussion should be the relation of church authority to authority outside the church. What about positions in government, or the corporate world, or the armed forces? Furthermore, the whole issue of authority needs further clarification. If the Bible bars women from the eldership, does that mean women never have authority over men? The idea is absurd when one considers that to be good at something, or to speak about it with competence, carries authority in and of itself.

Men's and women's leadership is an emotionally charged issue today. In an era too characterized by culture wars, there is imbalance on both sides. Many who are open to women's ordination to the eldership are rightly concerned for social justice and fair representation. They plausibly cite the places where the Bible stresses the essential equality between men and women, both God's image-bearers, both needing the other, both heirs of Christ in the same way (1 Cor. 11:11–12; Gal. 3:26–29). But they incorrectly suggest that such equality trumps every other way in which men and women relate, thus relativizing those passages that underscore male headship. They overlook some of the richer nuances involved in true justice and representation. Many who defend the traditional view plausibly look at the creation structures, as well as the apparently masculine nature of family and church leadership. But they wrongly ignore the rich scriptural material about women in ministry. They tend to flatten leadership into an authoritarian or military model. Some even fear the discussion, as though to raise questions is to threaten the order of the church and society. In so doing they tacitly endorse the status quo, which surely contains much that is unjust.

Both sides are in danger of accommodating the rule of Christ to various agendas. If we are truly willing to follow Christ, we will have to accept certain implications of discipleship that may not accord with our preferences. Experience shows that while some of these implications are puzzling at first, they often begin to make sense when followed faithfully. Should this not apply to the case of women in ministry?

Again, those who are more open to the ordination of women will be challenged by the more restrictive passages. At first, passages such as 1 Peter 3:1, which tells wives to submit to their husbands, even when they do not obey God's Word, seem patently unjust. But a closer look may defuse some of the difficulty. Is it not clear that the immediate concern for Peter is to challenge the accepted social conventions that winked at deceit and subversion under the guise of submission? In the big picture, that kind of behavior works against true liberation. Indeed, in a more ideal social context where proper authority structures are worked out, the effect is to promote everyone's gifts, not the reverse. Proper authority, in marriage and in the church, is far removed from a hierarchical authoritarianism. But finding out the way for loving leadership does not require abandoning a governing office.

Those who are closed to women's ordination will be challenged by Paul's calling Euodia and Syntyche fellow workers in the gospel (Phil. 4:2–3) and by the acceptance of women prophets and instructors, and perhaps even deaconesses, in the early church (Acts 21:9; 18:26; Rom. 16:1–2). But in the process, will they not discover that the full use of nonordained gifted people, women and men, is no threat to church order but an enhancement of it? A great deal of patience and humility is needed on both sides, until the day when there will be no sides but unity in submission to Christ (Eph. 4:13–16).

The Mother's Children

The Reformers did not hesitate to call the church our mother. John Calvin says that there is no other way to enter into life than through her. She is there to bring us up, to nurture and admonish us. She is there to favor and protect our work. He touchingly adds, "Our weakness does not allow us to be dismissed from her school until we have been pupils all our lives.[8]

The church has three purposes.

Worship

The first is to worship God. *Worship* means to render homage to God who is worthy (worth-ship). All of life, as we have said, is about

---

8. Calvin, *Institutes of the Christian Religion*, 4.1.4.

worship. Yet there are times to gather specifically for the worship of the divine Trinity. We may do this individually or in families and institutions. It is the mark of spiritually alive people that they hold regular devotional times, centered on the reading of Scripture and prayer. Prayer is difficult for fast-moving moderns, but it is commended in the Bible as a necessity and a privilege. Jesus gave us a model for the right balance in prayer's content in what we know as the Lord's Prayer. It is not easy to pray, because we are conversing with God. As New Testament Israelites ("wrestlers with God") we struggle before the Lord over issues like honesty, perseverance, and longing. If we are honest, we will admit to being far from adequate in prayer. As we have already seen, our prayers rise up to God having been perfected, silently, by the Holy Spirit, so that they accord with God's will (Rom. 8:26–27). The rewards of prayer are great, because God does answer, though we may be puzzled by his methods. One reason we are puzzled is that we restrict the realm of prayer to personal benefit. Much more is involved.

The relationship between the worshiper who prays and the God who answers is powerfully portrayed in Revelation 8:1–5. Here, an angel stands at a golden altar holding a golden censer. In it the prayers of the saints are mixed in with the smoke of incense and offered up (v. 3). As prayers and incense rise they reach the Lord (v. 4). The end result is that the censer is refilled with fire, which is visited upon the earth with a great noise (v. 5). These dramatic images illustrate the principle: when we pray in our distress, we are worshiping God, and he answers by his judgments. We are thus vindicated. Our prayers move God to change history!

The most significant occasion for worship is on Sunday, in church. It has generally been understood in the Christian outlook that the Old Testament Sabbath, the day of rest and feasting, has been transformed from the last day of the week to the first. This is because Christ rose from the dead on the first day. There is evidence that the churches founded by the apostles gathered on that day for worship. In the Reformed tradition, public worship is always regulated by the Word of God rather than human invention. The Lord gives us rules for coming into his presence, just as there might be conventions for coming to see a king or a dignitary. This rule is known as the "regulative principle," a concept that has sparked considerable controversy.[9] What is the proper order of worship? What sort of music is acceptable? May we bring innovations into the service that are not mentioned in Scripture?

The regulative principle is less a specific list of allowable practices than it is a guiding imperative. It says the Bible must determine the way we worship. The challenge is to decide what it says. Fundamentally, worship centers on two great principles, God's presence and human response. God is specially present by his Holy Spirit when we worship him. That the occasion is charged with grandeur is suggested by the supervision of angels during worship (1 Cor. 11:10; Heb. 12:22; Rev. 4:6). Specifically, that presence is represented by the reading and preaching of the Word and the administration of the sacraments. Our response is to listen to this Word, to observe the sacraments, and to pray to God. Our prayers may be in adoration and praise, in humiliation for our sins, or in requests for our needs and the needs of the world. There is obviously some flexibility here as to the content or elements of worship and their order. The service in Calvin's Geneva was rooted in the ancient liturgical tradition of the church but purged of what appeared to be the abuses in the Roman Catholic Mass:

> Confession
> Absolution
> Chant (of the first table of the law)
> Prayer for the law to be written on the heart
> Chant (of the second table of the law)
> Prayer for the Holy Spirit
> The Lord's Prayer
> Scripture reading
> Sermon
> Prayers of intercession
> Homily on the Lord's Prayer
> Psalm
> Aaronic Benediction

9. No one is sure of the exact origins of the term. The Anabaptists may have been the first to use it. In any case, here we simply mean "regulated by Scripture."

On Sundays when the Lord's Supper was celebrated, the Apostles' Creed was added but the chanting of the law and the Lord's Prayer were removed.[10] An offering may have been a feature in the service, or it may have been brought separately.[11] Nothing about an order of worship is sacrosanct, but the traditional pattern has much to commend it. A service without Scripture reading or biblical preaching would be outside the boundary of the regulative principle. There should be a good balance between liberality and the apostolic call that everything be done "decently and in order" (1 Cor. 14:40).

Music has always been a facet of worship with potential for great blessing but also for great contention. Calvin understood music to be a vehicle for prayers, particularly the psalms, which he believed to be the most appropriate prayer texts for worship. Various branches of the Reformed churches practice exclusive, or nearly exclusive, psalmody, disallowing harmony or instrumental accompaniment. It is their conviction that Christ has fulfilled the Old Testament with its ceremonies and choirs, so that the church is to be spiritual, not encumbered with such symbols. Reformed churches rightly sing the psalms. However, there are limits to them, not the least of which is that they do not proclaim a New Testament spirituality.

The Lutheran churches had from the beginning fewer scruples about using music in worship, making more frequent use of hymns, instruments, and choirs than Reformed churches, though not nearly as much as do most modern Protestant churches. In the contemporary worship format of many evangelical churches, music style resembles the popular repertoire. It tends to use a good many biblical texts ("Scripture songs") but also newly composed praise songs that relate to various themes for worship. No style is in itself incompatible with

---

10. See Francis Higman, *La diffusion de la Réforme en France* (Geneva: Labor et Fides, 1992), 119–20. Calvin had wanted the Lord's Supper every Sunday, but the church council thought this would resemble the Mass too closely, so the Lord's Supper was celebrated about once per month. The order of worship in the Morning Prayer section of the Anglican Book of Common Prayer is an excellent rendering of the Reformed ideal.

11. One could argue from texts like 1 Corinthians 16:2 that it is appropriate to take up an offering on the Lord's day, and presumably this could occur in the service of worship.

worship music. However, church leaders ought to be sensitive to people's associations, which do matter. That is not to say they ought to be driven by them or that strong leadership and education should not be involved.

Properly speaking, music in the church ought to combine several characteristics, the combination of which is not always easy to respect. The list should include the high aesthetic standards worthy of the God of all glory, the clarity required for human understanding, proper sensitivity to the culture of those worshiping as well as of guests in the church, and, finally, an appropriateness (fittingness) to the elements of worship (sober music for confession, joyful music for praise, meditative for the times of reflection).

Edification

Three times the risen Christ asked Peter if he loved him. Three times the answer was affirmative. Three times Jesus told Peter to show his love by feeding his sheep (John 21:15–17). The church is the primary place for this nurture. If Christ is the source of the nurture and his pastors the main conduits for it, yet edification is also mutual. The image of an edifice conveys this priority directly. We do not worship simply for our own sake but for the sake of brothers and sisters. The Corinthian church had a problem with the selfish use of gifts. They were calloused about the need to use their extraordinary gifts for the sake of the others gathered there, and especially for the guests in the church (1 Cor. 14:16, 25). The point is made each time the gifts and offices of the church are put into a list. They are "for building up the body of Christ" and "to serve one another" (Eph. 4:12; 1 Peter 4:10). Gifts are given in order that we function as one body, using diversity in the service of unity (Rom. 12:3–8).

Edification is not limited to teaching or learning biblical theology. Serving one another means just that. We take special consciousness of our debt to our fellow believers. We ought to "bear one another's burdens, and so fulfill the law of Christ" (Gal. 6:2). This can mean supplying someone's physical need. It can mean encouraging a brother or sister. It can even mean admonishing or correcting someone who errs. Naturally, we must do this with love, always ready to find fault first with ourselves. We fail equally in our love for a Christian friend when we ignore his or her error as when we ignore his or her need. James forcefully tells us that true religion before God is to visit orphans and widows in their affliction (James 1:27).

But true edification is even more. Ultimately we commune with one another even as we commune with the Lord. Our unity transcends social and racial barriers (Gal. 3:28). We are one in the Spirit, so that there is one body, with one hope (Eph. 4:4). Our unity with one another is nothing less than a communion like (and because of) the communion between the Father and the Son (John 17:21). This is why without love, nothing else matters, but with love, we have the greatest and most enduring of all the virtues (1 Cor. 13:13). With love, then we grow into our true head, Jesus Christ (Eph. 4:16).

Missions

Our Lord spoke to his disciples about his activity as the Good Shepherd. It is to lay down his life for the sheep. He stressed having "other sheep that are not in this fold" and the need to "bring them also," so that there would be one flock (John 10:16). Again, the risen Christ told his disciples, "As the Father has sent me, even so I am sending you" (John 20:21). He then breathed the Holy Spirit on them, in anticipation of Pentecost, and gave them declarative authority over the church's souls (John 20:22–23). The church is thus an outgoing group. The classic statement of the missions mandate in Matthew specifies that the church is to make disciples of all the nations, by going out to them (Matt. 28:19). The Book of Acts records the work of spreading the good news by the Holy Spirit through the apostles first to Jerusalem, then to Samaria, but then to all the ends of the earth (Acts 1:8). It ends with Paul in Rome. But Paul's letters state his desire to spread the gospel to every place on earth, a task not given to him or to his colleagues in their lifetimes alone (Rom. 1:13; 15:20–21; 2 Cor. 10:16).

The outreach of the church is actually an ingathering. As the mission of the church spreads to more and more people around the world, a larger and larger group is coming together to worship God in the heavenly Jerusalem. They are coming to Christ. Speaking of his death but with implications far beyond, Jesus told his disciples, "And I, when I am lifted up from the earth, will draw all people to myself" (John 12:32). Jesus is the great reconciler who not only brings people to communion in himself but also mends everything that was ever broken, "reconciling to himself all things, whether on earth or in heaven, making peace by the blood of his cross" (Col. 1:20).

The message the church brings to this broken world is that Jesus is the great reconciler (2 Cor. 5:15). He is the ransom of which his ministers are the appointed preachers (1 Tim. 2:6–7). His death and resurrection are the good news, the power of God unto salvation for every kind of person (Rom. 1:16–17). This gospel is received by faith. The world has always needed this message, but it has become particularly urgent in our times. As we saw previously, a concern for social justice must ride in tandem with the gospel message. In the Old Testament, the whole message of God's liberation was condensed to include justification and justice. In the New Testament we learn more clearly that justification is first of all an acquittal before God. Yet the gospel is far more than personal justification. The message of the kingdom is comprehensive.

When Jesus preached his first message, he received two responses. At first the people spoke well of him. Then the tide changed, and the congregation began to be disturbed, even furious at him, seeking to kill him. Why? Here is what he preached, from Isaiah:

> The Spirit of the Lord is upon me,
>   because he has anointed me
>   to proclaim good news to the poor.
> He has sent me to proclaim liberty to the captives
>   and recovery of sight to the blind,
>   to set at liberty those who are oppressed,
> to proclaim the year of the Lord's favor. (Luke 4:18–19)

Jesus had proclaimed the arrival of the long-awaited year of Jubilee (Lev. 25:11–17). It was truly good news to the poor because in this celebration year, all wrongs were made right, all property restored, all debts paid. Of course, the message had a fundamental significance in restoring the relationship between God and his people (justification). But an integral part of that restoration necessarily included justice. The congregation, made up of Jewish leaders who had turned their religion into an instrument of oppression, was angry because it was exposed.

Ideally, no tension should be present between salvation and justice. But the church has often slid over into one extreme or the other. Some evangelicals tend to stress personal salvation to the neglect of the issues of social justice. At best they have looked at changing society as the fruit of saved people, not part of the message. At the other extreme, various forms of liberation theology have neglected the personal and spiritual issues addressed by the gospel. Some people go so far as to change structures without seeking to change the heart. The right balance can be achieved only when the church looks at the message handed down from the apostles, the message of the kingdom of God. With Paul, we preach justification by faith, not meritorious works. Yet, with him, we address the needs of widows and the poor of Jerusalem, and we hold up the state as having a right to reward the good and punish evil. With James, we recognize grace, but we find evidence for it in the faith and the good works of its beneficiaries. With him, we refuse to let entitlements and privileges gain a foothold in the church. With John we know we need an advocate who pleads our case before the Father, based on his finished work at Calvary. But with John we also insist that any claim to love God and be his children without loving his other children is empty.

The church should not be confused with the state. In the time of Moses, considerable overlap existed between the power of the word and the power of the sword. In Christ's administration, the two are separated. He told Peter to put up his sword, when the hostile crowds came threatening them, for his kingdom is not of this world (Luke 22:51; John 18:11, 36). By this he did not mean his kingdom was otherworldly, for he is king over all (Heb. 1:4; Col. 2:15). But his glorious salvation is achieved through his death and resurrection, not by political conquest. The church, in one sense, is the community (the *polis*) of saints belonging to the kingdom of God, which represents Christ's authority over all things. The church has powerful authority to open and shut the doors with the keys of the kingdom. But it does so by preaching the Word and exercising discipline. No country today can claim to be Christian, even less to have the mission to shine its holy light on other peoples.

At the same time, legitimate government is also appointed by God to rule over society, to the end of establishing justice and punishing evil (Rom. 13:1–7). Caesar's face is on the coin, and he is due our honor and tax moneys. The civil magistrate may use the sword denied to the church. Christians are explicitly told to submit to the government, even when it may be corrupt. Furthermore, Christians may legitimately participate in government, including the armed forces, since it is an important place for service. They cannot use the government to enforce confessional allegiance to Christ. They may, and must, seek to legislate and rule fairly, which means biblically. The Bible tells us that we are in the time of God's patience and that God makes the sun to shine and the rain to fall on the just and the unjust (Matt. 5:45). Therefore a certain pluralism in society, together with religious freedom and equal access to the law, is not a grudging concession to an unfortunate realism. It is good government. That is why we pray for kings and rulers, so that "we may lead a peaceful and quiet life, godly and dignified in every way" (1 Tim. 2:2).

When the corruption of government reaches the dangerous level of persecuting Christians for their faith, they are not without recourse. Turning the other cheek is not a blanket *mot d'ordre* for every context (Matt. 5:39). Government is not above reproach or reform. Jesus called Herod a "fox," and Paul appealed to Rome. Many policies may be fought for, the press and media may be alerted, companies may put pressure on clients, churches may ask for more awareness. International cooperation can help put the right kind of pressure on particular countries slow to recognize human rights. When such appeals fail, there may be no other solution than to suffer, sometimes unto death. That is the tragic plight of many Christians around the world. Still, there are circumstances when it can be legitimate to engage in civil disobedience, as long as it is not vigilante justice or personal revenge. It ought always to be done through authorized channels. Calvin talked of enlisting the authority of the "lower magistrate" against the higher one if need be. Revolution is never a biblical option. Reformation is!

Do This in Remembrance of Me

The Word of God is a privileged vehicle for the presence of God in worship, and the response we bring is accordingly one of understanding and rational persuasion. At the same time, the Lord has provided for a visible manifestation of his saving presence, which confirms and enhances the verbal expression. In the Reformed view there are two such signs, baptism and the Lord's Supper. Although there is no biblical term for them, they are known as sacraments, from the Latin word for a soldier's sacred oath of fidelity. In the Roman Catholic tradition many things, natural and ritual, are considered sacramental, because they are signs of God's presence. Stress is on the analogy of nature to grace, culminating in the incarnation of the second person into human form. In medieval times, the Roman Catholic Church named seven sacraments, including marriage, ordination, penance, and the like. But Protestant theology is less concerned with analogies and more concerned with the utter difference between Creator and creature. Significantly, it then becomes all the more remarkable that the Lord should have singled out two special moments for the church to enact, as visible confirmations of a spiritual truth, sealed to our hearts.

Sacraments, then, are not just any natural manifestation of the supernatural. They are divinely instituted signs that make the gospel not only audible but also visible. A sacrament is the appointed means for participation in God's saving grace. In the classical language, it is a "sign and seal" of the covenant of grace (see Westminster Confession of Faith 27.1). A sacrament is a ceremony ordained by the Lord Jesus Christ for use in the church. Of baptism, he said, "Go therefore and make disciples of all nations, baptizing them in the name of the Father and of the Son and of the Holy Spirit" (Matt. 28:19). Of the Lord's Table, he said, "Do this in remembrance of me" (Matt. 26:26–28; Luke 22:19–20; 1 Cor. 10:15–21).

As such, the sacraments are a ceremony involving words of institution; elements, that is, the water for baptism and the bread and wine for the Lord's Table; and observance in the church meeting. The two ceremonies are a means of grace. The biblical authors go quite far. They consider participating in them to be the equivalent of receiving their inward and spiritual meaning (Rom. 6:4; 1 Peter 3:21–22). Christ not only ordained the sacraments, but is the center of their meaning. Reformation thinking seeks to match the Old Testament's highlighting of two great moments, circumcision and the Passover meal. But it also seeks to recognize the appointment of new signs for God's people, which no longer have blood as their theme. The New Testament rites of baptism and the Lord's Supper are the proper fulfillment of the Old Testament ordeals of cutting off skin and sprinkling blood. Christ is our circumcision; he is our Passover (Col. 2:11; 1 Cor. 5:7).

The sacraments refer to the past: in them we remember what Christ has done. They have a present reference: we are cleansed from sin; we feed on the Lord for our strength. And they look forward, to the future: Jesus explicitly told the disciples he would personally drink the wine with them in the Father's kingdom (Matt. 26:29). As *verba visibile* (visible words) the sacraments are meant to drive home the spiritual truth signified and strengthen the faith of believers by appealing to the senses. Much more, they are the occasion for a special work of grace to be exhibited and applied. It does not occur by magic but by the real presence of the Holy Spirit. When the ceremony is properly conducted, including instruction as to its purpose, relating it to the gospel, and with proper encouragements and warnings, then great blessing is promised to its recipients. This blessing, like all others, is received by faith, not automatically.[12]

12. All of the principal Reformers agreed that grace was not forthcoming *ex opere operato*, as the Roman Catholic Church had taught. But they differed over the way in which the Spirit seals the sacraments. In the Lutheran tradition the Spirit is present "with and under" the elements. In Zwingli's view, at least in some of his writings, the sacraments have almost purely symbolic value, without being a means of grace. Calvin and many Reformed thinkers asserted the presence of the Spirit to be real, yet not confused with the elements, and to be received by faith.

Baptism

Baptism signifies the purification needed for entry into the kingdom of God. In the Old Testament, ceremonial purging by water and by blood exhibited the connection between human cleansing and atonement (Heb. 9:10; Lev. 8:5–6; 14:8–9; 15:5). It meant judgment and justification. In view of the imminence of judgment, John the Baptist preached and administered the baptism of repentance for the forgiveness of sin (Mark 1:4). He was the forerunner of Jesus, who would baptize with the Spirit and fire, the true cleansing by the ordeal of his death. He took judgment on himself. From heaven at Pentecost, Jesus poured out his cleansing Spirit on his people, who in turn repented and believed for the forgiveness of their sins. Henceforth, baptism is a sign not of preparation or of judgment but of belonging to the Father, Son, and Holy Spirit (Matt. 28:18–19). Baptism with water especially signifies the age of the Holy Spirit.

Baptism is now the great sign given to the church by which the children of God are recognized. As such it is the equivalent of circumcision in the Old Testament. The cutting of the foreskin signified belonging to God by covenant, which term carries "cutting" as one of its meanings. Not to be circumcised makes one liable to being cut off from covenant life (Gen. 17:14). In the New Testament, the ceremony of water carries a similar meaning, since water can be the judgment by deluge and the life-giving Spirit (1 Peter 3:21; 1 Cor. 10:2; John 4:14; Titus 3:5). The proper response of God's people is commitment to keep the covenant. Sinless Jesus came to John for baptism, identifying with sinful Israel to pledge his covenant commitment (Matt. 3:13–17).[13] Again, this weighs against any idea of an automatic blessing, such as baptismal regeneration. In Roman Catholic teaching baptism is the cleansing from original sin. In reality it is far more; it is the sign and seal of our ingrafting to Christ.

The great majority within the Reformed faith recognizes the propriety of baptizing believers and their children. If circumcision is the precursor of baptism, then it makes sense to baptize infants, just as

---

13. It is likely that the baptism of Jesus was also his ordination as prophet, priest, and king.

eight-day-old males were circumcised in Israel. Paul explicitly connects circumcision and baptism in Colossians 2:11–12. The Lord does not isolate individuals from their offspring but claims them for his covenant. Paul calls the children of a believing spouse holy, not because they are presumed believers and certainly not because they are sinless, but because they are set apart, claimed for the covenant (1 Cor. 7:14). Baptism can be no less than circumcision; it is far more. Male and female are baptized. Peter makes it clear that repentance and baptism in the name of Christ is a promise "for you and for your children and for all who are far off, everyone whom the Lord our God calls to himself" (Acts 2:39).

The concern of those who cannot accept infant baptism is that there is too much distance between the sign and the reality. In the worst of cases the infant may grow up and not believe. They argue, further, that no one verse in Scripture explicitly tells us to baptize children. It appears to them as though baptism is always by immersion, as in John's practice to invite the penitent down "in the river Jordan" (Matt. 3:6). The concern is right, but the conclusion is misplaced. First, there is always some distance between the sign and the reality, even for adults. And adults too may reveal a heart of unbelief, despite efforts to determine the sincerity of their faith by the elders of the church. Second, it may be true that no verse explicitly teaches or describes infant baptism, but then no verse instructs us to wait, or describes an adult baptism of a grown son or daughter from a believing family. In fact, the Book of Acts describes several cases of households being baptized (Acts 16:15, 33; 18:8). These were family churches where the place of children would have been understood in continuity with the Old Testament model. Third, arguments for a particular mode of baptism, such as immersion rather than sprinkling, are not convincing. The purging with hyssop in the Old Testament was a sprinkling. Further, anyone who has visited the Jordan River must agree that it is shallow, and the expression "in the river Jordan" more likely refers to standing on the banks, possibly in the shallow water.

Children do grow up and reject the faith. In this case, baptism is still a sign not of the cleansing of forgiveness but of judgment to come. The fact that we cannot be sure any given child will continue in the faith is no reason to neglect the sign of promise, any more than we should neglect any sign of God's blessing on the entire family. Jesus reminded his skeptical followers that the kingdom of heaven belongs to little children as well as to adult believers (Luke 18:15–17). Also in continuity with the Old Testament, fathers are commanded to bring their children up in the discipline and instruction of the Lord (Eph. 6:4). They are not outsiders, but covenant children. When we say grace at meals or say the Lord's Prayer, our children are not observers but participants.

Many Reformed churches have a rite of passage called confirmation by which children who have become old enough to receive solid biblical teaching and embrace the faith on their own are recognized as adult members. This may be during the teen years or later. What is universally recognized is the need to instruct children in God's ways. Just as the Passover was used in the Old Testament as a mnemonic device to spark questions from young Jewish lads, so the sacraments ought to provoke questions and teaching opportunities in the church today.

If children may be baptized, some would ask, why should they not also participate in the Lord's Supper? It seems that children old enough to eat food were at the Passover meal in the Old Testament (Exod. 12:26). The answer given in the Reformed tradition is that the two sacraments differ in one important manner. In the Lord's Supper, believers are performing the sacrament as well as receiving it. They are expected to understand its meaning, so that they do not inveigh judgment on themselves by partaking thoughtlessly or in an unrepentant mood (1 Cor. 11:23–24). The Westminster Larger Catechism points out that only those "such as are of years and ability to examine themselves" ought to participate in the Lord's Supper (A. 177).

The Lord's Table

The second sacrament is a covenant meal. It is the Passover of the New Testament. The great events of the exodus were to be remembered at a meal, where a perfect, slain lamb was eaten. We understand the Lord's Supper to be the proclamation of Christ's death until he comes (1 Cor. 11:26). In it, we look back at his finished work, his broken body and shed blood, far more precious than that of any sacrificial lamb (1 Peter 1:19). And we look forward to the final banquet table of the new heavens, the marriage supper of the Lamb (Rev. 19:17; Isa. 34:6; Zech. 14:16). There is joy at the table. But there is solemnity, because the heart of it is the remembrance of Christ's death.

In the Lord's Supper we are nourished. While baptism initiates us into communion with Christ, the Supper signifies the continuing fellowship we have with him. It is a sign and seal of our death and resurrection with Christ. Jesus, the Bread of Life, called his flesh and blood true food and drink. If we partake, we abide in him and he in us (John 6:55–56). Many images convey the reality of our utter dependence on Jesus, dead and raised again. But eating and drinking are powerful reminders of our constant need for heavenly nourishment. This is one of the reasons the Reformed view recommends the regular and frequent celebration of the Lord's Supper.

The imagery has also been the occasion for enormous controversy over the precise way in which the spiritual truths are conveyed in earthly signs. In medieval times it was thought that the body and blood of Christ were substantially present in the bread and wine. From an Aristotelian distinction between substance and accident a doctrine known as transubstantiation emerged, wherein the reality of Jesus Christ was transferred into the accidents of bread and wine.[14] While the more sophisticated theologians, such as Thomas Aquinas, guarded against "materialization" of the body and blood into the accidents, this subtlety was lost on most participants. The ceremony of the Mass builds up to the high point of consecration, when Christ changes into the elements. The priest alone may say the Mass. Each element is considered to contain body and blood, so that if the wine is withheld from the laypeople, Christ's whole presence is still in the bread. The Mass is a sacrifice, and as such propitiatory. Since Christ is identified with the elements, they can be saved for later use and should be adored.

14. Augustine's view held that Christ was present spiritually. Theologians such as Ratramnus and Berengar continued in that tradition, but others, such as Radbertus, argued for a miracle in the Mass, which view won over, becoming official in 1059. The term *transubstantiation* was first used officially in the Fourth Lateran Council of 1215.

The Protestant Reformers rejected this view. They understood the risen Christ, the bodily Christ, to be seated at the right hand of God. He would not transfer his substance to an earthly accident. None denied the reality behind the symbols, but all rejected any suggestion of re-sacrifice. Christ was received by faith, not physically. At the same time, the Reformers differed among themselves on the manner of Christ's presence in the sacrament. For Luther, Christ is present bodily. While not identical with the elements, he is "in, with and under" them. This view is known as consubstantiation.[15] Luther could not see any other way of understanding Jesus saying, "This is my body." Thus, when we partake, we receive Christ's body "truly and physically." The Swiss Reformer Ulrich Zwingli went to the other extreme, denying any meaningful connection between the sign and the reality. For him, "This is my body" must be figurative, since Christ had gone to heaven. He argued that in John 6, where the Lord spoke of eating his body and drinking his blood, the key is verse 63: "It is the Spirit who gives life; the flesh is of no avail." His view is sometimes called the memorial view, since the Supper is purely symbolic, a reminder but not a means of grace.

John Calvin developed a third approach, not really to balance Luther's and Zwingli's, but one that is distinctive. The Supper is certainly a means of grace, whereby Christ nourishes us. His body and blood are truly received but spiritually, that is, by the Holy Spirit. Christ is ascended in glory and cannot become corrupted into earthly elements. Nor can he be several places at once with respect to his humanity. But the Holy Spirit will take of his virtues and apply them to the believer in the sacrament. The power of the body and blood of Christ is communicated to us. All of this depends upon the proper preaching of the Word and the correct administration of the sacrament. There is great mystery here, and Calvin so much as admits it is

15. Luther's view is no doubt connected to his belief in the ubiquity of Christ. Luther believed there was a communication of attributes between Christ's divine and human natures, such that the human is absorbed into the divine. Thus, Christ's human nature could be omnipresent (ubiquity) through the divine nature. Calvin rejected this as a violation of Chalcedon's affirmation that human and divine natures, though joined in the one person, were not confused nor intermingled.

beyond his comprehension, adding that he experiences it without understanding it.[16]

The presence of Christ in the Lord's Table is signified by the minister's words of institution. In addition to the sermon, these words remind the congregation of the grace offered in the sacrament and the grace of the gospel, and they warn of the danger of approaching the table casually. By a practice known as fencing the table, it is customary in Reformed churches to invite all those who are baptized and walking in faith to partake while admonishing the unrepentant to stay away. Generally, though not uniformly, underage children do not partake of the Lord's Supper, because they are unable to examine themselves in preparation for the meal (1 Cor. 11:28–29).

It is good to remember some of the insights of the Reformers surrounding the Lord's Supper. First, they stressed that it is a covenant meal, not a ritualistic consecration. Second, the Lord's Supper is a Eucharist, an offering of thanks. Often the prayers on this occasion are closer to theological textbooks than to joyful praise. Third, this sacrament is epicletic, that is, an invocation. The Reformers at Strasbourg and Geneva integrated a special prayer of intercession into the celebration of the Lord's Supper. It signified asking God to sanctify the church through the work of the Holy Spirit. Finally, the service of Holy Communion is a most appropriate occasion for diaconal commitment. Because of the unique sacrifice of Christ, signified in the sacrament, the believer must sacrifice all to him (Rom. 12:1). And so, it is most appropriate to present offerings after the service specially destined for service to others.[17]

In much Protestant worship today the Lord's Supper tends to be an addendum. This is a shame, for there is clear indication that the New Testament church administered it regularly. Reactions against the sacerdotal approach in Roman Catholicism or the casual approach of some evangelicals are understandable, but this should not justify reducing the sacrament's importance. Some Reformed churches go

16. Calvin, *Institutes of the Christian Religion*, 4.17.32.

17. These priorities are nicely set forth in Hughes Oliphant Old, *Worship Reformed according to Scripture* (Louisville: Westminster John Knox Press, 2002), 173–74.

to the extreme of celebrating the Supper only once or twice a year, usually with very strict discipline. The result is that the sacrament becomes an intimidating onus. Instead, the Lord's Supper ought to be a time for sober celebration. It ought to signify our utter need for feeding on our Lord and Savior. It ought to express our essential unity as believers. It ought to nurture our expectation of that great day when all of God's people will "come shouting to Zion" and sit down at the great wedding feast of the Lamb, with Jesus presiding.

11

ALL TO THE GLORY
OF GOD

~~~~~~~~~~~~~~~~

Two Mandates, One Calling

We have come a long way from the idea of reformation, through the history of the Reformed faith, and to the elements of Reformed theology. Understanding of the world and of life according to the Reformed faith centers on the three momentous realities, creation, fall, and redemption. God's good world has become corrupt. Yet he has not abandoned the world but brought life to it. He so loved the world that he sent his only Son to become incarnate, to suffer, to die, and then to be raised up, so that, believing in him, we could have life, in communion with him forever.

Just as the fall affected the entire cosmos, so does redemption. It is comprehensive. The new heaven and new earth will not be a place for souls only, but also for a remade humanity living in a new cosmos. The city of Jerusalem has Jesus Christ, the slain Lamb, at its center. By his light "will the nations walk, and the kings of the earth will bring their glory into it" (Rev. 21:24).

If this is true, how shall we live today? How does our understanding of the blight of evil on the world, together with the sure expectation of the resurrection, inform our walk? How do we live in the world while yet not being of the world (John 17:13–19)? How do we relate to the surrounding culture?

The Reformed outlook has always stressed the profound harmony between missions and justice, between conversion and social change. The Bible clearly teaches that we should not make such investments on earth, "where moth and rust destroy" (Matt. 6:19). At the same time, evangelism and missions cannot be so narrowly defined that they "despise all vanities on earth," to quote the subtitle of the Thomas à Kempis classic, *The Imitation of Christ*. The world and its lusts may be passing away, but the earth is still the Lord's and ought to be cared for. Thoughts should be captive (2 Cor. 10:5), magistrates supported (Rom. 13:1–7), food and drink consumed, and everything done to God's glory (1 Cor. 10:31). Whatever is true, honorable, and lovely should be held in honor and nurtured (Phil. 4:8). This way, Christ is preeminent in all things, whether earthly or heavenly (Col. 1:20).

We do not have to choose between the so-called spiritual and the so-called cultural. To choose is to set up an unwanted dichotomy. As one author has put it, the first view is heaven-centered. It prays, "Thy will be done in heaven, and so on earth." The second is world-centered. It prays, "Thy will be done, on earth, your heaven." Both views end up splitting the human being into two contradictory attributes. In the first, we are a disincarnate soul. In the second, we are a bunch of physical material, just a body. He wryly adds, a soul without a body is a ghost; and a body without a soul is a corpse.[1] The truth is both–and.

Perhaps the best way to look at the profound harmony of the two is to consider the relation between the two great mandates the Lord addressed to humankind. We have considered the matter earlier, but let us state things a bit more emphatically. The two great commandments are, first, what is known as the cultural mandate, to multiply, to subdue, and to have dominion over the earth (Gen. 1:26–30), and, second, the Great Commission, Jesus' order to make disciples of the nations (Matt. 28:18–20). How are they related?

---

1. Harvie M. Conn, *Evangelism: Doing Justice and Preaching Grace* (Grand Rapids: Zondervan, 1982), chap. 4.

On one view, the cultural mandate was abrogated because of the fall. Because people have lost the right to subdue the earth, God has now given us quite another task, that of missions. Culture now must take a back seat to the urgent call to evangelize. But a second look reveals a different picture. There is no compelling evidence that the cultural mandate was abrogated after the fall. Culture continues, despite the corruption of the human race (Gen. 4:17–22). Culture developed not only in the unbelieving race of Cain's descendants, but in Israel too, under the leadership of God's redeemed people. Psalm 8 describes human identity in almost the same terms as the cultural mandate (Ps. 8:6–8). Even the exiled Israelites could have children, build houses, grow crops, and pray for the welfare of the city (Jer. 29:4–7).

Furthermore, the New Testament, far from dismissing the cultural mandate, specifically identifies Christ as the cultural man of Psalm 8 (Heb. 2:6–9). Christ leads the new humanity in a renewed vocation. The Great Commission is not a narrow call to evangelize. It is an intensive and extensive call to make disciples and teach everything Christ prescribed. The significant difference between the two mandates is not that one replaces the other but that they both express God's covenant requirement in ways appropriate to the particular stage of history where they are enacted. The cultural mandate was the comprehensive commandment to the human race to engage all of life, from the family to the wider society, to scientific, political, and artistic life. It was appropriate before the fall. Its form, but not its content, is modified after the fall. The Great Commission is the great New Testament *mot d'ordre*. Like the cultural mandate, it centers on the covenant. But in addition to the first commission, this second one carries the grace of God in Christ needed to fulfill it. That explains its terms: because of his death and resurrection, Jesus Christ was given all authority in heaven and on earth; and because of his lordship over history he is with us until the end of time. Christ's people still go forth to have dominion and subdue the earth, but it is by making disciples. Not only does the command to engage in every area for God's glory still stand, but now, at this stage in the history of redemption, we accomplish the task by making disciples, by the authority and in the presence of the risen Christ.

The creation ordinances are still operative. We still participate in the three great aspects of the first calling: worship, family, and work. Yet our worship is now not only by resting in God's blessing (Gen. 2:3), but also by coming to the final rest of the heavenly Sabbath (Heb. 4:10). Not only is family life the mandate to be one with our vis-à-vis and multiply and fill the earth (Gen. 1:28; 2:24), but now we do so with regard to the total needs of human society in the world, fallen, yet being emancipated. We not only continue to have our own children, but also preach the gospel and thus fill the world with spiritually gifted people (Acts 2:33; Eph. 4:10). Each of us must still work. We continue to tend the garden and engage in every legitimate kind of labor, but now we do so as those concerned for the world's improvement, for salvation, for the poor, for social justice, for every aspect required by the love of our neighbor (Eph. 4:28).

Worthy of the Calling

In view of this larger picture, Reformed believers ought to be fully conscious of their calling in every legitimate area of life. To put it another way, Reformed theology issues in a Reformed ethic, one that is meant to be comprehensive. What is the best way to summarize this ethic? Remembering what we said about sanctification, with its nonmoralistic, already–not yet, grace-filled character, we could begin almost anywhere.

Though they come from the Old Testament, the Ten Commandments still provide a marvelous foundation for walking with the Lord that has much to commend it for our times. No doubt this is why the great Reformed creeds and confessions often used them as an outline for the Christian life. Far from being abrogated in the New Testament, they are given new depth and meaning in the new covenant.

As the preamble signifies, the Ten Commandments remind us that grace is the beginning, as well as the means and the end of our ethics. We have been delivered not only from Egypt but also from every house of bondage by the Lord God, who calls us to do everything for his glory, to the end of living before him, and for his sake, in every area of life. The commandments are life and health, a rule for the Christian life that, far from encouraging any self-sufficiency, are the expression of our gratitude to the God who loves us. They are the embodiment of the love we should practice for our God and for our neighbor (Rom. 13:8–10). What are they, and what do they mean for us today?

1. To have no other gods before God means to live before his wonderful face, to do all things not in secret but in fellowship with him. It means to acknowledge that God is one and to love him with all our heart, soul, mind, and strength. It means to recognize that all things are from him and through him and to him and that he and his glory have no rivals (Rom. 11:36). The Lord is spoken of as a jealous God, not because he is fitfully protective but because he knows that his name is the only one that brings truth and health to our bones. No room for Western secularism here, because the earth is the Lord's and the fullness thereof. No room for syncretism with other religious systems or with other gods here, because only he has the words of eternal life. Jesus is the way, the truth, and the life, because he alone went to such an extent for the love of his people. We may suffer for his name's sake, but we will never be let down by him or put to shame. So many Christians are persecuted for their faith today, in China, in North Africa, and throughout the world. Their faith, and the faith of all others, will emerge like gold, refined by fire (1 Peter 1:7). God's providential care will always show the way to safety, despite any imminent harm.

2. To refuse carved images means to deny the power of idols. There is nothing wrong with images in themselves or with symbols of all kinds. What is wrong is to promote ways of worshiping God that are not according to his regulations. Jesus Christ, the radiance of the Father's glory and the exact imprint of his nature, is the supreme image authorized by revelation fit for worship (Heb. 1:3). Whereas our ancestors worshiped in the temple of the city of Jerusalem, filled with images, we worship in Spirit and in truth (John 4:24). Images may help us understand the truth, but while we wait for the coming of the New Jerusalem in the new heaven and the new earth, we cannot confuse them for the

real thing. Images and artistic allusions may help us understand the invisible, but they cannot in themselves provide any true power. Money, masks, relationships, magisterial reason, and leaders, good in themselves, can never substitute for the true God, who is wholly other in his transcendence and wholly present in Jesus Christ. Him alone may we worship.

3. To refrain from using God's name in vain means to give all honor to God as he is and as he has revealed himself. False claims, false prophecies, ideologies, and alien systems are so many vain attempts to signify and accomplish what only God can stand for and achieve. This is why the early Christians refused to burn the torch to Caesar. While they were ready to honor him as emperor, they would not confuse his name and power with God's. In countries where animism was recently practiced, Christians will not engage in casting spells, using hexes, or even taking the name of God and claiming special power from it. Only the name of Jesus saves. The sin against the Holy Spirit is to attribute evil to the name of God (1 John 5:16). Oaths and vows, even in the name of God or his Scripture, are good in themselves. Contracts are honorable. But it is better to keep silent than to make an untenable vow (Matt. 5:33–37). Certain ill-conceived vows, such as celibacy or unreasonable pledges, are regrettable but not irreversible. They are not magically binding. God's grace is sufficient to undo a wrong vow and lead us to freedom.

4. To honor the Sabbath means to place all of life under the sign of hope. From the beginning, life had a goal. Even our first parents in the Garden were not to worship, procreate, and labor as ends in themselves. They did so by looking forward to the day of consummate bliss. In Western postindustrial societies, rest has been confused with leisure. The entertainment industry has given us more and more toys and sounds for our distraction. We can easily bargain first things away. The biblical Sabbath is very different. In the Old Testament, it told God's people to celebrate, in joy, after the hard work of the week. In the New Testament, we begin with the celebration, the permanent Sabbath of the Lord's day. Rest from our sins does not mean we can now abandon the pattern of work and rest intended in the commandment. Rather, the gospel gives it new depth and meaning (Heb. 4:9–10). We

now work for the sake of the kingdom. We earn treasure in order to give it away. We rest, we worship and pray, especially on the first day, the Lord's day, as a countercultural statement of our hope in a frenzied, distracted world.

5. To honor parents means just that. Father and mother, that privileged social institution, have a special meaning in the Scriptures. Children are honored to grow up in families and to respect their elders. Parents likewise are honored to nurture their children and to educate them in the wise ways of the Lord. Such mutual honor not only ensures the solidarity of this and other social units but also shows forth the particular virtues of the kingdom of God (Eph. 6:1–4). Among other things, future generations are the sign of hope for the coming of the kingdom. Strikingly, modern individualism is especially incompatible with the biblical stress on family solidarity. Idolizing the family is equally misguided. Children are not asked to obey their parents slavishly, particularly if they are told to do something immoral. Conflict legitimately arises within families when the gospel divides its members (Matt. 10:34–39). Allegiance to Christ ought to trump every other allegiance. Still, the norm is filial respect.

Secondarily, and by implication, the fifth commandment carries over to all legitimate governance, to whom honor is due—from magistrates to chief executive officers to department heads. Ultimately, all legitimate authority is from God (Rom. 13:1; 1 Peter 2:13–17). For this reason Christians ought to have no compunction about serving in public office, even in politics or the military. They are legitimate spheres of calling in this world. Governors may be corrupt, but government is of God.

6. To refrain from slaying means to respect the life of God's image-bearers. But it is more than that. Only God is the giver of life, and thus he is the one who has authority over it. Life as a substance is not sacred. We do not worship some sort of *élan vital* that is worthy of preservation at all costs. Nor are we religious vegetarians. Animals may have rights but not because of an abstraction called life, and certainly not at a level equivalent to human rights. Human life is precious, because it is specially made by God, after his likeness. This is so much so that in the Old Testament, the only appropriate sanction for its illegal ter-

mination is losing the privilege of living (Gen. 9:6). In our day we are threatened by therapeutic abortions, infanticide, assisted suicide, and euthanasia. The world is full of cruelty. Slavery, child abuse, and religious persecution are widespread. We also hear about justified rage, legitimate revenge, and vigilante justice. But our Lord made it clear that all of these are tantamount to murder.

At the same time, the Bible does not advocate pacifism. It makes room for the sadly necessary occasions when enemies of society may have to receive the sharp edge of the sword (Rom. 13:4). The government rightly defends its people from aggression. If force is needed for that purpose, it should never stem from vigilante justice or private revenge but must be authorized by the magistrate. Even in rare cases of legitimate civil disobedience, allegiance to a proper authority must be tantamount. If war is necessary, then there are rules even for the right engagement in conflict. The rules of war include keeping civilians from harm, treating prisoners humanely, and never seeking to gain more than is threatened. Christ came to give abundant life, and so we ought to love it as we love our neighbor.

7. Not to commit adultery means to hold faithfulness in highest regard, first within marriage and then in every commitment. Marriage is not for everyone. In the economy of the new covenant, singleness may be a most legitimate calling. The call to celibacy is appropriate in certain cases, and the church must pay more heed to singles. But for those called into marriage, connubial faithfulness not only echoes God's covenant faithfulness to his people; it is the precondition for the fulfillment of God's intention for order in human society. Marriage is a high estate wherein a man and a woman are joined as covenant companions (Prov. 2:17). Husband and wife are one flesh. It is the one legitimate occasion for sexual enjoyment (1 Cor. 7:3–5). It is the foyer for procreation and the nurturing of future generations for God's sake. To live faithfully in the marriage bond is to work out the proper relation between a man and a woman (Eph. 5:22–33). In many traditional societies the man claims unrightfully to dominate his wife. How can he lead without falling into abusive entitlements? Should submission be mutual? Who is responsible to earn the bread? Who is the

primary caregiver of the children? These areas are top items for consideration by the church today.

Is divorce ever legitimate? Seeking sexual adventure outside of marriage is so serious that it is one of the two legitimate grounds for divorce (Matt. 19:9). The other ground is desertion, which means something like the fundamental incompatibility of a believer and an unbeliever. If an unbeliever wants to leave, he or she is losing enormous privileges. Yet the believer is not bound (1 Cor. 7:15). Adultery can be literal but also in attitude. Included in the sin of adultery is to wish for someone else as spouse, to look lustfully at illicit pictures, and even to be captivated by seductive suggestion. One of the blights on many advanced societies today is easily available pornography, sexual tourism, and the like.

To be sure, the family is not the only social institution in God's world. For Christians, the church is the highest bond of fellowship. Other social units are instituted of God as well: the school, the government, corporations. But all are bound to the rule of faithfulness, just as God in Christ has pledged faithfulness to his covenant.

8. Not to steal means to acknowledge God's right to distribute his gifts to whom he will. He has providentially assigned a great diversity of blessings to people in various places around the world. The primary intention of any gift of God is for it to be used faithfully and productively, and to hold all things in with a light hand. Strictly speaking, we do not own anything but are keepers of God's gifts. As such we are meant to use them with gratitude and for service in God's kingdom. Thus, to steal is to usurp this plan, as if we know better what to do with our gifts than does the Lord. When we are not satisfied with what we have, we challenge God's wisdom. Envy, resentment, and unhealthy desires have the same background as the actual deed of burglary.

Of course, there is terrible poverty and injustice in the human and circumstantial distribution of wealth in this fallen world. Such injustice should not be allowed to stand. It is right to fight for true equality. This does not translate into either radical socialism, which is utopian and attempts to force the redistribution of wealth in an equitable way, or unbridled market economies, which on the surface ally hard work and rewards but underneath the surface end up rewarding the privileged. The Bible has nothing against possessions, as long as they are not ends in themselves (1 Tim. 6:9–10). Our money is for giving away as well as enjoying. Many countries harbor unfair taxes, enforced bribery, or entitlements of all kinds. But, whether corporately or individually, hoarding wealth is incompatible with our fundamental poverty, our complete lack of resources before Christ, who made himself poor that we may be rich in him (James 2:5–6).

9. To bear false witness means to destroy the neighbor we are meant to protect. Love requires that we not keep lists, that we not enjoy wrongdoing, but that we rejoice in the truth (1 Cor. 13:4–7). It is not always easy to speak the truth. Some neighbors are particularly unsavory, not candidates for protection, in our judgment. But our judgment is substandard when we justify defaming or subverting the neighbor. Lying can be overt, but more often it is subtle. The lie can range from keeping certain facts from surfacing to slanting a story in a certain way. Bragging is a form of lying. Even rudeness qualifies as a type of prevarication, because it does not protect one's neighbor (Gal. 5:15; Eph. 4:29). Some lies are big, such as government cover-up for corruption or organized crime's double life. Others are small, at least apparently, such as failing to report income on a tax form or making fun of someone.

Are all lies a breach of the ninth commandment? Not necessarily. The commandment requires truth in a lawful testimony. Not all testimonies are rightful. In war, for example, deception is necessary for the sake of good strategy. Thus, Rahab was not violating the commandment when she lied about the whereabouts of Israel's spies (Josh. 2:5). Protecting those wrongly pursued may require justified lying, as was the case in the Second World War, when many sought to harbor Jews otherwise doomed to deportation.

Truth-telling is not only the accurate uncovering of data but the wise stewardship of words. Truth-telling is not simply yielding the facts but grace-giving, words "seasoned with salt" (Col. 4:6). What is truth, asked Pilate? He had it right before him, in Christ who kept silence when he could have judged and spoken in order to set us free (John 18:37–38).

10. Not to covet means to have kingdom priorities in everything we do and think. Just as the first commandment summarizes all the others by placing us before the face of God, so the last commandment

encapsulates the others by testing our motives before our redeemer God. On the surface, we covet when we want something we should not have, such as our neighbor's goods. Under the surface, covetousness is idolatry. It invests in this world and its goods, a world with its lusts, a world that is passing away.

The test of covetousness comes when we hear Jesus asking us if we are willing to give up everything we have—goods, property, relationships, position—in order to follow him (Luke 14:15–24). If we cannot, then we are in an unhealthy relation to these things, many of them good in themselves. What is seductive is not the things but their conflict with the kingdom of God. Nothing in the Bible militates against possessions, even less against having sufficient food and clothing. Christians who pray "give us this day our daily bread" are doing nothing wrong, unless they forget first to pray, "your kingdom come, your will be done" (Matt. 6:10–11). Nothing is wrong with desiring satisfaction, as long as it comes just as easily in plenty and in want.

Much in the world, from Marxism to television advertising, pledges material comfort and upward mobility. Not only can they not humanly be delivered without injustice, but also they are out of synch with the great principles of the kingdom of God, which aim is to establish the Lord's kindly rule in a realm of his righteousness.

Bringing in the Glory

Holding to the Reformed faith today means avoiding nostalgia for the past while building on the legacy of our heritage. To the extent that Reformed theology is truly biblical, it ought not only to stand the test of time but also to help set the agenda. To use Martin Luther King Jr.'s metaphor, it will be more of a thermostat than a thermometer. We must build on our heritage. Many things have been so well established, sometimes with blood, sweat, and tears, that it would be arrogant to start afresh. Still, there is a great deal of work to be done. The agenda is more than full. It is not possible to be comprehensive here. But we can suggest five areas that need our attention from a Reformed standpoint. They represent a beginning. The discussion is open-ended.

Building on Our Theological Foundation

As we have seen, the heritage is considerable. And yet, more work is still to be done in the most fundamental areas of theology. In three areas, among many, questions can be raised.

Interpreting Scripture. There is plenty of work to be done in the field of biblical interpretation, or hermeneutics. One example is the question of the already–not yet. We have seen how helpful this approach is to understanding Christian ethics. We are already dead to sin and alive to Christ, but then we ought to live in that reality. How does this key open up the Bible to us even more? How does it help us understand the love command in relation to the law, for example (1 John 2:7–8)? How does it help us against antinomianism (Rom. 6:1)? Another example is the New Testament use of the Old. Sometimes this is quite straightforward. But at other times, it is not clear how the New Testament authors arrive at their interpretation of the Old Testament. For example, what does Paul mean when he talks of the rock that followed the people of Israel being Christ (1 Cor. 10:4)? How does he make use of the creation narrative in order to discuss gender relations (1 Cor. 11:7–12; 1 Tim. 2:13–15)? What procedure does the author of Hebrews use to apply Psalm 8 to Jesus Christ (Heb. 2:6–9)? Yet another example is the vast field of literary criticism and biblical hermeneutics. Narrative theology has rightly noticed that the Bible is not a consistently propositional book. While numerous passages are capable of being rendered into propositions, others are more challenging. Biblical poetry, proverbial wisdom, and historical narrative are among several genres that God used as he inspired the Scriptures for our edification. But how exactly do they translate into biblical authority? How does a book like Ecclesiastes speak infallibly?

Relating union with Christ to other doctrines. We have already noted that justification by faith is one of the major spokes attached to the central hub of union with Christ. But how so? How can we safeguard the doctrine that stands so much at the center of Reformed theology, namely, justification by faith alone, while at the same time fully recognizing the centrality of the mystical union? Much is at stake in getting this right.

The gospel message can come to the world in full force only if it proclaims the full pardon for sins as God's declaration to those who come in faith. At the same time, justification is neither the only virtue in the order of salvation nor the central one. Debates rage today over the proper way to understand the New Testament polemic against the Jewish interpretation of religion. Some people equate every modern Protestant polemic against the Roman Catholic Church as a matter of understanding the relation of good works to faith. Is it enough simply to state that the only enemy of the gospel is legalism? Or is the problem also not in understanding how union with Christ informs every other head of doctrine?

Developing the doctrine of the Trinity. Robert Letham helpfully points out that properly understood, the Trinity is an alternative to postmodernism and to Islam.[2] In the postmodern condition diversity is let loose. There is no overarching meaning, no metanarrative that pulls things together. The biblical view of God begins with his simple unity. In Islam, by contrast, there is unity but no significant diversity. Allah controls all things and speaks his law for every occasion and for all times in the Arabic language. The biblical view of God is that he is three. But the Trinity has apologetic value in our present circumstances. This is who God is. Everything in life reflects him. Our worship is less than fulfilled if we cannot center it on the God who is one and three. Our knowledge is less than true if we cannot confess the equal ultimacy of unity and diversity. Christian apologetics can develop many persuasive arguments to commend the faith if it could more fully recognize the unique nature of God as a starting point in a world that would like to deny every distinction between Creator and creature.

Theology in Partnership

Much has changed even in the years since the end of the Cold War. For example, it would appear the center of gravity of true and lively Christian faith has moved to the Southern Hemisphere. It would also appear that since the toppling of the Berlin Wall the West faces not

2. Robert Letham, *The Holy Trinity: In Scripture, History, Theology, and Worship* (Phillipsburg, N.J.: P&R, forthcoming).

one but many different pretenders to power. Some of them are explicitly religious, including the Islamic world in resurgence, while others are explicitly secular or purely economic, such as the emerging European economic community. How will the Reformed faith respond?

It has been gratifying to witness the emergence of theological voices from the Southern Hemisphere. Emphases and perspectives not highlighted in the creeds of the West are not only fitting for the local context but also biblical. Often two-thirds–world theologies help us rediscover a theme in the Bible hitherto not well known. At the same time, these non-Western approaches to theology are sometimes unprepared to grapple with modernity. As a result they either reject it, often rejecting the Western Reformed heritage in the bargain, or uncritically embrace certain parts of it, not realizing the problems involved. A few examples tell the tale.

Africa. In various sub-Saharan African theologies, we sometimes find a greater sense of the connectedness of all things than in certain Western approaches. This thinking has no doubt benefited from traditional African religions, where God is omnipresent, although not always easy to access. Humanity relates to him as an entire community, not simply individually. Spirits and demons not only exist but also play a significant role in the affairs of human life. While rejecting the system of traditional religion, many African Christian theologies rightly carry over a vivid sense of human solidarity. The sin of Adam, so difficult for modern Westerners to understand, is an obvious explanation for the presence of evil in the African understanding. Principalities and powers are all too real. And so, to acknowledge Jesus Christ as having nailed them to the tree and as being supreme over every power in life is the strongest possible statement of his preeminence.[3] This is a way to accentuate Christ's lordship in Reformed theology.

At the same time, it is incumbent on African theology to be wise in its reception of modernization and urbanization. As the pendulum

---

3. Wilbur O'Donovan, *Pour un christianisme biblique en Afrique* (Abidjan: Centre de Publications Bibliques, 1998), 292; Emefie Ikenga Metuh, *God and Man in African Religion* (London: Geoffrey Chapman, 1981), 109.

swings, some thinkers have been tempted to identify all modernization as evil, being the carrier of Western domination. To be sure, a good deal of globalization, even as it translates into development for southern countries, has been destructive. But the African church ought to recognize the inevitability of modernity. It will not just go away, however much the developing nations try to resist it. And the church ought to be at the forefront of development, precisely in order to interact critically and biblically with it.[4] Here, the West still has a contribution to make. For Reformed theology has interacted (to be sure, with mixed success) with the typical facets of modernity for a long time: secularization, market economies, work and rest, technology and science. Because of the peculiar journey of Western philosophy, questions of biblical interpretation have been asked and answered in ways that have deepened our understanding of the Bible and of God's revelation. Western apologetics has interacted with the prevailing culture, highbrow and popular, to good advantage. The results are uneven, but the benefit of experience is decisive. In partnership with African theologians, then, Western ones can help not only face modernity but also guide it in a salutary direction.

Japan. Since the Second World War, the church and the state in Japan have been separated. The Constitution of 1946, article 20, was influenced by the United States' model, which in turn owes much to a Reformed Christian idea of the separation of the spheres. Formerly, the Tenno was the high priest of Shintoism and the political ruler of the people. The change to separate religion from the state is liberating, as far as it goes. But the change has not seeped down into the heart of Japanese culture as radically as in various Western countries. And this change came with great suffering. Defeat at war was deeply humiliating as well as deeply painful for the Japanese people. It is no surprise that here and in many other countries, theology has been sensitive to questions of honor and suffering. For example, Kazoh Kitamori has written extensively about God's humiliation for the sake of

---

4. William Dyrness, *Learning about Theology from the Third World* (Grand Rapids: Zondervan, 1990), 68–70.

the kingdom.[5] When Christians are persecuted and tortured, they may take deep comfort in Christ's refusal to send legions of angels against his accusers but to let his face be spat upon.

Kitamori's student, Kosuke Koyama, traveled to Thailand, where he wrote on *Waterbuffalo Theology*.[6] On his way to a country church, Koyama watched the water buffalo and was put in remembrance of the issues facing the farmers: rain and drought, roofs that leak, rice that is sticky, unfair supervisors. He suggests more theology be done from the point of view of an empty stomach. Often, he notes, Western theological reflection presupposes a full stomach. Its method is consequently well ordered. Suffering is the exception. But in Asia, suffering is the norm. Asian theologians tend to understand the privilege as well as the pain of persecution better than most.

And yet, there is a problem. Certain Asian theologies are weak in two ways. First, they tend to glorify suffering. So much is the humiliation of believers connected to the humiliation of Christ in this view that Christ's sovereignty and victory may be obscured. The Lord is acquainted with grief. But he is also the victor, and he has triumphed over all evil, including that channeled through the state. Proper balance is difficult during persecution, but it is healthful. Second, sometimes there is not a proper sense of what political power may and may not do in Asian theologies. The result is either to blame government for every problem or to resign oneself to an inevitable secular force. Here, in partnership with the West, there is something to be learned from the Reformed tradition. Rather than drawing insights from the pre-Christian world, the culture of the West carries an important principle. As Nobuo Watanabe puts it, "Whereas in the Christian world and especially in the Reformed church people insist on the right to resist, in the non-Christian world people do not know such a fundamental right."[7] To which we might add, more than the right of resistance, a whole view of statecraft is available for consideration.

5. Kazoh Kitamori, *A Theology of the Pain of God* (Richmond: John Knox, 1965).
6. Kosuke Koyama, *Waterbuffalo Theology* (Maryknoll, N.Y.: Orbis, 1974).
7. Nobuo Watanabe, "Reformed Theology in East and West," in *Toward the Future of Reformed Theology: Tasks, Topics, Traditions*, ed. David Willis and Michael Welker (Grand Rapids: Eerdmans, 1999), 54.

China. There is a fascinating contradiction to behold in China. On the one hand, the house churches are illegal and heavily persecuted. On the other hand, a scholarly movement known as Cultural Christianity is promoting the Christian worldview as holding great promise for the future of China. Intellectuals, university professors, and scholars are looking to Europe for models that will help that great country to become a civil society. One of the ironies here is that this interest coincides with one of the most self-critical denials of anything Western by Westerners. No doubt the cultural Christians incorrectly pin too much hope on all things European, without fully addressing the great failures of that continent, sometimes failures because of oppressive measures in the name of Christ. But they rightly see some of the connections between the gospel and such advances as great art, democracy, science, and technology. It is an opportune moment for Christian theologians to join forces and develop a richer understanding for East and West. May we say it is particularly important for a robust, Reformed outlook to be shared with Asian believers, even as they have much to teach us about persevering joyfully under unspeakable hardship?

Our Call to Stewardship

Our calling to responsible lifestyles, particularly good stewardship of the environment, deserves attention and development. The church's life in the world raises issues far beyond ways of doing theology in a contextual fashion. A whole range of matters is at stake. How to be in the world but not of it? The Reformation helped us understand that vocation was not only for priests but also for all of God's people. Theologians like Abraham Kuyper helped us to apply the notion of calling to every sphere of life, including the political, the scientific, and the artistic spheres. Yet although Reformed people are good at discussing and theorizing about full involvement in every realm of life, their record of going out and doing so is mixed. They have been strong in education. Many of the great universities have had a Reformed character. So, too, have they helped foster a Christian school movement that teaches children the many skills and disciplines needed for participation in the world, but from a Christian point of view. The

Reformed stress on family life has generally been healthy. The Protestant work ethic has meant many Reformed people have taken the call to labor seriously. Many have done well but have not hoarded their goods, and so they have become generous and compassionate.

Despite some progress in understanding the plurality of vocations, there is still a widespread bias in the church, in the West and in the non-West, that elevates the pastoral ministry and missionary calling above all others. It is as though the medieval view still holds sway. Christians often think of themselves as having their primary identity in the church, not in the surrounding culture, either in professional spheres such as business and government or in other fields like farming, the arts, engineering, and so forth. A popular view of the church has it that it is a healing community, with little connection to the rest of society. But, biblically, every area of life is subject to the normative rule of Christ. And Christians are equally in their place whether in the ministry or in the many places of service outside of the orbit of the organized church. Calling is a comprehensive notion. It reminds us that God puts each of us where we can do the most good, and be of service. A number of areas need attention.

The environment. One of the most urgent issues on the agenda is the environment. On the whole, Reformed people have been slow to respond aggressively to the needs of the environment. Some of the more conservatively minded assume that ecology is a liberal fabrication. In fact, the creation groans in the decay of its bondage (Rom. 8:20–22), and so we should not be surprised at an environmental crisis. Indeed, we groan with the creation as we both wait for full redemption (v. 23). Further, we are the main contributors to the geo-crisis. As Calvin DeWitt puts it, "The pieces of this puzzle do not fit! One piece says, 'We honor the Great Master!' The other piece says, 'We despise his great masterpieces!' "[8] The issues are not always simple. But the idols of efficiency and productivity have seduced even Christians into becoming violators of the environment. Clean air, respon-

8. Calvin DeWitt, *Caring for Creation: Responsible Stewardship of God's Handiwork* (Grand Rapids: Baker, 1998), 16.

sible waste management, and the beautification of cities are not luxuries for those who believe in the proper dominion of the earth.

Business ethics. Corporate ethics is in need of serious attention from Reformed Christians. Honesty and transparent accounting are at a premium these days. Corrupt business practices are not the unique province of the Southern Hemisphere. They are found in Europe and North America in alarming degrees. Believers have a primary responsibility to conduct business according to the high standards required in biblical ethics. But more than that, the direction of the business, the choice of products, and the relations between employer and employee should be thought through from a biblical perspective. It is not enough for the manner to be transparent. The direction also should make a positive contribution to the welfare of humanity.

Arts and media. It is important to paint, sculpt, or program with integrity. In their expressions, that is, in the narrative of artistic production a true balance must be kept between realism about the corruption of this world and joy in the hope of redemption. In contrast, some art is pessimistic, because it is without hope. Some is optimistic, because it fails to address the reality of sin. The trouble with both attitudes is that they are not strong enough! Pessimism is dark, certainly, but escapist, and so not dark enough. It refuses to see how bad things really are! Optimism is hopeful but not fully aware of how complete the reconciliation of all things through Jesus Christ is. It refuses to see how good God's grace really is! If artwork could strike the proper balance, it would not have to be caught in the endless cycle of rebellion against the previous style and revolutionary statements of the new. In addition, we ought to say that more believers need to be present in the arts and media. Christians often blame the arts and media for slanting the facts. But they have not often wrestled with the issues from the inside.

Worship. Many other areas could be cited. Worship, once the front line of Protestant concerns, is in a state of some confusion today. There is a serious need to look closely at the regulative principle and ask what it requires for today. Reformed worship on the whole is quite verbal, not to say verbose. While correctly emphasizing the sermon, it sometimes neglects the nonverbal aspects of worship, whether the sacraments in their full meaning or music and art. American churches have less a sense of the simplicity of the liturgy than European ones. Two-thirds–world churches tend to have more spontaneity and exuberance, though sometimes at the expense of order and the proper sequence of events. Also, a great deal needs to be worked out in relating local culture to the timeless elements of worship. How can we use the ingredients of local music in our hymns and songs without falling into accommodation? How can we honor the cultural norms of a particular people group without diminishing the catholicity of the church?

The private dimension of worship needs attention as well. Spirituality and devotional styles are vastly popular, but how much of that is the thermometer rather than the thermostat? In the West, there is a restlessness about spirituality. Often legitimate questions are being raised about certain formal yet aesthetically empty inherited styles. Some are looking to the arts or to disciplines of meditation for fulfillment. Others insist that small groups within the church will give them the intimacy and the mutual support not possible in a larger body. But finding the right balance between proper devotional life and proper life in the world is a critical issue for the Reformed outlook today.

Personal energies. Social commentator Jacques Attali has recently described the prototypical resident of the twenty-first century as the nomad.[9] Working at home, not in an office, Attali's nomads include not only urban dwellers and virtual denizens but also migrant workers, political refugees, and the homeless. They are usually free, they travel light, they are connected, far too connected (the cell phone and e-mail are the symbols of connectedness). They may be vigilant and cautious but never far from just plain fear. Reformed Christians should be asking, How does a healthy spiritual life develop in these conditions? How can the church be a stabilizing force for such a mobile and global set?

9. Jacques Attali, *Dictionnaire du XXIe siècle* (Paris: Fayard, 1998), 243.

What does private worship look like in such a world? And what happens to our energies?

The average family in many parts of the world moves several times in its lifetime. How much is the decision to move dictated by upward mobility rather than wise stewardship of every gift? Families will move because one spouse gets a better job. But they will not think about giving up schools, friends, neighbors, doctors, let alone church, until it is too late. Companies will move because of a tax advantage in a new location. But they will not think about the stress on their workers, the possibility of disrupting the new place, or such things as environmental issues, until it is too late. Moving is not just a matter of picking up stakes and changing locations. The West, and increasingly the non-West, are marked by the mentality of mobilization. We are restless, always changing. This is one of the reasons for a high divorce rate and the frequency of midlife crises that destroy more than they build up. A Reformed approach to family and church will have to put a far greater emphasis on roots, stability, and wisdom in relation to our earthly pilgrimage.

Toward a More Just World

This is an enormous issue. To put things in perspective, it should be said at the outset that Christians have often been at the forefront of social justice. More than any other group, they have fought for the reversal of evil practices and for the establishment of fair ones. Yet, here too there is much work to be done. Gary Haugen of the International Justice Mission (IJM) describes firsthand the horrors of the massacres in Rwanda: mass graves at Kibuye, with hundreds of dead Tutsi victims of Hutu violence, a far different reality from the pictures seen on television. He reports poignantly, "We would never number all the mothers' children in these mass graves, but their Father in heaven had numbered even the very hairs of their heads."[10] Part of the work of IJM is to meet many surviving children and to remind them and us of God's hatred of injustice. Then it asks someone to "stand in

10. Gary Haugen, *Good News about Injustice* (Downers Grove, Ill.: InterVarsity, 1999), 28ff.

the breach" and seek justice in the midst of cruelty (Ps. 11:5, 7; Ezek. 22:25, 27, 30). The IJM helps with the capture and indictment of the Kibuye leaders but also with the protection of their victims.[11]

The IJM is a drop in the bucket, compared with the needs in the world. The call to effect justice should not be limited to specialists or committed heroes and heroines on the battlefront for integrity. That such brave men and women are doing good work is gratifying. But no individual believer should be deaf to the cry of the poor and the groaning of a world steeped in cruelty:

> Women are raped in Zion,
>   young women in the towns of Judah.
> Princes are hung up by their hands;
>   no respect is shown to the elders.
> Young men are compelled to grind at the mill,
>   and boys stagger under loads of wood.
> The old men have left the city gate,
>   the young men their music.
> The joy of our hearts has ceased;
>   our dancing has been turned to mourning. (Lam. 5:11–15)

If we feel overwhelmed by the stark reality of a world where everything is upside down, we are not alone. Despair is understandable, but it is not constructive.

The only sound answer to such drastic conditions is, first, to remember who God is. He loves justice. He hates cruelty and shows no partiality toward the oppressors in favor of the victim. But what is justice? It is the right exercise of power. "God is the ultimate power and authority in the universe, so justice occurs when power and authority is exercised in conformity with his standards."[12] This means, concomitantly, that injustice is the abuse of power. "Again I saw all the oppressions that are done under the sun. And behold, the tears of the oppressed, and they had no one to comfort them! On the side of their

11. Ibid., 33.
12. Ibid., 71.

oppressors there was power, and there was no one to comfort them" (Eccl. 4:1). Every day corrupt authorities endorse embezzlement and rob children of their childhood. Every day landowners extort property from its rightful owners. Problems multiply. Many will not believe the plight of victims. Women will be afraid to report aggressors. But God sees all, and he will not remain silent.

And then, second, if we remember who God is, we will be able to face the many forms of injustice in the world and make a difference. From bonded slavery to forced prostitution to dire poverty to the seemingly more mundane matters of the plight of the elderly and the sexual harassment of women in the workplace, our world is full of victims. Everyone can do something. The Reformed outlook in principle presents a balanced, whole-souled set of answers for the oppressed. Reformed Christians, with their memory of standing firm against the centralizing forces of a baroque monarchy, ought to be in the forefront and have the resilience to fight against oppression. Are we? Do we?

Such a battle will have different objects in different societies. In the non-West, victims are often disadvantaged because of government oppression or traditional entitlements. In the West, it is racial minorities, single mothers, the unborn, the elderly, and the disabled who are likely to be the oppressed. The field of bioethics is emerging and becoming one of the most significant battlefronts for justice.

A heroine to many of us in North America is Joni Eareckson Tada. She is a quadriplegic, having broken her neck in a diving accident as a young woman. Today, she is one of the most effective advocates for the disabled. Behind her unique work on their behalf is a spiritual conviction as a Reformed Christian. Her belief is that God's power and love are best manifested through weakness. Thus, she is far more than a humanitarian, though she certainly is that. She asks us to look again at the forces of good and evil and to learn something poignant about God's ways with humanity.

As Dr. Tada likes to put it, white canes, walkers, and wheelchairs are a glaring and obtrusive presence for an insensitive world. She sees her wheelchair as a kind of spotlight that illuminates the dark places of prejudice against weaker citizens of the world. In truth, her work illuminates the ways of God with all of humankind, weakened either visibly or more subtly. She wants to reflect the One who works for long-term victory, who shows tough love, with no easy answers but with a deep understanding that grace is made perfect through weakness. She says:

> The words of Jesus in Luke 14:12–14; 23–24 are a mandate to us to go out, find the disabled, and bring them in. And why do we do this? Because the Father wants His house full of "weaker members." Why? Because God underscores time and again in His Word that His power always shows up best through weakness. People with disabilities can be God's best audio-visual aids to the rest of the Body, reminding us that we are all richer when we recognize our poverty; we are all stronger when we acknowledge our weaknesses; and it is the lowly, not the proud, who will inherit the Kingdom of Heaven.[13]

The dreadful events of September 11, 2001, have brought another form of injustice, international terrorism, close to home. To some extent this has changed the rules, since there is no identifiable national enemy, but only an elusive series of clandestine groups. Often tied to extremist versions of Islam, these groups are bent on carrying out vengeful reprisals against their perceived adversaries, whether countries like Spain and the United States or ideals such as Western secularism. The Christian struggle for a just world will need to understand the mind-set of these groups and learn to apply biblical principles of legitimate opposition to such enemies, while at the same time being fair and patient with countries that may sympathize with them.

Of course, the battle for justice is not always so public and visible. It is waged in homes and offices and schools. It is fought wherever distortions and unkindness have made victims of the weak. The gospel is the free offer of unconditional grace. It is for anyone who comes to ask the mercy of Christ. But it always addresses the poor and

13. Joni Eareckson Tada, e-mail message to author, July 21, 2004.

the oppressed, literally and figuratively. A theology without a concern for justice is dead.

Trusting God's Providence

Reformed believers, though they have a rich heritage of reflections on God's providence, will want to devote more attention to submitting to God's ways in their lives. As we saw, God is not only the Creator but also the governor of the universe. He is also the one who ordains every step we take. At times this will be pure comfort to us. We will understand that in adverse conditions and through trials and difficulties, God is there; his rod and his staff comfort us (Ps. 23:4). At other times this will raise questions about his ways.

Sometimes the questions are on a cataclysmic scale. Where was God in the terror of ethnic cleansing in the Balkans? Where was he in the genocide at Rwanda? Where was God in the decimation of New York's Twin Towers and Washington's Pentagon by jet planes turned into live bombs? The problem of evil will not go away, no matter how much progress is made in matters of social justice and of theological clarity. No doubt such catastrophes will continue to haunt our planet. Reformed theology ought to have some helpful answers here. With due admission of mystery, it ought to be able to place everything under the sign of a sovereign God, who corrects human schemes and means it for good (Gen. 50:20).

Sometimes, though, the questions are more ordinary, yet with no less poignancy. Why must we grow older and become more frail, dependent on loved ones and social services? How can we handle disappointments in life, especially when things do not turn out as we had hoped? When we have invested so much energy in the work of God's kingdom, why are there so few measurable results? Many leaders have engaged in a lifetime of frenetic work to effect change but have not witnessed much of it. As soon as one victory is gained, other defeats follow.

At such times we need to develop and apply a deeper, richer view of God's providence. The Old Testament looks forward to the coming of the kingdom. The New Testament speaks of its fulfillment. Jesus, the son of David, is the king of Israel (Matt. 22:42). When he casts out demons by the Holy Spirit, then the kingdom is truly come (Matt. 12:28). In the reality of the kingdom the strong become weak, the powerful tumble, and little children take the place of the entitled elite (Matt. 8:28–34). Yet the rule of Christ is not one of brute force. He rules by the power of providence over all things. The Lamb is the Lord of lords and King of kings (Rev. 17:14). We need have no fear because Christ has overcome the entire world (John 16:33).

What are we to make of the events and trends in history? We dare not look to the finger of God in various historical events for justification of our actions, as if the events represent a direct message from him assuring us that he is on our side. This approach, sometimes known as providentialism, defends human actions because of what God has foreordained. The church ought to recoil from justifying strategies and measures on that basis. While nothing is outside of God's providence, his express will for us is found in his commandments, wisely applied, rather than in an insider's knowledge of his secret will. God's revealed will in Scripture equips us to evaluate events and trends as they unfold.

Since he announced his intentions to subdue all things under his feet, we should expect to see some evidence of that in world history (Gen. 3:15; 1 Cor. 15:27–28). What we have, then, is the ability to make critical decisions about how society should live and how government should legislate. Just as Augustine could react against the Romans for their pagan views of the city, so may we denounce various forms of paganism in our own cities. Just as Gamaliel asked for patience with Christians, we ought to plead for fair-mindedness by the powers that be in view of a Christian presence.

The central fact of history is not the establishment of any human government, however just and however favorable it might be to the gospel. The central fact of history is the death and resurrection of Jesus Christ in its relation to fallen humankind. How can we assert this and make it the surety of our hope for the history of the world? The disciples on the road to Emmaus had the same question. Concerning the life and death of Jesus, "we had hoped that he was the one to redeem Israel. Yes, and besides all this, it is now the third day since these things happened" (Luke 24:21). Then their mysterious companion revealed himself. Jesus Christ showed himself as the resurrected one, igniting their hearts to faith and admonishing them for such a slow reckoning with the truth. Then they went out and turned the world upside down. If we begin here, our calling in the world will make sense—sense enough to hope in Christ the Lord of the seals of history and to proclaim him until the day dawns and the morning star rises in every redeemed heart (Rev. 5:6–8; 2 Peter 1:19).

The agenda is more than full. Our God is more than able.

FOR FURTHER READING

This bibliography is for readers who want to make further investigations into the Reformed faith. It is organized into categories. It is hardly exhaustive but will afford the opportunity to explore some of the deeper dimensions of what was only surveyed in this volume.

Classics of Reformed Theology

Bavinck, Herman. *Gereformeerde Dogmatiek.* 4 vols. 4th ed. Kampen: Kok, 1928. A translation of the whole is in progress, Dutch Reformed Translation Society, Baker Books. Vols. 1–2 are in print.

———. *Our Reasonable Faith: A Survey of Christian Doctrine.* Translated by Henry Zylstra. Grand Rapids: Eerdmans, 1956.

Berkhof, Louis. *Manual of Christian Doctrine.* Grand Rapids: Eerdmans, 1933.

———. *Reformed Dogmatics.* 3 vols. Grand Rapids: Eerdmans, 1932.

———. *Systematic Theology.* Grand Rapids: Eerdmans, 1996. A new edition with preface by Richard Muller.

Berkouwer, G. C. *Studies in Dogmatics.* 20 vols. Grand Rapids: Eerdmans, 1955.

The Book of Common Prayer.

Calvin, John. *Institutes of the Christian Religion.* Edited by John T. McNeill. Translated by Ford Lewis Battles. Philadelphia: Westminster Press, 1960.

Contours of Christian Theology. Gerald Bray, gen. ed. Downers Grove, Ill.: InterVarsity Press, 1993–.

So far, the following have been published: *The Doctrine of God,* Gerald Bray; *The Work of Christ,* Robert Letham; *The Providence of God,* Paul Helm; *The Church,* Edmund P. Clowney; *The Doctrine of Humanity,* Charles Sherlock; *The Holy Spirit,* Sinclair B. Ferguson; *The Person of Christ,* Donald MacLeod; *The Revelation of God,* Peter Jensen. We await *The Last Things,* whose author is not yet announced.

Dabney, Robert Lewis. *Lectures in Systematic Theology.* 2 vols. 1868. Grand Rapids: Zondervan, 1972.

Ferguson, Sinclair B. *Know Your Christian Life: A Theological Introduction.* Downers Grove, Ill.: InterVarsity Press, 1981.

Heppe, Heinrich. *Reformed Dogmatics.* Translated by G. T. Thomson. Grand Rapids: Baker, 1979.

Hodge, Charles. *Systematic Theology.* 3 vols. Reprint ed. Grand Rapids: Eerdmans, 1979.

Kuyper, Abraham. *Encyclopaedie der Heilige Godgeleerdheid.* 3 vols. Amsterdam: J. A. Wormser, 1894.

Lindberg, Carter, ed. *The Reformation Theologians: An Introduction to Theology in the Early Modern Period.* Oxford: Blackwell, 2002.

Machen, J. Gresham. *Christianity and Liberalism.* Grand Rapids: Eerdmans, 1923.

Monod, Adolphe. *Les Adieux.* Lausanne: Eds Groupes Missionnaires, 1856/1978. Available in English as *Living in the Hope of Glory.* Edited and translated by Constance K. Walker. Phillipsburg, N.J.: P&R, 2002.

Packer, J. I. *Knowing God.* Downers Grove, Ill.: InterVarsity Press, 1977.

Ridderbos, Herman. *The Coming of the Kingdom.* Philadelphia: Presbyterian and Reformed, 1962.

Thornwell, James Henley. *The Collected Writings.* 4 vols. Edinburgh/Carlisle, Pa.: Banner of Truth, 1974.

Turretin, Francis (François Turretini). *Institutes of Elenctic Theology.* 3 vols. Edited by James T. Dennison Jr. Translated by George Musgrave Giger. Phillipsburg, N.J.: P&R, 1992–97.

Vos, Geerhardus. *Biblical Theology: Old and New Testaments.* Grand Rapids: Eerdmans, 1948.

Warfield, B. B. *Biblical and Theological Studies.* Edited by Samuel G. Craig. Philadelphia: Presbyterian and Reformed, 1952.

————. *The Person and Work of Christ.* Edited by Samuel G. Craig. Philadelphia: Presbyterian and Reformed, 1950.

————. *Selected Shorter Writings.* 2 vols. Edited by John E. Meeter. Nutley, N.J.: Presbyterian and Reformed, 1970, 1973.

The Reformed Creeds and Confessional Standards

Cochrane, Arthur C., ed. *Reformed Confessions of the Sixteenth Century.* Philadelphia: Westminster Press, 1966.

Schaff, Philip, ed. *The Creeds of Christendom.* Vol. 3. Revised by David Schaff. Grand Rapids: Baker, 1977, 1983.

The Westminster Standards: An Original Facsimile. Audubon, N.J.: Old Paths, 1997.

References and Resources

Benedetto, R., D. L. Gruder, and D. K. McKim. *Historical Dictionary of Reformed Churches.* Landham, Md.: Scarecrow, 1999.

Consult certain websites for further material; for example, Still Waters Revival Books and New Puritan Bookshelf CD series at http://www.swrb.com/puritan-books.

Introductions to Reformed Theology

Boice, James M., and Philip G. Ryken. *The Doctrines of Grace: Rediscovering the Evangelical Gospel.* Wheaton, Ill.: Good News/Crossway, 2002.

DeWitt, Richard John. *What Is the Reformed Faith?* Carlisle, Pa.: Banner of Truth, 1981.

Godfrey, W. Robert. *An Unexpected Journey: Discovering Reformed Christianity.* Phillipsburg, N.J.: P&R, 2004.

Hesselink, I. John. *On Being Reformed: Distinctive Characteristics and Common Misunderstandings.* Ann Arbor, Mich.: Servant, 1983.

Leith, John H. *Introduction to the Reformed Tradition.* Rev. ed. Atlanta: John Knox, 1981.

McKim, Donald K. *Introducing the Reformed Faith.* Louisville, Ky.: Westminster John Knox Press, 2001.

History and Theology of the Reformation: General Level

Bainton, Roland. *Here I Stand: A Life of Martin Luther.* New York: Mentor, 1957.

Bousma, William J. *John Calvin: A Sixteenth-Century Portrait.* New York: Oxford University Press, 1988.

Cameron, Euan. *The European Reformation.* Oxford: Clarendon, 1991.

Dickens, A. G. *The German Nation and Martin Luther.* New York: Harper & Row, 1974.

Higman, Francis. *La diffusion de la Réforme en France, 1520–1565.* Geneva: Labor et Fides, 1992.

———. *La Réforme: pourquoi?* Geneva: Labor et Fides, 2001.

Lindberg, Carter. *The European Reformations.* Oxford: Blackwell, 1996.

Ozment, Steven. *Protestants: The Birth of a Revolution.* New York: Doubleday, 1992.

Parker, T. H. L. *Calvin's Preaching.* Louisville, Ky.: Westminster John Knox Press, 1992.

———. *John Calvin.* London: J. M. Dent & Sons, 1975, 1982.

Pettegree, Andrew, ed. *The Reformation World.* London and New York: Routledge, 2000.

Reid, W. Stanford, ed. *John Calvin: His Influence in the Western World.* Grand Rapids: Zondervan, 1982.

Scribner, R. W. *The German Reformation.* Atlantic Highlands: Humanities Press International, 1986.

Trueman, Carl R. *Reformation: Yesterday, Today and Tomorrow.* Dundas, Ont.: Joshua Press, 2000.

History and Theology of the Reformation: Specialized

Bainton, Roland. *Women of the Reformation: in Germany and Italy.* Minneapolis: Augsburg, 1971.

―――. *Women of the Reformation: in France and England.* Minneapolis: Augsburg, 1973.

―――. *Women of the Reformation: from Spain to Scandinavia.* Minneapolis: Augsburg, 1977.

Edwards, Mark U. *Luther and the False Brethren.* Stanford, Calif.: Stanford University Press, 1975.

Guggisberg, H. R., and G. Krodel, eds. *The Reformation in Germany and Europe: Interpretations and Issues.* Gütersloh: Gütersloher Verlagshaus, 1993.

Huizinga, Johan. *The Waning of the Middle Ages.* Garden City, N.Y.: Anchor, 1956.

Maltby, William S., ed. *Reformation Europe: A Guide to Research.* St. Louis: Center for Reformation Research, 1992. See also the earlier volume, edited by Steven Ozment, 1982.

McKim, Donald K., ed. *The Cambridge Companion to John Calvin.* Cambridge: Cambridge University Press, 2004.

Oberman, Heiko A., ed. *Forerunners of the Reformation.* New York: Holt, Rinehart & Winston, 1966.

Ozment, Steven. *The Reformation in the Cities.* New Haven, Conn.: Yale University Press, 1975.

Pettegree, Andrew, et al. *The Early Reformation in Europe.* Cambridge: Cambridge University Press, 1992.

Zahl, Paul F. M. *Five Women of the English Reformation.* Grand Rapids: Eerdmans, 2001.

Post-Reformation History and Theology

Johnson, William S., and John H. Leith, eds. *A Reformed Reader: Sourcebook in Christian Theology.* Vol. 1, *Classical Beginnings 1519–1799.* Louisville, Ky.: Westminster John Knox Press, 1993.

Kingdon, Robert M. *Geneva and the Consolidation of the French Protestant Movement, 1564–1572.* Geneva: Droz, 1967.

McNeill, John T. *The History and Character of Calvinism.* New York: Oxford University Press, 1967.

Muller, Richard A. *Post-Reformation Reformed Dogmatics.* 2 vols. Grand Rapids: Baker, 1987.

Pettegree, Andrew, et al. *Calvinism in Europe 1540–1620.* Cambridge: Cambridge University Press, 1994.

World Reformed Theology

Bauswein, Jean-Jacques, and Lukas Vischer, eds. *The Reformed Family Worldwide.* Grand Rapids: Eerdmans, 1998.

Hoogstra, Jacob, ed. *American Calvinism: A Survey.* Grand Rapids: Baker, 1957.

Noll, Mark A., ed. *The Princeton Theology.* Grand Rapids: Baker, 2001.

Wells, David F., ed. *Dutch Reformed Theology.* Grand Rapids: Baker, 1989.

―――, ed. *The Princeton Theology.* Grand Rapids: Baker, 1989.

————, ed. *Reformed Theology in America*. Grand Rapids: Eerdmans, 1985.

————, ed. *Southern Reformed Theology*. Grand Rapids: Baker, 1989.

Worship and Devotion

Calvin, John. *Heart Aflame: Daily Readings from Calvin on the Psalms*. Phillipsburg, N.J.: P&R, 1999.

Marshall, Paul, with Lela Gilbert. *Heaven Is Not My Home: Living in the Now of God's Creation*. Nashville: Word, 1998.

Old, Hughes Oliphint. *Leading in Prayer: A Workbook for Worship*. Grand Rapids: Eerdmans, 1995.

————. *Worship: Reformed according to Scripture*. Rev. ed. Louisville: Westminster John Knox Press, 2002.

Rice, Howard L., and Lamar Williamson Jr., eds. *A Book of Reformed Prayers*. Louisville: Westminster John Knox Press, 1998.

Spirit of the Reformation Study Bible. Grand Rapids: Zondervan, 2003.

Tada, Joni Eareckson. *Glorious Intruder: God's Presence in Life's Chaos*. Portland, Ore.: Multnomah, 1989.

Special Developments in Reformed Theology

Begby, Jeremy S. *Voicing Creation's Praise: Towards a Theology of the Arts*. Edinburgh: T & T Clark, 1991.

Brand, Hilary, and Adrienne Chaplin. *Art and Soul: Signposts for Christians in the Arts*. Carlisle, Pa.: Piquant; Downers Grove, Ill.: InterVarsity Press, 2001.

Carter, Anthony J. *On Being Black and Reformed: A New Perspective on the African-American Christian Experience*. Phillipsburg, N.J.: P&R, 2003.

Conn, Harvie M. *Eternal Word and Changing Worlds: Theology, Anthropology, and Mission in Trialogue*. Grand Rapids: Zondervan, 1984.

————. *Evangelism: Doing Justice and Preaching Grace*. Grand Rapids: Zondervan, 1982.

————, and Manuel Ortiz. *Urban Ministry: The Kingdom, the City, and the People of God*. Downers Grove, Ill.: InterVarsity Press, 2001.

Ferguson, Sinclair B. *The Holy Spirit*. Downers Grove, Ill.: InterVarsity Press, 1996.

Frame, John M. *The Doctrine of the Knowledge of God*. Phillipsburg, N.J.: P&R, 1987.

Gaffin, Richard B., Jr. *Resurrection and Redemption: A Study in Paul's Soteriology*. 2d ed. Phillipsburg, N.J.: P&R, 1987.

Keller, Timothy J. *Ministries of Mercy: The Call of the Jericho Road*. 2d ed. Phillipsburg, N.J.: P&R, 1997.

Mouw, Richard J. *He Shines in All That's Fair: Culture and Common Grace*. Grand Rapids: Eerdmans, 2001.

Niebuhr, H. Richard. *Christ and Culture*. New York: Harper & Row, 1951.

Packer, J. I. *Evangelism and the Sovereignty of God*. 2d ed. Downers Grove, Ill.: InterVarsity Press, 1991.

Phillips, Richard D. *Turning Back the Darkness: The Biblical Pattern of Reformation.* Wheaton, Ill.: Crossway, 2002.

Plantinga, Alvin. *Warranted Christian Belief.* New York: Oxford University Press, 2000.

Powlison, David. *Seeing with New Eyes: Counseling and the Human Condition through the Lens of Scripture.* Phillipsburg, N.J.: P&R, 2003.

Rice, Howard L., and James C. Huffstuter. *Reformed Worship.* Louisville, Ky.: Geneva Press, 2001.

Ridderbos, Herman. *Redemptive History and the New Testament Scriptures.* 2nd rev. ed. Phillipsburg, N.J.: P&R, 1988.

Seerveld, Calvin. *Bearing Fresh Olive Trees.* Toronto: Tuppence Press; Nottingham: Piquant, 2000.

———. *Rainbows for the Fallen World.* Toronto: I.R.S.S., 1980.

Skillen, James W. *The Scattered Voice: Christians at Odds in the Public Square.* Grand Rapids: Zondervan, 1990.

Van Til, Cornelius. *The Defense of the Faith.* 3rd rev. ed. Nutley, N.J.: Presbyterian and Reformed, 1976.

Wolters, Albert M. *Creation Regained: Biblical Basics for a Reformational Worldview.* Grand Rapids: Eerdmans, 1985.

INDEX OF SCRIPTURE

INDEX OF SUBJECTS
AND NAMES

William Edgar is professor of apologetics at Westminster Theological Seminary in Philadelphia, where he has served on the faculty since 1989. Born in North Carolina, Dr. Edgar has lived much of his life in France and Switzerland. Before coming to Westminster, he served as a professor of the Faculté Libre de Théologie Réformée in Aix-en-Provence, France.

Edgar serves on several boards, including the Huguenot Fellowship (president). He is on the editorial committee of *La Révue Réformée*. He regularly participates as co-moderator at the Trinity Forum Seminars. He also serves on the Institutional Review Board and Medical Ethics Committee of Chestnut Hill Hospital.

He is author of *The Face of Truth, Reasons of the Heart,* and *La carte protestante*, as well as articles on cultural apologetics, Huguenot history, and African-American music. He also edited the newly annotated edition of Cornelius Van Til's *Christian Apologetics.*

Edgar received a B.A. from Harvard University, an M.Div. from Westminster Theological Seminary, and a D.Th. from the University of Geneva in Switzerland.